T0092680

Lecture Notes in Computer Science

Lecture Notes in Artificial Intelligence   14318

Founding Editor

Jörg Siekmann

Series Editors

The series Lecture Notes in Artificial Intelligence (LNAI) was established in 1988 as a topical subseries of LNCS devoted to artificial intelligence.

The series publishes state-of-the-art research results at a high level. As with the LNCS mother series, the mission of the series is to serve the international R & D community by providing an invaluable service, mainly focused on the publication of conference and workshop proceedings and postproceedings.

Roberto Basili · Domenico Lembo ·
Carla Limongelli · Andrea Orlandini
Editors

AIxIA 2023 – Advances in Artificial Intelligence

XXIInd International Conference
of the Italian Association for Artificial Intelligence
AIxIA 2023, Rome, Italy, November 6–9, 2023
Proceedings

 Springer

Editors
Roberto Basili ⓘ
Università degli Studi Tor Vergata
Rome, Italy

Domenico Lembo ⓘ
Sapienza Università di Roma
Rome, Italy

Carla Limongelli ⓘ
Università degli Studi Roma Tre
Rome, Italy

Andrea Orlandini ⓘ
Consiglio Nazionale delle Ricerche
Rome, Italy

ISSN 0302-9743   ISSN 1611-3349 (electronic)
Lecture Notes in Artificial Intelligence
ISBN 978-3-031-47545-0   ISBN 978-3-031-47546-7 (eBook)
https://doi.org/10.1007/978-3-031-47546-7

LNCS Sublibrary: SL7 – Artificial Intelligence

Preface

This volume contains the proceedings of the 22nd International Conference of the Italian Association for Artificial Intelligence (AIxIA 2023), the primary scientific event of the Associazione Italiana per l'Intelligenza Artificiale (AIxIA). AIxIA is a non-profit organization, dedicated to promoting the advancement of artificial intelligence (AI) within academic, social, and production contexts. The association established the series of international conferences in 1991, initially organizing an event every two years, and then maintaining an annual schedule from 2015 onwards. Over the years, the conference has visited many cities throughout the national territory, as reported in the LNCS proceedings of the various editions (https://link.springer.com/conference/aiia).

AIxIA 2023 was held in Rome, Italy, during November 6–9, hosted by the University of Roma Tre. The event took place on the occasion of the centenary of the foundation of the National Research Council of Italy (CNR) and was curated by CNR and the three main public universities of Rome, La Sapienza, Tor Vergata and Roma Tre.

The conference received 53 submissions for the regular research papers track. Each paper was carefully reviewed by at least three members of the Program Committee, and finally 33 papers were accepted for publication in these proceedings and presentation at the conference. Besides regular papers, the conference also received the submission of 15 discussion papers, i.e. position papers or extended abstracts of articles recently published in premier international conferences and journals related to AI. After a dedicated review process, 13 discussion papers were accepted for presentation at the conference.

AIxIA 2023 featured renowned keynote speakers. Specifically, three keynote talks were presented: 'The Evolution of Artificial Intelligence in Italy: A Personal Journey' by Luigia Carlucci Aiello, 'Artificial Intelligence: Some Thoughts?' by Stuart J. Russell, and 'Chatting with a Generative AI: A Personal Review', by Bernardo Magnini. The conference agenda also included two tutorials by Pietro Liò and Chiara Ghidini, a Doctoral Consortium, award events, a panel dedicated to FAIR, the largest AI project in Italy financed by the Italian Ministry for Universities and Research through the National Recovery and Resilience Plan (PNRR), and two satellite events: a public gathering titled 'Artificial Intelligence: Instructions for Use', focused on the impact of generative AI on schools and younger generations, and an event dedicated to the connections between AI and the business and industrial world.

Besides the main track, AIxIA 2023 encompassed a wide range of theoretical and applied AI aspects, with 19 co-located workshops dedicated to specific topics, bringing together AI communities with related interests:

- 7th Workshop on Advances in Argumentation in Artificial Intelligence (AI)
- 3rd Italian Workshop on Artificial Intelligence and Applications for Business and Industries (AIABI)
- 1st International Workshop on AI for Quantum and Quantum for AI (AIQxQIA)
- 10th Italian Workshop on Artificial Intelligence and Robotics (AIRO)
- 4th Italian Workshop on Artificial Intelligence for an Ageing Society (AIxAS)

- 1st International Workshop on High-Performance Artificial Intelligence Systems in Education (AIxEDU)
- 2nd Workshop on Artificial Intelligence for Human-Machine Interaction (AIxHMI)
- 1st Workshop on Artificial Intelligence for Perception and Artificial Consciousness (AIxPAC)
- 2nd Workshop on Bias, Ethical AI, Explainability and the Role of Logic and Logic Programming (BEWARE)
- 2nd Workshop on Artificial Intelligence & Creativity (CREAI)
- 2nd AIxIA Workshop on Artificial Intelligence for Healthcare (HC@AIxIA)
- 2nd Workshop on Artificial Intelligence for Cultural Heritage (IAI4CH)
- 11th Italian Workshop on Planning and Scheduling (IPS)
- 12th Italian Workshop on Machine Learning and Data Mining (MLDM)
- 7th Workshop on Natural Language for Artificial Intelligence (NL4AI)
- 5th Workshop on Artificial Intelligence and fOrmal VERification, Logic, Automata, and sYnthesis (OVERLAY)
- 30th Workshop of the Working group on Knowledge Representation and Automated Reasoning (RCRA)
- 2nd Workshop on Strategies, Prediction, Interaction, and Reasoning in Italy (SPIRIT)
- 4th Italian Workshop on Explainable Artificial Intelligence (XAI.it)

We express our gratitude to the various institutions and sponsors who supported AIxIA 2023, the AIxIA Executive Board for its steadfast assistance, the Rector of Roma Tre University, Massimiliano Fiorucci, for granting us the opportunity to host the conference in the facilities of the Department of Civil Engineering, Computer Science, and Aeronautical Technologies. We also want to thank all authors for submitting high-quality reearch papers, the members of the Program Committee and the additional reviewers for their efforts to produce fair and thorough evaluations of the submitted papers. Our heartfelt thanks also go to the Workshop and Tutorial chairs, Andrea Brunello and Danilo Croce, and the Doctoral Consortium chairs, Valentina Poggioni and Silvia Rossi, for their invaluable contributions in shaping an exciting program for AIxIA 2023. Finally, we would like to express our gratitude to all those who, in various capacities, contributed to the success of AIxIA 2023.

September 2023

Roberto Basili
Domenico Lembo
Carla Limongelli
Andrea Orlandini

Organization

General Chair

Andrea Orlandini   Consiglio Nazionale delle Ricerche, Rome, Italy

Program Committee Chairs

Roberto Basili   Università degli Studi Tor Vergata, Italy
Domenico Lembo   Sapienza Università di Roma, Italy
Carla Limongelli   Università degli Studi Roma Tre, Italy

Workshop and Tutorial Chairs

Andrea Brunello   Università degli Studi di Udine, Italy
Danilo Croce   Università degli Studi Tor Vergata, Italy

Doctoral Consortium Chairs

Valentina Poggioni   Università degli Studi di Perugia, Italy
Silvia Rossi   Università di Napoli Federico II, Italy

Sponsorship Chair

Marco Maratea   Università della Calabria, Italy

Registration Chair

Gabriella Cortellessa   Consiglio Nazionale delle Ricerche, Rome, Italy

Web Chair

Alessio Ferrato   Università degli Studi Roma Tre, Italy

Student Grant Committee

Valentina Poggioni	Università degli Studi di Perugia, Italy
Riccardo Rasconi	Consiglio Nazionale delle Ricerche, Rome, Italy
Marta Sanzari	Università degli Studi Roma Tre, Italy

Program Committee

Marco Baioletti	Università degli Studi di Perugia, Italy
Matteo Baldoni	Università di Torino, Italy
Luca Barbierato	Politecnico di Torino, Italy
Adriano Barra	Università del Salento, Italy
Sebastiano Battiato	Università di Catania, Italy
Stefano Berretti	Università di Firenze, Italy
Domenico Bloisi	Università della Basilicata, Italy
Guido Boella	Università di Torino, Italy
Stefano Borgo	Consiglio Nazionale delle Ricerche, Trento, Italy
Stefano Cagnoni	Università di Parma, Italy
Francesco Calimeri	Università della Calabria, Italy
Alberto Casagrande	Università di Trieste, Italy
Antonio Chella	Università di Palermo, Italy
Federico Chesani	Università di Bologna, Italy
Flavio S. Correa Da Silva	University of São Paulo, Brazil
Stefania Costantini	Università dell'Aquila, Italy
Dario Della Monica	Università degli Studi di Udine, Italy
Claudio Di Ciccio	Sapienza Università di Roma, Italy
Francesco M. Donini	Università della Tuscia, Italy
Aldo Franco Dragoni	Università Politecnica delle Marche, Italy
Stefano Ferilli	Università degli Studi di Bari Aldo Moro, Italy
Donatella Firmani	Sapienza Università di Roma, Italy
Enrico Giunchiglia	Università di Genova, Italy
Johannes K. Fichte	Linköping University, Sweden
Alberto Finzi	Università di Napoli Federico II, Italy
Fabio Fioravanti	Università di Chieti-Pescara, Italy
Andrea Formisano	Università di Udine, Italy
Giancarlo Fortino	Università della Calabria, Italy
Fabio Gasparetti	Università degli Studi Roma Tre, Italy
Marco Gavanelli	Università di Ferrara, Italy
Gianluigi Greco	Università della Calabria, Italy
Giorgio Grisetti	Sapienza Università di Roma, Italy
Ernesto Jimenez-Ruiz	City, University of London, UK

Francesca Alessandra Lisi	Università degli Studi di Bari Aldo Moro, Italy
Marin Lujak	University Rey Juan Carlos, Spain
Bernardo Magnini	Fondazone Bruno Kessler, Trento, Italy
Dario Malchiodi	Università degli Studi di Milano, Italy
Fabio Mercorio	Università di Milano-Bicocca, Italy
Alessio Micheli	Università di Pisa, Italy
Marina Mongiello	Politecnico di Bari, Italy
Marco Montali	Libera Università di Bozen-Bolzano, Italy
Roberto Navigli	Sapienza Università di Roma, Italy
Filippo Palumbo	Consiglio Nazionale delle Ricerche, Pisa, Italy
Francesco Ponzio	Politecnico di Torino, Italy
Luigi Portinale	Università del Piemonte Orientale A. Avogadro, Italy
Luca Pulina	Università di Sassari, Italy
Alessandra Raffaetà	Università Ca' Foscari Venezia, Italy
Riccardo Rasconi	Consiglio Nazionale delle Ricerche, Rome, Italy
Andrea Roli	Università di Bologna, Italy
Marco Rospocher	Università degli Studi di Verona, Italy
Marco Roveri	Università di Trento, Italy
Salvatore Ruggieri	Università di Pisa, Italy
Emanuel Sallinger	TU Wien, Austria
Giuseppe Sansonetti	Università degli Studi Roma Tre, Italy
Luigi Sauro	Università di Napoli Federico II, Italy
Domenico Fabio Savo	Università di Bergamo, Italy
Francesco Scarcello	Università della Calabria, Italy
Filippo Sciarrone	Universitas Mercatorum, Italy
Alessandro Sperduti	Università di Padova, Italy
Marco Temperini	Sapienza Università di Roma, Italy
Eloisa Vargiu	CETaqua Water Technology Center, Spain
Serena Villata	CNRS, Sophia Antipolis, France

Additional Reviewers

Manuel Borroto
Andrea Brunello
Alessandro Castelnovo
Simona Colucci
Riccardo De Benedictis
Michele Fontanesi
Michele Ianni
Lanzino Romeo
Giovanni Melissari

Corrado Mencar
Cataldo Musto
Sergey Paramonov
Luca Pedrelli
Giuseppe Primiero
Alessandro Quarta
Mattia Setzu
Laura State
Mauro Vallati

Contents

Robotics and Perception

Hybrid AI

Applications of AI

Argumentation and Logic Programming

ABALearn: An Automated Logic-Based Learning System for ABA Frameworks

Cristina Tirsi[1]([✉]), Maurizio Proietti[2][ID], and Francesca Toni[1][ID]

[1] Imperial College London, London, UK
{ct519,f.toni}@ic.ac.uk
[2] IASI-CNR, Rome, Italy
maurizio.proietti@iasi.cnr.it

Abstract. We introduce ABALearn, an automated algorithm that learns Assumption-Based Argumentation (ABA) frameworks from training data consisting of positive and negative examples, and a given background knowledge. ABALearn's ability to generate comprehensible rules for decision-making promotes transparency and interpretability, addressing the challenges associated with the black-box nature of traditional machine learning models. This implementation is based on the strategy proposed in a previous work. The learnt ABA frameworks can be mapped onto logic programs with negation as failure. The main advantage of this algorithm is that it requires minimal information about the learning problem and it is also capable of learning circular debates. Our results show that this approach is competitive with state-of-the-art alternatives, demonstrating its potential to be used in real-world applications where low user expertise is available. Overall, this work contributes to the development of automated learning techniques for argumentation frameworks in the context of Explainable AI (XAI) and provides insights into how such learners can be applied to make predictions.

Keywords: Logic-based learning · Assumption-based argumentation · Logic program transformation

1 Introduction

Within the field of artificial intelligence (AI), *computational argumentation* is a very powerful tool as it can be used to improve the performance and explainability of AI systems [1]. In general, argumentation is valuable through its interdisciplinary applications, such as legal and practical reasoning, game-theory, decision-theory, and philosophy. It uses formal logic to manipulate and reason about arguments, which provides a clear and comprehensible explanation for the reasoning behind a conclusion [2]. Recently, there has also been a renewed interest in logic-based learning, as it works with less data, human knowledge can be easily injected, and, most importantly, it is explainable [3].

Assumption-Based Argumentation (ABA) is a popular structured argumentation used for knowledge representation and reasoning [4]. In ABA frameworks,

R. Basili et al. (Eds.): AIxIA 2023, LNAI 14318, pp. 3–16, 2023.
https://doi.org/10.1007/978-3-031-47546-7_1

the focus is on the assumptions underlying arguments built from rules, rather than the arguments themselves, and it uses contraries of assumptions to determine attacks between arguments. The acceptability of an argument is determined by the acceptability of its assumptions.

On this basis, *ABA learning* [5] (a novel methodology to learn ABA frameworks) has been proposed as a solution to support logic-based learning through the means of computational argumentation.

The main idea is that it extends the knowledge, which is represented as an ABA framework, by introducing new rules or modifying existing ones following transformation rules. Currently, there is no existing algorithm that manages to automate ABA learning. However, a strategy has been proposed [5] to give an intuition on how such an algorithm could work, but it is not deterministic and there is no actual implementation of it.

We are interested in automating the ABA learning process. To this aim, we introduce ABALearn, an automated system using an algorithm based on the above mentioned strategy [5].

Additionally, we explore a potential solution to increase the interpretability of the learned ABA frameworks that makes use of Large Language Models [10].

We are also interested in assessing how our system compares with related existing learners. In this regard, we conduct an evaluation against two state-of-the-art logic-based learning systems, ILASP [11] and FOLD-RM [12], and discuss the results.

2   Background

2.1   Assumption-Based Argumentation Frameworks

An assumption-based argumentation (ABA) framework is a tuple $\langle \mathcal{L}, \mathcal{R}, \mathcal{A}, \overline{} \rangle$ where

- $\langle \mathcal{L}, \mathcal{R} \rangle$ is a *deductive system*, with $\mathcal{L}$ being the **language** and $\mathcal{R}$ a set of (inference) **rules**;
- $\mathcal{A} \subseteq \mathcal{L}$ is a (*non-empty*) set of **assumptions**;
- $\overline{}$ is a *total mapping* from $\mathcal{A}$ into $\mathcal{L}$, where $\overline{a}$ is the **contrary** of a, for $a \in \mathcal{A}$ [6].

The elements of $\mathcal{L}$ can be any sentences, but in this paper we will only focus on *ground atoms*. For sake of simplicity, however, we will use *schemata* for rules, contraries and assumptions. We will also assume $\mathcal{L}$ is *finite*. Additionally, we focus on **flat** ABA frameworks as they can be mapped onto logic programs.

Example 1 (ABA Framework). Consider the following components:
$\mathcal{L} = \{p(X), q(X), r(X), s(X), t(X), v(X) - X \in \{a, b\}\}$

$$\mathcal{R} = \{\rho_1 : p(X) \leftarrow s(X), \qquad \rho_4 : t(b) \leftarrow s(b), v(b),$$
$$\rho_2 : q(X) \leftarrow r(X), \qquad \rho_5 : t(a) \leftarrow,$$
$$\rho_3 : q(X) \leftarrow t(X), \qquad \rho_6 : v(b) \leftarrow\}$$

$$\mathcal{A} = \{r(X), s(X)\} \qquad\qquad \overline{r(X)} = p(X) \quad \overline{s(X)} = q(X)$$

Then, $\langle \mathcal{L}, \mathcal{R}, \mathcal{A}, {}^{-} \rangle$ is an ABA framework.

An **argument** for (the claim) $\sigma \in \mathcal{L}$ supported by $A \subseteq \mathcal{A}$ and $R \subseteq \mathcal{R}$ (denoted $A \vdash_R \sigma$) is a finite tree with nodes labelled by sentences in $\mathcal{L}$ or by *true*, the root labelled by σ, leaves either *true* or assumptions in A, non-leaves σ' with, as children, the elements of the body of some rule in R with head σ', and A is the set of all assumptions labelling the leaves [7].

Example 2. Arguments $\{\} \vdash_{\{\rho_5\}} t(a)$, $\{s(b)\} \vdash_{\{\rho_4, \rho_6\}} t(b)$, and $\{r(a)\} \vdash_{\{\}} r(a)$ are some of the arguments accepted by the ABA framework defined in Example 1.

An argument $A_1 \vdash_{R_1} \sigma_1$ **attacks** argument $A_2 \vdash_{R_2} \sigma_2$ iff $\overline{a} = \sigma_1$ for some $a \in A_2$ [6].

We look at attacks to decide the acceptability of arguments.

In order to decide which arguments are 'winning' we characterise the semantics of ABA through extensions (sets of arguments).

Given a flat ABA framework $\langle \mathcal{L}, \mathcal{R}, \mathcal{A}, {}^{-} \rangle$, let *Args* be the set of all accepted arguments. Then, a set of arguments A is:

- *stable* iff it is conflict-free (i.e. no attacks between its elements) and it attacks all arguments it does not contain;
- *admissible* iff it is conflict-free and attacks all arguments that attack it;
- *complete* iff it is admissible and it includes all arguments it defends, where a set of arguments A defends an argument α iff A attacks all arguments that attack α;
- *grounded* iff it is $\subseteq$-minimally complete [8].

For any flat ABA framework $\langle \mathcal{L}, \mathcal{R}, \mathcal{A}, {}^{-} \rangle$, there is a unique grounded extension and 0, 1 or multiple stable extensions [9].

An ABA framework $\langle \mathcal{L}, \mathcal{R}, \mathcal{A}, {}^{-} \rangle$ is said to **cover** a sentence $\sigma \in \mathcal{L}$ *under the grounded semantics* (denoted as $\langle \mathcal{L}, \mathcal{R}, \mathcal{A}, {}^{-} \rangle \models_{\mathcal{G}} \sigma$) if σ is the claim of an argument $\alpha \in G$, where G is the grounded extension of $\langle \mathcal{L}, \mathcal{R}, \mathcal{A}, {}^{-} \rangle$.

Example 3. For $\langle \mathcal{L}, \mathcal{R}, \mathcal{A}, {}^{-} \rangle$, as defined in Example 1, the grounded extension is $G = \{\{\} \vdash t(a), \ \{\} \vdash q(a), \ \{\} \vdash v(b), \ \{r(a)\} \vdash q(a), \ \{r(a)\} \vdash r(a)\}$, as it is the minimal set that attacks all the arguments that attack it, is conflict-free and contains all the arguments it defends.

Therefore $\langle \mathcal{L}, \mathcal{R}, \mathcal{A}, {}^{-} \rangle$ covers $t(a), q(a), v(b)$, and $r(a)$.

Similarly, we can define the coverage under credulous semantics:

An ABA framework $\langle \mathcal{L}, \mathcal{R}, \mathcal{A}, {}^{-} \rangle$ is said to *credulously (bravely)* **cover** a sentence $\sigma \in \mathcal{L}$ under the stable semantics if, there is a stable extension $\mathcal{S}$ of $\langle \mathcal{L}, \mathcal{R}, \mathcal{A}, {}^{-} \rangle$, such that σ is the claim of an argument $\alpha \in \mathcal{S}$.

If a sentence is not the claim of any argument accepted under the chosen semantics, then we say the sentence is **not covered**.

There is a *correspondence* between assumption-based argumentation frameworks and logic programs. Consider an ABA framework that: (i) is *flat*; (ii) $\mathcal{L}$ is a set of *atoms*; (iii) $\overline{}$ is a *one-to-one* mapping (i.e. there are no two distinct assumptions that are mapped to the same contrary); (iv) none of the contraries are assumptions (i.e. $\forall \alpha \in \mathcal{A}, \overline{\alpha} \notin \mathcal{A}$). Then there is a *one-to-one* mapping between the *ABA framework* and a *logic program*.

To Transform an ABA Framework to a Logic Program: For all contraries $\overline{\alpha(X)} = p(X)$, replace $\alpha(X)$ with *not p(X)*, in the set of rules $\mathcal{R}$ and remove it from the language $\mathcal{L}$ to obtain the Herbrand Base.

To Transform a Logic Program to an ABA Framework: For every negated atom in the logic program *not p(X)*, replace it with a new atom $\alpha(X)$, add $\alpha(X)$ to the Herbrand Base to obtain the language $\mathcal{L}$, add it to the set of assumptions $\mathcal{A}$ and add the contrary mapping $\overline{\alpha(X)} = p(X)$.

Example 4. The logic program corresponding to the ABA framework in Ex. 1:

$$p(X) \leftarrow not\ q(X) \qquad\qquad t(b) \leftarrow not\ q(b), v(b)$$
$$q(X) \leftarrow not\ p(X) \qquad\qquad t(a) \leftarrow$$
$$q(X) \leftarrow t(X) \qquad\qquad\quad v(b) \leftarrow$$

2.2 ABA Learning

Definition 1. *An ABA learning problem [5] that aims to learn the concept $p(X)$ (where p is a predicate with arity $n \geq 0$ and $X = X_1, X_2, ..., X_n$) consists of:*
- *Two disjoint sets representing the **training data**: a (non-empty) set of positive examples $\mathcal{E}^+$ and a set of negative examples $\mathcal{E}^-$ for predicate p*
- *A flat ABA framework $\langle \mathcal{R}, \mathcal{A}, \overline{} \rangle$ representing the **background knowledge**.*

Example 5 (ABA learning problem). The following is an example of an ABA learning problem, whose goal is to learn the concept of *robber(X)*:

$$\mathcal{R} = \{\rho_1 : seenAtBank(X) \leftarrow wasAtWork(X),$$
$$\rho_2 : wasAtWork(X) \leftarrow banker(X),$$
$$\rho_3 : banker(jane),$$
$$\rho_4 : banker(david),$$
$$\rho_5 : seenAtBank(ann),$$
$$\rho_6 : seenAtBank(taylor),$$
$$\rho_7 : wasAtWork(matt)\}$$
$$\mathcal{E}^+ = \{robber(matt), \quad robber(ann), \quad robber(taylor)\}$$
$$\mathcal{E}^- = \{robber(jane), \quad robber(david)\}$$

Definition 2 (Completeness). *An ABA framework $\langle \mathcal{L}, \mathcal{R}, \mathcal{A}, \overline{} \rangle$ satisfies **completeness**, if it covers all the positive examples $e \in \mathcal{E}^+$ under the chosen ABA semantics.*

Definition 3 (Consistency). *An ABA framework $\langle \mathcal{L}, \mathcal{R}, \mathcal{A}, \overline{} \rangle$ satisfies **consistency**, if it covers none of the negative examples $e \in \mathcal{E}^-$ under the chosen ABA semantics.*

The goal of ABA learning [5] is that the resulting framework should satisfy the properties of completeness and consistency.

The proposed methodology [5] for achieving this ABA framework is using five transformation rules as follows (see [5] for formal definitions and intuitions):

- `Rote Learning`: Given a positive example $p(a)$, generate the rule $\rho : \ p(X) \leftarrow X = a$.
- `Equality Removal`: Remove one of the equalities from the body of the rule.
- `Folding`: Consider two rules $\rho_1 : \ H_1 \leftarrow Eqs_1, B1, B2$ and $\rho_2 : \ H_2 \leftarrow Eqs_1, Eqs_2, B_1$. Then, replace ρ_1 by $\rho_3 : \ H_1 \leftarrow Eqs_2, H_2, B_2$.
- `Subsumption`: Allows the removal of a rule that is subsumed by other rules in the background knowledge.
- `Assumption Introduction`: Introduces a (possibly) new assumption in the body of a rule, and updates $\mathcal{A}$ and the contrary mapping accordingly.

The template in Fig. 1 is adapted from the proposed strategy [5] and describes how to apply the transformation rules such that by the end of the learning process the ABA framework should satisfy the goal of ABA learning.

3 The ABALearn System Algorithm

To explore the potential of ABA learning, we introduce ABALearn, an automated logic-based learning system. Its algorithm is based on the proposed strategy in Fig. 1, by adjusting it such that termination is enforced and there are no arbitrary choices at any point in the learning process. The source code of the system is available on GitHub at https://github.com/CristinaGTW/ABALearn.

For this section, when we talk about coverage (and implicitly about completeness and consistency), we imply that it is meant under the grounded semantics.

Termination Condition. The system keeps repeating the iteration consisting of five steps until the resulting ABA framework is complete and consistent. It is worth mentioning that the completeness and consistency checks are carried out against the *initial* sets of examples.

Training Data Maintenance and Exceptional Termination. At the end of every iteration, part of the training data gets removed. However, we want to always keep the initial positive examples that are not yet covered and the initial negative examples that are covered. Thus, at the start of every iteration we ensure those are still in the training data, and, if they are not, we reintroduce them. At this stage, we must also verify if the algorithm should trigger an exceptional termination. The two situations that could trigger that are:

Input: Background knowledge: ABA framework $\langle \mathcal{R}, \mathcal{A}, \overline{} \rangle$
                Training data: $\mathcal{E}^+$ and $\mathcal{E}^-$, with $\mathcal{E}^+ \cap \mathcal{E}^- = \emptyset$
Strategy:
Repeat until $\langle \mathcal{R}, \mathcal{A}, \overline{} \rangle$ is both complete and consistent:
  ***Step 1** [Select target for current iteration]* Choose a predicate p such that $\exists c. \ p(c) \in E^+$;
  ***Step 2** [Generate rules for p]* For each example $p(c) \in \mathcal{E}^+$ apply `Rote Learning`;
  ***Step 3** [Generalise]* For each rule ρ in $\mathcal{R}$, perform one of the following:
  – Find rule ρ' that subsumes ρ and apply `Subsumption`;
  – Repeatedly apply `Folding` and then `Equality Removal` until all constants are removed from ρ;
  ***Step 4** [Learn exceptions]* Repeat until for all $p(d) \in \mathcal{E}^-$, $\langle \mathcal{R}, \mathcal{A}, \overline{} \rangle \not\models p(d)$:
  1. Select $p(d) \in \mathcal{E}^-$;
  2. Select from $\mathcal{R}$ a rule $\rho : \ p(X) \leftarrow Eqs, B$. (w.l.o.g. $X \subseteq vars(B)$) such that we can construct an argument for $p(d)$ with ρ as top rule;
  3. Construct a set $A = \{a_1(Y_1), ..., a_k(Y_k)\} \subseteq B$ that can generate two ground instances A^+ and A^- ($A^+ \cap A^- = \emptyset$) such that:
      (a) For every example $p(e) \in \mathcal{E}^+$, we can build an argument for $p(e)$ with ρ as top rule and the ground atoms in A^+ are children of $p(e)$;
      (b) For every example $p(e) \in \mathcal{E}^-$, we can build an argument for $p(e)$ with ρ as top rule and the ground atoms in A^- are children of $p(e)$;
  4. Apply `Assumption Introduction` by adding the (new) assumption $\alpha(Y_1, ..., Y_k)$ with contrary $c\_\alpha(Y_1, ..., Y_k)$ to the body of the rule ρ;
  5. Add $c\_\alpha(consts(A^+))$ to $\mathcal{E}^-$. Add $c\_\alpha(consts(A^-))$ to $\mathcal{E}^+$.
  ***Step 5** [Remove examples]* Remove all examples for predicate p from training data.

Fig. 1. ABA Learning Strategy Template

1. The algorithm has just completed re-targeting each possible predicate, and at no point throughout that run has the ABA framework been complete.
2. The target in the previous iteration was the goal predicate and, we have reintroduced all the examples we have removed at the end of the previous iteration.

Both cases indicate that the system will not be able to make any more progress towards achieving the goal, thus it stops the learning process here.

Step 1 - Target Selection. Each iteration requires a target predicate to learn. The program selects it by looking at the positive examples in the current training data and selecting the predicate for which it has the most examples as it should provide more opportunity for learning. The program also keeps track of all the predicates that have been targeted previously and avoids choosing them as long as it can (i.e. as long as there are positive examples for predicates that have not been targeted yet). If it cannot find an unused target, it will go through the list of already used ones in order.

Step 2 - Generating rules. This step is carried out in accordance with the indication in Fig. 1: the program applies `Rote Learning` for each positive example of the target predicate.

Step 3 - Generalising. The program goes through every rule in the background knowledge and if its head uses the target predicate, it finds all other rules it can be folded with. It ultimately performs the optimal folds based on the following criteria:

1. Minimises the number of introduced variables;
2. Favours double folding (i.e. it tries to fold the resulting rule of a fold with another rule, if it does not introduce any additional variables);
3. Maximisies the number of covered positive examples and the number of not covered negative examples.

The system removes all equalities from the resulting rules using `Equality Removal`. Finally, the program goes through every new rule and checks if it can find any that is subsumed, such that it can apply the `Subsumption` rule and remove it.

Step 4 - Learning Exceptions. The program finds the top rules of all the arguments that have as a claim a negative example of the target predicate. Then, for each of these rules it does the following:

1. It constructs the two sets of constants $consts(A^+)$ and $consts(A^-)$, as described in Fig. 1, by taking into consideration the variables of every atoms in the body of the current rule;
2. Performs `Assumption Introduction` on the current rule by introducing a new assumption α_0 with contrary c_α_0;
3. It checks if there is any previously introduced assumption α_1 with contrary c_α_1 for which the same sets $consts(A^+)$ and $consts(A^-)$ have been used, in which case it considers α_0 equivalent to α_1, and proceeds to replace α_0 with α_1;
4. If no equivalent assumption has been found, it adds examples for the contrary c_α_0 to the training data using the sets $consts(A^+)$ and $consts(A^-)$.

Step 5 - Removing Examples. The program goes through the training data and removes all the examples for the target predicate of the current iteration.

Simplifying the ABA Framework. After the system has exited the learning loop, it will try to simplify the resulting framework. To do this it attempts removing redundant assumptions and performing some additional `Folding`.

Enumeration. If the learning process was stopped before achieving completeness, it will perform `Rote Learning` for the initial positive examples that remained uncovered. This guarantees completeness through enumeration.

Force-Attack. If the learning process was stopped before achieving consistency, the system finds the initial negative examples that are still covered, along with the top rules of their arguments. Then, ABALearn applies `Rote Learning` on the contraries of the supporting assumptions of these arguments to give rise to attacks.

4   Explainability

Logic-based learners have the advantage of producing interpretable learning output. ABALearn, although it shares this attribute, for assumptions and their contraries, it generates uninterpretable identifiers (e.g. `alpha1(A)` and `c_alpha1(A)`), potentially hindering explainability. To address this, we propose choosing more suggestive names for the predicates generated by the system. Achieving this would require semantic prediction of exceptional scenarios. We have considered leveraging the capabilities of large language models[1]. To explore this idea further, we conducted a simple experiment using OpenAI's ChatGPT [10]. The following is a transcript of the experiment[2]:

   Q: *"Consider the following logic program:*
flies(X) ← bird(X), not c_alpha1(X)
c_alpha1(X) ← feathered(X), not c_alpha2(X)
c_alpha2(X) ← bird(X), not c_alpha3(X)
c_alpha3(X) ← brokenwings(X)
   Can you come up with more suggestive names for the predicates
c_alpha1, c_alpha2 and c_alpha3 such that the rules are more intuitive
for a human reading them?"
   A: *"Certainly! Here are some alternative names for the predicates*
c_alpha1, c_alpha2, and c_alpha3 that might make the rules more
intuitive:
flies(X) ← bird(X), not incapable(X)
incapable(X) ← feathered(X), not can_fly_well(X)
can_fly_well(X) ← bird(X), not injured(X)
injured(X) ← brokenwings(X)
With these alternative names, the rules become more human-readable
and easier to understand in terms of bird behavior and wing conditions."

   This outcome goes to show that there is potential in making use of readily available LLMs to mitigate the potential obstacles in logic-based learners' explainability. Implementing this would most likely make use of OpenAI's GPT-4 API. The API is (at the time of writing) yet to be released, therefore further work in this direction is not possible at the current time.

---

[1] A large language model (LLM) consists of an artificial neural network, trained on large quantities of text using self-supervised or semi-supervised learning.

[2] We provided ChatGPT with the equivalent logic program, given that it deals better with that, as it does not need to handle the concept of contraries.

5   Evaluation

There are no other argumentation system we can compare with and no other implementation of ABA learning. However, as discussed before, there is a mapping between logic programs and ABA frameworks. Additionally, there is a correspondence between grounded extensions and well-founded models, and between stable extensions and stable models. Therefore, we have chosen ILASP and FOLD-RM to evaluate against.

ILASP [11] is a system that learns answer set programs and to do that is mostly uses inductive logic programming techniques. FOLD-RM [12] is an algorithm that learns stratified logic programs. It was designed to be highly efficient and scalable, and it is concerned with multi-category classification tasks.

5.1   Ease of Use

Looking at the input required by each system, there are some significant differences. ABALearn only requires essential information about a learning task (background knowledge and training data, as in Example 5) and is even able to define the learning problem on its own from tabular data. ILASP requires similar information, but, in addition, it also needs to be provided with the mode bias (e.g. specifying which predicates can go in the head or body, as well as the number of occurrences allowed), which we would argue represents a higher amount of cognitive demand from the user. FOLD-RM also has high cognitive complexity, as the user has to modify the source code to map any input (restricted to tabular data only, and excluding in particular rich, rule-based background knowledge) it does not have already prepared into a suitable internal representation. Given these considerations, we would argue ABALearn is the easiest to set up and run in contexts where low user expertise is available.

5.2   Response Time and Scalability

We will look at the execution time[3] of all three systems for both small learning tasks with a more complex background knowledge from a structural point of view, and larger learning tasks with the background knowledge consisting of just facts.

Small Learning Tasks. For this category, we have run all three systems on the same set of simple inductive tasks[4]. The execution times are shown in Fig. 2. We notice that at this scale ABALearn is slightly faster than ILASP in all tasks. FOLD-RM outperforms both by a high margin.

---

[3] All learning processes on all systems have been run on the same machine with AMD Ryzen 7 3700U @ 2.3 GHz and 16 GB RAM.

[4] The ABALearn input files for these tasks are available on the GitHub repository.

Input	ABALearn	ILASP	FOLD-RM
flies_1	0.1	0.11	0.0003
flies_2	0.21	0.32	0.0007
flies_3	0.27	0.31	0.0004
path	0.1	0.51	N/A*
robber	0.07	0.1	0.0002
free	0.15	0.3	N/A*

* The background knowledge could not be represented as tabular data.

Fig. 2. Mean execution times (over 10 runs) in seconds on different inputs

Dataset	Input Data Shape		ABALearn Input		Execution time (seconds)		
	Rows	Columns	BK	E^+	ABALearn	ILASP	FOLD-RM
krkp	63	37	682	33	333.24	25.84	0.008
krkp	15	37	155	7	4.45	11.91	0.005
krkp	14	37	141	7	4.9	15.65	0.003
krkp	10	37	100	5	2.3	6.55	0.003
krkp	7	37	73	3	0.96	5.94	0.001
acute	60	6	154	31	30.36	0.12	0.002
acute	30	6	72	15	3.2	0.09	0.001
acute	20	6	57	11	1.65	0.09	0.001
acute	13	6	33	9	0.68	0.08	0.0003
acute	10	6	24	5	0.19	0.08	0.0007

Fig. 3. Mean execution times (over 5 runs) in seconds on different subsets of *krkp* and *acute* datasets 'Rows' and 'Columns' specify the number of rows and columns in the input CSV file; 'BK' and E^+ specify the number of facts in the background knowledge and the number of initial positive examples of the equivalent ABALearn learning task.

Learning Tasks from Non-noisy UCI Datasets. For this part of the evaluation we have picked a couple of UCI datasets (which are perfectly labelled) and pruned them in order to be able to create inputs for all three systems as fairly as possible. Thus, we have only kept columns containing discrete values and have picked different-sized subsets of the datasets. The results of this experiment can be seen in Fig. 3.

As the input size increases, it is interesting to observe how ILASP compares with ABALearn. We notice that for the *acute* dataset ILASP outperforms ABALearn in almost all subset sizes, with significant differences for the three largest subsets. However, for the *krkp* dataset, ABALearn outperforms ILASP up until a certain size. If we look at the structure of the two inputs we notice that the *acute* dataset only uses 5 predicates in the given background knowledge, while the *krkp* one uses 36. Therefore, although ABALearn does not generally scale well as the size of the input increases (in terms of number of rules in the background knowledge and number of positive examples), it does scale with the size of the language in the given background knowledge better than ILASP. FOLD-RM outperforms both by a high margin, as expected.

5.3   Reliability

By 'accuracy' in this section we mean the result of computing $(TruePositives + TrueNegatives) \div Number\ of\ examples$, where $TruePositives$ is the number of positive examples that can be inferred by the learned rules, and $TrueNegatives$ is the number of negative examples that cannot be inferred by the learned rules.

For this section, we have measured the accuracy of each solution for each system over 10 consecutive runs of the same input. The inputs used are the same as in the previous section (both the small examples and the UCI datasets). We can see the outcomes of a couple of the experiments in Fig. 4 where we have plotted the mean accuracy along with its standard deviation.

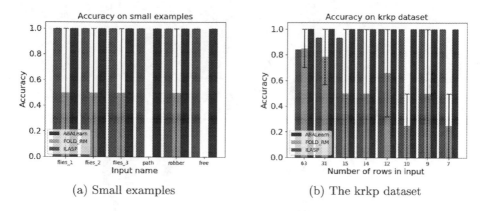

(a) Small examples   (b) The krkp dataset

Fig. 4. Accuracy measurements

We first observe both ABALearn and ILASP are deterministic, returning the same solution for the same input (thus a standard deviation of 0). On the other hand, FOLD-RM has very high standard deviations, even fluctuating from 0% to 100% accuracy for some inputs.

Another observation is that ABALearn managed to constantly achieve 100% accuracy across all runs. ILASP has achieved high accuracies as well, with 100% accuracy in most runs.

These measurements go to show that both ABALearn and ILASP are more reliable than FOLD-RM, in the sense that they return accurate solutions that are replicable.

5.4   Range of Applicability

Non-stratified, Circular Debates. One of the main advantages of ABALearn is that it manages to handle learning tasks that require to conduct circular debates. To illustrate consider the Nixon-diamond example [13]. For this learning task, ABALearn achieves its goal under *credulous* reasoning with this solution.

ILASP also manages to successfully learn rules to reason about this circular debate (but using ABALearn's solution as a basis for the mode bias).

For FOLD-RM, we gave it the equivalent input, using the same heuristics as in the small examples. It did not manage to learn any rule.

Handling Noise. For this aspect, we took a few of the tabular data inputs we used in Sects. 5.2 and 5.3 and introduced a few more duplicate rows with opposite labeling, which introduces noise given that identical properties result in different outcomes.

We will only compare ABALearn with FOLD-RM for this category[5].

To measure how well each system handles the noise, we looked again at accuracies. The results of the experiments can be seen in Figs. 5. We notice ABALearn generally achieves higher accuracies than FOLD-RM.

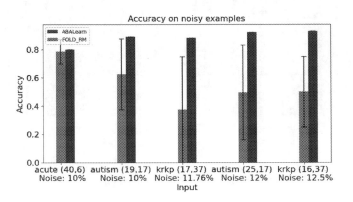

Fig. 5. Outcome of experiments with noisy inputs

6   Conclusion

We have introduced a novel system, called ABALearn, that implements an algo-rithm for learning ABA frameworks by extending the knowledge through trans-formation rules. We have explored the idea of integrating our system with LLMs to improve its explainability. We have conducted both observational and empir-ical evaluation, which prove the potential of ABALearn, but also acknowledge its limitations.

Overall, this report has brought significant insights into the potential of ABA learning and, more generally, of XAI. The development of ABALearn represents more exciting proof that we can closely model human-like methods of logical

---

[5] While we know that ILASP is capable of handling noise, the heuristics of generating equivalent inputs would have resulted in too much overhead for our aims.

reasoning, which shows that computational argumentation is truly powerful. While there are still undeniable limitations to our algorithm, we believe that there are good prospects that, with more research and development, it can have real-life applications under reasonable ethical considerations.

Future Work. While we did manage to make significant progress in coming up with an implementation of the proposed learning strategy for ABA frameworks, there are still improvements that can be made. The first one would be to improve the coverage checker. The current coverage checker is a prototype of a Python implementation, which is more scalable than an alternative Prolog one, but it does have a lot of limitations in terms of complexity of the rules it can deal with. Then, we also believe that there are optimisations that can be done to increase scalability. More specifically, the current bottleneck is in the generalising step of the learning process where we try to find the optimal folds to perform. Then, on the more technical side, the software is not currently packaged, so it requires some more work on that side in order to reach a releasable state. Lastly, it would be very exciting to implement the integration with LLMs.

Acknowledgements. We thank the support from the Royal Society, UK (IEC \ R2 \ 222045 - International Exchanges 2022). Proietti is a member of the INDAM-GNCS research group. Toni was partially funded by the ERC under the EU's Horizon 2020 research and innovation programme (grant agreement No. 101020934) and by J.P. Morgan and the Royal Academy of Engineering, UK, under the Research Chairs and Senior Research Fellowships scheme.

References

1. Atkinson, K., et al.: Towards artificial argumentation. AI Mag. **38**(3), 25–36 (2017). https://doi.org/10.1609/aimag.v38i3.2704
2. Cyras, K., Rago, A., Albini, E., Baroni, P., Toni, F.: Argumentative XAI: a survey. In: Zhou, Z.: Proceedings of the Thirtieth International Joint Conference on Artificial Intelligence, IJCAI 2021, Virtual Event/Montreal, Canada, 19–27 August 2021, pp. 4392–4399. ijcai.org. (2021). https://doi.org/10.24963/ijcai.2021/600
3. Law, M., Russo, A., Broda, K.: Logic-based learning of answer set programs. In: Krötzsch, M., Stepanova, D. (eds.) Reasoning Web. Explainable Artificial Intelligence. LNCS, vol. 11810, pp. 196–231. Springer, Cham (2019). https://doi.org/10.1007/978-3-030-31423-1_6
4. Cyras, K., Fan, X., Schulz, C., Toni, F.: Assumption-based argumentation: disputes, explanations, preferences. In: FLAP, vol. 4, no. 8 (2017). http://www.collegepublications.co.uk/downloads/ifcolog00017.pdf
5. Proietti, M., Toni, F.: Learning assumption-based argumentation frameworks. In: Proceedings of ILP 2022, LNCS. Springer, Heidelberg (2023). DOI: https://doi.org/10.48550/arXiv.2305.15921
6. Dung, P.M., Kowalski, R.A., Toni, F.: Assumption-based argumentation. In: Simari, G., Rahwan, I. (eds.) Argumentation in Artificial Intelligence, pp. 199–218. Springer, Boston (2009). https://doi.org/10.1007/978-0-387-98197-0_10
7. Fan, X., Toni, F.: A general framework for sound assumption-based argumentation dialogues. Artif. Intell. **216**, 20–54 (2014). https://doi.org/10.1016/j.artint.2014.06.001

 8. Toni, F.: A tutorial on assumption-based argumentation. Argument Comput. **5**(1), 89–117 (2014). https://doi.org/10.1080/19462166.2013.869878
 9. Bondarenko, A., Dung, P.M., Kowalski, R.A., Toni, F.: An abstract, argumentation-theoretic approach to default reasoning. Artif. Intell. **93**, 63–101 (1997). https://doi.org/10.1016/S0004-3702(97)00015-5
10. OpenAI. ChatGPT (May 24 Version) [Large Language Model] - personal communication (2023). https://chat.openai.com
11. Law, M., Russo, A., Broda, K.: The ILASP system for inductive learning of answer set programs. CoRR, vol. abs/2005.00904 (2020). https://arxiv.org/abs/2005.00904
12. Wang, H., Shakerin, F., Gupta, G.: FOLD-RM: a scalable, efficient, and explainable inductive learning algorithm for multi-category classification of mixed data. Theory Pract. Log. Program. **22**(5), 658–677 (2022). https://doi.org/10.1017/S1471068422000205
13. Reiter, R., Criscuolo, G.: On interacting defaults. In: Hayes, P.J. (ed.) Proceedings of the 7th International Joint Conference on Artificial Intelligence, IJCAI 1981, Vancouver, BC, Canada, 24–28 August 1981, pp. 270–276. William Kaufmann (1981). http://ijcai.org/Proceedings/81-1/Papers/054.pdf

Deriving Dependency Graphs from Abstract Argumentation Frameworks

Stefano Bistarelli[ID] and Carlo Taticchi[✉][ID]

Department of Mathematics and Computer Science, University of Perugia,
Perugia, Italy
{stefano.bistarelli,carlo.taticchi}@unipg.it

Abstract. Abstract Argumentation Frameworks (AFs) are used, in the field of Artificial Intelligence, to evaluate the justification state of conflicting information, thus allowing the development of automatic reasoning techniques and systems. Complex argumentative processes such as decision-making and negotiation, which take place over time, can be modelled through the Concurrent Language for Argumentation, a formalism for handling concurrent interactions between intelligent agents that use an AF as shared memory. In this paper, we first show how AFs can be interpreted as dependency graphs by exploiting the relation between arguments induced by the attacks. Then, we describe a methodology for obtaining a procedure that generates the given AF. Such a procedure allows to dynamically represent dialogues and other forms of interaction that brought to the instantiation of the specified AF.

1 Introduction

Applications that make use of artificial intelligence techniques provide results that do not always appear clear and credible, thus decreasing the trust that users place in them. Providing convincing explanations on how and why a certain result was achieved has therefore become of fundamental importance, especially in critical contexts such as health and finance. Argumentation Theory [9] deals with the problem of representing and reasoning with conflicting information. In this context, Argumentation Frameworks constitute the basic tool for studying complex phenomena like the cognitive processes through which humans draw conclusions from a set of premises. The logic underlying the single arguments is neglected in Abstract Argumentation Frameworks (AFs) [8], which can be represented as directed graphs where nodes and edges are interpreted as arguments and attacks, respectively. On the one hand, abstracting the internal structure of arguments entails the possibility of automating tasks such as the selection of acceptable conclusions. On the other hand, AFs only provide information regarding the relations between arguments, and not about the arguments themselves. This limits the understanding we can have of the argumentative process which leads to the instantiation of a given AF, an understanding that is crucial for achieving real-world results [11].

© The Author(s), under exclusive license to Springer Nature Switzerland AG 2023
R. Basili et al. (Eds.): AIxIA 2023, LNAI 14318, pp. 17–29, 2023.
https://doi.org/10.1007/978-3-031-47546-7_2

The purpose of this paper is twofold. Firstly, we interpret argumentation frameworks (AFs) as dependency graphs by examining the dependency relation between the arguments induced by attacks. Attacking arguments will depend on the attacked ones. This approach helps us understand the evolution of AFs and determine the order in which arguments are presented, to gain insight into the instantiation process of the AF itself. Secondly, we show how AFs can be generated using the Concurrent Language for Argumentation (CLA). This language enables intelligent agents to interact, communicate, and reason through a shared AF. This work is a continuation of a preliminary study conducted in [5] that was limited to acyclic graphs. Acyclic AFs closely represent dependency graphs, where a correct evaluation order for the elements can always be found. However, it is not possible to straightforwardly study the dependency between arguments when cycles are present in the topology under consideration. Also, notice that the same AF can have many correct evaluation orders. The program we provide in the CLA language represents all the possible "correct" evaluation orders.

2 Preliminaries

In this section, we briefly recall the fundamental notions of AFs and argumentation semantics, together with (part of) the CLA syntax and operational semantics that we use for deriving our procedure.

2.1 Computational Argumentation

Argumentation Theory aims at understanding and modelling the natural human fashion of reasoning, allowing one to deal with uncertainty in non-monotonic (defeasible) reasoning. In his seminal paper [8], Dung defines the building blocks of abstract argumentation.

Definition 1 (AFs). *An Abstract Argumentation Framework is a pair $\langle Arg, R \rangle$ where Arg is a finite set of arguments and R is a binary relation on Arg.*

For two arguments $a, b \in Arg$, the notation $(a, b) \in R$ represents an attack from a against b. Moreover, we denote as a^+ and a^- the sets of arguments that respectively are attacked by and attack a. Given an AF, we want to identify subsets of *acceptable* arguments which are selected by applying criteria called argumentation semantics. Non-accepted arguments are rejected. Different kinds of semantics have been introduced that reflect desirable qualities for sets of arguments. Among the most studied ones, we find the admissible, complete, stable, semi-stable, preferred, and grounded semantics [1,8] (denoted with *adm*, *com*, *stb*, *sst*, *prf* and *gde*, respectively). To operatively find acceptable arguments, we can resort to labelling-based semantics [7], an approach that associates with an AF a subset of all the possible labellings.

Definition 2 (Labelling). *A labelling of an AF $F = \langle Arg, R \rangle$ is a total function $L : Arg \rightarrow \{\mathsf{in}, \mathsf{out}, \mathsf{undec}\}$. Moreover, L is an admissible labelling for F when $\forall a \in Arg$*

- $L(a) = $ in $\implies \forall b \in Arg \mid (b,a) \in R.L(b) = $ out;
- $L(a) = $ out $\iff \exists b \in Arg \mid (b,a) \in R \wedge L(b) = $ in.

In other words, an argument is labelled in only if all its attackers are labelled out, and it is labelled out when at least one in node attacks it. In all other cases, the argument is labelled undec. In particular, in arguments are acceptable, while the others will be rejected. Similar criteria to that shown in Definition 2 can be used to capture other semantics [7].

2.2   Concurrent Language for Argumentation

The Concurrent Language for Argumentation (CLA) [3,4,6] is a framework for modelling concurrent interactions between agents that reason and take decisions through argumentation processes. Agents communicating through CLA constructs share a knowledge base, represented by an AF, to perform reasoning tasks. This shared store can be accessed and updated by the various agents via specifically designed operators that are also able to change the underlying AF. We refer the reader to [3,6] for a complete overview of the language.

A shortened version of the syntax is presented in Table 1: P denotes a generic process, C a sequence of clauses, A is a generic agent and E a generic guarded agent. In a CLA process $P = C.A$, A is the initial agent to be executed in the context of the set of declarations C. The operational model of P can be formally described by a transition system $T = (Conf, \rightarrow)$, where $Conf$ is a pair consisting of a process and an AF $F = \langle Arg, R \rangle$ representing the common knowledge base.

Table 1. Part of CLA syntax

$$P ::= C.A$$
$$C ::= p(x) :: A \mid C.C$$
$$A ::= success \mid add(Arg, R) \rightarrow A \mid E \mid A \| A$$
$$E ::= check^w(Arg, R) \rightarrow A \mid E + E$$

In Table 2, then, we give the definitions for the transition rules of addition (Add), check with waiting (Chw), parallelism (Par) and nondeterminism (Ndt) operators. The transition relation $\rightarrow \subseteq Conf \times Conf$ is the least relation satisfying those rules, and it characterises the system's evolution. In particular, $\langle A, F \rangle \rightarrow \langle A', F' \rangle$ represents a transition from a state in which we have the process $P = C.A$ and the AF F to a state in which we have the process $P = C.A'$ and the AF F'. An $add(Arg', R')$ results in the addition of a set of arguments Arg' and a set of attacks R' into the shared memory. The operation $check^w(Arg', R')$ is used to verify whether the specified arguments and attacks are contained in the knowledge base, without introducing any further change. If the check is positive, the operation succeeds; otherwise, it suspends. The parallel operator $\|$ enables the specification of concurrent agents following the interleaving approach. This means that only one action is executed at a time in accordance with a scheduling imposed by the processor. $A_1 \| A_2$ results in two possible outcomes: it succeeds when both actions succeed and suspends otherwise. Finally, any agent composed through nondeterminism (+ operator) is chosen if its guards succeed. In detail, a guarded agent E_1 transits to agent A_1 whenever it can do so (first rule for (Ndt)); otherwise, both guarded agents are sent one step forward (second rule for (Ndt)). Indeed, a guarded agent can be followed by more guarded agents, all of whom must be satisfied for the operation to succeed. Until E_1 transits to A_1 (or E_2 to E_2), both guarded agents are run simultaneously to ensure true concurrency during execution.

Table 2. CLA operational semantics: add, check and parallel operators

$$\langle add(Arg', R') \to A, \langle Arg, R \rangle \rangle \longrightarrow \langle A, \langle Arg \cup Arg', R \cup R'' \rangle \rangle \qquad \text{Add}$$
$$\text{with } R'' = \{(a,b) \in R' \mid a, b \in Arg \cup Arg'\}$$

$$\frac{Arg' \subseteq Arg \wedge R' \subseteq R}{\langle check^w(Arg', R') \to A, \langle Arg, R \rangle \rangle \longrightarrow \langle A, \langle Arg, R \rangle \rangle} \qquad \text{Chw}$$

$$\frac{\langle A_1, F \rangle \longrightarrow \langle A_1', F' \rangle}{\langle A_1 \| A_2, F \rangle \longrightarrow \langle A_1' \| A_2, F' \rangle} \qquad \frac{\langle A_1, F \rangle \longrightarrow \langle success, F' \rangle}{\langle A_1 \| A_2, F \rangle \longrightarrow \langle A_2, F' \rangle} \qquad \text{Par}$$
$$\langle A_2 \| A_1, F \rangle \longrightarrow \langle A_2 \| A_1', F' \rangle \qquad \langle A_2 \| A_1, F \rangle \longrightarrow \langle A_2, F' \rangle$$

$$\frac{\langle E_1, F \rangle \longrightarrow \langle A_1, F \rangle}{\langle E_1 + E_2, F \rangle \longrightarrow \langle A_1, F \rangle} \qquad \frac{\langle E_1, F \rangle \longrightarrow \langle E_1', F \rangle, \langle E_2, F \rangle \longrightarrow \langle E_2', F \rangle}{\langle E_1 + E_2, F \rangle \longrightarrow \langle E_1' + E_2', F \rangle} \qquad \text{Ndt}$$
$$\langle E_2 + E_1, F \rangle \longrightarrow \langle A_1, F \rangle$$

A web interface running a CLA interpreter [4] is also available.[1] To comply with the syntax of the tool, we will denote $check^w(Arg, R)$ by checkw(Arg,R) and $E + \cdots + E$ by sum(E,...,E).

3   AFs as Dependency Graphs

Attacks between arguments model conflicts in AFs and establish a dependency relationship between the arguments themselves. Consider an AF $F = \langle Arg, R \rangle$ with two arguments $a, b \in Arg$ and the attack relation $(b, a) \in R$. We interpret this attack as a conflict between the two arguments, knowing that b is the argument starting the attack on a. It is reasonable to assume that b is introduced into the framework to contrast argument a and undermine its validity. If a was not already in the framework, then there would have been no reason for adding b. Therefore, we can identify a dependency relation between a and b. In our example, the existence of a is preliminary to that of b, so we can say that b depends on a.

---

[1]   CLA web interface: https://conarg.dmi.unipg.it/cla/.

Following these considerations, an AF can be interpreted as a **dependency graph**, i.e. a directed graph representing the dependencies of various elements (in our case, arguments). A dependency graph is a couple $D = (S, T)$ where S is a set of elements and T is the transitive reduction of a relation $R \subseteq S \times S$. In a dependency graph, one can look for an *evaluation order* respecting the given dependencies. A correct evaluation order is a numbering that orders two elements a and b in such a way that if a is evaluated before b, then a must not depend on b.

Definition 3 (Correct Evaluation Order). *Let $G = (S, R)$ be an acyclic graph where S is a set of nodes and $R \subseteq S \times S$ a set of edges. A correct evaluation order for G is a numbering $n : S \to \mathbb{N}$ such that $\forall a, b \in S$ the following holds: $n(a) < n(b) \Rightarrow (a, b) \notin R$.*

For example, the element corresponding to argument a in Fig. 1 should come before b and c in a correct evaluation order, while b should come before d and after both a and c.

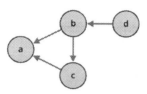

Fig. 1. Example of a directed graph that can be interpreted both as an AF and a dependency graph. Edges obtainable by transitive closure are not represented.

Finding a correct evaluation order for a dependency graph amounts to reconstructing the reasoning process that leads to the generation of an AF superseding the same graph. Indeed, AFs represent conflicting information and can be seen as the instantiation of an argumentative process between intelligent agents. In the real world, such processes take place over time and can be imagined as a succession of statements made by one or more counterparties, with the various statements referring to (attacking) each other. However, a correct evaluation order cannot be found when the graph has cycles of dependencies (also called *circular dependencies*) since none of the objects in the cycle can be evaluated first. Figure 2 shows an example of circular dependencies generated by arguments b, c and d, which are in a cycle. Although we cannot determine which elements involved in the cycle should be presented first, we can still argue that a should come before b and d before e, just by looking at the edges between them.

To solve the undecidability induced by the presence of cycles in the graph, we propose to treat any cycle as an agglomeration of nodes whose internal order cannot be evaluated and for which only connections with adjacent nodes are taken into account. Referring again to the graph in Fig. 2, we want to obtain an evaluation order such that b, c and d come after a and before e, while the order

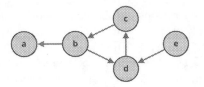

Fig. 2. Example of an AF containing a cycle.

between the arguments in the cycle is not influential (any of the six permutations of (b, c, d) can be used). We call this ordering a *feasible evaluation order*.

Definition 4 (Feasible Evaluation Order). *Given a graph $G = (S, R)$, we call cycle any subset of S whose elements form a cycle in G. Then, we denote with Cycles(G) the set of all cycles in G, and with $CiDep(a) = \{c \in S \mid \exists Cycle \in Cycles(G).a, c \in Cycle\}$ the set of nodes in circular dependences with a. A feasible evaluation order for the graph G is a numbering $n : S \to \mathbb{N}$ such that $\forall a, b \in S \mid a \notin CiDep(b)$ the following holds: $\forall \overline{a} \in \{a\} \cup CiDep(a), \overline{b} \in \{b\} \cup CiDep(b).n(a) < n(b) \Rightarrow (\overline{a}, \overline{b}) \notin R$.*

Proposition 1. *A feasible evaluation order for an acyclic graph G is a correct evaluation order for G.*

Proof. Follows from Definitions 3 and 4, observing that for any node a belonging to an acyclic graph, $CiDep(a) = \emptyset$.

We can verify that (a, b, c, d, e) and (a, c, b, d, e) are feasible evaluation orders for the graph of Fig. 2. In the next section, we show how an AF can be generated through a CLA procedure which adds arguments (and the associated attacks) following a feasible evaluation order.

4   A CLA Program for Building AFs

Our goal is to obtain a CLA procedure able to manipulate the shared store in such a way to obtain a desired AF. We also want to respect the constraints on the order in which arguments and attacks can be introduced. It is natural to think that a dialogue between intelligent agents is initiated by one of the counterparts with the assertion of an argument. This first argument can be then attacked by other, freshly introduced arguments, also giving a sense of temporal execution of actions by the agents. The sequence of actions (addition of arguments and attacks) performed to generate the AF will be described by our CLA procedure.

Consider, for example, the AF F in Fig. 2. Starting from an empty AF $G = \langle \emptyset, \emptyset \rangle$, we want to obtain a framework identical to F by gradually adding arguments and attacks in an order respecting the dependency relationship. In our example, we want to add argument a first since it is the only one that does not attack any others and can be seen as the starting point of the debate. Once a has been added, we realise that no other argument of the AF in Fig. 2 can be inserted in the framework under construction: b would require both a and d to be already in G, c and d requires b and c, respectively, and e depends on d. The source of the problem is the cycle formed by arguments b, c and d, which makes it impossible to establish an order for adding those arguments. To overcome this inconvenience, we select one of the three arguments through a nondeterministic choice and add it to G. We apply this technique also when the underlying graph has no leaf node (i.e. a node with no outgoing edges) because all the arguments in the AF are involved in some cycle. In our example, adding any argument among b, c and d allows us to resume the construction of G. For instance, if we choose to add b, then also c can be inserted, together with the attack (c, b). Next, we can add d and (d, c) since we know that c is already in G. At any moment after the addition of d, we can also add the attacks (b, a) and (b, d). Indeed, since b was inserted before d to break the cycle, we could not add all its outgoing attacks. Last, we insert e and the attack (e, d). At this point, G corresponds to the AF F we wanted to build. The sequence (a, b, c, d, e) of arguments added in G is a feasible evaluation order. In fact, even if we cannot determine which among b, c and d needs to come first, we know that a must be considered before b, c and d, while e must be considered after b, c and d.

The sequence of arguments and attacks additions described in the example above can be obtained as the output of the CLA procedure given in Listing 1.

```
1    add({a},{}) -> success ||
2    checkw({a,d},{}) -> add({b},{(b,a),(b,d)}) -> success ||
3    checkw({b},{}) -> add({c},{(c,b)}) -> success ||
4    checkw({c},{}) -> add({d},{(d,c)}) -> success ||
5    checkw({b,c,d},{}) -> add({e},{(e,d)}) -> success ||
6    sum(checkw({a},{}) -> add({b},{}) -> success,
7        checkw({a},{}) -> add({c},{}) -> success,
8        checkw({a},{}) -> add({d},{}) -> success);
```

Listing 1. CLA program for the AF of Figure 1.

From line 1 to 5, we add in parallel, one by one, all the arguments of F, together with their outgoing attacks. For instance, add(b,(b,a),(b,d)) adds to the shared store G the argument b and the attacks (b, a) and (b, d). Before the addition of an argument, we check that all the arguments it attacks are already in the framework. For example, before adding b, we execute checkw(a,d,). Since e attacks an argument in a cycle (namely, d), we also need to check if all the other arguments in the cycle are already in G (thus obtaining checkw(b,c,d,)). Note that the check is not required in case of no outgoing attacks, as happens for argument a at line 1. Finally, to break any possible cycle that would prevent the check conditions from ever being satisfied, we use the operator sum for making a nondeterministic choice among arguments b (line 6), c (line 7) and d (line 8). Since argument b, within the cycle, attacks a, we want a to be present in G before adding any argument among b, c and d. The sum operation is executed in parallel with all the other branches of lines 1–5 so that the program always terminates.

Algorithm 1: generate CLA program from AF

Data: AF $F = \langle Arg, R \rangle$
Result: string S

```
1  procedure gen_cla_prog(F):
2  │   S = ""
3  │   Cycles = find_cycles(F)                      // Cycles: set of cycles
4  │   foreach a in Arg do
5  │   │   if a is not the first element in Arg then
6  │   │   │   S = S + " || "
7  │   │   Dep = find_dep(Cycles, a)                 // Dep: set of arguments
8  │   │   S = S + "checkw(Dep, {}) -> "
9  │   │   S = S + "add({a}, {(a,b) | b ∈ a⁺}) -> "
10 │   │   S = S + "success"
11 │   foreach Cycle in Cycles do                    // Cycle: set of arguments
12 │   │   S = S + " || sum("
13 │   │   Cat = find_cat(Cycles, Cycle)            // Cat: set of arguments
14 │   │   foreach a in Cycle do
15 │   │   │   if a is not the first element in Cycle then
16 │   │   │   │   S = S + ", "
17 │   │   │   S = S + "checkw(Cat, {}) -> "
18 │   │   │   S = S + "add({a}, {}) -> "
19 │   │   │   S = S + "success"
20 │   │   S = S + ")"
21 │   S = S + ";"
```

In lines 8 and 9, the superscript appears as a^+.

In the following, we provide a procedure for automatically obtaining a CLA program that builds an AF taking into account a feasible evaluation order derived from attack relations. The procedure is illustrated in Algorithm 1.   Our input is an AF $F = \langle Arg, R \rangle$, while the output is a string corresponding to a CLA program. In the procedure gen_cla_prog, we first initialise an empty string S (line 2), and then we execute a subroutine find_cycles that returns a set of cycles with no permutations (line 3). We exclude permutations since we are only interested in identifying sets of arguments forming a cycle and not in the order in which they appear in the cycle. For instance, we do not need to distinguish the permutation (a, b, c) from (a, c, b). In lines 4–10, we generate the CLA code to add all arguments and attacks of F in the (initially empty) shared store. To ensure that each argument is inserted in respect of its dependencies, we resort to the procedure find_dep of line 7 that, given an argument a, returns a set of arguments Dep that must be added before a. This procedure is defined in Algorithm 2, and further details on its functioning will be provided later in this section. At line 8, we generate a check operation based on the set Dep, followed at line 9 by the addition of a and its attacks. If F is acyclic, the gen_cla_prog procedure terminates, and the resulting string is a correct CLA program. Otherwise, the case in which F contains cycles is handled in the remaining lines from 11 to 20. For each cycle $Cycle$ of F (line 11), we build a nondeterministic choice composed of

---

Algorithm 2: find argument dependencies

Data: set of cycles *Cycles*, argument a
Result: set of arguments *Dep*
1 **procedure** find_dep(*Cycles, a*):
2    $Dep = a^+$
3   **foreach** b *in* a^+ **do**
4   **if** $\nexists\ C$ *in Cycles* $|\ a, b \in C$ **then**
5   **foreach** *Cycle in Cycles* $|\ b \in Cycle$ **do**
6   **foreach** c *in Cycle* **do**
7            $Dep = Dep \cup \{c\}$

Algorithm 3: find cycle attacks

Data: set of cycles *Cycles*, set of arguments *Cycle*
Result: set of arguments *Cat*
1 **procedure** find_cat(*Cycles, Cycle*):
2    $Cat = \{\}$
3   **foreach** a *in Cycle* **do**
4   **foreach** b *in* a^+ **do**
5   **if** $\nexists\ C$ *in Cycles* $|\ a, b \in C$ **then**
6          $Cat = Cat \cup \{b\}$

---

the keyword "sum" (line 12) and a list of check and add operations. To ensure that arguments added in this way retain dependencies from other arguments outside the cycle, we execute the procedure find_cat of line 13. This procedure, described in Algorithm 3, returns the set *Cat* used at line 17 to generate the check operations preceding the additions.

Algorithm 2 describes the procedure we use to find the set of arguments on which a given argument a depends. We begin by initialising a set *Dep* with the arguments attacked by a (line 2). Then we look for any argument b attacked by a (line 3) which is not in a cycle with a (line 4), and we add to *Dep* all the arguments belonging to the same cycles as b (lines 5–7).

If an argument a in a cycle *Cycle* attacks another argument b which is in turn not part of the same cycle, we want b to be added before any other argument in *Cycle*. Algorithm 3 takes in input the set of all cycles of F and a cycle *Cycle*.

In the procedure find_cat, we initialise an empty set *Cat* and then, for all arguments a in *Cycle*, we go through the list of arguments b attacked by a. If no cycle exists containing both a and b, then we add b to the set *Cat*. In this case, we do not want to check if other arguments of the cycle have already been added before a because it would cause the CLA program to never terminate.

The program obtained as the result of Algorithm 1 lets us manipulate the shared store between CLA agents to shape it into a desired AF. In doing so, arguments are added considering the dependency relations derived by attacks in the framework, and respecting, in particular, a feasible evaluation order. Since the program includes nondeterministic operations, more than one distinct execution can be obtained, giving rise to different orderings for adding arguments. These orderings represent feasible evaluation orders for arguments in F.

Theorem 1. *Let $F = \langle Arg, R \rangle$ be an AF. The* CLA *program returned as output by the procedure* **gen_cla_prog**(F) *satisfies the following properties:*

1. *the program terminates;*
2. *the shared store obtained at the end of the execution corresponds to F;*
3. *arguments are added into the store in a feasible evaluation order.*

Proof. Below is the proof for all the properties listed above.

1. We use four kinds of operations: addition, check, parallelism and non-determinism. Among them, only the check can suspend the execution until its condition is satisfied. Hence, for the program to terminate, all the checks need their conditions to eventually become true. At line 8 of Algorithm 1, we resort to check operation to ensure that an argument a is only inserted after all arguments in Dep, which includes: i) all arguments b attacked by a and ii) all arguments c in the same cycle of b and not in the same cycle of a. If a and any c appear together in a cycle, the operation $checkw(Dep, \{\})$ would suspend. To prevent this behaviour, we add in separate parallel branches (which are executed regardless of the success of the operation above) one argument from each cycle (Algorithm 1, lines 11–20). The addition of those arguments is, in turn, regulated by another check operation (Algorithm 1, line 17), this time only accounting for attacked arguments outside the cycle. Therefore, the condition on every check will eventually be satisfied, and the program will always terminate.

2. The program adds all arguments of F into the shared store, together with their outgoing attacks (Algorithm 1, line 9). Following property 1, the program always terminates, implying the execution of all these parallel additions. Note that an argument a can be considered in more than one add operation, for instance, those in lines 9 and 18 of Algorithm 1 if a belongs to a cycle. However, the store will never contain duplicates since the CLA addition exploits the set union, as shown in Table 2.

3. Suppose that the sequence of additions executed by the program does not follow a feasible evaluation order for F. In this case, referring to Definition 4, we should find two arguments a and b with $a \notin CiDep(b)$ and $n(a) < n(b)$ for which $\exists \overline{a} \in \{a\} \cup CiDep(a), \overline{b} \in \{b\} \cup CiDep(b) \mid (\overline{a}, \overline{b}) \in R$. Four cases arises: i) a attacks b; ii) a attacks another argument in the circular dependences of b; iii) an argument in the circular dependences of a attacks b; iv) an argument in the circular dependences of a attacks another argument in the circular dependences of b. In all this cases, both check operations in lines 8 and 17 of Algorithm 1 would prevent adding a before b. Therefore, we reach a contradiction and the program adds arguments in a feasible evaluation order.

After running the CLA procedure generating a given AF F, we can read the execution trace (the ordered set of operations produced during the execution of the program) to analyse the argumentative process that leads to the instantiation of F. For example, a possible trace produced by executing the program in

Listing 1 contains, besides the various checks, addition operations in the following order: add({a},{}), add({b},{}), add({c},{(c,b)}), add({d},{(d,c)}), add({b},{(b,a),(b,d)}), add({e},{(e,d)}). We remark that different traces can be obtained according to how the nondeterministic choice between arguments in the cycle (b, d, c) is made, and how the interleaving parallelism is handled by the processor.[2] The trace reported above contains information regarding the temporal development of the AF. We can see, for instance, that argument c is inserted after b and before d, while e is the last proposed in the framework. With this knowledge, we can study the AF during its evolution, that is, while the underlying debate takes place.

5   Discussion

We studied AFs from the perspective of dependency between arguments. First, we showed how dependency can be derived from the attack relations, allowing us to interpret an AF as a dependency graph in which arguments depend on those they attack. Second, we resorted to CLA constructs for obtaining a program which generates a desired AF. By reading the trace of the CLA program, it is possible to study the AF's evolution and explain why a specific argument was introduced.

In the future, we plan to extend this study in several directions. The traces of the program we generate can be used to extract explanation trees from AFs. For example, considering the feasible evaluation order (a, b, c, d, e), which leads to the construction of the AF in Fig. 3, we are able to break the cycle b, d, c by removing the attack (b, d) and thus find an explanation for the justification state of argument a, which is reinstated by e.

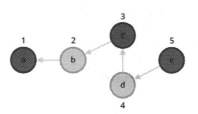

Fig. 3. Example of explanation tree obtained from the program in Listing 1. The arguments are highlighted according to a grounded labelling: the green arguments are labelled in and the red out (Color figure online).

The procedure we defined for generating AFs through CLA constructs can be optimised to avoid the execution of non-functional operations, such as the

---

[2] An alternative option is to use maximum parallelism [6], for which processes composed through ‖ are executed at the same time. However, this approach may result in the numbering assigned to arguments by the feasible evaluation order not being unique.

redundant addition of certain arguments. These operations have no effect but do impact the execution time of the program, especially for frameworks with many cycles. Contextually, we want to provide a working implementation and a formal analysis of the computational cost for the generating algorithm. By the rules of CLA, we only add an attack if both arguments involved are present in the AF. To deal with practical cases, however, it may be useful to consider hidden attacks in the manner of [2], where it is assumed that attacks are explicitly added between visible arguments at the time an argument is added. In the future, we also want to study this possibility and integrate it into the rules of the language. We also plan to investigate other models for concurrent execution (like Petri nets) to study how argumentative processes can be represented and interpreted to extract meaningful information. Then, we want to study dependency in more general frameworks, including, for instance, those where multiple arguments must be combined to undermine the validity of another [10]. Finally, it would be interesting to conduct a comparative study with existing approaches for the computation of argumentation semantics in order to understand the connections between the traces we obtain and the notion of acceptability.

Acknowledgments. Stefano Bistarelli and Carlo Taticchi are members of the INdAM Research group GNCS and Consorzio CINI. This work has been partially supported by: INdAM - GNCS Project, CUP E53C22001930001; Project FICO, funded by Ricerca di Base 2021, University of Perugia; Project GIUSTIZIA AGILE, CUP J89J22000900005; Project BLOCKCHAIN4FOODCHAIN, funded by Ricerca di Base 2020, University of Perugia; Project VITALITY, CUP J97G22000170005, funded by NRRP-MUR.

References

1. Baroni, P., Caminada, M., Giacomin, M.: An introduction to argumentation semantics. Knowl. Eng. Rev. **26**(4), 365–410 (2011). https://doi.org/10.1017/S0269888911000166
2. Baumann, R., Dvořák, W., Linsbichler, T., Spanring, C., Strass, H., Woltran, S.: On rejected arguments and implicit conflicts: The hidden power of argumentation semantics. Artif. Intell. **241**, 244–284 (2016)
3. Bistarelli, S., Taticchi, C.: A concurrent language for argumentation. In: Fazzinga, B., Furfaro, F., Parisi, F. (eds.) Proceedings of the Workshop on Advances in Argumentation in Artificial Intelligence 2020 co-located with the 19th International Conference of the Italian Association for Artificial Intelligence (AIxIA 2020), Online, November 25–26, 2020. CEUR Workshop Proceedings, vol. 2777, pp. 75–89. CEUR-WS.org (2020). http://ceur-ws.org/Vol-2777/paper67.pdf
4. Bistarelli, S., Taticchi, C.: Introducing a tool for concurrent argumentation. In: Faber, W., Friedrich, G., Gebser, M., Morak, M. (eds.) JELIA 2021. LNCS (LNAI), vol. 12678, pp. 18–24. Springer, Cham (2021). https://doi.org/10.1007/978-3-030-75775-5_2
5. Bistarelli, S., Taticchi, C.: Deriving dependency graphs from abstract argumentation frameworks: a preliminary report. In: Confalonieri, R., Porello, D. (eds.) Proceedings of the 6th Workshop on Advances in Argumentation in Artificial Intelligence 2022 co-located with the 21st International Conference of the Italian Association for Artificial Intelligence (AIxIA 2022), Udine, Italy, November 28, 2022.

CEUR Workshop Proceedings, vol. 3354. CEUR-WS.org (2022). https://ceur-ws. org/Vol-3354/short6.pdf
6. Bistarelli, S., Taticchi, C.: A concurrent language for modelling arguing agents. Argument & Computation (2023). (to appear)
7. Caminada, M.: On the issue of reinstatement in argumentation. In: Fisher, M., van der Hoek, W., Konev, B., Lisitsa, A. (eds.) JELIA 2006. LNCS (LNAI), vol. 4160, pp. 111–123. Springer, Heidelberg (2006). https://doi.org/10.1007/11853886_11
8. Dung, P.M.: On the acceptability of arguments and its fundamental role in non-monotonic reasoning, logic programming and n-person games. Artif. Intell. **77**(2), 321–358 (1995). https://doi.org/10.1016/0004-3702(94)00041-X
9. Dutilh Novaes, C.: Argument and Argumentation. In: Zalta, E.N. (ed.) The Stanford Encyclopedia of Philosophy. Metaphysics Research Lab, Stanford University, Fall 2022 edn. (2022)
10. Nielsen, S.H., Parsons, S.: A generalization of dung's abstract framework for argumentation: arguing with sets of attacking arguments. In: Maudet, N., Parsons, S., Rahwan, I. (eds.) ArgMAS 2006. LNCS (LNAI), vol. 4766, pp. 54–73. Springer, Heidelberg (2007). https://doi.org/10.1007/978-3-540-75526-5_4
11. Prakken, H., Winter, M.D.: Abstraction in argumentation: Necessary but dangerous. In: Modgil, S., Budzynska, K., Lawrence, J. (eds.) Computational Models of Argument - Proceedings of COMMA 2018, Warsaw, Poland, 12–14 September 2018. Frontiers in Artificial Intelligence and Applications, vol. 305, pp. 85–96. IOS Press (2018). https://doi.org/10.3233/978-1-61499-906-5-85

ReConf: An Automatic Context-Based Software Reconfiguration Tool for Autonomous Vehicles Using Answer-Set Programming

Tobias Kain$^{(\boxtimes)}$ and Hans Tompits

Institute of Logic and Computation, Knowledge-Based Systems Group E192-03,
Technische Universität Wien, 1040 Vienna, Austria
{kain,tompits}@kr.tuwien.ac.at

Abstract. A significant challenge in the domain of autonomous vehicles is to ensure a reliable and safe operation in a multitude of contexts. As a consequence, autonomous vehicles must be capable of handling various context changes, such as changing weather conditions as well as software and hardware faults, without human support. To address this issue, we introduce a context-based software configuration tool for autonomous vehicles, called ReConf, which is embedded into Aptus, a generic framework for extending system architectures of autonomous vehicles with a self-managing functionality proposed in previous work. ReConf reconfigures the autonomous driving system in case the context changes by means of a reasoning component based on answer-set programming in order to determine system configurations that fulfill the requirements of the current context.

Keywords: Autonomous Vehicles · Answer Set Programming · Software Reconfiguration

1 Introduction

The development of autonomous vehicles in accord to SAE level 4 and 5 [25] brings various challenges due to their complexity. The latter challenge is imposed by the requirement of handling different contexts [22], such as changing illumination and weather conditions, as well as various operation modes, where each such mode may demand different applications [19]. A further complication is that unpredictable system context changes, like ones triggered by hardware or software faults, must be handled to counteract safety-critical situations [1]. Importantly, autonomous vehicles need to deal with such situations without the help of an intervening driver or passenger. This necessitates mechanisms for reconfiguring the autonomous driving system based on the current context.

In this paper, we introduce ReConf, a context-based software configuration tool for autonomous vehicles. ReConf is integrated into the generic framework

© The Author(s), under exclusive license to Springer Nature Switzerland AG 2023
R. Basili et al. (Eds.): AIxIA 2023, LNAI 14318, pp. 30–43, 2023.
https://doi.org/10.1007/978-3-031-47546-7_3

APTUS [17] for extending system architectures of autonomous vehicles with a self-managing functionality.[1] APTUS defines three layers, viz., the *context layer*, the *reconfiguration layer*, and the *component layer*, whereby RECONF is embedded into the former two layers.

The task of RECONF is to analyze the current context the vehicle is experiencing and to determine configurations that fulfill the requirements imposed by it. In particular, RECONF implements this task using two interconnected components, viz., C-SAR (standing for "context-based software architecture requirements") and AP^{2}S (standing for "application-placement problem solver"). The former component is responsible for analyzing the current context and determining the implied configuration requirements, while the latter computes so-called *configurations*, i.e., assignments of applications to computing nodes that satisfy the given configuration requirements.

Overall, RECONF and its two components are implemented in Python, while C-SAR and AP^{2}S employ *answer-set programming* (ASP) [2,6,10–12] for representing and processing their underlying reasoning tasks. In particular, C-SAR uses ASP to specify the interconnection of context information the vehicle can generally experience and to determine configuration requirements necessary for the current context. On the other hand, AP^{2}S employs ASP to solve our version of the so-called *application-placement problem* [26], which is NP-hard in general [15,18].

The general concept of RECONF builds on the idea of *autonomic managers*, as introduced by IBM [14]. Autonomic managers implement a control loop consisting of a *monitor*, an *analyzer*, a *planner*, an *executor*, and a shared *knowledge base* to control resources, such as hardware and software components. A similar approach to RECONF was introduced by Zeller et al. [28], where software components, system objectives, and requirements are grouped into so-called *clusters*, whereby an autonomic manager controls each cluster. However, a drawback of their approach compared to RECONF are longer reconfiguration times. Another related approach was presented by Weiss and Struss [27]. Their idea is to activate or deactivate advanced driver assistance systems according to current context information. Compared to RECONF, a less complex reasoning is required due to the limitation to non-autonomous vehicles.

The paper is organized as follows: Section 2 explains the general architecture of RECONF and provides some basics on answer-set programming. Sections 3 and 4 contain the main part of our paper, detailing C-SAR and AP^{2}S, respectively. Section 5 concludes the paper with a brief summary and outlook.

2   General Architecture of RECONF

We start our discussion with a general overview about RECONF. As mentioned before, RECONF is implemented in Python and embedded into the generic framework APTUS [17] for extending system architectures of autonomous vehicles with

---

[1] Note that the name "APTUS" was not used previously [17] and is newly introduced here.

a self-managing functionality. RECONF consist of two components, C-SAR and AP^{2}S, which comprise several components. Since a key element of both of them is answer-set programming (ASP) [11,12], we first recapitulate some basic elements of it. Afterwards, we give a brief overview of APTUS and describe the embedding of RECONF into APTUS, as well as outline the architecture of RECONF.

Preliminaries on Answer-Set Programming. By an *answer-set program*, or *program* for short, we understand a finite set of rules of form

$$a_1 \vee \cdots \vee a_m \; :- \; b_1, \ldots, b_k, \text{not } b_{k+1}, \ldots, \text{not } b_n, \tag{1}$$

where $a_1, \ldots, a_m, b_1, \ldots, b_n$ are *literals* over a first-order vocabulary, i.e., atoms possibly preceded by the *strong negation* symbol $\neg$, $\vee$ denotes *disjunction*, and "not" stands for *default negation*. We refer to $a_1 \vee \cdots \vee a_m$ as the *head* and $b_1, \ldots, b_k, \text{not } b_{k+1}, \ldots, \text{not } b_n$ as the *body* of (1). A rule with an empty body is a *fact*, whilst a rule with an empty head is a *constraint*.

The semantics of a program is given in terms of *answer sets*, which are defined as minimal models of the *Gelfond-Lifschitz reduct* [11,12]. Prominent answer-set solvers are, e.g., clasp [8], which is used by clingo [7], and DLV [20].

We will employ the following aggregate functions: #*count* for counting elements satisfying certain properties, #*max* and #*min* for determining the maximum and minimum of elements, respectively, and #*sum* for calculating the sum of a set of elements. Furthermore, we use the optimization statement #*minimize* to find the answer set which minimizes a certain variable.

The APTUS *Framework.* APTUS [17] is a generic self-managing framework for autonomous vehicles in the sense that it does not require a specific underlying vehicle architecture. In particular, APTUS targets to extend arbitrary system architectures of autonomous vehicles with a self-managing functionality.

Following the general three-layered architecture as introduced by Gat [4] that is widely applied in the field of robotics, APTUS consists of three logical layers, viz., (i) a *context layer*, (ii) a *reconfiguration layer*, and (iii) a *component layer*. These layers implement various properties that are required for a system to be considered self-managing [13,24], whereby the key properties implemented by APTUS are (i) *context-awareness*, (ii) *self-configuring*, and (iii) *self-healing*.

The context layer achieves the context-awareness property. In particular, the context layer is responsible for deriving a set of configuration requirements, which constitute the input for the reconfiguration layer. The latter layer is required to determine reconfiguration actions., i.e., the reconfiguration layer implements the self-configuring property. Finally, the component layer implements the self-healing property by monitoring the system components and performing fault-tolerance measures to handle occurring faults.

In this paper, we focus on the context and the reconfiguration layer. In particular, C-SAR is embedded into the former whilst AP^{2}S is part of the latter.

The general purpose of RECONF is to determine *configurations* for an autonomous vehicle that fulfill the requirements of the current context, whereby we define configurations as assignments of applications to computing nodes.

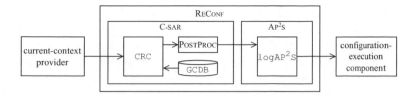

Fig. 1. The architecture of RECONF.

Computing such configurations can be separated into two successive tasks, referred to as T_1 and T_2 in what follows, respectively. Task T_1 is responsible for analyzing the current context and determining the derived configuration requirements, while T_2 takes care for computing a valid configuration that satisfies the given configuration requirements. The latter task is an instance of the general *application-placement problem* [26], which is NP-hard in general [15, 18].

The overall architecture of RECONF is depicted in Fig. 1. Tasks T_1 and T_2 are implemented by two separate components of RECONF, viz. C-SAR and AP^{2}S, whereby T_1 is realized by C-SAR and T_2 by AP^{2}S. C-SAR and AP^{2}S, in turn, consist of several subcomponents: C-SAR is composed of the *general context-database*, GCDB, the *context-reasoning component*, CRC, and the *post-processing component*, POSTPROC. Furthermore, AP^{2}S contains the logAP^{2}S solver for computing the application-placement problem.

These components serve the following purposes: (i) GCDB specifies the interconnection of context information the vehicle can generally experience. This information is provided at design time by the vehicle engineers and might be updated, e.g., in case the vehicle's features are extended. (ii) CRC determines, on the basis of the general context model as given by GCDB and the current context as provided by various components referred to as *current-context providers*, tasks which are requested by the current context as well as a collection of applications which can feasibly execute these tasks. (iii) Following the postprocessor POST-PROC, which adds applications that shall be executed as redundant instances, logAP^{2}S is responsible for finding a configuration that fulfills the received configuration requirements.

CRC, GCDB, and logAP^{2}S are implemented in terms of three answer-set programs, P_{CRC}, P_{GCDB}, and P_{logAP^2S}. As well, the current context is also represented by an answer-set program, viz. by a set P_{CC} of facts. To embed these answer-set programs into RECONF, we use clyngor [21], a Python wrapper for the ASP system clingo [7], which uses GrinGo [9] as a grounder and clasp [8] as a solver. Unlike the other subcomponents, POSTPROC is implemented in Python. The reason for this is that POSTPROC requires the implementation of a multilevel sort algorithm which can be realized more efficiently in Python than in ASP.

The output of CRC is the first answer set, A_{CR}, of the program $P_{CC} \cup P_{GCDB} \cup P_{CRC}$, containing the configuration requirements that need to be fulfilled in the current context. In case no answer set is found, the vehicle is transferred into a safe state by the component layer of APTUS. Then, A_{CR} is taken by POST-

PROC as input and extends it to A'_{CR} by adding applications that are executed as redundant instances, as mentioned before. Afterwards, A'_{CR} is handed over to logAP^{2}S which calculates a configuration that fulfills the received configuration requirements. The output of P_{logAP^2S} is the first answer set of the program $A'_{CR} \cup P_{logAP^2S}$. This answer set specifies the assignment of applications to specific computing nodes for execution. If $A'_{CR} \cup P_{logAP^2S}$ is not satisfiable, the component layer of APTUS ensures that the vehicle is transferred into a safe state. Finally, the output of logAP^{2}S is transferred to the so-called *configuration-execution component*, which is responsible for executing the determined requirement (note that both the configuration-execution component and the current-context provider are not part of RECONF).

A real-world example illustrating the interplay of C-SAR, logAP^{2}S, and the other components of APTUS can be found in the dissertation of the first author [16].

3   The Component C-SAR

In what follows, we provide details on the components of C-SAR, in particular on the answer-set programs P_{GCDB} and P_{CRC} of the context database GCDB and the context reasoning component CRC, respectively.

3.1   The General Context-Database GCDB

We define context as any information relevant to the vehicle's system configuration, where the context information is categorized into *system-context information, operational-context information, user-context information,* and *environmental-context information.*

The system context includes information about the vehicle system, including, e.g., the available applications and computing nodes, the currently applied configuration, as well as occurring hardware and software errors. The operational context includes the so-called *vehicle-operation mode*, which describes how the vehicle is operated, e.g., *fully autonomous* or *manual.* Additionally, *operation properties* can further describe these modes. Parameters that describe the requirements of the vehicle users, e.g., the type of the ordered entertainment package, are contained in the user context. Finally, the environmental context contains information about the external conditions of the vehicle, including, e.g., the roadway type, the current traffic rules, and the weather conditions.

The program P_{GCDB} is given by $DB_{sys} \cup DB_{op} \cup DB_{usr} \cup DB_{env}$, where its subprograms, detailed below, correspond to the above discussed context categories, containing the context information in terms of facts.

(1) *The Database DB_{sys}.* We define tasks as general functions, e.g., localization, sensor fusion, or motion control, that are implemented by applications, i.e., applications are concrete implementations of tasks. Tasks are declared by the predicate *task*/1, where its argument defines the task's unique name.

Multiple diverse applications can implement the same task. Applications and their relation to a specific task are modeled using the predicate $app/2$. The first argument of this predicate specifies the application's unique name and the second defines the task the application implements.

Additional parameters further define tasks and applications. For each task, the following parameters need to be specified: (i) the redundancy level, (ii) the diversity level, and (iii) the separation level. These parameters are expressed by the predicates $red/2$, $div/2$, and $sep/2$. The first argument of these predicates indicates the task, and the second argument defines the parameter value.

The redundancy level specifies the minimum number of redundant applications that need to be executed. We refer to redundantly executed applications as *active-hot applications*. On the other hand, the applications which primarily execute the task are called *active applications*.

Furthermore, the diversity level defines the number of redundant applications that have to be diverse, and the separation level defines on how many different computing nodes the applications have to be executed. Note that the redundancy, diversity, and separation parameters allow for increasing the safety and reliability of applications.

Applications have different demands regarding their execution, whereby we consider the following application parameters: (i) the memory demand, (ii) the performance demand, and (iii) a list of required supporting software.

The memory demand and performance demand are modeled by the predicates $mem/2$ and $perf/2$, respectively. The first argument of those predicates defines the application, and the second argument the parameter value.

For modeling supporting software, e.g., runtime environments like Python and Java, or libraries such as CUDA [26], the predicate $sup\_sw/1$ is used. To indicate whether an application requires a particular supporting software, we use the predicate $req\_sup\_sw/2$, where the first argument defines the application and the second specifies the supporting software that this application demands.

(2) *The Database DB_{op}.* Vehicle-operation modes and operation properties are expressed using the predicate $veh\_op\_mode/1$ and $op\_prop/1$, respectively, whereby their argument defines the unique name.

Each vehicle-operation mode and operation property requires that certain tasks are executed. Thus, these entities are linked to tasks. To express which tasks the individual vehicle-operation modes, operation properties, and user contexts demand, the predicate $req\_task/2$ is used. The first argument defines the vehicle-operation mode or the operation property and the second one the task.

(3) *The Database DB_{usr}.* User contexts are defined by the predicate $user\_cx/1$, whereby its argument defines the unique name of the user contexts. Like vehicle-operation modes and operation properties, a specific user context can require that certain tasks are executed by the vehicle. The above introduced predicate req_task is used to express this dependency.

(4) *The Database DB_{env}.* We introduce *environmental-context values* and *environmental-context sets* to concretely define the environment, including, for

instance, weather and lighting conditions. As applications can be designed for certain environmental contexts, they are linked to the environmental-context values and the environmental-context sets.

Context values are defined via the predicate $env\_cx\_val/1$, whereby its argument specifies the unique name of the context value. Conceivable environmental-context values are, for instance, highway, rainy, and dark.

The relation between environmental-context values and applications is defined via the predicate $env\_cx\_impl/3$. The first argument refers to the application, the second to the environmental-context value, and the third specifies the so-called *environmental-context rating*. The latter defines the suitability of an application in a given environment.

The performance of an application can also be rated for a more specific environmental context, i.e., a combination of environmental-context values. For instance, a sensor fusion application can be rated for urban driving in clear weather or for nightly journeys on highways while it is raining. Therefore, the definition of environmental-context sets, which are groups of environmental-context values, is supported. Environmental-context sets are specified by the predicate $env\_cx\_set/1$, which holds as its argument the unique name of the set. Environmental-context values can be added to sets using the predicate $env\_cx\_set\_mbr/2$, whereby the first argument refers to the environmental-context value and the second to the environmental-context set. The relation between environmental-context sets and applications is defined by the predicate env_cx_impl, similar to the relationship between values and applications.

3.2 The Context-Reasoning Component CRC

The component CRC is implemented by the answer-set program $P_{CRC} = P_{CRC\_1} \cup P_{CRC\_2} \cup P_{CRC\_3}$, where P_{CRC_1} is responsible for choosing the tasks that are requested by the current context, P_{CRC_2} takes care of selecting, for each chosen task, one active application, and P_{CRC_3} identifies the feasible diverse applications for each task. Details about these programs are given in what follows.

(1) P_{CRC_1}: *Task Selection.* As mentioned before, CRC takes as input the program P_{CC}, which specifies the current context. The latter is composed of one vehicle-operation mode and a set of operation properties, user contexts, and environmental-context values, whereby this set can be empty. To express the current context, we introduce the predicate $cur\_cx/1$, whose single argument can be the name of a vehicle-operation mode, an operation property, a user context, or an environmental-context value.

To determine the tasks that are required in the current context, the following rule is introduced:

$$r_1: \quad sel\_task(T) :- task(T), cur\_cx(C), req\_task(C, T).$$

The predicate $sel\_tas/1$ marks those tasks that are required in the current context. Note that a task is selected if it is required by the current vehicle-operation mode, the current operation properties, or the current user context.

r_2: $spec\_lvl(A, EC, SL)$:− $env\_cx\_impl(A, EC, \_)$, $SL = \#count\{X :$
$env\_cx\_set\_mbr(X, EC)\}$, $HITS = \#count\{X : env\_cx\_set(EC)$,
$env\_cx\_set\_mbr(X, EC)$, $cur\_cx(X)\}$, $SL = HITS$.

r_3: $spec\_lvl(A, EC, 1)$:− $cur\_cx(EC)$, $env\_cx\_impl(A, EC, \_)$,
$env\_cx\_val(EC, \_)$.

r_4: $max\_spec\_env\_cx(A, EC)$:− $spec\_lvl(A, EC, SL)$,
$SL = \#max\{X : spec\_lvl(A, \_, X)\}$.

r_5: $cx\_app\_rat(A, R)$:− $app(A, \_)$, $max\_spec\_env\_cx(A, EC)$,
$env\_cx\_impl(A, EC, R)$, $R = \#min\{X : max\_spec\_env\_cx(A, EC')$,
$env\_cx\_impl(A, EC', X)\}$.

r_6: $feas\_rat\_app(A, T)$:− $sel\_task(T)$, $app(A, T)$, $max\_spec\_env\_cx(A, EC)$,
$spec\_lvl(A, EC, SL)$, $SL = \#max\{X : app(A', T)$,
$max\_spec\_env\_cx(A', EC')$, $spec\_lvl(A', EC', X)\}$.

r_7: $feas\_non\_rat\_app(A)$:− $app(A, T)$, $sel\_task(T)$, $not\ env\_cx\_impl(A, \_, \_)$,
$not\ feas\_rat\_app(\_, T)$.

r_8: $max\_rat\_app(A)$:− $feas\_rat\_app(A, T)$, $cx\_app\_rat(A, R)$
$R = \#max\{X : feas\_rat\_app(A', T)$, $cx\_app\_rat(A', X)\}$.

r_9: $act\_app(A, 0)$:− $app(A, T)$, $max\_rat\_app(A)$,
$A = \#min\{X : max\_rat\_app(X)$, $app(X, T)\}$.

r_{10}: $act\_app(A, 0)$:− $app(A, T)$, $feas\_non\_rat\_app(A)$,
$A = \#min\{X : feas\_non\_rat\_app(X)$, $app(X, T)\}$.

Fig. 2. The Program $P_{\text{CRC\_2}}$.

(2) $P_{\text{CRC\_2}}$: *Active Application Selection.* Program $P_{\text{CRC\_2}}$, comprising rules r_2–r_{10} and depicted in Fig. 2, distinguishes between the selection of applications for which environmental-context ratings exist or not exist. Applications of the former kind are referred to as *rated applications*, while *non-rated applications* denote applications that do not depend on the environmental context. Generally, rated applications are preferred over non-rated ones. In particular, $P_{\text{CRC\_2}}$ selects applications with the most specific and highest rating to be active applications. Thus, the so-called *specialization level* has to be determined, which corresponds to the number of environmental-context values that are members of this set. Note that environmental-context values have specialization level 1.

The specialization level is defined by the predicate $spec\_lev/3$, whereby the first argument specifies the application, the second the environmental-context set or environmental-context value, and the last argument specifies the specialization level. Rule r_2 determines the specialization levels of environmental-context sets, while rule r_3 those of environmental-context values.

For each rated application, the most specific environmental-context values or sets, which are fully covered by the current context, are identified using the predicate $max\_spec\_env\_cx/2$, whereby the first argument defines the name of the application and the second argument the most specific environmental-context value or set. We introduce the rule r_4 for this predicate.

Rule r_5 determines, based on the predicate $max\_spec\_env\_cx$, the rating of an application in the current context. This rating is expressed by the predicate $cx\_app\_rat/2$, whereby the first argument defines the application name and the second argument the determined rating. In case multiple environmental-context values and sets associated with an application have the same specialization level, P_{CRC_2} acts conservatively and chooses the lower rating, which is determined using the aggregate $\#min$.

Next, for each selected task, the applications with the highest specialization level are identified. To indicate which applications are a feasible choice for a task, we define the predicate $feas\_rat\_app/2$, whereby the first argument defines the application and the second the task. Furthermore, all non-rated applications implementing a selected task for which no rated application exists in the current context are identified using the predicate $feas\_non\_rat\_app/1$, whereby its argument identifies the non-rated application. The predicates $feas\_rat\_app$ and $feas\_non\_rat\_app$ are determined by rule r_6 and rule r_7, respectively.

As multiple applications which implement the same task can have the same specialization level, the application with the highest rating is selected using the predicate $max\_rat\_app/1$, where its argument holds the name of the application. The predicate max_rat_app is determined by the rule r_8.

Finally, for each selected task, the application with the highest rating, which is the first in alphabetically ascending order regarding its name, is selected as active application. If only non-rated applications exist for a selected task, the one which is first in the alphabetically ascending order is selected.

To indicate that an application is selected as active application, we introduce the predicate $act\_app/2$. The first argument of this predicate specifies the name of the application, and the second term holds the so-called *redundancy-instance number*. We associate the application name and the redundancy-instance number to identify active and active-hot applications uniquely. Note that the redundancy-instance number of the active applications is 0. The active applications are determined by rule r_9 and rule r_{10}.

(3) P_{CRC_3}: *Diverse Application Determination.* As mentioned in Subsect. 3.1, tasks can require the execution of active-hot applications. Additionally, tasks can require these active-hot applications to be diverse from the active application. Therefore, it is required to identify those applications which are feasible choices for diverse applications. P_{CRC_3} comprises the rules r_{11} and r_{12} described below.

A rated application is classified as a feasible diverse application for a selected task if the application has not been selected as active application, and the predicate $max\_spec\_env\_cx$ is defined for this application. To identify feasible diverse applications, we introduce the predicate $feas\_div\_app/3$. The first argument of this predicate identifies the application, whilst the second one specifies the maximum specialization value. The third argument specifies the rating of the application in the current context. The latter two arguments are subsequently used by POSTPROC to decide which feasible diverse application shall be selected. Rule

r_{11}, given below, determines the feasible diverse applications:

r_{11}: $feas\_div\_app(A, SL, R)$ $:-$ $app(A, T), sel\_task(T),$

$max\_spec\_env\_cx(A, EC), cx\_app\_rat(A, R), spec\_lvl(A, EC, SL),$

$SL = \#max\{X : spec\_lvl(A, \_, X)\}, not\ act\_app(A, \_).$

A non-rated application is classified as a feasible diverse application for a selected task if the application is not selected as active application. As before, *feas_div_app* is used to indicate that a non-rated application is a feasible diverse application, whereby the specialization level and the rating are set to 0. Rule r_{12} determines non-rated applications that are feasible diverse applications as follows:

r_{12}: $feas\_div\_app(A, 0, 0)$ $:-$ $app(A, T), sel\_task(T),$

$not\ env\_cx\_impl(A, \_, \_), not\ act\_app(A, \_).$

3.3   The Post-processing Component PostProc

Based on the answer set A_{CR} computed by CRC, PostProc determines for each selected task the required set of active-hot applications. Active-hot applications are either of the same instance as the active application or are diverse. Therefore, as a first step, PostProc determines for each task whether the redundancy level of a task is greater than the diversity level. If this is the case, PostProc adds active-hot applications that are of the same instance as the active application using the predicate $act\_hot\_app/2$. The first term of this predicate specifies the name of the application, and the second term holds the redundancy-instance number.

In order to select for each task the required diverse active-hot applications, the feasible diverse applications (i.e., the applications for which the predicate *feas_div_app* holds) are sorted by their specialization level and their rating. Finally, the applications with the highest specialization level and rating are selected as diverse active-hot applications and added to the answer set. The resulting extended answer set, A'_{CR}, is forwarded to logAP^{2}S.

Performance tests showed that C-SAR can generate an output in around 10 ms to 20 ms for problem instances that include 15 tasks, 20 applications, 15 environmental-context values and sets, as well as 100 ratings. These values are in conformance to real-world parameters. The hardware used to generate this output was equipped with an Apple M2 chip with 8 cores and 8 GB memory.

4   The AP^{2}S Component of RECONF

The answer set A'_{CR} is used as input for logAP^{2}S. Based on this answer set, logAP^{2}S aims to determine a valid configuration, where the latter is the output of the application-placement problem, which is an NP-hard problem [18]. The input of this problem is a set A of applications and a set N of computing nodes, and the goal is to find a configuration that maps each application $a \in A$ to exactly one node $n \in N$ such that the following conditions are satisfied:

r_{13}: $\{asgmt(A, I, CN) : cn(CN)\} = 1 \ :- \ act\_app(A, I).$

r_{14}: $\{asgmt(A, I, CN) : cn(CN)\} = 1 \ :- \ act\_hot\_app(A, I).$

r_{15}: $:- \ cn(CN), mem(CN, MEM), \#sum\{M, A, I : mem(A, M),$
$app(A, \_), asgmt(A, I, CN)\} > MEM.$

r_{16}: $:- \ cn(CN), perf(CN, CPU), \#sum\{C, A, I : perf(A, C),$
$app(A, \_), asgmt(A, I, CN)\} > CPU.$

r_{17}: $:- \ asgmt(A, \_, CN), \ req\_sup\_sw(A, S), \ not \ prov\_sup\_sw(CN, S).$

r_{18}: $:- \ sel\_task(T, \_), sep(T, S), \#count\{CN : app(A, T), asgmt(A, \_, CN)\} < S.$

r_{19}: $displ\_cnt(CNT) \ :- \ CNT = \#count\{A : asgmt(A, CN),$
$cur\_asgmt(A\_CUR, CN\_CUR), A = A\_CUR, CN \neq CN\_CUR\}.$

r_{20}: $\#minimize\{CNT : displ\_cnt(CNT)\}.$

Fig. 3. The Program $P_{\text{logAP}^2\text{S}}$.

(C_1) An application has to be executed by exactly one computing node.
(C_2) The sum of the memory (resp., performance) demands of all applications running on a computing node cannot exceed the memory (resp., performance) capacity of that node.
(C_3) An application runs only on such a computing node that offers the software required by that application.
(C_4) For each task, the separation level has to be satisfied.

To discriminate among a potentially large number of solutions, we utilize an optimization function that aims to find those configurations that minimize the number of applications that have to be displaced compared to the current configuration, i.e., the configuration that the vehicle currently applies.

The configuration requirements determined by CRC constitute the input of logAP^{2}S. Furthermore, logAP^{2}S takes as input the set of currently available computing nodes as well as their memory and performance capacity. The available computing nodes are defined by the predicate $cn/1$, which holds as its argument the unique name of the computing node. Furthermore, the memory and performance capacity are specified similarly to the memory and performance demands of applications using the predicates $mem/2$ and $perf/2$, respectively. In addition, we introduce the predicate $prov\_sup\_sw/2$ to specify which supporting software is installed on the individual computing nodes. This predicate has two arguments: the first identifies the computing node, and the second specifies the corresponding supporting software.

Besides the software-architecture requirements and the specification of the available computing nodes, logAP^{2}S also considers the application placement of the current system state as an additional input parameter. Therefore, we introduce the predicate $cur\_asgmt/2$. The first argument of this predicate holds the name of an application, the second defines the redundancy-instance number, and the third indicates which computing node executes this application.

Table 1. Average solving time of $\mathtt{logAP^2S}$.

Problem-Size Class	Solving Time
$|N| = 3, |A| = 30$	6.3 ms
$|N| = 3, |A| = 60$	8.9 ms
$|N| = 3, |A| = 90$	11.4 ms
$|N| = 3, |A| = 120$	14.7 ms

As mentioned, the configuration that is determined by $\mathtt{logAP^2S}$ consists of assignments of active-hot and active applications to computing nodes. Those assignments are expressed using the predicate $asgmt/3$, which, like cur_asgmt, holds three arguments. The first two arguments identify the application, and the third argument indicates which computing node shall execute the application.

Figure 3 depicts the program $P_{\mathtt{logAP^2S}}$ which implements the configuration task of $\mathtt{logAP^2S}$. The rules r_{13} and r_{14} of $P_{\mathtt{logAP^2S}}$ implement condition (C_1). Note that we use *guards* in the head to ensure that each active and active-hot application is only assigned to one computing node. Condition (C_2) is implemented by rules r_{15} and r_{16}, while conditions (C_3) and (C_4) are taken care of by rules r_{17} and r_{18}, respectively. To implement the optimization function, we introduce the auxiliary predicate $displ\_cnt/1$, which counts the number of displaced applications. Rule r_{19} defines this predicate, which is then used as input for the optimization statement in rule r_{20}.

To evaluate the performance of $\mathtt{logAP^2S}$, we conducted tests with varying problem sizes. In particular, four realistic problem-size classes were defined, each consisting of 1000 randomized test cases, where the number of computing nodes remained fixed at 3 while the number of applications ranged from 10 to 40. The results are shown in Table 1 and reveal average solving times of a few milliseconds, which are well within an acceptable range for such a configuration [23].

5 Conclusion

In this paper, we introduced RECONF, a context-based software configuration tool for autonomous vehicles that is integrated into APTUS [17], a generic framework for extending system architectures of autonomous vehicles with a self-managing functionality. RECONF comprises the two submodules C-SAR and $\mathrm{AP^2S}$, which employ ASP for task solving. Our implementations of C-SAR and $\mathrm{AP^2S}$ illustrate that ASP is a viable approach for creating a software configuration tool for autonomous vehicles since answer-set programs are compact, comprehensible, and practicably efficient in their performance.

Concerning future work, we plan to extend the functionality of RECONF. In particular, we aim to enhance the data model implemented by GCDB and to integrate additional optimization functions into $\mathtt{logAP^2S}$. Furthermore, we plan to investigate the use of ASP-based stream reasoning [3,5].

References

1. APTIV, Audi, Baidu, BMW, Continental, Daimler, FCA, HERE, Infineon, Intel, Volkswagen: Safety First for Automated Driving (2019). White paper
2. Baral, C.: Knowledge Representation. Reasoning and Declarative Problem Solving. Cambridge University Press, Cambridge (2003)
3. Beck, H., Eiter, T., Folie, C.: Ticker: a system for incremental ASP-based stream reasoning. Theory Pract. Logic Program. **17**(5–6), 744–763 (2017)
4. Gat, E.: Three-Layer Architectures, pp. 195–210. AAAI Press, Washington (1998)
5. Gebser, M., Grote, T., Kaminski, R., Obermeier, P., Sabuncu, O., Schaub, T.: Stream reasoning with answer set programming: Preliminary report. In: Proceedings of the Thirteenth International Conference on Principles of Knowledge Representation and Reasoning (KR 2012), pp. 613–617 (2012)
6. Gebser, M., Kaminski, R., Kaufmann, B., Schaub, T.: Answer Set Solving in Practice. Intelligence and Machine Learning, Morgan & Claypool Publishers, Washington (2012)
7. Gebser, M., Kaminski, R., Kaufmann, B., Schaub, T.: Multi-shot ASP solving with clingo. Theory Pract. Logic Program. **19**(1), 27–82 (2019)
8. Gebser, M., Kaufmann, B., Neumann, A., Schaub, T.: *clasp*: a conflict-driven answer set solver. In: Baral, C., Brewka, G., Schlipf, J. (eds.) LPNMR 2007. LNCS (LNAI), vol. 4483, pp. 260–265. Springer, Heidelberg (2007). https://doi.org/10.1007/978-3-540-72200-7_23
9. Gebser, M., Schaub, T., Thiele, S.: GrinGo: a new grounder for answer set programming. In: Baral, C., Brewka, G., Schlipf, J. (eds.) LPNMR 2007. LNCS (LNAI), vol. 4483, pp. 266–271. Springer, Heidelberg (2007). https://doi.org/10.1007/978-3-540-72200-7_24
10. Gelfond, M., Kahl, Y.: Knowledge Representation, Reasoning, and the Design of Intelligent Agents: The Answer-Set Programming Approach. Cambridge University Press, Cambridge (2014)
11. Gelfond, M., Lifschitz, V.: The stable model semantics for logic programming. In: Proceedings of the 5th International Conference and Symposium on Logic Programming (ICLP/SLP 1988), pp. 1070–1080. MIT Press (1988)
12. Gelfond, M., Lifschitz, V.: Classical negation in logic programs and disjunctive databases. New Gener. Comput. **9**, 365–385 (1991)
13. Horn, P.: Autonomic Computing: IBM's Perspective on the State of Information Technology (2001). White paper
14. IBM: An Architectural Blueprint for Autonomic Computing (2005). White paper
15. Kain, T.: Towards a Reliable System Architecture for Autonomous Vehicles,: Master's Thesis. Technische Universität Wien, Institute of Logic and Computation (2020)
16. Kain, T.: Towards a Generic Framework for Extending System Architectures of Autonomous Vehicles with a Self-Managing Functionality. Dissertation, Technische Universität Wien (2023). In preparation
17. Kain, T., Müller, J.S., Mundhenk, P., Tompits, H., Wesche, M., Decke, H.: Towards a reliable and context-based system architecture for autonomous vehicles. In: Proceedings of the 2nd International Workshop on Autonomous Systems Design (ASD 2020), pp. 1:1–1:7 (2020)
18. Kain, T., Tompits, H., Müller, J.S., Wesche, M., Martinez Flores, Y.A., Decke, H.: Optimizing the placement of applications in autonomous vehicles. In: Proceedings of the 30th European Safety and Reliability Conference (ESREL) (2020)

19. Kampmann, A., et al.: A dynamic service-oriented software architecture for highly automated vehicles. In: Proceedings of the 2019 IEEE Intelligent Transportation Systems Conference (ITSC 2019), pp. 2101–2108 (2019)
20. Leone, N., et al.: The DLV system for knowledge representation and reasoning. ACM Trans. Comput. Log. **7**(3), 499–562 (2006)
21. Lucas Bourneuf: clyngor. https://github.com/Aluriak/clyngor
22. Mallozzi, P., Pelliccione, P., Knauss, A., Berger, C., Mohammadiha, N.: Autonomous vehicles: state of the art, future trends, and challenges. In: Automotive Systems and Software Engineering, pp. 347–367. Springer, Cham (2019). https://doi.org/10.1007/978-3-030-12157-0_16
23. Orlov, S.: AutoKonf: Forschung und Technologie für automatisiertes und vernetztes Fahren. Talk presented at the Fachtagung "Automatisiertes und vernetztes Fahren", Berlin (2017)
24. Parashar, M., Hariri, S.: Autonomic computing: an overview. In: Banâtre, J.P., Fradet, P., Giavitto, J.L., Michel, O. (eds.) UPP 2004. LNCS, vol. 3566, pp. 257–269. Springer, Berlin (2005). https://doi.org/10.1007/11527800_20
25. SAE International: Taxonomy and Definitions for Terms Related to Driving Automation Systems for On-Road Motor Vehicles (2021). SAE Standard J3016
26. Tang, C., Steinder, M., Spreitzer, M., Pacifici, G.: A Scalable application placement controller for enterprise data centers. In: Proceedings of the 16th International Conference on World Wide Web (WWW 2007), pp. 331–340 (2007)
27. Weiss, G., Grigoleit, F., Struss, P.: Context modeling for dynamic configuration of automotive functions. In: Proceedings of the 16th International IEEE Conference on Intelligent Transportation Systems (ITSC 2013), pp. 839–844 (2013)
28. Zeller, M., Weiss, G., Eilers, D., Knorr, R.: A multi-layered control architecture for self-management in adaptive automotive systems. In: Proceedings of the 2009 International Conference on Adaptive and Intelligent Systems (ICAIS 2009), pp. 63–68 (2009)

Mining Contrast Sequential Patterns with ASP

Francesca Alessandra Lisi[1]([⊠])[iD] and Gioacchino Sterlicchio[2][iD]

[1] DIB and CILA, University of Bari Aldo Moro, Bari, Italy
FrancescaAlessandra.Lisi@uniba.it
[2] DMMM, Polytechnic University of Bari, Bari, Italy
g.sterlicchio@phd.poliba.it

Abstract. In this paper we address an extension of the sequential pattern mining problem which aims at detecting the significant differences between frequent sequences with respect to given classes. The resulting problem is known as contrast sequential pattern mining, since it merges the two notions of sequential pattern and contrast pattern. For this problem we present a declarative approach based on Answer Set Programming (ASP). The efficiency and the scalability of the ASP encoding are evaluated on two publicly available datasets, iPRG and UNIX User, by varying parameters, also in comparison with a hybrid ASP-based approach.

Keywords: Declarative Pattern Mining · Contrast Sequential Pattern Mining · Answer Set Programming

1 Introduction

In recent times there is an increasing availability of data that contain sequences of events, items, or tokens organized according to an ordered metric space. The requirement to detect and analyze frequent subsequences has therefore become a common problem. Sequential Pattern Mining (SPM) arose as a subfield of pattern mining just to address this need (see, e.g., [18] for a survey). More precisely, the typical task in SPM consists in finding frequent and non-empty temporal sequences, called *sequential patterns*, from a dataset of sequences. Another interesting class of pattern mining problems goes under the name of Contrast Pattern Mining [4]. Here, the typical task is about detecting statistically significant differences/similarities, called *contrast patterns*, between two or more disjoint datasets (or portions of the same dataset). Sequential and contrast pattern mining are known to have a higher complexity than, e.g., itemsets mining. However, they have broad applications, e.g., the analysis of patient care pathways, education traces, digital logs (web access for client profiling, intrusion detection from network logs), customer purchases (rules for purchases recommendations), text and bioinformatic sequences. In this paper we consider to merge the concepts of sequential pattern and contrast pattern in order to find significant differences between frequent sequences with respect to given classes.

R. Basili et al. (Eds.): AIxIA 2023, LNAI 14318, pp. 44–57, 2023.
https://doi.org/10.1007/978-3-031-47546-7_4

This gives rise to the concept of *contrast sequential pattern*. The resulting problem of Contrast Sequential Pattern Mining (CSPM) is not new. However, it has been little addressed so far (see [3] for a recent survey).

In this paper we address the CSPM task by means of a declarative approach. In particular, we resort to Answer Set Programming (ASP) [2,14], a well-established computational logic paradigm for declarative problem solving. Declarative approaches are generally desirable in application domains where the requirements of transparency, verifiability and explainability of the AI techniques employed are of paramount importance, such as bio-informatics. For this reason a novel stream of research called Declarative Pattern Mining (DPM) has been proposed which can be more useful and appropriate in such contexts. To the best of our knowledge, no DPM approach exists that supports intensive knowledge-based contrast sequence mining. We have developed a concise and versatile ASP encoding for CSPM and for managing complex preferences on patterns. In particular, we have extended previous work on ASP-based SPM with the necessary code for checking which frequent sequential patterns out of the discovered ones highlight significant differences with respect to two classes. We have evaluated the encoding on two real-world public datasets of sequences (iPRG and UNIX User) which are enriched with information about the class of reference for each sequence. For a comparative evaluation, we have chosen a hybrid ASP-based approach that combines a first step with a traditional algorithm for SPM and a second step with ASP.

The paper is organized as follows. In Sect. 2 we overview the current research in CSPM and DPM. In Sect. 3 we provide the necessary background on ASP and CSPM. In Sect. 4 we describe our ASP enconding for the CSPM task and in Sect. 5 we report the experimental results obtained on the chosen datasets. Section 6 concludes the paper with final remarks.

2 Related Works

Sequential and Contrast Pattern Mining are challenging tasks in data mining and play an important role in many applications. Notably, *PrefixSpan* is an optimized algorithm for mining sequences [11]. The notion of contrast is deeply discussed by Dong in [4]. *Chen et al.* [3] provide an up-to-date comprehensive and structured overview of the research in Contrast Pattern Mining which includes also the case of contrast sequential patterns. In particular, *Zheng et al.* [23] present a CSPM method for taxpayer behaviour analysis, and *Wu et al.* [22] propose a top-k self-adaptive CSPM solution.

DPM covers many pattern mining tasks such as sequence mining [5,19] and frequent itemset mining [7,12]. In [19], the authors organize the constraints on sequential patterns in three categories: 1) constraints on patterns, 2) constraints on patterns embeddings, 3) constraints on pattern sets. These constraints are provided by the user and capture his background knowledge. Then, they introduce two formulations based on Constraint Programming (CP). *Jabbour et al.* [12] propose SAT based encodings of itemset mining problems to overcome space complexity issue behind the competitiveness of new declarative and flexible models. In [7], *MiningZinc* is presented as a declarative framework for constraint-based data mining.

Besides SAT and CP, ASP is also widely used in DPM. The first proposal is described by *Guyet et al.* [9]. The authors explore a first attempt to solve the SPM problem with ASP and compare their method with a dedicated algorithm. Next, in [5] *Gebser et al.* use ASP for extracting condensed representation of sequential pattern. They focus on closed, maximal and skyline patterns. *Samet et al.* in [21] show a method for mining meaningful rare sequential patterns with ASP, whereas in [8] *Guyet et al.* propose to apply an ASP-based DPM approach to investigate the possible association between hospitalization for seizure and antiepileptic drug switch from a french medico-administrative database. *Guyet et al.* [10] present the use of ASP to mine sequential patterns within two representations of embeddings (fill-gaps vs skip-gaps) and various kinds of patterns: frequent, constrained and condensed. *Besnard and Guyet* [1] address the task of mining negative sequential patterns in ASP. A negative sequential pattern is specified by means of a sequence consisting of events to occur and of other events, called negative events, to be absent. In [15,16] Guyet's ASP encodings for SPM are adapted in order to address the requirements of an application in the digital forensics domain: The analysis of anonymised mobile phone recordings. Motivated by the same application, *Lisi and Sterlicchio* present an ASP-based approach to contrast pattern mining in [17].

Whereas all the works mentioned so far are pure ASP-based DPM solutions, particularly interesting is the hybrid ASP-based approach proposed by *Paramonov et al.* [20] which combines dedicated algorithms for pattern mining and ASP. The authors show that such two-step approach outperforms one-shot ones.

3 Preliminaries

3.1 Answer Set Programming

ASP is a declarative and expressive programming language to resolve difficult research problems (e.g. security analysis, planning, configuration, semantic web, etc.) introduced at the end of the 90s [2]. Every ASP programs is made up of atoms, literals and logic rules. Atoms can be true or false and a literal is an atom a or its negation *not a*. An ASP general rule has the following form:

$$a_1 \vee \ldots \vee a_n \leftarrow b_1, \ldots, b_k, not\ b_{k+1}, \ldots, not\ b_m \tag{1}$$

where all a_i and b_j are atoms. The previous rule says that if $b_1, \ldots, b_k$ are true and there is not reason for believing that $b_{k+1}, \ldots, b_m$ are true then at least one of the $a_1, \ldots, a_n$ is believed to be true. The *not* statement is not the standard logical negation but it is used to derive *not p* (i.e. p is assumed not to hold) from failure to derive p. The left side of the $\leftarrow$ is called *head* while the right side *body*. Rules of the form "$a \leftarrow$" are called *facts* and they have no body. The head is unconditionally true and the arrow is usually omitted. Rules of the form

"$\leftarrow b_1, \ldots, b_k$" are called *constraints*. Adding a constraint in a program deletes answer sets that satisfy the constraint body. There are different ASP systems, the most important are Clingo [6] and DLV [13].

3.2   Contrast Sequential Pattern Mining

Sequential Pattern Mining [18] aims at identifying frequent subsequences within a sequences database $\mathcal{D}$. In the following, we briefly formalize the SPM problem. Throughout this article, $[n] = \{1, \ldots, n\}$ denotes the set of the first n positive integers. Let Σ be the alphabet, i.e., the set of items. An *itemset* $A = \{a_1, a_2, \ldots, a_m\} \subseteq \Sigma$ is a finite set of items. The size of A, denoted $|A|$, is m. A *sequence* s is of the form $s = \langle s_1 s_2 \ldots s_n \rangle$ where each s_i is an itemset, and n is the length of the sequence. A *database* $\mathcal{D}$ is a multiset of sequences over Σ. A sequence $s = \langle s_1 \ldots s_m \rangle$ with $s_i \in \Sigma$ is contained in a sequence $t = \langle t_1 \ldots t_n \rangle$ with $m \leq n$, written $s \sqsubseteq t$, if $s_i \subseteq t_{e_i}$ for $1 \leq i \leq m$ and an increasing sequence $(e_1 \ldots e_m)$ of positive integers $e_i \in [n]$, called an *embedding* of s in t. For example, we have $\langle a(cd) \rangle \sqsubseteq \langle ab(cde) \rangle$ relative to embedding $(1,3)$. Here, (cd) denotes the itemset made of items c and d. Given a database $\mathcal{D}$, the *cover* of a sequence s is the set of sequences in $\mathcal{D}$ that contain s: $cover(s, \mathcal{D}) = \{t \in D | s \sqsubseteq t\}$. The number of sequences in $\mathcal{D}$ containing s is called its *support*, that is, $supp(s, \mathcal{D}) = |cover(s, \mathcal{D})|$. For an integer *minsup* (that is often referred to as the *minimum support threshold*), the problem of *frequent sequence mining* is about discovering all sequences s such that $supp(s, \mathcal{D}) \geq minsup$. Each sequence that satisfies this requirement is called a *(sequential) pattern*. For $minsup = 2$ we can see how $\langle a \rangle$, $\langle b \rangle$, $\langle c \rangle$, $\langle a\ b \rangle$, $\langle a\ c \rangle$, $\langle b\ c \rangle$ and $\langle a\ b\ c \rangle$ are common patterns in the database $\mathcal{D}$ reported in Table 1 without considering the reference classes.

Table 1. Example of a sequence dataset, in tabular format (left) and encoded with ASP (right). Each sequence has a class label, that is used in CSPM.

ID	Sequence	Class
1	$\langle d\ a\ a\ c \rangle$	C_1
2	$\langle a\ c\ b\ c \rangle$	C_1
3	$\langle a\ c \rangle$	C_1
4	$\langle b \rangle$	C_1
5	$\langle a\ b\ c \rangle$	C_2
6	$\langle a\ b\ c \rangle$	C_2
7	$\langle c \rangle$	C_2

```
1    cl(1,c1). seq(1,1,d). seq(1,2,a). seq(1,3,a). seq(1,4,c).
2    cl(2,c1). seq(2,1,a). seq(2,2,c). seq(2,3,b). seq(2,4,c).
3    cl(3,c1). seq(3,1,a). seq(3,2,c).
4    cl(4,c1). seq(4,1,b).
5    cl(5,c2). seq(5,1,a). seq(5,2,b). seq(5,3,c).
6    cl(6,c2). seq(6,1,a). seq(6,2,b). seq(6,3,c).
7    cl(7,c2). seq(7,1,c).
```

A *contrast sequential pattern* is defined as a sequential pattern that occurs frequently in one sequence dataset but not in the others [3]. We start by introducing the concept of *growth rate*. Given two sequence datasets, $\mathcal{D}_1$ labelled with class C_1 and $\mathcal{D}_2$ labelled with class C_2, the growth rate from $\mathcal{D}_2$ to $\mathcal{D}_1$ of a sequential pattern s is defined as:

$$GR_{C_1}(s) = \frac{supp(s, \mathcal{D}_1)/|\mathcal{D}_1|}{supp(s, \mathcal{D}_2)/|\mathcal{D}_2|} \tag{2}$$

If $supp(s, \mathcal{D}_2) = 0$ and $supp(s, \mathcal{D}_1) \neq 0$ then $GR_{C_1}(s) = \infty$.

In the same way, the growth rate from $\mathcal{D}_1$ to $\mathcal{D}_2$ of s is defined as:

$$GR_{C_2}(s) = \frac{supp(s, \mathcal{D}_2)/|\mathcal{D}_2|}{supp(s, \mathcal{D}_1)/|\mathcal{D}_1|} \tag{3}$$

If $supp(s, \mathcal{D}_1) = 0$ and $supp(s, \mathcal{D}_2) \neq 0$ then $GR_{C_2}(s) = \infty$.

The *contrast rate* of s is denoted as:

$$CR(s) = max\{GR_{C_1}, GR_{C_2}\} \tag{4}$$

If $GR_{C_1}(s) = 0$ and $GR_{C_2}(s) = 0$ then $CR(s) = \infty$.

A sequence s in a sequences dataset is said to be a *contrast sequential pattern* if its contrast rate is not lower than the given threshold: $CR(s) \geq mincr$. Unlike frequent sequential pattern mining, contrast sequential pattern mining can discover the characteristics of different classes in sequences datasets, which has been widely used in sequential data analysis, such as protein/DNA dataset analysis, anomaly detection, and customer behavior analysis.

With reference to the dataset in Table 1, we split $\mathcal{D}$ into $\mathcal{D}_1$ and $\mathcal{D}_2$ according to the classes C_1 and C_2, respectively. For example, the sequence $s = \langle a\ c \rangle$ has $supp(s, \mathcal{D}_1) = 3$, $supp(s, \mathcal{D}_2) = 2$, $GR_{C_1}(s) = 1.125$, $GR_{C_2}(s) = 0.89$, and $CR(s) = 1.125$. Given $t = \langle a\ b\ c \rangle$, it has $supp(t, \mathcal{D}_1) = 1$, $supp(t, \mathcal{D}_2) = 2$, $GR_{C_1}(t) = 0.375$, $GR_{C_2}(t) = 2.67$, and $CR(t) = 2.67$. If, *e.g.*, $mincr = 1$, we can conclude that s and t are contrast sequential patterns for C_1 and C_2 resp., because $CR(s) \geq mincr$ and $CR(t) \geq mincr$.

4   ASP Encoding for Contrast Sequence Mining

In this section we describe the proposed ASP encoding and discuss the rationale behind. Since CSPM merges the two notions of sequential pattern and contrast pattern, it is necessary to first extract the frequent sequential patterns from the input sequences (see Sect. 4.1) and then check which of these regularities are actually contrast sequential patterns (see Sect. 4.2).

4.1   From Sequences to Sequential Patterns

The sub-problem of mining frequent sequential patterns is encoded according to the principles outlined in [5]. However, in our case, we need to consider also the reference class. In particular, $\mathcal{D}$ is represented as a collection of ASP facts of the kind *seq(s, p, i)* and *cl(s, c)*, where the *seq* predicate says that an item i occurs at position p in a sequence s while the *cl* predicate says that s is labelled with class c. Table 1 shows the ASP encoding of a sequence dataset.

Besides *minsup* and *mincr*, *maxlen* and *minlen* are introduced to denote the maximum and the minimum pattern length, respectively. Also, *c1* and *c2* stand for the classes C_1 and C_2, respectively. The lower the value of *minsup* and *mincr* the more patterns will be extracted; the lower the value of *maxlen*, the smaller the ground program will be. Therefore the parameters allow a tuning for the program efficiency. Finally, each answer set comprises a single pattern of interest. More precisely, an answer set represents a (contrast) sequential pattern $s = \langle s_i \rangle_{i \leq th \leq m}$ such that $1 \leq m \leq maxlen$ from atoms $pat(1, s_1), ..., pat(m, s_m)$. The first argument expresses the position of the item inside the pattern. For example the atoms $pat(1, a)$, $pat(2, b)$ and $pat(3, c)$ describe a contrast sequential pattern $\langle a\ b\ c \rangle$ for the database in Table 1.

For this sub-problem the basic "fill-gaps" encoding provided by [10] can be used with little modifications.

4.2   From Frequent Sequences to Contrast Patterns

The sub-problem of filtering contrast patterns out of the frequent sequences discovered by the encoding reported in Sect. 4.1 requires additional ASP rules.

```
1   card(Card, c1) :- Card = #count{T : cl(T, c1)}.
2   card(Card, c2) :- Card = #count{T : cl(T, c2)}.
3
4   sup(Sup, c1) :- Sup = #count{T : support(T), seq(T, _, _), cl(T, c1)}.
5   sup(Sup, c2) :- Sup = #count{T : support(T), seq(T, _, _), cl(T, c2)}.
6
7   gr_rate("inf", c1) :- sup(Sup1, c1), Sup1 != 0, sup(0, c2).
8   gr_rate("inf", c2) :- sup(Sup2, c2), Sup2 != 0, sup(0, c1).
9   gr_rate(@gr(Sup1, Card1, Sup2, Card2), c1) :- sup(Sup1, c1),
10      card(Card1, c1), sup(Sup2, c2), card(Card2, c2), Sup1 > 0, Sup2 > 0.
11  gr_rate(@gr(Sup2, Card2, Sup1, Card1), c2) :- sup(Sup1, c1),
12      card(Card1, c1), sup(Sup2, c2), card(Card2, c2), Sup1 > 0, Sup2 > 0.
13
14  contr_pat(yes, Class) :- gr_rate("inf", Class).
15  contr_pat(@csp(Cr, mincr), Class) :- gr_rate(Cr, Class),  Cr != "inf".
16
17  :- contr_pat(no, c1), contr_pat(no, c2).
```

In the code above Lines 1–2 compute the cardinality of the datasets $\mathcal{D}_1$ and $\mathcal{D}_2$ whereas Lines 4–5 compute the support of a pattern s in $\mathcal{D}_1$ and $\mathcal{D}_2$ respectively. Lines 9–10 calculate $GR_{C_1}(s)$ in accordance with the formula in Eq. (2), while Line 6 capture the case of $GR_{C_1}(s) = \infty$. ASP does not support the computation of formulas that return decimal values. For this reason, a Python script has been developed which can be called from within ASP (with the @ command followed by the function name). The result will no longer be treated in ASP as a constant but rather as a string. Analogously, Lines 12–13 encode the computation of GR_{C_2} according to Eq. (3) and Line 7 concerns the infinite case for GR_{C_2}. Finally, Lines 14–15 check if the sequence s in hand is a contrast pattern for either C_1 or C_2 by means of a Python function because it compares decimal numbers. If the growth rate is less than *mincr*, a constant *no* is returned, *yes* otherwise. Lines 14–15 set the first term of the *contrast_pattern* to *yes* in accordance with the formulas in Eq. (2) and (3), respectively. The constraint at Line 17 discards all answer sets that do not represent contrast patterns for any of the two classes.

Below, the same example of CSPM reported at the end of Sect. 3.2 is solved by running our ASP encoding over the ASP facts in Table 1 with $minsup = 20\%$ and $mincr = 1$.

```
1   pat(1,a) pat(2,c) gr_rate("0.89",c2) contr_pat(no,c2) gr_rate("1.125",c1) contr_pat(yes,c1)
2   pat(1,a) pat(2,b) pat(3,c) gr_rate("2.67",c2) contr_pat(yes,c2) gr_rate("0.375",c1) contr_pat(no,c1)
```

Table 2. Features of iPRG and UNIX User sub-datasets: The number of distinct symbols, the number of sequences, the total number of symbols in the dataset, the maximum sequence length, the average sequence length, and the density (calculated by $\frac{\|D\|}{|\Sigma|\|D|}$.)

Dataset	$|\Sigma|$	$|D|$	$\|D\|$	$\max|T|$	$\text{avg}|T|$	density
iPRG	21	8628	111,743	12	11.95	0.62
iPRG_25_25	20	50	657	12	11.88	0.64
iPRG_100_100	20	200	2591	12	11.83	0.64
iPRG_500_500	21	1000	12,933	12	11.92	0.62
iPRG_1000_1000	21	2000	25,841	12	11.91	0.61
UNIX	2672	9099	165,748	1256	18.22	0.01
UNIX_25_25	70	50	365	55	7.3	0.10
UNIX_100_100	178	200	2281	175	11.41	0.06
UNIX_500_500	420	1000	13,289	187	13.29	0.03
UNIX_755_755	540	1510	20,234	214	13.4	0.02

5   Experiments

In this section we examine the computational behavior of the ASP encoding described in Sect. 4. In pattern mining, it is usual to evaluate the effectiveness (number of extracted patterns) and the time and space efficiency of an algorithm. Moreover in ASP-based DPM approaches it is important to know the solver and grounder time. To this end, we conducted experiments on the following datasets:

- iPRG: each transaction is a sequence of peptides that is known to cleave in presence of a Trypsin enzyme,[1]
- UNIX User: each transaction is a sequence of shell commands executed by a user during one session.[2]

We have chosen these datasets because (i) they are suitable for the task considered in this paper (classified sequences), (ii) they have been already used in the DPM literature, in particular in [10,19] although for a different task, and (iii) they are publicly available. Notably, transactions in both datasets are labelled with one of two classes, *pos* and *neg*.

---

[1] https://dtai.cs.kuleuven.be/CP4IM/cpsm/datasets.html.
[2] https://archive.ics.uci.edu/ml/datasets/UNIX+User+Data.

In the following we report and discuss the results obtained from scalability tests on iPRG (Sect. 5.1) and UNIX User (Sect. 5.2). As a solver, we have used the version 5.4.0 of clingo, with default solving parameters. The timeout (TMO) has been set to 5 h. The ASP programs were run on a laptop computer with Windows 10 (with Ubuntu 20.04.4 subsystem), AMD Ryzen 5 3500U @ 2.10 GHz, 8 GB RAM without using the multi-threading mode of clingo. Multi-threading reduces the mean runtime but introduces variance due to the random allocation of tasks. Such variance is inconvenient for interpreting results with repeated executions.

As regards the comparison with alternative solutions to the CSPM problem in hand, it has not been possible to run experiments with dedicated algorithms like [22,23] since their code is not available. Thus, we have considered a hybrid ASP-based approach inspired by [20]. The results from the comparative evaluation are reported and discussed in Sect. 5.3.

Full code and detailed experimental results are available online.[3].

5.1 Scalability Tests on iPRG

In order to study the behaviour of the ASP encoding over iPRG, we have created several subsets of this dataset of increasing size (Table 2).

For each sub-dataset, we show runtime and memory behaviour of the encoding in two settings (see Table 3). On the left the minimum support threshold ($minsup$) varies from 10% to 50% while $mincr = 3$, $minlen = 2$, and $maxlen = 5$ remain fixed, and on the right the minimum contrast rate ($mincr$) varies from 1 to 5 while $minsup = 20\%$, $minlen = 2$, and $maxlen = 5$ remain fixed. When we increase $minsup$ and/or $mincr$, the number of patterns and the runtime decrease. The minimum support threshold at 20% represents a cut point as regards the number of patterns found. Obviously, as the size of the dataset increases, the runtime and memory parameters grow up but the grounding phase ($time - solv.\ t.$) not significantly. In the case of Table 3(e, f, g, h) the execution is interrupted as it exceeds the time limit of 5 h. Also, the choice of $minsup = 10\%$ influences the dimension of the program and consequently the execution time as shown in Table 3(e, g). We recall that these tests were conducted using a single thread for the reasons mentioned before. With more threads the total execution time will decrease. As regards memory usage, this grows up in proportion to the size of the input dataset but remains stable as $minsup$ or $mincr$ increases. Low $minsup$ values allow to find more patterns but at a higher runtime. In fact, the thresholds $minsup$ and $mincr$ have the pruning function, the former for frequent sequences and the latter for contrast sequences.

Below, as an illustrative example, we report some contrast sequential patterns found in iPRG_100_100 for $minsup = 10\%$ and $mincr = 3$.

```
1    pat(1,4) pat(2,5) pat(3,9) gr_rate("0.05",neg) contr_pat(no,neg) gr_rate("19.0",pos) contr_pat(yes,pos)
2    pat(1,9) pat(2,9) pat(3,2) pat(4,11) gr_rate("inf") contr_pat(yes,pos)
3    pat(1,11) pat(2,16) pat(3,8) gr_rate("12.0") contr_pat(yes,neg) gr_rate("0.08") contr_pat(no,pos)
4    pat(1,2) pat(2,16) pat(3,8) gr_rate("inf") contr_pat(yes,neg)
```

---

[3] https://github.com/mpia3/Contrast-Sequential-Pattern-Mining.git.

Line 1 describes the contrast pattern $\langle 4\ 5\ 9 \rangle$ that represents the sequence $\langle Q\ P\ N \rangle$ of peptides.[4] This pattern has high contrast rate for the *pos* class. Conversely, Line 3 shows a contrast pattern $(\langle 11\ 16\ 8 \rangle = \langle L\ D\ K \rangle)$ for the *neg* class. The patterns $\langle 9\ 9\ 2\ 11 \rangle = \langle N\ N\ I\ L \rangle$ and $\langle 2\ 16\ 8 \rangle = \langle I\ D\ K \rangle$ at Lines 2 and 4, respectively, have an important property. They occur only in the *pos* and *neg* classes respectively because the growth rate value is infinite.

Table 3. Number of patterns, runtime (seconds), solver time (seconds) and memory consumption (MB) on all iPRG sub-datasets. TMO means that the execution has exceeded the imposed 5-hour timeout.

(a) iPRG_25_25, mincr = 3

minsup	#pat	time	solv. t.	memory
10%	712	3.065	2.96	25.96
20%	24	1.550	1.35	23.89
30%	2	1.050	0.86	23.89
40%	0	0.480	0.34	23.89
50%	0	0.243	0.08	23.89

(b) iPRG_25_25, minsup = 20%

mincr	#pat	time	solv. t.	memory
1	0	0.085	0.00	22.31
2	0	0.076	0.00	21.93
3	0	0.086	0.00	21.67
4	0	0.086	0.00	22.31
5	0	0.086	0.00	22.18

(c) iPRG_100_100, mincr = 3

minsup	#pat	time	solv. t.	memory
10%	561	47.553	46.82	87.05
20%	15	22.585	21.43	60.05
30%	0	10.279	9.02	60.04
40%	0	5.474	4.34	60.00
50%	0	3.488	2.23	60.00

(d) iPRG_100_100, minsup = 20%

mincr	#pat	time	solv. t.	memory
1	72	20.290	19.12	59.16
2	37	21.855	20.74	61.77
3	15	21.974	20.73	60.05
4	9	18.289	17.15	60.04
5	8	18.338	17.11	59.98

(e) iPRG_500_500, mincr = 3

minsup	#pat	time	solv. t.	memory
10%	71	TMO	TMO	852.24
20%	12	3543.002	3524.08	852.24
30%	0	1712.463	1692.43	852.24
40%	0	140.521	120.08	852.24
50%	0	98.535	79.49	852.24

(f) iPRG_500_500, minsup = 20%

mincr	#pat	time	solv. t.	memory
1	71	TMO	TMO	852.24
2	20	403.259	383.63	859.90
3	12	3440.552	3421.60	852.24
4	8	606.101	586.90	851.83
5	4	TMO	TMO	1447.55

(g) iPRG_1000_1000, mincr = 3

minsup	#pat	time	solv. t.	memory
10%	12	TMO	TMO	3258.44
20%	3	TMO	TMO	3242.55
30%	0	7375.746	7284.13	3253.90
40%	0	2061.364	1972.19	3232.85
50%	0	TMO	TMO	3433.55

(h) iPRG_1000_1000, minsup = 20%

mincr	#pat	time	solv. t.	memory
1	12	TMO	TMO	3258.44
2	18	TMO	TMO	3166,26
3	3	TMO	TMO	3207.61
4	0	TMO	TMO	3172.99
5	0	TMO	TMO	3118.20

5.2   Scalability Tests on UNIX User

As regards the UNIX User dataset we have created several subsets of the same size as iPRG (see Table 2), except for one (namely, UNIX_755_755) where the rationale behind the size of 755 is the fact that the positive sequences are only 755 in the original dataset and we wanted to keep the two classes balanced.

---

[4] The meaning of each item can be found at the link where the dataset is published.

Analogously to the experiments conducted with iPRG, we report runtime and memory usage for two batches of tests (see Table 4). One concerns the variation of the minimum support threshold (*minsup*) from 10% to 50%, while keeping *mincr* = 3, *minlen* = 2, and *maxlen* = 5 fixed. The other concerns the variation of the minimum contrast rate (*mincr*) from 1 to 5 while leaving unchanged *minsup* = 20%, *minlen* = 2, and *maxlen* = 5. The particularity of the dataset lies in the size of its alphabet, clearly higher than iPRG. Such a size affects sequences with a higher average length. In fact the largest sequence, whatever the size of the dataset considered, is clearly larger than iPRG. This also affects the number of patterns found, lower than for iPRG because the single sequence has much more variance. Moreover, the alphabet size affects the overall time. From a comparison between Tables 3(e, f) and 4(e, f) it is clear the difference in magnitude of the time taken. All tables show the same behavior in memory as iPRG. When the data size is high, the overall time exceeds the timeout only when support threshold is less or equal than 20% (see Table 4(e, g, h)).

Table 4. Number of patterns, runtime (seconds), solver time (seconds) and memory consumption (MB) on all UNIX User sub-datasets. TMO means that the execution has exceeded the imposed 5-hour timeout.

(a) *UNIX_25_25, mincr = 3*

minsup	#pat	time	solv. t.	memory
10%	335	0.414	0.26	23.5
20%	1	0.105	0.02	22.93
30%	0	0.095	0.01	22.93
40%	0	0.086	0.01	22.93
50%	0	0.087	0.00	21.38

(b) *UNIX_25_25, minsup = 20%*

mincr	#pat	time	solv. t.	memory
1	1	0.132	0.01	22.94
2	1	0.103	0.02	22.94
3	1	0.099	0.02	22.93
4	1	0.104	0.02	22.93
5	1	0.103	0.02	21.21

(c) *UNIX_100_100, mincr = 3*

minsup	#pat	time	solv. t.	memory
10%	18	3.679	2.69	59.58
20%	0	1.792	1.02	59.57
30%	0	1.342	0.56	59.57
40%	0	0.973	0.24	37.48
50%	0	0.886	0.14	37.35

(d) *UNIX_100_100, minsup = 20%*

mincr	#pat	time	solv. t.	memory
1	0	2.409	1.4	59.4
2	0	1.841	1.10	59.55
3	0	0.818	1.03	59.57
4	0	1.789	1.04	59.53
5	0	1.753	1.04	59.56

(e) *UNIX_500_500, mincr = 3*

minsup	#pat	time	solv. t.	memory
10%	9	TMO	TMO	850.79
20%	1	129.941	110.99	850.79
30%	0	59.270	37.88	850.79
40%	0	50.735	30.39	850.79
50%	0	35.419	15.68	850.79

(f) *UNIX_500_500, minsup = 20%*

mincr	#pat	time	solv. t.	memory
1	1	74.553	53.96	855.96
2	1	123.825	104.54	846.29
3	1	123.167	103.68	848.51
4	1	125.537	106.22	850.38
5	1	128.747	109.14	850.38

(g) *UNIX_755_755, mincr = 3*

minsup	#pat	time	solv. t.	memory
10%	1	TMO	TMO	2653.12
20%	0	TMO	TMO	2642.25
30%	0	235.760	188.53	1849.92
40%	0	146.888	99.52	1850.01
50%	0	120.360	72.95	1850.00

(h) *UNIX_755_755, minsup = 20%*

mincr	#pat	time	solv. t.	memory
1	0	286.354	238.35	1848.77
2	0	13,709.513	13,661.11	1851.55
3	0	TMO	TMO	2642.25
4	0	TMO	TMO	1848.83
5	0	TMO	TMO	3766.38

Some contrast sequential patterns mined from UNIX_25_25 are shown below as an illustrative example. Each item represents a UNIX command.[5]

```
1   pat(1,12) pat(2,14) pat(3,15) pat(4,13) pat(5,12) gr_rate("inf",neg) contr_pat(yes,neg)
2   pat(1,103) pat(2,2611) pat(3,29) pat(4,2812) gr_rate("inf",pos) contr_pat(yes,pos)
```

Line 1 shows the sequence $\langle 12\ 14\ 15\ 13\ 12 \rangle = \langle fg\ |\ more\ finger\ fg \rangle$ that is a contrast pattern only for the *neg* class while Line 2 a sequence found only for the *pos* class: $\langle 103\ 2611\ 29\ 2812 \rangle = \langle quota\ emacs - nw\ netscape\ assoc.out \rangle$.

5.3   Comparison with a Hybrid ASP-Based Approach

As a baseline for a comparative evaluation we have considered a two-step approach that features an ASP filtering on top of a dedicated algorithm for SPM. In

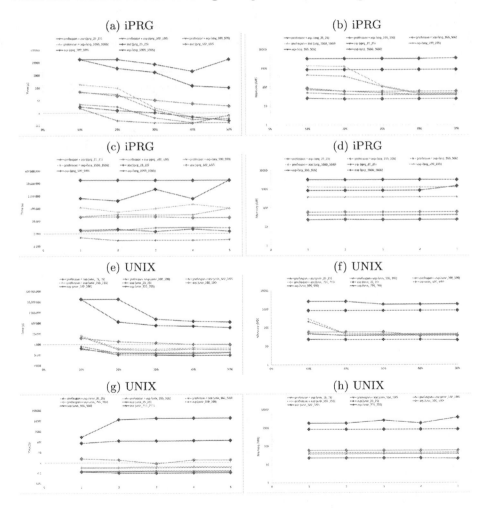

Fig. 1. Comparison between pure and hybrid ASP-based approaches.

---

[5] The reader can find the conversion table at the link where the dataset is published.

the first step, *PrefixSpan* [11] is applied to discover frequent sequential patterns, while in the second step, the patterns are post-processed by using the ASP rules reported in Sect. 4.2 to find the constrasting ones. The resulting hybrid *PrefixSpan+ASP* approach has been applied on the same datasets (see Table 2) and with the same parameters used in the scalability tests reported in the previous two sections. The results obtained with the pure ASP and the hybrid method as regards the time and memory dimensions are graphically presented in Fig. 1 in a comparative way.

It is interesting to note the behavior of the two approaches. For both iPRG and UNIX User, the one-shot approach performs slightly better than the two-step approach when the dataset size is not large (up to 100–100 sequences). This can be observed especially for memory usage (see Fig. 1 (b, d, f, h)).

6   Conclusions and Future Work

This article has presented a declarative approach to the CSPM task which is based on ASP. To the best of our knowledge, this is the first proposed ASP encoding for this task. It takes advantage of the Python interface for Clingo to design more complex ASP programs, e.g., numerical computation as in our case. The encoding has been extensively evaluated on real-world (publicly available) datasets to draw conclusions about the efficiency of the approach. Low *minsup* and *mincr* values allow to find more patterns. However, this comes with an increasing runtime. So, the results from the scalability tests are promising although they can not be considered conclusive about the validity of the approach. For this reason, a comparison with two-step approaches is particularly interesting. The results obtained with the hybrid PrefixSpan+ASP approach confirm and complement the conclusions of [20] concerning the advantages of hybrid approaches over pure approaches as regards time performance. Our contribution is the empirical evidence for a DPM task (namely, CSPM) that was not covered by [20]. In particular, the analysis of memory usage provides new hints on the behaviour of ASP-based DPM solutions.

Much work needs to be done for the future. In order to improve the performance, we intend to explore the extraction of condensed representations (e.g. maximal and closed patterns) in the context of CSPM. Also, further experiments are needed to complete the efficiency analysis of our ASP encoding, such as the ones aimed at studying the interplay between memory usage and pattern length as done in [10]. Another direction for future development of the present work is to consider other forms of contrast pattern as described in [3]. Our proposal is indeed general enough to enable the encoding of several types of constraints. The addition/deletion of constraints allows the modeling of problem variants. Overall, an advantage of DPM is that for most well-specified tasks, the development effort is significantly lower than for procedural approaches. We do not expect DPM to be competitive with dedicated algorithms, but to take advantage of the versatility of declarative frameworks to propose pattern mining tools that could exploit background knowledge during the mining process to extract less but meaningful patterns. To this aim, we plan to enrich the datasets for future experiments with domain knowledge, *e.g.*, chemistry or biology related constraints in the iPRG dataset.

Acknowledgments. This work was partially supported by the project FAIR - Future AI Research (PE00000013), under the NRRP MUR program funded by the NextGenerationEU.

References

1. Besnard, P., Guyet, T.: Declarative mining of negative sequential patterns. In: DPSW 2020–1st Declarative Problem Solving Workshop, pp. 1–8 (2020)
2. Brewka, G., Eiter, T., Truszczynski, M.: Answer set programming at a glance. Commun. ACM **54**(12), 92–103 (2011). https://doi.org/10.1145/2043174.2043195
3. Chen, Y., Gan, W., Wu, Y., Yu, P.S.: Contrast pattern mining: a survey. arXiv preprint arXiv:2209.13556 (2022)
4. Dong, G., Bailey, J.: Contrast Data Mining: Concepts, Algorithms, and Applications. CRC Press, Boca Raton (2012)
5. Gebser, M., Guyet, T., Quiniou, R., Romero, J., Schaub, T.: Knowledge-based sequence mining with asp. In: 25th International Joint Conference on Artificial Intelligence, IJCAI 2016, p. 8. AAAI (2016)
6. Gebser, M., Kaminski, R., Kaufmann, B., Schaub, T.: Clingo= ASP + control: preliminary report. arXiv preprint arXiv:1405.3694 (2014)
7. Guns, T., Dries, A., Nijssen, S., Tack, G., De Raedt, L.: Miningzinc: a declarative framework for constraint-based mining. Artif. Intell. **244**, 6–29 (2017)
8. Guyet, T., Happe, A., Dauxais, Y.: Declarative sequential pattern mining of care pathways. In: ten Teije, A., Popow, C., Holmes, J.H., Sacchi, L. (eds.) AIME 2017. LNCS (LNAI), vol. 10259, pp. 261–266. Springer, Cham (2017). https://doi.org/10.1007/978-3-319-59758-4_29
9. Guyet, T., Moinard, Y., Quiniou, R.: Using answer set programming for pattern mining. arXiv preprint arXiv:1409.7777 (2014)
10. Guyet, T., Moinard, Y., Quiniou, R., Schaub, T.: Efficiency analysis of ASP encodings for sequential pattern mining tasks. In: Pinaud, B., Guillet, F., Cremilleux, B., de Runz, C. (eds.) Advances in Knowledge Discovery and Management. SCI, vol. 732, pp. 41–81. Springer, Cham (2018). https://doi.org/10.1007/978-3-319-65406-5_3
11. Han, J., et al.: PrefixSpan: mining sequential patterns efficiently by prefix-projected pattern growth. In: proceedings of the 17th International Conference on Data Engineering, pp. 215–224. IEEE (2001)
12. Jabbour, S., Sais, L., Salhi, Y.: Decomposition based SAT encodings for itemset mining problems. In: Cao, T., Lim, E.-P., Zhou, Z.-H., Ho, T.-B., Cheung, D., Motoda, H. (eds.) PAKDD 2015. LNCS (LNAI), vol. 9078, pp. 662–674. Springer, Cham (2015). https://doi.org/10.1007/978-3-319-18032-8_52
13. Leone, N., et al.: Enhancing DLV for large-scale reasoning. In: Balduccini, M., Lierler, Y., Woltran, S. (eds.) LPNMR 2019. LNCS, vol. 11481, pp. 312–325. Springer, Cham (2019). https://doi.org/10.1007/978-3-030-20528-7_23
14. Lifschitz, V.: Answer sets and the language of answer set programming. AI Mag. **37**(3), 7–12 (2016)

15. Lisi, F.A., Sterlicchio, G.: Declarative pattern mining in digital forensics: preliminary results. In: Calegari, R., Ciatto, G., Omicini, A. (eds.) Proceedings of the 37th Italian Conference on Computational Logic, Bologna, Italy, 29 June–1 July 2022. CEUR Workshop Proceedings, vol. 3204, pp. 232–246. CEUR-WS.org (2022). http://ceur-ws.org/Vol-3204/paper_23.pdf
16. Lisi, F.A., Sterlicchio, G.: Mining sequences in phone recordings with answer set programming. In: Bruno, P., Calimeri, F., Cauteruccio, F., Maratea, M., Terracina, G., Vallati, M. (eds.) Joint Proceedings of the 1st International Workshop on HYbrid Models for Coupling Deductive and Inductive ReAsoning (HYDRA 2022) and the 29th RCRA Workshop on Experimental Evaluation of Algorithms for Solving Problems with Combinatorial Explosion (RCRA 2022) co-located with the 16th International Conference on Logic Programming and Non-monotonic Reasoning (LPNMR 2022), Genova Nervi, Italy, 5 September 2022. CEUR Workshop Proceedings, vol. 3281, pp. 34–50. CEUR-WS.org (2022). http://ceur-ws.org/Vol-3281/paper4.pdf
17. Lisi, F.A., Sterlicchio, G.: A declarative approach to contrast pattern mining. In: Dovier, A., Montanari, A., Orlandini, A. (eds.) AIxIA 2022. LNCS, vol. 13796, pp. 17–30. Springer, Cham (2023). https://doi.org/10.1007/978-3-031-27181-6_2
18. Mooney, C.H., Roddick, J.F.: Sequential pattern mining-approaches and algorithms. ACM Comput. Surv. (CSUR) 45(2), 1–39 (2013)
19. Negrevergne, B., Guns, T.: Constraint-based sequence mining using constraint programming. In: Michel, L. (ed.) CPAIOR 2015. LNCS, vol. 9075, pp. 288–305. Springer, Cham (2015). https://doi.org/10.1007/978-3-319-18008-3_20
20. Paramonov, S., Stepanova, D., Miettinen, P.: Hybrid ASP-based approach to pattern mining. Theory Pract. Log. Program. 19(4), 505–535 (2019). https://doi.org/10.1017/S1471068418000467
21. Samet, A., Guyet, T., Negrevergne, B.: Mining rare sequential patterns with ASP. In: ILP 2017–27th International Conference on Inductive Logic Programming (2017)
22. Wu, Y., Wang, Y., Li, Y., Zhu, X., Wu, X.: Top-k self-adaptive contrast sequential pattern mining. IEEE Trans. Cybern. 52(11), 11819–11833 (2022). https://doi.org/10.1109/TCYB.2021.3082114
23. Zheng, Z., Wei, W., Liu, C., Cao, W., Cao, L., Bhatia, M.: An effective contrast sequential pattern mining approach to taxpayer behavior analysis. World Wide Web 19, 633–651 (2016)

Ontologies

An Ontological Modelling of Reason-Based Preferences

Daniele Porello[(✉)][iD]

University of Genoa, Via Balbi 4, 1626 Genoa, Italy
daniele.porello@unige.it
https://www.danieleporello.net

Abstract. We present an ontological framework for the reason-based model of individual preferences introduced by F. Dietrich and C. List. According to this perspective, an agent prefers x to y if and only if the importance of the reasons motivating x outweighs the importance of the reasons motivating y. Firstly, we represent motivating reasons as concepts in Description Logic, to enable a rich ontological theory that provides a clear and shareable semantics of reasons. Secondly, we present a model to express preferences on combinations of reasons. Finally, we discuss how preferences on alternatives depend on preferences on motivating reasons. We present the framework in a knowledge-dependent way, meaning that the ontological background constrains the definable preferences on alternatives and reasons.

Keywords: property-based preferences · motivating reasons · knowledge-dependence · ontologies

1 Introduction

The theory of preference relations plays a fundamental role in various branches of economics, including game theory, decision theory, and social choice theory. Preferences are also a fundamental concept in computer science, particularly in multiagent systems and Artificial Intelligence. They contribute to defining the very notion of an agent—an entity typically endowed with beliefs, goals, desires, intentions, and preferences—and help understand and model scenarios such as coordination, negotiation, and competition among agents, including artificial ones.

The foundation of the theory of preference relations can be traced back to the work of Kenneth Arrow [2], where preferences are formalised as binary relations satisfying a number of desiderata, and to Amartya Sen [15], where preferences are inferred from observable choices. The debate on the nature of preferences and the question of 'where do preferences come from?' is, of course, too broad to be summarised here. We directly introduce a recent important contribution to the theory of preferences, that is at the origin of the proposed approach: the work of Dietrich and List, which construes preferences as based on motivating reasons, see [7] and [6]. A related logic-based view models preferences as grounded on agents' beliefs about the alternatives or on the properties of options, e.g. [9, 12].

© The Author(s), under exclusive license to Springer Nature Switzerland AG 2023
R. Basili et al. (Eds.): AIxIA 2023, LNAI 14318, pp. 61–73, 2023.
https://doi.org/10.1007/978-3-031-47546-7_5

The reason-based approach is interesting because it is quite general, it clearly (axiomatically) defines what it means for a preference to be reason-based, and it provides necessary and sufficient conditions that characterise preferences based on motivating reasons.

Therefore, this theory has interesting applications to the foundations of the problems *rationalisability* and *explicability* of individual preferences.

The modelling of reasons and preferences of Dietrich and List is semantical: preference are relations on a set of alternatives X, while reasons are properties of alternatives, that is, subsets of X. In fact, no formal language is explicitly introduced to model reasons and preferences. Moreover, the possible logical connections or conflicts between reasons—or, more generally, the meanings of reasons—remain somehow implicit in the applications of the approach.

The objective of this work is to develop the reason-based approach to preferences by leveraging the techniques of Knowledge Representation and Applied Ontology. In particular, we shall define a formal language to express reasons based on Description Logics ($\mathscr{DL}$s). To provide the information which is required to give contents to reasons, we shall introduce a methodology to place the reason-based approach within a rich ontological setting.

The semantic approach of Dietrich and List can be construed as if it were based on a single intended model of a theory. This option is often too demanding, as it forces the crisp agreement on any piece of information. We shall base our restatement of [7] on the models enabled by a formal theory. That is, the definitions that we shall develop (e.g. the satisfaction of a motivating reason) are to be intended as *knowledege-dependent*, in the sense explored in [8]. We also investigate how to express preferences on possible combinations of reasons. As we shall see, this task is related to the problem of defining preferences in combinatorial domains. To this task, we will adapt the setting in [16, 17] to the case of concepts in $\mathscr{DL}$s. Then, we shall model how the preferences defined on combinations of reasons affect the preferences on the alternatives that satisfy those reasons.

A delicate aspect that we encounter when defining preference on combination of reasons is the possible logical dependency or conflict between reasons, which constraint the definable preferences.

Two articles are specifically related to the proposed approach, they are in the area of multi-attribute decision making. In [14], weighted concepts in $\mathscr{DL}$ are used to define preferences on formulas. The main difference with the present approach is that we shall work with the class of models of a Knowledge Base, rather than with single models, besides, we are specifically interested in expanding the reason-based approach in an ontological setting. Secondly, in [1] weighted $\mathscr{DL}$s are used to model preferences and utility functions on options depending on the attributes that they satisfy. They do work with models of a Knowledge Base, the main difference with this works is that we are interested specifically in the reason-based approach of [7], and in discussing the compatibility between preferences and a Knowledge Base.

The remainder of this paper is organised as follows. In Sect. 2, we review the reason-based approach to preference proposed by Dietrich and List, [7]. In Sect. 3, we present our modelling of reason-based preferences in $\mathscr{DL}$s, specifically in $\mathscr{ALC}$. Then, we introduce a method to define utility functions and preferences on combinations of reasons. In Sect. 4, we approach the dependence of preference on motivating reasons and we discuss which preferences can be construed as reason-based, consistently with a Knowledge Base. Section 5 suggests applications, indicates future work, and concludes.

2 A Model of Reason-Based Preferences

In [7], the reason-based approach to preferences is presented "semantically", i.e. in terms of sets and relations. We rephrase it by means of a formal language. We refer here to a general predicative language $\mathscr{L}$ (e.g. a fragment of first-order logic), while in the next sections we will instantiate $\mathscr{L}$ with the language of Description Logics, i.e. $\mathscr{ALC}$.

Let X be a finite set of alternatives. As usual, a preference relation on X is a binary relation $\succeq \subseteq X \times X$ that is reflexive, transitive, and complete. The indifference relation is defined by $x \sim y$ iff $x \succeq y$ and $y \succeq x$.

A motivating reason is viewed by Dietrich and List as a property of the alternatives; hence, it is intended semantically as a subset of X. Here, we model properties as unary predicates and the preference relation as a binary predicate of the alphabet of $\mathscr{L}$. The preference relation is then supposed to satisfy the axioms corresponding to reflexivity, transitivity, and completeness (cf. [13]) to individuate the intended models. Abusing the notation, we stil use $\succeq$ for the relational symbol of the language.

We assume a (finite) designated set of unary predicates $\mathscr{R} = \{P_1, \ldots, P_m\}$ for representing reasons. We decide a model (X, I) to interpret the predicates, by selecting the set of alternatives X as domain. Thus, the predicates of $\mathscr{R}$ are interpreted as subsets of X: $I(P_i) \subseteq X$. A subset $M \subseteq \mathscr{R}$ represents a set of *motivating reasons* of a certain agent, cf. [7].

Definition 1 (Coherence of reasons). *A set M of reasons is* coherent *iff* $\bigcap_{P_i \in M} I(P_i) \neq \emptyset$ *(or, equivalently, iff $P_1 x \wedge \cdots \wedge P_n x$ is satisfiable in X, I).*[1]

We denote by $\mathscr{M} \subseteq 2^{\mathscr{R}}$ the set of all sets of motivating reasons. In [7], $\mathscr{M}$ is intended to abstractly represent the sets of motivating reasons of an agent in various circumstances. By setting $\mathscr{M} \subseteq 2^{\mathscr{R}}$, we may exclude implausible combinations of reasons, e.g. incoherent sets of reasons, if agents exhibit a modicum of rationality.

We assume a set of individual constants to refer to alternative in X. By slightly abusing the notation, we shall use the same letters for denoting the alternatives in X and the individual constants, we also endorse the unique-name assumption. We write $I \models Pa$ to state that the formula Pa is true in the model X, I.

We mildly restate the definition of property-based preference relations, cf. [7], in this setting.

Definition 2 (Property-based preference relations). *A family of preference relations $(\succeq_M)_{M \in \mathscr{M}}$ is* property-based *iff there exists a relation $\succeq$ defined on the set of (coherent*

---

[1] In [7], this property is termed consistency. We term it coherence, although it refers here to a single model, the one where P_is are interpreted. By contrast, the notion of coherence of a concept in $\mathscr{DL}s$ refers to the existence of a model where the concept is instantiated.

sets of) reasons ($\geq \subseteq \mathcal{M} \times \mathcal{M}$) *such that, for every a, b in X and for any motivating set of reasons* $M \in \mathcal{C}$, *the following equivalence holds:*

$$a \succeq_M b \text{ iff } \{P \in M \text{ s.t. } I \models Pa\} \succeq \{P \in M \text{ s.t. } I \models Pb\} \tag{1}$$

That is, a is preferred to b according to the motivating reasons M iff the reasons in M that a satisfies are "better" than the reasons in M that b satisfies (according to the relation $\succeq$). The relation $\succeq$ is termed a *weighing* relation, it compares the importance of every pair of sets of motivating reasons.[2]

In [7], property-based preferences are constrained by the following two axioms.

Axiom 1: If $\{P \in M \text{ s.t. } I \models Pa\} = \{P \in M \text{ s.t. } I \models Pb\}$ then $a \sim_M b$.

Axiom 2: For any a, b in X and any set M, M' of reasons in $\mathcal{M}$ with $M \subseteq M'$, if no P in M' is true of a and b, then $a \succeq_M b$ iff $a \succeq_{M'} b$.

Axiom 1 states that, if the properties of a are the same as the properties of b, then a is indifferent to b. That is, the only way to distinguish between a to b in terms of preferences is by proposing motivating reasons. Axiom 2 states that the reasons that do not apply to a nor to b cannot decide the ranking of a and b.

Dietrich and List proved that, if Axioms 1 and 2 hold, then it is possible to associate a single weighing relation $\succeq$ defined $\mathcal{M} \times \mathcal{M}$ to the family of preferences $(\succeq_M)_{\mathcal{M}}$. The weighing relation expresses the relevance of the combinations of reasons for the preference (cf. Theorem 1 in [7]) and every preference relation $\succeq_M$ can be generated by means of a weighing order on sets of reasons. We could say that any $\succeq_M$ is *rationalised* by a set of reasons M.

We conclude this section, by illustrating the reason-based setting by means of a toy example.

Example 1. Consider the purchase of a bicycle. Suppose that the motivationally salient reasons are, in times of inflation, "being a cheap bike" (represented by C) and "being a durable bike" (represented by D). Thus, we select a set of predicates for reasons $\mathcal{R} = \{C, D\}$. We select a domain X, consisting of four alternative bikes. $X = \{cd, c\bar{d}, \bar{c}d, \bar{c}\bar{d}\}$, where, e.g., cd denotes the element of the domain X which satisfies C and D, and $\bar{c}\bar{d}$ denotes an element of X which does not satisfy C nor D. By abusing the notation, we use the same symbols for the individual constants. Thus, we are interpreting C and D in X, so that we know which bikes are cheap and which bikes are durable: $I(C) = \{cd, c\bar{d}\}$ and $I(D) = \{cd, \bar{c}d\}$.

The possible sets of motivating reasons are then $2^{\mathcal{R}} = \{\emptyset, \{C\}, \{D\}, \{C, D\}\}$. Out of them, we can select the set $\mathcal{M} = \{\{C\}, \{D\}, \{C, D\}\}$, i.e. we exclude $\emptyset$, which amounts to assuming that preferences are always based on some combination of reasons. Notice that each set of reason is coherent in this case. The preference relations, based the various sets of motivating reasons, might be as follows.

---

[2] To avoid proliferation of symbols, we denote by $\succ_M$ the ordering of the alternatives, while $\succ$, with no index, indicates the ordering on sets of reasons.

$$M = \{C, D\} \qquad cd \succeq_M c\bar{d} \succeq_M \bar{c}d \succeq_M \bar{c}\bar{d}$$
$$M = \{C\} \qquad cd \sim_M c\bar{d} \succeq_M \bar{c}d \succeq_M \bar{c}\bar{d}$$
$$M = \{D\} \qquad cd \sim_M \bar{c}d \succeq_M c\bar{d} \succeq_M \bar{c}\bar{d}$$

Many preference relations can depend on those sets of reasons, the one above is just a case. However, the family of preference relations $\succeq_M$, for $M \in \mathcal{M}$, is *property-base*, cf. Definition 2. A weighing relation exists and meets the condition of Eq. (1):

$$\{C, D\} \succeq \{C\} \succeq \{D\}$$

3 Ontologies for Reason-Based Preferences

We rephrase the reason-based approach within an ontological setting. The motivations are essentially two and they provide the two objectives of this work. Firstly, we aim at introducing a semantical understanding of reasons. In Example 1, agents are supposed to have access to a single "intended" model, while usually agents' information is represented by (the models of) a Knowledge Base. The definitions of Sect. 2 were indeed phrased wrt. a single "intended" model. Moreover, Example 1 conveys a lot of implicit information about the alternatives and the motivating reasons. Bikes are physical objects, in particular, they are artifacts, usually produced by some factory, marketed by some company, etc. Durability is a property of physical object (in a technical ontological jargon, it may be construed as a *quality* or a *disposition*). Cheapness is also a property, which is related to having a low cost.

Secondly, we wish to explore the reason-based model of [7] in three directions: *i*) by proposing a general mechanism to express preferences on combination of reasons, *ii*) by proposing a general strategy for computing the weighing relation between sets of motivating reasons, *iii*) by investigating the dependence between the preferences definable on combinations of reasons and the logical connections between reasons.

The first task can be approached by selecting a suitable background theory—a Knowledge Base—where reasons are embedded in a network of constraints. That is, reasons are placed within a Tbox (a *terminological box*, i.e. a set of axioms), which makes the agent's information explicit. To provide a general language to express high-level ontological definitions (such as "objects", "events", "artifacts", "qualities", "social objects", etc.), the proposal is to include in the Tbox a *foundational ontology*, such as DOLCE [4, 10]. For an overview and a comparison of the main foundational ontologies and their modelling choices, see [5]. Usually foundational ontologies are expressed in rich logical language (e.g. first-order modal logics), while here we shall limit their expressive power by deploying their decidable counterparts in OWL, cf. [5].

The second task is approached by adapting the modelling of preferences in combinatorial domains of [16, 17] to $\mathcal{DL}s$.

While we do not enter the details of how to implement the first task, we stress that the next sections constraint the possibility of defining the reason-based approach in a knowledge-dependent way, that is, by considering the models of a given ontological theory. We shall delve into the task of extending the reason-based model with combination of reasons in the subsequent paragraphs. As we shall see, the possible preferences that are defined on sets of reasons shall depend on the intended semantics of reasons, i.e. on the Knowledge Base.

3.1 Description Logics

We use *Description Logics* ($\mathscr{DL}s$) as they are fundamental languages for representing *concepts*, i.e. unary predicates. Therefore, motivating reasons are here represented as concepts in DLs. We briefly introduce $\mathscr{ALC}$; for an exhaustive introduction, see [3]. We work with $\mathscr{ALC}$, however nothing prevents to apply the following definitions to richer $\mathscr{DL}s$. The syntax of $\mathscr{ALC}$ is based on three disjoint sets N_I, N_C, and N_R of *individual names*, *concept names*, and *role names*, respectively. The set of $\mathscr{ALC}$ *concepts* is generated by the following grammar, where $A \in N_C$ and $R \in N_R$.

$$C ::= A \mid \neg C \mid C \sqcap C \mid C \sqcup C \mid \forall R.C \mid \exists R.C$$

A *TBox* $\mathscr{T}$ is a finite set of *general concept inclusions* (GCIs) of the form $C \sqsubseteq D$ where C and D are concepts of $\mathscr{ALC}$. The TBox is used to store general terminological (semantic) knowledge about concepts and roles. An *ABox* is a finite set of formulas of the form Ca and Rab, which express knowledge about particular objects. A *Knowledge Base* $\mathscr{K}$ consists of a $\mathscr{T}$ and an $\mathscr{A}$.

The semantics of $\mathscr{ALC}$ is defined by means of *interpretations* $I = (\Delta^I, \cdot^I)$, where Δ^I is a non-empty set, the *domain*, and $\cdot^I$ is a function mapping every individual name in N_I to an element of Δ^I, each concept name in N_C to a subset of the domain, and each role name in N_R to a binary relation on the domain. Then, I extends from concepts in N_C to the full set of $\mathscr{ALC}$-concepts inductively, cf. [3].

We say that the interpretation I is a *model* of the TBox $\mathscr{T}$ ($I \models \mathscr{T}$) iff I satisfies all the GCIs in $\mathscr{T}$, i.e. for each $C \sqsubseteq D \in \mathscr{T}$, $C^I \subseteq D^I$. An interpretation I is *a model* of an ABox $\mathscr{A}$ ($I \models \mathscr{A}$) iff I satisfies every formula in $\mathscr{A}$, i.e. if $Ca \in \mathscr{A}$, then $a^I \in C^I$ and if $Rab \in \mathscr{A}$, $(a^I, b^I) \in R^I$. An interpretation I *is a model* of a Knowledge Base, $I \models \mathscr{K}$ iff $I \models \mathscr{T}$ and $I \models \mathscr{A}$. We say that $\mathscr{K}$ is *consistent* if there exists an interpretation I that is a model of $\mathscr{K}$.

Given two concepts C and D, we say that C is *subsumed* by D w.r.t. $\mathscr{K}$, $C \sqsubseteq_{\mathscr{K}} D$, iff $C^I \subseteq D^I$, for every model I of $\mathscr{K}$. We write $C \equiv_{\mathscr{K}} D$ when $C \sqsubseteq_{\mathscr{K}} D$ and $D \sqsubseteq_{\mathscr{K}} C$. A knowledge base $\mathscr{K}$ entails an Abox formula ϕ, $\mathscr{K} \models \phi$ iff, for every interpretation I that is a model of $\mathscr{K}$, I is a model of ϕ.

3.2 Concept Bases of $\mathscr{ALC}$

The approach developed in [16, 17] was designed to compactly represent utility functions over (finite) combinations of goods. In fact, goods are represented there by finite set of literals of a propositional language. To represent utility functions, the notion of a *goal base* is introduced: it is a set of weighted formulas of propositional logic (interpreted as goals) that allows for generating utility functions from sets of literals (representing goods) to (real) numbers.

In particular, we adapt [16,17] for concepts of $\mathscr{ALC}$, following the approaches in [14] and [1] for $\mathscr{DL}s$ and in [11] for first-order logic.

Let $\mathscr{R} = \{D_1, \ldots, D_m\} \subseteq N_C$ be a finite set of concept names of $\mathscr{ALC}$ (we exclude $\top$ and $\bot$) and assume that a Knowledge Base $\mathscr{K}$ is given. Let $\mathscr{ALC}_{\mathscr{R}}$ be the set of concepts of $\mathscr{ALC}$ constructed out of concept names in $\mathscr{R}$. $\mathscr{R}$ represents the set of motivating reasons, discussed in Sect. 2, while $\mathscr{K}$, and in particular its TBox, shall represent the background theory that constraints the meaning of the concepts in $\mathscr{R}$. We shall assume throughout the paper that the Tbox $\mathscr{T}$ is acyclic, cf. [3], and when we use a Knowledge Base $\mathscr{K}$ that includes $\mathscr{T}$, we assume that $\mathscr{K}$ is consistent.

A *weighted concept* is a pair (C, w) where C is a concept of $\mathscr{ALC}_{\mathscr{R}}$ and $w \in \mathbb{W}$ is a value in a suitable set of values (usually real numbers, but this is not important here).

We are ready to introduce the definition of a *concept base*, which is directly inspired by the notion of a goal base in [16,17].

Definition 3 (Concept base). *A concept base* C *is a finite set of weighted concepts*

$$C = \{(C_1, w_1), \ldots, (C_m, w_m)\}$$

The concept base allows for expressing preferences over possible combinations of reasons in $\mathscr{R}$. An example is $C = \{(D_1 \sqcap D_2, w_1), (D_1, w_2)\}$, where $w_1 > w_2$. In this case, an agent evaluates the conjunction of reasons $D_1 \sqcap D_2$ as more important than D_1 alone, while possibly not caring at all about D_2 alone, see also Example 2 below.

For each goal base C, we can define a (utility) function on any possible combination of reasons. That is, for every C, we can define a function $u_C : 2^{\mathscr{R}} \to \mathbb{W}$, that takes any set of reasons $M \in 2^{\mathscr{R}}$ and returns a value. To define u_C, we shall identify any set of reasons $\{D_1 \ldots, D_n\} \in 2^{\mathscr{R}}$ with their conjunction $\sqcap_{i \in \{1,\ldots,n\}} D_i$. In particular, we put $\sqcap \emptyset = \top$[3]. To compute the values of u_C, we take here the sum of the weights of the concepts in C that are entailed by M.[4] Summing up, u_C is defined as follows.

$$u_C(\{D_1, \ldots, D_m\}) = \sum \{w \mid (C, w) \in C \text{ and } D_1 \sqcap \cdots \sqcap D_m \sqsubseteq_{\mathscr{T}} C\} \tag{2}$$

As the following example shows, the value of u_C depends on $\mathscr{T}$. In fact, the adequate notation for such functions is $u_C^{\mathscr{T}}$. Since we shall consider one $\mathscr{T}$ at a time, we omit the superscript.[5]

Example 2. Let $C = \{(D_1 \sqcap D_2, w_1), (D_1, w_2)\}$. And assume that $\mathscr{R} = \{D_1, D_2\}$. The value $u_C(M)$ for $M \in 2^{\mathscr{R}}$ depends on $\mathscr{K}$, and in particular on $\mathscr{T}$. Consider $\mathscr{T} = \emptyset$. In this case, subsumptions $C \sqsubseteq_{\emptyset} D$ are assessed wrt. all possible models. Then, the graph of $u_C(M)$ is as follows.

---

[3] In a lattice, $\top$ is the infimum of the empty set.

[4] In this paper, we assume that weights are aggregated by means of the sum, but other choices are possible (e.g. products, [17]).

[5] This definition of the values returned by the concept base is termed "implication based" in [14].

M	$u_C(M)$
$\emptyset$	0
$\{D_1\}$	w_2
$\{D_2\}$	0
$\{D_1, D_2\}$	$w_1 + w_2$

The first line returns 0, because neither $\top \sqsubseteq_\emptyset D_1 \sqcap D_2$ nor $\top \sqsubseteq_\emptyset D_1$ hold.[6] The second line returns w_2 since $D_1 \sqsubseteq_\emptyset D_1$. The third line returns 0, because $D_2 \sqsubseteq D_1$ does not hold in every model. The fourth line returns $w_1 + w_2$, because $D_1 \sqcap D_2 \sqsubseteq_\emptyset D_1$ and $D_1 \sqcap D_2 \sqsubseteq_\emptyset D_1 \sqcap D_2$.

Consider the case of $\mathscr{T} = \{D_1 \sqsubseteq D_2\}$. In this case, the values of u_C are as follows.

M	$u_C(M)$
$\emptyset$	0
$\{D_1\}$	$w_1 + w_2$
$\{D_2\}$	0
$\{D_1, D_2\}$	$w_1 + w_2$

In the second line, since $D_1 \sqsubseteq D_2 \in \mathscr{T}$, $\mathscr{T}$ also entails that $D_1 \sqsubseteq D_1 \sqcap D_2$.

Notice that the notion of coherence of a set of reasons M in $2^{\mathscr{R}}$ (cf. Sect. 2, Definition 1) depends, in our ontological rendering, on $\mathscr{T}$. Intuitively, the elements of $\mathscr{R}$ are concept names in N_C, thus, they are just simple symbols and, if they are not logically connected by some axiom in $\mathscr{T}$, they cannot clash.

However, consider the case where $\mathscr{R} = \{D_1, D_2, D_3\}$ and $\mathscr{T} = \{D_1 \equiv \neg D_2\}$. In this case, the set $M_1 = \{D_1, D_2\}$ is not coherent, as there cannot be a $d \in D_1^I \cap D_2^I$, in any interpretation I that makes the TBox true. By contrast, $\{D_2, D_3\}$ is coherent (there are models I of $\mathscr{T}$ with a $d \in D_2^I \cap D_3^I$).

If $M \in 2^{\mathscr{R}}$ is incoherent wrt. $\mathscr{T}$, then $v_C(M) = \sum\{w \mid (C, w) \in C$ and $\bigsqcap M \sqsubseteq_\mathscr{T} C\}$ shall return the sum of all weights occurring in C (by *ex falso quodlibet*).

We discuss now which functions are representable, given a concept base C and a Tbox $\mathscr{T}$.

Definition 4. *We say that a function* $f : 2^{\mathscr{R}} \to \mathbb{W}$ *is represented by a concept base* C *iff* $f = u_C$ *(we may also say that* f *is generated by* C*).*

By tinkering Theorem 3.2 in [16], we could prove that every function from $2^{\mathscr{R}} \to \mathbb{W}$ can be *represented* by a concept base C, at least when $\mathbb{W} = \mathbb{R}$. We leave the details of the proof for a dedicated work. Notice however that the case of $\mathscr{DL}s$ is more delicate than the propositional case of [16]. The general representation result holds only for the case of an empty $\mathscr{T}$. That is, the set of functions that are representable depends on the Tbox $\mathscr{T}$, as the following example shows.

Example 3 (Representability). Let $\mathscr{R} = \{D_1, D_2, D_3\}$ and $\mathscr{T} = \{D_1 \equiv D_2\}$. Consider a function $f : 2^{\mathscr{R}} \to \mathbb{R}$ such that $f(\{D_1\}) \neq f(\{D_2\})$. We show that, in this case, f

---

[6] That is, it is not true that, in every model, $\Delta \subseteq D_1^I$ nor that $\Delta \subseteq (D_1 \cap D_2)^I$.

cannot be represented by any u_C. By contradiction, assume that there exists a C such that $f = u_C$. Thus, $u_C(\{D_1\}) \neq u_C(\{D_2\})$. That is,

$$\sum \{w \mid (C,w) \in C \text{ and } D_1 \sqsubseteq_{\mathscr{T}} C\} \neq \sum \{w \mid (C,w) \in C \text{ and } D_2 \sqsubseteq_{\mathscr{T}} C\}$$

The inequality implies that $\{C \text{ occurring in } C \mid D_1 \sqsubseteq_{\mathscr{T}} C\} \neq \{C \text{ occurring in } C \mid D_2 \sqsubseteq_{\mathscr{T}} C\}$. Thus, there must be a C_0 occurring in C such that, e.g., $D_1 \sqsubseteq_{\mathscr{T}} C_0$ and $D_2 \not\sqsubseteq_{\mathscr{T}} C_0$. That is, in every model I of $\mathscr{K}$, $D_1^I = D_2^I$ is both included in C_0^I and not included in C_0^I, which is a contradiction.

Therefore, f cannot be represented by any C. Other examples can be envisaged, e.g. when there are sets of reasons that are incoherent wrt. $\mathscr{T}$.

We shall therefore restrict to those utility functions on combinations of reasons that are compatible with the information conveyed by $\mathscr{T}$.

Definition 5 (Compatibility). *A function* $f : 2^{\mathscr{R}} \to \mathbb{W}$ *is compatible with the TBox* $\mathscr{T}$ *iff there exists a concept base* C *such that* f *is representable, i.e.* $f = u_C$.

Notice that, if $\mathscr{K}$ is consistent, then the $\mathscr{A}$ of $\mathscr{K}$ has no effect on which functions are representable. The motivation for the restriction to preferences and utility functions that are compatible with $\mathscr{T}$ is that $\mathscr{T}$ specifies the meanings of the reasons in $\mathscr{R}$, which is supposed to be acknowledged by the agents who are justifying their preferences in terms of motivating reasons.

In [16], it is possible to characterise several classes of utility functions in terms of the formulas occurring in the goal base. In the case of $\mathscr{DL}s$ this is not straightforward. E.g. if the TBox is empty and C contains only concept names $D \in \mathscr{R}$, then u_C is additive (i.e. $u_C(D_1, \ldots, D_n) = \sum_{i=1}^{i=n} u_C(\{D_i\})$). However, if the TBox is not empty, then we cannot ensure the independence of each D_i. While in the propositional case of [16], it suffices to constrain the language inside the goal base, in the case of $\mathscr{DL}s$ one needs to study the correspondence between the inferential features of the TBox and the definable classes of functions. We leave this interesting point for a future dedicated work.

4   Concept Bases and Reason-Based Preferences

Given a concept base C, by means of u_C, we can always define an ordering of sets of motivating reasons, as follows.

$$M \succeq_C M' \text{ iff } u_C(M) \geq u_C(M') \tag{3}$$

As $\succeq_C$ comes from $\geq$, it is always reflexive, transitive and complete. Moreover, since $\succeq_C$ comes from u_C it is always compatible with the TBox $\mathscr{T}$. By contrast, given an ordering $\succeq$ on $2^{\mathscr{R}}$, it is not the case that $\geq$ is always representable as $\succeq_C$, for some C and $\mathscr{K}$. Consider the following example.

Example 4. Let $\mathscr{R}$ and $\mathscr{K}$ as in Example 3. Define f such that $f(\{D_1\}) > f(\{D_2\})$ and $\succ$ such that $\{D_1\} \succ \{D_2\}$. Then, there is no concept base C such that $\succ = \succeq_C$.

Therefore, we shall confine to ordering on $2^{\mathscr{R}}$ which are compatible with $\mathscr{K}$, in the following sense.

Definition 6. *An order relation $\succeq \subseteq 2^{\mathscr{R}} \times 2^{\mathscr{R}}$ is compatible with $\mathscr{K}$ iff there exists a concept base* C *such that $\succeq = \succeq_{\text{C}}$, where $\succeq_{\text{C}}$ is defined by Eq. 3.*

We turn now to discussing how preferences on alternatives depend on their motivating reasons. Alternatives are here interpreted as individual names $a \in N_I$. Let $X \subseteq N^I$ be a finite set of alternatives. The utility of an alternative a, in a certain situation, is given by the sum of the weights of the motivating reasons that a satisfies in that situation.

A "situation" is modelled by means of a knowledge base $\mathscr{K}$, where the TBox $\mathscr{T}$ is given and the Abox $\mathscr{A}$ describes the (some) alternatives by the (some) reasons that they satisfy, i.e. $\mathscr{A}$ is a set of formulas of the form $D_i x$ for $x \in X$ and $D_i \in \mathscr{R}$. When $M \subseteq \mathscr{R}$, we denote by $\sqcap M$ the concept $\sqcap_i D_i$, for $D_i \in M$.

Definition 7 (Utility of alternatives). *The utility of $a \in X$, given a concept base* C, *a Knowledge Base $\mathscr{K}$, and a set of reasons $M = \{D_1, \ldots, D_m\} \subseteq \mathscr{R}$ is defined as follows.*

$$u_{\text{C}}^M(a) = \sum \{w \mid (C, w) \in \text{C}, \sqcap M' \sqsubseteq_{\mathscr{T}} C, \text{ for } M' \subseteq M, \text{ and } \mathscr{K} \models D_i a, \text{ for all } D_i \in M'\}$$

Thus, the utility of a given a concept base C, when the motivating reasons are M, is the sum of the weights of the concepts C such that: *i)* $(C, w) \in$ C, *ii)* C is entailed by some of motivating reasons in M', and *iii)* a satisfies those motivating reasons $D_i \in M'$.

Example 5. Let $X = \{a, b\} \subseteq N_I$, $\mathscr{R} = \{D_1, D_2, D_3, D_4\}$, $\mathscr{T} = \{D_1 \sqsubseteq D_2\}$. The ABox is $\mathscr{A} = \{D_1 a, D_2 b, D_3 b, D_4 a\}$. Let C $= \{(D_1 \sqcap D_2, w_1), (D_1 \sqcap D_3, w_2), (D_3, w_3), (D_4, w_4)\}$. Consider, for example, the case where $M = \{D_1, D_3\}$ are the sole motivating reason. The value $u_{\text{C}}^{\{D_1, D_3\}}(a)$ is then obtained as follows. We have that $D_1 \sqsubseteq_{\mathscr{T}} D_1 \sqcap D_2$ (given that $D_1 \sqsubseteq D_2 \in \mathscr{T}$) and $D_1 a$ is in $\mathscr{A}$, so the weight w_1 is obtained. The weight w_2 is not added, because $D_1 \sqcap D_3 \sqsubseteq_{\mathscr{T}} D_1 \sqcap D_3$, but $D_3 a$ is not in $\mathscr{K}$. Note that the weight w_4 is not added, even if $D_4 a \in \mathscr{K}$, because D_4 is not a motivating reason in this case.

By Definition 7, a preference order, that depends on M and C, on the set of alternatives can be defined.

$$a \succeq_M b \text{ iff } u_{\text{C}}^M(a) \geq u_{\text{C}}^M(b) \tag{4}$$

We claim that $a \succeq_M b$, for $M \in \mathscr{M}$, is a preference based on reasons, in the sense of [7]. That is, $a \succeq_M b$ satisfies Axiom 1 and 2, rephrased in this context.

Proposition 1. *Let $a \succeq_M b$, for $M \in \mathscr{M}$, defined as in Eq. 4. If $\{D \in M \mid \mathscr{K} \models Da\} = \{D \in M \mid \mathscr{K} \models Db\}$, then $a \sim_M b$.*

Proof. Suppose $\{D \in M \mid \mathscr{K} \models Da\} = \{D \in M \mid \mathscr{K} \models Db\}$. For any M and $M' \subseteq M$, we have that

$$\{C \mid (C, w) \in \text{C and } \sqcap M' \sqsubseteq_{\mathscr{T}} C \text{ and } \mathscr{K} \models D_i a\}$$

$$\overset{=}{\{C \mid (C,w) \in \mathsf{C} \text{ and } \bigsqcap M' \sqsubseteq_{\mathscr{T}} C \text{ and } \mathscr{K} \models D_i b\}}$$

Therefore, $u_{\mathsf{C}}^M(a) = u_{\mathsf{C}}^M(b)$, hence $a \sim_M b$.

Proposition 2. *Let* $a \succeq_M b$, *for* $M \in \mathscr{M}$, *defined as in Eq. 4. For any* $a, b \in X$ *and any* $M_1, M_2 \in \mathscr{M}$, *such that* $M_1 \subseteq M_2$, *if there is no* $D \in M_2 \setminus M_1$ *such that* $\mathscr{K} \models Da$ *or* $\mathscr{K} \models Db$, *then* $a \succeq_{M_1} b$ *iff* $a \succeq_{M_2} b$.

Proof. Assume that $M_1' \subseteq M_1$, $M_2' \subseteq M_2$. By assumption, $M_1 \subseteq M_2$ and there is no $D \in M_2 \setminus M_1$ such that $\mathscr{K} \models Da$ or $\mathscr{K} \models Db$. Therefore, we have that, for all $D_i \in M_2$:

$$\{C \mid (C,w) \in \mathsf{C}, \bigsqcap M_1' \sqsubseteq_{\mathscr{T}} C, \mathscr{K} \models D_i a\} = \{C \mid (C,w) \in \mathsf{C}, \bigsqcap M_2' \sqsubseteq_{\mathscr{T}} C, \mathscr{K} \models D_i a\}$$

$$\{C \mid (C,w) \in \mathsf{C}, \bigsqcap M_1' \sqsubseteq_{\mathscr{T}} C, \mathscr{K} \models D_i b\} = \{C \mid (C,w) \in \mathsf{C}, \bigsqcap M_2' \sqsubseteq_{\mathscr{T}} C, \mathscr{K} \models D_i b\}$$

Therefore $u_{\mathsf{C}}^{M_1}(a) \geq u_{\mathsf{C}}^{M_1}(b)$ iff $u_{\mathsf{C}}^{M_2}(a) \geq u_{\mathsf{C}}^{M_2}(b)$.

We can finally restate the definition of property-based preference relation (cf. Definition 2), to highlight the dependence on a $\mathscr{K}$.

Definition 8. *Let* $\mathscr{M} \subseteq 2^{\mathscr{R}}$. *A family of preference relations* $\succeq_M$ *for* $M \in \mathscr{M}$ *is property-based iff there exists a weighing relation* $\succ \subseteq \mathscr{M} \times \mathscr{M}$ *such that:*

$$a \succeq_M b \text{ iff } \{D \in M \mid \mathscr{K} \models Da\} \succeq \{D \in M \mid \mathscr{K} \models Db\}$$

We show that $\succeq_{\mathsf{C}}$ is indeed a weighing relation, for preferences $a \succeq_M b$ defined according to Eq. 4.

Proposition 3. *Given a Knowledge Base* $\mathscr{K}$, *for every family of preference* $\succeq_M$ *with* $M \in \mathscr{M}$ *defined as in Eq. 4,* $\succeq_{\mathsf{C}}$ *is a weighing relation for* $\succeq_M$.

Proof. We have the following sequence of equivalences: $a \succeq_M b$ iff $u_{\mathsf{C}}^M(a) \geq u_{\mathsf{C}}^M(b)$ iff

$$\Sigma\{w \mid (C,w) \in \mathsf{C}, \bigsqcap M' \sqsubseteq_{\mathscr{T}} C, \text{ for } M' \subseteq M, \mathscr{K} \models D_i a, \text{ for all } D_i \in M'\} \geq$$
$$\Sigma\{w \mid (C,w) \in \mathsf{C}, \bigsqcap M' \sqsubseteq_{\mathscr{T}} C, \text{ for } M' \subseteq M, \text{ and } \mathscr{K} \models D_i b, \text{ for all } D_i \in M'\}$$
$$\text{iff}^{(1)}$$
$$u_{\mathsf{C}}(\{D_1,\ldots,D_n\} \mid D_i \in M \text{ and } \mathscr{K} \models D_i a\}) \geq u_{\mathsf{C}}(\{D_1,\ldots,D_n\} \mid D_i \in M \text{ and } \mathscr{K} \models D_i b\})$$
$$\text{iff}^{(2)}$$
$$\{D \in M \mid \mathscr{K} \models Da\} \succeq_{\mathsf{C}} \{D \in M \mid \mathscr{K} \models Db\}$$

The step (1) is justified by noticing that $\{D_1,\ldots,D_n\}$ are concepts in $\bigsqcap M'$ that entail C, so the value of the sum of the weights of the Cs that are satisfied is $u_{\mathsf{C}}(\{D_1,\ldots,D_n\})$. Step (2) follows by definition of $\succeq_{\mathsf{C}}$, cf. Definition 3.

To sum up, we have restricted ourselves to preference and utility functions on alternatives in X that are compatible with a Knowledge Base by construction (cf. Definition 4). As we have shown, such preferences are reason-based and $\succeq_{\mathsf{C}}$ is an adequate weighing relation.

If we start from "any" family of preference relations $\succeq_M$ on alternatives in X (i.e. not defined using Definition 4) and then we apply Theorem 1 in [7], we could determine whether $\succeq_M$ is reason-based (i.e. if it satisfies Axiom 1 and 2). However, this would not guarantee compatibility with the Knowledge Base.

5   Conclusions and Future Work

We have shown that the reason-based approach proposed in [7] can be adapted for the case where: *i*) reasons are expressed as concepts of $\mathcal{ALC}$, *ii*) preference relations and utility functions on sets of reasons are defined by means of a concept base (cf. Definition 3), and *iii*) preferences on alternatives depend on preferences on sets of reasons (cf. Eq. 4).

The main feature of this setting is that it is knowledge-dependent, it relies on a Knowledge Base that confers meanings to the motivating reasons. To cope with the possible inconsistencies between the Knowledge Base and the preferences, we restricted to preferences and utility functions that are defined by means of concept bases, which are compatible with the Knowledge Base by design. In fact, this restriction does not limit the range of definable preferences, once we are willing to accept that an agent is rational, has a consistent Knowledge Base, and, consequently, has preferences that are compatible with it.

This framework paves the way for enriching the ontological side of the Knowledge Base with (the OWL version) of a foundational ontology, to improve the representation of motivating reasons and to enable the application to various domains of interest.

There are mainly three directions for future work. Firstly, as we mentioned previously, it is interesting to study the property of the TBox that enables defining classes of utility functions (e.g. superadditive, subadditive, k-additive, modular, cf. [16]).

Secondly, it is interesting to study preference aggregation based on motivating reasons. In this case, we could assume that agents agree on the Knowledge Base, i.e. on the meanings of the possible reasons, so that the ontological side of the Knowledge Base operates as a vocabulary that is shared among the agents. Agents' preferences may still be in conflict, as they are justified by different, and possibly conflicting, weighing relations.

Finally, we suggested the idea that the TBox captures the meanings of the motivating reasons. However, we depicted here a single-agent scenario. It is interesting to study reason-based preferences in the case of multiple agents, who have possibly contrasting views of reasons, namely, they might endorse possibly conflicting TBoxes. In this case, techniques of ontology integration, revision, alignment and aggregation are required to interact with the preferences defined in terms of motivating reasons.

Acknowledgements. This research is partially supported by Italian National Research Project PRIN2020 2020SSKZ7R. I would like to thank the anonymous reviewers for their valuable comments on the preliminary version of this paper.

References

1. Acar, E., Fink, M., Meilicke, C., Thorne, C., Stuckenschmidt, H.: Multi-attribute decision making with weighted description logics. IfCoLog J. Logics Appl. **4**(7), 1973–1996 (2017)
2. Arrow, K.: Social Choice and Individual Values. Yale University Press, New Haven (1963)
3. Baader, F., Calvanese, D., McGuinness, D., Nardi, D., Patel-Schneider, P.F.: The Description Logic Handbook: Theory, Implementation, and Applications. Cambridge University Press, Cambridge (2003)

4. Borgo, S., et al.: Dolce: a descriptive ontology for linguistic and cognitive engineering. Appl. Ontol. **17**(1), 45–69 (2022)
5. Borgo, S., Galton, A., Kutz, O.: Foundational ontologies in action. Appl. Ontol. **17**(1), 1–16 (2022). https://doi.org/10.3233/AO-220265
6. Dietrich, F., List, C.: A reason-based theory of rational choice. Nous **47**(1), 104–134 (2013)
7. Dietrich, F., List, C.: Where do preferences come from? Internat. J. Game Theory **42**(3), 613–637 (2013)
8. Galliani, P., Kutz, O., Porello, D., Righetti, G., Troquard, N.: On knowledge dependence in weighted description logic. In: Calvanese, D., Iocchi, L. (eds.) GCAI 2019. Proceedings of the 5th Global Conference on Artificial Intelligence, Bozen/Bolzano, Italy, 17–19 September 2019. EPiC Series in Computing, vol. 65, pp. 68–80. EasyChair (2019). https://doi.org/10. 29007/hjt1
9. Liu, F., et al.: Changing for the Better: Preference Dynamics and Agent Diversity. ILLC (2008)
10. Masolo, C., Borgo, S., Gangemi, A., Guarino, N., Oltramari, A.: Wonderweb deliverable d18. Technical report, CNR (2003)
11. Masolo, C., Porello, D.: Representing concepts by weighted formulas. In: Formal Ontology in Information Systems - Proceedings of the 10th International Conference, FOIS 2018, Cape Town, South Africa, 19–21 September 2018, pp. 55–68 (2018)
12. Osherson, D., Weinstein, S.: Preference based on reasons. Rev. Symbolic Logic **5**(01), 122–147 (2012)
13. Porello, D.: Ranking judgments in arrow's setting. Synthese **173**(2), 199–210 (2010)
14. Ragone, A., Noia, T.D., Donini, F.M., Sciascio, E.D., Wellman, M.P.: Weighted description logics preference formulas for multiattribute negotiation. In: Godo, L., Pugliese, A. (eds.) SUM 2009. LNCS, pp. 193–205. Springer, Berlin (2009). https://doi.org/10.1007/978-3-642-04388-8_16
15. Sen, A.K.: Choice functions and revealed preference. Rev. Econ. Stud. **38**(3), 307–317 (1971)
16. Uckelman, J., Chevaleyre, Y., Endriss, U., Lang, J.: Representing utility functions via weighted goals. Math. Logic Q. **55**(4), 341–361 (2009)
17. Uckelman, J., Endriss, U.: Compactly representing utility functions using weighted goals and the max aggregator. Artif. Intell. **174**(15), 1222–1246 (2010)

A Defeasible Description Logic for Abduction

Gian Luca Pozzato[(✉)][iD] and Marco Spinnicchia

Dipartimento di Informatica, Università di Torino, Turin, Italy
`gianluca.pozzato@unito.it, marco.spinnicchia@edu.unito.it`

Abstract. In this work we introduce a defeasible Description Logic for abductive reasoning. Our proposal exploits a fragment of a probabilistic extension of a Description Logic of typicality, whose semantics corresponds to a natural extension of the well established mechanism of rational closure extended to Description Logics. The presence of typicality assertions that can be non-monotonically inferred from a knowledge base, corresponding to those belonging to its rational closure, avoids the need of an explicit selection of abducibles.

1 Introduction

In AI logical formalisms have been developed to represent knowledge and draw new conclusions, even implicit or hidden ones, through automatic reasoning mechanisms. With a logic-based approach, one can encode some of the most usual "human" reasoning patterns, through syntactic manipulations of well-formed formulae (wffs) and the notion of logical consequence. Over the years, it became clear that reasoning in terms of individual elements would have moved away from capturing an abstraction that is both comprehensible to humans and capable of reflecting the underlying intuition behind symbolic representation. When knowledge began to be represented through concepts and relationships between concepts, the notion of ontology was born [7,30], shifting the focus from attributing properties to individual elements in an unambiguous manner, to attributing properties to concepts or individuals as instances of one or more concepts. The family of Description Logic (DLs) was developed to verify the presence of hierarchical relationships between classes, subsumption, or determining whether an element from the domain is an instance of a specific class [3].

Traditionally, a limitation of standard DLs is the impossibility of modeling defeasible inheritance in taxonomies, i.e. situations in which a child concept is subsumed by a parent concept, namely $SubConcept \sqsubseteq TopConcept$, it inherits some of the characteristics, while losing others. An exception is a reason for incompleteness in the ontology, and the lack of a formalism to represent and reason with exceptions, such as the monotonic $\mathcal{ALC}$ does, leads to "trivial" KBs. To overcome this limitation several non-monotonic extensions of DLs have been proposed [2,5,6,8–10], as well as the one introduced in [15,25], the non-monotonic extensions of $\mathcal{ALC}$ [11] called $\mathcal{ALC} + \mathbf{T_R}$, where prototypical properties are specified through a typicality operator $\mathbf{T}$. The basic idea is to also ascribe typical properties of a class, not holding for all the instances, but only for the "most normal" ones: for instance, $\mathbf{T}(Bird) \sqsubseteq Fly$ is used to express that, normally, birds fly, but we can have exceptions (e.g. penguins and ostriches), namely birds that do not fly. This proposal is the starting point of the present work.

© The Author(s), under exclusive license to Springer Nature Switzerland AG 2023
R. Basili et al. (Eds.): AIxIA 2023, LNAI 14318, pp. 74–87, 2023.
https://doi.org/10.1007/978-3-031-47546-7_6

In a complete, consistent and stable knowledge base, we talk about monotonicity, when no new fact can invalidate what is known or inferred before. But real-world domains change, and so the KB [29]. Non-monotonic reasoning deals with the incompleteness of a theory by making assumptions about missing knowledge. In particular, for abduction, from knowing the theory for which "if A then B" (Rule) and observing B (Fact), one can assume A (Case) as a possible explanation for B until consistency holds [23]. Deduction is a logical inference that explicates implicit knowledge, so adding conclusions to the KB does not correspond to increasing knowledge; in contrast, abductive reasoning has an intrinsic capacity to increase knowledge, as abductive hypotheses result in limiting models and thus reduce the ambiguity of KB, until proven otherwise.

In this work, we move a first step in the direction of providing a general approach for abduction in typicality Description Logics, through a restriction of a non-monotonic extension of $\mathcal{ALC} + \mathbf{T}_{\mathbf{R}}^{RaCl}$, equipped with probability to reflect the uncertainty behind a prototypical representation of "cause-and-effect" relationships. We aim to propose a mechanism to combine the expressive power of DLs, useful in case of complex domain representations, with the "exploratory" one of the abductive reasoning, which involves deriving new defeasible knowledge. Rather than explicitly specifying every detail of the abductive framework and identifying the abducibles within potentially vast application domains, this work would allow for a more systematic way. The basic idea is to consider as plausible explanations the set of typicality assertions that can be inferred from the initial knowledge base, by exploiting the rational closure mechanism characterizing the logic $\mathcal{ALC} + \mathbf{T}_{\mathbf{R}}^{\deg}$. In this respect, such typicality assumptions are the candidates for explanations, avoiding the need of explicitly defining abducibles. We can also show that performing abductive reasoning in such a Description Logic is essentially inexpensive, in the sense that it is in EXPTIME as the underlying, classical DL $\mathcal{ALC}$.

2   Description Logics of Typicality: The Logic $\mathcal{ALC} + \mathbf{T}_{\mathbf{R}}^{RaCl}$

In this section we quickly recall the main notions about the monotonic Description Logic of typicality $\mathcal{ALC} + \mathbf{T}_{\mathbf{R}}$ introduced in [11, 14, 15] underlying our approach.

The logic $\mathcal{ALC} + \mathbf{T}_{\mathbf{R}}$ is obtained by adding to standard $\mathcal{ALC}$ the typicality operator $\mathbf{T}$ [11]. The intuitive idea is that $\mathbf{T}(C)$ selects the *typical* instances of a concept C. We can therefore distinguish between the properties that hold for all instances of concept C ($C \sqsubseteq D$), and those that only hold for the normal or typical instances of C ($\mathbf{T}(C) \sqsubseteq D$). As an example, a TBox can contain *rigid* inclusions like $TeenAger \sqsubseteq Person$, representing that all teenagers are persons, as well as typical properties like $\mathbf{T}(TeenAger) \sqsubseteq Student$, saying that the prototype of a teenager is a student, but there can be exceptions to that.

From a semantic point of view, we refer to *rational models* [15], extending standard models of $\mathcal{ALC}$ by a preference relation $<$ among the elements of the domain of the discourse $\Delta^{\mathcal{I}}$: intuitively, $x < y$ means that x is "more normal" than y, then typical members of a concept C are the minimal elements of C with respect to this relation. An element $x \in \Delta^{\mathcal{I}}$ is a *typical instance* of some concept C if $x \in C^{\mathcal{I}}$ and there is no C-element in $\Delta^{\mathcal{I}}$ *more typical* than x. Formally:

Definition 1. *A model of $\mathcal{ALC} + \mathbf{T_R}$ is any structure $\mathcal{M} = \langle \Delta^{\mathcal{I}}, <, \cdot^{\mathcal{I}} \rangle$ where: $\Delta^{\mathcal{I}}$ is the domain; $<$ is an irreflexive, transitive, well-founded and modular (for all x, y, z in $\Delta^{\mathcal{I}}$, if $x < y$ then either $x < z$ or $z < y$) relation over $\Delta^{\mathcal{I}}$; $\cdot^{\mathcal{I}}$ is the extension function that maps each concept C to $C^{\mathcal{I}} \subseteq \Delta^{\mathcal{I}}$, and each role R to $R^{\mathcal{I}} \subseteq \Delta^{\mathcal{I}} \times \Delta^{\mathcal{I}}$. For concepts of $\mathcal{ALC}$, $C^{\mathcal{I}}$ is defined as usual. For the $\mathbf{T}$ operator, let $Min_<(C^{\mathcal{I}}) = \{x \in C^{\mathcal{I}} \mid \nexists y \in C^{\mathcal{I}} \text{ s.t. } y < x\}$, we define $(\mathbf{T}(C))^{\mathcal{I}} = Min_<(C^{\mathcal{I}})$.*

A model $\mathcal{M}$ can be equivalently defined by postulating the existence of a function $k_{\mathcal{M}} : \Delta^{\mathcal{I}} \longmapsto \mathbb{N}$, where $k_{\mathcal{M}}$ assigns a finite rank to each domain element: the rank function $k_{\mathcal{M}}$ and $<$ can be defined from each other by stating that $x < y$ if and only if $k_{\mathcal{M}}(x) < k_{\mathcal{M}}(y)$. Given standard definitions of satisfiability of a KB in a model, we define a notion of entailment in $\mathcal{ALC} + \mathbf{T_R}$:

Definition 2. *Given a query F (either an inclusion $C \sqsubseteq D$ or an assertion $C(a)$ or an assertion of the form $R(a, b)$), we say that F is entailed from a KB if F holds in all $\mathcal{ALC} + \mathbf{T_R}$ models satisfying KB.*

Even if the $\mathbf{T}$ operator itself is non-monotonic, in the sense that $C \sqsubseteq D$ does not imply that $\mathbf{T}(C) \sqsubseteq \mathbf{T}(D)$, the logic $\mathcal{ALC} + \mathbf{T_R}$ is monotonic. In order to perform useful non-monotonic inferences, in [15] the authors have strengthened the above semantics by restricting entailment to a class of minimal models. Intuitively, the idea is to restrict entailment to models that *minimize the untypical instances of a concept*. The resulting logic is called $\mathcal{ALC} + \mathbf{T_R}^{RaCl}$ and it corresponds to a notion of *rational closure* on top of $\mathcal{ALC} + \mathbf{T_R}$. Such a notion is a natural extension of the rational closure construction provided in [16] for Propositional Logic. The non-monotonic semantics of $\mathcal{ALC} + \mathbf{T_R}^{RaCl}$ relies on minimal rational models that minimize the *rank of domain elements*. Informally, given two models of KB, one in which a given domain element x has rank 2 (because for instance $z < y < x$), and another in which it has rank 1 (because only $y < x$), we prefer the latter, as in this model the element x is assumed to be "more typical" than in the former. Query entailment is then restricted to minimal *canonical models*. The intuition is that a canonical model contains all the individuals that enjoy properties that are consistent with KB. A model $\mathcal{M}$ is a minimal canonical model of KB if it satisfies KB, it is minimal and it is canonical[1]. A query F is minimally entailed from a KB if it holds in all minimal canonical models of KB. The notion of rational closure is further extended to the ABox. In [15] it is shown that query entailment in $\mathcal{ALC} + \mathbf{T_R}^{RaCl}$ is in ExpTime.

3 Extending DLs of Typicality with Probabilities

Let us now recall the main features of the logic called $\mathcal{ALC} + \mathbf{T_R}^{deg}$, extending and revising the DLs of typicality with probabilities and scenarios [24,25]. Here, typicality inclusion are equipped with a probability/degree and have the form

$$\mathbf{T}(C) \sqsubseteq_p D,$$

---

[1] In Theorem 10 in [15] the authors have shown that for any consistent KB there exists a finite minimal canonical model of KB.

where $p \in (0.5, 1)$. We then define a non-monotonic procedure whose aim is to describe alternative completions of the ABox obtained by assuming typicality assertions about the individuals explicitly named in the ABox: the basic idea is similar to the one proposed in [11], where a completion of an $\mathcal{ALC}+\mathbf{T}$ ABox is proposed in order to assume that every individual constant of the ABox is a typical element of the most specific concept it belongs to, if this is consistent with the knowledge base. This construction computes only *some* assumptions of typicality of individual constants, in order to describe alternative scenarios having different probabilities: different extensions/scenarios are obtained by considering different sets of typicality assumptions of the form $\mathbf{T}(C)(a)$, where a occurs in the ABox.

Given an inclusion $\mathbf{T}(C) \sqsubseteq_p D$, the higher the probability p the more the inclusion is "exceptions-free" or, equivalently, the less is the probability of having exceptional Cs not being also Ds. In this respect, the probability p is a real number included in the open interval $(0.5, 1)$: the probability 1 is not allowed, in the sense that an inclusion $\mathbf{T}(C) \sqsubseteq_1 D$ would correspond to a *strict* inclusion $C \sqsubseteq D$ (all Cs are Ds). Given another inclusion $\mathbf{T}(C') \sqsubseteq_{p'} D'$, with $p' < p$, we assume that this inclusion is less "strict" than the other one, i.e. the probability of having exceptional C's is higher than the one of having exceptional Cs with respect to properties D' and D, respectively[2]. In other words, the two inclusions are ordered, and $\mathbf{T}(C) \sqsubseteq_p D$ has a higher degree/is less uncertain with respect to $\mathbf{T}(C') \sqsubseteq_{p'} D'$. As an example in the direction of the DL for abduction that we will introduce in the following sections, if KB contains $\mathbf{T}(COVID) \sqsubseteq_{0.75} ShortnessOfBreath$ and $\mathbf{T}(COVID) \sqsubseteq_{0.6} Fever$, we have that, normally, both shortness of breath and fever are typical symptoms of COVID; however, the second inclusion has a lower rank with respect to the first one, that is to say it is believed that there could be more exceptions of COVID patients not having fever with respect to those not presenting shortness of breath.

Let us now introduce extensions of an ABox, in order to introduce implicit abducibles. Given a KB, as in [25] we define the finite set $\mathbb{C}$ of concepts occurring in the scope of the $\mathbf{T}$ operator, i.e. $\mathbb{C} = \{C \mid \mathbf{T}(C) \sqsubseteq_p D \in$ KB$\}$. Given an individual a explicitly named in the ABox, we define the set of typicality assumptions $\mathbf{T}(C)(a)$ that can be minimally entailed from KB in the non-monotonic logic $\mathcal{ALC} + \mathbf{T}_{\mathbf{R}}^{RaCl}$, with $C \in \mathbb{C}$. We then consider an ordered set $\mathbb{C}_{\mathcal{A}}$ of pairs (a, C) of all possible assumptions $\mathbf{T}(C)(a)$, for all concepts $C \in \mathbb{C}$ and all individual constants a in the ABox.

Definition 3 (Assumptions in $\mathcal{ALC} + \mathbf{T}_{\mathbf{R}}^{deg}$). *Given an $\mathcal{ALC} + \mathbf{T}_{\mathbf{R}}^{deg}$ KB = $(\mathcal{T}, \mathcal{A})$, let $\mathcal{T}'$ be the set of inclusions of $\mathcal{T}$ without probabilities, namely*

$$\mathcal{T}' = \{\mathbf{T}(C) \sqsubseteq D \mid \mathbf{T}(C) \sqsubseteq_p D \in \mathcal{T}\} \cup \{C \sqsubseteq D \in \mathcal{T}\}.$$

Given a finite set of concepts $\mathbb{C}$, we define, for each individual name a occurring in $\mathcal{A}$: $\mathbb{C}_a = \{C \in \mathbb{C} \mid (\mathcal{T}', \mathcal{A}) \models_{\mathcal{ALC}+\mathbf{T}_{\mathbf{R}}^{RaCl}} \mathbf{T}(C)(a)\}$. We also define $\mathbb{C}_{\mathcal{A}} = \{(a, C) \mid C \in \mathbb{C}_a$ and a occurs in $\mathcal{A}\}$ and we impose an order on its elements: $\mathbb{C}_{\mathcal{A}} = [(a_1, C_1), (a_2, C_2), \ldots, (a_n, C_n)]$. Furthermore, we define the ordered <u>multiset $\mathbb{P}_{\mathcal{A}} = [p_1, p_2, \ldots, p_n]$</u>, *respecting the order imposed on $\mathbb{C}_{\mathcal{A}}$, where*

---

[2] The meaning of probability/degree here is significantly different from those of the DISPONTE semantics in [26] and of the one used to define typicality in probabilistic DLs in [22].

$$p_i = \prod_{j=1}^{m} p_{ij} \text{ for all } \mathbf{T}(C_i) \sqsubseteq_{p_{i1}} D_1, \mathbf{T}(C_i) \sqsubseteq_{p_{i2}} D_2, \ldots, \mathbf{T}(C_i) \sqsubseteq_{p_{im}} D_m \text{ in } \mathcal{T}.$$

The ordered multiset $\mathbb{P}_{\mathcal{A}}$ is a tuple of the form $[p_1, p_2, \ldots, p_n]$, where p_i is the probability of the assumption $\mathbf{T}(C)(a)$, such that $(a, C) \in \mathbb{C}_{\mathcal{A}}$ at position i. p_i is the product of all the probabilities p_{ij} of typicality inclusions $\mathbf{T}(C) \sqsubseteq_{p_{ij}} D$ in the TBox.

We consider different extensions $\widetilde{\mathcal{A}}_i$ of the ABox and we equip them with a probability $\mathbb{P}_i$. Starting from $\mathbb{P}_{\mathcal{A}} = [p_1, p_2, \ldots, p_n]$, the first step is to build all alternative tuples where 0 is used in place of some p_i to represent that the corresponding typicality assertion $\mathbf{T}(C)(a)$ is no longer assumed (Definition 4). Furthermore, we define the *extension* of the ABox corresponding to a string so obtained (Definition 5). In this way, the highest probability is assigned to the extension of the ABox corresponding to $\mathbb{P}_{\mathcal{A}}$, where all typicality assumptions are considered. The probability decreases in the other extensions, where some typicality assumptions are discarded, thus 0 is used in place of the corresponding p_i. The probability of an extension $\widetilde{\mathcal{A}}_i$ corresponding to a string $\mathbb{P}_{\mathcal{A}_i} = [p_{i1}, p_{i2}, \ldots, p_{in}]$ is defined as the product of probabilities p_{ij} when $p_{ij} \neq 0$, i.e. the probability of the corresponding typicality assumption when this is selected for the extension, and $1 - p_j$ when $p_{ij} = 0$, i.e. the corresponding typicality assumption is discarded, that is to say the extension contains an exception to the inclusion.

Definition 4 (Strings of possible assumptions $\mathbb{S}$). *Given a KB = $(\mathcal{T}, \mathcal{A})$, let the set $\mathbb{C}_{\mathcal{A}}$ and $\mathbb{P}_{\mathcal{A}} = [p_1, p_2, \ldots, p_n]$ be as in Definition 3. We define the set $\mathbb{S}$ of all the strings of possible assumptions with respect to KB as*

$$\mathbb{S} = \{[s_1, s_2, \ldots, s_n] \mid \forall i = 1, 2, \ldots, n \text{ either } s_i = p_i \text{ or } s_i = 0\}$$

Definition 5 (Extension of ABox). *Let KB = $(\mathcal{T}, \mathcal{A})$, $\mathbb{P}_{\mathcal{A}} = [p_1, p_2, \ldots, p_n]$ and $\mathbb{C}_{\mathcal{A}} = [(a_1, C_1), (a_2, C_2), \ldots, (a_n, C_n)]$ as in Definition 3. Given a string of possible assumptions $[s_1, s_2, \ldots, s_n] \in \mathbb{S}$ of Definition 4, we define the extension $\widetilde{\mathcal{A}}$ of $\mathcal{A}$ with respect to $\mathbb{C}_{\mathcal{A}}$ and $\mathbb{S}$ as:*

$$\widetilde{\mathcal{A}} = \{\mathbf{T}(C_i)(a_i) \mid (a_i, C_i) \in \mathbb{C}_{\mathcal{A}} \text{ and } s_i \neq 0\}$$

We also define the probability of $\widetilde{\mathcal{A}}$ as $\mathbb{P}_{\widetilde{\mathcal{A}}} = \prod_{i=1}^{n} \chi_i$ *where* $\chi_i = \begin{cases} p_i & \text{if } s_i \neq 0 \\ 1 - p_i & \text{if } s_i = 0 \end{cases}$

It can be observed that, in $\mathcal{ALC} + \mathbf{T}_{\mathbf{R}}^{RaCl}$, the set of typicality assumptions that can be inferred from a KB corresponds to the extension of $\mathcal{A}$ corresponding to the string $\mathbb{P}_{\mathcal{A}}$ (no element is set to 0): all the typicality assertions of individuals occurring in the ABox, that are consistent with the KB, are assumed. On the contrary, in $\mathcal{ALC} + \mathbf{T}_{\mathbf{R}}$, no typicality assumptions can be derived from a KB, and this corresponds to extending $\mathcal{A}$ by the assertions corresponding to the string $[0, 0, \ldots, 0]$, i.e. by the empty set. It is easy to observe that we obtain a probability distribution over extensions of $\mathcal{A}$.

In [25], a notion of non-monotonic entailment in the Description Logic $\mathcal{ALC} + \mathbf{T}_{\mathbf{R}}^{\text{deg}}$ is provided. Intuitively, given KB and a query F, we distinguish two cases:

– if F is an inclusion $C \sqsubseteq D$, then it is entailed from KB if it is minimally entailed from KB' in the non-monotonic $\mathcal{ALC} + \mathbf{T}_{\mathbf{R}}^{RaCl}$, where KB' is obtained from KB by removing probabilities of exceptions, i.e. by replacing each typicality inclusion $\mathbf{T}(C) \sqsubseteq_p D$ with $\mathbf{T}(C) \sqsubseteq D$;

– if F is an ABox fact $C(a)$, then it is entailed from KB if it is entailed in the mono-tonic $\mathcal{ALC} + \mathbf{T_R}$ from the knowledge bases including the extensions of the ABox of Definition 5.

We provide both (i) a notion of entailment restricted to scenarios whose probabil-ities belong to a given range and (ii), similarly to [26], a notion of probability of the entailment of a query $C(a)$, as the sum of the probabilities of all extensions from which $C(a)$ is so entailed. Formally, given a knowledge base KB and two real numbers p and q, we write $KB \models_{\mathcal{ALC}+\mathbf{T_R^{deg}}}^{\langle p,q \rangle} F$ to represent that F follows – or is entailed – from KB restricting reasoning to scenarios whose probabilities range from p to q. When the query is an ABox assertion, we define:

Definition 6 (Entailment of an ABox inclusion in $\mathcal{ALC} + \mathbf{T_R^{deg}}$). *Given a $KB = (\mathcal{T}, \mathcal{A})$, given $\mathbb{C}$ a set of concepts, and given $p, q \in (0, 1]$, let $\mathcal{E} = \{\widetilde{\mathcal{A}_1}, \widetilde{\mathcal{A}_2}, \ldots, \widetilde{\mathcal{A}_k}\}$ be the set of extensions of $\mathcal{A}$ of Definition 5 with respect to $\mathbb{C}$, whose probabilities are such that $p \leq \mathbb{P}_1 \leq q, p \leq \mathbb{P}_2 \leq q, \ldots, p \leq \mathbb{P}_k \leq q$. Let $\mathcal{T}' = \{\mathbf{T}(C) \sqsubseteq D \mid \mathbf{T}(C) \sqsubseteq_r D \in \mathcal{T}\} \cup \{C \sqsubseteq D \in \mathcal{T}\}$. Given a query F which is an ABox assertion $C(a)$, we say that F is entailed from KB in $\mathcal{ALC} + \mathbf{T_R^{deg}}$ in range $\langle p, q \rangle$, written $KB \models_{\mathcal{ALC}+\mathbf{T_R^{deg}}}^{\langle p,q \rangle} F$, if $(\mathcal{T}', \mathcal{A} \cup \widetilde{\mathcal{A}_i}) \models_{\mathcal{ALC}+\mathbf{T_R}} F$ for all $\widetilde{\mathcal{A}_i} \in \mathcal{E}$. We also define the probability of the entailment of a query as $\mathbb{P}(F) = \sum_{i=1}^{k} \mathbb{P}_i$.*

When the query is a TBox assertion, probabilities p and q do not play any role: indeed, probabilities of scenarios are related to ABox extensions, that are not involved when we are reasoning about TBoxes. In this case entailment in $\mathcal{ALC} + \mathbf{T_R^{deg}}$ corre-sponds to entailment in the non-monotonic Description Logic $\mathcal{ALC} + \mathbf{T_R^{RaCl}}$. Therefore, we write $KB \models_{\mathcal{ALC}+\mathbf{T_R^{deg}}}^{\langle p,q \rangle} F$, if $(\mathcal{T}', \mathcal{A}) \models_{\mathcal{ALC}+\mathbf{T_R^{RaCl}}} F$, where $\mathcal{T}' = \{\mathbf{T}(C) \sqsubseteq D \mid \mathbf{T}(C) \sqsubseteq_r D \in \mathcal{T}\} \cup \{C \sqsubseteq D \in \mathcal{T}\}$. We can proceed as in [25] to show that entailment in $\mathcal{ALC} + \mathbf{T_R^{deg}}$ is EXPTIME-complete as for standard $\mathcal{ALC}$.

4   A Description Logic of Typicality for Abductive Reasoning

In this section, we present a general approach for abductive reasoning in defeasible DLs, in order to combine the expressive power of DLs of typicality with the reasoning capa-bilities offered by the rational closure, exploiting probabilities in the logic $\mathcal{ALC} + \mathbf{T_R^{deg}}$. All these ingredients allow us to perform abductive reasoning without the need to set up an abductive framework by domain expertise. Intuitively, the basic idea is to pro-vide an explanation of a set of symptoms (a set of ABox formulas) as an extension of the ABox in the logic $\mathcal{ALC} + \mathbf{T_R^{deg}}$, namely typicality assumptions that belong to the rational closure of the ABox and that can extend the initial knowledge in order to provide an explanation for the symptoms themselves. Those syntactic extensions of

$\mathcal{A}$ are generated by taking into account some plausible pairs $C(a) - \mathbf{T}(C)(a)$, from the set of abducibles, implicitly defined thanks to the modeling scheme itself. This process aims to seek an explanation for what is observed. For example if the $\mathcal{A}$ contains $\neg Euphoria(greg)$ and the $\mathcal{T}$ contains $\mathbf{T}(Depressed) \sqsubseteq \neg Euphoria$, assuming $\mathbf{T}(Depressed)(greg)$ in $\mathcal{ALC} + \mathbf{T}_{\mathbf{R}}^{RaCl}$ provides a plausible good explanation.

Let us first consider a restriction of the DL $\mathcal{ALC} + \mathbf{T}_{\mathbf{R}}^{deg}$ called R1. Intuitively, through specific modeling of the "cause-and-effect" relationships, underlying abductive reasoning, one can use $\mathbf{T}$ and non-monotonic $\mathbf{T}$-assumptions as conjectures to explain $\mathcal{G}$, the set of observations. So, $\mathbf{T}(Cause) \sqsubseteq Effect$ represents "a possible typical cause for the effect". Next, a syntax restriction of the language of $\mathcal{ALC} + \mathbf{T}_{\mathbf{R}}^{deg}$ is provided in order to facilitate the construction of an abductive reasoning strategy based on the study of minimal canonical models on a single individual a.

Definition 7 (R1 as restriction of $\mathcal{ALC} + \mathbf{T}_{\mathbf{R}}^{deg}$). *We consider an alphabet of concept names $\mathcal{C}$, and a single individual constant a. Given $A \in \mathcal{C}$, we define:*

$$C := A \mid \top \mid \bot \mid \neg C \mid C \sqcap C \mid C \sqcup C$$

$$D := A \mid \neg C \mid C \sqcap C \mid C \sqcup C$$

An $\mathcal{ALC} + \mathbf{T}_{\mathbf{R}}^{deg}$ knowledge base is a pair $(\mathcal{T}, \mathcal{A})$. $\mathcal{T}$ contains axioms of the form either $C \sqsubseteq C$, to represent taxonomies of only causes, or $\mathbf{T}(C) \sqsubseteq_p D$, to represent that "normally, C is a possible cause for D, and the probability of having exceptional instances of C not being correlated to D is $1 - p$", where $p \in \mathbb{R}, p \in (0.5, 1)$ and D does not occur in $\mathbf{T}$. $\mathcal{A}$ contains only assertions of the form $C(a)$.

$\mathcal{G}$ is a non empty set of assertions $C(a)$ where, due to the "abductive" modeling scheme $\mathbf{T}(Cause) \sqsubseteq Effect$, the concept C cannot occur in $\mathbf{T}$.

Example 1. Consider a domain for medical diagnoses. The TBox $\mathcal{T}$ contains $Pathology_B \sqsubseteq Pathology_A$ ("all patients of $Pathology_B$ are also patients of $Pathology_A$"), and $\mathbf{T}(Pathology_A) \sqsubseteq_p Symptom$ ("all typical $Pathology_A$ patients suffer/show $Symptom$ with a probability of having exceptions equals to $1 - p$"), where p is linked to the uncertainty of this prototypical description. Let the $\mathcal{A}$ contain $Pathology_A(john)$, denoting that "John suffers $Pathology_A$", or $Symptom(john)$, representing that "John has the symptom $Symptom$". As expected from the underlying $\mathcal{ALC} + \mathbf{T}_{\mathbf{R}}$, diseases are described in terms of the symptoms typically displayed by sufferers through $\mathbf{T}$-inclusions.

Let us now introduce the concept of abductive hypothesis under *rational closure*. By using the semantics of minimal canonical models combined with domain-specific modeling, the defeasible description logic for abduction seeks to take advantage of the implicit definition of abducibles from which abductive hypotheses can be formulated.

Definition 8 (Abducibiles in R1 as restriction of $\mathcal{ALC} + \mathbf{T}_{\mathbf{R}}^{deg}$). *Given a KB = $(\mathcal{T}, \mathcal{A})$ as in Definition 7, let $\mathfrak{Tip}$ be the set of abducibles, namely:*

$$\mathfrak{Tip} = \{C \mid \mathbf{T}(C) \sqsubseteq_p D \in \mathcal{T}\}$$

Two aspects must be considered: 1) not all assertions that can be instantiated from the set of possible abducibles are consistent with KB, and 2) if one supposes $C(a)$ but $\mathbf{T}(C)(a)$ is not minimally entailed in $\mathcal{ALC} + \mathbf{T}_{\mathbf{R}}^{RaCl}$, w.r.t. the modeling scheme $\mathbf{T}(Cause) \sqsubseteq Effect$, an unintended exception is introduced.

Let us now describe abducible hypothesis in the proposed logic. The main idea is to set up a strategy for generating abductive hypotheses that are *plausible* and for reasoning in a context of maximum typicality, according to *rational closure*, in which one can derive defeasible properties while searching for explanations for $\mathcal{G}$.

Let KB $= (\mathcal{T}, \mathcal{A})$ and let $\overline{KB}$ be the rational closure over KB. In R1, we restrict entailment to a class of minimal canonical models, where for each $C(a)$ conjectured, with $C \in \mathfrak{Tip}$, it should hold $(\mathcal{T}', \mathcal{A} \cup \{C(a)\}) \models_{\mathcal{ALC} + \mathbf{T}_{\mathbf{R}}^{RaCl}} \mathbf{T}(C)(a)$. It can be observed that, given an $\mathcal{ALC} + \mathbf{T}_{\mathbf{R}}$ model $\mathcal{M}$ satisfying KB, we have:

- the rank of a concept in a model is related to the rank of the most typical domain element belonging to the extension of that concept: $k_{\mathcal{M}}(C) = min\{k_{\mathcal{M}}(x) \mid x \in C^{\mathcal{I}}\}$, if $C^{\mathcal{I}} = \emptyset$ then $k_{\mathcal{M}}(C) = \infty$;
- as proved in [15,25], $\mathbf{T}(C) \sqsubseteq D$ is minimally entailed from the KB, if it holds in all minimal canonical models of KB. One can determine the rank of concept C through the computation of $\overline{\mathcal{T}}$, *rational closure* over $\mathcal{T}$, and when $\mathcal{M}$ is a canonical model minimizing the rank of domain elements, it holds in particular:
  - $\overline{\mathcal{T}} = \{\mathbf{T}(C) \sqsubseteq D \mid$ either $rank(C) < rank(C \sqcap \neg D)$ or $rank(C) = \infty\}$
  - $rank(C) = k_{\mathcal{M}}(C)$
- due to the equivalence between *rational closure* and the semantics based on rational models [15], the problem of deciding whether $\mathbf{T}(C)(a)$ is plausible, in addition to the assumption of $C(a)$, with $KB \cup \{C(a)\}$ consistent and $C \in \mathfrak{Tip}$, relies on: $KB \models_{\mathcal{ALC} + \mathbf{T}_{\mathbf{R}}^{RaCl}} \mathbf{T}(C)(a)$ iff $\mathbf{T}(C)(a) \in \overline{\mathcal{A} \cup \{C(a)\}}$. Then one can test all the rank assignments to the individual constant, $k_j(a)$, and evaluate different scenarios generated by the concepts that a would need to satisfy with that rank assigned: $\mu^j = \{(\neg C \sqcup D)(a) \mid \mathbf{T}(C) \sqsubseteq D \in \overline{\mathcal{T}}, k_j(a) = rank(C)\} \cup \{(\neg C \sqcup D)(a) \mid C \sqsubseteq D \in \mathcal{T}\}$. When $k_j(a)$ is minimal and consistent with $\mathcal{T} \cup \mathcal{A} \cup \{C(a)\} \cup \mu^j$, then $\mathcal{M}$ is a minimal canonical model, where a, the individual constant, can be mapped onto the most typical domain element w.r.t. C ($\mathbf{T}(C) \sqsubseteq_p D$), namely $k_j(a) = rank(C) = k_{\mathcal{M}}(C) = k_{\mathcal{M}}(a)$, therefore $a^{\mathcal{I}} \in Min_<(C^{\mathcal{I}})$, with $C \in \mathfrak{Tip}$ and $\mathcal{M}$ supporting the typicality assumption $a^{\mathcal{I}} \in (\mathbf{T}(C))^{\mathcal{I}}$.

Hence, proceeding with homogeneous rank is the most intuitive way to generate an abductive hypothesis in R1.

Definition 9 (Abductive hypothesis of rank r, in R1 as restriction of $\mathcal{ALC} + \mathbf{T}_{\mathbf{R}}^{deg}$). *Given a KB $= (\mathcal{T}, \mathcal{A})$ expressed as for Definition 7, a set of assertions on a, with rank r, can be instantiated as: $\Omega^r = \{C(a) \mid C \in \mathfrak{Tip}, rank(C) = r\}$, whereas the powerset for each rank is: $\mathcal{P}(\Omega^r) = \{\omega_l^r \mid \omega_l^r \in \Omega^r\}$, with $r \in \mathbb{N}_0$ and $l = 0, ..., 2^{|\Omega^r|} - 1$. An abductive hypothesis of rank r is a pair $\langle \omega_l^r, \mathfrak{Tip}_{\mathcal{A} \cup \omega_l^r} \rangle$ formed by:*

- *the assertions instantiated by the concepts occurring in $\mathbf{T}$, ω_l^r;*

– *the associated* $\mathbf{T}$*-assumptions, when consistent;*

$$\mathfrak{Tip}_{\mathcal{A}\cup\omega_l^r} = \{(a,C) \mid C(a) \in \omega_l^r \text{ and } (\neg C \sqcup D)(a) \in \mu^r\}$$

when $r = k_j(a)$*, and* $k_j(a)$ *is minimal and consistent with* $(\overline{\mathcal{T}}, \mathcal{A} \cup \omega_l^r)$.

Thanks to the "ad hoc" modeling schema and the rational closure in $\mathcal{ALC} + \mathbf{T_R}$ adapted in "abductive terms", the ABox reasoning procedure [15, 25] can be enriched with meaningful abductive hypothesis of rank r. Indeed when $\mathfrak{Tip}_{\mathcal{A}\cup\omega_l^r} \subseteq \overline{\mathcal{A} \cup \omega_l^r}$, if $C(a) \in \omega_l^r$ then $\mathbf{T}(C)(a) \in \mathfrak{Tip}_{\mathcal{A}\cup\omega_l^r}$.

Algorithm 1 generates "meaningful" $\langle \omega_l^r, \mathfrak{Tip}_{\mathcal{A}\cup\omega_l^r}\rangle$ and it is inspired by the procedure for computing $\overline{\mathcal{A}}$ in [15] and entailment in $\mathcal{ALC} + \mathbf{T_R^P}$ [24, 25]. In order to build sets of pairs $C_i^r(a)$ and $\mathbf{T}(C_i^r)(a)$, the algorithm starts from the concept rank range $[0, ..., k] \subseteq \mathbb{N}_0$ as in [15], considering concepts by homogeneous rank and testing minimal and consistent rank assignments for the individual constant a. Intuitively, the algorithm is used to check whether a new piece of information can be inferred for each conjectured fact, discarding ω_l^r when: (i) $\exists C_i^r(a) \in \omega_l^r$ t.c. $KB \cup \{C_i^r(a)\}$ unsatisfiable in $\mathcal{ALC} + \mathbf{T}_R$; (ii) there is at least one $\mathbf{T}$-assumption, related to ω_l^r, not minimally entailed in $\mathcal{ALC} + \mathbf{T_R^{RaCl}}$, through the calculation of $\overline{\mathcal{A} \cup \omega_l^r}$ and $\mathfrak{Tip}_{\mathcal{A}\cup\omega_l^r}$.

A simple strategy for composing abductive hypotheses is to combine the maximum number of assertions and $\mathbf{T}$-assertions, of concepts of different ranks, while maintaining the consistency of what can be assumed, namely:

$$\mathcal{T} \cup \mathcal{A} \cup \omega_l^x \cup \mathfrak{Tip}_{\mathcal{A}\cup\omega_l^x} \cup ... \cup \omega_m^z \cup \mathfrak{Tip}_{\mathcal{A}\cup\omega_m^z} \text{ consistent in } \mathcal{ALC} + \mathbf{T}_R$$

with $0 \leq x \leq z \leq k$, where k is the max rank of a concept in KB. Let us consider the reasoning procedure in $\mathcal{ALC} + \mathbf{T_R^{deg}}$ described in Sect. 3 we have the following adaptations: $\mathbb{C}_{\mathcal{A}\cup\omega_l^x\cup...\cup\omega_m^z} = \mathfrak{Tip}_{\mathcal{A}\cup\omega_l^x} \cup ... \cup \mathfrak{Tip}_{\mathcal{A}\cup\omega_m^z}$, where the *ordered multiset* $\mathbb{P}_{\mathcal{A}\cup\omega_l^x\cup...\cup\omega_m^z}$ and the possible extensions $\widetilde{\mathcal{A}_{\omega_l^x\cup...\cup\omega_m^z}} = \{\mathbf{T}(C_i^r)(a) \mid (a, C_i^r) \in \mathbb{C}_{\mathcal{A}\cup\omega_l^x\cup...\cup\omega_m^z}$ and $s_i \neq 0\}$ take into account the pairs, $C_i^r(a) - \mathbf{T}(C_i^r)(a)$, assumed and from which one wants to draw the most number of conclusions.

Intuitively, this approach results in non-monotonic reasoning through the inclusion of abductive hypotheses in syntactic extensions of the knowledge base. By examining different scenarios, we can investigate the probability distribution on models for the named individual a, under the assumption of different possible abductive hypotheses.

Definition 10 (Explanation in R1 as restriction of $\mathcal{ALC} + \mathbf{T_R^{deg}}$). *Given a* $KB = (\mathcal{T}, \mathcal{A})$ *expressed as for Definition 7, a finite and non empty set of facts on* a*,* $\mathcal{G}$*, when* $KB \nvDash_{\mathcal{ALC}+\mathbf{T_R^{RaCl}}} \mathcal{G}$ *and* $KB \cup \mathcal{G}$ *consistent in* $\mathcal{ALC} + \mathbf{T_R^{RaCl}}$ *one can seek for an explanation for* $\mathcal{G}$*. From Definition 6, we have:*

$$KB \cup \omega_l^x \cup ... \cup \omega_m^z \models_{\mathcal{ALC}+\mathbf{T_R^{deg}}}^{\langle p, r\rangle} \mathcal{G} \text{ when } (\mathcal{T}', \mathcal{A} \cup \omega_l^x \cup ... \cup \omega_m^z \cup \widetilde{\mathcal{A}_{\omega_l^x\cup...\cup\omega_m^z}}) \models_{\mathcal{ALC}+\mathbf{T_R}} \mathcal{G}$$

testing different scenarios generated by the abductive hypothesis assumed.

Example 2. Let us consider an example of medical diagnosis adapted from [24, 25]. Knowing that Greg belongs to the concept *Euphoria*, $\mathcal{A} = \{Euphoria(greg)\}$ and having a terminological knowledge of the domain as follows, we want to find, if possible, an explanation for Greg's symptoms, namely: $\mathcal{G} = \{MoodReactivity(greg)\}$.

Table 1. $\mathcal{T}$ from Example 2 in [25].

$$Bipolar \sqsubseteq Depressed \tag{1}$$
$$\mathbf{T}(Depressed) \sqsubseteq_{0.85} \neg MoodReactivity \tag{2}$$
$$\mathbf{T}(Depressed) \sqsubseteq_{0.65} \neg Euphoria \tag{3}$$
$$\mathbf{T}(Bipolar) \sqsubseteq_{0.7} MoodReactivity \tag{4}$$
$$\mathbf{T}(ProstateCancerPatient) \sqsubseteq_{0.6} MoodReactivity \tag{5}$$
$$\mathbf{T}(ProstateCancerPatient) \sqsubseteq_{0.8} Nocturia \tag{6}$$

Algorithm 1. Generating sets of couples $C_i^r(a) - \mathbf{T}(C_i^r)(a)$ in R1.

procedure GENERATEABDUCTIVEHYPOTHESESBYRANK$((\mathcal{T}, \mathcal{A}), \mathcal{T}', \mathfrak{Tip}, [0, ..., k])$
  $[...] \leftarrow \emptyset$ ▷ set of homogeneous sets by rank
  for each r in $[0, ..., k]$ **do**
    $\Omega^r \leftarrow \emptyset$
    for each $C \in \mathfrak{Tip}$ **do**
      if $rank(C) = r$ **then**
        $\Omega^r \leftarrow \Omega^r \cup \{C(a)\}$
    $[...] \leftarrow \Omega^r$ ▷ store sets of $C_i^r(a)$ by rank
  for each Ω^r in $[\Omega^0, ..., \Omega^k]$ **do**
    $\mathcal{P}(\Omega^r) \leftarrow \emptyset$ ▷ powerset of Ω^r
    for each $C(a) \in \Omega^r$ **do**
      for each $\{...\} \in \mathcal{P}(\Omega^r)$ **do**   ▷ iterate on each set in $\mathcal{P}(\Omega^r)$
        $\omega \leftarrow \emptyset$
        $\omega \leftarrow \{...\} \cup \{C(a)\}$
        $\mathcal{P}(\Omega^r) \leftarrow \mathcal{P}(\Omega^r) \cup \{\omega\}$
      $\mathcal{P}(\Omega^r) \leftarrow \mathcal{P}(\Omega^r) \cup \{\{C(a)\}\}$
    $[...] \leftarrow \mathcal{P}(\Omega^r)$ ▷ store powerset by rank
  ▷ Perform a selection of the "meaningful" abductive hypothesis by rank
  ▷ Remove ω_l^r when $(\mathcal{T}', \mathcal{A}) \cup \omega_l^r$ is inconsistent in $\mathcal{ALC} + \mathbf{T}_R$
  ▷ Remove ω_l^r associated to $\mathbf{T}$-assertions non minimally entailed in $\mathcal{ALC} + \mathbf{T}_R^{RaCl}$
  $\mathbb{X} \leftarrow \emptyset$ ▷ store abductive hypothesis as pair of set
  for each $\mathcal{P}(\Omega^r)$ in $[\mathcal{P}(\Omega^0), ..., \mathcal{P}(\Omega^k)]$ **do**
    for each $\omega_l^r \in \mathcal{P}(\Omega^r)$ **do**
      if $\mathcal{T}' \cup \mathcal{A} \cup \omega_l^r$ consistent in $\mathcal{ALC} + \mathbf{T}_R$ **then**   ▷ consistent with ω_l^r
        $\mathfrak{Tip}_{\mathcal{A} \cup \omega_l^r} \leftarrow \emptyset$
        for each $C(a) \in \omega_l^r$ **do**
          ▷ $\mathbf{T}$-assumption when $\mathcal{T}' \cup \mathcal{A} \cup \omega_l^r \cup \mu^r$ consistent in $\mathcal{ALC} + \mathbf{T}_R$
          if $(\mathcal{T}', \mathcal{A}) \cup \omega_l^r \models_{\mathcal{ALC}+\mathbf{T}_R^{RaCl}} \mathbf{T}(C)(a)$ **then**
            $\mathfrak{Tip}_{\mathcal{A} \cup \omega_l^r} \leftarrow \mathfrak{Tip}_{\mathcal{A} \cup \omega_l^r} \cup \{\mathbf{T}(C)(a)\}$ ▷ $\mathbf{T}$-assumption
        if $|\omega_l^r| = |\mathfrak{Tip}_{\mathcal{A} \cup \omega_l^r}|$ **then**   ▷ check all the $\mathbf{T}$-assumptions
          store $\langle \omega_l^r, \mathfrak{Tip}_{\mathcal{A} \cup \omega_l^r} \rangle$ in $\mathbb{X}$

Table 2. Assertions to be satisfied when rank assignments: $r = 0$ or $r = 1$, from $\overline{\mathcal{T}}$.

$$\mu^0 \qquad\qquad\qquad\qquad \mu^1$$

$(\neg Depressed \sqcup \neg MoodReactivity)(greg)$ $(\neg Bipolar \sqcup MoodReactivity)(greg)$
$(\neg Depressed \sqcup \neg Euphoria)(greg)$ $(\neg Bipolar \sqcup Depressed)(greg)$
$(\neg ProstateCancerPatient \sqcup Nocturia)(greg)$
$(\neg ProstateCancerPatient \sqcup MoodReactivity)(greg)$
$(\neg Bipolar \sqcup Depressed)(greg)$

We have that $\mathcal{G}$ is not entailed from KB, but KB $\cup \mathcal{G}$ is consistent. With a set of abducibiles as: $\mathfrak{Tip} = \{Depressed, Bipolar, ProstateCancerPatient\}$, and a computed rank of each concept as: $rank(Depressed) = rank(ProstateCancerPatient) = 0$ and $rank(Bipolar) = 1$, the possible rank assignments to the individual constant produce the assertions in Table 2. The "meaningful" abductive hypotheses by rank, from Table 3, are: $\langle \omega_2^0, \mathfrak{Tip}_{\mathcal{A} \cup \omega_2^0} \rangle$ and $\langle \omega_1^1, \mathfrak{Tip}_{\mathcal{A} \cup \omega_1^1} \rangle$, which can be combined, then we have: KB $\cup \omega_2^0 \cup \mathfrak{Tip}_{\mathcal{A} \cup \omega_2^0} \cup \omega_1^1 \cup \mathfrak{Tip}_{\mathcal{A} \cup \omega_1^1}$ is consistent in $\mathcal{ALC} + \mathbf{T_R}$. Moreover, we have $(greg, Bipolar)^{r=1}, (greg, ProstateCancerPatient)^{r=0}$ with $P = [0.7, 0.48]$. All the possible **T**-assumptions from $\omega_2^0 \cup \omega_1^1$ and the corresponding extensions of $\mathcal{A}$ with probabilities are shown in Table 4.

Table 3. Abductive hypotheses and **T** minimally entailed in $\mathcal{ALC} + \mathbf{T_R}^{RaCl}$.

abd. hypothesis by rank	assertions $C_i^r(\mathbf{a})$	T-assumptions $\mathbf{T}(C_i^r)(\mathbf{a})$
$\langle \omega_1^0, \mathfrak{Tip}_{\mathcal{A} \cup \omega_1^0} \rangle$	$Depressed(greg)$	$\emptyset$
$\langle \omega_2^0, \mathfrak{Tip}_{\mathcal{A} \cup \omega_2^0} \rangle$	$ProstateCancerPatient(greg)$	$\mathbf{T}(ProstateCancerPatient)(greg)$
$\langle \omega_3^0, \mathfrak{Tip}_{\mathcal{A} \cup \omega_3^0} \rangle$	$Depressed(greg)$ $ProstateCancerPatient(greg)$	$\emptyset$
$\langle \omega_1^1, \mathfrak{Tip}_{\mathcal{A} \cup \omega_1^1} \rangle$	$Bipolar(greg)$	$\mathbf{T}(Bipolar)(greg)$

Table 4. Plausible $\mathcal{A}$ extensions [25] (PCP stands for $ProstateCancerPatient$, B for $Bipolar$).

String	Extension	Probability
$[0.7, 0.48]$	$\mathcal{A}_{\omega_2^0 \cup \omega_1^1}^1 = \{\mathbf{T}(B)(greg), \mathbf{T}(PCP)(greg)\}$	$\mathbb{P}_{\widetilde{\mathcal{A}_{\omega_2^0 \cup \omega_1^1}^1}} = 0.7 \times 0.48$
$[0.7, 0.52]$	$\mathcal{A}_{\omega_2^0 \cup \omega_1^1}^2 = \{\mathbf{T}(B)(greg)\}$	$\mathbb{P}_{\widetilde{\mathcal{A}_{\omega_2^0 \cup \omega_1^1}^2}} = 0.7 \times 0.52$
$[0.3, 0.48]$	$\mathcal{A}_{\omega_2^0 \cup \omega_1^1}^3 = \{\mathbf{T}(CP)(greg)\}$	$\mathbb{P}_{\widetilde{\mathcal{A}_{\omega_2^0 \cup \omega_1^1}^3}} = 0.3 \times 0.48$
$[0.3, 0.52]$	$\mathcal{A}_{\omega_2^0 \cup \omega_1^1}^4 = \emptyset$	$\mathbb{P}_{\widetilde{\mathcal{A}_{\omega_2^0 \cup \omega_1^1}^4}} = 0.3 \times 0.52$
	$\mathbb{P}_{\widetilde{\mathcal{A}_{\omega_2^0 \cup \omega_1^1}^1}} + \mathbb{P}_{\widetilde{\mathcal{A}_{\omega_2^0 \cup \omega_1^1}^2}} + \mathbb{P}_{\widetilde{\mathcal{A}_{\omega_2^0 \cup \omega_1^1}^3}} + \mathbb{P}_{\widetilde{\mathcal{A}_{\omega_2^0 \cup \omega_1^1}^4}} =$	1

In R1 we have: $KB \cup \omega_2^0 \cup \omega_1^1 \models_{\mathcal{ALC}+\mathbf{T}_{\mathbf{R}}^{\mathrm{deg}}}^{\langle 0,1 \rangle} \mathcal{G}$ with a total probability of $\mathbb{P}(\mathcal{E}_{\omega_2^0 \cup \omega_1^1}) = 0.7$. Hence Greg's mood swings can be explained with a not trivial diagnosis [24,25] $(\mathbf{T}', \mathcal{A} \cup \omega_2^0 \cup \omega_1^1 \cup \widetilde{\mathcal{A}_{\omega_2^0 \cup \omega_1^1}^1}) \models_{\mathcal{ALC}+\mathbf{T}_{\mathbf{R}}} \mathcal{G}$, corresponding to the assumption of Greg as a typical person with bipolar disorder and prostate cancer with a probability of 34%, instead when $(\mathbf{T}', \mathcal{A} \cup \omega_2^0 \cup \omega_1^1 \cup \mathcal{A}_{\omega_2^0 \cup \omega_1^1}^2) \models_{\mathcal{ALC}+\mathbf{T}_{\mathbf{R}}} \mathcal{G}$, the scenario $\widetilde{\mathcal{A}_{\omega_2^0 \cup \omega_1^1}^2}$ could suggest that Greg is just a typical person with bipolar disorder, with a probability of 36%. Example 2 is a variation of that one in [25], to show how the assumption of the set $\omega_2^0 \cup \omega_1^1$ as "combined" abductive hypothesis, generates a scenario $\widetilde{\mathcal{A}_{\omega_2^0 \cup \omega_1^1}^3}$, with rank assignment $k(greg) = 0$, in which Greg cannot be an atypical person with bipolar disorder due to $\overline{\mathcal{A} \cup \omega_2^0 \cup \omega_1^1} \models_{\mathcal{ALC}+\mathbf{T}_{\mathbf{R}}} \mathbf{T}(Bipolar)(greg)$.

We conclude by observing that the whole procedure for abductive reasoning is essentially inexpensive, in the sense that it is in EXPTIME as the underlying, classic $\mathcal{ALC}$.

Theorem 1. *Abductive reasoning in R1 is in* EXPTIME.

5   Conclusions and Future Works

In this work, we have presented a general approach to defining a defeasible description logic for abductive reasoning, based on plausible typicality assumptions. The idea is to consider a restriction of $\mathcal{ALC} + \mathbf{T}_{\mathbf{R}}$ to TBoxes expressing that *typical X is a possible cause for effect Y*, $\mathbf{T}(X) \sqsubseteq Y$, in order to provide explanations for observed effects $\mathcal{G}$, while composing, indirectly, the set of abducibles as the concepts belonging to the scope of $\mathbf{T}$. Thanks to the notion of *rational closure* and through the computation of rank of concepts $C \in \mathfrak{Tip}$, one can determine when $\{\mathbf{T}(C) \sqsubseteq D\} \in \overline{\mathcal{T}}$, or the assertions $(\neg C \sqcup D)(a)$ to satisfy while finding a rank assignment for the named individual a, minimal and consistent with $(\overline{\mathcal{T}}, \mathcal{A} \cup \omega_l^x \cup ... \cup \omega_m^z)$ in $\mathcal{ALC} + \mathbf{T}_{\mathbf{R}}$, where $\omega_l^x \cup ... \cup \omega_m^z$ is one of the possible set of pairs $C_i^r - \mathbf{T}(C_i^r)$ of rank r, plausible to assume nonmonotonically as abductive hypothesis. In our approach, *scenarios* are inspired to *worlds* in Abductive Logic Programming [1,4]. In ALP_p, the integrity constraints $IC^p \cup IC^{np}$, probabilistic and non probabilistic, are criteria for selecting *worlds*, namely $KB \cup \Delta \models IC^{np}$ and $\forall (ic_i, \theta_j, 1) \in \sigma, KB \cup \Delta \models ic_i\theta_j$, under CWA with $(ic_i, \theta_j, 1)$ as the atomic choice for the i-th PIC. On the other hand, introducing integrity constraints in a defeasible description logic for abduction would lead to several limitations to tackle, among others: OWA, the main role of $\mathbf{T}$-assumption in drawing conclusions and the "all or nothing" behavior [15,24,25], avoiding to separately reason on different prototypical properties.

We evaluated two alternative notions of probability: the first one, called R1 and presented in this work, is based on considering different degrees of admissibility of exceptions with respect to $\mathbf{T}$-inclusions, where p represents the probability of (not) finding exceptional individual being Cs but not Ds. Sscenarios are syntactical extensions generated by assuming or not the typicality of the named individual with respect to concepts occurring in the scope of $\mathbf{T}$, when the associated $\mathbf{T}$-assertions are minimally entailed in the underlying $\mathcal{ALC} + \mathbf{T}_{\mathbf{R}}^{RaCl}$. Aside, we examined a defeasible description logic for abduction with probability more similar to the logics in [17,18], based on DISPONTE [27,28], which recently found several applications [19–21], to represent the uncertainty about information in KB. In this proposal, still under investigation, a probability distribution over the worlds is obtained by including (or not) formulas of the KB, each annotated with a probability, under the assumption that these are independent from each other. In this way, labeling with a probability – only – typicality inclusions, namely $p :: \mathbf{T}(C) \sqsubseteq D$ with $p \in (0.5, 1) \subseteq \mathbb{R}$, where p is a degree of belief in the truth of that inclusion, and one can reason on different *worlds* as syntactical manipulation of the terminological knowledge as in [18], surpassing the limit of "all-or-nothing".

In future research we aim at studying how to combine sets of pairs $C_i^r - \mathbf{T}(C_i^r)$ with different ranks in abductive hypotheses, entailing $\mathcal{G}$ under the greatest number of *plausible* assumptions and under the probabilistic distribution over those related *scenarios*. Moreover, we aim at developing an implementation of the proposed approach. Moreover, we aim at considering the use of low complexity DLs of typicality [12,13].

References

1. Azzolini, D., Bellodi, E., Ferilli, S., Riguzzi, F., Zese, R.: Abduction with probabilistic logic programming under the distribution semantics. Int. J. Approx. Reason. **142**, 41–63 (2022). https://doi.org/10.1016/j.ijar.2021.11.003
2. Baader, F., Hollunder, B.: Priorities on defaults with prerequisites, and their application in treating specificity in terminological default logic. J. Autom. Reason. (JAR) **15**(1), 41–68 (1995)
3. Baader, F., Calvanese, D., Mcguinness, D.L., Nardi, D., Patel-Schneider, P.F. (eds.): The Description Logic Handbook: Theory, Implementation and Applications. Cambridge University Press, Cambridge (2003)
4. Bellodi, E., Gavanelli, M., Zese, R., Lamma, E., Riguzzi, F.: Nonground abductive logic programming with probabilistic integrity constraints. Theory Pract. Logic Program. **21**(5), 557–574 (2021). https://doi.org/10.1017/S1471068421000417
5. Bonatti, P.A., Faella, M., Petrova, I., Sauro, L.: A new semantics for overriding in description logics. Artif. Intell. **222**, 1–48 (2015). https://doi.org/10.1016/j.artint.2014.12.010
6. Bonatti, P.A., Lutz, C., Wolter, F.: The complexity of circumscription in DLs. J. Artif. Intell. Res. (JAIR) **35**, 717–773 (2009)
7. Brachman, R.J., Levesque, H.J.: Chapter 9 - structured descriptions. In: Brachman, R.J., Levesque, H.J. (eds.) Knowledge Representation and Reasoning, The Morgan Kaufmann Series in Artificial Intelligence, pp. 155–186. Morgan Kaufmann, San Francisco (2004). https://doi.org/10.1016/B978-155860932-7/50094-7
8. Casini, G., Straccia, U.: Rational closure for defeasible description logics. In: Janhunen, T., Niemelä, I. (eds.) JELIA 2010. LNCS (LNAI), vol. 6341, pp. 77–90. Springer, Heidelberg (2010). https://doi.org/10.1007/978-3-642-15675-5_9
9. Casini, G., Straccia, U.: Defeasible inheritance-based description logics. J. Artif. Intell. Res. (JAIR) **48**, 415–473 (2013)
10. Donini, F.M., Nardi, D., Rosati, R.: Description logics of minimal knowledge and negation as failure. ACM Trans. Comput. Logics (ToCL) **3**(2), 177–225 (2002)
11. Giordano, L., Gliozzi, V., Olivetti, N., Pozzato, G.L.: ALC+T: a preferential extension of description logics. Fund. Inf. **96**, 341–372 (2009). https://doi.org/10.3233/FI-2009-185

12. Giordano, L., Gliozzi, V., Olivetti, N., Pozzato, G.L.: Prototypical reasoning with low complexity description logics: preliminary results. In: Erdem, E., Lin, F., Schaub, T. (eds.) LPNMR 2009. LNCS (LNAI), vol. 5753, pp. 430–436. Springer, Heidelberg (2009). https://doi.org/10.1007/978-3-642-04238-6_38

13. Giordano, L., Gliozzi, V., Olivetti, N., Pozzato, G.L.: Reasoning about typicality in low complexity dls: the logics elt_{min} and dl-lite$_c$ t_{min}. In: Walsh, T. (ed.) IJCAI 2011, Proceedings of the 22nd International Joint Conference on Artificial Intelligence, Barcelona, Catalonia, Spain, 16–22 July 2011, pp. 894–899. IJCAI/AAAI (2011). https://doi.org/10.5591/978-1-57735-516-8/IJCAI11-155

14. Giordano, L., Gliozzi, V., Olivetti, N., Pozzato, G.L.: A NonMonotonic description logic for reasoning about typicality. Artif. Intell. **195**, 165–202 (2013). https://doi.org/10.1016/j.artint.2012.10.004

15. Giordano, L., Gliozzi, V., Olivetti, N., Pozzato, G.L.: Semantic characterization of rational closure: from propositional logic to description logics. Artif. Intell. **226**, 1–33 (2015). https://doi.org/10.1016/j.artint.2015.05.001

16. Lehmann, D., Magidor, M.: What does a conditional knowledge base entail? Artif. Intell. **55**(1), 1–60 (1992). https://doi.org/10.1016/0004-3702(92)90041-U

17. Lieto, A., Perrone, F., Pozzato, G.L., Chiodino, E.: Beyond subgoaling: a dynamic knowledge generation framework for creative problem solving in cognitive architectures. Cogn. Syst. Res. **58**, 305–316 (2019)

18. Lieto, A., Pozzato, G.L.: A description logic framework for commonsense conceptual combination integrating typicality, probabilities and cognitive heuristics. J. Exp. Theor. Artif. Intell. **32**(5), 769–804 (2020)

19. Lieto, A., Pozzato, G.L., Striani, M., Zoia, S., Damiano, R.: DEGARI 2.0: a diversity-seeking, explainable, and affective art recommender for social inclusion. Cogn. Syst. Res. **77**, 1–17 (2023). https://doi.org/10.1016/j.cogsys.2022.10.001

20. Lieto, A., Pozzato, G.L., Zoia, S., Patti, V., Damiano, R.: A commonsense reasoning framework for explanatory emotion attribution, generation and re-classification. Knowl. Based Syst. **227**, 107166 (2021)

21. Lieto, A., et al.: A sensemaking system for grouping and suggesting stories from multiple affective viewpoints in museums. Human-Comput. Interact., 1–35 (2023). https://doi.org/10.1080/07370024.2023.2242355

22. Lukasiewicz, T.: Expressive probabilistic description logics. Artif. Intell. **172**(6–7), 852–883 (2008). https://doi.org/10.1016/j.artint.2007.10.017

23. Peirce, C.S.: Philosophical Writings of Peirce. Dover Publications, New York (1955)

24. Pozzato, G.L.: Reasoning in description logics with typicalities and probabilities of exceptions. In: Antonucci, A., Cholvy, L., Papini, O. (eds.) ECSQARU 2017. LNCS (LNAI), vol. 10369, pp. 409–420. Springer, Cham (2017). https://doi.org/10.1007/978-3-319-61581-3_37

25. Pozzato, G.: Typicalities and probabilities of exceptions in nonmotonic Description Logics. Int. J. Approx. Reason. **107**, 81–100 (2019)

26. Riguzzi, F., Bellodi, E., Lamma, E., Zese, R.: Probabilistic description logics under the distribution semantics. Semant. Web **6**(5), 477–501 (2015)

27. Riguzzi, F., Bellodi, E., Lamma, E., Zese, R.: Probabilistic description logics under the distribution semantics. Semant. Web **6**, 477–501 (2015). https://doi.org/10.3233/SW-140154

28. Riguzzi, F., Bellodi, E., Lamma, E., Zese, R.: Reasoning with probabilistic ontologies. In: Yang, Q., Wooldridge, M. (eds.) Proceedings of IJCAI 2015, pp. 4310–4316. AAAI Press (2015). https://ijcai.org/proceedings/2015

29. Strasser, C., Antonelli, G.A.: Non-monotonic logic. In: Zalta, E.N. (ed.) The Stanford Encyclopedia of Philosophy. Stanford University, Metaphysics Research Lab (2018)

30. Studer, R., Benjamins, V., Fensel, D.: Knowledge engineering: principles and methods. Data Knowl. Eng. **25**(1), 161–197 (1998). https://doi.org/10.1016/S0169-023X(97)00056-6

Ontology-Based Data Management in Healthcare: The Case of the Italian Arthroplasty Registry

Riccardo Valentini[1,2]([⊠]) [iD], Eugenio Carrani[2] [iD], Marina Torre[2] [iD], and Maurizio Lenzerini[1] [iD]

[1] Sapienza University of Rome, Piazzale Aldo Moro 5, 00185 Rome, Italy
{valentini,lenzerini}@diag.uniroma1.it
[2] Istituto Superiore di Sanitá, Viale Regina Elena 299, 00161 Rome, Italy
{carrani,torre}@iss.it

Abstract. Italian Arthroplasty Registry (Registro Italiano Artro-Protesi, RIAP) is organized as a federation of regional registries, involved on voluntary basis, with the purpose of collecting data to monitor joint prostheses safety and quickly recall patients in case of adverse events. Data collection flows may differ among the participating regions, therefore data have to be properly integrated in a single omnicomprehensive data repository. The aim of this paper is to report on the application of the Ontology Based Data Management (OBDM) approach in order to integrate, standardize and prepare data for analyses and for extracting pieces of information from the different flows converging to RIAP. From the point of view of Data Management, one of the distinguishing features of OBDM is to provide well-founded methods for data quality assessment, which is crucial also for subsequent machine learning tasks. From the knowledge representation point of view, the ontology constitutes a fundamental asset for giving proper semantics to concepts, relationships and rules regarding the arthroplasty domain, as determined by the expertise of the stakeholders. Thus, the whole approach improves the RIAP capabilities of handling data, dealing with complex research questions in the healthcare domain and sharing information with the international community of Arthroplasty Registries. Finally, the availability of a SPARQL endpoint to connect the central relational database to the RIAP ontology paves the way for enabling RIAP to publish open data with proper semantics.

Keywords: knowledge representation · ontology · OBDA · OBDM · SPARQL · open data · healthcare · arthroplasty · registry · medical device · big data · data management

R. Basili et al. (Eds.): AIxIA 2023, LNAI 14318, pp. 88–101, 2023.
https://doi.org/10.1007/978-3-031-47546-7_7

1   Introduction

Italian Arthroplasty Registry (RIAP) project started in the 2006 with the ambitious aim of collecting and analyzing demographics and surgery data, in order to monitor joint prostheses safety and quickly recall patients in case of adverse events [17]. These healthcare data can be structurally divided into their administrative part (for example, patient's demographics and data about hospitalization) and the clinical part which is registry-specific and covers all the knowledge related to the arthroplasty domain [6]. Following this distinction, there exist two main data flows which have to be linked:

1. **hospital discharge data** (HDD), containing all the relevant information about the hospitalizations of patients in Italy.
2. **minimum dataset** (MDS), regarding more specific information about the arthroplasties performed during a hospitalization and the relevant implanted devices.

Establishing a tight collaboration between stakeholders, RIAP achieved to document a standardized and complete knowledge comprising all the relevant characteristics of the arthroplasty domain. This information is organized into documents called *recordsets*[1] (tracciati record) as follows: one recordset contains all the descriptions of the attributes of the HDD flow, while the other four deal with the **hip, knee, shoulder** and **ankle** joint MDS's.

The HDD recordset is composed by **41** attributes principally referencing to a hospitalization occurred in an Italian structure and the associated patient. In order to give some examples, it is possible to mention:

- **(1) hospital code, (2) hospital subcode** and **(3) hdd progressive**, uniquely identifying the healthcare structure in which a hospitalization occurs and its assigned progressive code within that hospital;
- **(8) patient code, (7) patient gender, (35) patient current age**, representing, respectively, the *SHA-256*[2] pseudonimization of the identification code of a patient, his/her gender and age at the time of the hospitalization;
- **(14–19)** the ICD9-CM[3] codes describing **diagnoses** characterizing that patient during the hospital stay;
- **(20–31)** the ICD9-CM codes describing the **procedures** (and their **dates**) performed on that patient during the hospital stay.

A MDS recordset (with few differences among hip, knee, shoulder and ankle) is composed by **27–29** attributes comprising all the relevant knowledge regarding the specific arthroplasty. Some notable examples to mention are:

- **(1) hospital code, (2) hospital subcode** and **(3) HDD progressive**, to link an arthroplasty to the corresponding HDD part;

---

[1] https://riap.iss.it/riap/it/strumenti/documenti-tecnici/tracciati-record-riap/.
[2] http://csrc.nist.gov/publications/fips/fips180-2/fips180-2withchangenotice.pdf.
[3] https://www.cdc.gov/nchs/icd/ICD9-CMcm.htm.

- **(6) joint, (7) side,(8) type of surgery, (9), (11) cause of primary or revision arthroplasty** and **(15) entry point**, dealing with relevant features of an arthroplasty;
- **(22–27)** expressing knowledge about the device implanted during the arthroplasty[4].

All RIAP recordsets contain not only a detailed description of the semantics of each attribute, but also the possible values an attribute can assume and their definition. This is because the large majority of those values are simply alphanumeric codes, needing for an associated meaning.

From the point of view of the data, since the Italian Healthcare system is **region-based**, each participant to the RIAP project has to supply both HDD and MDS. For this reason, RIAP provides them with tools capable of collecting those data with a single and standardized method [1,17]. However, some regions already had a local arthroplasty registry with data collection implemented with their own systems. Therefore, *information integration* [7,8] represents a real challenge for the national registry, requiring, on the one hand, formal agreements between Italian National Institute of Health (ISS) and each single local referent and, on the other hand, an engineering approach for managing data coming from those extremely heterogeneous sources.

In order to give an example of the complexity of handling these data, let us consider the following two cases: the referent of region **A** uses RIAP softwares to transmit data, while the referent of region **B** has the local registry tool for data governance. **Region A** data consist of three files: the first containing HDD data; the second containing, for each HDD record, one or more arthroplasties; the third containing, for each arthroplasty, one or more associated devices. **Region B** data consist of a single file, with a row for each device considered and the eventually repeated parts of arthroplasties and HDD data. Besides the highlighted differences, it has to be pointed out that even the same attribute (e.g., the hospital code of the structure in which an arthroplasty took place) could have different names in the two situations[5]. It is easily understandable how managing this kind of heterogeneity can be challenging.

To summarize the above, RIAP achieved to obtain an extremely precise documentation about the arthroplasty domain and its specificities within the Italian Healthcare system, but it has to deal with a complex information integration task, due to the voluntary nature of the project. Therefore, RIAP is challenged to improve data quality assessment and to better exploit the huge efforts carried out with documenting the domain knowledge.

The aim of this paper is to propose a technique for preparing data in a specific healthcare scenario, thus discussing its application to the RIAP project described so far. Our method is based on the **Ontology-based Data Management (OBDM)** paradigm, which involves a three-level architecture constituted by the following elements:

---

[4] For example, the class of the implanted device according to the National Classification of Medical Devices (CND) [10];.

[5] This example is based on real Italian regions, whose actual names are omitted.

1. **ontology**: a conceptual description of the relevant domain in the given context, encompassing concepts, concept attributes, concept relationships, and logical assertions that define the domain knowledge;
2. **data sources**: repositories where data related to the domain are stored, typically numerous, heterogeneous, and managed independently of each other;
3. **the mappings**: specifies the correspondence between the data in the sources and the elements of the ontology; they act as a reconciling structure between the two levels.

The main objective of an OBDM system is to deliver several information services to users by utilizing the conceptual description of the domain, modeled through the ontology. Rather than simply providing a data structure housing data from various sources, the system provides a comprehensive and meaningful representation of the pertinent domain concepts and their interconnections. This differentiation between the ontology and the data sources creates a division between the user-oriented conceptual level and the underlying levels of the information system stored in the sources.

By explicitly representing the domain, the ontology layer in the architecture facilitates a declarative approach to information integration and data governance. The ontology and its corresponding mappings provide a common foundation for further documenting all the data in the organization, offering advantages for information system administration and management. Furthermore, the ontology enables the reusability of acquired knowledge and allows for incremental integration: new data sources or elements can be added gradually as they become available or are needed, thereby spreading the cost of integration, which is not possible when the global schema is solely a unified description of the underlying data sources. Finally, the mapping layer explicitly defines the relationships between domain concepts and data sources: it is not only used for system operations, but also serves additional documentation purposes. Consequently, the overall design can be seen as an incremental process of understanding and representing the domain, the available data sources, and their relationships.

This article is organized as follows: **Sect.** 2 describes the data modeling, thus focusing on the ontology and database design choices; **Sect.** 3 details the process of information integration and data preparation, needed to improve the quality of data; **Sect.** 4 summarizes the design of the mappings between the RIAP database and the ontology; **Sect.** 5 discusses the results of the application of the OBDM methodology both in terms of overall benefits for the registry and objectives reached thanks to the novel system; finally, **Sect.** 6 draws conclusions and future developments.

2 Data Modeling

From an analysis of the literature surrounding *arthroplasty ontologies*, it comes out that the most relevant example of knowledge representation of this domain is a subset of SNOMED CT : a thorough, multilingual clinical vocabulary employed in electronic health records and promoting interoperability [2]. Even if it indeed comprises arthroplasty-related terminology (*joints, devices, hip arthroplasty, and so on*), the *business rules* stated in RIAP documentation expressed a clinical knowledge going beyond the facts stated in SNOMED CT. However, its ability to provide a valuable high-level perspective on the phenomenon could frame it more as a landmark for enhancing RIAP ontology's interoperability in the future.

Taking all this into account, the first step of data modeling has been the conceptualization of a novel *arthroplasty knowledge base* via an *owl ontology*, built through the usage of *Eddy* [11]. It is a specialized tool developed with the purpose of building ontologies in GRAPHOL, namely a fully visual ontology language that holds the same level of expressiveness as OWL 2 [14]. Consequently, Eddy enables the creation of ontologies by simply drawing diagrams, as opposed to the more common approach of writing formulas in popular ontology design and engineering environments [5]. The important fact to point out regarding this phase is its independence w.r.t. the analysis of the data sources and the mappings: *at that moment, it was crucial to analyze only the recordsets, in order to keep this conceptualization as general as possible*. Only after a comprehensive understanding of all the peculiarities of this domain, with tight collaboration with RIAP stakeholders, in order to avoid inconsistencies, it has been possible to properly model the ontology [21].

The second step of data modeling is focused on the design of a relational database on a **Microsoft SQL Server**, which could also accommodate low quality data and serve as *data source* to be mapped to the ontology [21]. The choice of a relational database is motivated by the structure of the data, more centred on the entities and their numerous attributes rather than having a high number of interconnections.

2.1   The Ontology at a Glance

The ontology is modeled following the OWL 2 formalization, using Eddy as a tool to represent concepts, relations, properties, individuals and axioms graphically. Table 1 sums up the most important metrics characterizing the ontology, while Fig. 1 pictures a partial representation of the RIAP ontology. In the conceptualization of such a complex domain as the one of the arthroplasties, *modularity* is not optional: interacting in a separate fashion with the various modules allows a clearer understanding of the expressed knowledge. In addition, allowing query answering on a subsection of the total ontology, when possible, could improve performances. These are the four modules of the ontology, each one serving a specific purpose:

1. the **patient** module encompasses all the pertinent information regarding the patients' demographics;
2. the **hospitalisation** module comprises all the relevant details pertaining to each hospital stay, including the hospital where it takes place, the discharge diagnoses, and the procedures performed;

3. the **surgery** module incorporates all the necessary information regarding both arthroplasty procedures and general surgical activities carried out during a hospitalisation;

4. the **devices** module models all the relevant knowledge regarding the arthroplasty implant devices utilized within a surgery activity.

One further interesting aspect about this division in modules is its dual role: if the ontology is taken as a whole, it conceptualizes the knowledge about *Italian* arthroplasties, while taking into account only modules 3 and 4, it models *general* knowledge about arthroplasties.

Table 1. General metrics characterizing OWL 2 RIAP Ontology.

Metric	n	Type of Axiom	n
Axioms	3163	Sub-class of	759
Classes	535	Disjoint classes	163
Data Properties	96	Sub object property of	60
Object properties	103	Class assertions	69
Individuals	123	Annotation assertions	513

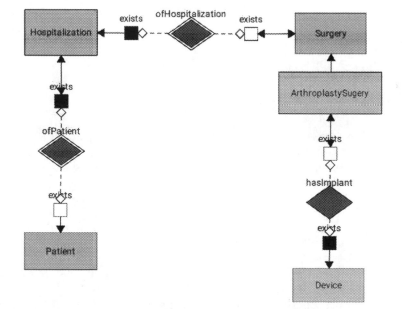

Fig. 1. A snippet of the ontology, represented through GRAPHOL as a diagram, showing the most relevant classes and their interconnections. Green rectangles represent *concepts*, while blue diamonds represent *relationships* between them.

During the design of some of the fundamental concepts (e.g., the ones expressing knowledge about *surgeries* and *hospitalizations*), it turned out that they have properties denoting a specialization of the described concept itself. This source of complexity has been tackled through both a **role participation**, capturing the associated characteristic, and an **ISA concept** representing the class specialization. This represents an example of the OWL 2 punning[6]: using the same name to describe both a class and an individual [12]. For example, a Hospitalization can be a DailyRegime or Ordinary. DailyRegime and Ordinary are modeled both as **sub concepts of** (ISA) Hospitalization and as individuals, being range of the relationship hasRegime, whose domain is the class Hospitalization. This modeling choice solves one type of integrity constraint (IC): *IC on the ranges of roles or on the domain of data properties*. In fact, it is sufficient to model the axiom on the interested sub-concept. Conversely, another type of IC, namely the *IC on the inter-relationship between concepts*, is more subtle, as it regards restrictions on the domain of a concept based on the range of a role. Consequently, those properties also resulted in ISA of concepts and ISA of relationships. For example, let us consider this piece of knowledge:

1. A hip arthroplasty (HA) can be *primary* (PHA) if performed for the first time or *revision* (RHA) if performed on a failed implant;
2. Every HA has a *cause* (CHA), linked with HA through the relationship hasCHA;
3. Every PHA has a cause, which is one among a well known subset of CHA (the same can be stated about every RHA).

Therefore, not only HA is specialized through the ISAs PHA and RHA, but also hasCHA has to be specialized through relationship ISAs, namely hasCPHA and hasCRHA, linking each one of the two subtypes of the parent domain concept (PHA and RHA) to different subsets of the parent range concepts.

2.2   The Relational Database at a Glance

The design of a relational database using the ontology modeled in the previous stage as a reference provides RIAP with a central repository, to store both data and metadata. Being a standard for dealing with large-scale data, the usage of a Microsoft SQL Server is a requirement of the organization [9][7]. The RIAP database is composed of **data** tables, covering the related key concepts of the ontology:

– arthroplasty: registry of the arthroplasties;
– device: registry of the prosthetic implants;
– diagnosis: links a hospitalization to the corresponding ICD9-CM diagnoses;
– hospitalization: registry of the RIAP hospitalizations;
– procedure: links a hospitalization to the corresponding ICD9-CM procedures;
– structure: registry of the Italian healthcare structures.

---

[6] http://www.w3.org/TR/owl2-new-features/#F12:_Punning.
[7] https://www.microsoft.com/en-us/sql-server/sql-server-2022.

The RIAP database also includes **metadata** tables with descriptions for each relevant attribute of `hospitalization` and `arthroplasty` tables and for ICD9-CM codes of `diagnosis` and `procedure`.

3   Information Integration and Data Preparation

A procedure has been designed and implemented in python as a pipeline through which, given a series of files containing RIAP source data described so far, the information integration and the population of the database can be executed automatically. The steps performed by the algorithm follow:

1. **information integration**: this is the core activity, i.e. where the actual disharmonious data sources are unified and integrated into a single dataset, representing all the dimensions of interest. This phase involves the RIAP attributes identification, the merging and possibly the joins between the two distinct parts of RIAP data sources (HDD and MDS);
2. **semantic ripartition**: during this phase, data are partitioned in several separated datasets, according to a semantic differentiation based on a specific subset of the identified ontology classes[8];
3. **target database population**: through this step, the algorithm actually populates the target database with all the data coming from the sources, produced in the previous step; this phase is eased by the previous one, which allowed to resemble the internal structure of the database tables;
4. **quality checks and data preparation**: this is the moment in which the differences between the heterogeneous data are uniformed through specific data preparation queries on the database[9]. Furthermore, during this phase, the quality metadata of the database are filled, assigning a quality score to each patient, hospitalization and arthroplasty record.

Please note that in the OBDM approach's depiction, the **RIAP database** plays the role of a *data source*, whereas, concerning the information integration performed on the raw files, it serves as the *target database*. The presence of this integration procedure is motivated by the complex nature of the project: data are sent annually by various partners and they can change. In this case, a central repository can act as an intermediate step of the OBDM mappings between the varying sources and the ontology.

3.1   Data Preparation of RIAP Data

In the step 4 of the described algorithm, we mentioned *specific data preparation* queries performed on the raw data in order to improve the general quality of the content of the RIAP database. It is extremely important to clarify the fact

---

[8] The following ontology concepts: `patient`, `hospitalization`, `diagnosis`, `procedure`, `arthroplasty` and `devices`.

[9] A more detailed description of this process will be provided in the following section.

that data, at this stage, are uniformed in terms of semantics: each attribute of a database table should have an unambiguous meaning, therefore its domain is well known and captured by the axioms of the modeled ontology. However, due to the heterogeneity of the content, there could potentially be a plethora of issues. Here is a list of the major sources of inconsistencies and errors, with the corresponding actions taken:

1. **format**: data have correct semantics, but wrong format; in this case, a single and standard format is chosen and used; for example, we found an extreme heterogeneity of the format of dates (i.e., MMDDYYYY, YYYYMMDD, and so on): the choice is to use YYYY-MM-DD;
2. **representation of the absence of information**: data with heterogeneous representations of NULL in some attributes; in this case, identifying all different representations and letting them all converge to NULL, is the straightforward solution; for example, NULLs are often coded as particular strings (i.e., X, # and so on);
3. **domain incongruousness**: values of an attribute not in the corresponding and well-known domain; in this case, those values are replaced by the correct one if it is possible to infer it from other information sources, otherwise they are simply replaced with a NULL; for example, some ICD9-CM diagnoses and procedures codes seem to be not existing, but often we found out that they contain unnecessary leading zeroes (i.e., a diagnosis of 02851 is indeed a 2851);
4. **quality**: values compliant with their domain, but not with an rule defined at the ontology level; in this case, those values are replaced by the correct ones if it is possible to infer them from other information sources, otherwise they are either replaced with a NULL, or they are kept, recording their quality. For example, a Hip Arthroplasty (HA) is recorded as *type* Primary and it has Infection as a *cause*. In this case, even if the type of surgery and the cause of surgery have both legit values, the ontology captures the rule stating that Infection **cannot be** a *cause* for a Primary hip arthroplasty.

Often, dealing with these inconsistencies is a subtle process. One example deserving to be mentioned is the one of the triplet (hospital code, hospital subcode, hdd progressive)[10]. There are cases in which not only the **format** (1), but also the **domain** (3) of one or more elements of the triplet have issues in some raw records. This is mostly due to the fact that hospital code and hospital subcode are subject to changes over the years, because of administrative choices of the healthcare structures in Italy. Fortunately, the table structure of the database keeps track of the temporal validity of the codes identifying a structure, thus in the large majority of cases it is possible to consistently update the quarantined records.

Finally, it should be worthy to highlight the fact that the **data preparation** and **cleaning** is a continuous process: the more the content of the database is explored broadly, the more some further sources of inconsistency could be found. This is a natural consequence of the integration of such a heterogeneous

---

[10] In Sect. 1, it is presented as the triplet which links MDS and HDD data flows.

information. However, the novel updates can be easily added incrementally to the data preparation queries of the step 4 of the algorithm presented in this section.

4 The Mappings

The output of the data modeling and preparation described by Sects. 2 and 3 represents the first two elements of the OBDM approach: the data sources, in our case unified by the relational database, and the ontology. In this section, we describe the third element: the process through which the mappings from the database to the ontology are carried out. **Monolith** [16] is the system used to accomplish this task, offering a unified environment that encompasses OBDM services, including ontology inspection, query answering, and data quality checking. Additionally, it enables querying of ontologies through a SPARQL endpoint[11], to ensure a proper *ontology-based data access* (OBDA).

In order to set up the SPARQL endpoint, we linked Monolith to the database and we loaded the ontology modeled through Eddy. At that point, the instances of each concept, role and data property of the ontology had been properly defined through views on the database. In this way, each SPARQL query on the RIAP Ontology is translated into the corresponding SQL query on the RIAP database at runtime. Each clinically relevant *business rule* in the documentation results in different combinations of values at the level of the *data source* and in a logical statement involving concepts and roles at the *ontological level*. It represented both a motivation for the usage of the OBDM approach and a subsequent challenge for the definition of the proper mappings to each element of the ontology.

In order to give an example, let us imagine one wants to count how many `hip arthroplasties` are in the registry. The SQL query on the database is the following:
```
select count(*) as num from arthroplasty where articulation = "A"
```

The SPARQL query on the ontology is the following:
```
select (count(?x) as ?num) where { ?x a riap:HipArthroplasty.}
```

In fact, even a non-clinician user could learn the semantics of the domain through the exploration of the ontology axioms, to then simply gather the desired data according to those semantics, without having any clue about the underlying representation (e.g., the fact that the attribute `articulation = "A"` of table `arthroplasty` identifies the entity `HipArthroplasty`).

The implementation of the SPARQL endpoint represents not only the last tile of the OBDM paradigm described in Sect. 1 of this work, but also a valuable opportunity to enhance RIAP capabilities of publishing *open data* about Italian arthroplasties and improving its interoperability within the International Society of Arthroplasty Registries (ISAR)[12].

---

[11] https://www.w3.org/TR/sparql11-protocol/.
[12] https://www.isarhome.org/.

5   Discussion

Healthcare data, by definition, have to be treated with particular attention to avoid incorrect or biased analyses [6,19]. However, they often come from heterogeneous sources, which could challenge the best practices of data engineering, as we outlined in the introduction of this paper. On the other hand, the knowledge surrounding the domain of these data is, equally often, clearly documented as it takes advantage of the expertise of the stakeholders [13]. Therefore, semantic technologies and, in particular, OBDM seems to push in the correct direction to exploit the valuable information provided by the clinicians to build proper knowledge bases, capable of framing those real-world data and, in parallel, correctly assessing their quality [15].

RIAP is a relevant example of the aforementioned statements: the application of the OBDM approach to the arthroplasty domain brings several benefits to the Italian Registry [20,22]. First of all, through the ontology-guided design of the database, was possible to integrate all the information gathered over fifteen years of activity in a central data repository. In addition, this overall process required to better explore the data and to clean and standardize them, improving their quality. The definition of proper metadata tables in the database let any analyses on the data to be more easily human-readable, while the ontology and the SPARQL endpoint provide RIAP with the possibility of producing machine-readable outputs. Finally, the clear separation between the *database* and the *ontology* allows to store data with a heterogeneous quality (from the semantic point of view) within the database, while implementing the documented rules governing them in a higher layer.

However, as stated in Sect. 3, data cleaning is a continuous process, and novel sources of inconsistencies can always come out. Furthermore, detecting an inconsistency does not necessarily mean solving it completely: some issues with data result in the deletion of a totally inconsistent record or to an update of a potentially useful dimension of the data to NULL. Moreover, the overall RIAP completeness[13] is around 28%, due to the fact that the participation to the project is voluntary. Given that one of the primary objectives of an arthroplasty registry is to perform *"survival analyses"* on implanted devices, in order to accurately identify issues with the orthopaedic surgeons' choice of implants, the data involved in this process also hold temporal significance [6]. In particular, RIAP aims to monitor the patients' history, specifically focusing on identifying arthroplasty revisions (i.e., implant failures). Unfortunately, achieving this task is currently unattainable at national level due to the insufficient level of completeness mentioned earlier, compounded by the unreliability of patient pseudonyms[14].

Despite these limitations, the OBDM approach brings the complete automation of the production of RIAP annual reports and allows the analyses to be cumulative, covering the entire lifetime of the registry. In addition, further

---

[13] The indicator measuring the ratio between the number of arthroplasties in the registry and the total number of arthroplasties in Italy.

[14] In some regions, the patient's code is not a real pseudonym, but only a progressive.

analyses are planned to compare the HDD ICD9-CM codes of `diagnoses` and `procedures` to the corresponding attributes in the MDS part of the data, to assess the quality of the HDD part from a clinical perspective [3,4,18]. Finally, if ever allowed by laws regulating the RIAP action, the entire HDD flow, coming from the Italian Ministry of Health, could be mapped to the ontology as an *additional data source* in order to partially cover the lack of information about the 72% of arthroplasty procedures that are not collected by the registry at the time being.

6   Conclusions

In our previous work, we already discussed the advantages of providing RIAP with an ontology [21,22] and we presented a poster about the information integration strategy and the perspective of a SPARQL endpoint as innovations for enhancing the capabilities of a medical registry [20]. This paper aims to give an integrated and detailed view of the RIAP data management strategy improvements through the OBDM. Specifically, this approach has been implemented in the context of the RIAP project to effectively organize, cleanse, and transform the HDD and MDS flows coming from the local healthcare structures into a valuable shared asset for future data analytics and machine learning tasks.

Notwithstanding the existence of RIAP standardized tools to upload data and an extremely clear documentation, significant efforts were invested in integrating and cleaning the RIAP dataset to achieve a stable state. Nevertheless, it has to be acknowledged the likelihood of additional cleaning requirements in the future, arising from the specific demands of forthcoming data analytics tasks centered around the dataset, as well as the inevitable need for future corrective maintenance due to the large size of the data.

As a result of the data modeling and preparation detailed in this paper, RIAP can shift its efforts away from managing its data flows and instead focus on its primary objective of monitoring the safety of joint prostheses through targeted data analytics. In fact, the presence of the relational database ensures to keep track of the content of the data sources from a centralized perspective, rather than analyzing an incremental set of csv files.

From the knowledge representation point of view, as already highlighted, the ontology and the SPARQL endpoint represent crowning achievements of the long-lasting process of knowledge elicitation carried out between RIAP and clinicians. Furthermore, the ontology can be seen as the complement of the database: it imposes rigid rules to be followed by the instances of concepts and relationships, in contrast with the database, which can accomodate also incomplete or lower quality data.

In conclusion, the OBDM approach could be particularly suitable for many healthcare domains, which share with the RIAP case study some characteristics such as the temporal relevance of the clinical events, the need for a clear set of metadata and a consistent documentation describing the domain. In these contexts, the ontology can really represent the machine-readable expression of the scientific expertise of the healthcare stakeholders.

Acknowledgements. This work has been partially supported by MIUR under the PRIN 2017 project "HOPE" (prot. 2017MMJJRE) and under the PNRR project PE0000013-FAIR, by the EU under the H2020-EU.2.1.1 project TAILOR, grant id. 95221 and under the H2020-EU.2.1.1 project TAILOR, grant id. 952215; the Italian Implantable Prostheses Registry (RIPI), that includes the Italian Arthroplasty Registry (RIAP), is supported by the Medical Devices and Pharmaceutical Service General Directorate of the Italian Ministry of Health.

References

1. Bacocco, D.L., Carrani, E., Ciciani, B., Di Sanzo, P., Leotta, F., Torre, M.: Design and implementation of the new Italian healthcare digital interoperable registry for implantable medical devices. Softw. Pract. Exp. **52**(11), 2368–2392 (2022). https://doi.org/10.1002/spe.3130. https://doi.org/onlinelibrary.wiley.com/doi/full/10.1002/spe.3130

2. Benson, T., Grieve, G.: SNOMED CT, pp. 293–324 (2021). https://doi.org/10.1007/978-3-030-56883-2_16

3. Bozic, K.J., Kurtz, S.M., Lau, E., Ong, K., Vail, T.P., Berry, D.J.: The epidemiology of revision total hip arthroplasty in the united states. J. Bone Joint Surg. **91**(1), 128–133 (2009). https://doi.org/10.2106/JBJS.H.00155

4. Bozic, K., Kurtz, S., Lau, E., et al.: The epidemiology of revision total knee arthroplasty in the united states. Clin. Orthop. Relat. Res. **468**, 45–51 (2010). https://doi.org/10.1007/s11999-009-0945-0

5. Calvanese, D., De Giacomo, G., Lembo, D., Lenzerini, M., Rosati, R.: Ontology-based data access and integration. In: Liu, L., Özsu, M.T. (eds.) Encyclopedia of Database Systems, 2nd edn. Springer, Heidelberg (2018). https://doi.org/10.1007/978-1-4614-8265-9_80667

6. Ciminello, E.: A Bayesian probabilistic record linkage method to perform survival analysis for joint prostheses when the operated side is not available. Phd thesis, Sapienza University of Rome, Dottorato di Ricerca in Scuola di dottorato in Scienze Statistiche, Rome, Italy (2023). https://iris.uniroma1.it/handle/11573/1665016#

7. Daraio, C., et al.: Data integration for research and innovation policy: an ontology-based data management approach. Scientometrics **106**, 857–871 (2015)

8. De Giacomo, G., Lembo, D., Lenzerini, M., Poggi, A., Rosati, R.: Using ontologies for semantic data integration. In: Flesca, S., Greco, S., Masciari, E., Saccà, D. (eds.) A Comprehensive Guide Through the Italian Database Research Over the Last 25 Years. SBD, vol. 31, pp. 187–202. Springer, Cham (2018). https://doi.org/10.1007/978-3-319-61893-7_11

9. Ilic, M., Kopanja, L., Zlatkovic, D., Trajkovic, M., Ćurguz, D.: Microsoft sql server and oracle: comparative performance analysis (2021)

10. Italy: Art. 57 legge finanziaria n.289 del 27.12.2002. Published into the "Gazzetta Ufficiale Serie Generale n.305 del 31.12.2002" (2002)

11. Lembo, D., Pantaleone, D., Santarelli, V., Savo, D.F.: Drawing owl 2 ontologies with eddy the editor. AI Commun. **31**, 97–113 (2018)

12. Lenzerini, M., Lepore, L., Poggi, A.: Metamodeling and metaquerying in owl2ql. Artif. Intell. **292**, 103432 (2021). https://doi.org/10.1016/j.artint.2020.103432

13. Maranghi, M., et al.: AI-based data preparation and data analytics in healthcare: the case of diabetes (2022)

14. Motik, B., et al.: Owl 2 web ontology language: structural specification and functional-style syntax (2008). https://doi.org/api.semanticscholar.org/CorpusID: 145268373
15. Pop, B., et al.: The role of medical registries, potential applications and limitations. Med. Pharm. Rep. **92**, 7–14 (2019)
16. Santarelli, V., Lepore, L., Namici, M., Ronconi, G., Ruzzi, M., Savo, D.F.: Monolith: an obdm and knowledge graph management platform. In: International Workshop on the Semantic Web (2019)
17. Torre, M., et al.: Monitoring outcome of joint arthroplasty in Italy: implementation of the national registry. Joints **5**(2), 70–78 (2017). https://doi.org/10.1055/s-0037-1603899. https://www.ncbi.nlm.nih.gov/pmc/articles/PMC5672872/pdf/10-1055-s-0037-1603899.pdf
18. Torre, M., et al.: Registro Italiano ArtroProtesi. Report Annuale 2021. Il Pensiero Scientifico Editore 2022 (2021). ISBN 978-88-490-0714-5
19. Valentini, R.: Bringing empowered and active telehealth: the modeling of a complex medical information system (2020). unpublished thesis
20. Valentini, R., Carrani, E., Bacocco, D., Torre, M., Lenzerini, M.: Ontology-based data integration and open data publication: the case of the Italian arthroplasty registry. In: Abstract Book ISAR 2022, Poster Presented at ISAR 2022, Dublin, Ireland (2022)
21. Valentini, R., Carrani, E., Torre, M., Lenzerini, M.: Ontology and data modeling for the Italian arthroplasty registry. In: Paper Presented at "Ontology Uses and Contribution to Artificial Intelligence" Workshop, Within KR2021 Virtual Conference (2021)
22. Valentini, R., Carrani, E., Torre, M., Lenzerini, M.: Ontology modelling for the Italian arthroplasty registry. In: Abstract Book ISAR 2021: Poster Hosted at ISAR 2021, Denmark (Virtual venue), Copenhagen (2021)

Planning

A Structure-Sensitive Translation from Hybrid to Numeric Planning

Francesco Percassi[1](✉)[iD], Enrico Scala[2](✉)[iD], and Mauro Vallati[1](✉)[iD]

[1] University of Huddersfield, Huddersfield, UK
{f.percassi,m.vallati}@hud.ac.uk
[2] Università degli Studi di Brescia, Brescia, Italy
enrico.scala@unibs.it

Abstract. PDDL+ is an expressive planning formalism that enables the modelling of hybrid domains with both discrete and continuous dynamics. However, its expressiveness makes this language notoriously difficult to handle natively. To address this challenge, translations from time-discrete PDDL+ into numeric PDDL2.1 have been proposed as a way to reframe the rich expressiveness of PDDL+ into a simpler and more manageable formalism. In this work, we first analyse existing translations and provide a means to compare them in terms of induced state space and the size of the reformulated tasks. Secondly, we propose a novel translation leveraging the structure of the problem to generate a compact reformulation. Our experimental results indicate that the novel translation outperforms the existing ones on a range of benchmarks.

Keywords: AI Planning · Hybrid Planning · Model Translation

1 Introduction

Automated planning is a solid branch of artificial intelligence that aims to design methodologies for synthesising a sequence of actions to reach a desired goal state, given a predictive model of the world and the initial state. Planning formalisms have been introduced to bridge the gap between theory and practical needs, allowing representation and reasoning for different problem classes [9,10,13].

Hybrid planning [22], involving discrete and continuous changes over time, is common in real-world applications. PDDL+ [10] is one of the planning formalisms for representing such systems, inspired by hybrid automata [14]. It combines an agent-oriented formalisation through actions with an explicit representation of the environment through processes and events. Processes describe how numeric variables evolve using ordinary differential equations, while events model instantaneous changes.

The expressive power of PDDL+ enabled its application in many domains, including traffic control [11,16], train dispatching [6], pharmacokinetic optimisation [1], and video games [21]. However, finding plans in PDDL+ remains challenging, also due to the limited number of planning engines supporting it.

To overcome this problem, a well-known approach is to translate the input problem into a more supported language (some recent examples [4,5,20]). Two

© The Author(s), under exclusive license to Springer Nature Switzerland AG 2023
R. Basili et al. (Eds.): AIxIA 2023, LNAI 14318, pp. 105–118, 2023.
https://doi.org/10.1007/978-3-031-47546-7_8

recent translations from time-discretised PDDL+ problems to numeric planning problems in PDDL2.1 [9] are the exponential (EXP) and polynomial (POLY) translations [19]. They incorporate environmental transitions into the agent's actions, requiring them to occur as time progresses. The EXP translation anticipates all possible processes, limiting the increase in the length of the compiled plans compared to the original ones, but resulting in an exponentially large representation. On the other hand, the POLY translation avoids exponential explosion at the cost of longer plans. Alternatively, the POLY$^-$ translation [17] combines the advantages of EXP while avoiding exponential blow-up by ignoring certain transitions. However, unlike EXP and POLY, POLY$^-$ is only sound and complete for a syntactic subclass of PDDL+ problems.

This paper takes the occasion to compare the theoretical properties of existing translations between PDDL+ and PDDL2.1, focusing the discussion on the induced state space and the size of numeric translated tasks. This analysis leads to a new translation, namely EXP$^{\mathcal{L}}$, that maintains soundness and completeness while limiting exponential blow-up. This is achieved by considering only necessary combinations of processes, resulting in exponential growth based on the largest set of processes affecting a single numeric variable. These considerations are supported by an experimental analysis that demonstrates the effectiveness of the proposed translation, considering a large set of well-known benchmarks.

2   Background

2.1   An Introductory Example: Linear-Car

The physics of a car is modelled using three numeric variables: position (x), velocity (v), and acceleration (a). At the start, the car is stationary at a specific position. The car's acceleration can be increased or decreased within defined bounds, i.e., $a_{min} \leq a \leq a_{max}$. The goal is to move the car from its initial position to a desired position by controlling its acceleration while position and velocity change continuously with $\dot{x} = v$ and $\dot{v} = a$ respectively, over time.[1] Variables can also be affected by events, causing instantaneous and deterministic changes when certain logical conditions are met. Events take priority over actions. For instance, in this domain, the car's velocity must not exceed a threshold speed v_{thresh} to prevent the engine from breaking down. Control over acceleration (a) is governed by two agent actions: *accelerate* and *decelerate*. The physical movement of the car is governed by the *displacement* process, while the potential engine failure is depicted by the *engineBlow* event. Figure 1 presents a PDDL+ encoding of these elements.

A possible solution plan (not optimal) for reaching a distance of $x = 30$ starting from $x = 0$ and stopping the car at $x = 30$, is the timestamped sequence $\langle\langle acc, 0\rangle, \langle dec, 4\rangle, \langle dec, 7\rangle, \langle acc, 10\rangle, \langle dec, 12\rangle, \langle acc, 13\rangle\rangle$ where *acc* and *dec* are the contraction of *accelerate* and *decelerate*, respectively. Such a plan must be executed within the interval $\langle 0, 13\rangle$.

---

[1] $\dot{x} = y$ denotes that the first derivative of x is y.

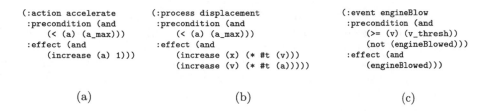

```
(:action accelerate          (:process displacement        (:event engineBlow
  :precondition (and            :precondition (and            :precondition (and
      (< (a) (a_max)))              (< (a) (a_max)))              (>= (v) (v_thresh))
  :effect (and                 :effect (and                      (not (engineBlowed)))
      (increase (a) 1)))            (increase (x) (* #t (v)))   :effect (and
                                    (increase (v) (* #t (a))))))    (engineBlowed)))
```

(a)   (b)   (c)

Fig. 1. PDDL+ encoding of an action (1a), process (1b) and event (1c). The snippet
(increase (x) (* #t (v))) means $\dot{x} = v$.

2.2 Problem Formalisation

A PDDL+ planning problem, denoted by Π, is a tuple $\langle F, X, I, G, A, E, P \rangle$, where
F is a set of Boolean variables and X is a set of numeric variables taking values
from $\{\top, \bot\}$ and $\mathbb{Q}$, respectively. These variables can be used in propositional formulas with numeric and Boolean conditions. Numeric conditions are of the form
$\langle \xi \bowtie 0 \rangle$ where ξ is a numeric expression over X and $\mathbb{Q}$, and $\bowtie \in \{\leq, <, =, >, \geq\}$.
Boolean conditions are of the form $\langle f = b \rangle$ with $f \in F$ and $b \in \{\top, \bot\}$. A formula is therefore a propositional formula using standard connectives from logic
involving numeric and Boolean conditions. I is the description of the initial state,
expressed as a full assignment to all variables in X and F. G is the description
of the goal, expressed as a formula. A and E are the sets of actions and events,
respectively. An action or event is a pair $\langle p, e \rangle$ where p is a formula and e is a set
of conditional effects of the form $c \triangleright e$.[2] Each conditional effect is such that (i) c
is a formula and (ii) e is a set of Boolean and numeric assignments. A Boolean
assignment has the form $\langle f := b \rangle$ where $f \in F$ and $b \in \{\bot, \top\}$. A numeric
assignment has the form $\langle op, x, \xi \rangle$ where $op \in \{asgn, inc, dec\}$, $x \in X$, and ξ is
a numeric expression over X and $\mathbb{Q}$. Specifically, op can be the contraction of
the keywords $assign$ $(x := \xi)$, $increase$ $(x := x + \xi)$ and $decrease$ $(x := x - \xi)$.
P is a set of processes and a process is a pair $\langle p, e' \rangle$ where p is a formula and
e' is a set of continuous numeric effects (CNE) expressed as pairs $\langle x, \xi \rangle$ where
$x \in X$ and ξ is a numeric expression defined as above. In a CNE, ξ represents the
additive contribution to the first derivative of x as time flows continuously. In
the discrete context, that is the scope of this work, ξ is the additive contribution
to the discrete change of x.

Let $a = \langle p, e \rangle$ be an action, event, or process, we use $pre(a)$ to refer to the
precondition p of a, and $eff(a)$ to the effect e of a. In the following, we will use
a, ρ, and ε to refer to a generic action, process, and event, respectively.

A PDDL+ plan π_t is a pair $\langle \pi, t_e \rangle$ where $\pi = \langle \langle a_1, t_1 \rangle, ..., \langle a_n, t_n \rangle \rangle$ is a sequence
of timestamped actions and $t_e \in \mathbb{Q}_{\geq 0}$ is the makespan within the plan π is
executed. Notably, the timestamps of π are ordered and bounded within $[0, t_e]$,
ensuring that for every i in $\{1, ..., n - 1\}$, $0 \leq t_i \leq t_{i+1} \leq t_e$ holds.

---

[2] Conditional effects are an important feature in planning formalisms in which the
effects of an action are state-dependent [2, 12].

A state s is a full assignment of the variables $X \cup F$. An action a (event ε) is applicable (is triggered) in a state s iff $s \models pre(a)$ ($s \models pre(\varepsilon)$). For describing how a state changes when an action (event) is executed (triggered) we use the transition function $\gamma(s, a)$. Given a state s and an action a (event ε), $\gamma(s, a)$ ($\gamma(s, \varepsilon)$) denotes the state resulting from the application of a (ε) in s accordingly to the effect of the action $eff(a)$ ($eff(\varepsilon)$). For a detailed explanation of the transition function, the interested reader should refer to [19]. The difference between actions and events is that the former prescribe *may transitions* under the control of the agent and can be executed if the current state meets the preconditions, while the latter prescribe *must transitions*, i.e., events are triggered immediately if their preconditions are met in a state.

A traditional way to handle PDDL+ problems is via discretisation [7]. Following [19] and [24], we formalise the PDDL+ discrete semantics through the notion of time points, histories and plan projection. A discretisation step $\delta \in \mathbb{Q}_{>0}$ is used to discretise the timeline. A time point, denoted by T, is a pair $\langle t = \delta \cdot n, n' \rangle$ where $n \in \mathbb{N}$ and $n' \in \mathbb{N}$; t denotes the clock of T while n' its counter. Time points in $\mathbb{Q} \times \mathbb{N}$ are ordered lexicographically. A history, denoted by $\mathbb{H}$, over an interval $\mathcal{I} = [T_s, T_e]$ maps each time point in $\mathcal{I}$ to a situation. A *situation at time point* T is represented by the tuple $\mathbb{H}(T) = \langle \mathbb{H}_A(T), \mathbb{H}_s(T) \rangle$, where $\mathbb{H}_A(T)$ is the action executed at time point T and $\mathbb{H}_s(T)$ is a state, which is an assignment of values to all variables in X and F at time point T. $\mathbb{H}_s(T)[v]$ and $\mathbb{H}_s(T)[\xi]$ represent the value of variable $v \in F \cup X$ and the value of a numeric expression ξ, respectively, in state $\mathbb{H}_s(T)$ at time T. $E_{trigg}(T)$ is a sequencing of the events triggered at time T. A time point T is considered a significant time point (STP) when it is associated with an instantaneous or temporal transition. Instantaneous transitions occur when an action is applied ($\mathbb{H}_A(T) \neq \langle \rangle$) or a non-empty sequence of events is triggered ($E_{trigg}(T) \neq \langle \rangle$), while temporal transitions relate to the discrete passage of time by a quantity δ. Additionally, time points resulting from these two types of transitions are also considered STPs.

According to [10], we assume that PDDL+ problems are *event-deterministic* (meaning that if multiple events are triggered in a given state, they can be sequenced arbitrarily and always produce the same outcome) and have *finite complexity*, which means that the problem induces a finite number of spontaneous changes over an interval. [8] described how these properties can be guaranteed.

To formally define when a plan π_t is a solution for a PDDL+ problem under discrete semantics, we need to introduce the notion of (discrete) PDDL+ plan-projection, which describes how π_t is projected onto a history, taking into account the effects of actions and changes yielded by events and processes. The plan projection is defined using a set of rules that describe how history progresses over time. In the following definition, R1 states that if at least an event is triggered at a specific time point, a successor state must exist with the same clock time and an increased counter. R2 states the same for actions. R3 ensures that the actions in a PDDL+ plan are projected over history while preserving their original ordering. R4 describes how numeric variables change over time when time advances by a discrete quantity δ. When time progresses, the successor state is determined by adding the CNEs of all active processes, whose preconditions are satisfied in the current state, and these effects are discretised using the formula $\Delta(\xi, \delta) = \xi \cdot \delta$.

Definition 1 (Discrete PDDL+ Plan Projection). *Let $\delta \in \mathbb{Q}_{>0}$ be a discretisation step, $\mathbb{H}$ a history, I an initial state and π_t a PDDL+ plan. We say that $\mathbb{H}$ is a discrete projection of π_t which starts in I iff $\mathbb{H}$ induces the STPs $T_{\mathbb{H}} = \langle T_0 = \langle 0, 0 \rangle, ..., T_m = \langle t_e, n_m \rangle \rangle$ where either $t_{i+1} = t_i + \delta$ or $t_{i+1} = t_i$ and, for all $i \in \{0, ..., m\}$, the following rules hold:*

R1 [Instantaneous Transition (events)]
$E_{trigg}(T_i) \neq \langle \rangle$ iff $\mathbb{H}_s(T_{i+1}) = \gamma(\mathbb{H}_s(T_i), E_{trigg}(T_i))$, $\mathbb{H}_A(T_i) = \langle \rangle$, $t_{i+1} = t_i$ *and $n_{i+1} = n_i + 1$;*

R2 [Instantaneous Transition (actions)]
$\mathbb{H}_A(T_i) \neq \langle \rangle$ iff $\mathbb{H}_s(T_{i+1}) = \gamma(\mathbb{H}_s(T_i), \mathbb{H}_A(T_i))$, $E_{trigg}(T_i) = \langle \rangle$, $t_{i+1} = t_i$ *and $n_{i+1} = n_i + 1$;*

R3 [Actions Ordering] *for each $\langle a_i, t_i \rangle, \langle a_j, t_j \rangle$ in π, with $i < j$ and $t_i = t_j$ there exists T_k, T_z in $T_{\mathbb{H}}$ such that a_i in $\mathbb{H}_A(T_k)$ and a_j in $\mathbb{H}_A(T_z)$ where $t_k = t_z = t_i$ and $n_k < n_z$;*

R4 [Temporal Transitions] *for each pair of contiguous STPs $T_i = \langle t_i, n_i \rangle$, $T_{i+1} = \langle t_{i+1}, n_{i+1} \rangle$ such that $t_{i+1} = t_i + \delta$, we have that $n_{i+1} = 0$ and the value of each numeric variable $x \in X$ is updated as:*

$$\mathbb{H}_s(T_{i+1})[x] = \mathbb{H}_s(T_i)[x] + \sum_{\substack{\langle x', \xi \rangle \in eff(\rho), \ x' = x \\ \rho \in P \ such \ that \ \mathbb{H}_s(T_i) \models pre(\rho)}} \mathbb{H}_s(T_i)[\Delta(\xi, \delta)]$$

and values of unaffected variables remain unchanged (frame-axiom).

Definition 2 (Discrete Valid PDDL+ Plan). *Let π_t be a PDDL+ plan and let $\mathbb{H}$ be the plan discrete projection of π_t for $\delta \in \mathbb{Q}_{>0}$; π_t is said to be a valid plan for Π under δ discretisation iff $\mathbb{H}_s(T_m) \models G$ and the sequence of actions $\mathbb{H}_A(T)$ is applicable in $\mathbb{H}_s(T)$ for each T in $T_{\mathbb{H}}$.*

A PDDL2.1 problem can be seen, with a certain degree of approximation, as a PDDL+ problem in which events and processes are not specified, therefore in which the exogenous component is absent. Said so, a PDDL2.1 is a tuple $\Pi = \langle F, X, I, G, A \rangle$ where each element is specified as the PDDL+ definition. A PDDL2.1 plan is simply a sequence of actions $\pi = \langle a_1, ..., a_n \rangle$. A PDDL2.1 plan π is said to be valid iff each action is applicable one after the other, and at the end, the plan achieves G.

3 From Discretised PDDL+ to PDDL2.1

Before introducing the new translation $\text{EXP}^{\mathcal{L}}$, in this section, we describe in detail the EXP translation and an overview of the polynomial translations (POLY and POLY^-). For the sake of conciseness, here we focus our attention on event-free PDDL+ problems; the discussed translations can be straightforwardly extended to handle events [19].

3.1   Exponential Translation

Given an event-free PDDL+ problem $\Pi = \langle F, X, I, G, A, \emptyset, P \rangle$, we define a context $\mathcal{C}$ to be a non-empty subset of processes and denote with $\mathcal{P}^+(P)$ the set of non-empty subsets of P, that is the set of all possible contexts.

For an event-free PDDL+ problem Π, the exponential translation generates a PDDL2.1 problem $\Pi_{\mathrm{EXP}} = \langle F, X, I, G, A \cup \{SIM\} \rangle$, discretised in δ. Π_{EXP} is almost identical to Π but for the absence of processes and the presence of the special action SIM playing the role of the simulator, i.e., what changes when time goes forward. SIM is defined as follows:

$$pre(SIM) = \top$$

$$eff(SIM) = \bigcup_{\mathcal{C} \in \mathcal{P}^+(P)} \{contpre(\mathcal{C}) \triangleright conteff(\mathcal{C})\}$$

$$contpre(\mathcal{C}) = \bigwedge_{\rho \in P \setminus \mathcal{C}} \neg pre(\rho) \wedge \bigwedge_{\rho \in P \cap \mathcal{C}} pre(\rho)$$

$$conteff(\mathcal{C}) = \bigcup_{x \in X} \{\langle inc, x, \sum_{\substack{\langle x', \xi \rangle \in eff(\rho),\ x' = x \\ \rho \in \mathcal{C}}} \Delta(\xi, \delta) \rangle\}.$$

Intuitively, the action SIM organises all possible contexts within a unique action, delegating to each conditional effect (i) the conditions under which a context is triggered and (ii) the consequences that such a context has on the state after some time δ has passed. Point (i) is formalised by conjoining two conjunctions: the first ensures that no other process of some other context has its precondition satisfied ($\bigwedge_{\rho \in P \setminus \mathcal{C}} \neg pre(\rho)$); the second ensures that all the preconditions of a given context are satisfied ($\bigwedge_{\rho \in P \cap \mathcal{C}} pre(\rho)$). Let x be some numeric variable of our problem, point (ii) is obtained by summing the contribution of each process within the context.

3.2   Polynomial Translations

As shown in [19], it is possible to translate a discretised PDDL+ problem into a PDDL2.1 problem that is only polynomial w.r.t. the size of the input. The idea is that POLY avoids the exponential representation by translating all CNEs of each process into the set of actions A_P. Given a process ρ and a CNE $ne = \langle x, \xi \rangle \in eff(\rho)$, there is an action $a_{ne} \in A_P$. This action applied in a state s modifies x according to the discretised effect of ne, i.e., $\langle inc, x, \Delta(\xi, \delta) \rangle$, iff $s \models pre(\rho)$. The simulation of the advancement of time is realised by the execution of the sequence of actions $\langle start, seq(A_P), end \rangle$, where $start$ initialises the simulation, $seq(A_P)$ is an arbitrary total order over actions from A_P. Finally, end closes the simulation. Such a sequence incrementally produces a state that is consistent with what is expected by R4 of Definition 1. Overall, POLY prevents the exponential blow-up of the problem's size but makes the search tree much deeper.

The idea of POLY has been further refined into POLY$^-$ [17]. Intuitively, POLY$^-$ leverages the advantages of EXP, using a single action for simulating the advance of a discrete quantum of time, and avoids the exponential blow-up with a schema that ignores some of the possible transitions. Specifically, all transitions in which at least two processes act simultaneously on the same numeric variable are removed from the model. This results in an approach that, differently from both EXP and POLY (which are both sound and complete), is sound but complete only for a syntactic subclass of PDDL+ tasks. This class, namely *mono left-hand side* PDDL+ problem (shortened in *1-lhs*) requires that each numeric variable is influenced by at most one process.

4   Making EXP Sensitive to the Structure of the Problem

Translations that involve performing a single action to simulate the passage of discrete time, such as EXP and POLY$^-$, are ideally more desirable than translations where simulation involves executing a sequence of actions, as seen in the case of POLY. What limits the practical utility of EXP and POLY$^-$ is that the former, generating an exponential number of conditional effects relative to the number of processes, becomes unfeasible when $|P|$ is large. The second approach, while highly efficient in certain situations, carries a general risk of making the problem unsolvable.

We propose a new translation, namely EXP$^{\mathcal{L}}$ ($\mathcal{L}$ stands for local), which has the same convenience in terms of search effort of EXP and POLY$^-$, but mitigates their negative aspects. Compared to POLY$^-$, EXP$^{\mathcal{L}}$ provides guarantees of soundness and completeness in the general case while, compared to EXP, it produces numeric tasks that are generally more feasible by exploiting the structure of the problem. Finally, for *1-lhs* tasks, EXP$^{\mathcal{L}}$ produces numeric problems structurally equivalent to what is produced by POLY$^-$.

The basic idea of EXP consists of enumerating all the possible non-empty contexts $\mathcal{C}$, and, for each of them, generating a conditional effect that will be activated individually when *SIM* is applied. As it is possible to note, this approach can become quickly inapplicable with problems having a large number of processes. EXP$^{\mathcal{L}}$ overcomes this weakness by enumerating, for each numeric variable $x \in X$, all the contexts in which only the processes that affect x are considered. To present this translation we need to introduce two new definitions.

Definition 3. *Let $x \in X$. We define the following sets:* $\mathbb{E}(x) = \{\langle\langle\xi, \rho\rangle \mid \langle x', \xi\rangle \in eff(\rho), \rho \in P, x' = x\}$ *and* $\mathbb{E}_P(x) = \{\rho \mid \langle x, \rho\rangle \in \mathbb{E}(x)\}$.

$\mathbb{E}(x)$ is the set of all the CNEs of Π affecting x together with the associated process. $\mathbb{E}_P(x)$ is the processes view of $\mathbb{E}(x)$. Let $x \in X$, $\mathcal{C} \subseteq \mathbb{E}_P(x)$ is what we call the *local context relevant to* x.

For an event-free PDDL+ problem $\Pi = \langle F, X, I, G, A, \emptyset, P\rangle$, EXP$^{\mathcal{L}}$ generates a PDDL2.1 problem $\Pi_{\text{EXP}^{\mathcal{L}}} = \langle F, X, I, G, A \cup \{SIM\}\rangle$, discretised in δ where:

$$pre(SIM) = \top$$

$$eff(SIM) = \bigcup_{x \in X} \bigcup_{\mathcal{C}_x \in \mathcal{P}^+(\mathbb{E}_P(x))} \{contpre(\mathcal{C}_x, \mathbb{E}_P(x)) \triangleright \{\langle inc, x, \sum_{\substack{\langle\xi, \rho\rangle \in \mathbb{E}(x), \\ \rho \in \mathcal{C}_x}} \Delta(\xi, \delta)\rangle\}\}.$$

SIM has a set of conditional effects for each numeric variable $x \in X$. Each set enumerates all the possible local contexts relevant to x, i.e., $\mathcal{C}_x \subseteq \mathbb{E}_P(x)$. The function used for generating a logical condition consistent with a given local context is $contpre(\mathcal{C}, P')$, with $\mathcal{C} \subseteq P' \subseteq P$. Such a function is a slightly revised version of the $contpre(\mathcal{C})$ function provided for the EXP translation and it is formally defined as:

$$contpre(\mathcal{C}, P') = \bigwedge_{\rho \in P' \setminus \mathcal{C}} \neg pre(\rho) \wedge \bigwedge_{\rho \in P' \cap \mathcal{C}} pre(\rho)$$

Each of these conditional effects generated is mutually exclusive and has in its effect a singleton with a single numeric assignment that collects the contribution of all the discretised CNEs affecting x within $\mathcal{C}_x$. Note that if $\mathcal{P}^+(\mathbb{E}(x)) = \emptyset$, then no conditional effects are generated since x cannot be affected by processes.

Theorem 1 (Soundness and Completeness of *EXP$^\mathcal{L}$*). *Let Π be a* PDDL+ *problem with no events ($E = \emptyset$), and let $\Pi_{\mathrm{EXP}^\mathcal{L}} = \langle F, X, I, G, A \cup \{SIM\}\rangle$ be the* PDDL2.1 *problem obtained by using* EXP$^\mathcal{L}$ *translation discretised in δ. Π admits a solution under δ discretisation iff so does $\Pi_{\mathrm{EXP}^\mathcal{L}}$.*

Proof. ($\Rightarrow$) Let $\pi_t = \langle \pi, t_e \rangle$ be a solution for Π under δ discretisation. And let $\pi_{\mathrm{EXP}^\mathcal{L}}$ be a PDDL2.1 plan constructed such that: (i) for each $\langle a, t \rangle$ in π, a' is in $\pi_{\mathrm{EXP}^\mathcal{L}}$ (where a' is the compiled version of a); (ii) for each $\langle a_i, t_i \rangle, \langle a_j, t_j \rangle$ with $a_i \prec a_j$ (a_i precedes a_j) in π, $a_i' \prec a_j'$ holds in $\pi_{\mathrm{EXP}^\mathcal{L}}$; and (iii) a sequence, possibly empty, of *SIM* actions has to be placed before each action a_i' in $\pi_{\mathrm{EXP}^\mathcal{L}}$ and at the end of $\pi_{\mathrm{EXP}^\mathcal{L}}$ with the structure $\pi_{\mathrm{EXP}^\mathcal{L}} = \langle \langle SIM \rangle \times \frac{t_1}{\delta}, a_1', \langle SIM \rangle \times \frac{t_2 - t_1}{\delta}, ..., a_n', \langle SIM \rangle \times \frac{t_e - t_n}{\delta} \rangle$, where $\langle SIM \rangle \times k$ represents k repetitions of *SIM*.

In order to prove that $\pi_{\mathrm{EXP}^\mathcal{L}}$ is a valid solution for $\Pi_{\mathrm{EXP}^\mathcal{L}}$, it suffices to show that, let $\tau = \langle \mathbb{H}_s(T_0), ..., \mathbb{H}_s(T_m) \rangle$ be the sequence of states associated to each STP of $\mathbb{H}$, and $\tau' = \langle s_0, ..., s_m \rangle$ be the sequence of states generated by iteratively executing $\pi_{\mathrm{EXP}^\mathcal{L}}$, $\mathbb{H}_s(T_i)$ and s_i are equivalent (agree on all values for $F \cup X$) for each $i \in \{0, ..., m\}$. We prove this by induction on τ (τ'). Note that $|\tau| = |\tau'|$ since for each action in π there is an action in π', there are no events and for each temporal transition in $\mathbb{H}$ there is a *SIM* action in π.

The base case ($i = 0$) is true as $\mathbb{H}_s(T_0) = I$ and $s_0 = I$. For the induction step, we assume the statement is true for some $i < |\tau|$ and prove it for $i + 1$ by examining the two types of transitions that occur between two consecutive STPs in $\mathbb{H}$, i.e., the *instantaneous transition* (i), caused by the execution of an action, and *temporal transition* (ii), caused by the advancement of time by δ.

(i) Let $T_i = \langle t_i, n_i \rangle$ and $T_{i+1} = \langle t_i, n_i + 1 \rangle$ be two STPs of $\mathbb{H}$. R2 of Definition 1 implies $\mathbb{H}_A(T_i) = \langle a_j \rangle \neq \langle \rangle$, with $j \in \{1, ..., n\}$. As π_t is a valid solution for Π, we know $\mathbb{H}_s(T_i) \models pre(a_j)$, therefore, by the inductive hypothesis, $s_i \models pre(a_j')$. Since a_j and a_j' represent the same action, it is easy to see that the outcomes of the transitions $\gamma(\mathbb{H}_s(T_i), a_j)$ and $\gamma(s_i, a_j')$ are equivalent.

(ii) Let i be an index such that $T_i = \langle t_i, n_i \rangle$ and $T_{i+1} = \langle t_i + \delta, 0 \rangle$ are two STPs of $\mathbb{H}$. Note that *SIM* features a set of conditional effects that individually affect a single numeric variable. Since the semantics of conditional effects prescribes that these are evaluated in parallel, we can restrict the proof to only a single numeric variable and then generalise the result for the remaining ones. Let $x \in X$ such that $\mathbb{E}(x) \neq \emptyset$. Given $\mathbb{E}_P(x)$, i.e., the set of processes possibly affecting x, the action SIM features a conditional effect for each possible local context relevant to x, i.e., for each $\mathcal{C}_x \in \mathcal{P}^+(\mathbb{E}_P(x)))$. By definition of $contpre(\cdot, \cdot)$, each conditional effect is mutually exclusive with the others and at most one of them is activated; in particular, the local context active in s_i is $\mathcal{C}'_x = \{\rho \in \mathbb{E}_P(x) \mid s_i \models pre(\rho)\}$. We can rephrase SIM as SIM_j by removing the conditional effects that are not triggered in s_i, that is: $SIM_j = \langle \top, \{\langle inc, x, \sum_{\substack{\langle \xi, \rho \rangle \in \mathbb{E}(x), \\ \rho \in \mathcal{C}'_x}} \Delta(\xi, \delta) \rangle\}, ... \rangle$.

By the inductive hypothesis we know that $s_i = \mathbb{H}_s(T_i)$ and then the local contexts induced in s_i and $\mathbb{H}_s(T_i)$ are equivalent, i.e., $\mathcal{C}_x = \{\rho \in \mathbb{E}_P(x) \mid \mathbb{H}_s(T_i) \models pre(\rho)\} = \mathcal{C}'_x$. By these considerations, it is easy to see that SIM_j applied to s_i produces the same effect as those produced by R4 of Definition 1 applied to $\mathbb{H}_s(T_i)$ w.r.t. x. For the remaining variables $x \in X$ such that $\mathbb{E}_P(x) = \emptyset$, note that these are left untouched by SIM. Then, we conclude that $s_{i+1} = \mathbb{H}_s(T_{i+1})$.

$(\Leftarrow)$ Let $\pi_{\text{EXP}^{\mathcal{L}}} = \langle \langle SIM \rangle \times \frac{t_1}{\delta}, a'_1, \langle SIM \rangle \times \frac{t_2 - t_1}{\delta}, ..., a'_n, \langle SIM \rangle \times \frac{t_e - t_n}{\delta} \rangle$ be a plan solving $\Pi_{\text{EXP}^{\mathcal{L}}}$ structured alternately with an agent's action and a sequence (possibly empty) of SIM actions. A valid PDDL+ plan $\pi_t = \langle \pi, t_e \rangle$ can be constructed as follows: (i) for each action a'_i in $\pi_{\text{EXP}^{\mathcal{L}}}$ such that $a'_i \neq SIM$, $\langle a_i, t_i \rangle$ is included in π where t_i is equal to δ multiplied by the number of occurrences of SIM in $\pi_{\text{EXP}^{\mathcal{L}}}$ before a'_i; (ii) for each a'_i, a'_j such that $a'_i \prec a'_j$ in $\pi_{\text{EXP}^{\mathcal{L}}}$, $\langle a_i, t_i \rangle \prec \langle a_j, t_j \rangle$ holds in π; and (iii) t_e is equal δ multiplied by the number of SIM in $\pi_{\text{EXP}^{\mathcal{L}}}$.

To demonstrate the validity of π_t thus obtained, we consider its discrete projection $\mathbb{H}$. Every action $\langle a_j, t_j \rangle$ in π is paired with an STP T_i such that $\mathbb{H}_A(T_i) = \langle a_j \rangle$, with $i \in \{0, ..., m\}$, which implies an STP $T_{i+1} = \langle t_i, n_i + 1 \rangle$ and $\mathbb{H}_s(T_{i+1}) = \gamma(\mathbb{H}_s(T_i), a_j)$. Between each pair of consecutive actions $\langle a_j, t_j \rangle$ and $\langle a_{j+1}, t_{j+1} \rangle$, there are k STPs associated with temporal transitions, where $k = \frac{t_{j+1} - t_j}{\delta}$. The number of such STPs equates to the number of SIM actions between a'_j and a'_{j+1}. After constructing $\mathbb{H}$, we generate τ and, since $\pi_{\text{EXP}^{\mathcal{L}}}$ is valid for $\Pi_{\text{EXP}^{\mathcal{L}}}$, proceed by induction over τ and τ' similarly to the opposite direction. $\square$

5   Properties

In this section, we study the properties of the presented and existing translations to provide a means for theoretically comparing them.

We evaluate all the schemata in terms of the size of the translated numeric task, and the structure of the induced search space. More precisely, given a PDDL+ task Π, we define $N_{max} = \max_{x \in X} |\mathbb{E}(x)|$ and $N_{tot} = \sum_{x \in X} |\mathbb{E}(x)|$. N_{tot} is the overall number of CNEs of Π, while N_{max} is the maximum number of CNEs that could affect a single numeric variable.

Let Π be an event-free PDDL+ problem and let $Z \in \{\text{EXP}, \text{POLY}, \text{POLY}^-, \text{EXP}^{\mathcal{L}}\}$, we denote with $\Pi_Z = \langle F_Z, X_Z, I_Z, G_Z, A_Z \rangle$ the numeric task obtained using Z.

For all $Z \in \{\text{EXP}, \text{POLY}^-, \text{EXP}^{\mathcal{L}}\}$, Z generates a numeric task Π_Z in which $|A_Z| = |A| + 1$, $|F_Z| = |F|$ and $|X_Z| = |X|$. This is due to the fact that these schemata add a single action, i.e., SIM, and do not add any new variable.

POLY adds an action for each CNE of Π, and two actions to initialise and close the simulation; therefore $|A_{\text{POLY}}| = |A| + N_{tot} + 2$. Then, POLY only adds predicates $pause$ and $done$. Therefore, $|F_{\text{POLY}}| = |F| + |D| + 1 = |F| + N_{tot} + 1$ with D being the set of $done$ predicates. Finally, to ensure that the simulation sequence $\langle start, seq(A_P), end \rangle$ produces an outcome consistent with the PDDL+ semantics, POLY doubles the numeric variables; therefore $|X_{\text{POLY}}| = 2 \cdot |X|$.

To have a clearer picture of the actual size of the problem, we also consider the number of conditional effects of Π_Z, denoted by $|\mathcal{W}_Z|$.

POLY associates a conditional effect to each $a \in A_P$, which in turn is associated with a single CNE of Π. Hence, $|\mathcal{W}_{\text{POLY}}| = \sum_{x \in X} |\mathbb{E}(x)| = N_{tot}$. On the other hand, POLY$^-$ associates a conditional effect for each process. These conditional effects are part of the effects of the SIM action, thus $|\mathcal{W}_{\text{POLY}^-}| = |P|$.

EXP generates a conditional effect for each possible global context $\mathcal{C} \in \mathcal{P}^+(P)$, resulting in $|\mathcal{W}_{\text{EXP}}| = 2^{|P|} - 1$. For EXP$^{\mathcal{L}}$, a set of conditional effects for each $x \in X$ is added to the effects of the SIM action. The size of each set is equal to the number of local contexts related to x. Hence, $|\mathcal{W}_{\text{EXP}^{\mathcal{L}}}| = \sum_{x \in X} 2^{|\mathbb{E}(x)|} - 1$.

Note that EXP$^{\mathcal{L}}$ can generate up to $2^{|P|} - 1$ whenever at least one variable is affected by all processes. Yet, as we will see in the experimental section, we have observed that this is quite a rare situation, i.e., we often observe that $2^{N_{max}} \ll 2^{|P|}$.

Table 1 provides an overview of the main theoretical properties of the translations and gives an intuition on the size of the translated planning tasks.

Table 1. Properties of *soundness* and *completeness* and size of the numeric translated tasks obtained through $Z \in \{\text{POLY}, \text{EXP}, \text{POLY}^-, \text{EXP}^{\mathcal{L}}\}$ for a event-free PDDL+ task Π.

	POLY	EXP	POLY$^-$	EXP$^{\mathcal{L}}$
soundness	✓ Lemma 2 ($\Leftarrow$) in [19]	✓ Lemma 1 ($\Leftarrow$) in [19]	✓ Prop. 1 in [17]	✓ Thm 1 ($\Leftarrow$)
completeness	✓ Lemma 2 ($\Rightarrow$) in [19]	✓ Lemma 1 ($\Rightarrow$) in [19]	✗ in the general case Prop. 2 in [17] ✓ if Π is *1-lhs* Prop. 3 in [17]	✓ Thm 1 ($\Rightarrow$)
$|F_Z|$	$|F| + N_{tot} + 1$	$|F|$	$|F|$	$|F|$
$|X_Z|$	$2 \cdot |X|$	$|X|$	$|X|$	$|X|$
$|A_Z|$	$|A| + N_{tot} + 2$	$|A| + 1$	$|A| + 1$	$|A| + 1$
$|\mathcal{W}_Z|$	N_{tot}	$2^{|P|} - 1$	$|P|$	$\mathcal{O}(2^{N_{max}})$

6   Experimental Analysis

To corroborate the above theoretical considerations from an empirical standpoint we tested our translations with ENHSP20 [23], an automated planning system that allows solving numeric planning tasks with non-linear dynamics. We consider two optimal search settings: h^{blind} and h^{max}. We focus on optimal search because it is more systematic and can crisply shed some light on the relative usefulness of the translations. We compare the performance over the translated numeric problems obtained with EXP, POLY, POLY$^-$ and EXP$^{\mathcal{L}}$ used with $\delta = 1$ followed by the (unchanged) translation that handles events (whose documentation is provided in [19]). All experiments were run on an Intel Xeon Gold 6140M CPU with 2.30 GHz. For each instance, we allotted 1800 seconds and limited memory to 8 GB. We consider the following linear domains: SOLAR-ROVER (ROVER), LINEAR-CAR (LIN-CAR), LINEAR-GENERATOR (LIN-GEN), URBAN-TRAFFIC-CONTROL (UTC) from [25], BAXTER from [3] and OVERTAKING-CAR (OT-CAR). We also include two non-linear domains: DESCENT and HVAC. The benchmark suite and the translator are available at https://bit.ly/30gMyNW. Out of the considered benchmark domains, 4 satisfy the *1-lhs* property: ROVER, LIN-CAR, OT-CAR and HVAC. The remaining domains, i.e. LIN-GEN, UTC, BAXTER and DESCENT, do not satisfy the mentioned property. The obtained plans were validated using the methodology described in [18].

Table 2 reports on the performance of the optimal search with all the possible translations when the two heuristics are used. UTC has been omitted because none of the approaches manages to solve any instance. It is easy to notice that (i) EXP$^{\mathcal{L}}$ is preferable for both heuristics in terms of coverage, and (ii) POLY, due to the numerous transitions required to make time flow, is penalised compared to all other approaches. Indeed, all approaches except POLY allow a significant coverage increase when h^{max} is used in place of h^{blind}. It can also be noted that in all the *1-lhs* domains the performance in terms of expanded nodes is substantially equivalent among POLY$^-$, EXP and EXP$^{\mathcal{L}}$.

Considering h^{max}, EXP performs well in terms of coverage in almost all the domains because they all have on average few processes, except for BAXTER, which has an average of 56. Indeed, EXP does not solve any instance on this domain. EXP$^{\mathcal{L}}$ manages to handle this domain quite well. BAXTER has in fact the following structure: $\mu(N_{max}) = 9$, $min(N_{max}) = 6$ and $max(N_{max}) = 12$. Notably, POLY$^-$ allows achieving good coverage performance when h^{max} is used. Except for DESCENT, where no instance is solved, the incompleteness of the translation did not turn out to be a problem in terms of solvability.

The results seem to support the theoretical considerations. In domains characterised by few processes, *SIM*-based methods are preferable to POLY and are roughly equivalent. Conversely, when the PDDL+ tasks include numerous processes, as in BAXTER, EXP becomes infeasible while EXP$^{\mathcal{L}}$ allows delivering the best performance. Finally, the incompleteness of POLY$^-$, although often advantageous in terms of speedup, may lead to cases wrongly detected as unsolvable.

Table 2. Performance achieved by h^{blind} (*upper*) h^{max} (*lower*) when run on models generated using the compared translations with $\delta = 1$. Results are presented in terms of coverage (number of solved instances), average runtime, and average number of nodes expanded during the search process. Averages are calculated on instances solved by all approaches. "—" indicates that no instances can be considered for the average calculation. ✗ denotes domain models that do not satisfy the *1-lhs* property.

h^{blind}	Coverage				Time				Exp. Nodes ($\times$ 1000)			
Domain	POLY	POLY$^-$	EXP	EXP$^{\mathcal{L}}$	POLY	POLY$^-$	EXP	EXP$^{\mathcal{L}}$	POLY	POLY$^-$	EXP	EXP$^{\mathcal{L}}$
ROVER (20)	1	1	1	1	61.2	**20.3**	33.7	21.1	12012.8	**3622.3**	**3622.3**	3630.7
LIN-CAR (10)	10	10	10	10	3.3	3.0	2.9	**2.7**	199.9	**27.1**	**27.1**	**27.1**
LIN-GEN (10) ✗	1	1	1	1	3.1	3.2	3.3	**2.7**	83.9	24.7	**22.7**	23.7
BAXTER (20) ✗	4	7	0	6	51.3	**9.2**	—	10.4	1294.4	**122.7**	—	177.6
OT-CAR (20)	5	5	5	5	16.8	**3.7**	4.6	5.9	2643.7	**252.3**	**252.3**	**252.3**
DESCENT (20) ✗	2	0	3	3	19.6	—	**8.5**	9.6	443.6	—	**134.1**	166.0
HVAC (20)	0	0	0	0	—	—	—	—	—	—	—	—
Σ	23	24	20	**26**								

h^{max}	Coverage				Time				Exp. Nodes ($\times$ 1000)			
Domain	POLY	POLY$^-$	EXP	EXP$^{\mathcal{L}}$	POLY	POLY$^-$	EXP	EXP$^{\mathcal{L}}$	POLY	POLY$^-$	EXP	EXP$^{\mathcal{L}}$
ROVER (20)	1	1	1	1	121.8	28.7	54.1	**24.9**	11898.0	**3512.7**	**3512.7**	3518.8
LIN-CAR (10)	10	10	10	10	3.2	**2.9**	3.3	3.1	39.2	**25.1**	27.1	**25.1**
LIN-GEN (10) ✗	1	2	2	3	3.5	2.7	**2.6**	**2.6**	83.9	5.0	**2.0**	**2.0**
BAXTER (20) ✗	4	7	0	7	44.8	**6.5**	—	11.6	1041.4	**68.2**	—	161.4
OT-CAR (20)	5	5	5	5	16.2	**5.2**	5.5	5.5	1270.7	**277.6**	**277.6**	**277.6**
DESCENT (20) ✗	2	0	3	3	13.6	—	**8.7**	9.2	246.2	—	**112.1**	152.8
HVAC (20)	0	16	16	16	—	**3.5**	**3.5**	**3.5**	—	**6.9**	**6.9**	**6.9**
Σ	23	41	37	**45**								

7   Conclusion

In this paper, we have investigated a range of translations from discrete hybrid planning to numeric planning. Our objective was to enhance our understanding of their characteristics and provide a basis for comparing not only the existing translations but also potential future ones. The analysis performed guided us to design a new translation, named EXP$^{\mathcal{L}}$. EXP$^{\mathcal{L}}$ shares the benefits of both EXP and POLY$^-$. However, unlike EXP, which exhibits exponential behaviour w.r.t. $|P|$ regardless of the problem's structure, EXP$^{\mathcal{L}}$ generates numeric tasks that show exponential behaviour w.r.t. a constant of the problem, i.e., N_{max}. The worst-case scenario for EXP$^{\mathcal{L}}$ in practical domains arises when all processes affect all numeric variables, but this scenario is rare. Generally, it is likely that $N_{max} \ll N_{tot}$ holds when P is large. It follows that, statistically, EXP$^{\mathcal{L}}$ will generate more feasible problems than its structure-insensitive EXP counterpart. However, in some contexts, N_{max} could be very large and EXP$^{\mathcal{L}}$ may still be infeasible. We see two main avenues for future work. Firstly, we are interested in exploring the online selection of a translation to be used according to the structure of the problem considered, in a similar fashion to algorithms selection approaches [15]. Secondly, we plan to investigate the possibility of automatically combining different translations on the same problem, to further mitigate the weaknesses of existing translations.

Acknowledgements. Francesco Percassi and Mauro Vallati were supported by a UKRI Future Leaders Fellowship [grant number MR/T041196/1]. Enrico Scala has been partially supported by AIPlan4EU, a project funded by EU Horizon 2020 research and innovation programme under GA n. 101016442.

References

1. Alaboud, F.K., Coles, A.: Personalized medication and activity planning in PDDL+. In: Proceedings of ICAPS, pp. 492–500 (2019)
2. Anderson, C.R., Smith, D.E., Weld, D.S.: Conditional effects in graphplan. In: Proceedings of AIPS, pp. 44–53. AAAI (1998)
3. Bertolucci, R., Capitanelli, A., Maratea, M., Mastrogiovanni, F., Vallati, M.: Automated planning encodings for the manipulation of articulated objects in 3D with gravity. In: Proceedings of AIxIA 2019, pp. 135–150 (2019)
4. Bonassi, L., De Giacomo, G., Favorito, M., Fuggitti, F., Gerevini, A.E., Scala, E.: Planning for temporally extended goals in pure-past linear temporal logic. In: Proceedings of ICAPS, vol. 33, pp. 61–69 (2023)
5. Bonassi, L., Gerevini, A.E., Scala, E.: Planning with qualitative action-trajectory constraints in PDDL. In: Proceedings of IJCAI, pp. 4606–4613 (2022)
6. Cardellini, M., Maratea, M., Vallati, M., Boleto, G., Oneto, L.: In-station train dispatching: a PDDL+ planning approach. In: Proceedings of ICAPS, pp. 450–458 (2021)
7. Della Penna, G., Magazzeni, D., Mercorio, F.: A universal planning system for hybrid domains. Appl. Intell. **36**, 932–959 (2012)
8. Fox, M., Howey, R., Long, D.: Validating plans in the context of processes and exogenous events. In: Proceedings of AAAI, pp. 1151–1156 (2005)
9. Fox, M., Long, D.: PDDL2.1: an extension to PDDL for expressing temporal planning domains. JAIR **20**, 61–124 (2003)
10. Fox, M., Long, D.: Modelling mixed discrete-continuous domains for planning. JAIR **27**, 235–297 (2006)
11. Franco, S., Lindsay, A., Vallati, M., McCluskey, T.L.: An innovative heuristic for planning-based urban traffic control. In: Proceedings of ICCS, pp. 181–193 (2018)
12. Gazen, B.C., Knoblock, C.A.: Combining the expressivity of UCPOP with the efficiency of Graphplan. In: Steel, S., Alami, R. (eds.) ECP 1997. LNCS, vol. 1348, pp. 221–233. Springer, Heidelberg (1997). https://doi.org/10.1007/3-540-63912-8_88
13. Gerevini, A., Haslum, P., Long, D., Saetti, A., Dimopoulos, Y.: Deterministic planning in the fifth international planning competition: PDDL3 and experimental evaluation of the planners. AIJ **173**(5–6), 619–668 (2009)
14. Henzinger, T.A.: The theory of hybrid automata. In: Proceedings 11th Annual IEEE Symposium on Logic in Computer Science, pp. 278–292 (1996). https://doi.org/10.1109/LICS.1996.561342
15. Kerschke, P., Hoos, H.H., Neumann, F., Trautmann, H.: Automated algorithm selection: survey and perspectives. Evol. Comput. **27**(1), 3–45 (2019)
16. Percassi, F., Bhatnagar, S., Guo, R., McCabe, K., McCluskey, L., Vallati, M.: An efficient heuristic for AI-based urban traffic control. In: Proceedings of MT-ITS (2023)

17. Percassi, F., Scala, E., Vallati, M.: A sound (but incomplete) polynomial translation from discretised PDDL+ to numeric planning. In: Proceedings of AIxIA 2021 (2021)
18. Percassi, F., Scala, E., Vallati, M.: The power of reformulation: from validation to planning in PDDL+. In: Proceedings of ICAPS, vol. 32, pp. 288–296 (2022)
19. Percassi, F., Scala, E., Vallati, M.: A practical approach to discretised PDDL+ problems by translation to numeric planning. JAIR **76**, 115–162 (2023)
20. Percassi, F., Scala, E., Vallati, M.: Fixing plans for PDDL+ problems: theoretical and practical implications. In: Proceedings of ICAPS, vol. 33, pp. 324–333 (2023)
21. Piotrowski, W., Sher, Y., Grover, S., Stern, R., Mohan, S.: Heuristic search for physics-based problems: angry birds in PDDL+. In: Proceedings of ICAPS, pp. 518–526 (2023)
22. Say, B.: Robust metric hybrid planning in stochastic nonlinear domains using mathematical optimization. In: Proceedings of ICAPS, vol. 33, pp. 375–383 (2023)
23. Scala, E., Haslum, P., Thiébaux, S., Ramírez, M.: Subgoaling techniques for satisficing and optimal numeric planning. JAIR **68**, 691–752 (2020)
24. Shin, J., Davis, E.: Processes and continuous change in a SAT-based planner. AIJ **166**(1–2), 194–253 (2005)
25. Vallati, M., Magazzeni, D., Schutter, B.D., Chrpa, L., McCluskey, T.L.: Efficient macroscopic urban traffic models for reducing congestion: a PDDL+ planning approach. In: Proceedings of AAAI 2016, pp. 3188–3194 (2016)

Intrinsically Motivated High-Level Planning for Agent Exploration

Gabriele Sartor[1]([✉])[ID], Angelo Oddi[2][ID], Riccardo Rasconi[2][ID],
and Vieri Giuliano Santucci[2][ID]

[1] University of Turin, Turin, Italy
`gabriele.sartor@unito.it`
[2] Institute of Cognitive Sciences and Technologies (ISTC-CNR), Rome, Italy
{`angelo.oddi,riccardo.rasconi,vieri.santucci`}`@istc.cnr.it`

Abstract. This paper proposes a new open-ended learning framework which aims at implementing an autonomous agent using intrinsic motivations (IM) at two different levels.

At the first level, the IM paradigm is exploited by the agent to learn new operational skills, described in terms of sub-symbolic *options*. After discovering the options, the agent iteratively: (1) executes them to explore the world, collecting the necessary data and (2) automatically abstracts the collected data into a high-level representation of the domain, expressed in PPDDL language.

At the second level, the IM paradigm is used to exploit the abstracted representation of the domain by identifying particular symbolic states deemed *promising* according to a specific criterium, which in the present work is the farthest distance covered by the agent (i.e., the most promising states are those that rest at the *frontier* of the visited space). Once these states are identified, they can be successively reached through an internally generated high-level plan and used as promising starting points for discovering new knowledge.

The presented framework is tested in the so-called Treasure Game domain described in the recent literature. The tests we have performed show that the proposed idea of implementing intrinsic motivations at two different levels of abstraction facilitates the discovery of new knowledge, compared to a previous approach proposed in the literature.

Keywords: Intrinsic Motivations · Open-ended learning · Planning

1 Introduction

Reinforcement Learning (RL, [37]) demonstrated to be an important method to make agents autonomously learn complex behaviours and solve a wide range of tasks. In the last decades, it has been extensively proved that temporally-extended actions [38], also called *options*, are a good abstraction for flexible duration behaviours which can speed up the learning of different tasks in both simulated and real environments [14,20].

© The Author(s), under exclusive license to Springer Nature Switzerland AG 2023
R. Basili et al. (Eds.): AIxIA 2023, LNAI 14318, pp. 119–133, 2023.
https://doi.org/10.1007/978-3-031-47546-7_9

While "standard" RL focuses on the acquisition of policies that maximise the achievement of assigned tasks (through reward maximisation), the field of intrinsically motivated open-ended learning (IMOL, [33]) tackles the problem of developing agents whose aim is to improve their capabilities to interact with the environment, without any specific assigned task. More precisely, Intrinsic Motivations (IMs, [1,24]) are a class of self-generated signals that have been used to provide robots with an autonomous guidance for several different processes, from state-and-action space exploration [3,12], to the autonomous discovery, selection and learning of multiple goals [5,8,32]. In general, IMs guide the agent in the acquisition of new knowledge independently (or even in the absence) of any assigned task: this knowledge will then be available to the system to solve user-assigned tasks [35] or as a scaffolding to acquire new knowledge in a cumulative fashion [11,29,36] (similarly to what has been called curriculum learning [4]).

The option framework has been combined to IMs and "curiosity-driven" approaches to drive option learning [36] and option discovery [19,23]. In the hierarchical RL [2] setting, where agents need to chunk together different options to properly achieve complex tasks, IMs have been used to foster sub-task discovery [15,22] and the exploration of the environment [3]. Autonomously learning and combining different skills is a crucial problem for agents acting in complex environments, where task solving consists of reaching several (possibly unknown) intermediate sub-tasks that are dependent on each other. An increasing number of works are tackling this problem using different approaches [5,25,28], most of them focused on low-level, sub-symbolic policy learning, in turn combined in a hierarchical manner using some sort of meta-policy. While promising, these approaches necessarily face the problem of exploration, which, as the space of states and actions increase, becomes slower and less efficient.

As opposed to the previous sub-symbolic methods, symbolic approaches and planning [21] allow the utilization of higher-level objects (symbols, indeed) that guarantee faster execution and facilitate the combination of complex sub-task sequences, *provided that the high-level representation of the planning domain is properly given in advance.* The need to be provided with an *ad-hoc* symbolic representation of the environment limits the utilization of high-level planning for artificial agents in unknown or highly unstructured settings, where the acquisition of new knowledge and new skills is a progressive result of the agent's autonomous exploration of the environment. Recently, some ideas have appeared in the literature that propose methodologies for the online learning of how to properly ground a provided abstract planning domain expressed in PDDL formalism [13], in the environment in which the agent operates [7,17,18]. Differently from the previous works, [16] proposes a methodology for creating from scratch a PDDL-based symbolic abstraction of the information acquired by an exploring agent at low level, which allows to explicitly describe all the context necessary to execute an action on the current state making use of the produced PDDL symbols.

From all of the above, and inspired by [16], in this paper we devise an artificial agent that, virtually starting with no previous knowledge, is capable of:

(i) autonomously acquiring new information and learning new skills at low-level, through the direct interaction with the environment guided by intrinsic motivations (e.g., curiosity), (ii) exploring the environment and collecting knowledge about the transitions between the visited states, (iii) triggering a knowledge abstraction process, thus autonomously creating a symbolic representation of the environmentexpressed in PPDDL [39] formalism, (iv) utilizing this representation to autonomously reach new objectives (i.e., high-level goals) selected on the basis of a different declination of the intrinsic motivations, ultimately maximizing the environment exploration capabilities and accelerating the knowledge acquisition process.

The simulated environment used in this work to test the agent's capabilities is the so-called Treasure Game (see Fig. 1), originally presented in [16], in which the agent's overall objective is to find a treasure and take it to the the starting location on top of the maze.

Fig. 1. The Treasure Game environment: a maze-like environment 672×624 pixels divided in 182 blocks, 13 rows by 14 columns.

In such environment, an agent can explore a maze-like space by moving through corridors and doors, climbing stairs, interacting with handles (necessary to open/close the doors), bolts, keys (necessary to unlock the bolts) and a treasure. The agent starts its activity from the ladder on top of the maze (home location) and its overall task is to find the treasure and to bring it back to the starting location. In all our experiments, described in Sect. 4, the agent starts endowed with no previous knowledge about the possible actions that can be executed in the environment; the agent is only aware of the basic motion primitives at its disposal $A = \{$go_up, go_down, go_left, go_right, interact$\}$, respectively used to move the agent up, down, left or right by 2–4 pixels (the exact value is randomly selected with a uniform distribution) and to interact with the closest object. The interaction with a lever changes the state (open/close) of the doors associated to that lever (both on the same floor or on different floors), the interaction with the key and/or the treasure simply collects the key and/or the treasure inside the agent's bag, while the interaction with a bolt opens the treasure's room *provided that the agent owns the key*; otherwise it has no effect.

The paper is structured as follows: Sect. 2 provides some background information on both the option-based and the abstract representation of the information used in this paper, Sect. 3 provides a thorough description of the presented framework, Sect. 4 presents a preliminary analysis of the obtained results and performance of the framework, and Sect. 5 provides some concluding remarks.

2   Background

The model of the environment follows the Markov Decision Process (MDP) formalism described by the tuple (S, A, R, T, γ) where: (i) S is the set of all possible states in high-dimensional space, (ii) A the set of all the possible primitive actions, (iii) R the reward function return a scalar value after executing an action $a \in A$ from the state $s \in S$ resulting in $s' \in S$, the transition function $T(s'|s, a)$ describing the distribution over the states in which the agent can be after executing a from s, γ a discount factor. In order to deal with the complexity of the space, primitives are combined to create more complex behaviors called *options* [38]. Options are temporally-extended actions which are defined by a tuple (I_o, π, B_o), where I_o is the set of states where the option $o \in O$ can start, π is the option policy to be executed and B_o is the termination condition of the policy π. Passing from primitives to options, results in moving from MDP to semi-Markov Decision Process (SMDP) framework.

High-level planning uses symbols to describe the state of the environment. In particular, in *set theoretic representation* a set of propositions $P = \{p_0, ..., p_n\}$ is used to define the feature of the environment. When a proposition p_i has the boolean value *True* means that the characteristic described by p_i is present in the environment, *False* otherwise. Then, each action $a_i \in A$ is defined by the tuple $(prec_i, eff_i^+, eff_i^-)$ where $prec_i \subseteq P$ are the propositions which have to be *True* to execute the action a_i, $eff_i^+ \subseteq P$ the propositions *True* after the execution of a_i and $eff_i^- \subseteq P$ the propositions *False* after the execution of a_i. Recently, it has been proved that the experience collected executing options can be translated into such symbolic representation [16]. The solution proposed in literature it is used in the framework described in this article to provide the agent a way to represent its goals, generated by its IMs, and chase them.

3   Framework Description

In this paper we propose a framework that, by leveraging IMs, allows to interleave the exploration, abstraction and planning phases with the ultimate goal of efficiently exploring the environment (see Fig. 2), starting from virtually no previous knowledge and/or capabilities, with the only exception of a number of basic movements/interaction primitives, as described in the remainder of the paper.

Basically, the framework is based on the utilization of the intrinsic motivations as the basis for the exploratory behaviour of the agent, declined at

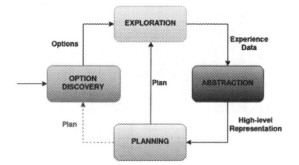

Fig. 2. The idea of the framework. Four modules: (i) option discovery, finding new options, (ii) exploration, using the learned options to collect data in the environment, (iii) abstraction, converting the collected data into a high-level representation and (iv) planning, to reach any sub-goal which can be described.

two different levels of abstraction, namely at the *Option Discovery* (i.e., pre-abstraction) level and at the *Planning* (post-abstraction) level. The overall result is the introduction of an exploration paradigm that allows the agent to use *curiosity* to steer both the option discovery phase and the high-level goal synthesis phase. What we also intend to demonstrate is that the agent's ability to abstract the acquired sub-symbolic information into a symbolic representation that lends itself to being efficiently reasoned upon, remarkably facilitates the environment's exploration by allowing rational decision-making as opposed to a purely randomic approach.

We begin the system's description by analyzing Algorithm 1, matching the execution loop depicted in Fig. 2. Such execution loop is intended to implement the agent's life-cycle for a determined number of *cycles* (line 7); in each cycle, the agent's overall objective is to pursuing the acquisition of new knowledge through a direct interaction with the environment.

Once the necessary initialization steps are performed (lines 2–6) the execution loop starts (line 9). At the beginning of the loop, the *Option Discovery* step is performed (line 8), in which the agent learns a set O of structured skills (i.e., the *options*) starting from a set of elementary motion and/or interaction primitives. The new options O_{new} are added to the previously collected options O, which will be available during the exploration phase. This step will be more thoroughly described in Sect. 3.1, as it represents the procedure where the IMs are used to drive the option learning mechanism at a lower level of abstraction.

***Exploration - Data Collection (line** 10–12).* The agent starts exploring the environment acquiring knowledge about the feasibility of executing the options $\in O$ from the current state, and the knowledge about the state transitions triggered by executing such options, through the *Collect_Data()* procedure. The exploration consists in executing *dpa_eps* episodes, where each episode is composed of a number of steps equal to *dpa_steps*. At each step, an option $o \in O$ is randomly selected and its execution is attempted from the state s the agent

Algorithm 1. Discover-Plan-Act algorithm

```
1: procedure DISCOVER_PLAN_ACT(cycles, dpa_eps, dpa_steps, d_eps, d_steps)
2:      c ← 0 //Cycle initialization
3:      O ← {} //Option set initialization
4:      ID ← {} //Initiation Data initialization
5:      TD ← {} //Transition Data initialization
6:      ω^EX ← {} //Initially, the high-level plan is empty
7:   while c < cycles do //For each cycle
8:          O_new ← DISCOVER(d_eps, d_steps, ω^EX) //Learning the available options
9:          O ← O ∪ O_new
10:         ID_new, TD_new ← Collect_Data(dpa_eps, dpa_steps, O, ω^EX)
11:         ID ← ID ∪ ID_new
12:         TD ← TD ∪ TD_new
13:         D ← Create_PPDDL(ID, TD)
14:         s_target ← Get_Target_State()
15:         P_target ← Generate_PPDDL_Problem(s_target)
16:         ω^EX ← Plan(D, P_target)
17:         Check_PPDDL_Validity(D)
18:         c ← c + 1
```

is currently in (the scenario is reset to the initial state at the beginning of each episode, which brings back the agent in its "home" location). Every time an option o is executed from the state s, two data tuples are saved in the new_data repository, the $initiation\ data$ tuple and the $transition\ data$ tuple. The $initiation\ data$ tuple takes the following structure $(s, o, f(s, o))$, where the function $f(s, o)$ returns the feasibility of executing o from s ($True$ if $s \in I_o$ and $False$ otherwise). The $transition\ data$ tuple takes the following structure (s, o, r, s', g, m, O') tuples, where s' is the state reached after executing option o from the state s, g is a flag saying if the final objective of the game has been reached, m is the $mask$[1] of the option and O' is a list defining the options that can be feasibly executed from s'. When all the steps of the episode have been executed, the environment is reset and the next episode is started until the maximum number of episodes is reached, in which case the $Collect\_Data()$ procedure terminates, and the stored data are added to the overall data repository $data$ (line 11–12).

As will be better clarified in the remainder on the paper, a very important role for the exploration process is played by the plan ω^{EX} produced by the planner, used as an input parameter of the $Collect\_Data()$ procedure. In case ω^{EX} is not empty (i.e., it has $length\ \delta(\omega^{EX}) > 0$) it will be used to guide the agent towards a specific goal state before the exploration commences, as follows; each episode will first execute the plan starting from the "home" location, hence setting the environment in some desired state s_{target}, and then the exploration will proceed from s_{target}. Conversely, if $\omega^{EX} = \{\}$, each episode will perform $n = dpa\_steps$ option executions, each starting from the "home" location.

Data Abstraction (line 13). The data collected in the previous step is then used as input for the function $Create\_PPDDL()$, which returns a symbolic representation of the agent's current knowledge expressed in PPDDL formalism (PPDDL domain). The main advantage of the obtained PPDDL representation is that it makes explicit the causal correlations between operators that would have

---

[1] The $mask$ is the list of state variables changed by a specific option [16].

remained implicit at option level. A thorough description of the data abstraction algorithm is beyond the scope of this paper; for further details, the reader is referred to [16]. In the following, we provide a summary description of the abstraction procedure.

The procedure basically executes the following five steps:

1. **Option partition**: this step is dedicated to partitioning the learned options in terms of *abstract subgoal options*. This operation is necessary as the (P)PDDL operators are characterized by a single precondition set and a single effect set; therefore, options that have multiple termination conditions starting from the same initiation set cannot be correctly captured in terms of (P)PDDL operators. As a consequence, before launching the abstraction procedure it is necessary to generate a set of options each of which is guaranteed to produce a single effect (*partial subgoal option*). This operation utilizes the *transition data* set collected before, as they capture the information about the domain segment the option modifies. Option partition is ultimately obtained by properly clustering the *transition data* through the DBSCAN algorithm [10] present in the scikit-learn toolkit [27].

2. **Precondition estimation**: this step is dedicated to learning the symbols that will constitute the *preconditions* of the PPDDL operators associated to all the options. This operation utilizes the *initiation data* set collected, and is performed utilizing the support vector machine [9] classifier implementation in scikit-learn.

3. **Effect estimation**: analogously, this step is dedicated to learning the symbols that will constitute the *effects* of the PPDDL operators. The effect distribution was modelled through the Kernel density estimation [26,30].

4. **PPDDL Domain synthesis**: finally, this step is dedicated to the synthesis of the PPDDL domain, characterized by the complete definition of all the operators associated to the learned options, in terms of preconditions and effect symbols.

As described in the previous section, the produced PPDDL domain can be used to potentially reach any subgoal that can be expressed in terms of the available generated symbols at any point during the Discovery-Plan-Act (DPA) loop. One interesting aspect of the proposed DPA framework is that the semantic precision of the abstract representation increases as the DPA cycles proceed, as will be described in the experimental section.

Planning (lines 14–16). Mapping the Planning module of Fig. 2 onto the Algorithm 1 breaks down into three different steps: 1) selecting one promising state from which to continue the exploration of the environment in the next cycle, 2) translating the selected state in terms of a PPDDL goal, and finally 3) launching the planner to reach such goal.

Target State Selection (line 14). After the exploration, one of the most promising states s_{target} is returned by the $Get\_Target\_State()$ function. As previously said, s_{target} will be the on the border of its synthesized knowledge, and therefore the state the new exploration cycle will start from. This strategy is called *Distance-based Goal Babbling* in the rest of the paper. Obviously, different and more complex criteria may be devised to identify the most promising states, hence suggesting different implementations of the agent's curiosity. Thanks to the information abstraction process previously finalized, the agent is now able to rationally reach that state by planning on the currently obtained PPDDL domain.

Target problem generation (line 15). In this step of the algorithm, the state s_{target} has to be converted in symbols, needed to define a high-level planning problem. The function *Generate_PPDDL_Problem()* is in charge of creating the problem description in PPDDL. In order to find the symbols needed to describe the s_{target} as a goal, the system finds the combination of symbols which represent better the goal s_{target}.

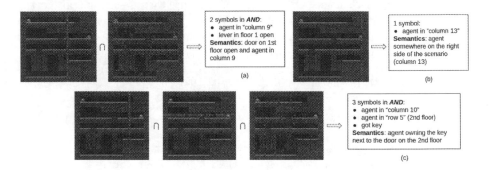

Fig. 3. Visualization of three target state examples synthesized by the agent over different iterations.

Figure 3 shows three examples of target states selected by the agent in different iterations, expressed in symbolic form. In iteration 1 (a) the agent is interested in opening the door on the 1st floor, remaining somewhere in column 9 of the environment, in iteration 7 (b) the agent wants to move somewhere towards the right side of the environment, and in iteration 11 (c) the agent wants to be on the second floor, owning the key.

Plan generation (line 16). Taking into consideration $\mathcal{D}$ and $\mathcal{P}_{target}$, respctively generated in line 13 and 15 of the Algorithm 1, it is generated the plan ω^{EX} to reach s_{target} in the successive cycle of the loop to facilitate the exploration.

3.1   Option Discovery

As anticipated at the beginning of Sect. 3, the agent starts exploring the environment by randomly executing a number of basic motion primitives, trying to learn the necessary skills that will allow it to explore the same environment more efficiently, through the *Discover()* procedure at line 8 of Algorithm 1.

Algorithm 2. Option Discovery

```
 1: procedure OPTION_DISCOVERY(d_eps, d_steps, ω^EX)
 2:     O_new ← {}
 3:     ep ← 0
 4:     while ep < d_eps do //For each episode
 5:         T ← 0
 6:         Reset_Game()
 7:         for option in ω^EX do // Execute IM plan
 8:             Execute(option)
 9:         while T < d_steps do //For each step
10:             s ← Get_State()
11:             a^p ← Get_Available_Primitive()
12:             while Is_Available(a^p) and not (New_Available_Prim()) do
13:                 Execute(a^p)
14:                 s' ← Get_State()
15:             if s ≠ s' then
16:                 if New_Available_Prim() then
17:                     a^t ← Get_New_Available_Prim()
18:                     o ← Create_New_Option(a^p, a^t)
19:                 else
20:                     o ← Create_New_Option(a^p, {})
21:                 O_new ← O_new ∪ o
22:             T ← T + 1 //End For each step
23:         ep ← ep + 1 //End For each episode
24:     return O_new
```

In this section, we will analyze the *Discover*() procedure in greater details with the help of the pseudocode depicted in Algorithm 2. By executing the algorithm, the agent is able to discover a set of options O from scratch; these options are generated by repeatedly executing a certain primitive a among the available ones, and collecting the produced changes in the environment.

In more details, the agent creates new options considering a particular definition of option $o(a^p, a^t, I, \pi, \beta)$ where a^p is the primitive used by the execution of π, a^t is the primitive which stops the execution of π when becomes available, π is the policy applied by the option, consisting in repeatedly executing a^p until a^t is available or a^p can no longer be executed, I is the set of states from which a^p can run; β is the termination condition of the action, corresponding to the availability of the primitive a^t or to the impossibility of further executing a^p. For the sake of simplicity, the option's definition will follow the more compact syntax $o(a^p, a^t)$ in the remainder of the paper.

Algorithm 2 describes the option discovery procedure previously cited. For a maximum number of episodes and steps, the agent save the current state s and randomly selects a primitive a^p which can be executed in s (line 9-11). a^p is repeatedly executed until state s' where a^p is not available or new primitives becomes available. If $s \neq s'$, the procedure creates a new option $o(a^p, a^t)$ whether a new option a^t has been enabled, or $o(a^p, \{\})$ if there are not new primitives enabled. For example, given the Treasure Game domain of Fig. 1, let us suppose that $a_p = $ go_right and the agent is on a floor where the path at the agent's right is free until reaching the wall (i.e., there is no object to interact with or stairs to climb). In this case, the option $o($go_right$, \{\})$ is generated. Conversely, if $a_p = $ go_left and the agent is on a floor where the path at the agent's left leads to a key it can interact with, then the option $o(\texttt{go\_left}, \texttt{interact})$ is generated. In either case, o is added to the set of collected options if it has not been discovered before. It is important to note that the options are independent on the state where the agent is, but it is defined by the primitives' availability. This definition makes options reusable in different floors and with different objects, just depending on the agent's abilities.

4   Experimental Analysis

This section describes the behaviour of our system in the Treasure Game simulated environment depicted in Fig. 1. As described in Algorithm 1, our experimental setting is for the agent to discover a set of options from scratch (Algorithm 2) and iteratively use them to collect data from the environment, generate a PPDDL representation, and plan to move towards particularly promising states expressed as symbolic goals synthesized according to some criteria that encode the intrinsic motivations *at high level*. In particular, the agent will be mostly interested at those states that are the farthest from its starting location, as they are the current *frontier* of the explored environment and thus represent good states from which to reprise the exploration. The selected PPDDL planner to perform the planning process is Mgpt [6]. In the following sections, the approach implemented by Algorithm 1 will be referred to as *Distance-based Goal Babbling (DB)*, to distinguish it from: (i) *Action Babbling (AB)*, in which the IMs are only used to discover the initial set of options and no abstract representation of the environment is used to guide the exploration, and (ii) *Goal Babbling (GB)*, in which the IMs are only used to discover the initial set of options and the exploration is guided by random abstract goals.

Generated Options. All the strategies execute Algorithm 2 to collect some options exploiting the agent's primitives at the beginning of each iteration. In the Treasure Game environment selected for this work, the agent executes $d\_eps = 1$ episodes each composed of $d\_steps = 200$ primitive actions. The result is the following set of learned options (11 in total) expressed as primitives pairs (a^p, a^t), as described in Sect. 3.1:

```
O = {(go_up,{}), (go_down,{}), (go_left,{}), (go_left,go_up), (go_left,
     go_down), (go_left,interact), (go_right,{}), (go_right,go_up),
     (go_right,go_down), (go_right,interact), (interact,{})}
```

For example, the option (go_left, go_up) has the following meaning: *"keep going left until it is possible to go up"*. It is important to note that in general, the discovered options are not all the possible options but only the ones experienced by the agent during the exploration. This procedure is incremental, adding options to the set O each iteration of the Algorithm 1.

Exploration. After the options are generated, the data collection is performed; in our experimental setting, $dpa\_eps = 4$ episodes are executed each composed of $dpa\_steps = 800$ option runs, at each main cycle. Consequently, at each cycle the agent executes 800 options. If at the beginning of the cycle $\omega^{EX} \neq \{\}$, at each episode the agent will first execute the δ *planned options* (where δ is the *plan*'s length), and then it will execute the remaining *dpa_steps* $- \delta$ options randomly. Successively, the accumulated data on the previous step are translated into a PPDDL representation; this is a very important step, as it is where the causal correlations between options are made explicit. Relatively to this aspect, it is very interesting to observe that the symbolic abstraction process also follows an iterative refinement path; initially, the agent abstracts the concepts which are easier to be experienced (i.e. the positions of the levers, position of the agent in the higher floors, etc.) and their correlated operators, while the concepts that require a deeper exploration of the environment (e.g., "bolt unlocked" and "got treasure") are abstracted later.

High-Level Exploration Strategies. As previously stated, the main difference between the exploration strategies lies in the different target state selection method. More precisely, AB is the simplest strategy consisting of a pure random walking of the agent. In fact, according to lines 14–16 in Algorithm 1, if $s_{target} = NULL$, then no plan is generated and executed in the next exploration. Instead, both *Goal Babbling* and *Distance-based Goal Babbling* select a s_{target} to be reached through planning, choosing a random state and the most distant state from "home", respectively.

Result Analysis. The most interesting results that we have obtained in our experiments are shown in Fig. 4. The figure depicts two fundamental aspects of the system such as the plan generation (Fig. 4a) and success rate (Fig. 4b) across the iterations of Algorithm 1 for all the strategies.

Figure 4a shows on the y-axis the length of the plan generated by all the strategies for each cycle in a specific trial. The red dotted line represents the length of the optimal plan to solve the game and the circles on the plot the successful plans. Of course, no plan whose length is shorter than the optimal plan's can be successful; similarly, plans whose length is bigger than the optimal one are not necessarily valid plans. This occurs because of the stochasticity of the abstraction process which can produce noisy domain representations, thus leading to plans that do not reach the desired goal.

In the case depicted in the figure, only the DB strategy finds valid plans (in the cycles 11, 12, 13, 15) focusing on the last cycles, after collecting enough data. Figure 4b depicts a cumulative representation, showing the success rate of ten trials over 15 iterations. As anticipated by Fig. 4a, DB strategy reveals particularly effective on solving the problem, reaching 90% of success rate at cycle 15, while GB and AB stop, respectively, at 30% and 20%.

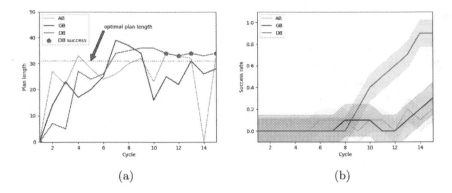

Fig. 4. (a) The plan length of different strategies over time for a trial and (b) the success rate of planning for each cycle.

5   Conclusions and Future Work

In this paper we have described a new open-ended learning framework proposing an innovative approach for using intrinsic motivations (IMs) at two different levels of abstraction. The presented framework is tested in the so-called Treasure Game [16] and our empirical analysis gives a preliminary evidence that the proposed idea facilitates the discovery of new knowledge compared to a baseline approach described in the literature [34].

The proposed framework opens several directions of future research work. One is the exploration of new strategies for the definition of target *promising* states, proposing more complex criteria beyond the visiting frequency. A second research track could explore the idea of using classical reinforcement learning algorithms [37] (e.g., SARSA) to drive the process of data collection within Algorithm 1. Furthermore, since option discovery plays a fundamental role in our framework, in the future our intention is to study a more flexible approach to discover new options using more sophisticated sub-symbolic methods (e.g. neural networks). In general, we observe that the use of an incremental version of the framework, which extends the set of training/learned data at each cycle, poses the problem of limiting the size of the stored data in order to bound the complexity of the learning process. Last but not least, the possibility of using a different language for abstracting the discovered options. In particular, one possibility may be to substitute PPDDL with RDDL [31]. The latter is becoming a more standard choice in the probabilistic planning community and can express all PPDDL domains (but not vice versa) with some additional features, like concurrent actions or independent exogenous stochastic events that could be considered for the future version of our framework.

Acknowledgements. This work has been supported by the European Union's Horizon 2020, research and innovation programme under GA 101070381 ('PILLAR-Robots - Purposeful Intrinsically motivated Lifelong Learning Autonomous Robots') and PNRR MUR project PE0000013-FAIR.

References

1. Baldassarre, G., Mirolli, M.: Intrinsically Motivated Learning in Natural and Artificial Systems. Springer, Heidelberg (2013). https://doi.org/10.1007/978-3-642-32375-1

2. Barto, A.G., Mahadevan, S.: Recent advances in hierarchical reinforcement learning. Disc. Event Dyn. Syst. **13**(1), 41–77 (2003)

3. Bellemare, M., Srinivasan, S., Ostrovski, G., Schaul, T., Saxton, D., Munos, R.: Unifying count-based exploration and intrinsic motivation. Adv. Neural Inf. Process. Syst. **29** (2016)

4. Bengio, Y., Louradour, J., Collobert, R., Weston, J.: Curriculum learning. In: Proceedings of the 26th Annual International Conference on Machine Learning, pp. 41–48 (2009)

5. Blaes, S., Vlastelica Pogančić, M., Zhu, J., Martius, G.: Control what you can: intrinsically motivated task-planning agent. Adv. Neural Inf. Process. Syst. **32** (2019)

6. Bonet, B., Geffner, H.: MGPT: a probabilistic planner based on heuristic search. J. Artif. Int. Res. **24**(1), 933–944 (2005)

7. Campari, T., Lamanna, L., Traverso, P., Serafini, L., Ballan, L.: Online learning of reusable abstract models for object goal navigation. In: 2022 IEEE/CVF Conference on Computer Vision and Pattern Recognition (CVPR), pp. 14850–14859 (2022). https://doi.org/10.1109/CVPR52688.2022.01445

8. Colas, C., Fournier, P., Chetouani, M., Sigaud, O., Oudeyer, P.Y.: Curious: intrinsically motivated modular multi-goal reinforcement learning. In: International Conference on Machine Learning, pp. 1331–1340. PMLR (2019)

9. Cortes, C., Vapnik, V.: Support-vector networks. Mach. Learn. **20**(3), 273–297 (1995)

10. Ester, M., Kriegel, H.P., Sander, J., Xu, X.: A density-based algorithm for discovering clusters in large spatial databases with noise. In: Proceedings of the Second International Conference on Knowledge Discovery and Data Mining, KDD 1996, pp. 226–231. AAAI Press (1996)

11. Forestier, S., Portelas, R., Mollard, Y., Oudeyer, P.Y.: Intrinsically motivated goal exploration processes with automatic curriculum learning. arXiv preprint arXiv:1708.02190 (2017)

12. Frank, M., Leitner, J., Stollenga, M., Förster, A., Schmidhuber, J.: Curiosity driven reinforcement learning for motion planning on humanoids. Front. Neurorobot. **7**, 25 (2014)

13. Ghallab, M., et al.: PDDL–the planning domain definition language (1998). http://citeseerx.ist.psu.edu/viewdoc/summary?doi=10.1.1.37.212

14. Jong, N.K., Hester, T., Stone, P.: The utility of temporal abstraction in reinforcement learning. In: AAMAS, no. 1, pp. 299–306. Citeseer (2008)

15. Konidaris, G., Barto, A.G.: Skill discovery in continuous reinforcement learning domains using skill chaining. Adv. Neural Inf. Process. Syst., 1015–1023 (2009)

16. Konidaris, G., Kaelbling, L.P., Lozano-Perez, T.: From skills to symbols: learning symbolic representations for abstract high-level planning. J. Artif. Intell. Res. **61**, 215–289 (2018). http://lis.csail.mit.edu/pubs/konidaris-jair18.pdf

17. Lamanna, L., et al.: Planning for learning object properties. In: Williams, B., Chen, Y., Neville, J. (eds.) Thirty-Seventh AAAI Conference on Artificial Intelligence, AAAI 2023, Thirty-Fifth Conference on Innovative Applications of Artificial

Intelligence, IAAI 2023, Thirteenth Symposium on Educational Advances in Artificial Intelligence, EAAI 2023, Washington, DC, USA, 7–14 February 2023, pp. 12005–12013. AAAI Press (2023). http://ojs.aaai.org/index.php/AAAI/article/view/26416

18. Lamanna, L., Serafini, L., Saetti, A., Gerevini, A., Traverso, P.: Online grounding of symbolic planning domains in unknown environments. In: Kern-Isberner, G., Lakemeyer, G., Meyer, T. (eds.) Proceedings of the 19th International Conference on Principles of Knowledge Representation and Reasoning, KR 2022, Haifa, Israel, 31 July–5 August 2022 (2022). http://proceedings.kr.org/2022/53/

19. Machado, M.C., Bellemare, M.G., Bowling, M.: A laplacian framework for option discovery in reinforcement learning. arXiv preprint arXiv:1703.00956 (2017)

20. Mann, T.A., Mannor, S., Precup, D.: Approximate value iteration with temporally extended actions. J. Artif. Intell. Res. **53**, 375–438 (2015)

21. Nau, D., Ghallab, M., Traverso, P.: Automated Planning: Theory & Practice. Morgan Kaufmann Publishers Inc., San Francisco (2004)

22. Niel, R., Wiering, M.A.: Hierarchical reinforcement learning for playing a dynamic dungeon crawler game. In: 2018 IEEE Symposium Series on Computational Intelligence (SSCI), pp. 1159–1166. IEEE (2018)

23. Oddi, A., et al.: Integrating open-ended learning in the sense-plan-act robot control paradigm. In: ECAI 2020, the 24th European Conference on Artificial Intelligence (2020)

24. Oudeyer, P.Y., Kaplan, F., Hafner, V.: Intrinsic motivation systems for autonomous mental development. IEEE Trans. Evol. Comput. **11**(2), 265–286 (2007)

25. Parisi, S., Dean, V., Pathak, D., Gupta, A.: Interesting object, curious agent: learning task-agnostic exploration. Adv. Neural. Inf. Process. Syst. **34**, 20516–20530 (2021)

26. Parzen, E.: On estimation of a probability density function and mode. Ann. Math. Stat. **33**(3), 1065–1076 (1962)

27. Pedregosa, F., et al.: Scikit-learn: machine learning in python. J. Mach. Learn. Res. **12**(null), 2825–2830 (2011)

28. Romero, A., Baldassarre, G., Duro, R.J., Santucci, V.G.: Analysing autonomous open-ended learning of skills with different interdependent subgoals in robots. In: 2021 20th International Conference on Advanced Robotics (ICAR), pp. 646–651. IEEE (2021)

29. Romero, A., Baldassarre, G., Duro, R.J., Santucci, V.G.: Autonomous learning of multiple curricula with non-stationary interdependencies. In: 2022 IEEE International Conference on Development and Learning (ICDL), pp. 272–279. IEEE (2022)

30. Rosenblatt, M.: Remarks on some nonparametric estimates of a density function. Ann. Math. Stat. **27**(3), 832–837 (1956)

31. Sanner, S.: Relational dynamic influence diagram language (rddl): language description (2010). http://users.cecs.anu.edu.au/~ssanner/IPPC_2011/RDDL.pdf

32. Santucci, V.G., Baldassarre, G., Mirolli, M.: Grail: a goal-discovering robotic architecture for intrinsically-motivated learning. IEEE Trans. Cogn. Dev. Syst. **8**(3), 214–231 (2016)

33. Santucci, V.G., Oudeyer, P.Y., Barto, A., Baldassarre, G.: Intrinsically motivated open-ended learning in autonomous robots. Front. Neurorobot. **13**, 115 (2020)

34. Sartor, G., Zollo, D., Mayer, M.C., Oddi, A., Rasconi, R., Santucci, V.G.: Autonomous generation of symbolic knowledge via option discovery. In: Proceedings of the 9th Italian workshop on Planning and Scheduling (IPS 2021), vol. 3065. CEUR Workshop Proceedings. CEUR-WS.org (2021)

35. Seepanomwan, K., Santucci, V.G., Baldassarre, G.: Intrinsically motivated discovered outcomes boost user's goals achievement in a humanoid robot. In: 2017 Joint IEEE International Conference on Development and Learning and Epigenetic Robotics (ICDL-EpiRob), pp. 178–183 (2017)
36. Singh, S., Barto, A.G., Chentanez, N.: Intrinsically motivated reinforcement learning. In: Proceedings of the 17th International Conference on Neural Information Processing Systems, NIPS 2004, pp. 1281–1288. MIT Press, Cambridge (2004)
37. Sutton, R.S., Barto, A.G.: Reinforcement Learning: An Introduction. MIT press, Cambridge (2018)
38. Sutton, R.S., Precup, D., Singh, S.: Between MDPS and semi-MDPS: a framework for temporal abstraction in reinforcement learning. Artif. Intell. **112**(1), 181–211 (1999)
39. Younes, H., Littman, M.: PPDDL1.0: An Extension to PDDL for Expressiong Planning Domains with Probabilistic Effects. Technical report, Carnegie Mellon University, CMU-CS-04-167 (2004)

Natural Language Processing

Mining Argument Components in Essays at Different Levels

Roberto Demaria[1]([✉]) [iD], Davide Colla[3] [iD], Matteo Delsanto[1] [iD],
Enrico Mensa[1] [iD], Enrico Pasini[2] [iD], and Daniele P. Radicioni[1] [iD]

[1] Dipartimento di Informatica, Universitá degli Studi di Torino, Turin, Italy
roberto.demaria@unito.it
[2] Istituto per il Lessico Intellettuale Europeo, ILIESI/CNR - Roma, Roma, Italy
[3] Dipartimento di Studi Storici, Universitá degli Studi di Torino, Turin, Italy

Abstract. The research of arguments in student essays has long been
the subject of automatic approaches to argument mining. The task has
been mostly modeled as a sequence tagging problem, where the text is
either analyzed in its entirety or split into smaller homogeneous units,
such as sentences or paragraphs. However, previous research has highlighted how the various essay sections may fulfill different functions, and
thereby how the position of specific argument components obeys precise
structural dependency criteria. Based on such underpinning we propose
an approach that exploits such structural information: in this work we
present a hybrid training approach that takes into account the specific
structural components of the essays, in order to be able to mine different
types of argument components at different levels. Our hybrid approach
achieves an improvement over essay-level and paragraph-level training,
in particular in the extraction of some specific argument components.

Keywords: Argument Mining · Argument Component Classification ·
Persuasive essays · Natural Language Processing · Transformers ·
Machine Learning

1 Introduction

Argumentation is a linguistic realization of the human reasoning [15], and is
employed to justify a viewpoint about a controversial issue [35]. One fundamental problem with the definition and formal description of argumentation and
argumentative paths is that there is no agreement among theorists about a universal an uniquely accepted theory. As Van Eemeren et al. [13] state in their
recent survey of the field:

> *As yet, there is no unitary theory of argumentation that encompasses the*
> *logical, dialectical, and rhetorical dimensions of argumentation and is uni-*
> *versally accepted. The current state of the art in argumentation theory is*
> *characterized by the coexistence of a variety of theoretical perspectives and*
> *approaches, which differ considerably from each other in conceptualization,*
> *scope, and theoretical refinement.*

ⓒ The Author(s), under exclusive license to Springer Nature Switzerland AG 2023
R. Basili et al. (Eds.): AIxIA 2023, LNAI 14318, pp. 137–150, 2023.
https://doi.org/10.1007/978-3-031-47546-7_10

While the lack of theories covering all possible argumentative structures affects computational applications, where we observe a gap between theoretical and computational models, a taxonomy of argumentation models has been proposed addressing three different categories —micro-level models (or monological models), macro-level models (or dialogical models), and rhetorical models—, intended to formalize conversations such as discussions, debates, or negotiations by introducing rules on how arguments interact [7].

Argument Mining (AM) is a specific area of Natural Language Processing aimed at mining arguments from natural language texts [21]. AM initially started with the aim at analyzing structured texts in the legal domain, and at a later time it was extended to more heterogeneous and unstructured sources from the web. When dealing with well-structured texts, we are in a paradigm called *closed-domain discourse-level AM* [33]. This task has been typically arranged into three main sub tasks [31]:

- *Argument Identification*, that is, the recognition and localization of arguments within a text;
- *Argument Classification*, which is concerned with the categorization of arguments and their argument components;
- *Structure Identification*, targeted to the reconstruction of the relations connecting the arguments.

All such tasks have been extensively studied in AM, and state-of-the-art approaches adopt supervised learning and transformer-based architectures such as BERT or LONGFORMER [6,11].

Among the many kinds of structured texts, we single out persuasive essays. A persuasive (or argumentative) essay is a text written to argue about a controversial topic while following a particular structure. This makes such kind of texts an excellent playground to test AM tasks [8]. An open issue, in this setting, is whether to treat arguments as a closed (or at least discrete) system with local fragments of text influenced by an isolated set of considerations, or to consider them as an open system within a broader spectrum of influence [28]. In analyzing student essays (a class of persuasive essays) this has resulted in considering a paragraph-level or an essay-level perspective when approaching the learning phase. In some cases the former perspective turned out to be preferable: for example, analyzing student essays at paragraph-level lead to better AM performances than essay-level [12], but contrasting evidence is also reported in literature [20], and there seems to be some intertwining with the model used.

In previous work we reported about differences stemming from learning at such different levels [10]; more specifically, we showed that, when employing a BERT-based model, the essay-level approach is preferable in order to deal with argument identification, whilst the paragraph-level approach is better when categorizing arguments. This boils down to the conclusion that mining arguments at a fine-grained level also needs a fine-grained learning approach. But we are not sure that the difficulty in mining argument components at essay-level does not actually depend on BERT limitations, in particular on the size of its memory window when considering long texts: so we presently employ LONGFORMER as well, to investigate whether it may be beneficial in overcoming such limitation.

Another point, then, is that the argument classification task is not scale-independent [37], since different argument components operate at different levels. Even though essay- and paragraph-level are popular partitions, these are not, in principle, the only ones that can be taken into account. Our hypothesis is that such approaches are too simplistic, and fail to capture some intrinsic and relevant structural characteristics of the argumentative essays, and that a hybrid-level separation during the training phase might be more suited and efficient to classify argument components. We explore such hypothesis by using both a BERT-based classifier and LONGFORMER-based classifier. Furthermore, using LONGFORMER we also improved the essay-level classification, which was particularly lacking with respect to the paragraph-level classification based on BERT, showing that in this case the two approaches have analogous accuracy. Finally, we implemented two variants of the hybrid-level (called *hybrid+* and *hybrid++*), covering some shortcoming of the basic approach and we registered further improvements when testing using LONGFORMER.

These are the main contributions of this paper: *i)* We report evidence that employing LONGFORMER leads to better results when training at essay-level, and show that a larger window may be helpful in mitigating performance differences compared to performing training at the paragraph-level; *ii)* We introduce a novel hybrid-level approach for learning, showing that it is possible to increase the performance of Argument Classification by mining the argument components at different levels; *iii)* Finally, we show that there exists a different model dependency among the three learning approaches and that not only the hybrid one is better, but it also reduces model dependency.

The paper is structured as follows: in Sect. 2 we survey related work that precedes and inspires our research. Section 3 provides more details on the Argument Classification task. In Sect. 4 we present our result and discuss them along with their implications. Section 5 contains conclusions and an outlook on future work.

2   Related Work

This paper mainly lays its foundations in the AM research. AM on structured texts has a long history: among the different application domains we mention news articles [5], scientific articles [1], legal documents [21], healthcare [17] and student essays [31]. Most relevant to our work are those approaches that focus on the classification of argument components in natural language texts. The first approach to identify the argument microstructure were carried out by [21]. They chose the simplest definition of argument as "a set of propositions, being all of them premises, except maximum one, which is a conclusion". So they used premises and conclusions as argumentative units. Research has continued uninterrupted, also with the help of the advances in machine learning and deep neural architectures: former approaches focused on feature-based models [23,24], but with the advances in machine learning and deep neural network techniques, new approaches were proposed using contextualised word embeddings [29] and adopting the transformers architecture [17] that alleviate the burden of developing *ad hoc* feature selection steps.

In our research we used the Argument Annotated Essay Corpus (AAEC) developed by Stab and Gurevych, containing 402 student essays annotated with argumentative information [31]. The argumentative structure is represented here as a tree, which is a simplified but realistic and useful abstraction for computational applications. This corpus has been extensively studied in subsequent research, that has attempted to improve the performances in AM tasks by using more advanced techniques, and also qualitative accounts have been considered in literature [9,32]. Essays are acknowledged to have a recurrent structure [30,36,38], and there are also proper guidelines to annotate them [31]. It is also important to note that essays considered in the AAEC are written by university students. As demonstrated by [3], 'middle school students' (11–14 years old) essays are quite different due to shortcomings in argumentation quality and conventions.

Eger et al. developed a neural end-to-end model addressing all the AM subtasks using the AAEC corpus [12], and this LSTM-ER model remained the state-of-the-art for a long time [19]. In their work they also compared the essay- and paragraph-level approach, showing that the paragraph-level was able to obtain better results in an easier way, which is also consistent with our own previous results [10]. However, the fact that text sequences are much longer when training at essay-level could also be a shortcoming when dealing with systems who struggle to keep a long memory on these long sequences of text. By contrast, paragraphs are shorter and contain an argumentative integrity that can be at least partly analyzed separately like a watertight compartment, since the argumentation structure in this case is completely contained within a paragraph. We will show in fact that using LONGFORMER when training at essay-level substantially dampens this disparity.

Mayer et al. [18] annotated randomized controlled trials for clinical decision making, and used the same components as Stab and Gurevych [31] but with a different logic: while major claims are usually defined as a stance of the author in the AM literature, here they are defined more as general/introductory claims about properties of treatments or diseases (a general hypothesis to be tested or an observation of a previous study to be confirmed), which is supported by a more specific claim, which is instead a concluding statement made by the author about the outcome of the study. Finally, a premise/evidence is an observation or measurement (observed facts, empirical evidence or comparisons) in the study, which supports or attacks another argument component (usually a claim). In this setting also the absence of change in outcomes plays an important role for clinical decision making, and is thus considered as an evidence in favour of the argumentation.

Bao et al. proposed a transition-based model [4] which can perform argument classification and relation identification simultaneously, increasingly constructing an argumentation graph [4]. The best F1-score were obtained by testing at the token-level on the argument classification task experimenting on the AAEC, while other relevant results include those obtained with the Multi-Task Argument Mining approach [20]. What emerges from the structural analysis of essays is that different types of argument components work at different levels within an essay. Based on this observation, the authors of the work in [37] argue that different types of argumentation components should be mined at different levels: this model obtained a significant improvement on mining major claims and claims with respect to previous models that only worked at essay- or paragraph-level for all the components. Our hybrid-level approach was developed by elaborating on this intuition.

Finally, we have to mention that state-of-art models are cast in a supervised learning fashion; however, some unsupervised approaches have been devised to cope with under-resourced settings. Persing and Ng [25] recently obtained interesting results compared with state-of-art supervised models: this research was concerned with avoiding argument-annotated data, and makes use of heuristics to bootstrap a small set of labels to self-train a model. These findings are relevant, and suggest to reconsider the unsupervised approach, also in the light of how difficult and expensive it may be to handcraft annotated data.

3   Methodology

In this paper we propose a novel learning approach for the *Argument Component Classification* (ACC) task, which is central to the field of Argument Mining. Specifically, ACC consists in the detection of specific argument components in an argumentative text. It is often treated as a supervised text classification problem: given a taxonomy describing the argumentative components, an annotated dataset is exploited to train a system that will perform their automatic recognition on previously unseen data. The kind of argumentative texts together with the adopted components taxonomy can affect the shape of the task. Concerning the taxonomy, most approaches in literature adopt a simplified claim premise model [22], while other works rely on more complex component definitions [14], such as those by Toulmin [34].

In this work we take in consideration the Argument-Annotated Essays Corpus (AAEC) developed by Stab and Gurevych [30,31], which is to date one of the most widely adopted corpora to experiment on this task. The authors adopt a model that includes major claim, claim and premise to classify argument components in persuasive student essays.

3.1   The Hybrid Approach

In order to explain the intuition behind our approach, we take into consideration the prototypical structure of a student essay, shown in Fig. 1. An essay usually begins with an *Introduction*, that describes the controversial topic of the argumentation, and as such is not argumentative itself. The introduction often illustrates the 'Major Claim', which is the author's stance towards the topic of the argumentation. The actual argumentation thus begins after the introduction,

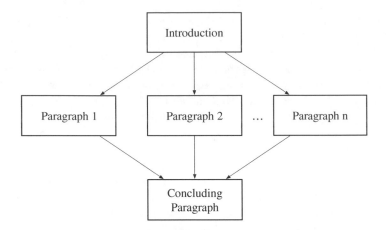

Fig. 1. The general structure of an essay. An essay typically starts with an *Introduction* where the Major Claim (MC) is stated; a set of *Body Paragraphs* follow, containing Premises (P) and Claims (C); finally a *Concluding Paragraph* possibly containing a restatement of the MC, summarizes and ends up the essay.

and is developed in a set of *Body Paragraphs*, each containing an argument in favour or against the major claim. Each such paragraph has an internal structure containing a 'Claim', which is the central component of each argument, and one or more 'Premises', either supporting or attacking the claim. Finally, we typically have a *Concluding Paragraph*, which often summarizes the highlights of the essay, restating the major claim and sometimes providing recommendations for future directions (which are also not argumentative themselves). The importance of the structure is also highlighted by other studies on other corpora, such as [36]: authors herein found that, similarly to Stab and Gurevych, the first paragraph usually begins with non argumentative sentences and contains an introduction together with the major claim (called thesis in their research). They also highlight the special roles of the first and last paragraph of an essay.

Systems proposed in literature are trained either at *essay-level* or at *paragraph-level*. In the former case the text of the essay is given in input to the system, and the model is concerned with recognizing all possible argumentative components. In this case the model has access to the entire structure of the essay, to its tags, and context. In the latter case, instead, paragraphs are the input unit for the tagger, which has to recognize argumentative components within much shorter sequences, and without knowing the entire context of the essay: in fact, if the paragraph is the unit, the model cannot distinguish between paragraphs from different essays, and can only access structure, tags and context within individual paragraphs.

We conjecture that both approaches can be improved by exploiting the structural information available in student essays. In fact, the essay-level training has to deal with the greater variability in the location of the components and may encounter difficulties arising from structural components (in particular MC and

C); the paragraph-level, conversely, may fail to recognize the specific role played by the individual paragraphs (paragraphs are not structurally equivalent), e.g., missing the specificity of introduction and conclusion, that intrinsically differ from the central paragraphs. Our hypothesis is therefore that we might guide the system to better trace these components developing an approach to capture the best of the two previous approaches. We call this approach *hybrid-level* training. We have considered three variants: in the basic one (referred to simply as *hybrid*), we have arranged the essay into three parts and then trained the system by feeding it with these three blocks: the introduction, the set of body paragraphs, and the concluding paragraph. Then, in the first variant (referred to as *hybrid+*) we have guided the system to recognize also the boundaries between the internal body paragraphs by inserting a separator —tagged with a specific label— between each of them; in the second variant (referred to as *hybrid++* we have inserted another separator (also with its own specific tag) between introduction and body paragraphs and body paragraphs and conclusion, which allows the essay to be seen again in its entirety as at the essay-level (and no longer split into three blocks), but with structure boundaries this time.

4   Experiments and Discussion

In previous work we investigated the task of Argument Identification and Argument Classification [10]; more precisely, we fine-tuned a BERT-model originally devised by [39]. We presently extend that approach by also employing LONGFORMER [6] to investigate the impact of a longer window for the subword tokenizer and test the effectiveness of competing learning approaches on different models. We cast the task to a span classification problem, using the BIO labeling system as sequence labeling strategy [27]. In this setting, every token is labeled according to the position within or outside an argument component: the tag '*B*' indicates the first token of the argument component, '*I*' is used to label tokens included within a component, and '*O*' is used to mark tokens outside argument components. Since the ACC task involves recognizing different unit types, the B-I-O tags are associated to each component: thus [B,I]-MC, [B,I]-C, [B,I]-P, and O tags for Major Claim, Claim, Premise and Other, respectively. Nevertheless, when testing we only consider 4 tags (one for each component) and we do not distinguish between B and I when calculating accuracy metrics, since they both identify the same component. This means that, at evaluation time, B and I tags are interchangeable for identifying a given component.

Three different training schemes were employed essay-level, paragraph-level and hybrid-level, and experiments were carried out in 5-fold cross-validation; a randomly-chosen 80% of the corpus was used for training and 20% for testing. We recorded F1-scores using both a token-level and the 'α-level matching' method proposed in [24]; this method considers the matching of spans instead of tokens, and allows considering both exact (100% α−level) and approximate (over 50%) matches. In this setting, two text spans are considered an exact match if they are featured by same boundaries, whilst they are considered as an approximate

Table 1. Results (F1-scores) on the Argument Classification Task using BERT.

		Essay	Paragraph	Hybrid
Major Claim	Token	65.36	70.74	**76.09**
	α 50%	77.20	79.11	**84.33**
	α 100%	51.59	59.78	**70.71**
Claim	Token	50.93	**58.64**	57.55
	α 50%	56.10	**65.31**	63.43
	α 100%	38.89	**51.80**	51.16
Premise	Token	86.28	87.25	**87.44**
	α 50%	87.74	**89.59**	88.91
	α 100%	75.82	76.00	**76.16**
Other	Token	**88.18**	85.99	87.78
	α 50%	**96.28**	95.07	95.09
	α 100%	**93.54**	90.82	91.08

match if they share over half tokens. This more lenient evaluation metrics is customarily used also to assess human annotators agreement, which is not always full in complex tasks, such as in the present one.

Let us start by introducing the results obtained when employing the BERT-based model. The results on the ACC task obtained by training at essay-, paragraph- and hybrid-level are illustrated in Table 1. In this case, for the sake of brevity, we have only considered the hybrid approach in its basic form; the models *hybrid+* and *hybrid++* were only tested using LONGFORMER as performances are generally better than BERT. The three metrics essentially reveal the same pattern. The MC is the component that benefits more from the hybrid approach, revealing that separating introduction and conclusion from the body paragraphs during the training helps in classifying such component. We obtain a 5% improvement with respect to the paragraph-level in classifying MC at token level, and a 5% and 10% improvement at the 50% and 100% α-level, respectively. Conversely, the C classification only loses 1% with respect to the paragraph-level, and also the classification of P registers the best results (by a reduced margin, though) in terms of F1 Score in 2 out of 3 metrics. The essay-level is less appropriate in classifying MC and C: our results unveil the difficulty of the BERT-based model to handle the whole essay, while it is surprisingly effective in classifying O. In general we observe that C is the hardest component to classify, probably because it varies to a greater extent (please also refer to results in [10]). In fact, training at the paragraph-level is the most suitable perspective for C, since we have a smaller degree of variability within a single paragraph with respect to an essay or all the body paragraphs gathered together. This is also supported by literature: e.g., in [36] regularities were found in the argumentation flow within body paragraphs, showing that students tend to first state a claim and then argue for it; also, it was showed that there is a tendency

Table 2. Results (F1-scores) on the Argument Classification Task using LONG-FORMER.

		Essay	Paragraph	Hybrid	Hybrid+	Hybrid++
Major Claim	Token	77.50	75.78	78.49	**78.97**	78.27
	α 50%	82.71	83.83	85.48	**86.21**	85.15
	α 100%	70.57	71.31	72.88	73.75	**74.11**
Claim	Token	57.51	61.24	60.89	**63.97**	60.12
	α 50%	62.64	67.23	66.62	**68.48**	65.58
	α 100%	53.81	58.77	57.02	**61.01**	57.19
Premise	Token	88.23	88.12	88.55	**89.29**	88.83
	α 50%	89.62	90.10	89.85	**90.60**	90.15
	α 100%	80.13	78.10	78.0	79.29	**81.03**
Other	Token	**89.74**	87.05	88.55	88.88	89.71
	α 50%	**96.07**	94.60	95.11	95.45	96.01
	α 100%	**93.72**	90.61	90.75	91.66	93.41

to state the central claim of a paragraph in the very first sentence, followed by the end of the text [22]. Such tendency to state the central claim at the beginning of a paragraph seems to be a peculiarity of the English language (and of Anglo-Saxon cultures, more in general), since other studies show that in documents authored by Asian people the claim is mostly found at the end [16,26]. Even MC can be either posited at the beginning of the essay or pushed into the middle, mostly when it contains background information about the discussion topic. In this case, having the introduction separated and more identifiable from the other paragraphs gives to the model less ambiguity to identify the MC using semantic and syntactic information.

Table 3. Averaged results (F1-scores) on Argument Classification using BERT and LONGFORMER.

	BERT			LONGFORMER				
	Essay	Paragraph	Hybrid	Essay	Paragraph	Hybrid	Hybrid+	Hybrid++
Token	72.69	75.66	**77.21**	78.25	78.05	79.12	**80.28**	79.23
α 50%	79.33	82.27	**82.94**	82.76	83.94	84.26	**85.26**	84.22
α 100%	64.96	69.60	**72.28**	74.56	74.70	74.68	76.37	**76.44**

The results recorded by employing LONGFORMER (presented in Table 2) show improved results with respect to those of BERT. Even in this case the hybrid-level brings a significant improvement for MC, and is in general more favorable than the other two approaches, as also confirmed in Table 3. More specifically, we can see that the results obtained by employing LONGFORMER

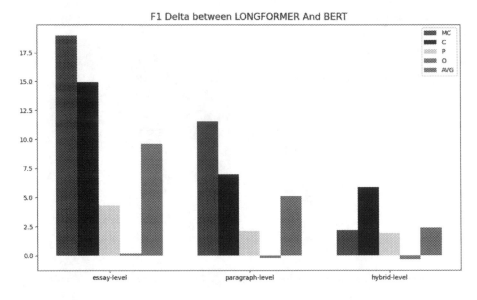

Fig. 2. Difference in F1-score when passing from BERT to LONGFORMER (F1-delta) using the three different approaches (case exact match).

improve over those obtained through the BERT-based models around 2% at token-level, 1.5% at 50% α-level and 2.5% at 100% α-level for the hybrid-level. Even more consistent is the improvement for the essay-level which increase 6%, 3.5% and 10% respectively, revealing the relevance of long-memory cutting. Also the paragraph-level registers improvements in the order of 3.5%, 1.5% and 5%. In general, the exact-matching is the perspective which benefits the most from passing from BERT to LONGFORMER, probably due to the fact that it is easier to improve a lower performance.

Figure 2 shows the F1-delta scores by passing from BERT to LONGFORMER in the case of exact match; for the sake of brevity, we report the figures for exact match condition only testing with the the basic hybrid level; token- and approximate-levels also reveal the same trend. Higher bars illustrate experimental conditions where LONGFORMER ensures higher improvements with respect to BERT. This plot also shows that the hybrid approach, in addition to higher accuracy, also exhibits a lower dependence on the model, since the F1-delta is the lowest one, while it is clear how the essay-level is highly dependent on the model in this case. That is, the reduced difference between LONGFORMER and BERT when adopting the hybrid approach may be explained by a simple effect: the shorter the text excerpts being processed, the lesser the benefits deriving from employing a longer memory window (in such a case, almost all texts could be processed through BERT with little loss). The results obtained experimenting with LONGFORMER at essay-level are also of interest: the classification of MC is improved by 12%, 5.5% and 19% for token-level, approximate and exact match, respectively, when passing from BERT to LONGFORMER; the classification of C is improved by 6.5%, 6.5% and 15% instead. Such results illustrate how the larger memory window of LONGFORMER impacts on the ACC of argumentative essays.

To complete the assessment, we need to mention that the three approaches and the two models are also featured by different computational properties. LONGFORMER requires more computational resources than BERT and the same holds for the paragraph-level, since there are more chunks of text to analyse.[1] This involves that using the hybrid-level is also beneficial in saving computational resources and, since it has less model dependency, using BERT hybrid-level also ensures a good computational gain with a loss in accuracy in the order of 2%. Finally, guided by the encouraging results obtained with the basic hybrid approach, we developed two variants called *hybrid+* and *hybrid++* in order to overcome some shortcoming of the basic hybrid approach, and whose results are reported in Tables 2 and 3. In the first case (*hybrid+*) we still have a partitioning of the essay in introduction, body paragraphs and conclusion but we have informed the system about the boundaries of the internal paragraphs through the insertion of a specific separator (tagged as *P-Sep*); thanks to this arrangement we were able to reach a consistent improvement on each component and in particular on C. In the second case (*hybrid++*) we used the same separators as in *hybrid+*, but instead of considering a partitioning into three blocks we returned to consider the essay in its entirety (since this allows to save computational resources) and we inserted another separator, tagged as *IC-Sep*, between the introduction and the body paragraphs and the body paragraphs and the conclusion (thus two of these separators for each essay). The last setting is particularly beneficial when considering the exact matching; it also helps improving the classification of O, which seams particularly good when considering the whole essay.

Finally, even though our main concern was not to overcome state-of-the-art accuracy, but rather to compare different learning strategies to investigate strengths and weaknesses of each one when applying LONGFORMER associated to our hybrid++ model, we obtained a 76.44 F1 for the exact matching, which closely approaches the 76.55 F1 obtained by [20] which is, to the best of our knowledge, the highest reported accuracy on the corpus. For the approximate matching at 50% level-alpha, we are not aware of recent results in this setting (except for our own results, [10]) so the 85.26 F1 obtained using the hybrid+ model is currently the highest accuracy obtained on this corpus.

5 Conclusions and Future Work

In this work we have been experimenting on the Argument Component Classification task: we introduced a novel level (the hybrid level) to train the models, and compared and commented results obtained through models based on

---

[1] Experiments were performed on machinery provided by the Competence Centre for Scientific Computing [2]; nodes employed were equipped with 8VCPU, 1x NVIDIA Tesla T4 GPU and 64GB Memory. Running experiments with LONGFORMER took 11.5 h to complete 15 epochs at essay-level, while BERT only took 4 h. At paragraph-level instead, LONGFORMER took 28 h, BERT 9.5.

BERT and LONGFORMER. In so doing, different strategies were employed to train the models: in the essay-level setting we used entire essays, and in the paragraph-level one we arranged the essays into their paragraphs, following two popular approaches from the literature. We then introduced a novel strategy named *hybrid-level* and two variants: in the basic form we differentiate introduction, set of body paragraphs, and conclusion; the first variant also considers separators between internal body paragraphs; the second variant abandons the partition into three blocks and considers the entire essay, but with two specific separators to better mark the structure of the essay and speed up the computation. It is noteworthy that such hybrid approaches all have in common the goal to better fit the essay structure of components when mining them. We found that this learning perspective is beneficial with respect to the classical essay- and paragraph-level when performing argument classification, using both BERT and LONGFORMER. Then, comparing the two transformers models, we found that the results obtained through LONGFORMER consistently improve on those obtained with BERT, in particular when training at the essay-level: this fact shows that the longer memory-window of LONGFORMER ensures better results when analysing text sequences. Finally, we provided experimental evidence supporting the intuition that argumentation, in particular within structured texts like argumentative essays, typically follows a particular and recurrent structure that can be exploited to facilitate the learning phase. Since our hybrid-level strategy is a model-free solution, we hope that these findings can be helpful for further research.

Future directions will consider different aspects. For example, in the classification of claims we recorded lower accuracy with respect to the other components, showing that this step is harder and still needs further efforts. Furthermore, to enhance the robustness of this technique there is also the necessity to test the hybrid approach on state-of-the-art systems and on further types of argumentative texts featured by an underlying recurring structure. This is a first exploratory step in this direction which has shown encouraging prospects.

References

1. Accuosto, P., Saggion, H.: Mining arguments in scientific abstracts with discourse-level embeddings. Data Knowl. Eng. **129**, 101840 (2020)
2. Aldinucci, M., Bagnasco, S., Lusso, S., Pasteris, P., Rabellino, S., Vallero, S.: OCCAM: a flexible, multi-purpose and extendable HPC cluster. J. Phys: Conf. Ser. **898**(8), 082039 (2017)
3. Alhindi, T., Ghosh, D.: Sharks are not the threat humans are: argument component segmentation in school student essays. arXiv preprint arXiv:2103.04518 (2021)
4. Bao, J., Fan, C., Wu, J., Dang, Y., Du, J., Xu, R.: A neural transition-based model for argumentation mining. In: Proceedings of the 59th Annual Meeting of the Association for Computational Linguistics and the 11th International Joint Conference on Natural Language Processing (Volume 1: Long Papers), pp. 6354–6364 (2021)

5. Basile, P., Basile, V., Cabrio, E., Villata, S.: Argument mining on Italian news blogs. In: Third Italian Conference on Computational Linguistics (CLiC-it 2016) & Fifth Evaluation Campaign of Natural Language Processing and Speech Tools for Italian. Final Workshop (EVALITA 2016) (2016)
6. Beltagy, I., Peters, M.E., Cohan, A.: Longformer: the long-document transformer. arXiv preprint arXiv:2004.05150 (2020)
7. Bentahar, J., Moulin, B., Bélanger, M.: A taxonomy of argumentation models used for knowledge representation. Artif. Intell. Rev. **33**(3), 211–259 (2010)
8. Cabrio, E., Villata, S.: Five years of argument mining: a data-driven analysis. In: IJCAI, vol. 18, pp. 5427–5433 (2018)
9. Carlile, W., Gurrapadi, N., Ke, Z., Ng, V.: Give me more feedback: annotating argument persuasiveness and related attributes in student essays. In: Proceedings of the 56th Annual Meeting of the Association for Computational Linguistics (Volume 1: Long Papers), pp. 621–631 (2018)
10. Demaria, R., et al.: Shuffling-based data augmentation for argument mining. In: CEUR WORKSHOP PROCEEDINGS, pp. 1–17. CEUR (2022)
11. Devlin, J., Chang, M.W., Lee, K., Toutanova, K.: BERT: pre-training of deep bidirectional transformers for language understanding. arXiv preprint arXiv:1810.04805 (2018)
12. Eger, S., Daxenberger, J., Gurevych, I.: Neural end-to-end learning for computational argumentation mining. arXiv preprint arXiv:1704.06104 (2017)
13. Haaften, T.: Frans H. van Eemeren, Bart Garssen, Erik C.W. Krabbe, A. Francisca Snoeck Henkemans, Bart Verheij and Jean H.M. Wagemans: Handbook of Argumentation Theory. Argumentation **30**(3), 345–351 (2015). https://doi.org/10.1007/s10503-015-9381-3
14. Habernal, I., Gurevych, I.: Argumentation mining in user-generated web discourse. Comput. Linguist. **43**(1), 125–179 (2017)
15. Hinton, M.: Evaluating the Language of Argument. AL, vol. 37. Springer, Cham (2021). https://doi.org/10.1007/978-3-030-61694-6
16. Kaplan, R.B.: Cultural thought patterns in inter-cultural education. Lang. Learn. **16**(1–2), 1–20 (1966)
17. Mayer, T., Cabrio, E., Villata, S.: Transformer-based argument mining for healthcare applications. In: ECAI 2020, pp. 2108–2115. IOS Press (2020)
18. Mayer, T., Marro, S., Villata, S., Cabrio, E.: Enhancing evidence-based medicine with natural language argumentative analysis of clinical trials. Artif. Intell. Med. **118**, 102098 (2021). https://doi.org/10.1016/j.artmed.2021.102098. https://hal.science/hal-03264761
19. Miwa, M., Bansal, M.: End-to-end relation extraction using LSTMS on sequences and tree structures. arXiv preprint arXiv:1601.00770 (2016)
20. Morio, G., Ozaki, H., Morishita, T., Yanai, K.: End-to-end argument mining with cross-corpora multi-task learning. Trans. Assoc. Comput. Linguist. **10**, 639 658 (2022)
21. Palau, R.M., Moens, M.F.: Argumentation mining: the detection, classification and structure of arguments in text. In: Proceedings of the 12th International Conference on Artificial Intelligence and Law, pp. 98–107 (2009)
22. Peldszus, A., Stede, M.: An annotated corpus of argumentative microtexts. In: Argumentation and Reasoned Action: Proceedings of the 1st European Conference on Argumentation, Lisbon, vol. 2, pp. 801–815 (2015)
23. Peldszus, A., Stede, M.: Joint prediction in MST-style discourse parsing for argumentation mining. In: Proceedings of the 2015 Conference on Empirical Methods in Natural Language Processing, pp. 938–948 (2015)

24. Persing, I., Ng, V.: End-to-end argumentation mining in student essays. In: Proceedings of the 2016 Conference of the North American Chapter of the Association for Computational Linguistics: Human Language Technologies, pp. 1384–1394 (2016)
25. Persing, I., Ng, V.: Unsupervised argumentation mining in student essays. In: Proceedings of the 12th Language Resources and Evaluation Conference, pp. 6795–6803 (2020)
26. Putra, J.W.G., Teufel, S., Tokunaga, T.: Parsing argumentative structure in English-as-foreign-language essays. In: Proceedings of the 16th Workshop on Innovative Use of NLP for Building Educational Applications, pp. 97–109 (2021)
27. Ramshaw, L.A., Marcus, M.P.: Text chunking using transformation-based learning. In: Armstrong, S., Church, K., Isabelle, P., Manzi, S., Tzoukermann, E., Yarowsky, D. (eds.) Natural Language Processing Using Very Large Corpora. Text, Speech and Language Technology, vol. 11, pp. 157–176. Springer, Dordrecht (1999). https://doi.org/10.1007/978-94-017-2390-9_10
28. Reed, C.: Argument technology for debating with humans (2021)
29. Reimers, N., Schiller, B., Beck, T., Daxenberger, J., Stab, C., Gurevych, I.: Classification and clustering of arguments with contextualized word embeddings. arXiv preprint arXiv:1906.09821 (2019)
30. Stab, C., Gurevych, I.: Identifying argumentative discourse structures in persuasive essays. In: Proceedings of the 2014 Conference on Empirical Methods in Natural Language Processing (EMNLP), pp. 46–56 (2014)
31. Stab, C., Gurevych, I.: Parsing argumentation structures in persuasive essays. Comput. Linguist. **43**(3), 619–659 (2017)
32. Stab, C., Gurevych, I.: Recognizing insufficiently supported arguments in argumentative essays. In: Proceedings of the 15th Conference of the European Chapter of the Association for Computational Linguistics: Volume 1, Long Papers, pp. 980–990 (2017)
33. Stab, C., Miller, T., Gurevych, I.: Cross-topic argument mining from heterogeneous sources using attention-based neural networks. arXiv preprint arXiv:1802.05758 (2018)
34. Toulmin, S.: The Uses of Argument. Cambridge University Press, Cambridge (1958)
35. Van Eemeren, F.H., Grootendorst, R., Johnson, R.H., Plantin, C., Willard, C.A.: Fundamentals of Argumentation Theory: A Handbook of Historical Backgrounds and Contemporary Developments. Routledge, Milton Park (2013)
36. Wachsmuth, H., Al Khatib, K., Stein, B.: Using argument mining to assess the argumentation quality of essays. In: Proceedings of COLING 2016, the 26th International Conference on Computational Linguistics: Technical Papers, pp. 1680–1691 (2016)
37. Wang, H., Huang, Z., Dou, Y., Hong, Y.: Argumentation mining on essays at multi scales. In: Proceedings of the 28th International Conference on Computational Linguistics, pp. 5480–5493 (2020)
38. Wang, X., Lee, Y., Park, J.: Automated evaluation for student argumentative writing: a survey. arXiv preprint arXiv:2205.04083 (2022)
39. Yang, X., Bian, J., Hogan, W.R., Wu, Y.: Clinical concept extraction using transformers. J. Am. Med. Inform. Assoc. **27**(12), 1935–1942 (2020)

Unraveling ChatGPT: A Critical Analysis of AI-Generated Goal-Oriented Dialogues and Annotations

Tiziano Labruna[1,2]([✉]) [iD], Sofia Brenna[1,2] [iD], Andrea Zaninello[1,2] [iD], and Bernardo Magnini[1] [iD]

[1] Fondazione Bruno Kessler, Trento, Italy
{tlabruna,sbrenna,azaninello,magnini}@fbk.eu
[2] Free University of Bozen-Bolzano, Bolzano, Italy

Abstract. Large pre-trained language models have exhibited unprecedented capabilities in producing high-quality text via prompting techniques. This fact introduces new possibilities for data collection and annotation, particularly in situations where such data are scarce, complex to gather, expensive, or even sensitive. In this paper, we explore the potential of pre-trained language models to generate and annotate goal-oriented dialogues, and conduct an in-depth analysis to evaluate their quality. Our experiments employ ChatGPT, and encompass three categories of goal-oriented dialogues (task-oriented, collaborative, and explanatory), two generation modes (interactive and one-shot), and two languages (English and Italian). Through extensive human-based evaluations, we demonstrate that the quality of generated dialogues is on par with those generated by humans. On the other side, we show that the complexity of dialogue annotation schema (e.g., for dialogue state tracking) exceeds the capacity of current language models, a task which still requires substantial human supervision.

Keywords: Large Language Models · Conversational Agents · Goal-oriented Dialogues

1 Introduction

Since its initial release in November 2022, ChatGPT has been tested on various AI tasks, including traditional NLP tasks, and on various domains such as medicine, computer programming, and even on neuro-psychological tests used for humans. In addition, some attention has been paid to ChatGPT's ability to produce annotated data for training purposes [11,18]. In this paper, we specifically aim to evaluate ChatGPT's ability to generate novel, human-like dialogues and to annotate them according to a predetermined semantic schema.

There are two main reasons motivating our work. First, generating high-quality training data remains essential for developing adaptable dialogue systems for various domains and conversational contexts. However, collecting human-like dialogues often requires complex and expensive settings (e.g., Wizard of Oz [20], Map Task [1, 41]), and reducing the cost of data collection while preserving their quality is of utmost importance. Second, although dialogue annotation is crucial for training dialogue models, this is a complex and costly process, as annotation schemas are often not standardized and human annotation is time-consuming and error-prone (see the various versions of the MultiWOZ dataset [4]). As a result, only a few annotated dialogue datasets are currently available, which cover limited dialogue types and domains, and with insufficient data.

Meanwhile, very large pre-trained language models (LLMs), such as, among the others, BERT [9], T5 [34], LaMDA [8], have demonstrated unparalleled ability to generate high-quality text via prompting strategies [23]. Particularly interesting for our purposes are instruction-tuned models (e.g. IstructGPT [29], LLama 2 [40]), which have been fine tuned to be aligned with human conversational preferences. While recent studies have examined the potential of LLMs as annotators [11, 15], this area remains largely unexplored, especially regarding dialogue generation and annotation. We investigate the ability of LLMs both to generate and to annotate different types of dialogues, in a multilingual setting, so that those data are ready to be used for training dialogue models without human intervention except for prompt optimization, an effort that unlike annotation is highly scalable as the same prompt can be reused to produce an indefinite amount of datasets. We consider three dialogue scenarios of varying complexity: (i) task-oriented dialogues involving a user with specific goals and an agent helping the user to achieve them; (ii) cooperative dialogues where two participants collaborate to achieve a shared goal; and (iii) explanatory dialogues aimed at providing clarifications and explanations on a specific topic through dialogue. To evaluate the quality of the generated dialogues, we conducted a crowd-sourced evaluation using a questionnaire based on a 6-point Likert scale, comparing both the dialogues generated by ChatGPT and corresponding human-generated dialogues. Additionally, we used standard measures (e.g., for dialogue state tracking) to evaluate the quality of the annotations performed by ChatGPT.

The contributions of the paper are as follows: (i) We report on the first experiment, to the best of our knowledge, aiming at generating complex, human-like dialogues through controlled prompting of a LLM. (ii) We show that the quality of automatically generated dialogues is comparable to that of reference human-generated dialogues. (iii) We show that the quality of the annotations generated by ChatGPT is still not comparable to human annotations and report a number of critical limitations, including the generation of hallucinations, which need to be considered in future research.

2　Background and Related Work

We consider three types of dialogues: (i) task-oriented dialogues, (ii) collaborative dialogues, and (iii) explanatory dialogues. As for LLM, for all experiments we use ChatGPT, a recent conversational model built upon a state-of-the-art GPT model.

2.1   Task-Oriented Dialogues

The objective of task-oriented dialogues [26] is to obtain specific pieces of information that meet the user's requirements, such as booking a restaurant, learning how to open a bank account, or checking tomorrow's weather. A typical task-oriented dialogue presumes that the user has a definite objective in mind, which is then identified by an operator during the conversation. The operator may pose questions to the user to narrow down the search space and pinpoint the objects that match the user's objectives. In some situations, the obtained information may be in the form of text, as is the case with Frequently Asked Questions (FAQ) retrieval. In other scenarios, information may consist of objects, such as movies or restaurants, that have been extracted from a knowledge base.

MultiWOZ 2.4. MultiWOZ [4] is a widely used task-oriented conversational datasets, consisting of over 10,000 dialogues, collected using the Wizard of Oz technique, spanning seven different domains, including restaurant reservations and train ticket purchases. Subsequent versions of the dataset brought incremental improvements, culminating in version 2.4 [44], which we use in our experiments. Semantic annotations in MultiWOZ follow a commonly used schema for training dialogue understanding [25] and dialogue state tracking [2] components. Annotations are based on triplets consisting of *domain* (e.g., RESTAURANT), *slot* (e.g., FOOD), and *slot-value* (e.g., ITALIAN), which are consistent with the domain ontology. Annotations are incremental, meaning that new slot-values mentioned in the dialogue are added to previous ones, enabling to maintain a full belief state of the user's requirements at each step of the conversation. A MultiWOZ dialogue with its annotations is reported in Appendix A.1.

2.2   Collaborative Dialogues

Collaborative dialogues require the cooperation of the interlocutors to follow the execution of a shared plan. For instance, when a user is planning a vacation with a travel operator, multiple steps must be taken, such as determining the vacation's time and location, reviewing various travel agent proposals, making decisions, and reserving transportation and lodging. Numerous command-based dialogues, in which one participant requests the other to complete a task (e.g., in a car, at home), with varying degrees of complexity, belong to the category of collaborative dialogues and are now prevalent in many personal assistants.

JILDA. We use the JILDA Corpus [38], a collection of 525 Italian dialogues between two humans in the job search and offer domain. Dialogues were gathered using the role-taking method [1] in a two-party online chat, where an Applicant seeks assistance from a Navigator, who is a job consultant. Compared to dialogues collected using the Wizard of Oz approach, JILDA exhibits greater lexical variety, syntactic complexity, conversational naturalness, and overall length. In JILDA, similarly to MultiWOZ, semantic annotations are based on domain specific dialogue acts and slot-value pairs associated with each dialogue utterance. A JILDA dialogue is reported in Appendix A.2.

2.3 Explanatory Dialogues

There is nowadays widespread agreement that explaining a concept is primarily a social and collaborative practice, which is often likened to a dialogue where both the explainer, typically an expert in the field, and the explainee work together to construct an understanding of a particular topic [5,27,36]. An example of such an explanatory dialogue can be observed between a patient and a medical doctor. Here, the doctor must explain the reasons for a particular diagnosis, while the patient can seek clarifications and additional information. However, despite the growing interest in such data, explanatory dialogue datasets are still rare.

WIRED 5 Levels. One of the few resources that cater to explanatory dialogues, which we used in our experiments, is the *WIRED 5 Levels* corpus by [41]. This corpus comprises transcriptions of dialogues from the WIRED video series 5 Levels, all in English, where a field expert (a university teacher) explains over 13 topics (from music harmony to machine learning) to five explainees with varying levels of proficiency (from children to colleagues). The corpus contains 65 dialogues, with a total of 1550 dialogue turns. Furthermore, each turn was manually labeled according to three dimensions: i. DISCUSSED TOPIC (*how is the discussed topic relevant to the main topic?*); ii. SPEAKER'S GOAL (*what goal does the speaker pursue with utterance in the given turn?*); iii. SPEAKER'S DIALOGUE ACT (*how is the goal being pursued in the turn?*). In our experiments, we used the 5-level dialogues (child, teenager, undergrad, postgrad, colleague) that deal with the topic of "machine learning". Refer to Appendix A.3 for an example of a WIRED dialogue.

2.4 Pre-trained LMs and Prompt-Learning

In recent years, LLMs have been the focus of extensive research, due to their ability to learn from large amounts of data in a self-supervised fashion and to achieve impressive results in various tasks [17,33]. One of the latest trends in utilizing LLMs is the development of prompt-based techniques, where a textual prompt is given to the model as input to generate the desired output. Such techniques have shown to be highly effective, especially for tasks that require specific outputs and have the advantage of (i) not requiring any parameter updates in the LLM; (ii) be human readable, and (iii) not requiring in-domain data, unlike fine-tuning techniques. An example of such a model is GPT-3 [3], a pre-trained language model that uses the Transformer architecture and an attention mechanism to generate natural language text. For an extensive survey on prompt-based techniques, refer to [24].

Given our focus on dialogue, we leverage the "gpt 3.5 turbo" model, which is the basis of the interactive interface of ChatGPT [28]. GPT 3.5 turbo is part of the InstructGPT family [30] based on the GPT-3 language model [3]. However, unlike standard GPT-3.5 models, InstructGPT models are optimized for interactive use, are particularly suited to take instructions as input prompts, and can "learn" from their mistakes throughout a dialogue, making them more aligned with users' requests. GPT 3.5 turbo is generally considered to offer the best price-performance ratio compared to other GPT versions. This is accomplished by a reward mechanism called Reinforcement Learning from Human Feedback (RLHF) [6] used to optimize the model. At training, human trainers engaged in conversations as both a user and an AI assistant. The model was then fine-tuned through supervised training, and the AI-generated suggestions were given to human trainers to produce their responses. The resulting dataset was combined with the InstructGPT dataset and transformed into dialogue format.

2.5   Related Work: LLMs as Annotators

Several recent contributions address the use of LLMs as annotators. [11] explores the potential of GPT-3 as a data annotator on two tasks, text classification (sentiment analysis) and named entity recognition. Findings show that employing GPT-3 annotations can achieve comparable results to those obtained from human-labeled datasets, at a 5% cost. [14] evaluates the efficiency and performance of ChatGPT in comparison to human crowd workers in annotating a dataset of about 2,400 tweets on 5 tasks with several classes, comparing both performances with trained human annotations as gold standard. The research findings show that zero-shot ChatGPT outperforms human annotators on 4 out of 5 tasks (relevance, stance, topics, and frames detection) at a cost about 20 times cheaper than using MTurk, while showing higher inter-coder agreement than both crowd workers and trained annotators. [39] adopts a similar methodology to test accuracy, reliability and bias of ChatGPT compared to crowd workers and expert annotators. This study evaluates 500 political tweets from American politicians during the 2020 elections and classifies them as originating from either Democratic or Republican side. For each tweet ten runs are conducted, with five at a temperature of 0.2 and five at a temperature of 1. Superior accuracy is demonstrated at a lower temperature setting. The authors argue that ChatGPT-4 outperforms human annotators in terms of accuracy and reliability, while demonstrating an equal or lesser extent of bias. Similarly, [46] reports a mean accuracy of 0.609 on 5 data annotation tasks on Twitter datasets, with the highest performance noted in sentiment analysis tasks. Despite promising results, significant room for improvement remains, as performance is reported to vary substantially across individual labels. Another critical issue of using ChatGPT for text annotation and classification is non-reproducibility of outputs, as noted by [35] that annotated 232 texts, employing different settings with temperatures at 0.25 and 1, and using 10 distinct instruction prompts. Varying temperatures and even slightly dissimilar prompts lead to inconsistent outputs, thus raising concerns regarding ChatGPT's reliability. Although multiple repetitions may alleviate this issue, it is advised against the deployment of LLMs for automated annotation in a wholly unsupervised manner and without any validation of the model's performance against human-generated labels, as [31] state.

3   Methodology

We propose a three-step methodology to investigate the generation and annotation of training dialogues. (i) We select a dialogue from an existing available repository, as the *reference dialogue*. We then prompt the language model to produce a *generated dialogue* that closely resembles the reference dialogue. (ii) Next, we prompt the language model to annotate the generated dialogue using the same annotation schema provided in the existing repository. This results in an *annotated dialogue*. (iii) Finally, we carry out an evaluation of both the generated dialogues (comparing them to the reference) and the annotated dialogues.

3.1   Dialogue Generation

Here the goal is to create appropriate prompts that can generate a dialogue which is similar in content to a reference dialogue. There are two ways to prompt a LLM for a dialogue: provide all the instructions in a single prompt and allow the LLM to generate the entire dialogue at once (*one-shot* approach), or, instruct the model to simulate the behavior of one participant only and obtain the dialogue through interaction with a human who plays the role of the other participant (*interactive* approach). For our purposes, i.e., collecting dialogues at a low cost, we are more interested in the *one-shot* approach, although the *interactive* approach can provide important feedback on the ability of the LLM to engage in a conversation with a real user. For both *one-shot* and *interactive* approaches, we follow a structured prompt format with the following content areas (more detailed examples are available in the Appendix):

1. High level instruction about the task to be executed. E.g., "Create a dialogue between a user and a system." (or in the case of the interactive setting: "Simulate to be a system and respond to a user").
2. Description of the dialogue context. E.g. "The user asks for information on restaurants in order to make a reservation and the system, called "Cambridge InfoTown" asks the user all the needed information, tells the user whether there is availability for the people, time and date requested and finally it makes the reservation, giving a random reference number. Every user message should be followed by a system message. Be polite and don't forget to say goodbye. Everything said by "Cambridge InfoTown" needs to be strictly coherent to the Domain Knowledge that I provide you".
3. Domain knowledge to be used in the dialogue. E.g., "name: pizza hut city centre, address: Regent Street City Centre, area: centre, food: italian, phone: 01223323737, postcode: cb21ab, pricerange: cheap".
4. Dialog-specific instructions to be followed by the user (only for the *one-shot* setting). E.g., "For the dialog that you have to generate, the instructions for the user are the following: You are looking for an Indian restaurant in the north [...]".
5. Instructions on how to simulate the system (only for the *interactive* setting. E.g., "I will start acting like a user needing information about restaurants in Cambridge starting from my next message".

We chose the GPT-3.5 turbo model, through OpenAI's API and the `ChatCompletion` method, which allows the model to keep track of previous turns, and empirically set *temperature* $= 0.8$ (the degree of randomness of the model) and *top_p* $= 0.1$ (the cumulative percentage of considered predictions) as this best reproduces the standard setting in the interactive web interface.

3.2 Dialogue Annotation

We now describe the methodology for annotating a dialogue through prompting the Large Language Model (LLM). All semantic annotations are added to a previously generated dialogue (either by humans or by a LLM), as we considered too complex the option where annotations are generated simultaneously with the dialogue generation. For the three dialogue types we are experimenting, we use the annotation schema as provided in the corresponding reference datasets (see in Sect. 2). The prompt for dialogue annotation has the following structure:

1. High level instruction about the task to be executed. E.g., "Write annotations about a dialogue that I will send you".
2. Instructions on annotations. E.g., "Add annotations of the intents and slots for each one of the dialog turns. The annotations have to follow this format: [...] The possible intents are: [...] The possible slots are: [...]
3. Dialogue to be annotated. E.g., "The dialogue that you have to annotate is the following: 1. User: [...] 2. System: [...]".

3.3 Evaluation Methods

According to the methodology described in Sect. 3.1, we have three versions of each dialogue we consider: a *reference dialogue*, a *one-shot generated dialogue* and a *interactive generated dialogue*. Here the goal is to assess the quality of the generated dialogues, in order to establish whether LLMs are capable of creating dialogues that are comparable to the ones collected by humans.

Evaluating dialogue quality. Although automatic metrics like BERT-score [45] exist for scoring the similarity of a text against a reference, such metrics are insufficient, as they do not capture the peculiarities of dialogue. To address the issue, we designed a questionnaire to collect human evaluations through crowdsourcing [7,13,22]. The questionnaire, reported below, assesses dialogue quality based on six criteria: consistency and quality of content (criteria 1 and 2), formality (3), politeness (4), naturalness (5), and successfulness (6).

Labelers are presented with each criterion as an affirmative declarative clause and asked to rate their overall agreement on a 6-item Likert verbal scale, ranging from "strongly disagree" to "strongly agree". Our Likert scale replicates the commonly used 7-point bipolar disagreement/agreement scale, with increasing agreement value from left to right. We chose not to provide a neutral middle option, which would allow respondents to avoid committing to a direction in

1. Requests and responses are consistent across the dialogue
2. The information that is exchanged by participants in the dialogue is realistic
3. The level of formality shown by the participants is consistent in the dialogue
4. Participants are respectful towards each other (e.g., no offensive language)
5. The participants' sentences sound spontaneous and natural in the dialogue
6. The dialogue comes to a conclusion

their opinion itetional commn comments and feedback.agraphDetecting hallucinations. To evaluate whether a dialogue generated by a LLM includes hallucinations (i.e., generated text that is "nonsensical or unfaithful to the provided source input" [19]), we analyze all system turns that reference the domain knowledge base. We request a domain expert to assess whether the information conveyed in these utterances is accurate or not, assigning a score equal to 0 if any of the information provided is inconsistent with the knowledge base, and 1 if all information is correct. Hallucination accuracy is then averaged across the entire dialogue (or set of dialogues).

Adherence to Instructions. Here we consider the instructions (i.e., prompts) related to the user goals in the dialogue (e.g. "user is looking for an Italian restaurant") and evaluate whether the generated dialogues comply with the given instructions. We only take into account utterances that are relevant to the instructions provided (e.g., utterances such as "Thank you for your help" are disregarded). For each utterance, a domain expert assigns a score equal to 0 if any of the information presented in the generated dialogue conflicts with the instructions, and 1 if there is no conflict. The scores for each utterance are then averaged to obtain the overall score for a dialogue (or for the set of dialogues).

Evaluating Dialogue Annotation Quality. In order to assess the quality of generated annotations, we rely on a domain expert that determines whether the annotations for the dialogues are correct. For WoZ and Jilda, we use Slot Accuracy (SA) and Joint Goal Accuracy (JGA) as quality metrics, as they are commonly used in the literature for dialogue annotation evaluation [10]. To compute SA and JGA, we ask the experts to define the sets of false negatives (FN) and false positives (FP) triplets (*domain, slot, slot-value*), such as "RESTAURANT-FOOD-ITALIAN", for each conversational utterance and its corresponding annotation. Then, we compute SA using the following formula:

$$SA = \frac{|S| - |FN| - |FP| + |P \cap Q|}{|S|}$$

where S is the set of unique (*domain, slot*) pairs in the dataset, P is the set of unique (*domain, slot*) pairs from FN, and Q is the set of unique (*domain, slot*) pairs from FP. Therefore, $P \cap Q$ represents the set of *domain-slot* pairs that are present in both FN and FP. JGA, instead, is a more strict measure and is computed by assigning a score equal to 0 to any annotation with at least one false negative or false positive, and 1 to annotations that are 100% correct. Finally, we take the average of both SA and JGA values for each conversational turn to obtain a score for the entire dialogue (or set of dialogues).

For Wired, we cannot rely on the same metrics because the rationale behind the annotation is different, as it is not constituted by *domain-slot-value* triplets. Therefore, following the baselines proposed by the original release paper [41], we report Macro F_1-score for each labelling dimension separately (*Topic, Goal, Dialogue act*) as the average of single F_1-scores for all the labels.

4   Experiments and Results

The experimental setup for our qualitative analysis comprises three different types of dialogues, with one dataset per type, a model (ChatGPT) that we utilized for dialogue generation and annotation, a quality assessment procedure for generated dialogues, based on a questionnaire created through Amazon Mechanical Turk (AMT), two expert evaluations to gauge ChatGPT's ability to avoid hallucinations and follow instructions, and a quality assessment method for dialogue annotations.

Table 1. Qualitative assessment for dialogue generation via AMT. Scores assigned through a questionnaire in a Likert scale (inter-rater reliability equal to Krippendorff's $\alpha = 0.47$ [21] computed via the R package *"irr"* [32] [12]). [†] indicates scores that are not statistically different from the correspondent reference quality score (*p-value* > 0.05). *Jilda dialogues are in Italian.

Dataset	Reference (humans)	Generated: One-shot	Generated: Interactive	Avg.
MULTIWOZ	1.81	1.60	1.83[†]	**1.75**
JILDA*	2.47	2.38[†]	2.31[†]	**2.39**
WIRED	1.61	1.78[†]	1.38[†]	**1.59**
Avg.	**1.96**	**1.92**	**1.84**	**1.91**

4.1   Dialogues Generation

We randomly selected five reference dialogues from each of the considered datasets: MultiWOZ[1], JILDA[2], and WIRED. Using the *one-shot* and *interactive* dialogue generation methods described in Sect. 3.1, we prompted ChatGPT to produce two additional versions of each reference dialogue, resulting in 10 generated dialogues per dataset and a total of 45 dialogues including the reference

---

[1] SNG0548, SNG01611, SNG01425, SNG0524 and SSNG0007.

[2] b2, b3, b4, b5 and b22, since they all share the same knowledge base of job offers.

dialogues. We asked 10 AMT workers to evaluate the overall quality of each dialogue using the questionnaire described in Sect. 3.3. For rating the JILDA dialogues, we created an Italian version of the questionnaire. Additional details are provided in Appendix B, which includes an example of how evaluators were presented with the task. To facilitate results analysis, we converted the verbal scale to numerical values ranging from -3 (corresponding to "strongly disagree") to $+3$ (corresponding to "strongly agree"). Table 1 presents the average quality scores for the three datasets, including the reference dialogue and the two versions generated by ChatGPT (one-shot generation and interactive generation). Notably, the quality of both human dialogues (score $= 1.96$) and dialogues fully generated by ChatGPT (score $= 1.92$) was perceived by our annotators as substantially equivalent. This result was consistent across the six dimensions considered in the questionnaire. Additionally, the quality of dialogues generated through interaction between ChatGPT and a human (score $= 1.84$) was substantially equivalent to that of human-generated dialogues. We conducted a test to determine whether the difference in quality between the one-shot and interactive generations was statistically significant with respect to the corresponding reference dialogues. Results, reported in Table 1, show that there was no significant difference in quality score for almost all of generated dialogues (the only exception is for MultiWoz one-shot), confirming ChatGPT's capacity to generate human-like dialogues. As expected, task-oriented dialogues in MultiWOZ and JILDA collaborative dialogues achieved higher quality than WIRED, likely due to the simpler structure of the dialogues (e.g., fewer turns). We also observe that the use of Italian for JILDA does not affect the quality of ChatGPT generation. The results obtained for the Italian dialogues are comparable to those obtained for the English dialogues, since language does not play as much of a role as the dialogue type in the experiment.

4.2   Assessing Hallucinations

We now assess the extent to which ChatGPT generates dialogues with hallucinating characteristics (see Sect. 3.3). Since the presence of hallucinations is judged by comparison against domain knowledge, we did not conduct the evaluation on the WIRED dataset, as it does not come with a knowledge base. For MultiWOZ and JILDA we considered both the one-shot and interactive versions. Results, Table 2, column "Hallucination Accuracy", show a relatively high adherence to the domain knowledge base, with only a few instances of hallucinations. As an example, in the MultiWOZ one-shot experiment, the user requested a Chinese restaurant, but the system suggested a Modern European one; in the interactive setting, ChatGPT mentioned two restaurants that were not included in the domain knowledge. While ChatGPT remains adherent to the provided knowledge base in most of the cases, in a few cases (approximately three out of every 20 utterances), it returns responses that are highly incorrect. As future work, we plan to explore other types of hallucinations beyond those related to domain knowledge, such as hallucinations concerning annotations.

Table 2. Qualitative assessment of dialogue annotations: slot accuracy, joint goal accuracy, adherence to domain knowledge and to instructions for the MultiWoz and Jilda datasets; topic accuracy, goal accuracy, dialogue act accuracy, and average accuracy for the Wired dataset.

Dataset	Slot Accuracy	Joint Goal Accuracy	Halluc. Accuracy	Instructions Adherence
MultiWOZ_one-shot	0.88	0.50	0.89	0.83
MultiWOZ_Interactive	0.93	0.52	0.89	–
JILDA_one-shot	0.71	0.03	1	0.92
JILDA_Interactive	0.73	0.05	0.82	–
Dataset	Topic Macro-F1	Goal Macro-F1	Dial. act Macro-F1	Average Macro-F1
WIRED_one-shot	0.93	0.29	0.20	0.47
WIRED_Interactive	0.88	0.21	0.35	0.48

4.3 Evaluating Instruction Adherence

We followed the methodology described in Sect. 3.3 to measure ChatGPT's ability to adhere to prompt instructions related to the user goals. The WIRED dataset could not be used for this evaluation, as it does not provide specific instructions. Similarly, we could not consider dialogues generated through the interactive method, as the user's turns are not generated by ChatGPT. While results (Table 2 column "Instruction Adherence") confirm that prompting can properly condition the model generation (MultiWOZ 0.83, JILDA 0.92) we report the presence of macroscopic and critical errors. For example, in JILDA, one of the generated dialogues had the user claiming to possess certain skills that were not mentioned in the instructions. In another case, in MultiWOZ, the user made a reservation for a date and time that did not correspond to what was specified in the instructions.

4.4 Dialogue Annotations

To assess ChatGPT's ability to generate proper semantic annotations we used the metrics described in Sect. 3.3. Table 2 shows the results of generated annotations both for the one-shot and interactive dialogues previously generated by ChatGPT (Sect. 3.1). As for MultiWOZ, slot-filling accuracy (i.e., 0.88 and 0.93 for, respectively, one-shot and interactive) is still relatively lower than current state of art of recent DST systems, which is around 0.99 [16, 42, 43].

As for JILDA dialogues, slot accuracy is considerably lower than MultiWoz. Slot filling hardly ever succeed in comprehensively identify each required slot and in correctly assigning each of the required values, resulting in extremely low JGA measure. Also the F1 measure for slot annotation (i.e., 0.49 and 0.43 for, respectively, one-shot and interactive) is significantly lower than those obtained by the model proposed in [37], which achieves 71.46. The discrepancy with MultiWoZ may be due to the longer length of the JILDA's dialogues, greater lexical variety and syntactic complexity, and the more intricate annotation schema.

Similarly, we believe the complexity of the annotation schema and the inherent difficulty of the dialogue metadata annotation task to motivate a discrepancy in results compared to [14] and [39], where ChatGPT is reported to outperform human annotators; however, the tasks there concerned, namely tweet classification and text classification are relatively simple, compared to the proposed dialogue annotation tasks.

As for Wired dialogues, we notice a discrepancy between the "Topic" dimension, which achieves very high scores, and the other two dimensions ("Goal" and "Dialogue act"). The "Topic" dimension beats the best performing model reported by [41] (0.52). This is certainly due to the smaller number of classes in the first dimension (4 vs. 10 classes) and also to the relative simplicity of detecting the relationship of a dialogue turn to the main topic, as opposed to the other tasks, where our experiments do not achieve SOTA results, but still perform much higher than a simple "majority" heuristic baseline, which would be 0.06 as reported by [41]. We hypothesize that prompt optimization, which would also include a clearer explanation of the single classes, would result in higher scores, but we leave a more in-depth analysis of this aspect as future work.

5   Conclusion

We presented an extensive human-based evaluation aimed at assessing both the quality of dialogues and of semantic annotations generated by ChatGPT. This is, to be the best of our knowledge, the first qualitative analysis that has been conducted on fully automatically generated dialogues. The experimental setup included three types of dialogues (task-oriented, collaborative, and explanation-based), two generation methods (interactive and one-shot), and two languages (English and Italian). Our findings demonstrate that the quality of the generated dialogues is comparable to corresponding human generated reference dialogues in available datasets. In this respect, ChatGPT can be considered as a good alternative to more expensive dialogue collection approaches, such as Wizard of Oz. On the other side, although dialogue annotation has shown a number of relevant limitations (some hallucinations, some instruction failing cases), we believe that such automatically annotated training data could be an excellent option for creating silver-data at low-cost, for a number of approaches, including data augmentation and domain adaptation techniques.

A   Appendix: Dialogue Examples

A.1   MultiWOZ Example

USER: "I am looking for an expensive Italian restaurant".

metadata: {"restaurant": {"pricerange": "expensive", "food": "Italian"}}

SYSTEM: "There is an expensive Italian restaurant named Frankie and Bennys at Cambridge Leisure Park Clifton Way Cherry Hinton. Would you like to go there or choose another?"

USER: "Great yeah that sounds great can you book a table for 5 people at 11:30 on Sunday?"

metadata: {"restaurant": {"pricerange": "expensive", "food": "Italian", "people": "5", "time": "11:30", "day": "Sunday"}}

SYSTEM: "Unfortunately there are no tables available, please try another day or time slot".
USER: "How about 10:30 on sunday ? And may I have a reference number?"

metadata: {"restaurant": {"pricerange": "expensive", "food": "Italian", "people": "5", "time": "10:30", "day": "Sunday"}}

SYSTEM: "I was able to book a table for 5 at 10:30 on Sunday. Your reference number is MBC9E6AL. Is there anything else I can help you with today?"
USER: "No, that is all. Thank you so much for your help".

metadata: {"restaurant": {"pricerange": "expensive", "food": "Italian", "people": "5", "time": "11:30", "day": "Sunday"}}

SYSTEM: "You're welcome. Good - bye".

A.2   JILDA Example

SYSTEM: "Buongiorno"
USER: "Buongiorno!"
SYSTEM: "Ciao, sono Giulia! Oggi sono qui per farti da Navigator. Di cosa sei alla ricerca?:)"
USER: "Ciao! Sto cercando lavoro come ricercatore".
SYSTEM: "Interessante! Dimmi, in quale settore sei specializzato?"
USER: "Sono specializzata in informatica e robotica, vorrei trovare lavoro in questi settori se possibile".
SYSTEM: "Sei alla ricerca di uno stage o preferiresti una posizione lavorativa più stabile?"
USER: "Preferirei una posizione più stabile, a tempo determinato o indeterminato".
SYSTEM: "Molto bene. Dimmi, hai già esperienze lavorative nel settore?"
USER: "Purtroppo non ho esperienze in azienda, ma ho un dottorato in Ingegneria Robotica".
SYSTEM: "Perfetto! Puoi dirmi quali sono i linguaggi di programmazione e i software con cui hai più confidenza?"
USER: "Certo! So programmare molto bene in C++, java e PhP".
SYSTEM: "Ok, hai conoscenze di javascript, MySQL e bash Linux?"
USER: "Li conosco molto superficialmente".
SYSTEM: "Ok, dalle informazioni che mi hai dato ho trovato un lavoro che potrebbe interessarti. Un'azienda estera sta cercando una persona che ricopra il ruolo di software engineer. L'annuncio specifica che preferirebbero una persona con esperienze lavorative pregresse in questo settore, saresti comunque interessato a candidarti?"

USER: "Sì, potrebbe interessarmi. Di che cosa si occupa l'azienda?"

SYSTEM: "Non viene specificato. Tuttavia il ruolo che dovresti ricoprire consisterebbe nello sviluppare un nuovo progetto in tutte le sue fasi (Design + Coding + Test + Packaging + Delivery) oltre ad aggiornare i progetti esistenti. Specificano comunque che il lavoro offre la possibilità ai lavoratori di esprimere la propria creatività rispetto a prodotti usati ogni giorno da milioni di persone".

USER: "Interessante. Come si chiama l'azienda?"

SYSTEM: "Il nome dell'azienda è Jobtome, una start up formata da circa 50 persone. Vuoi che ti dia il loro contatto?"

USER: "Sì, grazie. Così poi posso contattarli direttamente io".

SYSTEM: "info@azienda.com. Hai bisogno di altre informazioni?"

USER: "Al momento no, grazie".

SYSTEM: "Spero di esserti stata d'aiuto! Buona giornata:)"

USER: "Sì, sei stata molto gentile! Buona giornata anche a te:)"

A.3   WIRED Example

EXPERT: Hi.

CHILD: Hi.

EXPERT: I'm Hilary, what's your name?

CHILD: I'm Brynn.

EXPERT: Do you know what machine learning means? Have you heard that before?

CHILD: No.

EXPERT: So machine learning is a way that we teach computers to learn things about the world by looking at patterns and looking at examples of things. So can I show you an example of how a machine might learn something?

CHILD: Sure.

EXPERT: [Hilary] So is this a dog or a cat?

CHILD: It's a dog.

EXPERT: And this one?

CHILD: A cat.

EXPERT: And what makes a dog, a dog and a cat, a cat?

CHILD: Well, dogs are very playful, I think, more than cats. Cats lick themselves more than dogs, I think.

EXPERT: That's true. Do you think, if we look at these pictures, do you think maybe we could say, Well, they both have pointy ears, but the dogs have a different kind of body and the cats like to stand up a little different.? Do you think that makes sense?

CHILD: Yeah. Yeah.

EXPERT: What about this one?

CHILD: A dog. A cat. I think, a cat? Because it's more skinny. And also, its legs are like really tall and its ears are a little pointy.

EXPERT: This one's a jackal. And it's actually a kind of dog. But you made a good guess. That's what machines do too. They make guesses. Is this a cat or a dog?

CHILD: [Brynn] None.

EXPERT: [Hilary] None. What is it?

CHILD: It's humans.

EXPERT: And how did you know that it's not a cat or a dog?

CHILD: Because cats and dogs... Because they walk on their paws and their ears are like right here, not right here, and they don't wear watches.

EXPERT: And so, you did something pretty amazing there. Because we asked the question, Is it a cat or a dog? And you said, I disagree with your question. It's a human. So machine learning is when we teach machines to make guesses about what things are based on looking at a lot of different examples. And I build products that use machine learning to learn about the world and make guesses about things in the world. When we try to teach machines to recognize things like cats and dogs, it takes a lot of examples. We have to show them tens of thousands or even millions of examples before they can get even close to as good at it as you are. Do you have tests in school?

CHILD: Yeah, I have. After every unit, we have a review and then we have a test.

EXPERT: Are those like the practice problems you do before the test?

CHILD: Well, just like everything that's gonna be on the test is on the review.

EXPERT: Which means that in the test, you're not seeing any problems that you don't know how to solve. As long as you did all your practice, right?

CHILD: Yeah.

EXPERT: So machines work the same way. If you show them a lot of examples and give them practice, they'll learn how to guess. And then when you give them the test, they should be able to do that. So we looked at eight pictures and you were able to answer really quickly. But what would you do if I gave you 10 million examples? Would you be able to do that so quickly?

CHILD: No.

EXPERT: So one of the differences between people and machines is that people might be a little better at this, but can't look at 10 million different things. So now that we've been talking about machine learning, is this something you want to learn how to do?

CHILD: Kind of. Because I kind of want to become a spy. And we used to do coding, so I may be kind of good at it.

EXPERT: And machine learning is a great way to use all those math skills, all those coding skills, and would be a super cool tool for a spy.

B   Appendix: Questionnaire Used to Assess Dialogue Quality: Statements and Verbal Tags

B.1   English Version

Statements:

1. Requests and responses are consistent across the dialogue.
2. The information that is exchanged by participants in the dialogue is realistic.

3. The level of formality shown by the two participants is consistent throughout the dialogue.
4. Participants are respectful towards each other (no offensive/discriminatory language is used).
5. The participants' sentences sound spontaneous and natural in the dialogue.
6. The dialogue comes to a conclusion.

Items:

Strongly disagree, Disagree, Somewhat disagree, Somewhat agree, Agree, Strongly Agree.

B.2 Italian Version

Affermazioni:

1. Le richieste e le risposte nel dialogo sono coerenti.
2. Le informazioni che i partecipanti si scambiano nel dialogo sono realistiche.
3. Il livello di formalità dei due partecipanti è mantenuto costante per tutto il dialogo.
4. I partecipanti sono rispettosi l'uno verso l'altro (non usano linguaggio offensivo o discriminatorio).
5. Le frasi dei partecipanti sono spontanee e naturali nel contesto del dialogo.
6. Il dialogo arriva ad una conclusione.

Items:

Fortemente in disaccordo, In disaccordo, Leggermente in disaccordo, Leggermente d'accordo, D'accordo, Fortemente d'accordo.

C Appendix: Prompts Used for Dialogue Generation

C.1 One-Shot Approach

JILDA Create a dialogue between a user and a system in Italian. The user asks for information on job offers in order to find a suitable one for himself or herself and the system, called Navigator, asks the user all the needed information, tells the user whether there is availability for the skills, requests of the user and finally matches the job offer, giving the company e-mail address as contact. Every user message should be followed by a system message. Be polite and don't forget to say goodbye. Everything said by the system needs to be strictly coherent to the knowledge base that I provide you, and everything said by the user needs to be strictly coherent to the user's CV that I provide you.

Knowledge base:
Job offers:

1. job_description1
2. job_description2
3. job_description3

4. job_description4
5. job_description5

User CV:
user_cv_D1

WIRED Create a dialogue between an Explainer (a University teacher) and an Explainee. The Explainer and the Explainee hold a conversation on a topic where the Explainer is an expert. The dialogue is a spoken dialogue. The dialogue is explanatory: this means that each turn has a relation to the main topic (e.g. main topic, subtopic, related topic, ...), performs a dialogue act (e.g. check question, agreeing statement, informing statement, ...), and makes an explanation move (e.g. test understanding, request explanation, provide explanation, ...).

The dialogue needs to comply to the knowledge base that I provide to you.

Knowledge base: Explainer is a machine learning scientist. Explainee is a computer scientist named Claudia. Explainee asks about: the Explainer's view on the democratization of machine learning and avaialbility of tools, open questions in the ethics of machine learning, applications of machine learning in fields like agriculture, Explainer asks about: things that are holding back from applying machine learning to fields useful to society Explainer talks about: democratization and accessibility of tools in machine learning, representativeness of data, reproducibility, future of machine learning Explainee talks about: transparency in machine learning, biases in data, students nowadays

The dialogue should be friendly, informative, and provide details and examples. It should be around 15 turns, and turns can be somehow long. Don't forget to greet at the beginning.

C.2 Interactive Approach

JILDA Simulate to be a system and respond to a user in Italian. The user asks for information on job offers in order to find a suitable one for himself or herself and the system, called Navigator, asks the user all the needed information, tells the user whether there is availability for the skills, requests of the user and finally matches the job offer, giving the company e-mail address as contact. Every user message should be followed by a system message. Be polite and don't forget to say goodbye. Everything said by the system needs to be strictly coherent to the knowledge base that I provide to you.
Knowledge base:
Job offers:

1. job_description1
2. job_description2
3. job_description3
4. job_description4
5. job_description5

User CV:
user_cv_D1
I will start acting like a user needing of information about job offers starting
from my next message.

WIRED Let's play a roleplay. We simulate a dialogue between a system, called
the Explainer (pretending to be a University teacher) and an Explainee. You
play the system (the Explainer), and start with the first turn, and I play the
Explainee. Please DO NOT write sentences for both turns: you must ONLY play
the Explainer, and start the conversation. Then you wait for me to respond.

We hold a conversation on a topic where you are an expert. The dialogue
is explanatory: this means that each turn has a relation to the main topic (e.g.
main topic, subtopic, related topic, ...), performs a dialogue act (e.g. check question, agreeing statement, informing statement, ...), and makes an explanation
move (e.g. test understanding, request explanation, provide explanation, ...).
The dialogue needs to comply to the following information:

Explainer (you): "machine learning scientist". Explainee (me): "computer
scientist" named Claudia. Possible topics: democratization and accessibility of
tools in machine learning, representativeness of data, reproducibility, future of
machine learning, applications of machine learning to fields useful to society,
transparency in machine learning, biases in data, students nowadays, the democratization of machine learning, availability of tools, ethics of machine learning,
applications of machine learning in socially relevant fields.

D   Appendix: Prompts Used for Dialogue Annotation

JILDA Write annotations about a dialogue that I will send you. The annotations
have to follow this format: metadata: {slot_name1: slot_value1, slot_name2:
slot_value2, slot_value3, slot_name3, ...}
The possible slots are: "job_description" (description of the job offered), "contract" (type of contract of the job offer), "duties" (the main duties of the job
position), "skills" (skills requested for the job), "past_experience" (past experience required for the job), "degree" (degree or qualification required for the job),
"age" (age required for the job), "language" (knowledge of foreign languages),
"area" (the field where the company operates), "company_name" (the name of
the company), "company_size" (the number of workers in the company), "location" (the place where the company is).
The annotations are cumulative and need to keep track of all information that
has been provided or selected only by the User until that moment of the conversation.
Example of dialog:
example_dialogue
Example of annotations:
example_annotation
The dialogue that you have to annotate is the following:

dialogue_ D1
Annotate only the User's turns.

References

1. Anderson, A.H., et al.: The HCRC map task corpus. Lang. Speech **34**(4), 351–366 (1991). https://doi.org/10.1177/002383099103400404
2. Balaraman, V., Sheikhalishahi, S., Magnini, B.: Recent neural methods on dialogue state tracking for task-oriented dialogue systems: a survey. In: Proceedings of the 22nd Annual Meeting of the Special Interest Group on Discourse and Dialogue, pp. 239–251. Association for Computational Linguistics, Singapore and Online (2021). https://aclanthology.org/2021.sigdial-1.25
3. Brown, T.B., et al.: Language models are few-shot learners (2020). https://doi.org/10.48550/ARXIV.2005.14165, https://arxiv.org/abs/2005.14165
4. Budzianowski, P., et al.: MultiWOZ - a large-scale multi-domain Wizard-of-Oz dataset for task-oriented dialogue modelling. In: Proceedings of the 2018 Conference on Empirical Methods in Natural Language Processing, pp. 5016–5026. Association for Computational Linguistics, Brussels, Belgium (2018). https://doi.org/10.18653/v1/D18-1547, https://aclanthology.org/D18-1547
5. Cawsey, A.: Explanatory dialogues. Interact. Comput. **1**(1), 69–92 (1989). https://doi.org/10.1016/0953-5438(89)90008-8, https://www.sciencedirect.com/science/article/pii/0953543889900088
6. Christiano, P.F., Leike, J., Brown, T., Martic, M., Legg, S., Amodei, D.: Deep reinforcement learning from human preferences. In: Advances in Neural Information Processing Systems, vol. 30 (2017)
7. Chyung, S.Y., Roberts, K., Swanson, I., Hankinson, A.: Evidence-based survey design: the use of a midpoint on the Likert scale. Perform. Improv. **56**(10), 15–23 (2017)
8. Cohen, A.D., et al.: LaMDA: language models for dialog applications. arXiv (2022)
9. Devlin, J., Chang, M.W., Lee, K., Toutanova, K.: BERT: pre-training of deep bidirectional transformers for language understanding. arXiv preprint arXiv:1810.04805 (2018)
10. Dey, S., Kummara, R., Desarkar, M.S.: Towards fair evaluation of dialogue state tracking by flexible incorporation of turn-level performances. arXiv preprint arXiv:2204.03375 (2022)
11. Ding, B., Qin, C., Liu, L., Bing, L., Joty, S., Li, B.: Is GPT-3 a good data annotator? (2022). https://doi.org/10.48550/ARXIV.2212.10450, https://arxiv.org/abs/2212.10450
12. Gamer, M., Lemon, J., Fellows, I., Singh, S.: Various coefficients of interrater reliability and agreement (2019). https://CRAN.R-project.org/package=irr. R package version 0.84.1
13. Garland, R.: The mid-point on a rating scale: is it desirable. Mark. Bull. **2**(1), 66–70 (1991)
14. Gilardi, F., Alizadeh, M., Kubli, M.: ChatGPT outperforms crowd-workers for text-annotation tasks. arXiv preprint arXiv:2303.15056 (2023)
15. Gilardi, F., Alizadeh, M., Kubli, M.: ChatGPT outperforms crowd workers for text-annotation tasks. Proc. Natl. Acad. Sci. **120**(30), e2305016120 (2023). https://doi.org/10.1073/pnas.2305016120, https://www.pnas.org/doi/abs/10.1073/pnas.2305016120

16. Guo, J., Shuang, K., Zhang, K., Liu, Y., Li, J., Wang, Z.: Learning to imagine: distillation-based interactive context exploitation for dialogue state tracking. In: Proceedings of the AAAI Conference on Artificial Intelligence, vol. 37, pp. 12845–12853 (2023)
17. Howard, J., Ruder, S.: Universal language model fine-tuning for text classification. arXiv preprint arXiv:1801.06146 (2018)
18. Huang, F., Kwak, H., An, J.: Is ChatGPT better than human annotators? Potential and limitations of ChatGPT in explaining implicit hate speech. ArXiv abs/2302.07736 (2023)
19. Ji, Z., et al.: Survey of hallucination in natural language generation. ACM Comput. Surv. **55**, 1–38 (2022)
20. Kelley, J.F.: An empirical methodology for writing user-friendly natural language computer applications. In: Proceedings of the SIGCHI Conference on Human Factors in Computing Systems, CHI 1983, pp. 193–196. Association for Computing Machinery, New York (1983). https://doi.org/10.48550/ARXIV.2005.14165, https://arxiv.org/abs/2005.14165
21. Krippendorff, K.: Computing Krippendorff's alpha-reliability (2011)
22. Lietz, P.: Research into questionnaire design: a summary of the literature. Int. J. Mark. Res. **52**(2), 249–272 (2010)
23. Liu, P., Yuan, W., Fu, J., Jiang, Z., Hayashi, H., Neubig, G.: Pre-train, prompt, and predict: a systematic survey of prompting methods in natural language processing. CoRR abs/2107.13586 (2021). https://arxiv.org/abs/2107.13586
24. Liu, P., Yuan, W., Fu, J., Jiang, Z., Hayashi, H., Neubig, G.: Pre-train, prompt, and predict: a systematic survey of prompting methods in natural language processing. ACM Comput. Surv. (CSUR) **55**, 1–35 (2021)
25. Louvan, S., Magnini, B.: Recent neural methods on slot filling and intent classification for task-oriented dialogue systems: a survey. In: Proceedings of the 28th International Conference on Computational Linguistics, pp. 480–496. International Committee on Computational Linguistics, Barcelona (Online) (2020). https://doi.org/10.18653/v1/2020.coling-main.42, https://aclanthology.org/2020.coling-main.42
26. McTear, M.: Conversational AI: dialogue systems, conversational agents, and chatbots. Synthesis Lect. Hum. Lang. Technol. **13**(3), 1–251 (2020)
27. Moore, J.D.: Participating in Explanatory Dialogues: Interpreting and Responding to Questions in Context. MIT Press, Cambridge (1994)
28. OpenAI: Introducing ChatGPT. OpenAI Blog (2022). https://openai.com/blog/chatgpt
29. Ouyang, L., et al.: Training language models to follow instructions with human feedback (2022). https://doi.org/10.48550/ARXIV.2203.02155, https://arxiv.org/abs/2203.02155
30. Ouyang, L., et al.: Training language models to follow instructions with human feedback. arXiv preprint arXiv:2203.02155 (2022)
31. Pangakis, N., Wolken, S., Fasching, N.: Automated annotation with generative AI requires validation. arXiv preprint arXiv:2306.00176 (2023)
32. R Core Team: R: A language and environment for statistical computing. R Foundation for Statistical Computing, Vienna, Austria (2021). https://www.R-project.org/
33. Radford, A., et al.: Language models are unsupervised multitask learners. OpenAI Blog **1**(8), 9 (2019)

34. Raffel, C., et al.: Exploring the limits of transfer learning with a unified text-to-text transformer. J. Mach. Learn. Res. **21**(140), 1–67 (2020). http://jmlr.org/papers/v21/20-074.html
35. Reiss, M.V.: Testing the reliability of ChatGPT for text annotation and classification: a cautionary remark. arXiv preprint arXiv:2304.11085 (2023)
36. Rohlfing, K.J., et al.: Explanation as a social practice: toward a conceptual framework for the social design of ai systems. IEEE Trans. Cogn. Dev. Syst. **13**(3), 717–728 (2021). https://doi.org/10.1109/TCDS.2020.3044366
37. Sucameli, I., De Quattro, M., Eshghi, A., Suglia, A., Simi, M.: Dialogue act and slot recognition in Italian complex dialogues. In: Proceedings of the Workshop on Resources and Technologies for Indigenous, Endangered and Lesser-resourced Languages in Eurasia within the 13th Language Resources and Evaluation Conference, pp. 51–60 (2022)
38. Sucameli, I., Lenci, A., Magnini, B., Speranza, M., Simi, M.: Toward data-driven collaborative dialogue systems: the JILDA dataset. Ital. J. Comput. Linguist. **7**, 67–90 (2021)
39. Törnberg, P.: ChatGPT-4 outperforms experts and crowd workers in annotating political twitter messages with zero-shot learning. arXiv preprint arXiv:2304.06588 (2023)
40. Touvron, H., et al.: Llama 2: open foundation and fine-tuned chat models (2023)
41. Wachsmuth, H., Alshomary, M.: "Mama always had a way of explaining things so I could understand": a dialogue corpus for learning to construct explanations. In: Proceedings of the 29th International Conference on Computational Linguistics, pp. 344–354. International Committee on Computational Linguistics, Gyeongju (2022). https://aclanthology.org/2022.coling-1.27
42. Xie, H., et al.: Correctable-DST: mitigating historical context mismatch between training and inference for improved dialogue state tracking. In: Proceedings of the 2022 Conference on Empirical Methods in Natural Language Processing, pp. 876–889 (2022)
43. Ye, F., Feng, Y., Yilmaz, E.: ASSIST: towards label noise-robust dialogue state tracking. arXiv preprint arXiv:2202.13024 (2022)
44. Ye, F., Manotumruksa, J., Yilmaz, E.: MultiWOZ 2.4: a multi-domain task-oriented dialogue dataset with essential annotation corrections to improve state tracking evaluation. arXiv preprint arXiv:2104.00773 (2021)
45. Zhang, T., Kishore, V., Wu, F., Weinberger, K.Q., Artzi, Y.: BERTScore: evaluating text generation with BERT. arXiv preprint arXiv:1904.09675 (2019)
46. Zhu, Y., Zhang, P., Haq, E.U., Hui, P., Tyson, G.: Can ChatGPT reproduce human-generated labels? A study of social computing tasks. arXiv preprint arXiv:2304.10145 (2023)

Scaling Large Language Models to the Extreme: Neural Semantic Processing of Multiple Tasks in Italian

Claudiu D. Hromei[1(✉)], Danilo Croce[1(✉)], Valerio Basile[2(✉)], and Roberto Basili[1(✉)]

[1] University of Rome, Tor Vergata, Rome, Italy
hromei@ing.uniroma2.it, {croce,basili}@info.uniroma2.it
[2] Università di Torino, Turin, Italy
valerio.basile@unito.it

Abstract. This paper explores the potential of utilizing a unified neural model to tackle multiple and complex semantic processing tasks in the Italian language. We applied a state-of-the-art instruction-tuned Decoder-only Large Language Model to the recent EVALITA 2023 [17] challenge, which encompassed 13 different tasks and 22 subtasks across diverse semantic dimensions, such as Affect Detection, Authorship Analysis, Computational Ethics, Named Entity Recognition, Information Extraction, and Discourse Coherence. Our approach focuses on representing tasks using natural language instructions, for which prompts to the model are designed able to define the process as well as the desired responses. Notably, this single neural model achieved first place in 41% of the subtasks and demonstrated top-three performance in 64% of them. A dedicated experiment was also conducted to investigate the degree of linguistic generalization achieved by the LLM specifically, through instruction-tuning it with limited sets of training data. Results suggest that instruction-tuning is still required to capture dependencies between input and output even in such LLMs.

Keywords: Large Language Models · Multi-task Learning · Semantic Processing Task · Affect Detection · Authorship Analysis · Computational Ethics · Named Entity Recognition · Information Extraction · and Discourse Coherence

1 Introduction

Over the past few years, there has been significant interest in Large Language Models (LLMs) due to their exceptional performance across a wide range of natural language processing (NLP) tasks. Not only have LLMs like T5 [26], mT5 [38], IT5 [33], and FlanT5 [10] achieved state-of-the-art results in individual tasks, but they have also demonstrated remarkable capabilities in solving various tasks individually and collectively through multi-task training methods, even in a zero-shot learning scenario [31]. Simultaneously, models such as GPT [25] and GPT3 [7], known for their generative power, as well as the emergence of foundational models like LLaMA [35], have opened up new possibilities for utilizing the concept of "prompting". This approach allows

R. Basili et al. (Eds.): AIxIA 2023, LNAI 14318, pp. 172–186, 2023.
https://doi.org/10.1007/978-3-031-47546-7_12

inductive tasks to be modeled linguistically, using natural language queries or instructions, enabling accurate responses from the model. By combining the strengths of LLMs and the prompting technique, the need for task-specific neural architectures or ad hoc feature engineering can be alleviated. In this paper, we introduce `ExtremITA`, an approach applied to the whole set of EVALITA 2023 [17] challenges. It consists in adopting a unique model and making it capable of addressing a diverse set of tasks by training a Decoder-only model on the combined datasets available for the challenge. Through multi-task learning, we assess the effectiveness of a single model in solving multiple tasks simultaneously. The EVALITA challenge provided an ideal context for evaluating the capabilities of LLMs across various tasks over texts in Italian, with no specific architectural requirements. We prompt the model with task-specific queries such as *"Does this text mention any conspiracy? Answer yes or no"* or *"On a scale of 0 to 5, how much coherent is the following paragraph?"*. An in-depth analysis of the resulting model allows us to evaluate the ability of such LLMs to effectively solve different tasks under different scenarios (e.g. increasing amount of available training examples). The tasks in which the `ExtremITA` approach participated cover an overall wide range of semantic dimensions, including Affect Detection, Authorship Analysis, Computational Ethics, Named Entity Recognition, Information Extraction, and Discourse Coherence: *i)* EMit - Categorical Emotion Detection in Italian Social Media [3]; *ii)* EmotivITA - Dimensional and Multi-dimensional emotion analysis [13]; *iii)* PoliticIT - Political Ideology Detection in Italian Texts [28]; *iv)* GeoLingIt - Geolocation of Linguistic Variation in Italy [27]; *v)* LangLearn - Language Learning Development [2]; *vi)* HaSpeeDe 3 - Political and Religious Hate Speech Detection [16]; *vii)* HODI - Homotransphobia Detection in Italian [21]; *viii)* MULTI-Fake-DetectiVE - MULTImodal Fake News Detection and VErification [6]; *ix)* ACTI - Automatic Conspiracy Theory Identification [29, 30]; *x)* NERMuD - Named-Entities Recognition on Multi-Domain Documents [23]; *xi)* CLinkaRT - Linking a Lab Result to its Test Event in the Clinical Domain [1]; *xii)* WiC-ITA - Word-in-Context task for Italian [9]; *xiii)* DisCoTEX - Assessing DIScourse COherence in Italian TEXts [8]. Among the 13 tasks and 22 subtasks, `ExtremITA`, a single monolithic architecture based on LLaMA [35], achieved first place in 9 subtasks (41%) and ranked within the top three in 14 subtasks (64%): this demonstrates its effectiveness and large applicability. Recent work [11] further confirms this evidence on other languages.

The rest of the paper is organized as follows: Sect. 2 presents the related work. Section 3 describes the LLMs used in our approach. Section 4 presents the results along with a brief error analysis. Finally, Sect. 5 provides the conclusions.

2   Related Work

Several studies, such as [7], have demonstrated the few-shot learning capabilities of the Language Models. These models exhibit the ability to generalize information from a limited number of input examples given through prompting, producing coherent and accurate output. Motivated by these findings and those of a recent work [4], we investigate here the training of a unique Transformer-based model in a multi-task setting to solve a wide range of tasks by extremely increasing the number of tasks they are trained on. The Transformer architecture [36] can be divided into two main components, each giving rise to distinct families of models. The encoder, represented by BERT [12], RoBERTa [19], and DeBERTa [14], is responsible for encoding input sequences and generating meaningful representations (embeddings) using the self-attention mechanism. On the other hand, the decoder, exemplified by models like GPT [25], GPT3 [7], and LLaMA [35], generates output sequences in an auto-regressive manner based on the input and previously generated output tokens. BLOOM [37] is a particular Decoder-only Transformer Language Model that was trained in multitask-prompted scenarios in order to achieve strong performance on a variety of benchmarks. Additionally, there exists another family of models, the Encoder-Decoder models, such as T5 [26] and BART [18], which combine the strengths of both the encoder and decoder components. These models maintain the integration of the two aforementioned blocks and are typically used in tasks like machine translation, summarization, and question-answering, where complex input understanding and transduction are required. A notable application of an Encoder-Decoder architecture in a multi-task scenario is presented in [26]. Specifically, the pre-training process of the T5 model involves training it on a diverse text corpus derived from various sources, including books, articles, and websites, as well as texts related to machine translation, classification, and regression tasks. During pre-training, T5 employs a denoising objective, similar to other popular Transformer-based models like BERT and GPT. The model is trained to reconstruct masked or corrupted input text, aiding in the learning of meaningful representations and the capture of contextual information. T5's key strength lies in its versatility: by formulating different NLP tasks in a text-to-text format, it can be fine-tuned for a specific task by simply providing a prefix that describes the task and appropriate input-output pairs during fine-tuning. In practice, this architecture can be exploited by concatenating the task name with an input text, generating the expected solution in the output, such as a class label in a classification task or a text span that answers a question. This flexibility eliminates the need for task-specific architectures or modifications, making it easier to apply T5 in various scenarios. Recently, this model has been applied to hundreds of tasks in [11], while [10,31] demonstrate its effectiveness in "zero-shot" or "few-shot" learning scenarios. On the other hand, Decoder-only models are typically trained to be triggered by text, such as natural language requests or text intended for processing. These models generate text step by step, producing output that can serve as an answer to a question or a solution to given tasks or requests. The ability to effectively follow instructions is exemplified by the recent release of ChatGPT[1]. This characteristic holds greater appeal as tasks can be linguistically described using prompts, where the input sentence provides contextual information. InstructGPT [22] is an extension of the GPT [7] language model specifically designed to excel in multi-task scenarios when used with prompts. It combines the power of language models with the ability to follow instructions provided in the form of natural language prompts. Unlike conventional language models that generate text freely, InstructGPT is fine-tuned using human feedback to understand and generate text based on a given prompt and select the best sequence that humans would prefer. The process of following instructions is also known as *instruction-tuning*. Another language model that employs this instruction-tuning technique is Alpaca [34],

---

[1] https://openai.com/blog/chatgpt.

which builds upon the LLaMA [35] foundational models. In the case of Alpaca, the authors created 175 sets of English instructions, input sentences, and corresponding outputs. These were then used as seeds to generate variations using GPT 3.5, resulting in a collection of approximately 52, 000 instruction examples. The LLaMA model was further fine-tuned using this extensive dataset, a process referred to as instruction-tuning to produce Stanford Alpaca. More recently, an Italian counterpart called Camoscio [32] underwent a similar instruction-tuning process to Alpaca but using Italian data, effectively serving as the Italian equivalent. It is based on the same LLaMA model and was instruction-tuned using the 52, 000 instructions that were automatically translated into Italian using ChatGPT. As the size of these models continues to grow, reaching trillions of parameters, there is a need to effectively fine-tune them using modest GPU resources. The technique adopted in this paper, known as Low-Rank Adaptation (LoRA) [15], involves freezing the weights of the pre-trained model and introducing smaller trainable rank decomposition matrices into each layer of the Transformer architecture. This approach significantly reduces the number of trainable parameters for downstream tasks while avoiding additional inference latency.

3   Multi-task Instruction Tuning in ExtremITA

The approach adopted here for the EVALITA challenge focuses on efficiently modeling all available tasks using a single monolithic architecture, namely extremITLLaMA. This is an instruction-tuned Decoder-only model built upon the LLaMA foundational models[2], with a total of 7 billion parameters. The initial model was trained using the LoRA technique on Italian translations[3] of Alpaca instruction data, similar to the process undergone by Camoscio. This training enables the model to comprehend and follow instructions in Italian. After training the additional matrices, they are merged into the original model to create an instruction-based model (using the "merge" procedure from [15]). Finally, this model is further fine-tuned using LoRA on instructions that reflect the EVALITA task. For each example from EVALITA, an input text is paired with a manually crafted question simulating an instruction to be solved, accurately representing the specific task. The next section details how the 22 subtasks in EVALITA are encoded as prompts to fine-tune the architecture.

Prompt Engineering in ExtremITA. The methodology employed in this study takes inspiration from the original LLaMA foundational models. Similar to that approach, each instance used for training is transformed into a specific format consisting of an instruction, an input, and an output. In the case of extremITLLaMA, which is pre-trained to execute instructions, it utilizes a structured prompt containing a textual description of the task and the desired output format specification. For example, when applied to the ACTI task, the instruction provided is as follows: *"In this text, does the subject matter involve a conspiracy? Answer yes or no."*. The subsequent sentence to be evaluated is appended to this instruction. A comprehensive set of such instructions can be found in Table 1.

---

[2] https://huggingface.co/decapoda-research/llama-7b-hf.
[3] https://github.com/teelinsan/camoscio/tree/main/data.

Table 1. List of the natural language instruction definition for all tasks for the `extremITLLaMA` model.

Task Name	Natural language instruction
EMit A	*"Quali emozioni sono espresse in questo testo? Puoi scegliere una o più emozioni tra'rabbia','anticipazione','disgusto','paura','gioia','amore','tristezza','sorpresa','fiducia', o'neutro'."*
EMit B	*"Di cosa parla il testo, tra'direzione','argomento','entrambi','non specificato'?"*
EmotivITA	*"Scrivi quanta valenza è espressa in questo testo su una scala da 1 a 5, seguito da quanto stimolo è espresso in questo testo su una scala da 1 a 5, seguito da quanto controllo è espresso in questo testo su una scala da 1 a 5."*
PoliticIT	*"Scrivi se l'autore del testo è'uomo' o'donna', seguito dalla sua appartenenza politica tra'destra','sinistra','centrodestra','centrosinistra'."*
GeoLingIt	*"Scrivi la regione di appartenenza di chi ha scritto questo testo, seguito dalla latitudine, seguita dalla longitudine."*
LangLearn	*"Questi due testi separati da [SEP] sono presentati nell'ordine in cui sono stati scritti? Rispondi sì o no."*
HaSpeeDe 3	*"In questo testo si esprime odio? Rispondi sì o no."*
HODI A	*"In questo testo si esprime odio omotransfobico? Rispondi sì o no."*
HODI B	*"Con quali parole l'autore del testo precedente esprime odio omotransfobico? Separa le sequenze di parole con [gap]."*
MULTI-Fake -DetectiVE	*"L'evento riportato nel testo è'certamente vero','probabilmente vero','probabilmente falso', o'certamente falso'?"*
ACTI A	*"In questo testo si parla di una cospirazione? Rispondi sì o no."*
ACTI B	*"Di quale teoria cospirazionista parla questo testo, tra'Covid','Qanon','Terrapiattista','Russia'?"*
NERMuD	*"Scrivi le menzioni di entità nel testo, indicandone il tipo: [PER] (persona), [LOC] (luogo), [ORG] (organizzazione)."*
CLinkaRT	*"Trova i risultati dei test e delle misurazioni nel testo. Per ogni risultato, scrivi'[BREL]', seguito dal risultato seguito da'[SEP]', seguito dal test, seguito da'[EREL]'. Se non trovi nessun risultato, scrivi'[NOREL]'."*
WiC-ITA	*"La parola compresa tra [TGTS] e [TGTE] ha lo stesso significato in entrambe le frasi? Rispondi sì o no."*
DisCoTEX 1	*"Le due frasi precedenti, separate da'[SEP]', sono coerenti tra loro? Rispondi sì o no."*
DisCoTEX 2	*"Quanto è coerente questa frase, su una scala da 0 a 5?"*

The output varies depending on the specific task. For a comprehensive collection of outputs, please refer to Table 2. In binary classification tasks such as LangLearn, HaspeeDe 3, HODI A, ACTI A, WiC-ITA, and DisCoTEX 1, the model is expected to respond with either *"Yes"* or *"No"*. For instance, for the input *"Hanno votato tutti obbligo vaccinale, green pass, persecuzioni varie"* in the ACTI A task, the output would be *"Yes"* as the input text reflects a conspiracy theory. In classification tasks involving a single label, such as EMit B, MULTI-Fake-DetectiVE, and ACTI B, the output simply represents the label of the target class. For the same aforementioned input, the output for the ACTI B task would be *"Covid"* as it pertains to the Covid conspiracy theory. In certain tasks like PoliticIT [28], where a text is expected to be associated with the gender and political inclination of the author, multiple labels representing these different dimensions are used, e.g., *"male left center-left"*. In EMit A [3], where multiple emotions can be evoked, these emotions are provided as a sequence of labels. In regression tasks such as EmotivITA [13] and DisCoTEX 2 [8], the output is a number that needs to be predicted within a specific range. In GeoLingIt [27], the models are asked to detect the author's geographical region and the corresponding coordinates (latitude and longitude), solely based on the tweet. For example, the given prompt is: *"Write the region to which the author of this text belongs, followed by the latitude, followed by the longitude"*. If the input sentence is *"Daje che je'a famo!"*, the model should provide the answer *"Lazio 41.8984164 12.54514535"*, considering the use of typical Roman dialect. This particular task combines both multi-label classification and regression since it requires determining the region (classification) and providing precise coor-

Table 2. Output templates for `extremITLLaMA`. In EMit A the model is requested to generate one or more labels from the first set ($^{+}$) or the text *"Neutrale"* if no emotion is expressed.

Task	Output Templates
EMit A	{*"Rabbia"*, *"Anticipazione"*, *"Disgusto"*, *"Paura"*, *"Gioia"*, *"Amore"*, *"Tristezza"*, *"Sorpresa"*, *"Fiducia"*}$^{+}$ ∨ *"Neutrale"*
EMit B	{*"Direzione"*, *"Argomento"*, *"Entrambi"*, *"Non specificato"*}
EmotivITA	*"Valenza: {0–5} Stimolo: {0–5} Controllo: {0–5}"*
PoliticIT	*"Gender:* {*"Uomo"*, *"Donna"*} *PIB:* {*"Sinistra"*, *"Destra"*} *PIM:* {*"Sinistra"*, *"Destra"*, *"Centro Sinistra"*, *"Centro Destra"*}*"*
GeoLingIt	*"Regione:* {*Abruzzo, ..., Veneto*} *Latitudine:* {} *Longitudine:* {}*"*
LangLearn	{*"Sì"*, *"No"*}
HaSpeeDe 3	{*"Sì"*, *"No"*}
HODI A	{*"Sì"*, *"No"*}
HODI B	<HOMOTRANSPHOBIA_MENTION>
MULTI-Fake -DetectiVE	{*"Certamente Falso"*, *"Probabilmente Falso"*, *"Probabilmente Vero"*, *"Certamente Vero"*}
ACTI A	{*"Sì"*, *"No"*}
ACTI B	{*"Terrapiattista"*, *"Covid"*, *"Qanon"*, *"Russia"*}
NERMuD	[<ENTITY_TYPE>] <ENTITY_MENTION>
CLinkaRT	*"[BREL]* <RML_ENTITY_MENTION> *[SEP]* <EVENT_ENTITY_MENTION> *[EREL]"*
WiC-ITA	{*"Sì"*, *"No"*}
DisCoTEX 1	{*"Sì"*, *"No"*}
DisCoTEX 2	{0–5}

dinates (regression) simultaneously. In HODI B [21], where the objective is to extract the span of the offending text, the output simply consists of that span. In NERMuD [23], the expected list of Named Entities is reported as a sequence of text spans, each associated with the corresponding entity type. CLinkaRT [1] focuses on extracting the names of medical tests performed on patients from an input text and linking them to the corresponding test results, treating it as a Relation Extraction problem. Here, the relations are encoded using a slightly more complex form to summarize a list of relations, each associating an EVENT with a corresponding measure (or RML). As an example, the sentence *"Il PSA aumentava da 2 a 62 ng/ml."* is associated with *"[BREL] 2 [SEP] PSA [EREL] [BREL] 62 ng/ml [SEP] PSA [EREL]"* (where 2 and 62 represent the RML while PSA is the test event).

4   Experimental Evaluation

Experimental Setup. The training of the model utilized PyTorch and the Huggingface library, along with the PEFT [20] packages, to implement the LoRA [15] technique. The training was performed on a unified dataset that included all the tasks of EVALITA [17]. In general, each example in an EVALITA task corresponded to an example in our learning setup, with a few exceptions. For the ACTI task, the dataset was expanded, in order to increase its number in the overall training data, by incorporating some[4] sentences from dataset B, and vice versa. This resulted in an increase in the number of examples from 460 to 1,909 for ACTI A and from 300 to 777 for ACTI B. In the case of CLinkaRT, only long documents were available, so we segmented the medical reports

---

[4] Only the positive examples, i.e. the ones that involved any conspiracy theory, are added from the dataset A to B or vice versa.

into smaller parts for computational purposes using the Spacy library. The segmentation process respected sentence boundaries and resulted in a dataset expansion from 83 large documents to 3, 903 shorter sentences. Additionally, we augmented this dataset with examples from the dataset provided in TESTLINK@IberLEF 2023[5], which contained medical reports in Spanish. Although the language was different, these texts exhibited similar phenomena related to events and measures that are generally language invariant. This augmentation process recovered over 95% of annotated relations. For the EMit task, we converted emoji representations into textual descriptions to enhance compatibility with language models. In GeoLingIt, we modified the task to solve both task A and task B simultaneously, enabling a single prediction for both, as we thought that the model would benefit from the end-to-end prediction. In HODI B, we only considered sentences expressing homotransphobia, because we modeled this task as a rewriting process of spans of the input: if the sentence does not contain any homotransphobia content, there is no span to rewrite. The process resulted in a reduction from 5, 000 to 1, 914 examples. The dataset for the LangLearn task was truncated into sentences with a maximum of 100 tokens, for computational purposes. We also added additional examples with inverted sentence pairs, augmenting the dataset from 3, 377 to 6, 438 examples, in order to enhance the model capability of solving this task. In MULTI-Fake-DetectiVE, we disregarded images and removed duplicate examples with the same text but different images as we are dealing with Language Models, that are uni-modal. The process resulted in a decrease from 1, 058 examples to 860. The NERMuD task was transformed into a sequence-to-sequence task from its original token classification format to enhance compatibility with language models. For PoliticIT, each text was divided into sentences with a maximum length of 200 tokens for computational purposes, and a voting strategy was applied at classification time to select the final class for gender and political ideas, grouping sentences by the same author. Finally, the WiC-ITA dataset was expanded by including examples[6] with inverted sentence pairs while preserving the same label, resulting in an increase from 5, 610 to 6, 600 examples. The complete dataset consisted of a total of 134, 018 examples. The `extremITLLaMA` model underwent 2 epochs of training (over 144 hours) with a learning rate of $3 \cdot 10^{-4}$ and a batch size of 32. To optimize the model's performance, a linear scheduler with warmup was utilized, using a warmup ratio of 0.1. The training process employed LoRA to refine the transformer's W_q, W_k, W_v, and W_o modules, as in [15]. The LoRA matrices had a matrix rank R of 8 and a parameter α of 16. The training was performed on a single Tesla T4 GPUs with 16GB of memory. This is particularly interesting as we have implied the smallest available model, i.e. with 7-billion-parameters, to demonstrate that it can be used even on standard architectures. It doesn't rule out the possibility of evaluating larger models like LLaMA $30B$ or LLaMA $65B$, but currently, they require such computational power that would limit their applicability in real-world scenarios, due to their extensive training duration and memory requirements. Initially, the training data was split into a 95% training set and a 5% validation set for hyper-parameter optimization. The source code for reproducing the experiment and dataset generation is available on GitHub[7].

---

[5] https://e3c.fbk.eu/testlinkiberlef.

[6] Only the positive examples underwent sentence order flipping in order to rebalance the class distribution.

[7] https://github.com/crux82/ExtremITA.

Table 3. Performance and rank of our `extremITLLaMA` instruction-tuned model, the *0-shot Camoscio* model, and the *Best Competitor* (either that won or placed higher in the ranking) model for the task of EVALITA 2023. Here each task is divided into the subtasks we participated in. In bold the rank and the scores of the winning systems. The HM* measure for the DisCoTEX task refers to the Harmonic Mean between Pearson's and Spearman's correlations. The *"na"* value is due to missing the official evaluation scripts for the specific tasks at the time of paper writing.

Task	SubTask	Eval metric	extremITLLaMA Score	Rank	0-shot Camoscio Score	Best Competitor Score	Rank
EMit	A	F1	**0.6028**	**1**	0.0092	0.4994	3
	B	F1	**0.6459**	**1**	0.1325	0.6184	3
EmotivITA	B	Pears Val	**0.8110**	**1**	0.0000	0.8110	2
		Pears Aro	**0.6330**		0.0931	0.6520	
		Pears Dom	**0.6300**		0.0000	0.6540	
PoliticIT	-	F1	0.7719	3	0.2965	**0.8241**	**1**
GeoLingIt	A	F1	0.3818	11	0.0205	**0.6630**	**1**
	B	Avg Km	145.15	9	280.14	**97.74**	**1**
LangLearn	COWS	F1	0.5500	8	na	**0.7500**	**1**
	CITA	F1	0.6100	8	na	**0.9300**	**1**
HaSpeeDe 3	A	F1 - text	0.9034	3	0.3333	**0.9128**	**1**
		F1 - context	0.9034	3	0.3333	**0.9128**	**1**
	B	F1 - xRel	**0.6525**	**1**	0.4558	0.6461	2
		F1 - xPolitic	0.9034	3	0.3333	**0.9128**	**1**
HODI	A	F1	0.7942	5	0.3284	**0.8108**	**1**
	B	F1	**0.7228**	**1**	0.4790	0.7051	2
Multi-Fake -Detective	A	F1	0.5070	2	0.3800	**0.5120**	**1**
	ATD	F1	**0.4640**	**1**	0.2900	0.4600	2
ACTI	A	F1	0.8565	2	0.3306	**0.8571**	**1**
	B	F1	0.8556	5	0.1603	**0.9123**	**1**
NERMUD	DAC	F1	**0.8900**	**1**	na	na	na
CLinkaRT	-	F1	0.5916	2	na	**0.6299**	**1**
Wic-Ita	A	F1 it-it	0.5100	10	0.3333	**0.7300**	**1**
		F1 it-en	0.5400	8	0.3333	**0.7400**	**1**
	B	F1 all	0.5100	10	0.3333	**0.7300**	**1**
DisCoTEX	1	Acc	**0.8150**	**1**	na	0.7200	2
	2	HM*	**0.6500**	**1**	na	0.6300	2

Results Discussion. The experimental results are reported in Table 3. We presented the tasks categorized by sub-task, followed by the specific evaluation metric, and the scores and ranks achieved by the `extremITLLaMA` model, the 0-shot application of Camoscio (as this is the base of our model) and the best competitor. The best-performing method in terms of score and ranking for each subtask is highlighted in bold. Our system ranked first in 9 out of 22 subtasks (i.e., 41% of subtasks) in EVALITA 2023, and it ranks in the top-three position in 14 subtasks, i.e., 64% of all tasks. However, we faced challenges in tasks such as GeoLingIt, LangLearn, and WiC-Ita, where our monolithic architecture demonstrated limitations. These tasks specifically require a system to detect and analyze changes in the author's writing style or the contextual meaning of words. Our models are primarily designed for sentence classification or rewriting spans of input text to justify previous decisions (e.g., HODI). There are also important considerations regarding the computational cost of both training and inference. Training `extremITLLaMA` on the entire EVALITA dataset took over 144 hours. In terms of inference, it processes only 2 or 3 sentences per second. This significant delay in processing speed makes the `extremITLLaMA` model less practical using "standard" computational resources, despite its performance across a wide range of tasks. Overall, the above results are quite impressive, especially when considering that no task-specific architectural choice was applied. Instead, a single LLM was utilized, demonstrating competitive performance across almost all tasks. The key to achieving such results seems to lie in properly prompting the model with natural language requests or employing task-specific encoding techniques for the outputs. On the other hand, the 0-shot application of Camoscio showed poor performance in all tasks. This is to be expected as the model is not tuned but it is used as is, with the original instruction-tuning on the $52,000$ instructions from Alpaca. Most of the time, this model predicted the most frequent class or hallucinated by rewriting parts of the input text. It suggests, thus, that instruction-tuning using the natural language descriptions of the task is indeed necessary to guide the model in the generation of the answer. To conduct a more comprehensive evaluation and optimization, it would have been beneficial to explore a wider range of architectures and investigate all the hyper-parameters of the models. The estimation of these parameters was done hastily due to the time constraints imposed by the EVALITA deadlines and the extensive commitment required for the 13 tasks.

The Impact of Different Training Set Sizes. The `extremITLLaMA` model is trained using about one hundred thousand examples, with a significant portion (30-40%) com-

Table 4. Scores of different `extremITLLaMA` models, where 0, 100, 500 and *All* refer to the number of examples the models were trained on. Not all the tasks from EVALITA are reported in this table as some official evaluation scripts are missing at the time of paper writing and thus the evaluation could not be performed.

Task	SubTask	Eval metric	TOTAL examples	0	100	500	1000	All
EMit	A	F1	5688	0.0092	0.2438	0.3526	0.4440	0.6028
	B	F1		0.1325	0.4013	0.5797	0.4450	0.6459
EmotivITA	B	Pears Val	7608	0.0000	0.2115	0.6399	0.7043	0.8110
		Pears Aro		0.0931	-0.0218	0.3447	0.4398	0.6330
		Pears Dom		0.0000	0.1836	0.4441	0.5627	0.6300
PoliticIT	-	F1	16047	0.2965	0.3129	0.5956	0.5548	0.7719
GeoLingIt	A	F1	13669	0.0205	0.1163	0.1351	0.1523	0.3818
	B	Avg Km		280.14	277.32	281.14	267.48	145.15
LangLearn	COWS	macro-F1	320	0.3347	0.5428	0.4875	0.4804	0.5739
	CITA	macro-F1	307	0.3326	0.3725	0.4845	0.4918	0.5954
HaSpeeDe 3	A	F1 - text	5340	0.3333	0.4212	0.7239	0.8498	0.9034
		F1 - context		0.3333	0.4212	0.7239	0.8498	0.9034
	B	F1 - xRel		0.4558	0.5079	0.6199	0.6500	0.6525
		F1 - xPolitic		0.3333	0.4212	0.7239	0.8498	0.9034
HODI	A	F1	4770	0.3284	0.3653	0.6126	0.6606	0.7942
	B	F1	1914	0.4790	0.4831	0.5782	0.6122	0.7228
Multi-Fake- Detective	A	F1	860	0.3800	0.4200	0.4400	0.4700	0.5070
	ATD	F1		0.2900	0.4200	0.3900	0.4700	0.4640
ACTI	A	F1	1909	0.3306	0.6129	0.7850	0.7944	0.8565
	B	F1	777	0.1603	0.3691	0.8471	0.8440	0.8556
WiC-ITA	A	F1 it-it	5610	0.3333	0.3333	0.3333	0.3333	0.5100
		F1 it-en		0.3333	0.3378	0.3333	0.3333	0.5400
	B	F1 all		0.3333	0.3333	0.3333	0.3333	0.5100

ing from the NERMUD dataset. While LLaMA and its derived models, Alpaca and Camoscio, are intended to be used in a 0-shot manner, we conducted additional instruction tuning using the EVALITA data. In order to evaluate the model's generalization capabilities across these domains and its reliance on specific data, we conducted an experiment to analyze its learning curve based on different training set sizes. For this experiment on the EVALITA data, we followed the methodology outlined in Sect. 3 for instruction-tuning. We utilized up to 100, 500, and 1000 examples for each task, whenever available. Additionally, we used the 0-shot application of Camoscio as is, i.e. using 0 examples with no additional instruction-tuning. Table 4 displays the results for selected tasks, for which official evaluation scripts were available, categorized by the trained models: 0, 100, 500, 1000 and the "*All*" model, which corresponds to extremITLLaMA as it was trained using *all* the available data.

Unsurprisingly, the "*All*" model consistently outperforms the others. For instance, in the EMit task, where extremITLLaMA achieved first position in both subtasks, we observe an improvement in model performance as the training set size increases from 0 to 1000. This suggests that performance gains are directly linked to the size of the training set. This trend is observed in the majority of the tasks, such as EmotivITA, HaSpeeDe3, HODI, and ACTI. However, some tasks, such as WiC-ITA, seem to be more challenging, as the models often tend to produce responses aligned with the most frequent class. Tasks such as GeoLingIt show that even 1000 examples are not sufficient to capture the relations between the input and the output and the resulting performance is increasing, yet still poor. Note that for LangLearn we switched the evaluation metric from F1 of the positive class (used in the official script and in Table 3) to macro-average F1, to better capture the evaluation of biased models. In fact, the official metric for this task is artificially high for the 0-shot model even if it always outputs the positive label. Conversely, the 0-shot application of Camoscio performs the poorest. This model was developed to comprehend instructions, respond to queries, and fulfill requests using natural language, all while providing argumentation for its decisions. However, due to its design, it occasionally fails to strictly adhere to the provided instructions in the prompt before classifying examples. As a result, the generated text often deviates significantly from the intended output and the model struggles to accurately follow instructions and generate the desired output. This result highlights the significant challenges presented by EVALITA and emphasizes the continued importance of instruction-tuning for enhancing the performance of Large Language Models (LLMs) on complex tasks. Specifically, even with a Decoder-base and relatively smaller, more computationally efficient models like LLaMa 7B (as discussed in this paper), instruction-tuning applied to a consistent number of representative examples remains essential. Another interesting idea is to assess the few-shot learning capabilities of Language Models by leveraging a limited number of input-output pairs within the prompt. To evaluate this, we selected only the "HaSpeeDe 3" and "ACTI" tasks (due to space and time constraints, but this can be expanded in the future). "HaSpeeDe 3" involves binary classification to detect if the input text contains any form of hate speech. We utilized the Camoscio model without instruction-tuning but made modifications to the prompt by adding two examples, one randomly-selected example from the training set for each class. The resulting prompt, combined with the original task description (see Table 1), included a description of the examples as follows: "*This text contains hate:* <POSITIVE EXAMPLE>*, and* *you should answer yes. This text does not contain hate:* <Negative Example>, *and you should answer no.".* We then added the current example to be predicted. This few-shot version achieves an F1 measure of 0.4486, surpassing the fine-tuned version on 100 examples by more than 2%. This result confirms the few-shot learning capabilities of LLMs as they exhibit a remarkable ability to capture dependencies and relationships with just a few examples. Moreover, we evaluated the use of prompts by the 2-shot strategy over the model instruction-tuned on 100, 500, and 1000 examples, with results of 0.60, 0.67, and 0.83, respectively: this thus shows that a good increase in performance is observed at 100 examples (from 0.42 to 0.60) but then slightly poorer performances are obtained. We then applied the same strategy on the "ACTI" task, which involves detecting if a text concerns a conspiracy theory and the results are different: the 2-shot model shows an increase achieving 0.4819, while all the other versions (100, 500 and 1000) show a drop in performance. One reason could be that recognizing conspiracy aspects over a brief text may require capabilities that these models still lack, even in a few-shot scenario. To validate these findings conclusively, further comprehensive experimentation is necessary. However, we believe that this paves the way for diverse evaluations and prompting engineering tests of such models.

Error Analysis. Since our team participated in all the tasks, it would be unfeasible to provide a deeper analysis of each individual result in this report. However, in order to gain some insight into the inner working of the model, here we present some error analysis carried out on two tasks. We selected a successful task where our systems ranked very high, and another one with a much lower ranking.

In the LangLearn task, our system ranked quite low, specifically 8th place. LangLearn is a text pair classification task where the most informative features are expected to be stylistic, rather than semantic, for capturing the text author's development in language learning. With this premise, we were anticipating a subpar performance by our model from the beginning. However, one relative challenge of this task is the text length. For computational limitations, in EVALITA we had to cut input texts to 100 tokens or less, therefore neglecting a significant portion of the data — we

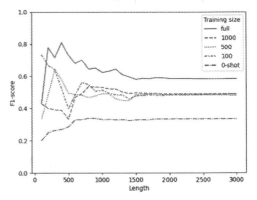

Fig. 1. F1-measure of our systems on the LangLearn test set, with texts removed that are longer than an increasing threshold (horizontal axis).

retained exactly 24.6% of the tokens from the two training sets combined. We checked the impact of text size on the performance of the `extremITLLaMA` prediction, under the hypothesis that longer texts in the test set (cut by our systems to a greater extent) are penalized due to lack of information. The plot in Fig. 1 shows the F1-measure of our system, with varying portions of the test set, where texts were filtered by length. The number on the horizontal axis is thus a threshold on the maximal allowed size in terms

of characters of the two texts forming an instance. The downward trend of the performance of the fully fine-tuned system indicates that its predictions are more accurate
on shorter text pairs, while more and more errors are made on longer, thus underrepresented, texts. The trend is similar, albeit noisier, in the different training size settings,
indicating a greater gain in performance on relatively shorter texts due to the additional
training examples.

Table 5. Performance in terms of Precision, Recall and F1-measure of our system on the EMit A
task. The last column (Support) is the number of positive instances per label in the test set.

Label	0			100			500			1000			All			Sup.
	Pr.	R.	F1	Pr.	R.	F1	Pr.	R.	F1	Pr.	R.	F1	Pr.	R.	F1	
Anger	.077	.018	.029	.111	.018	.031	.488	.357	.412	.500	.268	.349	.759	.393	.518	56
Antic	.000	.000	.000	.310	.106	.158	.542	.376	.444	.621	.424	.503	.675	.612	.642	85
Disgust	.480	.073	.126	.476	.412	.442	.632	.333	.437	.586	.455	.512	.674	.588	.628	165
Fear	.071	.077	.074	.500	.077	.133	.000	.000	.000	.750	.231	.353	.636	.538	.583	13
Joy	.068	.240	.106	.675	.270	.386	.571	.360	.442	.588	.470	.522	.648	.590	.618	100
Love	.190	.039	.065	.571	.078	.137	.882	.146	.250	.683	.272	.389	.745	.398	.519	103
Neutral	.000	.000	.000	.364	.495	.419	.400	.824	.538	.513	.743	.607	.657	.757	.704	210
Sadness	.244	.305	.271	1.000	.105	.190	.742	.242	.365	.667	.358	.466	.750	.537	.626	95
Surprise	.081	.157	.107	.000	.000	.000	1.000	.039	.075	.382	.333	.356	.632	.422	.506	102
Trust	.339	.618	.438	.429	.735	.542	.556	.570	.563	.648	.562	.602	.698	.673	.685	272

EMit is a multi-label classification problem, where the labels are eight emotions
defined by Plutchik [24] plus "love" and a label for neutral texts. Table 5 reports the
performance of our system broken down by labels. It is interesting to notice that the
advantage shown by `extremITLLaMA` on the aggregated result comes from addressing successfully some underrepresented labels. In particular, while the least represented
labels (Fear and Anger) are predicted with less consistency, other labels at the lower
end of the representation spectrum like Anticipation and Sadness are predicted quite
reliably. While the overall performance of `extremITLLaMA` on the EMit task is competitive, the figures show how it is also strongly dependent on fine-tuning. In fact, the
difference between the performance even in the 1000-instances instruction-tuning setting is significantly lower than that with access to the full EMit training set, for all
labels.

5   Conclusions

In a recent position paper with a provocative title, "*is EVALITA done?*" [5], the author
raises concerns about the impact of LLMs and Zero-Shot approaches on the evaluation campaign in NLP. The results presented in this paper confirm that EVALITA
continues to provide a valuable platform for understanding and developing language
resources and tools for the Italian language, as evidenced by the variability in ranking
obtained by our Transformer-based models, despite the huge number of parameters or
the extensive instruction-tuning. Nevertheless, the effectiveness of `extremITLLaMA`,

requiring only minor adjustments and instruction-tuning, undeniably pushes the boundaries of certain tasks, particularly those involving text classification that relies on text semantics. Notably, the performance of the "smaller" model used here, i.e., based on LLaMA composed of 7 billion parameters, even with zero-shot and instruction-tuning approaches, highlights the need for a significant amount of training data to achieve competitiveness with state-of-the-art methods. While these smaller models offer sustainability advantages by requiring less computation, they still rely on a substantial amount of training data. These findings underscore the potential of LLMs in real-world scenarios, while also highlighting the importance of striking a balance between model size, computational resources, and the different usage of training data between fine-tuning and prompting. Further research can explore approaches that optimize the use of limited training data, such as zero or few-shot learning through prompt engineering while considering the sustainability aspect of the models.

Acknowledgments. We would like to thank the "Istituto di Analisi dei Sistemi ed Informatica - Antonio Ruberti" (IASI) for supporting the experimentations. Claudiu Daniel Hromei is a Ph.D. student enrolled in the National Ph.D. in Artificial Intelligence, XXXVII cycle, course on *Health and life sciences*, organized by the Università Campus Bio-Medico di Roma. We acknowledge financial support from the PNRR MUR project PE0000013-FAIR.

References

1. Altuna, B., Karunakaran, G., Lavelli, A., Magnini, B., Speranza, M., Zanoli, R.: CLinkaRT task overview: building links between clinical tests and their results. In: Proceedings of the Eighth Evaluation Campaign of Natural Language Processing and Speech Tools for Italian. Final Workshop (EVALITA 2023). CEUR.org, Parma, Italy (2023)
2. Alzetta, C., et al.: LangLearn at EVALITA 2023: Overview of the language learning development task. In: Proceedings of the Eighth Evaluation Campaign of Natural Language Processing and Speech Tools for Italian. Final Workshop (EVALITA 2023). CEUR.org, Parma, Italy (2023)
3. Araque, O., Frenda, S., Sprugnoli, R., Nozza, D., Patti, V.: EMit at EVALITA 2023: overview of the categorical emotion detection in Italian social media task. In: Proceedings of the Eighth Evaluation Campaign of Natural Language Processing and Speech Tools for Italian. Final Workshop (EVALITA 2023). CEUR.org, Parma, Italy (2023)
4. Aribandi, V., et al.: Ext5: Towards extreme multi-task scaling for transfer learning. In: The Tenth International Conference on Learning Representations, ICLR 2022, Virtual Event, 25–29 April 2022. OpenReview.net (2022). https://openreview.net/forum?id=Vzh1BFUCiIX
5. Basile, V.: Is EVALITA done? On the impact of prompting on the Italian NLP evaluation campaign. In: Nozza, D., Passaro, L.C., Polignano, M. (eds.) Proceedings of the Sixth Workshop on Natural Language for Artificial Intelligence (NL4AI 2022). CEUR Workshop Proceedings, vol. 3287, pp. 127–140. CEUR-WS.org (2022). https://ceur-ws.org/Vol-3287/paper13.pdf
6. Bondielli, A., Dell'Oglio, P., Lenci, A., Marcelloni, F., Passaro, L.C., Sabbatini, M.: Multi-fake-detective at EVALITA 2023: overview of the multimodal fake news detection and verification task. In: Proceedings of the Eighth Evaluation Campaign of Natural Language Processing and Speech Tools for Italian. Final Workshop (EVALITA 2023). CEUR.org, Parma, Italy (2023)

7. Brown, T.B., et al.: Language models are few-shot learners. CoRR abs/2005.14165 (2020). https://arxiv.org/abs/2005.14165

8. Brunato, D., Colla, D., Dell'Orletta, F., Dini, I., Radicioni, D.P., Ravelli, A.A.: DisCoTex at EVALITA 2023: overview of the assessing discourse coherence in Italian texts task. In: Proceedings of the Eighth Evaluation Campaign of Natural Language Processing and Speech Tools for Italian. Final Workshop (EVALITA 2023). CEUR.org, Parma, Italy (2023)

9. Cassotti, P., Siciliani, L., Passaro, L., Gatto, M., Basile, P.: WiC-ITA at EVALITA2023: overview of the EVALITA2023 word-in-context for Italian task. In: Proceedings of the Eighth Evaluation Campaign of Natural Language Processing and Speech Tools for Italian. Final Workshop (EVALITA 2023). CEUR.org, Parma, Italy (2023)

10. Chung, H.W., et al.: Scaling instruction-finetuned language models. CoRR abs/2210.11416 (2022). https://doi.org/10.48550/arXiv.2210.11416

11. Chung, H.W., et al.: Scaling instruction-finetuned language models (2022)

12. Devlin, J., Chang, M., Lee, K., Toutanova, K.: BERT: pre-training of deep bidirectional transformers for language understanding. In: Burstein, J., Doran, C., Solorio, T. (eds.) Proceedings of the NAACL 2019, pp. 4171–4186 (2019). https://doi.org/10.18653/v1/n19-1423

13. Gafà, G., Cutugno, F., Venuti, M.: Emoita: realizing and studying the Italian translation and annotation of an existing dataset for dimensional emotion analysis. In: Proceedings of the Eighth Evaluation Campaign of Natural Language Processing and Speech Tools for Italian. Final Workshop (EVALITA 2023). CEUR.org, Parma, Italy (2023)

14. He, P., Liu, X., Gao, J., Chen, W.: DeBERTa: decoding-enhanced BERT with disentangled attention. In: 9th International Conference on Learning Representations, ICLR 2021, Virtual Event, Austria, 3–7 May 2021 (2021). https://openreview.net/forum?id=XPZIaotutsD

15. Hu, E.J., et al.: LoRA: low-rank adaptation of large language models. CoRR abs/2106.09685 (2021). https://arxiv.org/abs/2106.09685

16. Lai, M., Celli, F., Ramponi, A., Tonelli, S., Bosco, C., Patti, V.: HaSpeeDe3 at Evalita 2023: overview of the political and religious hate speech detection task. In: Proceedings of the Eighth Evaluation Campaign of Natural Language Processing and Speech Tools for Italian. Final Workshop (EVALITA 2023). CEUR.org, Parma, Italy (2023)

17. Lai, M., Menini, S., Polignano, M., Russo, V., Sprugnoli, R., Venturi, G.: EVALITA 2023: overview of the 8th evaluation campaign of natural language processing and speech tools for Italian. In: Proceedings of the Eighth Evaluation Campaign of Natural Language Processing and Speech Tools for Italian. Final Workshop (EVALITA 2023). CEUR.org, Parma, Italy (2023)

18. Lewis, M., et al.: BART: denoising sequence-to-sequence pre-training for natural language generation, translation, and comprehension. CoRR abs/1910.13461 (2019). http://arxiv.org/abs/1910.13461

19. Liu, Y., et al.: RoBERTa: a robustly optimized bert pretraining approach. CoRR abs/1907.11692 (2019). http://arxiv.org/abs/1907.11692

20. Mangrulkar, S., Gugger, S., Debut, L., Belkada, Y., Paul, S.: PEFT: state-of-the-art parameter-efficient fine-tuning methods (2022). https://github.com/huggingface/peft

21. Nozza, D., Damo, G., Cignarella, A.T., Caselli, T., Patti, V.: HODI at EVALITA 2023: overview of the homotransphobia detection in Italian task. In: Proceedings of the Eighth Evaluation Campaign of Natural Language Processing and Speech Tools for Italian. Final Workshop (EVALITA 2023). CEUR.org, Parma, Italy (2023)

22. Ouyang, L., et al.: Training language models to follow instructions with human feedback (2022)

23. Palmero Aprosio, A., Paccosi, T.: NERMuD at EVALITA 2023: overview of the named-entities recognition on multi-domain documents task. In: Proceedings of the Eighth Evaluation Campaign of Natural Language Processing and Speech Tools for Italian. Final Workshop (EVALITA 2023). CEUR.org, Parma, Italy (2023)

24. Plutchik, R., Kellerman, H.: Theories of Emotion, vol. 1 (1980)
25. Radford, A., et al.: Improving language understanding by generative pre-training (2018)
26. Raffel, C., et al.: Exploring the limits of transfer learning with a unified text-to-text trans-former. J. Mach. Learn. Res. **21**, 140:1–140:67 (2020). http://jmlr.org/papers/v21/20-074.html
27. Ramponi, A., Casula, C.: GeoLingIt at EVALITA 2023: overview of the task on geolocation of linguistic variation in Italy. In: Proceedings of the Eighth Evaluation Campaign of Natural Language Processing and Speech Tools for Italian. Final Workshop (EVALITA 2023). CEUR.org, Parma, Italy (2023)
28. Russo, D., et al.: Overview of PoliticIT2023@EVALITA: Political Ideology Detection in Italian Texts (2023)
29. Russo, P., Stoehr, N., Ribeiro, M.H.: Subtask a- conspiratorial content classification (2023). https://kaggle.com/competitions/acti-subtask-a
30. Russo, P., Stoehr, N., Ribeiro, M.H.: Subtask b - conspiracy category classification (2023). https://kaggle.com/competitions/acti-subtask-b
31. Sanh, V., et al.: Multitask prompted training enables zero-shot task generalization. CoRR abs/2110.08207 (2021). https://arxiv.org/abs/2110.08207
32. Santilli, A., Rodolà, E.: Camoscio: an Italian instruction-tuned llama (2023). https://arxiv.org/abs/2307.16456
33. Sarti, G., Nissim, M.: IT5: large-scale text-to-text pretraining for Italian language understanding and generation. CoRR abs/2203.03759 (2022). https://doi.org/10.48550/arXiv.2203.03759
34. Taori, R., et al.: Stanford alpaca: an instruction-following llama model (2023). https://github.com/tatsu-lab/stanford_alpaca
35. Touvron, H., et al.: LLaMA: open and efficient foundation language models (2023)
36. Vaswani, A., et al.: Attention is all you need. CoRR abs/1706.03762 (2017). http://arxiv.org/abs/1706.03762
37. Workshop, B., et al.: Bloom: a 176b-parameter open-access multilingual language model (2023)
38. Xue, L., et al.: mT5: a massively multilingual pre-trained text-to-text transformer. In: Toutanova, K., et al. (eds.) Proceedings of the NAACL-HLT 2021, Online, 6–11 June 2021, pp. 483–498. Association for Computational Linguistics (2021). https://doi.org/10.18653/v1/2021.naacl-main.41

Named Entity Recognition and Linking for Entity Extraction from Italian Civil Judgements

Riccardo Pozzi[(✉)] [iD], Riccardo Rubini[iD], Christian Bernasconi[iD],
and Matteo Palmonari[iD]

University of Milano-Bicocca, Milan, Italy
riccardo.pozzi@unimib.it

Abstract. The extraction of named entities from court judgments is
useful in several downstream applications, such as document anonymization and semantic search engines. In this paper, we discuss the application of named entity recognition and linking (NEEL) to extract entities
from Italian civil court judgments. To develop and evaluate our work,
we use a corpus of 146 manually annotated court judgments. We use a
pipeline that combines a transformer-based Named Entity Recognition
(NER) component, a transformer-based Named Entity Linking (NEL)
component, and a NIL prediction component. While the NEL and NIL
prediction components are not fine-tuned on domain-specific data, the
NER component is fine-tuned on the annotated corpus. In addition, we
compare different masked language modeling (MLM) adaptation strategies to optimize the result and investigate their impact. Results obtained
on a 30-document test set reveal satisfactory performance, especially on
the NER task, and emphasize challenges to improve NEEL on similar
documents. Our code is available on GitHub.(https://github.com/rpo19/
pozzi_aixia_2023. We are not allowed to publish sensitive data and the
NER models trained on sensitive data.)

Keywords: Named Entity Recognition · Named Entity Linking · NIL
Prediction · Italian Civil Court Judgments · Legal · Domain
Adaptation

1 Introduction

Solutions to extract information from legal texts have a long tradition [37] and
are attracting even greater interest, also due to the performance boost on many
tasks that has been made possible by recent advances in natural language processing (NLP) technologies (see Sect. 2). The language in legal text and the
downstream application may differ significantly depending on the domain, a
broad spectrum of specific solutions have been proposed in a variety of domains,
e.g., from law to court judgments, from contracts to criminal investigations [3].

© The Author(s), under exclusive license to Springer Nature Switzerland AG 2023
R. Basili et al. (Eds.): AIxIA 2023, LNAI 14318, pp. 187–201, 2023.
https://doi.org/10.1007/978-3-031-47546-7_13

For example, many approaches have been proposed to extract legal terminology [5] and some approach has focused on named entities [37]. In this paper, we focus on a specific domain: the extraction of named entities from Italian court judgments, and, in particular, from judgments produced in the context of civil trials. The work discussed in this paper is part of activities conducted in two projects developed in cooperation with or funded by DGSIA, the body that manages information systems of the Ministry of Justice, and the Ministry of Justice itself.

Entity extraction is applied to enrich court judgment data to support three main target downstream applications: 1) semantic search, where stakeholders (mainly judges) can search for previous judgments, and use named entities therein to filter out results; 2) anonymization, where finding references, especially to people and organizations, is a prerequisite to anonymize the judgments; 3) calculate advanced statistical analyses, which can use variables that are not found in trial records and metadata, and can be found only in the actual text (e.g., average alimony by district). While additional NLP processing methods may be required for advanced statistical analyses, named entity extraction remains a crucial component for solutions targeting this application.

With entity extraction, we refer to a task that goes a bit beyond NER, as proposed in most of the previous approaches. In fact, for all or some of the above applications, it is valuable not only to find named entity mentions and classify them into a set of known classes, but also to consolidate these mentions into an entity-centric knowledge layer, which supports deeper data integration functionalities and related downstream functionalities. In particular, deeper integration can be achieved by: 1) reconciling the mentions of different entities and linking references to known entities described in background knowledge bases, e.g., Wikipedia entities (named entity linking - NEL); 2) reconciling different mentions of entities within a document (entity clustering). Observe that named entity linking contributes to entity clustering, where mentions with the same link are implicitly clustered together. Another reason to use NEL in the entity extraction process is that there are entities in court judgments that are known because described in background knowledge bases, which makes these links useful. In fact, in these projects, we developed an end-to-end entity extraction pipeline that performs the following tasks: NER; NEL; NIL prediction, which decides whether to link an entity mention to an entity in the KB (the one identified by NEL) or to consider that the correct entity is not in the KB, i.e., if a mention is respectively not NIL, or NIL ("not in lexicon"); NIL clustering, i.e., the task of clustering NIL mentions referring to the same entity. The pipeline is inspired by and shares some components of the approach described in previous work [24].

In this paper, we focus on discussing the performance that our neural algorithms achieve on named entity recognition and linking tasks (NEEL) including NIL prediction. To better illustrate the NEEL process, we provide an example in Fig. 1. We leave out of the focus of this paper the NIL clustering part, mainly for reasons of space.

In particular, we present a pipeline that combines a transformer-based named entity recognition (NER) component, a transformer-based Named Entity Linking

(NEL) component, and a NIL prediction component. While the NEL and NIL prediction components are not fine-tuned on domain-specific data, the NER component is fine-tuned on an annotated corpus of civil court judgments. In addition, we test different masked language modeling (MLM) [10] adaptation strategies, including adaptation with a larger corpus of civil court judgments from which the annotated corpus has been taken.

The paper is organized as follows: in Sect. 2 we discuss related work; in Sect. 3, we present our approach; in Sect. 4 we present the results of our experimental evaluation; finally, conclusion ends the paper in Sect. 5.

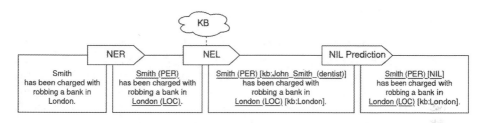

Fig. 1. Overview of NEEL with a NIL (*Smith*) and a ¬NIL mention (*London*). The correct entity for *Smith* is not present in the KB, indeed, NEL provides a wrong candidate, and NIL prediction classifies *Smith* as NIL.

2   Related Work

This section presents an overview of recent advancements in Named Entity Extraction and Linking (NEEL) techniques, including NIL prediction. We start by focusing on NEEL approaches in the legal domain, then we proceed with the status of NEEL for the Italian language. Finally, we briefly highlight recent developments in general-domain NEEL, additionally discussing the advancements achieved in the three subtasks of NEEL: named entity recognition (NER), named entity linking (NEL), and NIL prediction. NER identifies mentions of named entities and classifies them into a predefined set of classes, while NEL links these mentions to corresponding entities in a knowledge base.; 3) NIL prediction determines if the NEL candidate is correct or if the mention refers to an entity that is missing from the KB, i.e., an unlinkable entity mention or NIL ("not in lexicon") mention.

By examining the related works in these areas, we lay the foundation for our research and shed light on existing gaps in the field of NEEL with NIL prediction applied to Italian court judgments.

2.1   NEEL for Legal Documents

Most of the previous work on NEEL for legal documents has focused on the NER task only. The first NER approaches are based on handcrafted rules and statistical models [37], such as conditional random fields (CRFs) [19]. More recent approaches to NER started using BiLSTM-based models combined with CRFs for Brazilian and German legal texts [37]. After the advent of transformers [33] and BERT [10], which obtained impressive performance in multiple NLP tasks, LEGAL-BERT, specialized in the legal domain, has been released [7]. Later, some work compared LEGAL-BERT with previous approaches [16] for NER finding that LEGAL-BERT performance is comparable to simple models (LSTMs, CNNs).

A few approaches have studied NEL in legal texts. One of the first approaches applied NER and NEL on a corpus of judgments of the European Court of Human Rights [4]. As the background KB, they use a legal-specific ontology enriched with YAGO[1] after an alignment procedure. Another approach targets the NEL task only on the EUR-Lex law article dataset [11]. Their NEL system is trained using transfer learning. We study the end-to-end combination of NER, NEL, and NIL prediction, and we use a more recent NEL approach [35] trained on a large Italian Wikipedia corpus without fine-tuning on court judgment data. Another study combined BERT [10] with rule-based techniques for NER and coupled it with an off-the-shelves NEL service to extract entities from court decisions in the Finnish language [29]; NEL is performed with a popularity-based approach. This study is the most similar to ours; however, we focus on the NIL prediction problem, and we use a BERT-based NEL approach; also, in this paper, we discuss only the performance of neural algorithms.

Some work that studies NEL with NIL prediction is also evaluated on documents that are related to the legal domain [17] (the depositions of the 1641 Irish rebellion[2]). However, to the best of our knowledge, no prior work has investigated end-to-end NEEL considering the NIL prediction problem on recent legal data.

2.2   NEEL in the Italian Language

Italian datasets for NER include multilingual resources [22,30], and domain-specific datasets, such as [6] in the medical domain. Similarly, Italian NEL datasets comprise multilingual ones, i.e. VoxEL [26] and resources based on micro-posts [2].

Among the ready-to-use NEEL libraries for the Italian language, notable options are SpaCy[3] and Tint [23] for NER and DBpedia Spotlight [8] for both NER and NEL. SpaCy provides pre-trained NER models of different sizes (small, medium and large), but currently does not provide any pre-trained transformer-based model for Italian. Tint performs NER with a combination of CRFs taggers and rule-based systems for dates and money. DBpedia Spotlight is a ready-to-use tool that recognizes and links entity mentions to DBpedia[4].

---

[1] https://yago-knowledge.org/.
[2] http://1641.tcd.ie/.
[3] https://spacy.io.
[4] https://www.dbpedia.org/.

2.3   NEEL for General Domain

NEEL with NIL prediction dates back to the knowledge base population track (TAC-KBP) of the Text Analysis Conference[5] (TAC), which has included the NIL prediction task since 2009 [21]. Work focusing on end-to-end NEEL includes approaches that jointly perform the subtasks [1,18] and pipeline-based systems [13,15].

Follows a brief overview of the recent developments of the three subtasks.

NER. Recent DL approaches for NER include models based on recurrent neural networks (RNNs), convolutional neural networks (CNNs), and transformers [28], often combined with CRFs for the final prediction of sequence labels. Several studies highlighted the importance of word embeddings and character embeddings for NER, including non-contextualized embeddings and contextualized embeddings [10]. Indeed, the most effective approaches are based on this latter class of embeddings: the state-of-the-art on CoNLL2003 [31], an important benchmark for English NER, is detained by concatenating character-based, contextualized, and non-contextualized embeddings [34].

NEL. Since 2013, representation learning techniques for NEL have been explored to obtain dense representations of mentions and entities and calculate a similarity score (e.g. cosine similarity) to rank linking candidates [12,36]. The attention mechanism and transformers [33] have played a crucial role in enhancing dense representations, leading to the development of the bi-encoder and cross-encoder paradigms [14,35], which are widely used for dense-retrieval and candidate re-ranking, respectively. Recently, promising entity linking paradigms that better leverage the pre-training task of language models are emerging: autoregressive entity linking [9], and extractive entity linking [25].

NIL Prediction. NIL entities have been often ignored in the literature of entity linking: among the 38 approaches compared by the survey [28] only 8 considered NIL entities. NIL prediction strategies, several of which derive from the TAC-KBP, include applying a threshold to the entity linking score, representing NIL with an additional class, and using a binary classifier on top of the linking score and additional features [28].

3   Named Entity and Linking Algorithms

As discussed in Sect. 1, in this paper we focus on presenting our NEEL approach for extracting entities from civil court judgments and evaluating its performance on an annotated dataset. Our approach implements three tasks [24] in a pipeline: NER, NEL, and NIL prediction. For NER, we focus on neural NER algorithms,

---

[5] https://tac.nist.gov/.

Table 1. Statistics of ICCJ. Number of NIL annotations is indicated in parentheses.

	#Docs	#Ann	PER	ORG	LOC	DATE	MONEY	MISC
Train	102	11940	2997	2761	612	2088	791	2691
Validation	14	1688	308	369	77	350	84	500
Test(#NIL)	30	3006(2539)	722(653)	694(443)	195(58)	555	223	617

considering a transformer-based NER module that we fine-tune on an annotated corpus of court judgments. Given that the NER component can use different transformers, we also analyze the impact of domain adaptation, based on masked language modeling (MLM), on downstream performance. Since the classes of entities considered by NER are related to the annotated corpus, we organize this section as follows: we first introduce the Italian Civil Court Judgment Corpus; we discuss the classes used in the NER module; then we provide details about the NER component, the NEL algorithm, and the NIL prediction.

3.1   Italian Civil Court Judgment Corpus and NER Classes

The gold standard dataset we use for training and evaluation is composed of 146 annotated judgments derived from a corpus of 900,000 legal judgments, organized as follows: 102 documents as the training set, 14 for validation, and a test set of 30 documents. Unfortunately, we are unable to publish the corpus due to the sensitive nature of the data it contains. However, upon request, we are open to exploring the possibility of sharing it through bilateral agreements. The annotations in the corpus have been performed by two annotators. The inter-annotator agreement (IAA) has been calculated using the F1-measure to assess the coherence between the annotations in terms of both class and span and using Cohen's Kappa, obtaining respectively 80.8% and 66.2%.

All the documents have NER annotations considering the following classes: Person (*PER*), Organization (*ORG*), Location (*LOC*), Date (*DATE*), Money (*MONEY*), and Miscellaneous (*MISC*), that includes references to court judgments, law articles, court decrees, or any entity not covered by the above classes. In total, the dataset is composed of more than 16,000 annotations and each document counts on average ~1,900 words. Table 1 reports detailed statistics, including the number of annotations for each class.

The annotations for named entity linking (NEL) and NIL prediction are only available in the test set. These annotations are limited to the classes *PER*, *ORG*, and *LOC*. *DATE*, *MONEY*, and *MISC* mentions have not been annotated for NEL and NIL prediction because they are expected to be processed by rule-based algorithms that we do not cover in this work.

For the remainder of this work, we will refer to our annotated corpus of 146 documents as ICCJ (Italian Civil Court Judgment) and to the 900,000 legal judgment (without annotations) as ICCJ900k.

Table 2. NER backbones details with the applied MLM-adaptations (one model per column). Model names indicate the order of applied adaptations. Legal domain data used for the LGL adaptation vary: *3.7GB legal corpus from the National Jurisprudential Archive; **6.6GB legal corpus composed of civil and criminal cases.

	ITA	ITA+LGL+ICCJ900k	ITA+LGL	LGL+ICCJ900k	LGL
ITA	Y	Y	Y	-	-
LGL	-	Y*	Y*	Y**	Y**
ICCJ900k	-	Y	-	Y	Y

3.2 NER with MLM-Adaptation and Fine-Tuning

We use the library SpaCy-transformers[6] with the SpaCy transition-based parser to leverage contextualized token representations obtained from a transformer [33].

As the backbone transformer for the NER system, we evaluate five different BERT encoders that have been trained with one of three different MLM-adaptations or with a combination of them. They are further described in Table 2 where *ITA* (Italian) denotes the pre-training with MLM on general-domain Italian data, *LGL* (Legal) the MLM-adaptation to legal-domain data, and *ICCJ900k* to our corpus of 900,000 Italian civil court judgments. It is important to note that some models (*LGL* and *LGL+ICCJ900k*) are directly pre-trained on legal domain data using MLM.

As a baseline, we consider the general-domain model *ITA* (available pre-trained on huggingface[7]). Also, *ITA+LGL* [20] and *LGL*[8] are available pre-trained on huggingface, while for the *ICCJ900k* versions we perform the adaptation with MLM. For each backbone, we consider five models with a different random weight initialization.

Finally, each model has been fine-tuned for the NER task on ICCJ training set using the SpaCy library with early stopping on the validation set and AdamW as the optimizer with the initial learning rate set to 5×10^{-5}.

3.3 NEL with BLINK-ITA-Bi-encoder

For NEL we use the bi-encoder architecture of BLINK [35]. We initialize the bi-encoder with the weights from Italian BERT-base[9] [27], then we fine-tune them on $9M$ training samples from Italian Wikipedia hyperlinks, following the original work, for 5 epochs (in the last one we train with hard-negatives instead of random negatives) using AdamW optimizer with the initial learning rate set to 1×10^{-5} and a batch size of 20. As the linking KB, we use $\sim 1.5M$ entities obtained from Italian Wikipedia[10] after filtering out redirects and disambiguation pages.

---

[6] https://spacy.io/universe/project/spacy-transformers.
[7] https://huggingface.co/dbmdz/bert-base-italian-xxl-cased.
[8] https://huggingface.co/dlicari/Italian-Legal-BERT-SC.
[9] https://huggingface.co/dbmdz/bert-base-italian-uncased.
[10] https://it.wikipedia.org.

3.4   NIL Prediction

In the NIL prediction component, we use a *logistic regression classifier* that receives as input features 1) the score of the top-ranked entity given by the NEL system and 2) the difference between the top-ranked entity score and the second-best one [24], and produces an output $p \in [0,1]$, where 1 means the top-ranked entity is correct for linking the mention, while 0 means the opposite. In this latter case, we consider the mention NIL, assuming that if the correct entity is not in the top-ranked position, then it is not in the KB.

4   Experimental Evaluation

In order to evaluate the NEEL pipeline, we study the overall effectiveness of the pipeline and each component separately. By doing so, we have been able to independently study the behavior of the NER, the NEL, and the NIL prediction systems, and finally of NEL with NIL prediction combined. We would like to remind the reader that the NEL and NIL prediction components are applied only to mentions classified as *PER*, *ORG*, and *LOC* by the NER component. In our evaluation, we focus especially on the following objectives:

1. investigating the performance with different backbone transformers and the impact of different MLM adaptation strategies on the NER performance;
2. investigating which classes of entities are more challenging;
3. investigating the performance of NEL and NIL prediction in a best-case scenario, independently from the NER component;
4. investigating the performance of the end-to-end NEEL pipeline;
5. to discuss the main challenges.

4.1   Evaluation Settings and Measures

Please note that the ICCJ training set is only used to fine-tune the NER component. All results refer to the ICCJ test set.

NER. NER is evaluated using strong and partial matching measures, which is a quite common practice in evaluating NER approaches [32]. Both measures rigorously require that the predicted class matches the gold standard one, while they differ with respect to span detection: the former measure considers an annotation correct when the predicted boundaries perfectly match the gold standard, the latter when there is an overlap between them. Considering both measures is useful also for two other reasons: 1) we can investigate to what extent some correct annotations are returned by the algorithms, even when the span of the mention is not perfectly identified; 2) by considering the gap between strong and partial matching measures in a per-class performance analysis, we can investigate which classes are more affected by boundary identification issues. For each of the measures, as in a multiclass classification problem, we calculate *precision*, *recall*, and *F1-measure*, micro and macro-averaged on the class, and separately for each class.

Comparison of Backbone Transformers for NER. The comparison of backbone transformers for NER considers five different random weight initializations for each backbone. We calculate the mean and the standard deviation of the micro *precision*, *recall*, and *F1-measure* of the five initializations for each transformer. We identify the top-performing model based on its *F1-measure* and utilize it as the foundation of the NER component for subsequent evaluations.

NEL. We evaluate the NEL component in terms of *accuracy* and *recall@100*, similarly to recent work [35], on the ICCJ test set, additionally comparing to the news-based benchmark VoxEL [26].

It is important to remind that the NEL evaluation and the following ones (NIL prediction, and end-to-end NEEL) exclusively focus on the classes *PER*, *ORG*, and *LOC*.

NIL Prediction. The NIL prediction component is evaluated as a binary classifier with *precision*, *recall*, and *F1-measure* calculated for both classes (NIL and ¬NIL). It is important to emphasize that, to evaluate the NIL prediction independently from NEL errors, we consider it correct when the NIL prediction classifies as NIL the mentions incorrectly linked by the NEL component. We attribute a positive value to this behavior as it showcases the ability of the NIL prediction to effectively identify NEL errors, thereby mitigating their impact.

NEL and NIL Prediction. We evaluate NEL with NIL prediction independently from NER errors by calculating 1) the *recall* of the *mentions to link*, 2) the *recall* of *NIL mentions*, and 3) the *accuracy* of all the mentions.

NEEL End-to-End. Finally, we evaluate the end-to-end NEEL using strong and partial matching measures; in this case, an annotation is considered correct when 1) the predicted class matches the gold standard, 2) the span matches the gold standard according to the measure, and 3) the mention is linked to the correct entity (if ¬NIL) or correctly identified as NIL. We calculate *precision*, *recall*, *F1-measure* micro and macro-averaged for each class, exactly as in the NER evaluation.

4.2 Results

Comparison of Backbone Transformers. Table 3 shows the results for the comparison of the 5 backbone transformers for NER. Based on the sample mean, the encoder that gives the best results is ITA+LGL+ICCJ900k, while the worst one is LGL+ICCJ900k.

In order to properly analyze the presence of statistical differences based on the choice of the backbone transformer, we conducted an analysis of variance (ANOVA) test on the *F1-measure*. The results reveal a highly significant difference (with significance level $\alpha = 0.05$). To further investigate the pairwise differences, we conducted a Tukey's HSD test with a significance level of $\alpha = 0.05$. We

Table 3. Comparison of the backbone transformers (one per row) for NER on ICCJ test. Using strong matching we calculate mean ($\pm$ std) on 5 random initializations.

	Precision	Recall	F1 Score
ITA	81.96($\pm$0.76)	83.77($\pm$1.39)	82.76($\pm$0.63)
ITA+LGL+ICCJ900k	**82.08($\pm$0.87)**	**84.69($\pm$0.52)**	**83.36($\pm$0.41)**
ITA+LGL	81.11($\pm$1.00)	83.57($\pm$1.04)	82.41($\pm$0.55)
LGL+ICCJ900k	80.87($\pm$0.73)	82.62($\pm$1.55)	81.72($\pm$0.52)
LGL	79.90($\pm$1.05)	82.62($\pm$1.36)	81.23($\pm$0.47)

observe that *ITA*, the pre-training on general-domain Italian data, has a positive impact on performance: the models *ITA+LGL+ICCJ900k* and *ITA+LGL* tend to perform better than those trained from scratch on domain-specific data (*LGL* and *LGL+ICCJ900k*).

Surprisingly, the findings suggest that employing a domain-specific legal BERT does not result in a substantial enhancement in NER performance compared to a generic Italian BERT. This observation extends to the adaptation to the corpus of judgments (ICCJ900k) as well. Furthermore, we emphasize that the use of a pre-trained generic Italian BERT significantly reduces the effort required for adaptation in terms of time, costs, and environmental imprint.

NER. The evaluation results for the NER component, as shown in Table 4, are promising. All the strong matching measures exceed 80%, and all the partial matching measures surpass 90%, indicating overall proficiency in NER recognition. The classes *MONEY* and *PER* achieve high recognition rates, surpassing 90% with the strong matching measure. However, the performance for *MISC* is lower compared to other types. This discrepancy may be attributed to the intrinsic heterogeneity of the MISC class. Additionally, *MISC* exhibits the largest disparity between strong matching performance and partial matching performance. A significant difference (approximately 12%) between strong and partial matching outcomes also affects the class *ORG*, highlighting the difficulty in precisely detecting the boundaries of organization mentions.

We also consider the successful results achieved by the NER component indicative of the high quality of our annotated corpus ICCJ.

NEL and NIL Prediction. Table 5 reveals that the NEL and NIL prediction components do not exhibit the same level of effectiveness as the NER component. The independent evaluation of the NEL component ($NEL_\perp$) demonstrates a lower *accuracy* (73.52%) but achieves a *recall@100* of 90.81%, suggesting that the integration of a re-ranking system could potentially enhance our results. Additionally, the comparison with the outcomes obtained with the news-based VoxEL benchmark [26] further underscores the challenges presented by the ICCJ corpus. We also remind you that the NEL component has not been fine-tuned on

Table 4. NER evaluation with strong and partial matching on ICCJ test.

	Strong Match			Partial Match		
	Prec	Recall	F1	Prec	Recall	F1
DATE	83.49	80.18	81.80	92.12	87.84	89.93
LOC	86.34	84.62	85.49	94.24	92.31	93.26
MONEY	96.19	90.58	93.30	99.52	93.72	96.54
ORG	76.58	80.12	78.31	89.12	92.83	90.93
PER	90.37	91.00	90.68	95.77	95.43	95.10
MISC	73.97	70.02	71.94	91.27	85.14	88.10
Macro by Class	84.50	82.75	83.59	93.51	91.21	92.31
Micro	82.70	81.74	82.22	92.53	90.97	91.74

Table 5. NEL and NIL Prediction evaluation on ICCJ test. $\text{NEL}_\perp$ and NIL $\text{Pred}_\perp$ are independent from other tasks. NEL & NIL $\text{Pred}_\perp$ evaluate the two tasks independently from NER. *$\text{NEL}_\perp$ also reports results on VoxEL [26] for comparison.

$\text{NEL}_\perp$			NIL $\text{Pred}_\perp$				NEL & NIL $\text{Pred}_\perp$	
	Acc	Rec@100		Prec	Rec	F1	Link_{Rec}	52.95
ICCJ	73.52	90.81	NIL	92.15	86.51	89.24	NIL_{Rec}	86.31
sVoxEL-it*	88.89	96.83	¬NIL	58.45	72.02	64.53	Overall_{Acc}	76.85

ICCJ, and that the utilized knowledge base has not been restricted to domain-related entities. These two factors represent possibilities for enhancing this component.

The NIL prediction classifier ($\text{NIL}_\perp$) is effective in recognizing the NIL class, while it suffers with $\neg NIL$ mentions: the low precision of 58.45% highlights that several NIL mentions are wrongly predicted as $\neg NIL$.

During the evaluation of *NEL with NIL prediction*$_\perp$, we notice the *overall accuracy* is acceptable (76.85%) and the *recall* on the NIL mentions is satisfactory at 86.31%. However, we observe that the performance of ¬NIL mentions (Link_{Rec}), which should have been linked to the knowledge base (KB), is not up to the desired standard. The errors for this measure include both mentions linked to incorrect entities and mentions inaccurately identified as NIL. After the NIL prediction, indeed, only 52.95% of the ¬NIL mentions are correctly classified, whereas the accuracy of $\text{NEL}_\perp$ stands at 73.52%. This substantial 20% decline in performance can be attributed to the false-NIL predictions.

For these reasons, we consider the NIL prediction to be the most significant challenge in NEEL. It is important to further study and improve this component in order to enhance the overall performance and reliability of NEEL systems.

NEEL End-to-End. Lastly, Table 6 presents the comprehensive results for the end-to-end NEEL task. *PER* and *LOC* exhibit similar satisfactory performance levels. On the other hand, *ORG* entities appear to be more challenging.

Table 6. NEEL end-to-end evaluation of PER, LOC, ORG mentions on ICCJ test.

	Strong Match			Partial Match		
	Prec	Recall	F1	Prec	Recall	F1
LOC	75.92	74.36	75.13	80.10	78.46	79.27
ORG	51.10	53.46	52.25	60.61	63.22	61.88
PER	76.89	77.42	77.16	80.19	80.86	80.52
Macro by Class	67.97	68.41	68.18	73.63	74.18	73.89
Micro	65.39	66.73	66.05	71.53	72.95	72.24

Furthermore, the difference between strong and partial matching is limited for *PER* and *LOC*, but significant for *ORG*, confirming the difficulty in accurately detecting boundaries for *ORG* entities previously observed in the NER results. Additionally, the relatively modest overall difference of 6% between partial and strong matching, along with the disparity with NER-only results (72.24% vs 91.74%), highlights that the NEL and NIL prediction components are responsible for the majority of errors. This observation, combined with the fact that we fine-tuned only the NER component, suggests that fine-tuning the NEL and NIL prediction components on the data could potentially enhance the overall performance of the end-to-end NEEL system.

5   Conclusion

In this paper, we have presented the application of a NEEL pipeline to Italian civil court judgments and an evaluation of its performance. The experimental evaluation conducted on 30 annotated judgments suggests that the performance of our NEEL pipeline is encouraging, especially the performance of the NER component, and emphasizes some remaining challenges. Quite surprisingly, the gap in performance between models that use domain-specific transformers, adapted with masked language modeling, and those that use transformers trained on generic Italian text is quite limited and not statistically significant. The challenges concern especially the NEL and NIL prediction components, which so far we have not customized for or fine-tuned on domain-specific data. Fine-tuning these algorithms using limited data is a challenge that we plan to address in the future. Moreover, we plan to investigate strategies to support human-in-the-loop NEEL, by improving the extraction quality and minimizing the user effort during the annotation and validation phases. Finally, a prospective scenario for future development involves jointly performing NEL and NIL prediction within a unified module, as recent research indicates that consolidating multiple pipeline tasks in a single module can significantly reduce error propagation [18]. Despite the remaining challenges, we believe that the evidence discussed in the paper suggests that, with further improvements, end-to-end NEEL pipelines could be effectively applied to court judgments to disclose a variety of downstream applications.

Acknowledgements. This research has been partially funded by Cini in the context of the Italian project Datalake@Giustizia and by the project PON Next Generation UPP promoted by the Italian Ministry of Justice.

References

1. Ayoola, T., Tyagi, S., Fisher, J., Christodoulopoulos, C., Pierleoni, A.: ReFinED: an efficient zero-shot-capable approach to end-to-end entity linking. In: Proceedings of the 2022 Conference of the North American Chapter of the Association for Computational Linguistics: Human Language Technologies: Industry Track. Association for Computational Linguistics (2022)
2. Basile, P., Caputo, A., Gentile, A.L., Rizzo, G.: Overview of the EVALITA 2016 named entity recognition and linking in Italian tweets (NEEL-IT) task. In: of the Final Workshop, vol. 7 (2016)
3. Batini, C., Bellandi, V., Ceravolo, P., Moiraghi, F., Palmonari, M., Siccardi, S.: Semantic data integration for investigations: lessons learned and open challenges. In: 2021 IEEE International Conference on Smart Data Services (SMDS) (2021)
4. Cardellino, C., Teruel, M., Alemany, L.A., Villata, S.: A low-cost, high-coverage legal named entity recognizer, classifier and linker. In: Proceedings of the 16th Edition of the International Conference on Artificial Intelligence and Law. ICAIL 2017, Association for Computing Machinery (2017)
5. Castano, S., Falduti, M., Ferrara, A., Montanelli, S.: A knowledge-centered framework for exploration and retrieval of legal documents. Inf. Syst. **106**, 101842 (2022)
6. Catelli, R., Gargiulo, F., Casola, V., De Pietro, G., Fujita, H., Esposito, M.: Crosslingual named entity recognition for clinical de-identification applied to a COVID-19 Italian data set. Appl. Soft Comput. **97**, 106779 (2020)
7. Chalkidis, I., Fergadiotis, M., Malakasiotis, P., Aletras, N., Androutsopoulos, I.: LEGAL-BERT: the Muppets straight out of law school. In: Findings of the Association for Computational Linguistics: EMNLP 2020. Association for Computational Linguistics (2020)
8. Daiber, J., Jakob, M., Hokamp, C., Mendes, P.N.: Improving efficiency and accuracy in multilingual entity extraction. In: Proceedings of the 9th International Conference on Semantic Systems. I-SEMANTICS 2013, Association for Computing Machinery (2013)
9. De Cao, N., et al.: Multilingual autoregressive entity linking. Trans. Assoc. Comput. Linguist. **10**, 274–290 (2022)
10. Devlin, J., Chang, M.W., Lee, K., Toutanova, K.: BERT: pre-training of deep bidirectional transformers for language understanding. In: Proceedings of the 2019 Conference of the North American Chapter of the Association for Computational Linguistics: Human Language Technologies, Volume 1 (Long and Short Papers). Association for Computational Linguistics (2019)
11. Elnaggar, A., Otto, R., Matthes, F.: Deep learning for named-entity linking with transfer learning for legal documents. In: Proceedings of the 2018 Artificial Intelligence and Cloud Computing Conference. AICCC 2018, Association for Computing Machinery (2018)
12. He, Z., Liu, S., Li, M., Zhou, M., Zhang, L., Wang, H.: Learning entity representation for entity disambiguation. In: Proceedings of the 51st Annual Meeting of the Association for Computational Linguistics (Volume 2: Short Papers). Association for Computational Linguistics (2013)

13. Heist, N., Paulheim, H.: NASTyLinker: NIL-aware scalable transformer-based entity linker. In: Pesquita, C., et al. (eds.) The Semantic Web, ESWC 2023. Lecture Notes in Computer Science, vol. 13870, pp. 174–191. Springer, Switzerland (2023). https://doi.org/10.1007/978-3-031-33455-9_11

14. Humeau, S., Shuster, K., Lachaux, M.A., Weston, J.: Poly-encoders: Architectures and pre-training strategies for fast and accurate multi-sentence scoring. In: International Conference on Learning Representations (2019)

15. Kassner, N., Petroni, F., Plekhanov, M., Riedel, S., Cancedda, N.: EDIN: an end-to-end benchmark and pipeline for unknown entity discovery and indexing. In: Proceedings of the 2022 Conference on Empirical Methods in Natural Language Processing. Association for Computational Linguistics (2022)

16. Keshavarz, H., et al.: Named entity recognition in long documents: an end-to-end case study in the legal domain. In: 2022 IEEE International Conference on Big Data (Big Data) (2022)

17. Klie, J.C., Eckart de Castilho, R., Gurevych, I.: From zero to hero: human-in-the-loop entity linking in low resource domains. In: Proceedings of the 58th Annual Meeting of the Association for Computational Linguistics. Association for Computational Linguistics (2020)

18. Kolitsas, N., Ganea, O.E., Hofmann, T.: End-to-end neural entity linking. In: Proceedings of the 22nd Conference on Computational Natural Language Learning. Association for Computational Linguistics (2018)

19. Lafferty, J.D., McCallum, A., Pereira, F.C.N.: Conditional random fields: probabilistic models for segmenting and labeling sequence data. In: Proceedings of the Eighteenth International Conference on Machine Learning. ICML 2001, Morgan Kaufmann Publishers Inc., San Francisco, CA, USA (2001)

20. Licari, D., Comandè, G.: ITALIAN-LEGAL-BERT: a pre-trained transformer language model for Italian law. In: Companion Proceedings of the 23rd International Conference on Knowledge Engineering and Knowledge Management. CEUR Workshop Proceedings, vol. 3256. CEUR (2022)

21. McNamee, P., Dang, H.T.: Overview of the tac 2009 knowledge base population track. In: Second Text Analysis Conference (TAC 2009), vol. 2 (2009)

22. Nothman, J., Ringland, N., Radford, W., Murphy, T., Curran, J.R.: Learning multilingual named entity recognition from Wikipedia. Artif. Intell. **194**, 151–175 (2013)

23. Aprosio, A.P., Moretti, G.: Tint 2.0: an all-inclusive suite for NLP in Italian. In: Proceedings of the Fifth Italian Conference on Computational Linguistics CLiC-it, vol. 10 (2018)

24. Pozzi, R., Moiraghi, F., Lodi, F., Palmonari, M.: Evaluation of incremental entity extraction with background knowledge and entity linking. In: Proceedings of the 11th International Joint Conference on Knowledge Graphs. IJCKG 2022, Association for Computing Machinery (2023)

25. Procopio, L., Conia, S., Barba, E., Navigli, R.: Entity disambiguation with entity definitions. In: Proceedings of the 17th Conference of the European Chapter of the Association for Computational Linguistics. Association for Computational Linguistics (2023)

26. Rosales-Méndez, H., Hogan, A., Poblete, B.: VoxEL: a benchmark dataset for multilingual entity linking. In: Vrandečić, D., et al. (eds.) ISWC 2018. LNCS, vol. 11137, pp. 170–186. Springer, Cham (2018). https://doi.org/10.1007/978-3-030-00668-6_11

27. Schweter, S.: Italian BERT and Electra models. Zenodo (2020)

28. Sevgili, O., Shelmanov, A., Arkhipov, M.V., Panchenko, A., Biemann, C.: Neural entity linking: a survey of models based on deep learning. Semant. Web **13**, 527–570 (2020)
29. Tamper, M., Oksanen, A., Tuominen, J., Hietanen, A., Hyvönen, E.: Automatic annotation service APPI: named entity linking in legal domain. In: The Semantic Web: ESWC 2020 Satellite Events. Springer International Publishing (2020)
30. Tedeschi, S., Navigli, R.: MultiNERD: a multilingual, multi-genre and fine-grained dataset for named entity recognition (and disambiguation). In: Findings of the Association for Computational Linguistics: NAACL 2022. Association for Computational Linguistics (2022)
31. Sang, E.F.T.K., De Meulder, F.: Introduction to the CoNLL-2003 shared task: language-independent named entity recognition. In: Proceedings of the Seventh Conference on Natural Language Learning at HLT-NAACL 2003 (2003)
32. Tsai, R.T.H., et al.: Various criteria in the evaluation of biomedical named entity recognition. BMC Bioinform. **7**, 1–8 (2006)
33. Vaswani, A., et al.: Attention is all you need. In: Advances in Neural Information Processing Systems, vol. 30. Curran Associates, Inc. (2017)
34. Wang, X., et al.: Automated concatenation of embeddings for structured prediction. In: Proceedings of the 59th Annual Meeting of the Association for Computational Linguistics and the 11th International Joint Conference on Natural Language Processing (Volume 1: Long Papers) (2021)
35. Wu, L., Petroni, F., Josifoski, M., Riedel, S., Zettlemoyer, L.: Scalable zero-shot entity linking with dense entity retrieval. In: Proceedings of the 2020 Conference on Empirical Methods in Natural Language Processing (EMNLP). Association for Computational Linguistics (2020)
36. Yamada, I., Shindo, H., Takeda, H., Takefuji, Y.: Joint learning of the embedding of words and entities for named entity disambiguation. In: Proceedings of the 20th SIGNLL Conference on Computational Natural Language Learning. Association for Computational Linguistics (2016)
37. Çetindağ, C., Yazıcıoğlu, B., Koç, A.: Named-entity recognition in Turkish legal texts. Nat. Lang. Eng. **29**, 615–642 (2023)

Machine Learning

CENTAURO: An Explainable AI Approach for Customer Loyalty Prediction in Retail Sector

Giuseppina Andresini[1,2] , Annalisa Appice[1,2] , Pasquale Ardimento[1] ,
Andrea Antonio Brunetta[1], Antonio Giuseppe Doronzo[1], Giuseppe Ieva[3],
Francesco Luce[1], Donato Malerba[1,2] , and Vincenzo Pasquadibisceglie[1,2(✉)]

[1] Department of Informatics, Università degli Studi di Bari Aldo Moro,
via Orabona, 4, 70125 Bari, Italy
{giuseppina.andresini,annalisa.appice,pasquale.ardimento,
donato.malerba}@uniba.it
[2] Consorzio Interuniversitario Nazionale per l'Informatica - CINI, via Orabona, 4,
70125 Bari, Italy
vincenzo.pasquadibisceglie@uniba.it
[3] Lutech Group, Cinisello Balsamo, Italy
g.ieva@lutech.it

Abstract. Customer loyalty is a crucial factor for retail business success. This paper illustrates an AI approach, named CENTAURO, to learn customer loyalty prediction models that may help retailers to run powerful loyalty programs and take better decisions. In particular, the proposed approach learns a classification model from the Recency, Frequency and Monetary (RFM) value of historical customer shopping data. For this purpose, the RFM model is extended to monitor Recency, Frequency and Monetary both over time and over the various categories of products purchased. Experiments performed with a benchmark dataset explore the performance of the extended RFM model in combination with several classification algorithms (e.g., Logistic Regression, Multi-Layer Perceptron, Random Forest, Decision Tree and XGBoost). Finally, we use an eXplainable Artificial Intelligence (XAI) technique – SHAP – to explore the effect of RFM values on the customer loyalty profile learned through the classification model.

Keywords: Churn Prediction · Customer Loyalty · Classification · XAI

1 Introduction

In today's fiercely competitive markets, organizations are deeply concerned about retaining their customers and preventing customer churns. The ability to predict customer loyalty is crucial for business stakeholders who would identify potential churners early on, in order to employ effective, preventive strategies.

© The Author(s), under exclusive license to Springer Nature Switzerland AG 2023
R. Basili et al. (Eds.): AIxIA 2023, LNAI 14318, pp. 205–217, 2023.
https://doi.org/10.1007/978-3-031-47546-7_14

Particularly in sectors like retail and e-commerce, where customers are not bound by contracts, the occurrence of non-contractual churn is quite common due to the low switching costs associated with finding alternative services [9]. On the other hand, the acquisition of new customers is an expensive activity that may cost five times as much as retaining existing ones [7]. Therefore, the availability of accurate loyalty prediction services is crucial to enable retail companies to identify customer behaviours that show signs of churn and proactively persuade these customers to stay with the company [10].

In the AI literature, predictive models of customer loyalty are mainly learned by adopting the RFM (Recency, Frequency, Monetary) value to describe the customer behaviour. This is a marketing technique that measures: the recency as how much time has elapsed since a customer performed the last purchase, the frequency as the number of purchases made by a customer within a reference period, and the amount of money spent by the customer within a reference period. Several AI studies evaluate the performance of various classification algorithms, e.g., Logistic Regression and Random Forest [4,6]. However, they commonly compute a single RFM value per customer. This value is measured on the entire (or recent) purchase history of the customer without paying attention to represent how the purchase behavior of a customer changes over time. With the boom of deep learning, a few recent studies have also started the investigation of the accuracy performance of deep neural models, mainly Long Short-Term Memory Neural Networks (LSTMs) and Convolutional Neural Networks (CNNs), trained on customers' sequence data [5]. For example, [1] learns an LSTM for customer loyalty prediction from data sequences composed of average RFM values progressively incremented on intervals of growing length over time. On the other hand, some studies explore the accuracy performance of customer loyalty prediction models trained by enriching the RFM value of a customer with product-based information, e.g., the product category variance [2]. Although these studies account for information related to product categories, they neglect possible changes happening in which categories of products have been purchased over time. Finally, we note that despite several studies explore the accuracy performance of various classification models learned for predicting customer loyalty in several domains (e.g., telecommunication services, online gaming, multimedia streaming, banking and insurance agencies), only a few research studies focus on the problem of customer loyalty in retail. This may be due to the lack of public datasets. In fact, the Brazilian Olist dataset is one of the few public datasets recording purchase data for studying the problem of customer loyalty prediction in the retail sector. This dataset has been recently used in [8] to compare the performance of various classification algorithms used to learn a churn prediction models from demographic, geographic and purchase data of customers. Although this study describes the imbalanced condition of non-churn data, it is limited to consider a hypothetical balanced condition with equal number of churn and non-churn samples.

This work aims to define an XAI-based approach to predict customer loyalty in the retail sector with a good trade-off between accuracy and explainability. Hence, a contribution of this study is the definition of an approach named CENTAURO (An extended reCency frEquency moNeTary model for explAinable cUstomer pRedictiOn), that integrates an extended RFM model, to extract smart representation of how a customer's RFM value changes over both the time and the categories of products purchased. We consider the original data recorded in the Brazilian Olist dataset, to explore the effect of smart customer data extracted through the proposed extended RFM model on the accuracy performance of classification models trained with multiple classification algorithms (i.e., Logistic Regression, Multi-Layer Perceptron, Random Forest, Decision Tree and XGBoost). Another contribution is the study of how RFM values measured in a customer profile has an effect on the customer loyalty classification produced through a classification model. For this purpose, we use the SHAP explainer [3]. This is an eXplainable AI, model-agnostic technique that measures the Shapley values to explain model decisions. The analysis of SHAP explanations allow us to identify the main dimensions of the RFM model that has the higher effect on the recognition of churners.

The rest of the paper is organized as follows. Preliminary concepts are provided in Sect. 2. The customer loyalty prediction approach is described in Sect. 3, while the experimental results are discussed in Sect. 4. Finally, in Sect. 5, the conclusions are drawn.

2   Preliminary Concepts

In this section, we introduce the terminology referred to purchase basket, sale receipt, sale receipt stream, customer trace, RFM value, churn condition and churn classification model. Given a retail business company, a customer is a user who performs periodic purchases, while a sale receipt is a receipt associated with a purchase basket. According to this definition of a sale receipt, a sale receipt stream is a stream of timestamped sale receipts associated one-to-one with customers' purchase baskets. Let $\mathcal{C}$ be the set of all customer identifiers, $\mathcal{P}$ be the set of product categories that can be added to a purchase basket and $\mathcal{T}$ be the set of all timestamps. Timestamps are formatted as $Month.Day.Year\ Hours : Minutes : Seconds$. Let $CURRENT\ TIME$ denote the current timestamp. Let us consider $time \in \mathcal{T}$, $day(time)$ returns the calendar day of $time$, while $midnight(time)$ denotes the midnight of $day(time)$. For example, $day(05.07.23\ 20 : 01 : 05) = 05.07.23$, while $midnight(05.07.23\ 20 : 01 : 05) = 05.07.23\ 24 : 00 : 00$.

Definition 1 (Purchase Basket Item). *Given the purchase basket item universe $\mathcal{B} = (\mathcal{P} \times \mathbb{N}^+ \times \mathbb{R}^+)$, a purchase basket item $i \in \mathcal{B}$ is a triple $i = (p, q, a)$ that represents the purchase of q units of product category p at the price of a per unit.*

Definition 2 (Purchase Basket). *A purchase basket $b \in \mathcal{B}^*$ is a set of purchase basket items.*

Definition 3 (Sale Receipt). *Given the sale receipt universe $\mathcal{S} = \mathcal{C} \times \mathcal{T} \times \mathcal{B}^*$, a sale receipt $s \in \mathcal{S}$ is a triple $s = (c, time, b)$ that represents the purchase of basket b by customer c at timestamp $CURRENT\ TIME$.*

Table 1. An example of a sale receipt stream Σ

Sale Receipt Id	Customer	Timestamp	Purchase basket
s_1	Paul	05.01.23 12:00:23	[(apple,3,5), (pasta,2,7)]
s_2	Mary	05.01.23 12:00:23	[(apple,3,5), (disk,1,4)]
s_3	Elliot	05.01.23 20:00:01	[(disk,3,7)]
s_4	Paul	05.02.23 08:00:25	[(apple,5,6)]
s_5	Mary	05.03.23 09:00:25	[(book,3,2), (fish,2,6)]
s_6	Paul	05.03.23 19:01:05	[(meat,4,7), (fish,1,8)]
s_7	Paul	05.03.23 20:01:05	[(meat,2,7)]
s_8	Paul	05.04.23 20:01:05	[(flower,5,1)]
s_9	Mary	05.04.23 21:01:05	[(disk,2,1)]
s_{10}	Mary	05.06.23 11:21:00	[(disk,1,1),(apple,3,4)]
s_{11}	Elliot	05.07.23 19:00:05	[(flower,5,1)]
s_{12}	Elliot	05.07.23 20:01:05	[(apple,5,1),(book,2,4)]
$\ldots$	$\ldots$	$\ldots$	$\ldots$

Let us introduce the functions: $\Pi_{\mathcal{C}} : \mathcal{S} \mapsto \mathcal{C}$ such that $\Pi_{\mathcal{C}}(s) = c$, $\Pi_{\mathcal{T}} : \mathcal{S} \mapsto \mathcal{T}$ such that $\Pi_{\mathcal{T}}(s) = time$ and $\Pi_{\mathcal{B}^*} : \mathcal{S} \mapsto \mathcal{B}^*$ such that $\Pi_{\mathcal{B}^*}(s) = b$.

Definition 4 (Sale Receipt Stream). *A sale receipt stream Σ is an (infinite) sequence of sale receipts $\mathbb{N}^+ \mapsto \mathcal{S}$, that is, $\Sigma = s_1, s_2, \ldots, s_t, \ldots$ so that $\forall t \in \mathbb{N}^+$, $s_t \in \mathcal{S}$ and $\Pi_{\mathcal{T}}(s_t) \leq \Pi_{\mathcal{T}}(s_{t+1})$.*

Given a sale receipt stream Σ, the selection $\Sigma(t)$ is the t-sale receipt recorded in Σ. $size(\Sigma) \in \mathbb{N}^+$ is the number of sale receipts recorded in Σ.

Definition 5 (Customer Trace). *Given a sale receipt stream Σ and a customer $c \in \mathcal{C}$, the customer trace $\sigma(c, \Sigma)$ is the sequence $\mathcal{C} \times \mathbb{N}^+ \mapsto \mathcal{S}^*$ of sale receipts of customer c recorded in Σ, that is, $\sigma(c, \Sigma) = s_1, s_2, \ldots, s_n$, such that $\forall i = 1, 2, \ldots, n - 1$, $\Pi_{\mathcal{T}}(s_i) \leq \Pi_{\mathcal{T}}(s_{i+1})$ and $\forall i = 1, 2, \ldots, n$, $\exists t \in \mathbb{N}^+$ with $t \leq size(\Sigma)$ such that $\Sigma(t) = s_i$ and $\Pi_{\mathcal{C}}(s_i) = c$.*

Given a customer trace $\sigma(c, \Sigma)$, the operator $observe(\sigma(c, \Sigma)) \in \mathcal{S}$ returns the latest sale receipt recorded in $\sigma(c, \Sigma)$. For example, let us consider the sale receipt stream Σ reported in Table 1, and customer *Paul*,

$$\sigma(Paul, \Sigma) = (Paul, 05.01.23 \ 12:00:23, [(apple, 3, 5), (pasta, 2, 7)]),$$
$$(Paul, 05.02.23 \ 08:00:25, [(apple, 5, 6)]),$$
$$(Paul, 05.03.23 \ 19:01:05, [(meat, 4, 7), (fish, 1, 8)]),$$
$$(Paul, 05.03.23 \ 20:01:05, [(meat, 2, 7)]),$$
$$(Paul, 05.04.23 \ 20:01:05, [(flower, 5, 1)]),$$
$$observe(\sigma(Paul, \Sigma)) = (Paul, 05.04.23 \ 20:01:05, [(flower, 5, 1)]).$$

In this study, the RFM value is used to model the purchase pattern of a customer trace.

Definition 6 (RFM model). *Given a customer trace $\sigma(c, \Sigma) \in \mathcal{S}^*$. The Recency (R) is a function $\rho \colon \mathcal{S}^* \times \mathcal{T} \mapsto \mathbb{N}$ so that $\rho(\sigma(c, \Sigma), CURRENT\ TIME)$ measures the customer recency (i.e., how long ago, with respect to CURRENT TIME, he/she made a purchase in $\sigma(c, \Sigma)$). The Frequency (F) is a function $\phi \colon \mathcal{S}^* \mapsto \mathbb{N}$ so that $\phi(\sigma(c, \Sigma))$ measures the customer frequency (i.e., how often he/she makes purchases in $\sigma(c, \Sigma)$), and Monetary (M) is a function $\mu \colon \mathcal{S}^* \mapsto \mathbb{R}$ so that $\mu(\sigma(c, \Sigma))$ measures the customer monetary value (i.e., how much money he/she spends in $\sigma(c, \Sigma)$).*

For example, let us consider current $CURRENT\ TIME = 05.04.23\ 24 : 00 : 00$, then $\rho(\sigma(Paul, \Sigma), CURRENT\ TIME) = 0$, $\phi(\sigma(Paul, \Sigma)) = 5$ and $\mu(\sigma(Paul, \Sigma)) = (15+14)+30+(28+8)+14+5 = 114$. We note that the recency will increase by one for each new day that passes without Paul producing a receipt (e.g., $\rho(\sigma(Paul, \Sigma), CURRENT\ TIME) = 1$ on $CURRENT\ TIME = 05.05.23\ 24 : 00 : 00$).

Definition 7 (Churn status). *Given a sale receipt stream Σ, a churn time amount ΔT (in days), a customer c stays in a churn status in Σ if ΔT days have passed since the last sale receipt of c was stored in Σ, that is, $churn(c, \Sigma) = churn$ iff $CURRENT\ TIME - \Pi_T(observe(c, \Sigma)) \geq \Delta T$, non-churn otherwise.*

In this study, we assume that the churn status of a customer c is evaluated at midnight of each day. Hence, if $churn(c, \Sigma) = churn$, then $t = midnight(\Pi_T(observe(c, \Sigma))) + \Delta T$ denotes the timestamp at which the churn status of c started in Σ. Let us consider the sale receipt stream Σ reported in Table 1. Let us assume $\Delta T = 2$ days, the churn status of $Paul$ started on $05.06.23\ 24 : 00 : 00$, while the churn status of $Elliot$ started on $05.03.23\ 24 : 00 : 00$. We note that the churn status of a customer can be temporary. For example, the churn alert on $Elliot$, which starts on $05.03.23\ 24 : 00 : 00$, is cancelled as soon as a new sale receipt $(Elliot, 05.07.23\ 19 : 00 : 05, [(flower, 5, 1)])$ is recorded in Σ on $05.07.23\ 19 : 00 : 05$.

According to the formulated definition of churn status, there is a delay between when a sale receipt is recorded in a customer trace and when it will be known if the customer must be labeled as a churn case in the next future. A retail business company would know churn cases as soon as possible, if possible when the last sale receipt of the customer was recorded in the sale receipt stream. For example, the company would predict the churn of $Elliot$, started on $05.03.23\ 24 : 00 : 00$, as close as possible to $05.01.23\ 20 : 00 : 00$, that is the time of registration of the last sale receipt of $Elliot$ in Σ. This customer loyalty prediction problem can formulated as a binary classification problem with labeled samples produced for customer traces.

Definition 8 (Churn classification model). *A churn classification model is defined as a function $M_\Theta \colon \mathcal{S}^* \times \mathcal{T} \mapsto \{churn, non - churn\}$ with the real-valued parameters $\Theta \in \mathbb{R}^m$ learned from a churn training set D.*

Table 2. A portion of the labeled customer trace set extracted from the sale receipt stream Σ reported in Table 1. σ denotes the customer trace, t denotes the time and l denotes the churn label.

σ	t	l
$(Paul, 05.01.23\ 12:00:23, [(apple, 3, 5), (pasta, 2, 7)])$	$05.01.23\ 24:00:00$	$non-churn$
$(Mary, 05.01.23\ 12:01.23, [(apple, 3, 5), (disk, 1, 4)])$	$05.01.23\ 24:00:00$	$non-churn$
$(Mary, 05.01.23\ 12:01.23, [(apple, 3, 5), (disk, 1, 4)])$	$05.02.23\ 24:00:00$	$non-churn$
$(Elliot, 05.01.23\ 20:00:01, [(disk, 3, 7)])$	$05.01.23\ 24:00:00$	$churn$
$(Elliot, 05.01.23\ 20:00:01, [(disk, 3, 7)])$	$05.02.23\ 24:00:00$	$churn$
$(Paul, 05.01.23\ 12:00:23, [(apple, 3, 5), (pasta, 2, 7)]),$ $(Paul, 05.02.23\ 08:00:25, [(apple, 5, 6)])$	$05.02.23\ 24:00:00$	$non-churn$
$\ldots$	$\ldots$	$\ldots$

To create the training dataset for learning a churn classification model, we take into account that a new customer trace is available as soon as a new sale receipt of the customer is recorded in Σ. However, the label of this customer trace is unknown at the observation time. This label is known after some time, i.e., as soon as the customer makes a new purchase before the churn time passed (non-churn) or the churn time has passed without a new purchase being made by the customer (churn). In addition, as the passage of time since the last purchase modifies the customer RFM value (e.g., it has an effect on the Recency value) and, consequently, the prediction of churners based on RFM values, we produce multiple samples for the same customer trace to reproduce the passage of time. For each new day that has passed since the date of the last purchase, a new sample is produced with the customer trace associated with the midnight of that day.

Definition 9 (Churn training set). *Given a sale receipt stream Σ and a churn time amount ΔT, the churn training set $D \in \mathbf{P}(\mathcal{S}^* \times \mathcal{T} \times \{churn, non-churn\})$ is a set of triples composed of: a customer trace extracted from Σ, a time at which the RFM of the customer trace is measured to perform a prediction of the churn condition and the churn label of the customer trace. Let $\sigma(c, \Sigma)$ be a customer trace updated as soon as a new sale receipt of customer c is recorded in Σ. Let labelTime denote the timestamp at which the churn label l of $\sigma(c, \Sigma)$ is known in Σ so that $labelTime \geq \Pi_{\mathcal{T}}(observe(\sigma(c, \Sigma)))$. We distinguish two cases:*

1. *If $midnight(\Pi_{\mathcal{T}}(observe(\sigma(c, \Sigma)))) < midnight(labelTime)$, then a sequence of triples $(\sigma(c, \Sigma), t, l)$ is produced and added to D with $midnight(\Pi_{\mathcal{T}}(observe(\sigma(c, \Sigma)))) \leq t < midnight(labelTime)$ and $midnight(t) = t$.*
2. *If $midnight(\Pi_{\mathcal{T}}(observe(\sigma(c, \Sigma)))) = midnight(labelTime)$, then a single triple $(\sigma(c, \Sigma), t, l)$ is produced and added to D with $t = midnight(labelTime)$.*

Table 2 reports a portion of the churn training set D that is extracted from the sale receipt stream Σ shown in Table 1. Let us consider a churn classification model M_Θ and the customer trace $\sigma(c, \Sigma)$ whose last sale receipt has been stored in the sale receipt stream less than ΔT days ago, $M_\Theta(\sigma(c, \Sigma))$ can be used to predict the churn status of customer c within ΔT days of his/her last sale receipt will be recorded in Σ. We note that if ΔT days have passed since the last sale receipt stored for c in Σ, there is no reason to predict the churn status of c since the same has already occurred. For example, let us consider the sale receipt stream Σ in Table 1. At time stamp 05.07.23 08 : 01 : 05, we know that *Paul* has been already recognized as a churner on 05.06.23 24 : 00 : 00, while we are interested in using a churn classification model M_Θ to predict if either *Mary* will become a churner at midnight on 05.08.23 24 : 00 : 00 or *Elliot* will become a churner at midnight on 05.09.23 24 : 00 : 00.

3   The **CENTAURO** Approach

The CENTAURO approach allows us to learn a churn classification model for monitoring customer loyalty in retail sector problems. Let us consider a historical sale receipt stream Σ and a churn time amount ΔT. In the training stage, CEN-TAURO extracts the churn training set $D \in \mathbf{P}(\mathcal{S}^* \times \mathcal{T} \times \{churn, non - churn\})$ from Σ with churn period ΔT (see Definition 9) and learns parameters Θ of a churn classification model $M_\Theta : \mathcal{S}^* \times \mathcal{T} \mapsto \{churn, non - churn\}$ (see Definition 8) by minimizing a cost function on D. Any classification algorithm can be used to learn M_Θ. Regardless of the classification algorithm chosen, the classification algorithm is fueled with a smart feature vector representation of the raw customer traces associated with samples recorded in D. In CENTAURO, this feature vector representation is extracted through an extended RFM model. In the monitoring stage, CENTAURO uses the churn classification model M_Θ to monitor an online receipt purchase stream and perform customer loyalty predictions, in order to recognize churn cases from the time of the last purchase performed until the time at which the churn (or non-churn) case is finally verified.

The extended RFM model adopted in this study extends the traditional RFM model (see Definition 6), in order to disclose patterns on how the RFM values of a customer have changed over time and by the product categories purchased. For this purpose, the Recency, Frequency and Monetary features of the extended RFM model are extracted by processing a customer trace with both a temporal consumer and a product category consumer, respectively. Given a customer trace $\sigma(c, \Sigma) \in \mathcal{S}^*$ (see Definition 5), let us consider that the customer purchase habits may change over time, but the most recent purchase habits are more influential than the oldest purchase habits in assessing a customer's loyalty. Based upon these premises, we account for the sale receipts of $\sigma(c, \Sigma)$, which have been timestamped in the most recent $\Delta T \times n$ days, while we forget the oldest ones. n is a user-defined parameter that represents the number of periods. In the adopted formulation, each period is as long as a churn period.

Based on the period-based decomposition of $\sigma(c, \Sigma)$, two groups of features can be extracted:

- Temporal RFM: For each period $j = 1, \ldots, n$, the RFM values of a customer trace are extracted by consuming the sale receipts of $\sigma(c, \Sigma)$ recorded in period j. This schema produces a purchase profile of $\sigma(c, \Sigma)$ with $3 \cdot n$ features.

– Aggregated Temporal RFM: This schema determines the minimum, maximum, mean and standard deviation of Recency values, Frequency values and Monetary values measured for $\sigma(c, \Sigma)$ on the n periods considered in the Temporal RFM. It produces a purchase profile of $\sigma(c, \Sigma)$ with 12 features.

The two feature schemes reported above allow us to capture how values of Recency, Frequency and Monetary of a customer have evolved in the recent customer history. In this study, we further extend the RFM model, to account for differences in the product categories appearing in the purchase baskets of the sale receipts of a customer trace. To this aim, for each product category, the RFM values are extracted from the sale receipts recorded in $\sigma(c, \Sigma)$ by considering the purchase basket items that contain the product category considered. Let N be the number of distinct product categories. Based on the product-based decomposition of $\sigma(c, \Sigma)$, two groups of features can be extracted:

– Product-based RFM: For each period $j = 1, \ldots, n$, for each product category $p = 1, \ldots, N$, the RFM values of the customer trace are extracted by consuming the purchase basket items recorded for the product category p in the sale receipts of $\sigma(c, \Sigma)$ timestamped in period j. This schema produces a purchase profile of $\sigma(c, \Sigma)$ with $3 \cdot n \cdot N$ features.
– Aggregated Product-based RFM: This schemes determines, for each product category $p = 1, \ldots, N$, the minimum, maximum, mean and standard deviation of the Recency values, Frequency values and Monetary values extracted on the n periods for product category p with the Product-based RFM. This schema produces a purchase profile of $\sigma(c, \Sigma)$ with $12 \cdot N$ features.

Finally, CENTAURO integrates a post-hoc eXplainable AI technique to understand how the different characteristics of a customer purchase profile, extracted through the extended RFM model, can provide useful knowledge to monitor customer loyalty. These explanations may help in the root-cause-analysis of churn cases by disclosing useful information for planning effective alerting strategies to early recognize customer loyalty. For this purpose, CENTAURO integrates SHAP [3], an eXplainable AI technique for understanding both the global and local structure of predictive models. SHAP performs a theoretic game approach, to determine the contribution of each input feature to the prediction (relevance value) of a classifier as the average marginal contribution of a feature value for all possible predictions. Intuitively, if a feature is important, then randomly permuting its values will cause the loss to increase. By analyzing what features have greater relevance on decisions, we can identify the features that contribute the most to the characterization (and detection) of churn cases.

4   Experimental Results

We conducted a range of experiments on the Brazilian E-commerce public data set collected from the public repository on Kaggle.com, in order to evaluate the accuracy performance of CENTAURO. For the experimental study, we used the implementation of CENTAURO done in Python 3.9 - 64 bit version.

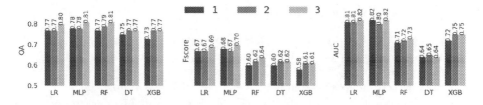

Fig. 1. OA, FScore and AUC of CENTAURO run with Temporal RFM schema by varying the number of periods n among 1, 2 and 3 and the classification algorithm among Logistic Regression (LR), Multi-Layer Perceptron (MLP), Random Forest (RF), Decision Tree (DT) and XGBoost (XGB)

4.1 Data and Experimental Setting

Brazilian E-commerce dataset[1] is a public dataset of real commercial data concerning sale receipts made at Olist Store. The dataset collects 100k sale receipts from 2016, October 7, to September 2, 2018 made at multiple marketplaces in Brazil. It contains data on purchase baskets, payments and product categories (for a total of 74 product categories). In this study, we considered customers who had made at least two different purchase transactions and we selected sale receipts produced by these customers. This allowed us to select 3345 sale receipts. We sorted the selected sale receipts by their timestamps and generated a sale receipt stream. We considered a churn period of 120 days, that is, the customer was regarded as a churner as he/she did not produce any sale receipt for consecutive 120 days. As we planned to test CENTAURO with RFM values extracted on customer trace histories composed of one period, two periods and three periods ($n = 1, 2, 3$), we considered the customer traces produced in 2017 between June 6 and October 6 for the training stage. We used the remaining customer traces produced between 2017 October 7 and 2018 September 9 for the evaluation stage. We adopted the temporal split in order to simulate the real-world scenario. We processed 34920 churn samples and 8041 non-churn samples in the training stage, and 305160 non-churn samples and 52156 churn samples in testing stage. We performed various experiments to analyse the accuracy performance of CENTAURO by considering the classification algorithms: Logistic Regression, Multi-Layer Perceptron, Random Forest, Decision Tree and XGBoost using the default hyperparameters configuration as implemented in Scikit-learn library[2]. For each configuration, we measured the Overall Accuracy (OA), Macro Fscore (Fscore) and Area Under the ROC (AUC). In addition, we used SHAP to explain which dimensions of the RFM model mainly contribute to produce decisions on churn customer traces.

4.2   Results and Discussion

We start this analysis by exploring the effect of the number of periods n on the accuracy of the churn classification model. For this purpose, we analyse the accuracy performance of churn classification models learned with input features extracted according to the Temporal RFM schema by varying the number of periods n among 1, 2 and 3. Results of OA, Fscore and AUC are reported in Fig. 1. These results show that monitoring RFM values measured on several periods of the recent history of customers aids in gaining accuracy, regardless of the classification algorithm. In any case, the highest accuracy performance is achieved with classification models learned with both Logistic Regression and Multi-Layer Perceptron.

We continue this analysis by using Logistic Regression and Multi-Layer Perceptron as classification algorithms and exploring the accuracy performance of classification models learned with these two algorithms by processing input features produced with: Temporal RFM, Aggregated Temporal RFM, Product-based RFM and Aggregated Product-based Temporal RFM with $n = 3$ (i.e., the best configuration reported in Fig. 1). Results of OA, Fscore and AUC are reported in Table 3. These results show that performing aggregations on the sequences of RFM values computed on customer traces allows us to produce a smarter representation of customers' purchase profiles. This representation boosts the learning of classification models that gain accuracy in the task of churn classification. Instead, computing customers' purchase profiles at the level of product categories lead us to learn a churn classification model that lacks in generality and, hence, achieves worse accuracy performance in correctly disentangling churn traces from non-churn traces. These conclusions can be drawn, regardless of the classification algorithm.

Finally, we analyse the effect of the input dimensions of customers' purchase profiles on decisions concerning customer traces in the classes: churn and non-churn. We perform this analysis on the classification model trained with Multi-Layer Perceptron using the input feature space produced with the Aggregated Temporal RFM schema and computing the Shapley values of the model decisions on the testing samples. Figure 2 shows the Shapley values grouped with respect to the ground-truth class. Positive Shapley values identify input dimensions which are relevant for the considered class. Features are ranked by the average of the measured Shapley value so that the top-ranked features are the most important dimensions for the class. This analysis discloses some interesting patterns on both churner and non-churner profiles. In particular, low values of both maximum Recency and mean Recency are the top-two relevant dimensions of the non-churn profile, while high values of Standard Deviation of both Monetary and Recency are the top-two relevant dimensions of the churn profile. Surprisingly, low values of minimum, maximum and mean Frequency have a relevant effect on the non-churn profile, while high values of minimum, maximum and mean Frequency have a relevant effect on the churn profile. This suggests that churners may appear abruptly in the e-commerce scenario.

Table 3. OA, Fscore and AUC of CENTAURO run with the feature schemes: Temporal RFM (RFM), Aggregated Temporal RFM (A-RFM), Product-based RFM (P-RFM) and Aggregated Product-based Temporal RFM (A-P-RFM) by wrapping Logistic Regression and Multi-Layer Perceptron as classification algorithm. All features schemes are computed with $n = 3$. The best results are in bold.

Features	Logistic Regression			Multi-Layer Perceptron		
	OA	Fscore	AUC	OA	Fscore	AUC
RFM	0.80	0.69	0.82	0.81	0.70	0.82
A-RFM	**0.84**	**0.73**	**0.85**	**0.85**	**0.74**	**0.84**
P-RFM	0.72	0.61	0.72	0.74	0.62	0.71
A-P-RFM	0.75	0.64	0.74	0.75	0.63	0.73
RFM+P-RFM	0.78	0.66	0.76	0.76	0.64	0.73
A-RFM+P-RFM	0.77	0.65	0.76	0.75	0.63	0.73
RFM+A-RFM	0.81	0.70	0.83	0.82	0.71	0.82
P-RFM+A-P-RFM	0.74	0.63	0.73	0.74	0.62	0.72
RFM+A-P-RFM	0.75	0.64	0.75	0.76	0.64	0.73
A-RFM+A-P-RFM	0.77	0.65	0.76	0.78	0.65	0.74
RFM+A-RFM+P-RFM	0.77	0.66	0.77	0.75	0.63	0.73
RFM+P-RFM+A-P-RFM	0.77	0.65	0.75	0.76	0.64	0.73
P-RFM+A-RFM+A-P-RFM	0.76	0.64	0.75	0.76	0.63	0.73
RFM + A-RFM+P-RFM	0.76	0.65	0.76	0.76	0.64	0.74
RFM+A-RFM+P-RFM+A-P-RFM	0.77	0.65	0.75	0.76	0.64	0.73

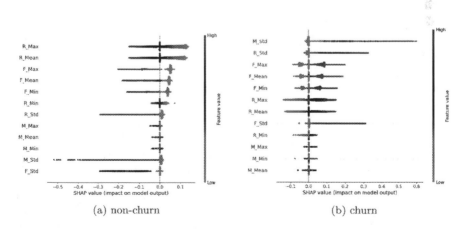

(a) non-churn   (b) churn

Fig. 2. Shapley values of the input dimensions of the Aggregated Temporal RFM schema for the classes: *churn* and *non − churn*. Shapley values are computed using the Multi-Layer Perceptron classification model on the testing samples, that have been grouped with respect to the ground-truth class.

5 Conclusion

This study illustrates an AI approach for customer loyalty monitoring in retail sector. The proposed approach allows us to learn a churn classification model from the RFM value of a customer. In particular, we introduce an extended RFM model to describe the possible variations in the RFM value of a customer over time and over various categories of products. Experiments performed with a benchmark dataset explores the effectiveness of the proposed approach by varying the classification algorithm. Finally, we use SHAP to explain the effect of the RFM value on the decisions of the churn classification model. As future work, we plan to extend this investigation to new datasets (collected outside the retail sector). In addition, we plan to extend the proposed approach to a data stream scenario, in order to detect and handle concept drifts in retail data.

Acknowledgment. The work of Giuseppina Andresini and Vincenzo Pasquadibisceglie was supported by the project FAIR - Future AI Research (PE00000013), Spoke 6 - Symbiotic AI, under the NRRP MUR program funded by the NextGenerationEU. The work of Annalisa Appice, Pasquale Ardimento, Donato Malerba and Giuseppe Ieva was in partial fulfilment of the research objectives of the Research Contract "LUTECH DIGITALE 4.0: Progetto di Tecniche di Machine Learning predittivo per la piattaforma di Loyalty Management" within the project "LUTECH DIGITALE 4.0".

References

1. Ahn, J., Hwang, J., Kim, D., Choi, H., Kang, S.: A survey on churn analysis in various business domains. IEEE Access **8**, 220816–220839 (2020)
2. Jha, N., Parekh, D., Mouhoub, M., Makkar, V.: Customer segmentation and churn prediction in online retail. In: Goutte, C., Zhu, X. (eds.) Canadian AI 2020. LNCS (LNAI), vol. 12109, pp. 328–334. Springer, Cham (2020). https://doi.org/10.1007/978-3-030-47358-7_33
3. Lundberg, S.M., Lee, S.I.: A unified approach to interpreting model predictions. In: Guyon, I., et al. (eds.) Advances in Neural Information Processing Systems, vol. 30. Curran Associates, Inc. (2017)
4. Martins, H.: Predicting user churn on streaming services using recurrent neural networks (2017)
5. Mena, C.G., De Caigny, A., Coussement, K., De Bock, K.W., Lessmann, S.: Churn prediction with sequential data and deep neural networks. a comparative analysis. arXiv preprint arXiv:1909.11114 (2019)
6. Mohammadzadeh, M., Hoseini, Z.Z., Derafshi, H.: A data mining approach for modeling churn behavior via RFM model in specialized clinics case study: a public sector hospital in Tehran. In: 9th International Conference on Theory and Application of Soft Computing, Computing with Words and Perception, ICSCCW 2017, pp. 23–30 (2017)
7. Slof, D., Frasincar, F., Matsiiako, V.: A competing risks model based on latent dirichlet allocation for predicting churn reasons. Decis. Support Syst. **146**, 113541 (2021)
8. Sweidan, D., Johansson, U., Gidenstam, A., Alenljung, B.: Predicting customer churn in retailing. In: 2022 21st IEEE International Conference on Machine Learning and Applications, (ICMLA), pp. 635–640 (2022)

9. Tamaddoni Jahromi, A., Sepehri, M.M., Teimourpour, B., Choobdar, S.: Modeling customer churn in a non-contractual setting: the case of telecommunications service providers. J. Strateg. Mark. **18**(7), 587–598 (2010)
10. Verbeke, W., Martens, D., Baesens, B.: Social network analysis for customer churn prediction. Appl. Soft Comput. **14**, 431–446 (2014)

Toward Novel Optimizers:
A Moreau-Yosida View of Gradient-Based Learning

Alessandro Betti[1(✉)], Gabriele Ciravegna[2], Marco Gori[1,3], Stefano Melacci[3],
Kevin Mottin[1], and Frédéric Precioso[1]

[1] Université Côte d'Azur, Inria, CNRS, Laboratoire I3S, Maasai Team, Nice, France
{alessandro.betti,kevin.mottin,frederic.precioso}@inria.fr
[2] Politecnico di Torino, Torino, Italy
gabriele.ciravegna@polito.it
[3] Department of Information Engineering and Mathematics, University of Siena,
Siena, Italy
marco.gori@unisi.it, mela@diism.unisi.it

Abstract. Machine Learning (ML) strongly relies on optimization procedures that are based on gradient descent. Several gradient-based update schemes have been proposed in the scientific literature, especially in the context of neural networks, that have become common optimizers in software libraries for ML. In this paper, we re-frame gradient-based update strategies under the unifying lens of a Moreau-Yosida (MY) approximation of the loss function. By means of a first-order Taylor expansion, we make the MY approximation concretely exploitable to generalize the model update. In turn, this makes it easy to evaluate and compare the regularization properties that underlie the most common optimizers, such as gradient descent with momentum, ADAGRAD, RMSprop, and ADAM. The MY-based unifying view opens to the possibility of designing novel update schemes with customizable regularization properties. As case-study we propose to use the network outputs to deform the notion of closeness in the parameter space.

1 Introduction

Gradient based optimization procedures are arguably one of the main ingredients of Machine Learning (ML). As a matter of fact, the success of deep learning strongly relies on the efficiency of Stochastic Gradient Descent (SGD) to solve large scale optimization problems [3]. It is pretty common to introduce the gradient descent method in Euclidean spaces, leveraging on the geometrical interpretation of the *direction of steepest descent* [5], that yields the definition of gradient descent by means of an iterative procedure. In particular, we are given a function f which we aim at minimizing, and which depends on some parameters $w \in \mathbb{R}^N$. If w^k are the values of the parameters at the k-th step of the gradient descent, their update scheme is given by

$$w^{k+1} = w^k - \tau \nabla f(w^k), \tag{1}$$

© The Author(s), under exclusive license to Springer Nature Switzerland AG 2023
R. Basili et al. (Eds.): AIxIA 2023, LNAI 14318, pp. 218–230, 2023.
https://doi.org/10.1007/978-3-031-47546-7_15

for some initial $w^0 = w_0 \in \mathbb{R}^N$ and $\tau > 0$ (learning rate, step size), being ∇f the gradient of f with respect to w. The ML literature includes several works aimed at providing adaptive values for τ, eventually considering a specific learning rate for each component of w, or introducing further terms in the update rule [7,10, 19,22]. Despite their large ubiquity in implementations of ML-based solutions, such works are inspired by different principles and they are presented starting from different problem formulations, that make it hard to quickly compare them. Moreover, simply looking at the final update rules they devise is not enough to fully grasp what are the expected effects they bring to the optimization. Delving into their details to trace connections among them is definitely possible, but it is not straightforward.

Motivated by these considerations, in this paper we propose to reconsider the aforementioned update rules, casting them all into a *unified view* in which w^{k+1} is presented as the solution of a newly introduced optimization problem with well-defined and clearly interpretable regularity conditions. Such conditions constrain the variation between w^k and w^{k+1}, thus making it easier to understand the expected properties of the solution (w^{k+1}) and to compare different approaches. Our idea is rooted on the so-called Moreau-Yosida (MY) approximation of a function [1], that we apply to the loss f, and it is motivated by evident analogies between the stationary points defining the MY approximation and update rules in the form of Eq. (1). It turns out that directly dealing with such approximation is not enough to recover the update scheme of Eq. (1), thus we investigate the first-order Taylor expansion of f in the MY approximation to devise a related optimization problem whose solution is indeed equivalent to Eq. (1) under certain regularity conditions. Beyond the benefits introduced by the interpretability of the proposed unified view, it is important to remark that our main goal is to provide researches with a formulation that more easily opens to the development of novel, more informed, optimizers. A related approach is well-known and exploited in the specific context of the online learning community [4], still not widely known to a wider ML audience.

In order to emphasize the usefulness of the proposed uniform view, we consider a case-study in which data is continuously streamed and learning proceeds in a continual manner [6,12,18]. Since our contribution is theoretical, our goal is to showcase the flexibility of the MY view in injecting problem-related prior knowledge in the update scheme, while proposing powerful experimentally-validated optimizers goes beyond the scope of this paper. In particular, we exploit the MY approximation to design a novel update scheme for the weights of a neural network , modulating the strength of the updates in function of the variations of the predictions over time. In the considered setting it is widely known that it is hard to find a good trade-off between plasticity and stability [18], and we follow the assumption for which strong output variations might be associated to significant changes in the data, thus they require the network to be more plastic in order to adapt to the novel information. Differently, small variations triggers less significant updates, preserving the already learned information, thus favouring stability. We notice that while the use of a regularization based on information from the output space of a model is a well-known principle behind Manifold Regularization [2,15], here we show how it can be exploited in continual learning by direct injection in the update rule of the model parameters. Moreover, recent approaches to continual learning exploited related heuristics to improve the quality of the learning process [13], even if without a clear theoretical formalization behind them.

The paper is organized as follows (see Fig. 1): Sect. 2 is devoted to the description of the MY approximation, its properties, the uniform view of gradient-based learning, and its relationships with proximal algorithms. Section 3 revisits commonly used optimization methods in Machine Learning in the context of the proposed uniform view, describing all of them in a unique, common, framework. In Sect. 4, we present a case-study based on an output-modulated update scheme. Section 5 concludes the paper with our final discussions.

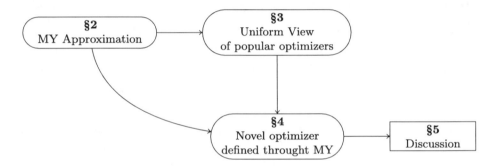

Fig. 1. Conceptual scheme of the organization of the article, that highlights the main theoretical contributions.

2   From Moreau-Yosida Approximations to Gradient-Based Learning

In this section we formally introduce the Moreau-Yosida (MY) approximation that we consider in the context of this paper, Definition 1. Then, we will exploit such notion to setup an update scheme, Eq. (9), based on a related optimization problem whose minima are described by the same recursive rule of gradient based methods. This fully connects the MY approximation and gradient-based learning, yielding a uniform view that we will exploit in the rest of the paper. For completeness, we also discuss its relations with proximal algorithms (Sect. 2.1).

Definition 1 (Moreau-Yosida Approximation). *Given a non-negative, lower semicontinuous function $f \colon \mathbb{R}^N \to \mathbb{R}$, such as for many implementations* *of the empirical risk in Machine Learning, the Moreau-Yosida approximation [1] of f evaluated in point w, referred to as $f_{\mathrm{MY}}(w)$, is[1]*

$$f_{\mathrm{MY}}(w) := \min_{w' \in \mathbb{R}^N} f(w') + \frac{1}{2\tau} \|w' - w\|^2, \tag{2}$$

where $\| \cdot \|$ is the Euclidean norm and $\tau > 0$.

The objective function in the optimization problem of Eq. (2) is composed of two terms: the left-most one is the value of f in w' (for example, a loss function aggregated over the available data), being w' the variable of the minimization problem, while the right-most term is a regularizer that penalizes strong variations between such w' and the target point of the approximation, i.e., w. As a result, given $w^\star$ that minimizes the objective of Eq. (2),

$$w^\star \in \arg \min_{w' \in \mathbb{R}^N} f(w') + \frac{1}{2\tau} \|w' - w\|^2, \tag{3}$$

we have that

$$f_{\mathrm{MY}}(w) = f(w^\star) + \frac{1}{2\tau} \|w^\star - w\|^2,$$

where smaller values of τ forces $w^\star$ and w to be closer (in the sense of standard Euclidean topology). See Fig. 2. In the case of hard-constrained optimization, the problem of Eq. (2) is conceptually equivalent to the following constrained optimization problem,

$$\min_{w' \in \mathbb{R}^N} f(w');$$

$$\text{s.t. } \|w' - w\| \leq \epsilon,$$

for some $\epsilon > 0$ (that increases when τ decreases), that makes evident the notion of spatial locality of the MY approximation.[2] When $f \in C^1(\mathbb{R}^N; \mathbb{R})$, the stationary points of the objective function in Eq. (2) are those $w^\star$ for which the gradient ∇f of f is null,[3] thus

$$\nabla f(w^\star) + \frac{1}{\tau}(w^\star - w) = 0, \tag{4}$$

from which we get

$$w^\star = w - \tau \nabla f(w^\star), \tag{5}$$

that is an alternative representation of Eq. (3).

---

[1] Notice that the minimum here exists since $f + \| \cdot -w\|^2/2$ is lower semicontinuous (because f is lower semicontinuous) and coercive since $f \geq 0$ and $\| \cdot -w\|^2/2$ is coercive (then the sublevels of $f + \| \cdot -w\|^2/2$ are contained in the sublevels of $\| \cdot -w\|^2/2$, which are compact). The existence of the minimum then follows from Weierstrass. .

[2] Of course, this formulation calls for Lagrange multiplier theory to be solved.

[3] Notice that in general in Eq. (2) such strong assumption on differentiability is not required, since the MY approximation is general and can be applied even in contexts, like functional analysis, where the notion of gradient could not be clear.

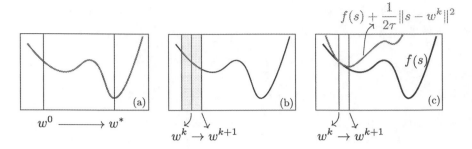

Fig. 2. Three different optimization steps. In (a) it is represented the global optimization step from w^0 to $w^{k+1} \in \arg\min_{w'} f(w')$. In (b) the global step is made local by
requiring that the minimization should be done around (magenta strip) the previous
step w^k as described in Eq. (2). In (c) we graphically show the equivalence between the
local step and the one induced by the MY regularization as it is described by Eq. (7).
Picture (b) and (c), as it is noted in Eq. (8), are equivalent to an implicit gradient
descent step.

Bridging Gradient-Based Learning. Let us consider the sequence of points
$(w^k)_{k \geq 0}$ defined by the classic recursive relation of gradient-based methods with
learning rate τ, as the one of Eq. (1),

$$\begin{cases} w^0 = w_0 \in \mathbb{R}^N; \\ w^{k+1} = w^k - \tau \nabla f(w^k), \quad k > 0. \end{cases} \tag{6}$$

where w_0 is a fixed initial point. We can exploit the MY approximation of f
in Eq. (2) and, in particular, the expression of the argument that minimizes
its optimization problem, Eq. (3), to devise another related recursive relation,
replacing w^* with w^{k+1} and w with w^k,

$$\begin{cases} w^0 = w_0 \in \mathbb{R}^N; \\ w^{k+1} \in \arg\min_{w' \in \mathbb{R}^N} f(w') + \frac{1}{2\tau}\|w' - w^k\|^2, \quad k > 0, \end{cases} \tag{7}$$

that, accordingly to Eq. (5), is equivalent to[4]

$$\begin{cases} w^0 = w_0 \in \mathbb{R}^N; \\ w^{k+1} = w^k - \tau \nabla f(w^{k+1}), \quad k > 0. \end{cases} \tag{8}$$

It is evident that Eq. (8) describes an *implicit* scheme, from which w^{k+1} cannot
be immediately computed, since it belongs to both the sides of the equation. This
is different from Eq. (6), that is indeed an *explicit* scheme. For ML application it
is critical to rely on explicit schemes, since solving the implicit Eq. (7) is usually
unfeasible. A further step can be done to recover the *explicit* gradient descent

---

[4] In the reminder of the paper we will omit to write explicitly the initialization of the
method $w^0 = w_0$ and we will just describe the recursion relation for $k > 0$.

method from MY approximation. The basic observation is that whenever f is smooth, at least in the neighbourhoods of w^k, we can approximate the value of f using a Taylor expansion truncated to the first order,

$$f(w') \approx f(w^k) + \nabla f(w^k) \cdot (w' - w^k),$$

where $\cdot$ is the standard scalar product in $\mathbb{R}^N$. Using this approximation in Eq. (7), and considering that $f(w^k)$ is a constant for the optimization problem reported in such an equation (thus it can be dropped), we get

$$w^{k+1} \in \underset{w' \in \mathbb{R}^N}{\arg\min} \, \nabla f(w^k) \cdot (w' - w^k) + \frac{1}{2\tau} \|w' - w^k\|^2, \quad k > 0. \tag{9}$$

Following the same procedure we already applied in Eq. (4), we can write down the equation of the stationary points of the newly introduced Eq. (9), that holds for $w' = w^{k+1}$, $\nabla f(w^k) + (w^{k+1} - w^k)/\tau = 0$, which ultimately yields $w^{k+1} = w^k - \tau \nabla f(w^k)$, that is exactly the *explicit* gradient descent method of Eq. (6). Equation (9) represents the MY view on gradient-based methods of Eq. (6). Figure 2 qualitatively depicts the connections between classic gradient descent and the MY view.

Uniform View. The MY scheme in Eq. (9) allows us to clearly spot the role of the variation between $w' = w^{k+1}$ and w^k, that is involved both in the squared regularizer (weighed by learning rate τ), and in the modulating term of the gradient of loss function f. Equation (9) is a powerful tool that is general enough to describe several variants of gradient-based updates, also referred to as optimizers. This is achieved by tweaking the regularizer $\|w' - w^k\|^2$ or adapting ∇f, thus clearly showing what are the expected properties of the resulting update rule, that is the topic covered in the following Sect. 3. Differently, in Sect. 4 we will use this framework to describe a case-study in which a new gradient-based method is introduced, as a proof-of-concept of the versatility of this view toward the design of novel optimizers.

2.1   Relations with Proximal Algorithms

In is interesting to formally analyze the relations of the MY view and proximal algorithms. A proximal algorithm is an algorithm that solves a *convex* optimization problem making use of the *proximal operator* of the objective function (see [17]). The simplest example of this class of methods, which is called "proximal minimization algorithm", defines a minimizing sequence that is obtained by the repeating application of the proximal operator $\text{prox}_{\tau f}$ (that we will formally define shortly) to an initial point w_0:

$$\begin{cases} w^0 = w_0 \in \mathbb{R}^N; \\ w^{k+1} = \text{prox}_{\tau f}(w^k), \quad k > 0. \end{cases} \tag{10}$$

Such method is closely related to the Moreau-Yosida approximation of the objective function f, once we provided and discuss the definition of the proximal operator. Let us suppose that f, in addition of being lower semicontinuous and non-negative (hence proper), is also convex (we recall that what we presented so far did not have such a requirement, introduced here only with the goal of discussing proximal algorithms). Then, the function $f(w') + 1/(2\tau)\|w' - w\|^2$ of which we are taking the minimum in Eq. (2) is strongly convex. This implies that the minimizer of Eq. (2), that we will denote as w'_w, is unique. The operator implementing the mapping $w \mapsto w'_w$ is called *proximal operator* or *proximation* (for more details, see [17,21]). In order to be able to write an explicit representation of this operator, let us recall from subdifferential calculus [21] that if f is convex, and if g is C^1 near w, being w a point that minimizes $f + g$, then

$$-\nabla g(w) \in \partial f(w),$$

where ∂f is the subdifferential of f. If we apply this result to $f(w') + 1/(2\tau)\|w' - w\|^2$ with $g(w') = 1/(2\tau)\|w' - w\|^2$ we immediately have

$$\partial f(w'_w) + \frac{1}{\tau}(w'_w - w) \ni 0,$$

which is the relation that uniquely characterizes w'_w and that, in particular, guarantees that the operator $\mathrm{prox}_{\tau f}$, implemented as

$$\mathrm{prox}_{\tau f}(w) := (I + \tau \partial f)^{-1}(w) \equiv w'_w,$$

is uniquely defined. It should now be apparent that the proximal operator and the MY approximation of Definition 1 are very closely related. For instance, when f is convex we can write

$$f_{\mathrm{MY}}(w) = f(\mathrm{prox}_{\tau f}(w)) + \frac{1}{2\tau}\| \mathrm{prox}_{\tau f}(w) - w\|^2,$$

and we can relate the gradient[5] of f_{MY} with the proximal operator as follows,

$$\mathrm{prox}_{\tau f}(w) = w - \tau \nabla f_{\mathrm{MY}}(w).$$

Finally we notice that in the convex case the arg min in Eq. (7) becomes a singleton and hence the algorithm in Eq. (7) coincides with the one in Eq. (10). For completeness, we mention that there exists scientific literature that studies proximal algorithms also in the non-convex case [9,11].

3   Moreau-Yosida View of Popular Optimizers

In this section we will discuss how the MY view of Eq. (9) is general enough to can describe several existing optimizers widely employed in the ML community. In particular, we will consider the case of Stochastic Gradient Descent (SGD)

---

[5] It is indeed a standard result that under the convexity assumption f_{MY} is differentiable.

[20], Heavy Ball method (gradient descent with momentum) [19], AdaGrad [7], RMSprop [22], and ADAM [10].

SGD. The largely popular Stochastic Gradient Descent method [20] is based on a stochastic objective that involves a fraction of the available data at each iteration. We use it as starting example to introduce further notation that will be helpful in the following, being it a pretty straightforward case to cast in the MY view. We consider a training set with n samples, and we assume that $f = (1/n) \sum_{i=1}^{n} f_i$, being f_i the loss evaluated on the i-th example. At each iteration of gradient descent, a mini-batch of independently (randomly) sampled data is considered. If we indicate with I_k the set of m indices of the examples in the k-th mini-batch, and with $(1/m) \sum_{i \in I_k} f_i(w^k)$ the loss function evaluted on it, then the standard update scheme in the SGD algorithm is

$$w^{k+1} = w^k - \tau \frac{1}{m} \sum_{i \in I_k} \nabla f_i(w^k), \quad k > 0.$$

The MY view is obtained without applying any changes to the squared regularized, as expected, and by simply replacing the term $\nabla f(w^k)$ in Eq. (6) with $(1/m) \sum_{i \in I_k} \nabla f_i(w^k)$,

$$w^{k+1} \in \arg\min_{w' \in \mathbb{R}^N} g_k \cdot (w' - w^k) + \frac{1}{2\tau} \|w' - w^k\|^2, \quad k > 0, \tag{11}$$

where we introduced the notation $g_k := (1/m) \sum_{i \in I_k} \nabla f_i(w^k)$, that we will keep using in the following, since it allows us to be general enough to go back to classic full-batch gradient descent by setting g_k to $\nabla f(w^k)$.

Heavy Ball Method. Also known as gradient descent with momentum [19], is based on an explicit formula that involves the latest variation $w^k - w^{k-1}$ between the learnable parameters,

$$w^{k+1} = w^k - \alpha g_k + \beta(w^k - w^{k-1}), \quad k > 0, \tag{12}$$

with $\alpha, \beta > 0$. The MY view be obtained introducing a higher order regularization term and by writing the constants α and β as $\alpha = \mu\tau/(\mu+\tau), \beta = \tau/(\mu+\tau)$,

$$w^{k+1} \in \arg\min_{w' \in \mathbb{R}^N} g_k \cdot (w' - w^k) + \frac{\|w' - w^k\|^2}{2\tau} + \frac{\|w' - 2w^k + w^{k-1}\|^2}{2\mu}, \quad k > 0.$$

Interestingly, the MY view clearly shows that, compared to vanilla gradient descent, here we also have an addition regularity term (weighed by $1/(2\mu)$), that enforces second-order information on the update step. An alternative definition of the method is sometimes given using exponential averages, that can still be cast in the MY view. Let $(a_k)_{k\geq 0}$ be a sequence, then the exponential moving average with discount factor δ of $(a_k)_{k\geq 0}$ is the sequence $(\langle a \rangle_k^\delta)_{k\geq 0}$ where the k-th term is computed as

$$\langle a \rangle_k^\delta := (1 - \delta) \sum_{j=0}^{k} \delta^{k-j} a_j. \tag{13}$$

Using such a notion, a popular alternative form of the update rule of Eq. (12) is $w^{k+1} = w^k - \tau \langle g \rangle_k^\beta$. In this case, using Eq. (13) we can rewrite the MY view as

$$w^{k+1} \in \arg\min_{y \in \mathbb{R}^N} \langle g \rangle_k^\beta \cdot (y - w^k) + \frac{1}{2\tau} \|y - w^k\|^2, \quad k > 0,$$

i.e., by replacing the gradient term g_k with its exponential moving average with decay factor β. The higher-order regularity is replaced by a smoothing operation on the gradient term g_k. We will use this alternative form also when describing the ADAM algorithm.

AdaGrad and RMSprop. Both methods (see [7] and [22]) can be cast in the MY view in a related manner. Their update schemes are defined as

$$w^{k+1} = w^k - \tau(H_k)^{-1} g_k, \quad k > 0.$$

where H_k is a diagonal matrix with the following elements in the diagonal,

$$(H_k)_{ii} := \begin{cases} \varepsilon + \sqrt{\sum_{n=0}^k (g_i^n)^2}; & \text{for AdaGrad} \\ \varepsilon + \sqrt{\sum_{n=0}^k \langle g_i^2 \rangle_n^\beta}, & \text{for RMSprop,} \end{cases}$$

where $\varepsilon > 0$, $i \in \{1, 2, \ldots, N\}$, g_i^k is the i-th component of the gradient and, for i fixed in $\{1, \ldots, N\}$, $((g_i^2)_n)_{n \geq 0}$ is the sequence of the square of the i-th component of the gradient, where $(g_i^2)_n := (g_i^n)^2$. The MY view can be described by changing the metric with which we assess the closeness of the next point with respect to the current value of w^k. In particular, both the methods are obtained from Eq. (11) with the substitution $\|w' - w^k\|^2/(2\tau) \longrightarrow (w' - w^k) \cdot H_k(w' - w^k)/(2\tau)$, that clearly emphasizes the change of metric induced by matrix H_k when evaluating the regularization term in the variation of the learnable parameters.

ADAM. As it is well known, ADAM [10] consists in a specific way to put together gradient descent with momentum and RMSprop. In order to see exactly how it can be expressed in the regularization approach à la Moreau-Yosida, first we need to introduce a further definition of normalized exponential moving average. Let $(\langle a \rangle_k^\gamma)_{k \geq 0}$ be the exponential moving average of the sequence $(a_k)_{k \geq 0}$ with discount factor δ, then we define

$$\widehat{\langle a \rangle}_k^\delta := \frac{\langle a \rangle_k^\delta}{1 - \delta^{k+1}}, \qquad k \geq 0. \tag{14}$$

The update scheme of ADAM is then,

$$w^{k+1} = w^k - \tau(\hat{H}_k)^{-1} \widehat{\langle g \rangle}_k^{\beta_1}, \quad k > 0,$$

where $\hat{H}_k$ is a diagonal matrix with

$$(\hat{H}_k)_{ii} = \varepsilon + \sqrt{\sum_{n=0}^k \widehat{\langle g_i^2 \rangle}_n^{\beta_2}}, \quad i \in \{1, \ldots, N\},$$

and β_1 and β_2 are the customizable parameters of the ADAM algorithm. Following the exact same procedure we described in the case of the Heavy Ball method, using Eq. (14) we can describe ADAM in the context of the MY view as

$$w^{k+1} \in \arg\min_{y \in \mathbb{R}^N} \widehat{\langle g \rangle}_k^{\beta_1} \cdot (y - w^k) + \frac{1}{2\tau}(y - w^k) \cdot \hat{H}_k(y - w^k), \quad k > 0, \quad (15)$$

where it can be easily noticed both (i.) the change of metric in the regularity term due to the role of matrix $\hat{H}_k$, and (ii.) the smoothing operation on g_k, that, as discussed in the case of the Heavy Ball method, indirectly introduces a higher-order regularity condition on the variation of the weights.

4   Case Study: Output-Modulated Update Scheme

When introducing the MY view of Sect. 2, we discussed essentially how a gradient step is equivalent to solving a local minimization problem on a risk f around the current step w^k. As a proof-of-concept of the versatility of this view toward the design of novel optimizers, we consider a specific use-case based on neural networks.

Scenario. Let $\nu(\cdot, w) \colon \mathbb{R}^d \to \mathbb{R}^p$ be a neural network that, given a set of weights $w \in \mathbb{R}^N$, maps some input data $x \in \mathbb{R}^d$ into an output $\nu(x, w) \in \mathbb{R}^p$. The risk f is a measure of the performance of the network ν. We focus on a continual learning scenario, in which the data samples are not i.i.d., for example due to the fact that tasks and task-related data are presented in a sequential manner, where the data distribution changes over time [8,14,18]. In this case, the learning process might be plagued by several similar/related samples streamed in neighboring steps, and by abrupt changes in the data when switching from one task to another. The plasticity of the model should then adapt over time, being the network more plastic when never-seen-before data is provided, while it should not be too prone to overfitting data that was already shown several times in the last time frame. We make the hypotetis that the variations in the network outputs could indirectly tell if we are in front of data that is similar to what was just observed, or if we are switching to different data. Of course, there are no attempts to solve catastrophic forgetting issues of to propose a novel continual learning algorithm, since what we are presentin is just a case-study to support the simplicity of injecting novel knowledge in the update procedure by working on the MY view.

Output-Based Modulation. In Eq. (7) the notion of closeness in the space of parameters is given by the term $\|w' - w^k\|^2/(2\tau)$. Here the general idea is to modify this natural Euclidean topology by taking into account the way in which the changes in the parameters, induced by learning, is affected by the variations of the outputs of the model. The simplest way in which we can achieve this is by introducing a *modulation function* $\psi(\nu)$ that takes into account the outputs of the network ν in order to appropriately weigh the regularization term in Eq. (7);

what we are proposing hence is to study variants of a gradient descent method that are obtained thought the following transformation of the "distance" term:

$$\frac{1}{2\tau}\|w' - w^k\|^2 \longrightarrow \frac{\psi(\nu)}{2\tau}\|w' - w^k\|^2. \tag{16}$$

The MY-view, by explicitly showing the regularizer of the variation of the weights, allows us to immediately connect the modulated term with its effects in the update rules, as we are going to investigate by providing the precise form and structure of $\psi(\nu)$. Since the output of the network depends on the input data other than the value of the parameters, we also need to define a protocol with which data is introduced to the learner. At each time step, we are given a mini-batch of data of size m, with sample indices collected in the already introduced I_k, and using the same definition of g_k we presented in the case of SDG, i.e., $g_k = \frac{1}{m}\sum_{i \in I_k} \nabla f_i(w^k)$. We are now in position to discuss our proposal for the modulation function ψ, that we select to be

$$\psi(\nu) := \frac{1}{\gamma_k}\left\|\frac{1}{m}\sum_{i \in I_k} \nu(x_i, w^k) - \frac{1}{m}\sum_{j \in I_{k-1}} \nu(x_j, w^{k-1})\right\|^{-2}, \tag{17}$$

being $\gamma_k > 0$ a normalization factor that can eventually vary over time (that is the reason for its subscript). When the average outputs of the network produced at step $k-1$ are similar to the ones at time k, then $\psi(\nu)$ is small, and vice-versa. The MY view is then

$$w^{k+1} \in \underset{w' \in \mathbb{R}^N}{\arg\min}\, g_k \cdot (w' - w^k)$$

$$+ \frac{1}{2\tau} \frac{\|w' - w^k\|^2}{\gamma_k\left\|\frac{1}{m}\sum_{i \in I_k} \nu(x_i, w^k) - \frac{1}{m}\sum_{j \in I_{k-1}} \nu(x_j, w^{k-1})\right\|^2}, \quad k > 0, \tag{18}$$

from which it is easy to compute the stationarity condition of the objective function to get

$$w^{k+1} = w^k - \tau\gamma_k\left\|\frac{1}{m}\sum_{i \in I_k} \nu(x_i, w^k) - \frac{1}{m}\sum_{j \in I_{k-1}} \nu(x_j, w^{k-1})\right\|^2 g_k,$$

for $k > 0$. The last equation shows the update rule of our newly designed optimizer, which embeds our knowledge/intuitions on the learning problem at hand. The whole process we followed in devising it, shows how the such knowledge was initially injected into the MY view having a clear understanding of the regularization properties we aimed at enforcing, and only afterwards we obtained the update rule, in which the gradient of the loss is shown jointly with what comes from the proposed regularization.

5   Conclusions and Future Work

In this work we discussed how Moreau-Yosida approximation can be a powerful tool to efficiently devise optimization methods for Machine Learning. We presented a framework that offers a unified view on many existing gradient-based methods, but that also gives new insights and suggests different interpretations of them. We used the Moreau-Yosida view in the context of a continual learning use-case, devising a customized output-modulated gradient-based step, with a mechanism that inhibits updates of the parameters in presence of stationary outputs of a neural network. Future works will focus on the usage of the Moreau-Yosida view of this paper to design novel optimizers for Machine Learning, injecting well-defined and understandable properties in the optimization problem that yields the update scheme of the model parameters. While this paper is focused on the theoretical aspects of the proposed approach, in future work we plan to experimentally investigate the impact of novel optimizers designed within our uniform view, also considering modern benchmarks and learning scenarios [16].

Acknowledgment. This work has been supported by the French government, through the 3IA Coôte d'Azur, Investment in the Future, project managed by the National Research Agency (ANR) with the reference number ANR-19-P3IA-0002.

References

1. Ambrosio, L., Gigli, N., Savaré, G.: Gradient Flows. In Metric Spaces and in the Space of Probability Measures. Springer, Basel (2005). https://doi.org/10.1007/b137080
2. Belkin, M., Niyogi, P., Sindhwani, V.: Manifold regularization: a geometric framework for learning from labeled and unlabeled examples. J. Mach. Learn. Res. **7**(85), 2399–2434 (2006). http://jmlr.org/papers/v7/belkin06a.html
3. Bottou, L.: Large-scale machine learning with stochastic gradient descent. In: Lechevallier, Y., Saporta, G. (eds.) Proceedings of COMPSTAT 2010, pp. 177–186. Springer, Cham (2010). https://doi.org/10.1007/978-3-7908-2604-3_16
4. Cesa-Bianchi, N., Orabona, F.: Online learning algorithms. Annual review of statistics and its application (2021)
5. Curry, H.B.: The method of steepest descent for non-linear minimization problems. Q. Appl. Math. **2**(3), 258–261 (1944)
6. Delange, M., et al.: A continual learning survey: defying forgetting in classification tasks. IEEE Trans. Pattern Anal. Mach. Intell. **44**, 3366–3385 (2021)
7. Duchi, J., Hazan, E., Singer, Y.: Adaptive subgradient methods for online learning and stochastic optimization. J. Mach. Learn. Res. **12**(7), 2121–2159 (2011)
8. French, R.M.: Catastrophic forgetting in connectionist networks. Trends Cogn. Sci. **3**(4), 128–135 (1999)
9. Gu, B., Wang, D., Huo, Z., Huang, H.: Inexact proximal gradient methods for non-convex and non-smooth optimization. In: Proceedings of the AAAI Conference on Artificial Intelligence, vol. 32 (2018)
10. Kingma, D.P., Ba, J.: Adam: a method for stochastic optimization. arXiv preprint arXiv:1412.6980 (2014)
11. Le, H., Gillis, N., Patrinos, P.: Inertial block proximal methods for non-convex non-smooth optimization. In: International Conference on Machine Learning, pp. 5671–5681. PMLR (2020)
12. Mai, Z., Li, R., Jeong, J., Quispe, D., Kim, H., Sanner, S.: Online continual learning in image classification: an empirical survey. Neurocomputing **469**, 28–51 (2022)

13. Marullo, S., Tiezzi, M., Betti, A., Faggi, L., Meloni, E., Melacci, S.: Continual unsupervised learning for optical flow estimation with deep networks. In: Conference on Lifelong Learning Agents, pp. 183–200. PMLR (2022)
14. McCloskey, M., Cohen, N.J.: Catastrophic interference in connectionist networks: the sequential learning problem. In: Psychology of learning and motivation, vol. 24, pp. 109–165. Elsevier (1989)
15. Melacci, S., Belkin, M.: Laplacian support vector machines trained in the primal. J. Mach. Learn. Res. **12**(3), 1149–1184 (2011)
16. Meloni, E., Betti, A., Faggi, L., Marullo, S., Tiezzi, M., Melacci, S.: Evaluating continual learning algorithms by generating 3D virtual environments. In: Cuzzolin, F., Cannons, K., Lomonaco, V. (eds.) Continual Semi-Supervised Learning. LNCS, pp. 62–74. Springer, Cham (2022)
17. Parikh, N., Boyd, S., et al.: Proximal algorithms. Found. Trends® Optim. **1**(3), 127–239 (2014)
18. Parisi, G.I., Kemker, R., Part, J.L., Kanan, C., Wermter, S.: Continual lifelong learning with neural networks: a review. Neural Netw. **113**, 54–71 (2019)
19. Polyak, B.T.: Some methods of speeding up the convergence of iteration methods. USSR Comput. Math. Math. Phys. **4**(5), 1–17 (1964)
20. Robbins, H., Monro, S.: A stochastic approximation method. Annals Math. Stat. **22**, 400–407 (1951)
21. Rockafellar, R.T.: Convex analysis, vol. 11. Princeton University Press, Princeton (1997)
22. Swersky, K., Hinton, G., Srivastava, N.: RMSProp: divide the gradient by a running average of its recent magnitude. Neural Networks for Machine Learning, COURSERA (2012)

Mastering the Card Game of Jaipur Through Zero-Knowledge Self-Play Reinforcement Learning and Action Masks

Cristina Cutajar[(✉)] and Josef Bajada[ID]

Department of Artificial Intelligence, Faculty of ICT, University of Malta,
Msida, Malta
{cristina.cutajar.20,josef.bajada}@um.edu.mt

Abstract. Jaipur is a challenging two-player score-based strategy game
where the players take turns to trade and sell cards for points, with the
objective of having more points than the opponent at the end of the
game. This game contains multiple factors which make self-play learning
challenging, such as being partially observable, having stochastic actions,
and having a very large action space of 25,469 possible discrete actions.
Moreover, the game contains both immediate and long-term rewards,
and the players have the possibility of adopting different strategies as
the game is adversarial. In this work we benchmark the state-of-the-art
PPO, A2C, DQN and DDQN reinforcement learning algorithms using
self-play without any domain knowledge and starting from random play.
Due to the large action space of the game, we propose to use action
masks. The policy generated by each algorithm was evaluated quantitatively against typical Jaipur scores, and also qualitatively by checking
which actions each agent was selecting. The results show that all the
algorithms converged to policies that played the game strongly, with the
PPO algorithm obtaining the best results.

Keywords: Reinforcement Learning · Multi-agent · Score-based ·
Large Action Space · Turn-based · Adversarial

1 Introduction

Reinforcement Learning has proven to be very successful in perfect-information
deterministic adversarial games such as Go, Chess and Shogi [20,21]. These techniques take advantage of such characteristics by rolling out a Monte Carlo Tree
Search (MCTS) to prune out less attractive search branches. However this approach becomes more challenging when the problem being solved is characterised
by partial-observability and stochasticity. If not all information about the current environment state is known, and the effect of an action cannot be predicted
reliably, or there is a significant number of possible outcomes (such as drawing
a card from a shuffled deck), modelling and solving the problem as a Partially
Observable Markov Decision Process (POMDP) can become intractable [13].

© The Author(s), under exclusive license to Springer Nature Switzerland AG 2023
R. Basili et al. (Eds.): AIxIA 2023, LNAI 14318, pp. 231–244, 2023.
https://doi.org/10.1007/978-3-031-47546-7_16

Having a large action space makes the problem even harder, increasing the complexity exponentially due to the high branching factor.

In literature, two different approaches to reduce the high branching factor have been proposed. The first of which is vector embedding, where the action space is encoded as a vector [29], similar to the embedding techniques used in Natural Language Processing (NLP). This approach is useful when several actions have similar effects, and the embedding process captures such similarities. The second approach is through the use of action masks, where inapplicable actions in a specific state are explicitly filtered out as part of the feedback to the reinforcement learning algorithm [30]. In this work, we adopt the latter approach in order to solve the partially-observable stochastic adversarial two-player score-based game of *Jaipur*[1].

The partial observability aspect comes from the fact that each player's hand is hidden from the opponent. Furthermore, it also makes use of a shuffled deck facing downward, making it hard to predict what cards will be drawn next from the deck. The game has a large action space, with a total of 25,469 possible discrete actions. By comparison, chess only has 4,672 possible moves [21]. Nevertheless, just like in Chess, not all actions are applicable in each state, making action masks a viable approach to reduce the branching factor and help the policy learning converge faster.

In this work, we propose a scheme to encode the state of the game from the perspective of each player. We use a multi-agent reinforcement learning approach so that each player has its own policy which only learns from the data observed by the respective player. The algorithms start with zero knowledge of the game, and the policies improve through self-play against each other. The reward function follows the score structure of the game. The action space represents all the possible actions that can be taken in the game, but through the use of action masking, any invalid actions can be filtered out. This approach was tested using the state-of-the-art PPO, A2C, DQN and DDQN reinforcement learning algorithms. Our results show that the learnt policies produced strong agent players that obtained high scores, comparable to those of human players.

2   The Jaipur Card Game

Jaipur is played by two players who take turns to trade or sell cards to get points. The game consists of two types of cards; Goods cards and Camel cards. There are six different types of Goods cards, in descending order of value: Diamond (D), Gold (G), Silver (Si), Cloth (C), Spice (Sp) and Leather (L). During gameplay, each player can have up to seven Goods cards in his 'hand' which are only visible to the respective player as well as any number of Camel cards in his 'herd' which are visible to both players. Moreover, the game consists of a 'marketplace', which contains five cards that are always visible to both players. The remaining cards are shuffled and assigned to the deck facing downwards, as shown in Fig. 1.

---

[1] Jaipur is a strategy card game created by Sébastien Pauchon and published by Space Cowboys (Asmodee).

Fig. 1. Screenshot of the Digital Jaipur Game

Whenever a player takes cards from the marketplace, it is replenished from the deck so that it contains five cards at all times. The game also has a set of tokens which carry points for when a Goods card is sold. The tokens are ordered highest value first, such that selling the Goods earlier in the game yields higher points. On the other hand, the game also has bonus tokens which are given to the player when sets of 3, 4 or 5 cards of the same Goods type are sold at once. This creates an opportunity for players to strategise whether to sell early, or wait until more cards of the same Goods type are in hand. Camel cards have no value during the game, except for currency to trade them with cards in the marketplace. However, at the end of the game, the player with the most Camel cards gets the Camel Bonus token which is worth 5 points. The game ends when either all tokens of three Goods types have been taken or when there are no more cards in the deck to replenish the cards taken from the marketplace. The player with the most points wins the game. In each turn, the player can choose to: i) take one Goods card from the marketplace, ii) take all the Camel cards present in the marketplace, iii) trade two or more cards from the player's hand or herd with the equivalent number of Goods cards from the marketplace, and iv) sell Goods cards of the same type for tokens.

There are some rules as to how trading can take place. Only Goods cards can be taken from the marketplace, and they must not be of the same type being traded by the player. The trade must consist of at least two cards. The player can also use Camel cards in the trade, as long as the hand does not result in more than seven cards. When selling Goods cards, the more valuable Goods types (Diamond, Gold and Silver) are restricted to only be sold in pairs, while the less valuable ones (Cloth, Spice and Leather) can be sold as single cards. For the latter, there are some strategic actions that one could adopt, such as selling the first card early to take the only 5-point token of that Goods-type, or selling cards of the same type one-by-one, instead of together, to purposely avoid risking putting new cards into the marketplace which could be beneficial for the opponent.

The game of Jaipur contains numerous factors which make the problem challenging and somewhat interesting for self-play reinforcement learning. While there are some strategies human players have suggested, there is no known dominant strategy. The fact that the opponent's hand is not known introduces an element of partial observability, where the belief state carries an element of uncertainty, depending on what prior information was available during the game. Furthermore, there is an element of chance, both from the players' initial hand, and also from what cards get dealt from the deck to replenish the marketplace, making the effect of the first two actions stochastic.

What makes this game particularly interesting from a Reinforcement Learning perspective is that the actions could have good immediate rewards but bad long-term consequences. Furthermore, strategically postponing actions that give an immediate reward can potentially lead to higher future rewards (for example, selling more cards of the same Goods type at one go), or lower future rewards (because the opponent sells cards of the same Goods type before and gets higher points). This aspect fits into the characteristics of Reinforcement Learning, which learns to choose actions that maximise the return (the sum of all discounted future rewards) rather than the immediate rewards [22].

3   Related Work

To our knowledge, there is very little research on implementing an AI agent to play this game, and this is the first study that provides an in-depth analysis of using Deep Reinforcement Learning techniques to learn how to play the game with no prior knowledge. In this section, we review work where problems with some of the aforementioned characteristics have been solved, with the intention of reusing some of the ideas available in this literature if applicable.

The agents developed to play DouDizhu and Go, which are both multi-agent board games, make use of the MCTS algorithm improved with deep learning [2,31,34]. While Go is a perfect-information fully deterministic game, DouDizhu has an element of partial observability and chance. For board game learning, training a neural network was also proposed [3,11,27], in combination with the TD algorithm to approximate a game-theoretic value of an action. Moreover, Huang et al. [6] discuss the use of the PPO and A2C algorithms in game AI for a diversity of games including board games and complex multi-agent games. Yu et al. [32] concluded that the PPO algorithm proved to be a good baseline for multi-agent reinforcement learning when tested on four different multi-agent games. Meanwhile, A2C had a satisfactory performance on Blood Bowl, which is a multi-player turn-based stochastic board game [7], albeit fully observable.

The DQN algorithm achieved great results, similar to those achieved by a professional human game player, when it was tested on various Atari games [15,16]. It outperformed the other learning algorithms that were tested and was considered to be the first AI agent capable of performing well on a variety of challenging games [16].

Various approaches have been proposed to deal with large-scale action spaces. The first of which involves combining multiple different actions into a single meta-action based on some similarity metric. When the actions are continuous, they can also be combined into a single discrete action. Alternatively, actions that are unlikely to lead to a good result can be pruned out [8,33]. Yao et al. [29] proposed the use of a Markov Decision Process to encode the action space for Axie Infinity by generating a small set of actions from all the possible actions, and selecting the most optimal action. Meanwhile, Dulac-Arnold et al. [1] proposed what they refer to as the Wolpertinger architecture, which combines action embedding with the Actor-Critic reinforcement learning architecture. Prior knowledge about the actions is embedded into a continuous space and the Deep Deterministic Policy Gradient algorithm is then used to perform policy iteration and train the policy and critic networks.

Tang et al. [23] proposed the use of action masking with the PPO algorithm to which the improved algorithm returned better results as the action mask specifies which actions are valid and which are invalid based on the state of the environment. The implementation of an action mask resulted in the algorithm converging quicker and obtaining a higher return value. The use of an action mask was also incorporated in MOBA games to enhance the efficiency of the algorithm's training by eliminating the irrational possibilities [30]. Moreover, Liu et al. [12] conducted a study regarding reinforcement learning on tactical driving decision-making where the use of an action mask was proposed to enhance the reinforcement learning process by filtering out the invalid actions immediately instead of waiting for the agent to potentially learn to avoid them.

4   Background

This section provides a detailed explanation of different reinforcement learning algorithms which are compatible with discrete action spaces.

4.1   Deep Q-Network (DQN)

A Deep Q-Network (DQN) is an example of a deep reinforcement learning value-based algorithm which is a combination of deep learning and Q-learning [17]. DQN makes use of two neural networks; the Q-network and the target Q-network [5,24]. The target Q-network is similar to the Q-network with the difference being that it has fixed weights which are updated periodically to be equal to the weights of the Q-network [16,24]. This algorithm makes use of the deep neural network, the Q-network, to approximate the Q-value of each action from the given state and then chooses the action with the highest Q-value [17]. To do this, DQN performs experience replay by storing the agent's past experiences; observations, actions and rewards for each time-step, in a replay buffer to sample from during learning [5,24]. During training, DQN makes use of the epsilon-greedy policy to either perform exploitation by choosing an action based on the Q-network's value prediction, or perform exploration by choosing a random action with probability ϵ [24]. The algorithm will calculate the target Q-value with the target update function shown in Eq. 1 [5]:

$$y_t^{DQN} = r_{t+1} + \gamma \max_a Q(s_{t+1}, a; \theta_t) \tag{1}$$

where r_{t+1} is the reward obtained from applying the last action a_t in state, s_t, at time step t, and θ_t refers to the weight parameters of the target Q-network, Q, at time step t, which predicts the value of each possible action, a, applied to the subsequent state, s_{t+1}. The discount factor, $\gamma \in [0, 1]$, influences the value of rewards obtained in the future with respect to instant rewards [5, 24]. Similar to conventional Q-Learning [25, 26], it chooses the action that maximises the state-action value.

To stabilize training, a separate target network is maintained that is only updated periodically, while the prediction network is updated after each time step. The loss function to train the Q-network is typically set to be the Mean Squared Error (MSE) [10] between the predicted network and target network, as shown in Eq. 2, which is used :

$$L(\theta) = [((r + \gamma \max_{a_{t+1}} Q(s_{t+1}, a_{t+1}; \theta^{target})) - Q(s, a; \theta^{pred}))^2] \tag{2}$$

The target network is then updated after a number of time steps to have the weights of the prediction network. Furthermore, Deep Q-Learning makes use of Experience Replay, where past state transitions are stored in a replay buffer and reused for training, thus increasing sample efficiency. Samples from the replay buffer are taken randomly, to break the sequential correlation. The use of a neural network function approximation enables this off-policy algorithm to work in environments with high-dimensional state spaces, while stabilising the deep reinforcement learning process [17].

4.2   Double Deep Q-Network (DDQN)

Similar to the conventional Q-Learning [25, 26], the DQN algorithm has a tendency to overestimate action values [17]. The Double Deep Q-Network (DDQN) algorithm [5] adopts the same concept of Double Q-Learning [4] to address this overestimation by evaluating the policy's value using a second set of weights.

Whilst DQN makes use of one neural network to update the target values, DDQN makes use of two neural networks; the target network and the online network [5]. The online neural network determines the greedy policy and is used to select the actions, whilst the target neural network estimates the target Q-values. Moreover, this algorithm performs the policy update by making use of two different sets of weights, θ for the online neural network and θ' for the target neural network. Hence, whereas DQN makes use of the target update function explained in Sect. 4.1 to update the Q-values, DDQN uses the modified update function shown in Eq. 3 to update the Q-values with the use of the target and online networks [5]:

$$y_t^{DDQN} = r_{t+1} + \gamma Q(s_{t+1}, \arg \max_a Q(s_{t+1}, a; \theta_t); \theta'_t) \tag{3}$$

4.3   Actor-Critic Algorithms

Actor-Critic algorithms were developed to combine policy-based methods and value-based methods in order to provide more stable and efficient reinforcement learning agents [22]. These algorithms consist of an actor component, which makes use of the policy-based method, and a critic component to perform the value-based method. The actor handles the policy of the algorithm and performs exploration and exploitation of actions. Meanwhile, the critic calculates the state or state-action value function to estimate how favourable the policy is and provides feedback, referred to as the TD error, to the actor in order to optimise the policy in terms of the expected cumulative reward.

The two popular actor-critic algorithms used in this work are Proximal Policy Optimisation (PPO) and Advantage Actor Critic (A2C). An explanation of both algorithms is provided below.

Advantage Function. The advantage function is used to stabilise the agent's learning as it reduces the policy networks' high variance [19,24]. It is used in both PPO and A2C. The advantage function provides an estimation of whether an action is better or worse when compared to the average value that would be returned for a particular state and is calculated as follows [24]:

$$A(s,a) = Q(s,a) - V(s) \qquad (4)$$

where $Q(s,a)$ is the expected state-action value of applying action a on state s, and $V(s)$ is the expected state value of s.

Alternatively, the advantage value can also be calculated using just one value function $V(s)$ together with the TD error calculated from the reward r, taking into account the discount factor γ [22]:

$$A(s,a) = r + \gamma V(s') - V(s) \qquad (5)$$

4.4   Proximal Policy Optimization (PPO)

The PPO algorithm [19] was designed to be an improvement on Trust Region Policy Optimisation (TRPO) [18]. It ensures that the policy updates are stable by implementing a "proximal" constraint on the updates to limit how much the policy can change from one update to another, lowering the variance of the updates. There are two variants of PPO which are PPO Penalty and PPO Clip. Typically, PPO Clip is more popular since it is easier to implement and performs better than PPO Penalty. The PPO Clip variant contains a restriction on how much the policy may change by specifying the clipping range and ignoring any advantages accomplished that are not within the specified range. To update and improve the policy, Schulman et al. [19] state that this PPO variant makes use of the following surrogate objective function:

$$L^{CLIP}(\theta) = \mathbb{E}_t[\min(r_t(\theta)A_t, clip(r_t(\theta), 1 - \epsilon, 1 + \epsilon)A_t)] \qquad (6)$$

where A is the advantage value which was estimated at each time step in the batch, θ refers to the policy's parameters, and $r(\theta)$ represents the probability ratio of the change between the old policy and the updated policy for each time step in the batch. Meanwhile, the hyper-parameter ϵ determines the clipping range. Furthermore, the first term of this equation inside the min function, $r_t(\theta)A_t$, maximizes the surrogate objective. However, the maximisation of this function would result in the policy update being extremely large. Therefore, the second part of the min function, $clip(r_t(\theta), 1 - \epsilon, 1 + \epsilon)A_t$, is used to clip the probability ratio from the surrogate objective. The minimum value from the calculated unclipped and clipped values is chosen. The expected value over a number of experiences, t, is taken. Schulman et al. [19] state that with this function, the probability ratio change only comes into play when it causes the objective to be worse, in order to avoid performing large policy changes which could have a negative impact on the policy's performance and lead to instability.

4.5   Advantage Actor Critic (A2C)

The A2C algorithm is a deep reinforcement learning actor-critic algorithm which was developed as a synchronous variant of the Asynchronous Advantage Actor Critic (A3C) algorithm [28], which was developed as an asynchronous actor-critic variant to perform better by making use of multiple independent actors learning in parallel, each on a different copy of the environment [9,14]. During learning, A3C performs optimisation of the deep neural network controllers with the use of the asynchronous gradient descent [14]. After an update is performed, each agent will reset their parameters to correspond to the parameters of the deep neural network, prior to continuing their independent training [9]. Mnih et al. [14] state that the A3C algorithm is very powerful, being very successful on both discrete and continuous action spaces along with being very efficient on 2D and 3D games, and stated that it was considered to be "the most general and successful reinforcement learning agent to date" [14].

However, the asynchronous updating strategy of A3C had a drawback of causing some of the agents to make use of the older version of the deep neural network parameters during training [9]. The synchronous version of the A3C algorithm, A2C, was developed in order to overcome this drawback. A2C also makes use of multiple agents during learning, but instead of the agents updating the deep neural network asynchronously, the algorithm will only update the deep neural network parameters and reset the agents when all the agents have finished their training segment [9]. Being an actor-critic algorithm, A2C combines features of both policy-based algorithms and value-based algorithms to perform optimisation on the deep neural network controllers [14]. Wu et al. [28] state that A2C is a first-order gradient algorithm which means that the actor neural network is updated with the use of the policy gradient. Moreover, the A2C algorithm also makes use of the advantage function, explained in Sect. 4.3, to learn the advantage values which will be used to improve the policy.

During interaction with the environment, for each time step, each agent will gather the necessary information such as the observations prior to and after an action is applied, the reward received and the action performed. The actor and critic are updated, with the use of the gathered environment information, as well as the calculated advantage values and the cumulative sum of rewards, either when a terminal state is encountered or when the maximum amount of time steps have been performed. Moreover, as explained in Sect. 4.3, since A2C is an actor-critic algorithm, it is able to learn in environments where the actions have both immediate and long-term rewards.

5   Methodology

Since there is no publicly available research on how the game should be implemented, the entire game and all its rules had to be implemented from scratch. The implementation takes care of maintaining the game state for the two players and offers the functions for each player to take actions, as described in Sect. 2. The code was developed in Python, and is available publicly on Github[2].

Since we are using self-play with two agents playing against each other, we have to have a reinforcement learning environment that partitions the states and rewards observed by each adversarial agent. A custom PettingZoo[3] environment was created with the appropriate action and observation spaces to perform multi-agent reinforcement learning on the game environment. In contrast with the conventional single-agent Gymnasium Environment[4], this environment allows for the agents to have their own reward, termination and truncation variables and their own observation and action spaces. It also allows the multiple agents to take turns to sequentially take in their observation, perform an action and receive the respective reward. Furthermore, each agent will have its own policy, trained from its respective actions and feedback. This environment provides a function which applies the chosen action, and returns the new reward from applying the action, the new observation (state information of the game), and additional information such as whether the new state is a terminal state (the game ended). An additional piece of information used in this work is the action mask, which indicates which actions are possible.

The four main action types that the player can choose from in this game were all split into more detailed actions, making up a total of 25,469 possible discrete actions, for the agent to be able to distinguish between them and learn. The action space for each agent was thus set to a Discrete space of size 25,469 to represent all the possible actions that an agent can choose from. The action mask for the current player's possible actions is also created as a NumPy array of 25,469 elements with each element set to 1 if the corresponding action is valid or 0 if the action is invalid.

The observation space was constructed as a Dict space (a set of key-value pairs, with each value corresponding to other data structures), with two Box (n-dimensional continuous space) spaces named 'observation' and 'action_mask'.

---

[2] https://github.com/Cristina0702/JaipurRL.
[3] https://pettingzoo.farama.org/.
[4] https://gymnasium.farama.org/.

The observation element represents the player's cards and score, the opponent's Camel cards, the marketplace cards and the remaining tokens. Meanwhile, the action_mask element contains the player's action mask which proved to be a crucial component for the algorithm to converge quickly since the action space is very large.

The RLlib[5] library was used to apply the chosen Reinforcement Learning algorithms, as it contains ready-made and tested algorithms that are compatible with PettingZoo environments. This library also contains multiple action masking models which can be used with the algorithms for action masking to be performed during training.

Since the custom PettingZoo environment makes use of a Discrete action space, algorithms which are compatible with Discrete action spaces were used. The PPO, A2C, DQN and DDQN algorithms were trained in this environment, with the RLlib action masking mechanism.

The PPO, DQN and DDQN algorithms were trained with 1 local worker whilst the A2C algorithm was trained with 2 rollout workers since this algorithm make use of multiple workers. Training of the A2C algorithm was performed with the Learning Rate set to 0.01 and the Gradients Clip set to a value of 30. For PPO, the KL Divergence coefficient was set to 0, the Gamma value was set to 0.9 and the Learning Rate was set to 0.01. For the DQN and DDQN algorithms, the replay buffer used was the MultiAgentPrioritizedReplayBuffer with size set to 1,000. The replay buffer's prioritized_replay_alpha was set to 0.6 and the prioritized_replay_beta was set to 0.4. Furthermore, the batch_mode was set to 'complete_episodes'. The listed hyper-parameters were set to the recommended default values while the remaining hyper-parameters of all the algorithms were left as the default values. This was performed as, at the time of writing, experimentation on the hyper-parameters was limited and impractical due to the very high training times of the algorithms.

For each of these algorithms, two different policies were trained so that each agent has its own policy, to ensure that the agents do not learn to help each other. The total number of steps trained, games played, which were all unique as the deck is shuffled randomly, and the training time taken for the final models are displayed in Table 1. All the final models were trained using an Intel Core i5 6th Generation processor and 16 GB RAM. The trained models were then evaluated quantitatively on 1000 unique games which were not part of the training set.

Table 1. Number of Steps Trained and Time Taken

Algorithm	Number of Steps Trained	Games Played	Time Taken
PPO	2,000,000	37,166	40 h
A2C	939,680	16,700	11 h
DQN	1,027,663	17,700	25 h
DDQN	2,055,485	36,200	50 h

---

[5] https://docs.ray.io/en/latest/rllib/index.html.

6   Results

All the algorithms were evaluated quantitatively, by comparing their scores with scores achieved by human players, and qualitatively, by checking which actions the policies were selecting. The algorithms were evaluated based on the minimum, mean and maximum rewards obtained per episode, and by each individual player. These metrics were selected as they give a clear indication of how each trained agent performs. These were also inspired from forums about the game[6][7][8], which are related to the Jaipur game where players were discussing their scores. From these sources, the data gathered was that most players' high score is around 80 to 100 with their average score being around 60 to 75 and players were getting scores as low as 16 points.

The quantitative results obtained from the trained algorithms after they were played for 1000 unique games, which were not part of the training set, are displayed in Figs. 2 and 3. From these figures, it can be seen that all the algorithms generated results similar to each other, with the PPO algorithm performing the best. Moreover, these figures also show that the results generated by all the algorithms are similar to the results discussed in the forums. Therefore, it can be concluded that quantitatively, all the algorithms perform well with this game environment. Furthermore, Fig. 4 displays the difference in the scores obtained by the trained Player 1 and Player 2 policies of all the algorithms, throughout the 1000 unique games. From this figure as well as from Figs. 2 and 3, it can be noted that for all the algorithms, the Player 2 policy performed better than the Player 1 policy. Therefore, the results show that the PPO Player 2 policy obtained the highest scores.

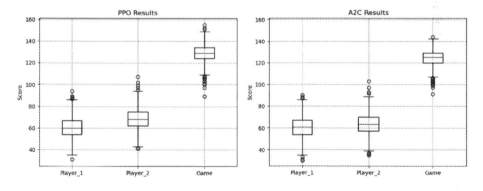

Fig. 2. PPO and A2C Results

---

[6] https://boardgamegeek.com/thread/702405/what-your-best-round-score-jaipur.

[7] https://www.reddit.com/r/boardgames/comments/dhxwa4/data_analysis_on_jaipur_games_between_my_wife_and/.

[8] https://imgur.com/gallery/GizBVGW.

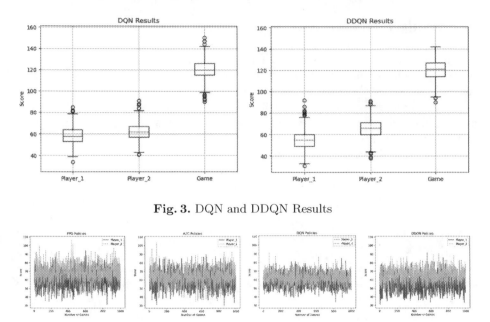

Fig. 3. DQN and DDQN Results

Fig. 4. PPO, A2C, DQN and DDQN Player 1 vs Player 2 Policies

The trained algorithms were also evaluated qualitatively, to check if the actions they were selecting were intelligent actions based on the game's state. During the qualitative testing, it was noted that the algorithms were all performing smart actions throughout the gameplay, similar to actions chosen by rational human players.

7   Conclusions and Future Work

This work presents four well-performing agents on the game of Jaipur. This game has some characteristics which make self-play reinforcement learning challenging, such as having a large-action space and being adversarial, which were addressed by implementing action masking and by training a separate policy for each player. From the results obtained from this work, we found that despite these challenges, the four deep reinforcement learning algorithms, PPO, A2C, DQN and DDQN, obtained good quantitative results and learned to perform smart actions with the PPO algorithm obtaining the best results.

For future work, this research could be taken further by evaluating the policies against professional human players. Furthermore, while for this work little hyperparameter optimisation was performed due to the significant time needed for training, performing such optimisations could result in even better policies. Finally, the use of action masking to reduce the action space could be compared with other techniques such as vector embedding of actions by similarity.

References

1. Dulac-Arnold, G., et al.: Deep reinforcement learning in large discrete action spaces. arXiv preprint arXiv:1512.07679 (2015)
2. Fujita, K.: AlphaDDA: strategies for adjusting the playing strength of a fully trained AlphaZero system to a suitable human training partner. PeerJ Comput. Sci. **8**, e1123 (2022)
3. Ghory, I.: Reinforcement learning in board games. Technical report 105, Department of Computer Science, University of Bristol (2004)
4. van Hasselt, H.: Double Q-learning. In: Advances in Neural Information Processing Systems, vol. 23 (2010)
5. van Hasselt, H., Guez, A., Silver, D.: Deep reinforcement learning with double Q-learning. In: Proceedings of the 30th AAAI Conference on Artificial Intelligence (AAAI 2016) (2016)
6. Huang, S., Kanervisto, A., Raffin, A., Wang, W., Ontañón, S., Dossa, R.F.J.: A2C is a special case of PPO. arXiv preprint arXiv:2205.09123 (2022)
7. Justesen, N., Uth, L.M., Jakobsen, C., Moore, P.D., Togelius, J., Risi, S.: Blood bowl: a new board game challenge and competition for AI. In: 2019 IEEE Conference on Games (CoG), pp. 1–8. IEEE (2019)
8. Kanervisto, A., Scheller, C., Hautamäki, V.: Action space shaping in deep reinforcement learning. In: 2020 IEEE Conference on Games (CoG), pp. 479–486. IEEE (2020)
9. Karagiannakos, S.: The idea behind actor-critics and how A2C and A3C improve them (2018). https://theaisummer.com/Actor_critics
10. Karunakaran, D., Worrall, S., Nebot, E.: Efficient statistical validation with edge cases to evaluate highly automated vehicles. In: 2020 IEEE 23rd International Conference on Intelligent Transportation Systems (ITSC), pp. 1–8. IEEE (2020)
11. Konen, W.: Reinforcement learning for board games: the temporal difference algorithm. Technical report, Research Center CIOP (Computational Intelligence, Optimization and Data Mining), TH Köln-Cologne University of Applied Sciences (2015)
12. Liu, J., Hou, P., Mu, L., Yu, Y., Huang, C.: Elements of effective deep reinforcement learning towards tactical driving decision making. arXiv preprint arXiv:1802.00332 (2018)
13. Liu, Y., Zheng, J., Chang, F.: Learning and planning in partially observable environments without prior domain knowledge. Int. J. Approximate Reasoning **142**, 147–160 (2022). https://doi.org/10.1016/j.ijar.2021.12.004
14. Mnih, V., et al.: Asynchronous methods for deep reinforcement learning. In: International Conference on Machine Learning, pp. 1928–1937. PMLR (2016)
15. Mnih, V., et al.: Playing atari with deep reinforcement learning. arXiv preprint arXiv:1312.5602 (2013)
16. Mnih, V., et al.: Human-level control through deep reinforcement learning. Nature **518**(7540), 529–533 (2015)
17. Plaat, A.: Deep Reinforcement Learning. Springer, Singapore (2022). https://doi.org/10.1007/978-981-19-0638-1
18. Schulman, J., Levine, S., Abbeel, P., Jordan, M., Moritz, P.: Trust region policy optimization. In: International Conference on Machine Learning, pp. 1889–1897. PMLR (2015)
19. Schulman, J., Wolski, F., Dhariwal, P., Radford, A., Klimov, O.: Proximal policy optimization algorithms. arXiv preprint arXiv:1707.06347 (2017)

20. Silver, D., et al.: Mastering chess and shogi by self-play with a general reinforcement learning algorithm. arXiv preprint arXiv:1712.01815 (12 2017)
21. Silver, D., et al.: A general reinforcement learning algorithm that masters chess, shogi, and go through self-play. Science **362**(6419), 1140–1144 (2018). https://doi.org/10.1126/science.aar6404
22. Sutton, R.S., Barto, A.G.: Reinforcement Learning: An Introduction, 2nd edn. MIT Press, Cambridge (2018)
23. Tang, C.Y., Liu, C.H., Chen, W.K., You, S.D.: Implementing action mask in proximal policy optimization (PPO) algorithm. ICT Express **6**, 200–203 (2020). https://doi.org/10.1016/j.icte.2020.05.003
24. Wang, Z., Schaul, T., Hessel, M., Hasselt, H., Lanctot, M., Freitas, N.: Dueling network architectures for deep reinforcement learning. In: International Conference on Machine Learning, pp. 1995–2003. PMLR (2016)
25. Watkins, C.J.: Learning from delayed rewards. Ph.D. thesis, King's College, Cambridge United Kingdom (1989)
26. Watkins, C.J., Dayan, P.: Q-learning. Mach. Learn. **8**, 279–292 (1992)
27. Wiering, M.A., Patist, J.P., Mannen, H.: Learning to play board games using temporal difference methods. Technical report UU-CS-2005-048, Utrecht University (2005)
28. Wu, Y., Mansimov, E., Grosse, R.B., Liao, S., Ba, J.: Scalable trust-region method for deep reinforcement learning using kronecker-factored approximation. In: Advances in Neural Information Processing Systems, vol. 30 (2017)
29. Yao, Z., et al.: Towards modern card games with large-scale action spaces through action representation. In: 2022 IEEE Conference on Games (CoG), pp. 576–579. IEEE (2022)
30. Ye, D., et al.: Mastering complex control in MOBA games with deep reinforcement learning. In: Proceedings of the 34th AAAI Conference on Artificial Intelligence (AAAI-20), pp. 6672–6679 (2020)
31. Yin, Q.Y., et al.: Ai in human-computer gaming: techniques, challenges and opportunities. Mach. Intell. Res. **20**, 1–19 (2023)
32. Yu, C., et al.: The surprising effectiveness of PPO in cooperative multi-agent games. Adv. Neural. Inf. Process. Syst. **35**, 24611–24624 (2022)
33. Zahavy, T., Haroush, M., Merlis, N., Mankowitz, D.J., Mannor, S.: Learn what not to learn: action elimination with deep reinforcement learning. In: Advances in Neural Information Processing Systems, vol. 31 (2018)
34. Zha, D., et al.: Douzero: Mastering doudizhu with self-play deep reinforcement learning. In: International Conference on Machine Learning, pp. 12333–12344. PMLR (2021)

Uncovering Bias in the Face Processing Pipeline: An Analysis of Popular and State-of-the-Art Algorithms Across Demographic Groups

Christian Galea[1,2(✉)] ⓘ, Chantelle Saliba[1,2] ⓘ, Matthew Sacco[1,2], Mark Bugeja[1,2] ⓘ,
Noel Buttigieg[3] ⓘ, and Dylan Seychell[4] ⓘ

[1] Beyond Museums R&D, Birkirkara, Malta
[2] SeyTravel Ltd, Msida, Malta
`{chris.galea,chantelle,matthew,mark}@seytravel.com`
[3] Institute for Tourism and Culture, University of Malta, Msida, Malta
`noel.buttigieg@um.edu.mt`
[4] Department of Artificial Intelligence, University of Malta, Msida, Malta
`dylan.seychell@um.edu.mt`

Abstract. Numerous algorithms process face images to perform tasks such as person identification and estimation of attributes such as the race and gender. While previous work has focused on biases in face recognition systems, relatively limited work has considered the full face processing pipeline to determine if other components also exhibit any biases related to a person's demographic attributes. An evaluation of popular and state-of-the-art methods in the face processing pipeline reveals that, although the overall performance may appear satisfactory, numerous differences are uncovered when digging deeper to consider the performance not just within a single demographic group, but also across different types of groups. Several avenues of future work are also provided.

Keywords: face recognition · face attribute estimation · bias · demographics · computer vision · machine learning · museums

1 Introduction

Facial images depicting one or more faces of human beings have been used for a number of tasks, including for Face Recognition (FR) [12] and for Face Attribute Estimation Systems (FAESs) [17,44], which estimate attributes such as a person's sex, race, age, and facial expression, among others.

These tasks tend to be used in important applications such as those related to security [3,15,16] or for customer behaviour analysis in museums and shops [32], which require accurate information about subjects of interest. Handling all subjects fairly, without any prejudices, is vital in such applications. However, face processing systems have often come into the limelight after it was noted that certain demographic groups might be handled differently than others [18,35]. This phenomenon has also been observed in the context of the human ability to recognise faces of people belonging in different

© The Author(s), under exclusive license to Springer Nature Switzerland AG 2023
R. Basili et al. (Eds.): AIxIA 2023, LNAI 14318, pp. 245–264, 2023.
https://doi.org/10.1007/978-3-031-47546-7_17

demographic groups to their own, known as the "other-race effect" [11, 14]. Indeed, it could be argued that automated systems could be leveraged to mitigate this problem.

The study of demographic bias has been considered in previous works, but this has often centered on face recognition systems. Whilst undoubtedly important, there are other types of algorithms that operate on faces and which could pose detrimental effects if found to be biased. Such algorithms include those used for pre-processing, such as face detectors, and algorithms to estimate the demographic attributes of a person, that could be used to filter out subjects not matching the desired criteria.

In this study, a number of popular and State-of-The-Art (SoTA) FR and FAES methods that are publicly available (and thus can easily be used by anyone) are evaluated. In the case of attribute estimation, the focus is on gender and race since they are typically among the most important types of information. In contrast to most evaluations, the choice of face detector that is often used as a pre-processing step to detect, crop, and normalise faces is also considered to determine whether it significantly affects the performance of subsequent steps.

The main contributions of this paper are thus as follows:

- The effect on demographic biases of each component in the processing pipeline (not Face Recognition Systems (FRSs) only) is investigated.
- It is shown that the face detector can significantly affect the downstream performance, highlighting the lingering sensitivity of machine learning methods to variances in the appearance of an image
- The investigation focuses on methods that are freely and readily available to use by anyone (even those who may not be well-versed with potential issues)
- It is shown that even a method designed for fairness may yield labels that are wildly different to the actual ones, with high confidence. This again indicates that some Machine Learning (ML) methods may not be truly learning the actual problem.

The rest of this paper contains an overview of existing literature in Sect. 2, followed by a description of the evaluation methodology in Sect. 3. Results are provided and discussed in Sect. 4, with concluding remarks and directions for future work finally given in Sect. 5

2   Literature Review

There exist numerous approaches that can perform face recognition and attribute estimation. An overview of popular and state-of-the-art methods will first be provided, followed by a discussion of existing work where biases across demographic groups have been considered.

2.1   Face Recognition Systems

Face recognition is a topic of research that has long attracted attention since the face is a biometric trait that is quite distinguishable among subjects and is easy to capture even without a person's direct cooperation. Methods capable of automatically identifying persons are referred to as Face Recognition Systems (FRSs).

Modern methods are primarily based on deep learning, with one of the pioneering approaches being the VGG-Face method [29] that was based on the VGG16 architecture [41] designed for object recognition and then tuned using face images in the VGG-Face dataset (also presented in [29]). VGG-Face was first trained for the task of classification and is then tuned using *triplet loss* to train a fully-connected layer tasked with yielding features that can be used for *verification*.

An extension of the work in [29] was performed in [6], whereby a new dataset called VGGFace2 was used to train models based on ResNet-50 [20] and SE-ResNet-50 [21]. It was demonstrated that SoTA performance was attained when using the IJB-A [24], IJB-B [45], and IJB-C [27] benchmarks.

The Additive Angular Margin Loss (ArcFace) function [10] improved on learning an embedding using triplet loss, by employing an arc-cosine-based function to increase feature discriminability and allowing for sub-classification within classes. It aims to minimise the distance between a sample and its corresponding sub-class while maximising the distance to other sub-classes. ArcFace achieved SoTA performance.

2.2 Attribute Estimation

There exist several attributes that can be used to describe humans, one of which is *sex*. Generally, the labels of 'male' and 'female' are utilised. *Race* and *ethnicity* are by far the hardest to quantify provided that it is difficult to segregate individuals into particular classes [26]. A race is generally described by society and is composed of people sharing distinctive physical traits, whereas ethnicity is based on cultural practices [4].

There exist several methods capable of estimating a person's attributes and which are also publicly available, thereby being easily accessible. For example, the Deep-Face (DF) library[1] contains implementations for a number of face detectors, FRSs [40], and models capable of estimating a person's gender, age, race, and facial expression/emotion [39]. The work in [36] served as inspiration to the models designed for age and gender [38]. These FAESs apply transfer learning to the pre-trained VGG-Face network [29], modified to output the required classes.

The FairFace dataset [22] aims to address racial bias by providing an equal representation of various races, namely 'White', 'Black', 'Latino', 'Middle Eastern', 'Indian', 'East Asian' and 'Southeast Asian'. An architecture trained on the FairFace dataset capable of classifying face, age, and gender was also proposed. This is denoted as Fair-Face (FF) in the rest of this paper. FF utilises the dlib library [23] to perform face detection using a Convolutional Neural Network (CNN)-based approach and the ResNet-34 [20] network as the backbone for all the attributes considered.

Lastly, the method in [46] employs the Face Recognition library[2] that is based on the well-known dlib library [23] to perform facial feature extraction. Specifically, the face encoding function from this library is used to represent the input as a face embedding vector, while the Histogram of Orientation Gradients (HOG)-based face localisation

---

[1] Available at: https://github.com/serengil/deepface.

[2] A facial recognition library that recognises and manipulates faces. Available at https://github.com/ageitgey/face_recognition.

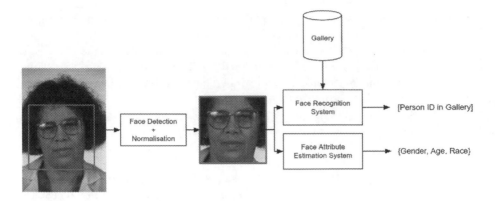

Fig. 1. Architecture of the evaluation pipeline used in this work

algorithm is used to perform face detection. The Multi-Layer Perceptron (MLP) classifier available in the scikit-learn package [30] is utilised to narrow down the input data sets to a set of appropriate outputs consisting of gender and race categories.

2.3 Biases in Face Processing Systems

Amidst a growing global concern on the use of FR and FAESs, various research works are exploring and evaluating the effects of biased and unfair algorithms [34] within different demographic groups. It is claimed that while ML has great commercial value, society is still not readily able to fully trust its widespread use, due to inherent biases. However, the authors of [34] also highlight the "other-race effect" [11, 14] where bias is not limited to ML systems but also found in human evaluations, after subjects demonstrated better recognition of persons within their own demographic.

Other works [9, 19] propose initial efforts that not only evaluate the level of bias, but also aim at mitigating it across different demographic groups. The de-biasing face recognition network (DebFace) proposed in [19] learns the disentangled representation for gender, race, age estimation, and face recognition simultaneously using adversarial learning, which in turn is used to reduce bias across the recognition and attribute estimate stages. The authors of [9] outline a similar concept using a multi-task CNN approach, by employing joint dynamic loss weight adjustment to minimise bias when predicting age, race, and gender.

The reader is also referred to the studies in [8, 11, 43], which contain several insights on biases in biometrics predominantly in face recognition.

3 Evaluation Methodology

The architecture of the evaluation pipeline is shown in Fig. 1. A face image is first processed by a face detector to (i) determine the coordinates of the face within the image, (ii) crop the image such that it depicts primarily the face of a subject, and (iii) optionally aligns and normalises the image, for example to reduce the angle between

Table 1. Statistics of the 866 subjects in the Color FERET dataset used in this study.

	MALE				FEMALE			
	ASIAN	BLACK	WHITE	ALL	ASIAN	BLACK	WHITE	ALL
# OF SUBJECTS	113	34	362	509	57	44	256	357
PERCENTAGE OF TOTAL	13.05	3.93	41.80	58.78	6.58	5.08	29.56	41.22

the eyes to zero degrees. Normalisation has been found to improve performance, e.g. in face recognition systems [29]. Hence, the effect of the face detector on performance will also be analysed to determine its importance in subsequent processing steps.

The face image output by the detector is then sent to two types of systems: (i) FRSs, to determine the identity of the subject from a *gallery* set of images having face photos of subjects with known identities, and (ii) FAESs, which can estimate attributes such as the age, gender, or race of the subject in the image. Some FAES methods may be capable of estimating more than one attribute at a time.

3.1 Dataset

It is hard to find a good dataset that was not used to train any of the models (to ensure no unfair advantage to any method). To this end, the Color FERET dataset [31] was used in this study. It contains a substantial number of good quality frontal images with variations across age and race. The use of good quality frontal images helps to ensure that any differences in performance among demographic groups are primarily due to such biases, rather than the image quality (thereby reducing potential confounding factors).

The demographic distribution of subjects is shown in Table 1, while some examples are shown in Figs. 1 and 4. There may be some shadows due to the lighting setup, striking a good balance between images that are neither too easy nor too difficult.

For most subjects in the dataset, there exist at least two frontal face images. One of these images is used in the *probe* set[3], for which the identity needs to be determined using a *gallery* set of images where the identities corresponding to the subject in each image are known. The gallery is composed of the second image of the subject.

In the case of the FAESs, the probe and gallery sets are merged such that each subject is represented by two images. The predicted attributes (gender, race) are then extracted for each subject and compared with the ground-truth labels.

It should be noted that some labels may not correspond exactly with the labels used to train a race estimation method. Moreover, some groups contain a relatively small number of subjects, which may yield unreliable results. Hence, only the subjects belonging to 'White', 'Black', and 'Asian' categories are used, which are also considered to be among the major divisions of the human race [1]. Most methods are capable of predicting all three groups since they were trained on datasets having these labels.

---

[3] Also known as a *query* set.

(a) dlib [23]   (b) MTCNN [47]   (c) OpenCV [5]

Fig. 2. Examples of the face detector outputs, for the image in Fig. 1

3.2   Methods and Evaluation Protocol

There exist two main types of methods, namely FRSs and FAESs, the latter which can be further sub-divided into methods performing estimations of gender and race. As mentioned in Sect. 3, a face image first needs to be processed by a face detection system to ensure that the subsequent face processing systems are provided images containing normalised faces. More information will now be given.

Face Detection. The first step in the pipeline of any FRS or FAES is typically a face detector. Hence, the performance of any methods utilising this image depends on the quality of the detector employed. To determine the extent of a detector's impact on performance, three methods are considered:

- Multitask Cascaded Convolutional Networks (MTCNN) [47], which outperformed SoTA methods across a number of benchmarks and was used for VGG-Face with the ResNet-50 backbone [6]
- OpenCV's Haar cascade method [5], the default detector for DF [39]
- dlib [23], where a CNN-based model is used by default for FF [22]. The method in [46] uses a HOG-based implementation in the 'face_recognition' library [2] that is based on dlib. The implementation in DF [39] uses dlib's default face detector that is also based on HOG, which is used for methods marked with 'dlib' in Sect. 4.

Examples of outputs for each face detector are shown in Fig. 2. The attributes estimated by DF [39] were predominantly considered for this evaluation, since the library in which they are provided also includes the implementations of the face detectors considered and thus ensures compatibility between the algorithms.

Face Recognition. The FRSs considered include:

- VGG-Face (VGG16): VGG-Face based on the VGG-16 architecture [29]
- VGG-Face (ResNet-50): ResNet-50 trained on the VGGFace2 dataset [6], a more modern variant of the original VGG-Face and attained SoTA performance
- ArcFace [10], which outperformed SoTA methods

The implementations in the DeepFace library are used for the VGG16-based VGG-Face and for ArcFace. It should be noted that the original implementation of VGG-Face was trained first for the task of classifying 2,622 subjects, followed by tuning for verification using the triplet loss to yield a feature embedding. However, the implementation in the DeepFace library yields 2,622-D vectors. Whilst this implementation is retained, an alternate implementation that appears to be more closely aligned with the original model described in [29] is also considered, available at [25][4] which is also used for the VGG-Face method using ResNet-50 as the backbone architecture.

The metrics used to evaluate FRS performance include (i) accuracy, representing how many subjects are correctly identified as the best match, (ii) the Equal Error Rate (EER) corresponding to the error rate at the Receiver Operating Characteristics (ROC) operating point where the False Match Rate (FMR) is equal to the False Non-Match Rate (FNMR), and (iii) the Area under Curve (AuC), denoting the area under the ROC curve. Accuracy and AuC should be maximised (maximal values of 100% and 1, respectively) whilst minimising the EER (minimal value of 0).

Attribute Estimation. The methods considered for attribute estimation (each capable of estimating both the race and gender) include:

- DeepFace (DF) [39]
- FairFace (FF) [22] trained on a dataset containing balanced demographic groups
- The implementation in [46], which also performs face detection

Evaluation of these methods was performed using the well-known accuracy, precision, recall, and F1-score metrics. An algorithm with a low recall but high precision is unable to detect a class well but is reliable when it does, while an algorithm with a high recall but low precision is capable of detecting the class well but then also includes incorrectly classified samples within that category.

The AuC is also computed since the methods considered additionally output confidence scores for each class, except for DF which does not output such values for gender labels. Furthermore, the following are also computed: (i) the probability/confidence score when the predicted class is correct (which should be high), (ii) the score when the predicted method is incorrect (which should be minimised), and (iii) the score for the correct class when the prediction is incorrect (which should be maximised). These values give an indication of the confidence of an algorithm when it is right and when it is wrong. Inspired by the field of *explainable AI*, this enables a glimpse into the black box that such algorithms (especially those based on deep learning) tend to be, and enable a better understanding and interpretation of their predictions [7,28].

The variant of FF that is capable of estimating four racial groups is chosen over the variant predicting seven groups since it is more closely aligned with the labels used in this study. Confusion matrices considering an additional number of labels that are present in the dataset and which can be predicted by the algorithm are also shown, to give a more complete picture of any biases involved and the main sources of confusion. Furthermore, these are combined with the gender to delve deeper into any biases between demographic groups.

---

[4] Available at: https://github.com/rcmalli/keras-vggface.

Table 2. Gender estimation methods performance, for each gender. All values in %. 'Prec.' and 'Rec.' denote 'Precision' and 'Recall', respectively.

METHOD	MALE			FEMALE		
	PREC.	REC.	F1	PREC.	REC.	F1
FF	96.85	99.90	98.35	99.85	95.38	97.56
[46]	88.19	99.80	93.64	99.65	80.90	89.30
OPENCV + DF	75.17	99.70	85.71	99.20	53.14	69.21
MTCNN + DF	77.99	99.90	87.60	99.77	59.80	74.78
DLIB + DF	76.31	100.00	86.56	100.00	55.68	71.53

Table 3. Performance of race estimation methods, for each racial group. All values in %.

METHOD	ASIAN			BLACK			WHITE		
	PRECISION	RECALL	F1	PRECISION	RECALL	F1	PRECISION	RECALL	F1
FF	96.62	98.47	97.53	96.73	100.00	98.33	99.83	99.00	99.41
[46]	92.86	80.29	86.12	83.53	91.61	87.38	96.60	99.03	97.80
OPENCV + DF	69.47	74.92	72.09	84.55	77.04	80.62	99.40	67.56	80.45
MTCNN + DF	63.87	97.16	77.07	94.55	70.75	80.93	99.37	89.12	93.97
DLIB + DF	95.35	94.99	95.16	92.00	97.18	98.87	99.53	98.87	99.20

4   Results

The results obtained for each method will now be provided and discussed, starting with an analysis of the face detector's effect on the performance of subsequent steps.

4.1   Effect of Face Detector on Performance

As shown in Tables 2 and 5 and Fig. 3b, the detector can affect the performance of the downstream gender attribute estimation methods. The default detector for DF, OpenCV [5], attains the worst overall performance across all metrics considered while MTCNN [47] generally enables the best performance. It was also noted that the OpenCV detector tends to struggle more than the other algorithms in detecting faces, despite utilising relatively high-quality images as found in the dataset considered in this study.

Differences in performance are more evident in the case of the race attribute estimations by DF, as shown in Table 6. The systems using OpenCV and MTCNN yield performance values that are quite similar with each other, but are significantly worse than the system using dlib.

There also exist differences among racial groups, as shown in Table 3 and Figure 3a. For example, the system using dlib attained a slightly higher value for precision than recall for 'Asian' subjects, in contrast to the other two detectors which also obtained significantly lower precision values. However, the OpenCV and MTCNN-based detectors also attained higher values for precision than recall for 'White' and 'Black' subjects.

The effect of the face detector on face recognition performance is also fairly evident, as shown in Table 4. For instance, ArcFace was able to correctly determine the identity of all subjects when using dlib, but its performance noticeably degraded when using OpenCV as the detector and normaliser. Similar observations can also be made when considering individual demographic groups, as shown in Tables 8 and 9.

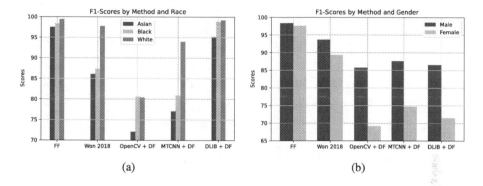

(a)   (b)

Fig. 3. F1-scores of the methods considered over different (a) race and (b) gender groups

The subsequent discussions will consider the performance using the default face detector for each architecture where applicable, as outlined in Sect. 3.2.

4.2 Face Recognition Performance

The choice of face detector affects the performance of FRSs. VGG-Face with ResNet-50 as the backbone architecture [6] is the least affected by the detector choice, consistently performing well as shown in Table 4. However, significant differences arise among demographic groups, as shown in Tables 8 and 9 and Figs. 5 and 6. For example, using the MTCNN detector leads to lower performance for 'Male' 'Asian' subjects.

VGG16-based VGG-Face achieves the best performance for "Male" "White" subjects, followed by "Male" "Asian" and "Male" "Black" subjects. This is a trend that is fairly consistent among all the face detection/recogniser systems considered, although it does not always hold. For example, ArcFace attains better performance for 'Male' 'Black' subjects than 'Male' 'Asian' subjects and is also superior to 'Male' 'White' subjects when utilising the OpenCV detector.

Gender differences are also observed, with ResNet-50-based VGG-Face performing better on "Female" subjects, while OpenCV and ArcFace perform better for 'Male' subjects. OpenCV-based pipelines yield inferior performance for 'Female' subjects. Performance is generally better for 'Female' 'Black' subjects than not only 'Male' 'Black' subjects, but also in many cases 'Female' 'Asian' and 'Female' 'White' subjects.

Some methods focus on external details like glasses, which may introduce biases. As an example, for the subject shown in Fig. 7, three of the top five best matching subjects (including the best match) are seen to wear glasses, as is the case for the subject in the query image. This suggests that the face recogniser might be using glasses as a means of discrimination, which is not entirely desirable given that it is very easy to wear or remove glasses and as such is not a discriminating factor of a person's identity.

Lastly, the DeepFace library's implementation of VGG-Face performs worse due to architectural differences (specifically the use of the classification layer rather than the feature embedding layer as originally recommended in [29]). This highlights the need to use methods as intended to ensure fair and valid comparisons.

Table 4. Performance for FRSs across all demographic groups. [DF] denotes that the method as implemented in the DeepFace library. The rest of the methods use the implementations in [25].

METHOD	ACC.	EER	AUC
MTCNN + VGG-FACE (RESNET-50)	98.69	0.30	0.999
OPENCV + VGG-FACE (RESNET-50)	97.41	1.14	0.995
DLIB + VGG-FACE (RESNET-50)	99.90	0.00	1.000
MTCNN + VGG-FACE (VGG16)	90.74	3.53	0.990
OPENCV + VGG-FACE (VGG16)	86.01	6.85	0.977
DLIB + VGG-FACE (VGG16)	95.16	1.51	0.999
MTCNN + VGG-FACE (VGG16) [DF]	89.02	5.75	0.976
OPENCV + VGG-FACE (VGG16) [DF]	85.91	7.26	0.976
DLIB + VGG-FACE (VGG16) [DF]	95.36	1.11	0.999
MTCNN + ARCFACE [DF]	98.99	0.60	0.998
OPENCV + ARCFACE [DF]	91.81	8.30	0.943
DLIB + ARCFACE [DF]	100.00	0.00	1.000

4.3 Attribute Estimation Performance

Focusing on the performance between different FAESs when using the default detectors, it can be observed in Table 5 that FF attains the best overall performance for gender estimation, followed by the method in [46] and DF.

However, delving deeper into the performance across genders reveals further insights. For instance, FF attains fairly consistent performance for both 'Male' and 'Female' subjects. However, FF is similar to the other approaches in attaining a higher recall than precision for 'Male' subjects, but then attaining higher precision than recall for 'Female' subjects. This means that the methods considered may struggle to detect 'Female' subjects but are quite reliable when they do, whereas they are capable of detecting almost all 'Male' subjects but may also incorrectly label 'Female' subjects as 'Male'. This can also be observed graphically in Fig. 8, particularly in the case of DF where it is clear that the model is able to correctly classify almost all 'Male' subjects but is then often confused in the case of 'Female' subjects and is hardly any better than the flip of a coin. This suggests that the models considered are more predisposed to classifying subjects as 'Male' than 'Female'.

In the case of race estimation, DF is also outperformed by the other methods, with FF generally attaining the best performance. However, the AuC for FF is marginally inferior to the approach in [46], indicating that the probability/confidence values generated by the latter are able to better distinguish between true matches and false matches.

More insightful observations can also be derived when considering individual demographic groups as shown in Table 3. In general, all methods perform better when considering 'White' subjects than the rest of the racial groups, except for some cases where the recall values are inferior to the other races. For instance, FF and DF with OpenCV attain higher recall for 'Black' subjects than 'White' subjects, with the latter also exhibiting a higher recall for 'Asian' subjects.

FF, which was trained on a balanced dataset, also exhibits overall lower performance for 'Asian' subjects. In terms of precision, the performance on 'White' subjects is noticeably higher than the other racial groups. However, as shown in Table 7, the confidence values when incorrectly classifying subjects as 'Asian' are generally quite high, indicating that the model is highly confident of making the correct prediction even when it is wrong. The confidences for 'White' subjects are also higher than the other methods, but lower than for the 'Asian' demographic. The values for 'Black' subjects could not be estimated since all incorrect predictions were classified as 'Indian' by FF, and were thus removed from evaluation. An example is shown in Fig. 4. While it could be argued that there are some similarities between the appearances of subjects in the two demographics, it would be expected that the confidences reflect this uncertainty.

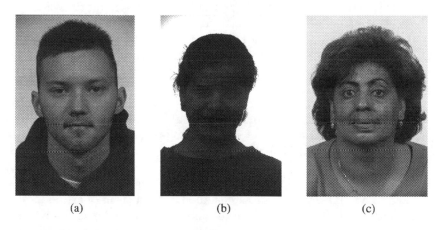

(a)   (b)   (c)

Fig. 4. Some incorrect results by FF: (a) actual race is 'White' but predicted race is 'Black' (59.47% confidence), (b) actual race and gender are 'White' 'Female', predicted are 'Indian' 'Male' with confidences of 77.94% and 96.12%, respectively, (c) 'Black' subject classified as 'Indian', with a 91.97% confidence (actual race given a score of just 7.91%).

All methods generally perform better on 'Black' subjects than 'Asian' subjects, although the difference is starker for DF while FF achieves a 100% recall. The method in [46] achieves lower precision for 'Black' subjects than 'Asian' subjects, indicating that it classifies several subjects as 'Black' but a number of them are actually incorrect.

Figure 4 shows some examples where FF is incorrect. In one case, both the gender and race are incorrect, with the model being 96.12% confident of having predicted the correct gender. However, it can be argued that the lighting in this image is sub-optimal, which might have affected the model. In the second case, the image has no such issues and the subject is clearly visible, but FF predicts the race to be 'Black' rather than 'White', albeit with a relatively low probability score of 59.47% with the true label having a score of 35.70%. However, as previously mentioned, the subject in the third example is given an incorrect label with a high probability score of 91.97%.

5   Conclusions and Future Work

This paper has presented and discussed performance differences across demographic groups of not only FRSs as is normally done, but also of FAESs. The considered methods (some of which have attained SOTA performance and all of which are freely available) generally attained good performance, which is unsurprising since the dataset was chosen to contain relatively good quality images. Nevertheless, the study in this work has exposed a number of cases where performance is lacking, particularly in terms of biases against demographic groups.

FF was designed to counteract the effect of biases, and generally exhibited the most consistent performance across demographic groups. This highlights the importance of using balanced datasets or techniques to counteract the issue of class imbalance. Nevertheless, it still showed several inconsistencies across demographic groups. A number of incorrect labels were also given high confidence values. This worrying behaviour underlines the need for more work to truly understand how machine learning models operate, in order to enable the design of approaches that counteract these issues [11, 13, 42].

It was also noted that performance differences across demographic groups may be further exacerbated by the choice of the face detector employed to crop and normalise face images that are then input to the attribute estimation methods and FRSs. Hence, care should be taken in the choice of pre-processing methods employed in order to maximise the performance potential of subsequent algorithms. It is also vital that anyone using such algorithms is aware of their weaknesses and ascertains that they are acceptable for the task at hand, lest there be undesired and potentially detrimental consequences.

Most methods consider a fairly limited spectrum of races (typically 'White', 'Asian', and 'Black'). It could be argued that the limited number of categories might artificially increase algorithms' performance, since the likelihood of choosing the correct category is higher. However, there do exist other labels that are more descriptive and which cater for a wider gamut of races (e.g. 'Hispanic', 'Middle-Eastern', etc.). This is arguably a severe limitation of most current approaches and is thus also an avenue of future work.

Future work can also consider the use of more datasets and techniques to make FAESs more robust across demographics, perhaps by using other network architectures, loss functions, and evaluation metrics. An analysis could also be done to determine the factors contributing the most to mitigating bias.

The reasons as to why the ML models can be highly affected across demographics, even by changes that appear small to the naked eye, need to be better understood. For example, techniques such as Grad-CAM [37] and LIME [33] could be used to visualise the salient regions as determined and used by the models.

ML models can be applied in numerous domains, such as computation of museum visitor statistics and attributes to enable the design of better exhibits. Whilst manual processes already exist, they may still be biased due to the 'other-race effect', subjectivity, and inconsistent practices. By transitioning to ML models, museums can streamline their data collection processes and improve efficiency. However, it is crucial to address the biases that can arise from these models. This work provides a framework and benchmark for evaluation of a wider spectrum of methods and datasets, to ensure that any models deployed in the real-world minimize biases in such sensitive applications.

Acknowledgements. This research was supported by the project REtics (Review Analytics), which is financed by the Malta Council for Science & Technology, for and on behalf of the Foundation for Science and Technology, through the FUSION: R&I Technology Development Programme LITE.

A   Appendix: Supplementary Information

This appendix contains additional images and tables that supplement the discussion in the main manuscript, as follows:

- Table 5 and Table 6 show the performance of the gender and race estimation methods, respectively, across all subjects.
- Table 7 contains the confidence scores for the race estimation methods, for each race considered.
- Table 8 and Table 9 contain the performance of the FRSs when evaluated on male and female subjects, respectively.
- Fig. 5 and Fig. 6 show the accuracy scores of the methods considered over different racial groups for male and female subjects, respectively
- Fig. 7 depicts examples of an incorrect match by OpenCV + VGG-Face (VGG16) [DF].
- Fig. 8 shows the confusion matrices for the gender and race estimation methods.

Table 5. Performance of the gender estimation methods, across all subjects. 'C' and 'I' refer to the mean confidence values output by the method when the prediction is correct and when the prediction is incorrect, respectively. 'A' represents the confidence score of the correct label when the prediction is incorrect. All values in %.

METHOD	ACCURACY	PRECISION	RECALL	F1	AUC	C	I	A
FF	98.04	98.09	98.04	98.03	99.05	96.21	82.61	13.02
[46]	92.02	92.91	92.02	91.86	99.30	79.15	23.16	6.40
OPENCV + DF	80.48	85.09	80.48	78.90	–	–	–	–
MTCNN + DF	83.37	86.97	83.37	82.31	–	–	–	–
DLIB + DF	81.74	86.07	81.74	80.37	–	–	–	–

Table 6. Performance of the race estimation methods, across all subjects. 'C' and 'I' refer to the mean confidence values output by the method when the prediction is correct and when the prediction is incorrect, respectively. 'A' represents the confidence score of the correct label when the prediction is incorrect. All values in %.

METHOD	ACCURACY	PRECISION	RECALL	F1	AUC	C	I	A
FF	99.01	99.03	99.01	99.01	96.22	96.21	66.97	24.15
[46]	94.68	94.70	94.68	94.57	96.96	79.15	23.16	6.40
OPENCV + DF	89.89	91.92	89.89	90.38	95.58	74.02	45.90	15.57
MTCNN + DF	88.82	92.20	88.82	89.50	95.70	75.18	43.12	15.52
DLIB + DF	98.02	98.05	98.02	98.03	97.02	77.61	54.92	13.93

Table 7. Confidence scores for race estimation methods, for each race. 'C' and 'I' denote confidence scores when the predicted label is correct and when the predicted label is incorrect, respectively. 'A' represents the confidence score of the correct label when the prediction is incorrect. All values in %.

METHOD	ASIAN			BLACK			WHITE		
	C	I	A	C	I	A	C	I	A
FF	98.25	81.95	0.30	–	–	–	95.70	61.98	32.10
[46]	81.24	19.62	2.69	61.23	26.00	12.08	80.77	39.83	20.96
OPENCV + DF	82.25	59.40	13.88	91.75	37.22	15.77	69.34	45.76	15.83
MTCNN + DF	83.08	63.41	8.39	88.01	41.80	14.44	71.50	42.21	16.41
DLIB + DF	84.51	66.40	9.19	88.53	52.80	22.92	74.55	43.19	16.07

Table 8. FRS performance for 'Male' subjects in each demographic group. [DF] denotes that the method as implemented in the DeepFace library. The rest of the methods use the implementations in [25]. 'Acc.' denotes 'Accuracy'.

METHOD	ASIAN			BLACK			WHITE			ALL		
	ACC.	EER	AUC	ACC.	EER	AUC	ACC.	EER	AUC	ACC.	EER	AUC
MTCNN + VGG-FACE (RESNET-50)	93.81	4.16	0.994	100.00	0.00	1.000	99.17	0.35	0.999	98.04	0.35	0.998
OPENCV + VGG-FACE (RESNET-50)	99.06	0.12	0.999	96.30	0.12	1.000	97.23	0.71	0.990	97.57	0.71	0.992
DLIB + VGG-FACE (RESNET-50)	100.00	0.00	1.000	100.00	0.00	1.000	99.72	0.12	1.000	99.80	0.12	1.000
MTCNN + VGG-FACE (VGG16)	84.96	7.05	0.976	79.41	7.28	0.953	90.61	4.39	0.988	88.61	5.55	0.983
OPENCV + VGG-FACE (VGG16)	86.79	5.11	0.975	74.07	10.82	0.951	86.70	5.83	0.979	86.03	7.73	0.976
DLIB + VGG-FACE (VGG16)	92.92	0.93	0.997	88.24	1.16	0.998	94.48	1.62	0.998	93.71	1.62	0.998
MTCNN + VGG-FACE (VGG16) [DF]	85.84	8.90	0.967	76.47	11.91	0.922	89.78	5.32	0.982	88.02	6.47	0.974
OPENCV + VGG-FACE (VGG16) [DF]	85.85	7.85	0.977	70.37	12.13	0.954	87.26	6.30	0.976	86.03	6.66	0.975
DLIB + VGG-FACE (VGG16) [DF]	93.81	2.20	0.998	85.29	1.39	0.999	94.48	1.39	0.999	93.71	1.39	0.999
MTCNN + ARCFACE [DF]	94.69	3.24	0.988	97.06	0.12	1.000	99.72	0.12	0.998	98.43	1.39	0.996
OPENCV + ARCFACE [DF]	93.40	2.02	0.966	96.30	0.12	0.969	95.84	0.12	0.971	95.34	2.02	0.970
DLIB + ARCFACE [DF]	100.00	0.00	1.000	100.00	0.00	1.000	100.00	0.00	1.000	100.00	0.00	1.000

Table 9. FRS performance for 'Female' subjects in each demographic group. [DF] denotes that the method as implemented in the DeepFace library. The rest of the methods use the implementations in [25]. 'Acc.' denotes 'Accuracy'.

METHOD	ASIAN			BLACK			WHITE			ALL		
	ACC.	EER	AUC	ACC.	EER	AUC	ACC.	EER	AUC	ACC.	EER	AUC
MTCNN + VGG-FACE (RESNET-50)	100.00	0.00	1.000	100.00	0.00	1.000	99.22	0.12	1.000	99.44	0.12	1.000
OPENCV + VGG-FACE (RESNET-50)	100.00	0.00	1.000	100.00	0.00	1.000	94.86	2.62	0.995	96.26	1.31	0.996
DLIB + VGG-FACE (RESNET-50)	100.00	0.00	1.000	100.00	0.00	1.000	100.00	0.00	1.000	100.00	0.00	1.000
MTCNN + VGG-FACE (VGG16)	92.98	1.50	0.999	93.18	1.27	1.000	92.58	1.85	0.996	92.72	1.50	0.997
OPENCV + VGG-FACE (VGG16)	84.21	6.18	0.990	97.37	1.31	1.000	80.24	9.87	0.963	82.76	7.73	0.971
DLIB + VGG-FACE (VGG16)	96.49	0.58	1.000	93.02	0.93	1.000	98.05	1.27	0.999	97.19	0.93	0.999
MTCNN + VGG-FACE (VGG16) [DF]	91.23	3.47	0.993	68.18	17.34	0.893	92.58	3.24	0.990	89.36	5.09	0.979
OPENCV + VGG-FACE (VGG16) [DF]	84.21	5.35	0.989	92.11	0.12	0.999	80.63	10.82	0.964	82.47	9.63	0.972
DLIB + VGG-FACE (VGG16) [DF]	100.00	0.00	1.000	93.02	0.93	0.999	97.66	0.35	1.000	97.47	0.81	1.000
MTCNN + ARCFACE [DF]	98.25	0.23	1.000	100.00	0.00	1.000	100.00	0.00	1.000	99.72	0.12	1.000
OPENCV + ARCFACE [DF]	87.72	0.59	0.899	94.74	0.12	0.975	82.21	8.92	0.876	84.48	8.92	0.891
DLIB + ARCFACE [DF]	100.00	0.00	1.000	100.00	0.00	1.000	100.00	0.00	1.000	100.00	0.00	1.000

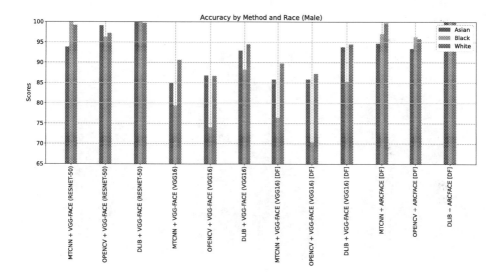

Fig. 5. Accuracy scores of the methods considered over different racial groups for male subjects

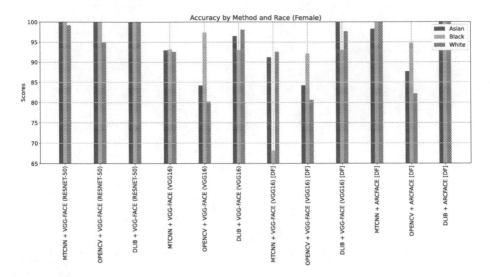

Fig. 6. Accuracy scores of the methods considered over different racial groups for female subjects

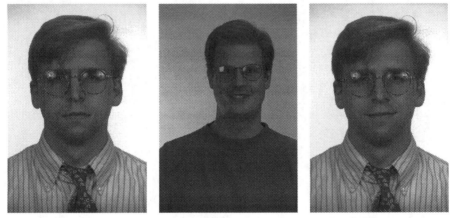

(a) Query image   (b) Best match   (c) True match

Fig. 7. Example of an incorrect match by OpenCV + VGG-Face (VGG16) [DF]. Three of the top five subjects wear glasses, like the query subject.

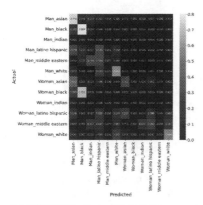

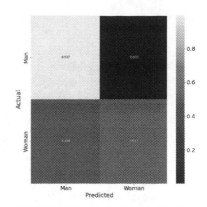

(a) DF [39] (+ OpenCV [5]) (Race and Gender)

(b) DF [39] (+ OpenCV [5]) (Gender)

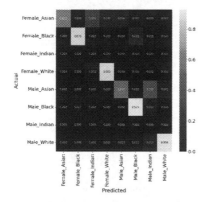

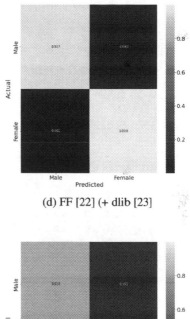

(c) FF [22] (+ dlib [23]) (Race and Gender)

(d) FF [22] (+ dlib [23]

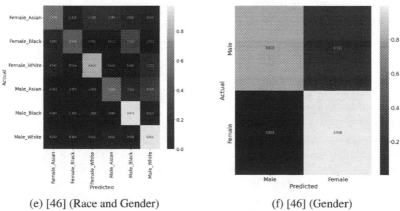

(e) [46] (Race and Gender)

(f) [46] (Gender)

Fig. 8. Normalised confusion matrices for the gender and race estimation methods. Labels the same as those used by the methods considered.

References

1. How many major races are there in the world? (2011). https://blog.world-mysteries.com/science/how-many-major-races-are-there-in-the-world/
2. Face recognition (2018). https://github.com/ageitgey/face_recognition/
3. Badave, H., Kuber, M.: Face recognition based activity detection for security application. In: 2021 International Conference on Artificial Intelligence and Smart Systems (ICAIS), pp. 487–491 (2021). https://doi.org/10.1109/ICAIS50930.2021.9395829
4. Blakemore, E.: Race and ethnicity: How are they different? https://www.nationalgeographic.com/culture/article/race-ethnicity (2019)
5. Bradski, G.: The OpenCV library. Dr. Dobb's J. Softw. Tools **25**(11), 120–123 (2000)
6. Cao, Q., Shen, L., Xie, W., Parkhi, O.M., Zisserman, A.: VGGFace2: a dataset for recognising faces across pose and age. In: 2018 13th IEEE International Conference on Automatic Face & Gesture Recognition (FG 2018), pp. 67–74. IEEE Computer Society, Los Alamitos, CA, USA (2018). https://doi.org/10.1109/FG.2018.00020
7. Cascone, L., Pero, C., Proença, H.: Visual and textual explainability for a biometric verification system based on piecewise facial attribute analysis. Image Vis. Comput. **132**, 104645 (2023)
8. Cavazos, J.G., Phillips, P.J., Castillo, C.D., O'Toole, A.J.: Accuracy comparison across face recognition algorithms: where are we on measuring race bias? IEEE Trans. Biometrics Behav. Identity Sci. **3**(1), 101–111 (2021). https://doi.org/10.1109/TBIOM.2020.3027269
9. Das, A., Dantcheva, A., Bremond, F.: Mitigating bias in gender, age and ethnicity classification: a multi-task convolution neural network approach. In: Proceedings of the European Conference on Computer Vision (ECCV) Workshops (2018)
10. Deng, J., Guo, J., Xue, N., Zafeiriou, S.: ArcFace: additive angular margin loss for deep face recognition. In: 2019 IEEE/CVF Conference on Computer Vision and Pattern Recognition (CVPR), pp. 4685–4694 (2019). https://doi.org/10.1109/CVPR.2019.00482
11. Drozdowski, P., Rathgeb, C., Dantcheva, A., Damer, N., Busch, C.: Demographic bias in biometrics: a survey on an emerging challenge. IEEE Trans. Technol. Soc. **1**(2), 89–103 (2020). https://doi.org/10.1109/TTS.2020.2992344
12. Du, H., Shi, H., Zeng, D., Zhang, X.P., Mei, T.: The elements of end-to-end deep face recognition: a survey of recent advances. ACM Comput. Surv. (CSUR) **54**(10s), 1–42 (2022)
13. Ferrari, C., Lisanti, G., Berretti, S., Del Bimbo, A.: Investigating nuisances in DCNN-based face recognition. IEEE Trans. Image Process. **27**(11), 5638–5651 (2018). https://doi.org/10.1109/TIP.2018.2861359
14. Furl, N., Phillips, P., O'Toole, A.J.: Face recognition algorithms and the other-race effect: computational mechanisms for a developmental contact hypothesis. Cogn. Sci. **26**(6), 797–815 (2002)
15. Galea, C., Farrugia, R.A.: Forensic face photo-sketch recognition using a deep learning-based architecture. IEEE Signal Process. Lett. **24**(11), 1586–1590 (2017). https://doi.org/10.1109/LSP.2017.2749266
16. Galea, C., Farrugia, R.A.: Matching software-generated sketches to face photographs with a very deep CNN, morphed faces, and transfer learning. IEEE Trans. Inf. Forensics Secur. **13**(6), 1421–1431 (2018). https://doi.org/10.1109/TIFS.2017.2788002
17. Galea, N., Seychell, D.: Facial expression recognition in the wild: dataset configurations. In: 2022 IEEE 5th International Conference on Multimedia Information Processing and Retrieval (MIPR), pp. 216–219 (2022). https://doi.org/10.1109/MIPR54900.2022.00045
18. Georgopoulos, M.: Bias in deep learning and applications to face analysis. Ph.D. thesis, Imperial College London (2022)

19. Gong, S., Liu, X., Jain, A.K.: Jointly de-biasing face recognition and demographic attribute estimation. In: Vedaldi, A., Bischof, H., Brox, T., Frahm, J.-M. (eds.) ECCV 2020. LNCS, vol. 12374, pp. 330–347. Springer, Cham (2020). https://doi.org/10.1007/978-3-030-58526-6_20

20. He, K., Zhang, X., Ren, S., Sun, J.: Deep residual learning for image recognition. In: Proceedings of the IEEE Conference on Computer Vision and Pattern Recognition, pp. 770–778 (2016)

21. Hu, J., Shen, L., Sun, G.: Squeeze-and-excitation networks. In: 2018 IEEE/CVF Conference on Computer Vision and Pattern Recognition, pp. 7132–7141 (2018). https://doi.org/10.1109/CVPR.2018.00745

22. Karkkainen, K., Joo, J.: FairFace: face attribute dataset for balanced race, gender, and age for bias measurement and mitigation. In: Proceedings of the IEEE/CVF Winter Conference on Applications of Computer Vision, pp. 1548–1558 (2021)

23. King, D.E.: Dlib-ml: a machine learning toolkit. J. Mach. Learn. Res. **10**, 1755–1758 (2009)

24. Klare, B.F., et al.: Pushing the frontiers of unconstrained face detection and recognition: iarpa janus benchmark a. In: 2015 IEEE Conference on Computer Vision and Pattern Recognition (CVPR), pp. 1931–1939 (2015). https://doi.org/10.1109/CVPR.2015.7298803

25. Malli, R.C.: keras-vggface (2019). https://github.com/rcmalli/keras-vggface

26. Mather, M., Jacobsen, L.A., Scommegna, P.: Population: an introduction to demography. Popul. Bull. **75**(1) (2021)

27. Maze, B., et al.: Iarpa janus benchmark - c: face dataset and protocol. In: 2018 International Conference on Biometrics (ICB), pp. 158–165 (2018). https://doi.org/10.1109/ICB2018.2018.00033

28. Neto, P.C., et al.: Explainable biometrics in the age of deep learning (2022)

29. Parkhi, O.M., Vedaldi, A., Zisserman, A.: Deep face recognition. In: British Machine Vision Conference (2015)

30. Pedregosa, F., et al.: Scikit-learn: machine learning in Python. J. Mach. Learn. Res. **12**, 2825–2830 (2011)

31. Phillips, P., Wechsler, H., Huang, J., Rauss, P.J.: The FERET database and evaluation procedure for face-recognition algorithms. Image Vis. Comput. **16**(5), 295–306 (1998). https://doi.org/10.1016/S0262-8856(97)00070-X

32. Popa, M., Rothkrantz, L., Yang, Z., Wiggers, P., Braspenning, R., Shan, C.: Analysis of shopping behavior based on surveillance system. In: 2010 IEEE International Conference on Systems, Man and Cybernetics, pp. 2512–2519. IEEE (2010)

33. Ribeiro, M.T., Singh, S., Guestrin, C.: "Why should i trust you?": explaining the predictions of any classifier. In: Proceedings of the 22nd ACM SIGKDD International Conference on Knowledge Discovery and Data Mining, KDD 2016, pp. 1135–1144. Association for Computing Machinery, New York, NY, USA (2016). https://doi.org/10.1145/2939672.2939778

34. Robinson, J.P., Livitz, G., Henon, Y., Qin, C., Fu, Y., Timoner, S.: Face recognition: too bias, or not too bias? In: Proceedings of the IEEE/CVF Conference on Computer Vision and Pattern Recognition Workshops (2020)

35. Rodríguez Spinelli, F.: Facing the bias: when face processing algorithms bump into diversity. SSRN 3823012 (2021)

36. Rothe, R., Timofte, R., Van Gool, L.: DEX: deep expectation of apparent age from a single image. In: 2015 IEEE International Conference on Computer Vision Workshop (ICCVW), pp. 252–257 (2015). https://doi.org/10.1109/ICCVW.2015.41

37. Selvaraju, R.R., Cogswell, M., Das, A., Vedantam, R., Parikh, D., Batra, D.: Grad-CAM: visual explanations from deep networks via gradient-based localization. In: 2017 IEEE International Conference on Computer Vision (ICCV), pp. 618–626 (2017). https://doi.org/10.1109/ICCV.2017.74

38. Serengil, S.I.: Apparent age and gender prediction in keras (2019). https://sefiks.com/2019/02/13/apparent-age-and-gender-prediction-in-keras/
39. Serengil, S.I., Ozpinar, A.: Lightface: a hybrid deep face recognition framework. In: 2020 Innovations in Intelligent Systems and Applications Conference (ASYU), pp. 23–27. IEEE (2020). https://doi.org/10.1109/ASYU50717.2020.9259802
40. Serengil, S.I., Ozpinar, A.: Hyperextended lightface: a facial attribute analysis framework. In: 2021 International Conference on Engineering and Emerging Technologies (ICEET), pp. 1–4. IEEE (2021). https://doi.org/10.1109/ICEET53442.2021.9659697
41. Simonyan, K., Zisserman, A.: Very deep convolutional networks for large-scale image recognition. In: Bengio, Y., LeCun, Y. (eds.) 3rd International Conference on Learning Representations, ICLR 2015, San Diego, May 7–9 2015, Conference Track Proceedings (2015). https://arxiv.org/abs/1409.1556
42. Terhörst, P., et al.: Reliable age and gender estimation from face images: stating the confidence of model predictions. In: 10th IEEE International Conference on Biometrics Theory, Applications and Systems, BTAS 2019, Tampa, FL, USA, 23–26 September 2019, pp. 1–8. IEEE (2019). https://doi.org/10.1109/BTAS46853.2019.9185975
43. Terhörst, P., et al.: A comprehensive study on face recognition biases beyond demographics. IEEE Trans. Technol. Soc. **3**(1), 16–30 (2022). https://doi.org/10.1109/TTS.2021.3111823
44. Thom, N., Hand, E.M.: Facial attribute recognition: a survey. Comput. Vis.: Ref. Guide, 1–13 (2020)
45. Whitelam, C., et al.: Iarpa janus benchmark-b face dataset. In: 2017 IEEE Conference on Computer Vision and Pattern Recognition Workshops (CVPRW), pp. 592–600 (2017). https://doi.org/10.1109/CVPRW.2017.87
46. Won, D.: Gender and race classification with face images (2018). https://github.com/wondonghyeon/face-classification
47. Zhang, K., Zhang, Z., Li, Z., Qiao, Y.: Joint face detection and alignment using multitask cascaded convolutional networks. IEEE Signal Process. Lett. **23**(10), 1499–1503 (2016). https://doi.org/10.1109/LSP.2016.2603342

A Multi-label Classification Study for the Prediction of Long-COVID Syndrome

Marco Dossena, Christopher Irwin, Luca Piovesan, and Luigi Portinale[✉]

Computer Science Institute (DiSIT), University of Piemonte Orientale,
Alessandria, Italy
{marco.dossena,christopher.irwin,luca.piovesan,luigi.portinale}@uniupo.it

Abstract. We present a study about the prediction of long-COVID sequelae through multi-label classification (MLC). Data about more than 300 patients have been collected during a long-COVID study at Ospedale Maggiore of Novara (Italy), considering their baseline situation, as well as their condition on acute COVID-19 onset. The goal is to predict the presence of specific long-COVID sequelae after a one-year follow-up. To amplify the representativeness of the analysis, we carefully investigated the possibility of augmenting the dataset, by considering situations where different levels in the number of complications could arise. MLSmote under six different policies of data augmentation has been considered, and a representative set of MLC approaches have been tested on all the available datasets. Results have been evaluated in terms of Accuracy, Exact match, Hamming Score and macro-averaged AUC; they show that MLC methods can actually be useful for the prediction of specific long-COVID sequelae, under the different conditions represented by the different considered datasets.

Keywords: multi-label classification · data augmentation · long-COVID syndrome

1 Introduction

In the last years, the intelligent analysis of clinical data has become a cornerstone of modern biomedical research. An increasing number of projects focus on the definition of biomedical databanks, and on their analysis through machine and deep learning techniques. Notably, databanks can be fed from different sources (e.g., electronic health records, clinical trial data, laboratory analysis results), which are usually updated over time. In such contexts, it is useful to provide practitioners with direct and easy access to sophisticated AI-driven data analysis.

In this paper, we move a step forward in such a direction, by studying how machine learning techniques can be adopted in order to work with a real-world databank. This work is part of the TECNOMED-HUB research project [1], which

R. Basili et al. (Eds.): AIxIA 2023, LNAI 14318, pp. 265–277, 2023.
https://doi.org/10.1007/978-3-031-47546-7_18

aims to build a research platform supporting the collection and intelligent analysis of *long-COVID* data, but with the long-term goal of being applicable to a wide range of other diseases. In particular, the goal of this study is to define a framework for predicting long-COVID sequelae, based on patients' clinical data collected during the acute phase of COVID infection.

Following the characterization in [15], post(long)-COVID-19 syndrome consists of signs and symptoms (sequelae) consistent with COVID-19 that are present beyond 12 weeks of the onset of acute COVID-19 infection, and not ascribable to alternative causes (i.e., other diseases). From the machine learning point of view, considering the syndrome to be defined as the persistence of at least one of such symptoms, the characterization of the problem can be viewed as a Multi-Label Classification problem (see Sect. 2), where instances are the patients' data collected at hospitalization, and the labels are the long-COVID symptoms persisting at follow-up.

Notably, such a kind of task characterizes a wide range of applications in the field of *individualized predictive modelling* where the onset of comorbidities is analyzed in a precise context; examples are reported for diabetes [26], heart failure [13] and dyspnea [3]. Notice that differently from these works, our study focuses on the prediction of specific symptoms, rather than on the risk of comorbidities, making the clinical context slightly different, since the physician suspecting the insurgence of a given symptom can directly take this into account (for instance with specific therapies avoiding undesirable effects of such symptoms).

Coping with individualized predictive modelling in real-world settings implies working in a low-data regime and unbalanced labels. As a consequence, upsampling techniques must be adopted. However, such an aspect conflicts with the evidence-based nature of the medical research field. To this end, one of the goals of our work is to evaluate which upsampling techniques can be considered a valid trade-off between the need for a more balanced dataset and keeping the synthetic data close to the real-world ones.

The results of the work described in this paper are twofold:

- from the medical point of view, we investigated the correlation between long-COVID syndrome and the patients' data, providing a framework to predict long-COVID sequelae;
- from the technological perspective, we defined a framework for the multi-label classification of symptoms working in a low-data regimen, that can be easily adapted for different tasks in the field of individualized predictive modelling.

The paper is organized as follows: Sect. 2 summarizes the MLC framework and the adopted algorithms and evaluation criteria; Sect. 3 presents the case study with the characterization of the collected data; Sect. 4 describes the experimental part whose results are reported in Sect. 5; finally conclusions are drawn in Sect. 6.

2   Multi-label Classification

Multi-Label Classification (MLC) can be defined as follows [6, 14]. Let us consider an instance space $\mathcal{X} = \{x_1, \ldots x_n\}$ where each $x_i \in \mathcal{X}$ is a tuple of size $D = |x_i|$, a label space $\mathcal{L} = \{\lambda_1, \ldots \lambda_Q\}$ of $Q = |\mathcal{L}|$ possible labels, a set of instances $E = \{(x_i, \mathcal{Y}_i)|x_i \in \mathcal{X}, \mathcal{Y}_i \subseteq \mathcal{L}, 1 \leq i \leq n\}$; a *quality criterion* q. The objective of MLC is to find a function $h : \mathcal{X} \to 2^{\mathcal{L}}$ that maximizes q. The goal is to obtain a function h able to predict the subset of labels associated with a given example. To this end, the problem is usually tackled by considering the set of labels represented as a binary vector of size Q, where 0 means that the label is absent (or not predicted) and 1 means the label is present (or predicted). The problem can be generalized to label ranking by learning a function $h : \mathcal{X} \times \mathcal{L} \to \mathcal{R}$ such that $h(x_i, \lambda_j) = r$ is the prediction score for label λ_j in the example x_i. Usually, the score is the probability of label λ_j given x_i, and the presence of the label can be predicted if it exceeds a given threshold (usually 0.5). Given an instance $(x_i, \mathcal{Y}_i) \in E$ we define $\mathcal{Y}_i$ as the *label-set* of x_i. Usually, the number of label-sets in a given instance space (dataset) is much less than $2^{|\mathcal{L}|}$, making the label-set space very sparse.

2.1   MLC Methods

MLC can be approached in two different ways: *problem transformation* and *algorithm transformation* [6]. Methods in the former category transform the multi-label dataset into one or more datasets that are then targeted using traditional single-label classification algorithms; they finally build one or multiple single-label models. Methods in the latter adapt traditional single-label algorithms to the multi-label setting such as decision trees, functional models (SVM or NN), instance-based models and probabilistic models.

In the present study we concentrate on the problem transformation category of approaches, which is the most widely adopted in MLC; in fact, most of the algorithm transformation methods actually rely on an internal problem transformation in order to solve the MLC task. Moreover, this allows in principle to experiment with a larger number of base classifiers.

Concerning problem transformation methods, they can further be divided into *binary*, *multi-class* or *ensemble* methods [6]. In binary methods, each pair of labels is considered to produce a quadratic number of single-target binary datasets following a one-vs-all strategy; the results is the construction of $|\mathcal{L}|$ binary classifiers one for each possible label. Methods belonging to this category are *Binary Relevance* (BR) [11] and different versions of *classifier chain* such as CC [18] or BCC [25]. Multi-class methods, on the contrary, build one single multi-class classifier: the target class has a set of possible values equal to the cardinality of the label-sets. The *Label Powerset* or *Label Combination* (LC) algorithm [11] and the *Pruned Set* (PS) method [19] are examples of this kind of approach. Finally, ensemble methods adopt ensemble-like techniques in order to train multiple single-label classifiers; important representatives of such methods are the *Conditional Dependency Network* (CDN) [12] and the *RAkEL* [24] algorithms.

2.2   MLC: Characterization and Evaluation Measures

MLC dataset characterization is a very important aspect, especially in terms of label distribution and balancing. Different measures can be used to characterize a dataset for MLC [23] starting from basic measures such as *number of instances, number of attributes, number of labels, number of distinct label-sets*. Another characterization can be given in terms of label distribution through measures such as *label cardinality* (average number of labels in the examples) and *label density* (the cardinality divided by the number of labels), as reported in Eq. 1.

$$Card(E) = \frac{1}{n}\sum_{i=1}^{n}|\mathcal{Y}_i|; \quad Dens(E) = \frac{1}{|\mathcal{L}|}Card(E) \qquad (1)$$

Imbalance level measures are also important in order to characterize how frequent or rare are certain labels. The most relevant measures are the *Imbalance Ratio per Label (IRLbl)* and the *Mean Imbalance Ratio (MeanIR)* which are reported in Eq. 2 and Eq. 3 respectively.

$$IRLbl(\lambda) = \frac{\max_{\lambda' \in \mathcal{L}}\sum_{i=1}^{n}h(\lambda', \mathcal{Y}_i)}{\sum_{i=1}^{n}h(\lambda, \mathcal{Y}_i)}; \quad h(\lambda, \mathcal{Y}_i) = \begin{cases} 1 & \text{if } \lambda \in \mathcal{Y}_i \\ 0 & \text{if } \lambda \notin \mathcal{Y}_i \end{cases} \qquad (2)$$

$$MeanIR = \frac{1}{|\mathcal{L}|}\sum_{\lambda \in \mathcal{L}}IRLbl(\lambda) \qquad (3)$$

IRLbl(λ) is the ratio between the occurrence of the majority label and the current label λ; *IRLbl* is ≥ 1 (1 only for majority labels), and the larger the value the greater the imbalance of the label. MeanIR characterises the level imbalance of the whole dataset. In addition, the standard coefficient of variation of *IRLbl* (*CVIR*, the ratio between standard deviation and mean) can be useful to measure if labels experience a similar level of imbalance or if there are large differences, in terms of imbalance, among them.

Finally, the SCUMBLE metric [8] provides a way to understand the level of concurrence between minority and majority labels; values are in the $[0, 1]$ range, and the higher the value the more instances sharing minority and majority labels exist in the dataset. It is based on the computation of the Atkinson index [2] over the *IRLbl* of the labels occurring in each instance; the final score is the average over all the instances of the dataset (see [8] for details). A small value of SCUMBLE (usually ≤ 0.1) denotes a low concurrency between minority and majority labels; this is a proxy for the possibility of adopting data augmentation techniques without the risk of increasing in a significant way the label imbalance. In particular, oversampling techniques such as MLSmote [7] are well justified and applicable when the dataset SCUMBLE is low [8,17].

Concerning evaluation measures for MLC, several metrics have been proposed with very different aims. They can be categorized as *bipartition-based* and *ranking-based* [11]. In our setting, bipartition-based are more significant, since the emphasis is on predicting the right set of long-COVID symptoms, rather than a correct ranking. In the present study, we then consider some of the most popular and natural bipartition-based metrics. Let $\mathcal{Y}_i$ be the ground-truth label-set of instance x_i, $\mathcal{Z}_i$ the predicted label-set and Δ the symmetric set difference operator:

HammingScore=1- HammingLoss where *Hamming Loss* evaluates how many times, on average, an example-label pair is misclassified.

$$HammingLoss = \frac{1}{n}\sum_{i=1}^{n}\frac{|\mathcal{Y}_i\Delta\mathcal{Z}_i|}{|\mathcal{L}|}$$

Accuracy or *Jaccard Index* evaluates the average proportion of labels correctly classified on the total number (predicted and actual) of labels, and averaged over all instances.

$$Accuracy = \frac{1}{n}\sum_{i=1}^{n}\frac{|\mathcal{Y}_i\cap\mathcal{Z}_i|}{|\mathcal{Y}_i\cup\mathcal{Z}_i|}$$

ExactMatch evaluates the percentage of label-sets that are correctly predicted as a whole

$$ExactMatch = \frac{1}{n}\sum_{i=1}^{n}\mathbb{1}(\mathcal{Y}_i = \mathcal{Z}_i)$$

Notice that the Hamming Score is somewhat lenient, since when several labels are absent in a label-set, the score may find several correct matches; however, it is an important metric since the correct prediction of an absent label should be relevant in several applications, as in our case study. On the contrary, Exact Match is a very strict measure, since partial predictions are completely ruled out. A somewhat intermediate metric is the Accuracy/Jaccard Index, where however, due to the nature of an MLC problem, one can hardly expect to get results close to 1 (as can be in the case of single-label classification). Jaccard Index of about 0.65/0.7 can be regarded as good results (see [14]).

We will finally consider the AUC (Area Under Roc Curve) in the macro-averaged version (the metric is computed independently for each label and then averaged). Since in our case all labels have the same importance (they should be treated equally as one of the symptoms of long-COVID), macro-average is preferred to micro-averaging (where the specific measures of each class are combined together).

3   The Case Study: Long-COVID Syndrome

3.1   Problem Characterization

The focus of the present paper refers to a long-COVID study realized at Ospedale Maggiore of Novara in Italy, where data about 324 patients, hospitalized for acute COVID-19 onset during the first three waves of the pandemic, have been collected [4,5]. As already reported in Sect. 1, a patient is considered suffering from long-COVID if she shows at least one sequela (symptom) of acute COVID-19 after a minimum of 12 weeks from the onset [15]. In the present study, we consider a follow-up time of about one year after the first hospitalization due to acute COVID-19, and we focus on some specific sequelae for which data has been collected. In particular, the following symptoms are considered: *arthromyalgia*, *asthenia, cough, diarrhea, dysgeusia, anosmia*. They are all represented as binary features denoting the absence/presence of the corresponding symptom at follow-up time. In addition, we also consider the results of the respiratory test *mMRC* (modified - British - Medical Research Council questionnaire), which is a reliable indicator for dyspnea. Clinicians have then summarized it into a binary variable (*mMRC_cat*) representing the absence/presence of severe dyspnea. In summary, we consider a total of 7 sequelae at follow-up.

Concerning patient characterization, *baseline* data indicate features of demographic and medical history of the patient, while *hospitalization* data refer to the patient's symptoms at hospitalization (acute COVID-19 onset). Baseline data are not directly related to COVID-19 infection but are important factors to take into account in order to make an accurate diagnosis or prediction. Features in the baseline data can be grouped in terms of demographic characteristics (sex, age, smoking attitude, ...) and of prior comorbidities (obesity, chronic liver disease, hypertension, anxiety and depression, ...). Hospitalization data include the patient's symptoms at COVID-19 onset (fever, cough, dyspnea, arthralgia, ...), drugs administered (hydroxychloroquine, monoclonal antibodies, glucocorticoids, antivirals, ...), and hospitalization information (duration, oxygen administration, ICU intubation, ..) All the baseline and hospitalization data result in a total of 57 features, among which 47 binary and 10 numeric.

The classification problem can then be described as follows: *predict the presence of specific long-COVID sequelae at follow-up, using baseline and hospitalization information*. This problem can be addressed as an MLC problem with $|\mathcal{L}| = 7$.

3.2   Dataset Analysis

The dataset produced in our long-COVID study (named *orig* in the following) resulted in $n = 324$ instances (324 different patients under study) with $D = 57$ features (47 binary features and 10 numeric features). No missing value was reported[1]. The cardinality of the label-set is $|\mathcal{L}| = 7$ since we consider 7 long-COVID sequelae (see Sect. 3.1).

Some distributions concerning label and instances are reported in Fig. 1, while the first row of Table 1 shows the main characterization measures. We can notice that the imbalance level (as measured by MeanIR) is significant, even if a low

---

[1] Actually the collected data concerned much more hospitalized patients, but we have been able to work only with those patients who decided to partecipate in the study and for which reliable data were available [5].

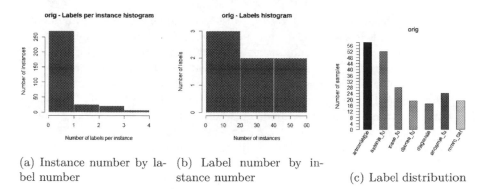

(a) Instance number by label number

(b) Label number by instance number

(c) Label distribution

Fig. 1. Original dataset

Table 1. Main features of considered datasets; n: number of instances, #ls: cardinality of label-set, #pl: number of label-set with more than one label

Dataset	n	#ls	#pl	Card	Dens	MeanIR	CVIR	Scumble
orig	324	36	54	0.670	0.096	2.303	0.417	0.012
k3I	424	36	54	0.592	0.085	2.173	0.415	0.009
k3R	424	38	79	0.814	0.116	1.762	0.373	0.007
k3U	424	48	154	1.752	0.250	1.566	0.239	0.008
k5I	424	36	54	0.512	0.073	2.303	0.417	0.009
k5R	424	36	54	0.599	0.086	2.089	0.466	0.008
k5U	424	48	154	1.745	0.249	1.602	0.311	0.009

$CVIR$ shows that there are similar level of imbalance among the labels. Moreover, the Scumble metric $S = 0.012$ is relatively low, showing a low level of interactions (concurrency) between minority and majority labels. This suggest that data augmentation techniques through resampling can be attempted, in order to get more significant data; this is very important in the present context, since the study was able to process just a few hundreds real patients, and the possibility of increasing the dataset size (even if with a limited increase of data) is considered as fundamental. We choose MLSmote [7], an oversampling technique producing new synthetic data by first identifying minority labes (using $IRLbl$ measures), followed by a kNN search and a feature generation from such search as in the standard SMOTE technique [9]. Finally, label-sets for the synthetic instances are generated, using 3 possible criteria: *Intersection (I)*: labels appearing in the reference sample and in all the neighbors are added to the new sample; *Union (U)* labels appearing in either the reference sample or in any of the neighbors are added to the new sample; *Ranking (R)*: labels present in more than half of the reference and neighbor samples are added to the new sample (majority voting).

We started from the original dataset (orig) and generated 6 data augmented datasets using MLSmote with $k = 3, 5$ (number of considered neighbors) and the intersection, union and ranking generation (datasets k3I, k3U, k3R, k5I, k5U, k5R respectively). The number of synthetic instances to introduce has been set to 100, in order to increment the available examples in a reasonable way (the increase is less than $\frac{1}{3}$ of the original size, but allows us to consider a situation with a significant number of additional potential patients). Table 1 shows a summary of the characterization measures for each considered dataset.

We can notice that the more aggressive the augmentation (U more aggressive than R more aggressive than I), the larger the number of label-sets and the presence of label-sets with several labels, as reflected by cardinality and density as well. This allows also to reduce the label imbalance, by also keeping the SCUMBLE index under control. To this end, considering a smaller number of neighbours in the instance generation ($k = 3$) seems to take the label imbalance more under control.

4   Experimental Framework

The experimental analysis has been performed using MEKA [20], a multi-label extension to WEKA [10]. We considered the following problem transformation approaches to MLC:

- BR (Binary Relevance): a set of 7 independent binary classification models (one for each possible label) has been built and results have been merged; label correlation information is completely neglected in this case.
- CC (Classifier Chain): labels are processed in a random order by a set of binary classifiers; each classifier predicts the presence of the corresponding label, by considering the classification produced by the previous ones, i.e., classifier C_i ($2 \leq i \leq 7$) uses problem features augmented with the label values predicted by classifiers C_j ($1 \leq j \leq i - 1$). Classifier C_1 uses only the problem features.
- BCC (Bayesian Classifier Chain): as the CC method, but the order in which labels are processed is not random; we tested two possible versions of BCC corresponding to different label ordering: BCC(I), where the label order is induced by the mutual information among labels, and BCC(C) where label ordering is determined by label co-occurrence counts.
- LC (Label Combination): the problem features are augmented with a class attribute taking discrete values in the range $[1, \#ls]$ where #ls is the cardinality of the label-sets; the problem is then solved as a standard single-label multi-class classification.
- PS (Pruned Set): first it prunes all examples having label-sets that occur less than p times in the training set (we set $p = 2$ in our analyses); then it subsamples the label-sets of these examples for label subsets that occur more frequently in the training data. It then attaches these label sets to the example, creating new examples and reintroducing them into the training set; after these steps, it trains a standard LC classifier.

– CDN (Conditional Dependency Network): it builds a fully-connected network where nodes are the labels, then it builds a set of binary classifiers (7 in our case) one for each label λ_j, predicting $p(\lambda_j|x_i, \lambda_1, \ldots \lambda_{j-1}, \lambda_{j+1}, \ldots \lambda_Q)$; inference is performed through Gibbs sampling [21] over a set of I iterations, and by collecting results from last I_c iterations (in our case we set $I = 500$ and $I_c = 100$).
– RAkEL (RAndom k-labEL Pruned Sets): it randomly draws M subsets of labels, each with k labels, from the set of labels, and trains PS upon each one (in our case we set PS as indicated above, $M = 10$ and $k = 3$).

The tested MLC methods are 4 binary methods (BR, CC and the two versions of BCC), 2 multi-class methods (LC and PS), and 2 ensemble methods (CDN and RAkEL). We tested the above methods with several base classifiers (from lazy classifiers, to neural nets, SVM and tree-based classifiers), and we have finally found that a 200-trees Random Forest provided the most interesting results. In the following, we will report results concerning the above transformation-based methods using this base classifier.

It is worth to remark that multi-class methods rely on the label-sets which are actually present in the data. A suitable data augmentation strategy could be really important to consider potential label-sets which are not occurring in the original dataset.

5   Results

This section presents the comparative results obtained by the MLC algorithms described in Sect. 4, on the considered datasets. We tested all the methods using 5 runs of 10-fold cross-validation, and we finally averaged the results. In the following tables, we highlight in bold the best results obtained for each considered dataset; the last row reports the average performance of each MLC method over all the datasets (in bold are shown the best results). Table 2 shows the Accuracy/Jaccard Index for the various datasets and tested methods. We can

Table 2. Accuracy (Jaccard Index)

Datasets	BCC(C)	BCC(I)	BR	CC	CDN	LC	PS	RAkEL
orig	0.604	**0.605**	0.420	0.604	0.415	0.604	**0.605**	0.604
k3I	0.646	0.647	0.507	0.649	0.503	0.653	**0.673**	0.651
k3R	0.615	0.615	0.546	0.613	0.527	**0.660**	0.643	0.652
k3U	0.637	0.639	0.577	0.638	0.537	0.637	0.624	**0.651**
k5I	0.666	0.666	0.488	0.669	0.466	0.646	**0.680**	0.641
k5R	0.645	0.648	0.499	0.645	0.496	0.648	**0.668**	0.647
k5U	0.651	0.649	0.582	0.649	0.552	0.648	0.637	**0.666**
Avg	0.638	0.638	0.517	0.638	0.500	0.642	**0.647**	0.645

Table 3. Exact Match

Datasets	BCC(I)	BCC(C)	BR	CC	CDN	LC	PS	RAkEL
orig	0.601	0.603	0.383	0.601	0.377	0.604	**0.605**	0.601
k3I	0.641	0.643	0.475	0.645	0.471	0.644	**0.668**	0.642
k3R	0.590	0.593	0.479	0.590	0.461	0.620	**0.623**	0.614
k3U	0.559	0.564	0.460	0.568	0.431	0.589	**0.594**	0.586
k5I	0.666	0.666	0.473	0.669	0.449	0.646	**0.680**	0.641
k5R	0.641	0.645	0.472	0.640	0.468	0.639	**0.664**	0.640
k5U	0.571	0.571	0.472	0.580	0.435	0.586	**0.594**	0.593
Avg	0.610	0.612	0.459	0.613	0.442	0.618	**0.633**	0.612

Table 4. Hamming Score

Datasets	BCC(I)	BCC(C)	BR	CC	CDN	LC	PS	RAkEL
orig	**0.904**	**0.904**	0.847	0.903	0.844	**0.904**	**0.904**	**0.904**
k3I	0.915	0.915	0.874	0.915	0.875	0.911	**0.922**	0.913
k3R	0.903	0.903	0.874	0.903	0.871	0.908	**0.910**	0.908
k3U	0.873	0.876	0.850	0.876	0.839	0.859	0.856	**0.876**
k5I	0.918	0.918	0.868	0.918	0.869	0.908	**0.922**	0.909
k5R	0.913	0.914	0.872	0.913	0.874	0.909	**0.922**	0.911
k5U	0.881	0.880	0.859	0.882	0.842	0.861	0.858	**0.883**
Avg	**0.901**	**0.901**	0.863	0.901	0.859	0.894	0.899	0.900

notice that multi-class methods have better performance, with chain classifiers showing very close results (independently from label ordering). The use of an ensemble (RAkEL) does not actually improve the basic PS version. As also outlined in Sect. 2.2, reported scores can be regarded as quite satisfactory results.

Similar considerations apply for the Exact Match score as well, where PS method is definitely the better (see Table 3). Since this metric is much more strict than Jaccard Index, the obtained results can be considered very satisfactory. Notice that augmented datasets produced with MLSmote(U) have a larger cardinality and density: this decreases the probability of getting and exact match as shown in the table.

The last bipartition-based metric we have considered is the Hamming Score and results are shown in Table 4. The obtained scores are in general very good, again with comparable performances of multi-class methods and classifier chains.

Finally, we computed the macro-averaged AUC as shown in Table 5. In this case, the results of all methods are comparable over all datasets; a slightly better performance can be noticed for basic BR method and for the ensemble algorithm CDN. This can be explained by the fact that in these approaches the contribution of labels more represented dominates on the aggregated ROC, disregarding the

Table 5. Area under ROC (macro-averaged)

Datasets	BCC(C)	BCC(I)	BR	CC	CDN	LC	PS	RAkEL
orig	0.504	0.504	0.543	0.503	**0.547**	0.501	0.500	0.501
k3I	0.535	0.537	0.574	0.533	**0.579**	0.563	0.560	0.550
k3R	0.621	0.618	0.727	0.622	**0.731**	0.673	0.639	0.666
k3U	0.763	0.765	**0.847**	0.768	0.836	0.746	0.724	0.778
k5I	0.496	0.496	0.452	0.496	0.459	0.490	**0.497**	0.491
k5R	0.529	0.531	0.544	0.532	**0.560**	0.553	0.551	0.550
k5U	0.785	0.784	**0.870**	0.787	0.846	0.760	0.737	0.797
Avg	0.605	0.605	**0.651**	0.606	**0.651**	0.612	0.601	0.619

contribution of some minority labels (that is usually better captured by multi-class methods).

In conclusion, the performances of MLC methods highlight the capability of a multi-label classifier to obtain interesting predictions concerning long-COVID syndrome on the collected data (baseline and hospitalization); such results can be improved with a suitable data augmentation, taking into careful consideration the main characteristics of the original data.

6   Conclusions

We have presented a study about the prediction of long-COVID sequelae through multi-label classification (MLC). We have initially considered data about more than 300 patients, considering their baseline situation, as well as their condition when hospitalized after contracting severe COVID-19 infection. The goal was to study the presence of specific long-COVID sequelae after a one year follow-up. Since the original set of patients under study was limited and could suffer of under-representativeness, we carefully investigated the possibility of augmenting the dataset, by considering situations where different levels in the number of complications could arise. MLSmote under six different policies of data augmentation has been considered, and a representative set of MLC approaches have been finally tested on all the available datasets.

Results have been evaluated in terms of Accuracy, Exact match, Hamming Score and macro-averaged AUC. They showed that MLC methods can actually be useful for the prediction of specific (label-based) long-COVID sequelae, under the different conditions represented by the different considered datasets. Multi-class MLC methods appear to be very promising, and binary approaches based on chains could be a valid alternative in order to take into account label correlation. Currently, we are integrating our approach with the TECNOMED-HUB databank. As future works, on the side of the long-COVID syndrome study, we aim at integrating additional clinical information such as the level of several cytokines, which are indicators of specific inflammatory processes supposed to be involved in the long-COVID syndrome. Moreover, on the side of the applicability of our approach to a general databank, we aim to test it with different diseases and to complement it with explanation techniques for MLC (see, e.g., [16,22]), to make our approach usable in practice by physicians.

Acknowledgments. M. Dossena and C. Irwin are supported by the National PhD program in Artificial Intelligence for Healthcare and Life Sciences (Campus Bio-medico University of Rome). We want to thank A. Chiocchetti and M. Bellan for having provided us with the long-COVID data and for several fruitful discussions about the case study. This work was funded by "Piano Riparti Piemonte", Azione n. 173 "INFRA-P. Realizzazione, rafforzamento e ampliamento infrastrutture di ricerca pubbliche—bando INFRA-P2-TECNOMED-HUB n.378-48".

References

1. TECNOMED-HUB webpage. https://www.tecnomedhub.it. Accessed 30 June 2023
2. Atkinson, A.: On the measurement of inequality. J. Econ. Theory **2**(3), 244–263 (1970)
3. Baarts, J., et al.: Multilabel classification of disease prediction in patients presenting with dyspnea. Eur. Respir. J. **58**(suppl 65) (2021)
4. Bellan, M., et al.: Long-term sequelae are highly prevalent one year after hospitalization for severe covid-19. Sci. Rep. **11**(1), 22666 (2021)
5. Bellan, M., Soddu, D., Balbo, P.E., Baricich, A., Zeppegno, P., et al.: Respiratory and psychophysical sequelae among patients with covid-19 four months after hospital discharge. JAMA Netw. **41**(1), e2036142 (2021)
6. Bogatinovski, J., Todorovski, L., Džeroski, S., Kocev, D.: Comprehensive comparative study of multi-label classification methods. Expert Syst. Appl. **203**, 117215 (2022)
7. Charte, F., Rivera, A., delJesus, M., Herrera, F.: MLSMOTE: approaching imbalanced multilabeled learning through synthetic instance generation. Knowl. Based Syst. **89**, 385–397 (2015)
8. Charte, F., Rivera, A., delJesus, M., Herrera, F.: Dealing with difficult minority labels in imbalanced mutilabel data sets. Neurocomputing **326–327**, 39–53 (2019)
9. Chawla, N.V., Bowyer, K.W., Hall, L.O., Kegelmeyer, W.P.: Smote: synthetic minority over-sampling technique. J. Artif. Intell. Res. **16**(1), 321–357 (2002)
10. Frank, E., Hall, M., Witten, I.: The WEKA workbench. In: Data Mining: Practical Machine Learning Tools and Techniques, 4th ed. (2016). (Online Appendix)
11. Gibaja, E., Ventura, S.: A tutorial on multilabel learning. ACM Comput. Surv. (CSUR) **47**(3), 1–38 (2015)
12. Guo, Y., Gu, S.: Multi-label classification using conditional dependency networks. In: Proceedings of the 22nd International Joint Conference on Artificial Intelligence (IJCAI 2011), pp. 1300–1305 (2011)
13. Huang, Y., et al.: A multi-label learning prediction model for heart failure in patients with atrial fibrillation based on expert knowledge of disease duration. Appl. Intell., 1–12 (2023)
14. Madjarov, G., Kocev, D., Gjorgjevikj, D., Džeroski, S.: An extensive experimental comparison of methods for multi-label learning. Pattern Recogn. **45**(9), 3084–3104 (2012)

15. Nalbandian, A., et al.: Post-acute covid-19 syndrome. Nat. Med. **27**(4), 601–615 (2021)
16. Panigutti, C., Guidotti, R., Monreale, A., Pedreschi, D.: Explaining multi-label black-box classifiers for health applications. In: Shaban-Nejad, A., Michalowski, M. (eds.) W3PHAI 2019. SCI, vol. 843, pp. 97–110. Springer, Cham (2020). https://doi.org/10.1007/978-3-030-24409-5_9
17. Rana, P., Sowmya, A., Meijering, E., Song, Y.: Imbalanced classification for protein subcellular localization with multilabel oversampling. Bioinformatics **39**(1), btac841 (2023)
18. Read, J., Pfahringer, B., Holmes, G., Frank, E.: Classifier chains for multi-label classification. Mach. Learn. **85**, 333–359 (2011)
19. Read, J., Pfahringer, B., Holmes, G.: Multi-label classification using ensembles of pruned sets. In: Proceedings of the 8th IEEE International Conference on Data Mining (ICDM 2008), pp. 995–1000 (2008)
20. Read, J., Reutemann, P., Pfahringer, B., Holmes, G.: MEKA: a multi-label/multi-target extension to Weka. J. Mach. Learn. Res. **17**(21), 1–5 (2016). http://meka.sourceforge.net/
21. Robert, C.P., Casella, G.: Monte Carlo Statistical Methods, 2nd edn. Springer, Cham (2004). https://doi.org/10.1007/978-1-4757-4145-2
22. Tabia, K.: Towards explainable multi-label classification. In: 2019 IEEE 31st International Conference on Tools with Artificial Intelligence (ICTAI), pp. 1088–1095 (2019). https://doi.org/10.1109/ICTAI.2019.00152
23. Tarekegn, A., Giacobini, M., Michalak, K.: A review of methods for imbalanced multi-label classification. Pattern Recogn. **118**, 107965 (2021)
24. Tsoumakas, G., Katakis, I., Vlahavas, I.: Random k-labelsets for multi-label classification. IEEE Trans. Knowl. Data Eng. **23**, 1079–1089 (2011)
25. Zaragoza, J., Sucar, L., Morales, E., Bielza, C., Larranaga, P.: Bayesian chain classifiers for multidimensional classification. In: Proceedings of the 22nd International Joint Conference on Artificial Intelligence (IJCAI 2011), pp. 2192–2197 (2011)
26. Zhou, L., Zheng, X., Yang, D., Wang, Y., Bai, X., Ye, X.: Application of multi-label classification models for the diagnosis of diabetic complications. BMC Med. Inform. Decis. Making **21**(1), 182 (2021)

PAUL-2: An Upgraded Transformer-Based Redesign of the Algorithmic Composer PAUL

Felix Schön[✉][iD] and Hans Tompits[iD]

Institute of Logic and Computation E192-03, Technische Universität Wien,
Favoritenstraße 9-11, 1040 Vienna, Austria
{schoen,tompits}@kr.tuwien.ac.at

Abstract. In this paper, we introduce PAUL-2, an algorithmic composer for two-track piano pieces of specifiable difficulty levels, as a ground-up redesign of its predecessor system PAUL. While PAUL was designed using a long short-term memory neural network, along with a sequence-to-sequence network, PAUL-2 is based on the state-of-the-art transformer architecture and makes use of relative attention. A shortcoming of PAUL was that it generated unsatisfying accompanying tracks and allowed for only few difficulty levels. PAUL-2 overcomes these limitations and theoretically supports an arbitrary number of difficulty classes due to the fact that it utilises an additional encoder for handling difficulty information. We also carried out a medium-scale survey which showed that the output of PAUL-2 was evaluated quite favourably by the participants.

Keywords: Algorithmic composition · Transformers · Music education

1 Introduction

Algorithmic composition (AC) refers to the process of composing music by means of formalisable methods. While this includes the creation of music by humans based on specific rules or algorithms, a method which exists already for centuries, modern AC techniques deal with the automated generation of music without direct human intervention. Many different approaches have been proposed in the literature to this end, like methods based on *Markov models* [3,8], *generative grammars* [10,15], *genetic algorithms* [3,5], *logic-based approaches* [20], *cellular automata* [19], *agent-based systems* [13,14], and *neural networks* [7,12,21]. Especially the latter approaches based on neural networks showed impressive results in recent years, like the Music Transformer [12], or OpenAI's MuseNet [21] and Jukebox [6], which are all based on the transformer architecture [26].

We would like to thank Wolfgang Schmidtmayr from the University of Music and Performing Arts Vienna and Geraldine Fitzpatrick from the Human-Computer Interaction Group at our university for their valuable input. We also would like to thank the anonymous reviewers for their helpful comments.

In this paper, we introduce the algorithmic composer PAUL-2 for two-track piano pieces, one track for representing the lead and the other for representing the accompaniment. The particular feature of PAUL-2 is that it allows to specify the *difficulty level* of the generated pieces, representing how challenging the pieces would be for a human pianist. This possibility of parameterising the output of PAUL-2 is essential for the designated usage of PAUL-2 as being part of an educational environment, teaching piano students how to *sight-read*.[1] Here, students would be provided with phrases generated by PAUL-2 that conform to their level of skill in order to challenge but not overwhelm them. Consecutive correctly played bars would result in them receiving harder prompts, while the opposite would reduce the difficulty of the provided music.

PAUL-2 itself is a complete redesign of the algorithmic composer PAUL [22, 24] which was designed for the same purpose as PAUL-2.[2] While PAUL is based on a *long short-term memory* (LSTM) network [11] to produce the lead track and a *sequence-to-sequence neural network* [25] for the realisation of the accompanying track, PAUL-2 makes use of an advanced transformer neural network architecture [26] and the enhancements introduced by Huang et al. [12] as part of the Music Transformer approach.

The redesign of PAUL was motivated by the fact that its output for the accompanying track was unsatisfactory and that it admits only three difficulty levels. PAUL-2 overcomes these limitations and produces output which is superior to that of PAUL and additionally supports a theoretically arbitrary number of difficulty levels. The latter property is achieved by using an encoder to inject information about the desired difficulty instead of training different versions of the network to produce pieces of a specific singular difficulty as done with PAUL. We furthermore introduce a *single-out mask* in order to efficiently attend over the desired difficulties, greatly reducing the computational complexity for this specific case.

Other works on algorithmic composition such as, e.g., Music Transformer [12] or MuseNet [21] are mostly concerned with creating either single-track music, or creating multiple tracks at the same time. Furthermore, their focus lies on generating pleasant sounding output alone. In contrast to these endeavours, with PAUL-2 we aim to create two separate tracks in sequential fashion that are not only musically interesting but inhibit good characteristics regarding being playable by a human. We also incorporate the aforementioned difficulty parameter, in order to make PAUL-2's output usable in an educational environment.

The paper is organised as follows: In the next section, we provide some background on music theory and the transformer architecture on which PAUL-2 is based upon. Then, in Sect. 3, we give the details of PAUL-2. Section 4 reports on the training of the networks as well as on an analysis and an evaluation of PAUL-2, and Sect. 5 concludes the paper.

---

[1] Sight-reading refers to the act of performing sheet music without having studied it beforehand.

[2] PAUL is named after the well-known Austrian pianist Paul Badura-Skoda (6th October 1927 - 25th September 2019).

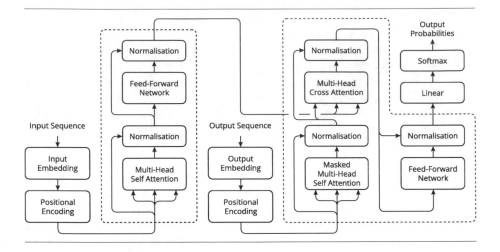

Fig. 1. A visual representation of the transformer architecture.

2   Background

Let us begin with some very basic terminology from music theory. For more information about this topic, we refer the reader to the well-known works of Benward [4], Aldwell [1], and Laitz [16].

In musical scores *notes* are used to denote pitch. The higher the note on the score, the higher the corresponding pitch will be. These notes have *values*, which tell the reader how long a note lasts. *Rests* are similar to notes in the sense that they have values, although they tell the player to pause for a specified amount of time. This, in combination with note values, allows for the construction of rhythm.

Relevant for our purposes is also the MIDI file format [18], which is an industry standard for connecting electronic music and audio devices. MIDI files contain a number of *note on* and *note off* messages, which represent, e.g., the pressing and releasing of a piano key. Furthermore, subsequent messages specify how many ticks (units of time) to wait between them.

Let us now turn to the *transformer architecture* which was introduced in 2017 by Vaswani et al. [26] and, in contrast to, e.g., LSTM-based networks [11], does not use any recurrent neural networks. Instead, a transformer relies on the use of the so-called *scaled dot-product attention mechanism* to model temporal dependencies within and in-between input sequences, as given by the function

$$sdpa(Q, K, V, M) := softmax\left(\frac{1}{\sqrt{dM}}QK^{T} + M\right)V,$$

where $Q, K, V \in \mathbb{R}^{sL \times dM}$ are matrices containing a set of *queries*, *keys*, and *values*, respectively, which are the result of linear transformations of the internal representation of the network, while $M \in \mathbb{R}^{sL \times sL}$ is a *mask* used to disregard the padding values. Here, sL and dM give the maximum sequence length and the size of the internal representation dimension, respectively. Moreover, K^{T} denotes the transpose of K and *softmax* is a function which produces a probability distribution matrix based on an input matrix $X \in \mathbb{R}^{m \times n}$ as follows: for $X = (x_{ij})$ and $softmax(X) = (y_{ij})$,

$$y_{ij} = \frac{e^{x_{ij}}}{\sum_{k=1}^{j} e^{x_{ik}}}, \quad \text{for } 1 \le i \le m, 1 \le j \le n.$$

This attention mechanism determines the importance and influence of all messages of the input sequence for the next prediction. *Self-attention* describes the practice of applying attention over a network's own previous outputs and allows the transformer to consider past predictions for future decisions. This approach facilitates the parallelisation of the training process, considerably reducing the time needed to train a network.

The transformer is based on the *encoder-decoder paradigm* [25], where an *encoder* generates a fixed-size representation from an input sequence, e.g., a musical lead sequence, and this representation is then fed to a *decoder*, which from it extrapolates information and produces an output sequence, e.g., an accompanying bass sequence.

Figure 1 shows a visual representation of the transformer architecture. Note that the dashed sections mark an encoder layer (or, respectively, a decoder layer) that can be stacked multiple times. Furthermore, *layer normalisation* [2] is applied after both attention and feed-forward layers, forming a so-called *residual block*. For more information on the transformer architecture, we refer to the work of Vaswani et al. [26].

3   The PAUL-2 System

As mentioned earlier, PAUL-2 is a transformer-based [26] algorithmic composer. It is capable of sequence-to-sequence translations where the sequences consist of either musical information or musical meta-information in the form of difficulty values.

3.1   Overview

PAUL-2 consists of two distinct models. Both of these models have different internal architectures and support a different set of hyperparameters. As well, they both need to be trained separately and have a different set of weights. The models of PAUL-2 are the following:

(i) P2L, a sequence-to-sequence transformer for composing polyphonic *lead tracks*, based on an input difficulty sequence, and

(ii) P2A, a multi-sequence-to-sequence transformer for composing polyphonic *accompanying tracks*, based on an input lead track and a difficulty sequence.

With the preceding system PAUL [24], six different models needed to be trained, since each model only supported a single difficulty level for a total of three distinct difficulty levels. This induced a large overhead and lowered the potential of the models, since only sequences that contained subsequent bars of the same assessed difficulty could be used to train the networks. With PAUL-2, however, we drop these constraints altogether, supporting a theoretically arbitrary amount of difficulty classes, settling on ten in practice. We argue that ten classes serve as a good starting point as this amount provides an adequate balance between being too finely and too coarsely grained.

For P2L, we use the encoder solely to encode the desired difficulty values of the output lead track, from which we then construct the generated sequence. For P2A, we were inspired by the enhancements introduced by Libovický, Helcl, and Marecek [17] to modify the transformer architecture to be able to generate accompanying sequences from both an input sequence consisting of difficulty values and an input sequence consisting of musical information representing the lead track. We also utilise the enhancements made by Huang et al. [12], who introduced the performant relative self-attention mechanism. Using this enhanced attention, the decoder of the transformer is able to better attend to its own input, i.e., the sequence generated so far. As a result, the structures of the sequences generated by the model contain better long-term dependencies. The source code of our project can be found at its git repository located at

https://github.com/FelixSchoen/PAUL-2.

3.2 Architecture

We now cover the structure of P2L and P2A. In order to produce musical pieces of varying difficulty levels, we use one encoder to encode a sequence of ten different difficulty values. Rather than encoding a single integer value, we opted to encode a sequence $difs_i := (dif_{i,1}, \ldots, dif_{i,\mathsf{sL}})$ having the same length as the desired output, consisting of exactly one difficulty value for each (potential) message (representing, e.g., the pressing or releasing of a key) of the output sequence, where $difs_i$ defines the difficulties of the ith musical sequence in a batch and $dif_{i,j}$ refers to the (integer) difficulty value of the jth message in this sequence. We conjectured that, this way, the network will be better able to learn to accurately generate pieces of the desired difficulty. We note that this approach would in theory allow for us to use any number of difficulty classes and to set difficulty values per message, although we did not make use of this in practice but rather only allowed for one difficulty class per bar.

We can use *masks* for the attention mechanism in order to prevent the model to attend to values it is not supposed to. In order to ensure that each message is only able to attend to its designated difficulty value, we introduce a *single-out mask* $M^{so} = (m^{so}_{ij})$ as follows:

$$m^{so}_{ij} := \begin{cases} 0 & \text{if } i = j, \\ 1 & \text{otherwise,} \end{cases}$$

for $1 \leq i, j \leq \mathsf{sL}$. Here, each element is only able to attend to the element sharing its index of the sequence to attend to.

In order to apply the mask to the product QK^{T}, it has to be scaled as follows:

$$scaleMask(\omega, M) := \omega M,$$

where $\omega = -10^9$ is used in order to approximate negative infinity. This way we can ensure that the subsequent application of the *softmax* function sets all those entries of QK^{T} to (a value close to) zero providing $m_{ij} = 1$, for $M = (m_{ij})$. More specifically, for

$$softmax\left(\frac{1}{\sqrt{\mathsf{dM}}}(QK^{\mathrm{T}} + scaleMask(\omega, M))\right) = (y_{ij}),$$

if $m_{ij} = 1$, then

$$\lim_{\omega \to -\infty} y_{ij} = 0.$$

Note that, as an immediate consequence of the previous equation, we get

$$\lim_{\omega \to -\infty} softmax\left(\frac{1}{\sqrt{\mathsf{dM}}}QK^{\mathrm{T}} + scaleMask(\omega, M^{so})\right) = I,$$

where $I \in \{0,1\}^{\mathsf{sL} \times \mathsf{sL}}$ is the identity matrix (recall that $V \in \mathbb{R}^{\mathsf{sL} \times \mathsf{dV}}$). Thus,

$$\lim_{\omega \to -\infty} softmax\left(\frac{1}{\sqrt{\mathsf{dM}}}QK^{\mathrm{T}} + scaleMask(\omega, M^{so})\right)V = V.$$

As a consequence, we obtain an improved formulation of the scaled dot-product attention when using a single-out mask together with a padding mask $M^p \in \{0,1\}^{\mathsf{sL} \times \mathsf{sL}}$, given by $sdpaSingleOut(V, M^p) = (v'_{ij})$, where

$$v'_{ij} = \begin{cases} v_{ij} & \text{if } m^p_{ij} = 0, \\ 0 & \text{otherwise}, \end{cases}$$

with $V = (v_{ij})$ and $M^p = (m^p_{ij})$. This reduces the time complexity of the operation to $\mathcal{O}(\mathsf{sL} \cdot \mathsf{dM})$, with no need for expensive matrix multiplications.

Figure 2 shows the simplified architecture of the lead and accompanying network. For the lead network, shown in Fig. 2a, we adapted an architecture similar to the standard transformer, utilising sinusoidal encodings, multi-head attention [26], and layer normalisation [2]. We use an encoder to encode the difficulties from which we create an output sequence using the decoder. The main differences include our usage of the relative attention mechanism [12] for the decoder's self-attention and the fact that we apply the single-out mask instead of a normal padding mask (which ignores padding-only messages) used in the original paper [26] for both the encoder's self-attention and the cross-attention of the decoder over the encoder's output values.

Figure 2b shows the simplified architecture of the accompanying network. We modified the standard transformer architecture to utilise a total of two encoders,

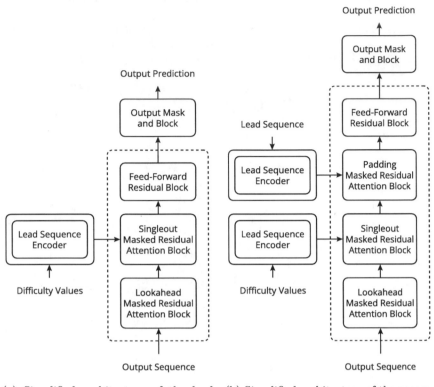

(a) Simplified architecture of the lead network comprising a difficulty encoder and an output sequence decoder.

(b) Simplified architecture of the accompanying network comprising a difficulty encoder, a lead sequence encoder, and an output sequence decoder.

Fig. 2. Architectures of P2L and P2A.

one encoding the desired difficulty of the piece while the other encodes the lead sequence to create an accompaniment for it.

For the self-attention of the lead sequence encoder, we use a padding mask as attending over future positions is valid here even during the generation stage. For the self-attention of the difficulty encoder, we apply the same single-out mask as we did with P2L. In order to incorporate the output of both encoders, we opted for a serial connection of two subsequent attention blocks in the decoder. Libovický, Helcl, and Marecek [17] state that the serial approach outperformed other architectures for multi-source machine translation tasks.

We initially apply single-out masked attention over the output of the difficulty encoder after which we apply regular padding masked attention over the output of the lead sequence. We experimented with the order of the cross-attention blocks and found that this configuration produced the best results. Finally, we apply an output mask to the output probabilities.

As part of the development of PAUL-2, we furthermore introduced S-Coda, a Python music preprocessing library. With S-Coda, we are able to create a list of musically valid next messages for an existing musical sequence, which we can utilise to create an output mask to restrict the next predicted output messages, which we use for both P2L and P2A. This ensures that all further predictions made by the network are based on a valid musical sequence. More information about both S-Coda and PAUL-2 can also be found in the first author's thesis [23]. Furthermore, S-Coda is publicly available at

www.github.com/FelixSchoen/S-Coda/.

As stated previously, the intended usage of PAUL-2 is to be used in a tutoring system, teaching piano students how to sight-read. Here, a balance between the current sight-reading skill of a student and the difficulty of the pieces has to be found and adjusted over the course of the learning process, which is where we imagine PAUL-2 to come in. In such a system, the students could use MIDI keyboards to perform the musical prompts, allowing for the system to judge their performances and based on these metrics adjust the difficulty of the pieces.

4   Training, Analysis, and Evaluation

We now discuss some details about the input data for the training of the underlying neural networks of PAUL-2. Afterwards, we briefly analyse the achieved results of PAUL-2, and lastly we report on a user study for assessing the musical quality of the generated music files of PAUL-2.

4.1   Retrieval and Processing of the Dataset

In order to train neural networks, large amounts of input data are necessary. Both the quality and quantity of the data are of great importance, as the network can only learn to make correct predictions if the data itself is valid and there is enough material to train on.

We used a combination of the *piano-midi.de* and *ADL Piano MIDI* [9] dataset, as they both contain the necessary sequenced MIDI files. Such files are created manually in a step-by-step process, inserting notes by hand. With this technique one can add information about, e.g., which tracks the inserted notes belong to, which is generally not possible when recording a MIDI performance. It is essential for the training of PAUL-2 that the MIDI files separate the sequences into the lead and the accompanying track. Since we want to be able to generate an accompanying track for a given input lead track, we need to provide the network with training data consisting of two separate tracks as well. In a preprocessing procedure, we sorted out any file that did not conform to our needs, e.g., having too few tracks or a too large number of empty bars.

This left us with a total of 2,147 MIDI files, almost a seventeen-fold increase over the dataset used for PAUL.

In order to be able to produce music of varying difficulty levels, the pieces of the dataset needed to be assigned such values beforehand. Using S-Coda, we were able to assign difficulty values to musical bars of the dataset based on seven different metrics. We settled on using ten difficulty levels as we believe that this serves as a good middle ground between being too finely- and too coarsely-grained. A fewer amount of levels could result in jumps between them being too substantial to be used in an educational environment, while using a too large amount could result in the network not being shown enough training data for each level.

The metrics we used to assess difficulties are the following: (i) the amount of concurrent notes and the amount of overall notes in a bar, (ii) the distances between notes, (iii) the key signature of a bar, (iv) the amount of note classes, (v) the note values of all the notes in the bar, (vi) the rhythm, and (vii) potential note patterns.

These metrics were designed based on multiple factors, such as correspondence with an expert on music theory, personal investigation and experience, and intuition. We note that although we are confident that the difficulty assessment reflects the difficulty of a piece rather accurately as shown with PAUL [24], at the moment it still serves as a proof of concept only. Our main goal was to show that our model is capable of producing pieces that conform to a specific difficulty assessment, not to make this assessment as accurate as possible.

4.2   Analysis of Results

For the training process, we utilised a set of two NVIDIA RTX 3090 GPUs, allowing us to greatly increase the capacity of the model compared to PAUL. As for the choice of hyperparameters, we settled on using 6 layers, 4 attention heads, a dropout rate of 0.2, 512 neurons per layer for the feed-forward networks, and a dimensionality of 256 and 512 for P2A and P2L, respectively. We used a combination of grid search and Bayesian optimisation to arrive at this combination of parameters. We note that due to the additional encoder used for P2A, we had to reduce the dimensionality due to hardware limitations.

We are able to report that the output of PAUL-2 is vastly superior to that of PAUL, both in terms of temporal structure and melodic quality. In contrast to PAUL which sometimes creates pieces with ten or more concurrent notes, PAUL-2 is able to compose humanly playable accompaniments. For the training of PAUL, only sequences of bars of the same assessed difficulty level could be used. This approach would not be feasible with PAUL-2 as the pieces are assigned one of ten different difficulty classes. This diversification would result in almost no sequences of consecutive bars containing more than a single bar, since the number of training samples per difficulty class would linearly decrease with the amount of classes.

Figure 3a shows a confusion matrix of the specified difficulty versus the generated difficulty of bars generated using the lead network. For each difficulty

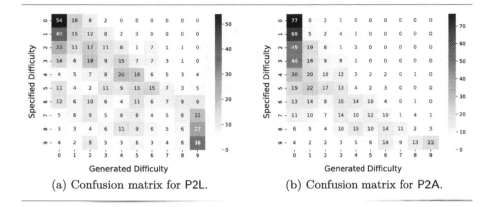

(a) Confusion matrix for P2L.   (b) Confusion matrix for P2A.

Fig. 3. Confusion matrices of specified difficulties versus generated difficulties of bars generated by P2L and P2A.

class, 80 bars were generated. For the easier difficulty classes, the network seems to perform quite well. Here, a correlation between specified and generated class is clearly visible. When it comes to the more difficult classes, the network tends to either produce bars of the most difficult class or bars that are substantially easier than specified.

Figure 3b shows the confusion matrix for the accompanying network, where we created pieces based on a lead sample from the test set. Interesting to note is the fact that the network tends to produce bars that are easier than specified, which could be attributed to the fact that accompanying sequences for piano music are often less difficult in general. Other than that, a clear correlation between specified and generated difficulty is visible again. Arguably, for the accompanying network, the difficulties are somewhat less scattered than for its lead counterpart.

Overall, the results shown by the confusion matrices are very promising. We note that the metrics used to assess the difficulty of the input pieces are very abstract and at the moment serve as a proof of concept only. Nonetheless, the networks are able to rather accurately produce pieces exhibiting the desired characteristics.

Figure 4 shows example outputs generated by PAUL-2 in score representation. We decided on providing samples of three different difficulty classes in order to highlight some of the differences induced by the difficulty specification. The output of PAUL-2 consists of valid musical pieces that can potentially be used in a tutoring environment. The sequences are characterised by their rhythmic validity.

Although a clear rhythmic dependence between lead and accompanying track is observable, sometimes the output of PAUL-2 lacks melodic consistency between the tracks. The system tends to create pieces that can sound unpleasant to the listener's ear due to dissonances between the notes of the two tracks. We note

(a) Score representation of output of difficulty 2.

(b) Score representation of output of difficulty 5.

(c) Score representation of output of difficulty 8.

Fig. 4. Three output samples of different difficulties generated by PAUL-2.

that the individual output of both tracks sound musically valid to our ears and we believe that the quality could be further improved with access to a larger dataset.

4.3   User Study

We conducted a medium-scale study with 60 participants in order to assess the musical quality of the output of PAUL-2. Participants were presented with 18 pairs of short musical phrases and asked to decide on a sample-by-sample basis whether they believed them to be genuine or computer-generated. Each of the questions consists of one sample generated by either P2L or P2A and one sample from the test dataset. At the end of the study, we asked participants to self-assess their level of musical proficiency, to rate how confident they were in their assessments, and to rate the quality of the samples they believed to be computer-generated.

Table 1 shows the main results of the study. With an overall score of 26% of the computer-generated samples having been selected as genuine ones, PAUL-2 does not yet pass our "Turing test", as ideally we would see values closer to 50%.

Table 1. Results of the study per self-reported musical proficiency. Values rounded to two decimal places. Standard deviation given in parenthesis.

Subset	Selected Generated	Quality Mean (σ)	Confidence Mean (σ)	Number Samples
Overall Results	26%	3.20 (1.05)	2.52 (1.07)	60
Proficiency 1	22%	3.44 (1.01)	2.56 (1.01)	9
Proficiency 2	29%	3.10 (1.10)	2.30 (1.06)	10
Proficiency 3	32%	3.57 (0.93)	2.43 (0.98)	21
Proficiency 4	23%	2.75 (1.13)	2.56 (1.15)	16
Proficiency 5	19%	2.75 (0.96)	3.25 (1.50)	4

The results obtained by the study still indicate that the quality of the output of PAUL-2 is quite good, which is especially impressive considering the drastically smaller datasets PAUL-2 was trained on compared to state-of-the-art approaches like MuseNet or Jukebox.

We asked the participants to rate the quality of the samples they believed to be computer-generated. With an average of 3.20, we argue that the musical quality of PAUL-2 shows good promise. We note that participants were never told which samples were genuine, which in turn means that it is likely that for this question participants will have only considered the worse of the two samples, independently of whether that sample was the computer-generated one or not, resulting in a downwards skew of the quality scores.

Participants were asked to report their confidence regarding their evaluations on a scale of one to five. We note that for proficiency levels one through four, these scores are quite low. This score is higher for level five although here the standard deviation is quite large. This leads to believe that even though the participants performed quite well regarding the separation of computer-generated and genuine samples, it could be the case that this was based on subconscious feelings alone rather than logical reasoning.

We would have assumed that the difficulty of the samples would also play a role in the percentage of the correctly classified ones. Contrary to our expectations, however, there seems to be only a small difference in the amount of wrongly categorised samples between the groups of different difficulties.

5   Conclusion

In this paper, we introduced PAUL-2, a transformer-based [26] algorithmic composer of two-track piano pieces capable of generating piano pieces that conform to a *difficulty specification* consisting of ten difficulty levels. In future work, we plan to compare different methods of representing musical sequences and to improve upon the relative attention mechanism. Furthermore, we want to implement an educational system utilising PAUL-2 which provides piano students with sight-reading prompts conforming to their skill.

References

1. Aldwell, E., Schachter, C., Cadwallader, A.: Harmony & Voice Leading, 5th edn. Cengage, Boston (2019)
2. Ba, L.J., Kiros, J.R., Hinton, G.E.: Layer normalization. arXiv:1607.06450 (2016)
3. Bell, C.: Algorithmic music composition using dynamic Markov chains and genetic algorithms. J. Comput. Sci. Coll. **27**(2), 99–107 (2011)
4. Benward, B., Saker, M.: Music in Theory and Practice: Volume 1, 8th edn. McGraw-Hill, New York (2009)
5. Biles, J.A.: Autonomous GenJam: eliminating the fitness bottleneck by eliminating fitness. In: Proceedings of the 3rd Annual Conference on Genetic and Evolutionary Computation (GECCO 2001) (2001)
6. Dhariwal, P., Jun, H., Payne, C., Kim, J.W., Radford, A., Sutskever, I.: Jukebox: a generative model for music. arXiv:2005.00341 (2020)
7. Eck, D., Schmidhuber, J.: Finding temporal structure in music: blues improvisation with LSTM recurrent networks. In: Proceedings of the 12th IEEE Workshop on Neural Networks for Signal Processing (NNSP 2002), pp. 747–756. IEEE (2002)
8. Eigenfeldt, A., Pasquier, P.: Realtime generation of harmonic progressions using constrained Markov selection. In: Proceedings of the 1st International Conference on Computational Creativity (ICCC 2010), pp. 16–25. Computationalcreativity.net (2010)
9. Ferreira, L.N., Lelis, L.H.S., Whitehead, J.: Computer-generated music for tabletop role-playing games. In: Proceedings of the 16th AAAI Conference on Artificial Intelligence and Interactive Digital Entertainment (AIIDE 2020), pp. 59–65. AAAI Press (2020)
10. Hamanaka, M., Hirata, K., Tojo, S.: FATTA: full automatic time-span tree analyzer. In: Proceedings of the 33rd International Computer Music Conference (ICMC 2007). Michigan Publishing (2007)
11. Hochreiter, S., Schmidhuber, J.: Long short-term memory. Neural Comput. **9**(8), 1735–1780 (1997)
12. Huang, C.A., et al.: Music transformer: generating music with long-term structure. In: Proceedings of the 7th International Conference on Learning Representations (ICLR 2019). OpenReview.net (2019)
13. Kirke, A., Miranda, E.R.: Emergent construction of melodic pitch and hierarchy through agents communicating emotion without melodic intelligence. In: Proceedings of the 37th International Computer Music Conference (ICMC 2011). Michigan Publishing (2011)
14. Kirke, A., Miranda, E.R.: A multi-agent emotional society whose melodies represent its emergent social hierarchy and are generated by agent communications. J. Artif. Soc. Soc. Simul. **18**(2), 16 (2015)
15. Kitani, K.M., Koike, H.: ImprovGenerator: online grammatical induction for on-the-fly improvisation accompaniment. In: Proceedings of the 10th International Conference on New Interfaces for Musical Expression (NIME 2010), pp. 469–472. Nime.org (2010)
16. Laitz, S.G.: The Complete Musician: An Integrated Approach To Tonal Theory, Analysis, and Listening, 3rd edn. Oxford University Press, Oxford (2012)
17. Libovický, J., Helcl, J., Marecek, D.: Input combination strategies for multi-source transformer decoder. In: Proceedings of the 3rd Conference on Machine Translation (WMT 2018), pp. 253–260. Association for Computational Linguistics (2018)

18. MIDI Manufacturers Association: The Complete MIDI 1.0 Detailed Specification (1996). https://midi.org/
19. Miranda, E.R.: Cellular automata music: from sound synthesis to musical forms. In: Miranda, E.R., Biles, J.A. (eds.) Evolutionary Computer Music, pp. 170–193. Springer, London (2007). https://doi.org/10.1007/978-1-84628-600-1_8
20. Opolka, S., Obermeier, P., Schaub, T.: Automatic genre-dependent composition using answer set programming. In: Proceedings of the 21st International Symposium on Electronic Art (ISEA 2015), pp. 627–632. ISEA International, Brighton (2015)
21. Payne, C.: MuseNet (2019). https://openai.com/research/musenet. Accessed 20 June 2023
22. Schön, F.: PAUL: an algorithmic composer of two-track piano pieces using recurrent neural networks. Bachelor's thesis, Technische Universität Wien, Institute of Logic and Computation, E192-03 (2020)
23. Schön, F.: PAUL-2: a transformer-based algorithmic composer of two-track piano pieces. Diploma thesis, Technische Universität Wien, Institute of Logic and Computation, E192-03 (2023)
24. Schön, F., Tompits, H.: PAUL: an algorithmic composer for classical piano music supporting multiple complexity levels. In: Marreiros, G., Martins, B., Paiva, A., Ribeiro, B., Sardinha, A. (eds.) EPIA 2022. LNCS, vol. 13566, pp. 415–426. Springer, Cham (2022). https://doi.org/10.1007/978-3-031-16474-3_34
25. Sutskever, I., Vinyals, O., Le, Q.V.: Sequence to sequence learning with neural networks. In: Proceedings of the 27th Annual Conference on Neural Information Processing Systems (NIPS 2014), pp. 3104–3112 (2014)
26. Vaswani, A., et al.: Attention is all you need. In: Proceedings of the 30th Annual Conference on Neural Information Processing Systems (NIPS 2017), pp. 5998–6008 (2017)

Robotics and Perception

Understanding the Effect of Deep Ensembles in LiDAR-Based Place Recognition

Matteo Vaghi[1(✉)], Fabio D'Elia[1], Augusto Luis Ballardini[2], and Domenico Giorgio Sorrenti[1]

[1] Universitá degli Studi di Milano - Bicocca, Milan, Italy
m.vaghi9@campus.unimib.it
[2] Universidad de Alcalá, Alcalá de Henares, Spain

Abstract. Place recognition, the task of recognizing a previously visited location, has a decisive role in the autonomous driving field since it enables rough global localization in GNSS-denied environments. In the last few years, LiDAR-based place recognition and deep learning approaches achieved outstanding results also within challenging scenarios. However, the use of DNN-based methods is still limited due to the safety-critical nature of the task and the difficulty in detecting potential model failures. Determining the uncertainty of DNN-based outputs is a useful technique to discover unreliable predictions. Among the existing approaches, Deep Ensemble represents a popular sampling method to estimate epistemic uncertainty by exploiting multiple models. However, an in-depth investigation of its application for LiDAR-based place recognition is missing and only one approach has been recently proposed [22]. Our ultimate goal is to gain a deeper understanding of the strengths and weaknesses of Deep Ensemble methods. To achieve this, we propose a Deep Ensemble strategy that uses a knowledge-distillation approach and we compare it to [22] by evaluating its recall and failure detection capabilities.

1 Introduction

Accurate localization is essential for the safe and efficient navigation of self driving cars. Among the many available techniques to perform localization, the recognition of previously visited locations offers a powerful alternative to standard Global Navigation Satellite System (GNSS) methods. This technique, known as place recognition, allows the car to achieve a global estimate based on previously mapped areas, retrieving the most likely location that matches its sensor readings. This can be particularly useful in environments where other localization methods, such as GNSS, may be unavailable or unreliable. In recent years, several Deep Neural Network (DNN) based approaches [2,9,16,25] have demonstrated outstanding performance in the retrieval task, making them valuable tools also for Simultaneouos Localization And Mapping (SLAM) systems [6]. Incorporating

R. Basili et al. (Eds.): AIxIA 2023, LNAI 14318, pp. 295–309, 2023.
https://doi.org/10.1007/978-3-031-47546-7_20

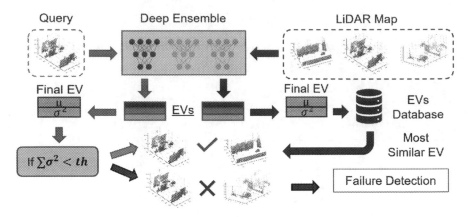

Fig. 1. In this work, we propose an ensemble-based method to address the LiDAR-based place recognition task. We train different models with a teacher-student training approach to produce similar feature spaces and to enable uncertainty estimation, that can be used to detect localization failures. Finally, we compare our approach with other ensemble-based strategies by exploring the advantages and flaws of each methods.

these approaches into production autonomous driving systems presents several challenges. One major issue is that neural networks provide estimates without any associated information about their reliability. Using this data without considering their potential uncertainty can lead to treacherous situations and have serious consequences when making decisions during navigation, endangering the safety of both passengers and other road users. Therefore, the ability to accurately estimate the uncertainty associated with the output of DNN models is of paramount importance for mitigating the risks inherent in the deployment of these technologies. This will allows us to make more informed decisions during navigation, reducing potential hazards. From a technical perspective, uncertainty refers to situations where information is incomplete or unavailable, often arising due to the inherent complexity of an environment or the limitations of a model in accurately representing a specific aspect of reality. As a result, uncertainty can be divided into the following two categories: aleatoric and epistemic. Aleatoric uncertainty arises from the inherent variability and randomness of data and is irreducible, representing the intrinsic property of observing the real world. On the other hand, epistemic uncertainty arises from the limitations of the procedure used for training neural networks, where a limited amount of data leads to incomplete knowledge of the world. This type of uncertainty can be reduced by incorporating more data during the training stage of a DNN model. In the specific context of place recognition, there have been relatively few approaches to estimate uncertainty, with the majority of these approaches focusing primarily on aleatoric uncertainty.

In this study, we introduce and assess a novel approach for accurately estimating uncertainty during the retrieval process. Our strategy incorporates multiple models that share a common feature space, as well as a threshold-based technique for eliminating unreliable observations. Figure 1 provides a visual representation of our place recognition pipeline. The first step involves multiple models generating distinct feature-based representations of input point clouds, from which we derive feature-wise uncertainty. Next, our method only performs localization if the total uncertainty falls below a specific threshold.

2   Related Work

2.1   LiDAR-Based Place Recognition

In the last decade, many deep learning-based approaches emerged to deal with the place recognition problem by exploiting observations gathered from different sensors. In the literature, we can identify techniques that use only image data [2], 3D data such as LIDAR [25], and multi-modal based methods [5].

Deep learning-based LiDAR place recognition demonstrated superior performance than other modalities by showing robustness across challenging scenarios [16,17,25,27]. Due to such promising results, we decided to focus on this category. One of the groundbreaking works in this field is PointNetVLAD [2], a DNN that combines PointNet [24] for extracting features and VLAD [11] for computing the final descriptor from a point cloud. More recently, Komorowski *et al.* [16] proposed MinkLoc3D, a DNN that exploits sparse convolutions to extract discriminative descriptors.

In this work, we decided to focus on those two methods with the idea of understanding the effect of ensembles on two different architectures which extract global features with different techniques.

2.2   Uncertainty Estimation Methods for DNNs

Nowadays, uncertainty estimation in neural network approaches represents a particularly discussed topic. One of the first attempts at modeling uncertainty is through Bayesian Neural Networks (BNNs) [8,23], where a prior is associated with each model's weight. However, their application is limited to light-weighted architectures due to the intractability of the posterior distribution.

To overcome the previous issue, Kingma et al. [14] and Lakshminarayanan et al. [19] proposed two sample-based strategies for estimating epistemic uncertainty: the former exploits dropout sampling, the latter uses a set of predictions provided by an ensemble. More recently, Amini et al. [1] proposed an approach for a direct estimation of uncertainty in DNN models named Deep Evidential Regression (DER). In particular, this approach can estimate both aleatoric and epistemic uncertainty with a single step.

2.3   Uncertainty Estimation in Place Recognition

In recent years, localization approaches that deal with the uncertainty estimation problem emerged [7,12,26] and more recently also in the place recognition field. For instance, Cai et al. [4] proposed STUN: a DNN-based approach that

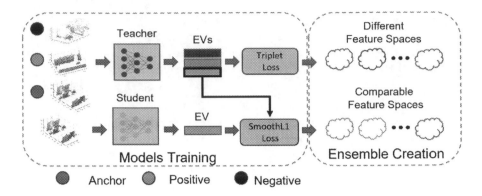

Fig. 2. Pipeline followed by our method to create ensemble members. Firstly, we train a teacher DNN with a standard metric learning approach (top-left), then we train a student model to imitate the teacher feature space (bottom-left). By doing that, we are able to train different ensemble members to which correspond similar feature spaces (bottom-right). As we will show later, when training different models with a standard triplet loss, we obtain unique feature spaces (top-right) where a direct aggregation of results leads to undesired effects.

exploits a knowledge-distillation technique for estimating aleatoric uncertainty in a visual place recognition task. Another notable work is proposed by Latoje et al. [18] by integrating an aleatoric uncertainty-aware visual place recognition model within a SLAM system. Please note, the previous approaches estimate aleatoric uncertainty, while we aim to model the epistemic component.

Regarding Light Detection And Ranging (LiDAR) based place recognition, Mason et al. [22] recently proposed an ensemble-based strategy for estimating epistemic uncertainty. In particular, they train multiple DNNs with different parameters initialization to extract discriminative point-cloud global descriptors. Then, they represent a navigation map as a set of n database copies, where n corresponds to the number of models used. For each model, they compute the similarity score between an input query and the corresponding database entries. Considering all models, the final match is the location with the highest average similarity score over the different copies.

To the best of our knowledge, only their work exploits an ensemble-based method for place recognition. However, such an approach presents some flaws that we aim to overcome. For instance, such a method requires different database replicas, and epistemic uncertainty corresponds to similarity variance rather than features variance, making more arduous to obtain a model introspection in presence of challenging inputs. As we will describe later, our method exploits a knowledge-distillation learning technique to allow us a direct comparison between feature spaces created by each model.

3   Method

3.1   Ensemble-Based LiDAR Place Recognition

In the context of place recognition, we achieve the main goal by generating a compact and discriminative representation of an input observation, such as an image or point cloud. This representation, commonly referred to as Embedding Vector (EV), is then used to find previously visited locations that have been encoded using the same strategy. From a technical perspective, an EV is a vector of m real numbers denoted as $v = (f_1, ..., f_m)$ designed to represent an input observation in such a way that observations belonging to the same location are positioned in close proximity within the feature space, while observations from different locations are more distant to each other. By generating accurate and robust EVs, it is possible to effectively match and retrieve previously visited locations, thereby facilitating effective navigation and localization. DNN models designed for place recognition are typically trained with a metric learning approach. This involves the use of a loss function that aims to create a discriminative feature space by comparing positive and negative pairs of samples. Positive examples consist of observations corresponding to the same place, while negative ones consist of samples belonging to different locations. In an ensemble-based approach, multiple networks are trained independently, and the output of the system is generated by aggregating the predictions of these individual networks. This allows for the computation of metrics such as mean and variance, which can be used to represent previously visited locations together with the associated epistemic uncertainty. For example, given a set of EVs $V = \{v_1, ..., v_n\}$, the output of an ensemble could be the mean and variance of each feature:

$$\mathbb{E}\left[\mu_v\right] = \frac{1}{n} \cdot \sum_{i=1}^{n} v_i, \quad Var[\mu_v] = \frac{1}{n} \cdot \sum_{i=1}^{n} (v_i - \mathbb{E}\left[\mu_v\right])^2 \qquad (1)$$

where i corresponds to the i-th member of the ensemble. While the application of an ensemble-based approach may appear straightforward in theory, it is important to note that the process of averaging features can sometimes lead to undesired results in practice. This is because a direct comparison of the vectors within the set V may not always be meaningful, and can result in inaccurate or unreliable estimates. One potential issue arises from the randomization processes that occur during a standard training procedure. Since metric learning is generally an unsupervised process, it is difficult to ensure that each member of the ensemble produces the same feature space and, although a ground-truth is used to build positive and negative sample pairs, it is not possible to explicitly control how each model learns the final feature space. As a result, even if two independent models are able to extract effective EVs from the same input observation, the actual values of the vectors may differ.

To address the issue of variability in the feature spaces generated by different members of an ensemble, we propose the use of a popular method known as knowledge distillation. This approach allows us to create an ensemble in which each member is capable of representing similar feature spaces. This is achieved through a two-step process. First, a DNN model, referred to as the *teacher*, is trained using the triplet loss function in Eq. (2) to produce a target feature space. In the equation, v is a generic EV, a, p, n refer to *anchor*, *positive* and *negative* samples respectively, d is a distance metric and m represents a margin:

$$\mathcal{L}^{triplet} = \sum_{i=1}^{n} [d(v_p, v_a) - d(v_n, v_a) + m]_+ \tag{2}$$

The target feature space serves as a reference for the other members of the ensemble, known as the *student*. Put differently, we train additional models with the goal of imitating the EVs generated by the teacher. To achieve this, we use the *teacher* network to produce ground-truth EVs of the training set. These ground-truth EVs are then used to train the different student models that will become part of the ensemble. By using the teacher-student approach, we employ the loss function in Eq. (3) to train each member of the ensemble.

$$\mathcal{L}^{ts} = d(f(p_i), g(p_i)) \tag{3}$$

This loss function is designed to optimize the performance of the ensemble members and ensure that they are able to accurately imitate the EVs generated by the teacher model. In the equation, f and g are the teacher and student model respectively, d is a distance measure computed over the output EVs, *e.g.*, smoothL1 in our case, and p_i is an input point cloud. Please note, only the student model $g(\cdot)$ is trained in this case, while the $f(\cdot)$ weights do not change. In Fig. 2, we show the difference between creating an ensemble where members are trained with a triplet loss and a knowledge-distillation approach.

3.2 Exploiting Ensemble Predictions

Once our ensemble is trained, we are able to extract features mean and variance from a generic set of predictions V by using Eq. (1). As desired from an ensemble-based approach, we expect to obtain an increment of the overall performance, that in the case of a retrieval system should result in a better recall. To match an input query with a map location, we simply compute the similarity between query and database EVs and choose the match with the highest similarity score:

$$s(EV_q, EV_{db}) = \frac{EV_q \cdot EV_{db}}{||EV_q|| \, ||EV_{db}||} \tag{4}$$

Moreover, we can take advantage of ensemble uncertainty to detect possible failures and decide to not exploit a particular prediction for localization. More practically, given the ensemble $EV = (v_\mu, v_{\sigma^2})$ we can compute the total amount of uncertainty u_{EV} as:

$$u_{EV} = \sum_{i=1}^{m} f_i^{\sigma^2} \tag{5}$$

where $f_i^{\sigma^2}$ represents the variance associated to feature i obtained from v_{σ^2}. Once obtained u_{EV}, we can decide to discard or not the associated predictions according to a threshold.

3.3   Comparison with Existing Approaches

To the best of our knowledge, only Mason et al. [22] recently proposed a deep ensemble method for addressing the task of LiDAR-based place recognition. However, there are some differences between their work and the approach proposed in this manuscript. In particular, we propose a method to produce feature-wise uncertainty estimates, while they represent uncertainty as a degree of accordance between ensemble members. From a technical perspective, their method produces n replicas of a query and database set, for each EV they compute a similarity score between a selected EV and each database entry, and then, given the database element with the highest average similarity, a possible representation of uncertainty is the similarity variance of EV copies. As we will describe in Sect. 4, the previous method has the advantage to considerably improve the overall recall capability at the expense of maintaining distinct database instances. Instead, our approach has the ability to encode ensemble predictions with a single representation and to better detect localization failures in order to improve the recall capability of the proposed system.

3.4   Training Details

A DNN architecture for place recognition comprises two main components: a feature extractor followed by a feature aggregation layer. Our experimental setup is based on the implementation of two widely used DNNs for 3D place recognition: MinkLoc3D [16] and PointNetVLAD [25]. MinkLoc3D requires a sparse voxelized representation of the scene as input and employs a Feature Pyramid Network architecture [20] to extract relevant features. On the other hand, PointNetVLAD [25] extracts features directly from a point cloud using PointNet as its feature extractor. For feature aggregation, MinkLoc3D uses a Generalized Mean Pooling (GeM) layer, while PointNetVLAD employs a VLAD layer [3]. No modifications were made to the architecture of either neural network considered in this study.

From a technical perspective and inspired by the training configuration of MinkLoc3D, we fixed the configuration settings for both the teacher-student and triplet-loss training methods as well as both DNNs. Specifically, the batch size expansion described by Komorowski et al. [16] was disabled and the batch size was fixed to 64. Moreover, due to limited memory space available on the GPU, the batch size for training MinkLoc3D and PointNetVLAD using the Knowledge-Distillation pipeline was reduced to 32 and 8 respectively. Initially, we trained models for 40 epochs, but we observed that halving the epochs improved the uncertainty quality for the teacher-student approach.

With regard to the training methods, for the triplet-loss function [10] we trivially used Eq. (2). However, the teacher-student method involves comparing the feature vector extracted by the student network with the corresponding ground-truth vector extracted by the teacher network. To evaluate the distance between these vectors, we used smoothL1 distance as the cost function.

Table 1. Triplet vs knowledge-distillation feature space interchangeability: from left to right, we represent the R@1 of MinkLoc3D trained using triplet loss (left) and knowledge-distillation (right) loss functions. Only the knowledge-distillation method allows us to exchange database and query sets across different student models.

		QUERY							QUERY			
		m1	m2	m3	m4	m5			m1	m2	m3	m4	m5
DATABASE	m1	92.37	0.75	0.25	0.28	1.40	DATABASE	m1	93.44	92.49	92.94	92.83	92.99
	m2	0.87	92.20	0.49	0.48	0.21		m2	92.93	93.36	93.09	93.07	93.14
	m3	0.58	1.31	91.86	0.74	0.49		m3	92.85	92.66	93.60	93.14	93.07
	m4	1.34	0.76	1.25	92.53	0.93		m4	93.05	92.89	93.30	93.48	93.23
	m5	0.98	0.55	0.77	0.14	92.07		m5	93.24	92.82	93.15	93.11	93.63

4 Experimental Activity

In the following section, we report our extensive experimental activity to compare the ensemble-based methods previously discussed. In particular, we compare our teacher-student ensemble with [22] and with a naive ensemble approach that follows a similar idea to our method but without using a knowledge-distillation technique. In particular, we evaluate the recall gain obtained by each ensemble modality and the capability of detecting localization failures according to a threshold-based strategy that exploits system uncertainty generated by the ensemble. Such an assessment is performed across different datasets never used during the training stage of ensemble members.

4.1 Datasets

To train DNN models and to validate our approach, we choose three popular automotive datasets: Oxford Robotcar [21], NUS InHouse [25] and MulRan [13]. Please note, for all the methods considered we used only the Oxford Robotcar dataset for training, while others were only used to validate our system.

Oxford and NUS InHouse datasets are characterized by urban scenes collected during multiple traversals of the city of Oxford and Singapore, respectively. Scenes depicted in these datasets can present tricky examples for a place recognition system due to the presence of external actors, *e.g.*, cars, bicycles, and pedestrians, that may occlude relevant scene constituents. Furthermore, the presence of different light and weather conditions causes an increasing recognition difficulty. Similarly, MulRan also comprises tricky environments characterized by repetitive scenarios, inducing perceptual aliasing.

Regarding Oxford Robotcar and NUS InHouse datasets, we exploit the benchmark provided by Uy et al. [25]. For the MulRan dataset, we considered DCC and Riverside locations by selecting two runs for each: one for building a database set and the other for a query set. In particular, we exploited the pre-processed point clouds provided by Knights *et al.* [15].

When training models with a triplet-loss, we consider positive correspondences as point clouds with a maximum distance of 10 m, whereas negative matches are point clouds situated more than 50 m apart. Differently, during evaluation, a match is positive if the retrieved database sample is at a maximum distance of 25 m from the query.

Point clouds belonging to each dataset are pre-processed by applying a set of transformations following the pipeline described by Uy et al. [25]. In particular, such transforms comprehend ground plane removal and $3D$ downsampling to obtain point clouds with 4096 points. Finally, points coordinates are re-scaled within a range of $[-1; 1]$.

4.2   Evaluation Strategy and Metrics

For the evaluation, we follow a similar method reported in [16,22,25]. We consider a dataset $D = \{d_1, d_2, ..., d_n\}$, where each element d_i corresponds to the $i - th$ traversal. We represent a query set as $Q = \{q_1, q_2, ..., q_n\}$, where q_j refers to the $j - th$ traversal. We compare each d_i with all the queries in Q by excluding q_j when $i = j$. The goal is to evaluate only queries recorded during a different traversal than d. We label a match as *correct* if the spatial distance between the query point cloud and database is within 25 m. To assess the retrieval capability of the approaches considered, we employ the recall R@1, R@5, and R@10. We use the recall measure also to highlight the feature spaces differences in the exchangeability test shown in the following subsection.

Finally, to understand if a method can detect localization failures, we observe the recall trend when progressively removing queries according to a dynamic threshold applied on u_{EV}. Ideally, higher uncertainties should correspond to a higher likelihood of prediction errors. For each step, the recall is computed only considering the number of queries considered reliable.

4.3   Feature Space Interchangeability: Triplet vs TS Ensemble

In the following experiment, we compare the feature spaces produced by each trained model. In particular, we aim to demonstrate that only using student models allows us to exchange feature spaces without altering recognition performance, that is features from different models are directly comparable. Considering a set of models $M = \{m_1, ..., m_n\}$, we employ the following protocol: we use one model m_k to create a set of EVs representing a database D_k, the remaining members to produce different query sets from Q_j and, finally, we observe the R@1 following the protocol described in Sect. 4.2. In Table 1, we demonstrate the comparability between the database built with a model and the query set obtained from another ensemble member when using a knowledge-distillation approach. In that case, we can achieve similar performance no matter how we build a pair (D_k, Q_j). Please note, experiments were performed on the test set of the Oxford dataset.

4.4 Recall Capability

In Table 2, we report the recalls R@1, R@5, R@10 of the baseline approaches [16,25] and the Δ recalls obtain by the other methods. Our evaluation scheme comprises a variation of the backbone architecture and the training method. In particular, columns indicated with T-S refers to the results obtained with a single network trained in a knowledge-distillation strategy, Naive Ensemble is an ensemble where members were trained with a standard triplet loss, and T-S Ensemble is the method proposed in this paper. Finally, we also report the performance obtained with an ensemble that relies on different query and database replicas [22]. At first glance, we can see a difference between the performance achieved with our method across the two different architectures. As explained in Sect. 3.4, we trained the teacher-student models by reducing the overall number of epochs since we noticed that model over-training leads to better recall in general but also to a lower uncertainty quality. With MinkLoc3D, we found the optimal trade-off between the number of training epochs and the recall performance. Unfortunately, we could not achieve similar results with PointNetVlad.

Table 2. In this table, we show different recalls r@1, r@5 and r@10 achieved by the baseline model [16] across different datasets. For the other approaches, we report the Δ recall with respect to the baseline method. All the methods reported were trained only on the Oxford Robotcar dataset

PNVlad	Baseline			T-S			Naive Ens.			T-S Ens. (ours)			Mason et al. [22]		
Datasets	R@1	R@5	R@10	Δ1	Δ5	Δ10	Δ1	Δ5	Δ10	Δ1	Δ5	Δ10	Δ1	Δ5	Δ10
Oxford	71.1	86.6	91.7	-2.9	-1.7	-1	0.7	0.3	0.3	-1.9	-1.1	-0.6	1.7	1.2	0.9
U.S.	66.8	84.3	90.2	0.3	-0.5	-0.6	1.2	-0.3	-0.1	1.2	0.4	0.5	2.1	0.2	-0.2
R.A.	62.7	80.5	85.6	-2.8	-1.8	-0.2	1.5	0	-0.1	-1.1	-1.2	-0.9	2	1.1	0.9
B.D.	63.8	81.7	87.2	-1.5	-3	-2	1.8	-0.2	0.2	-0.7	-1.1	-0.7	2.6	0.5	0.8
DCC	62.8	65.9	67.8	0	0.4	0.6	1.9	1.4	1.5	0.1	0.7	0.6	1.8	1.4	1.2
Riverside	54.9	67.4	72.3	-1.9	-1.4	-1.3	1.9	0.7	-0.1	-0.6	-0.1	-0.2	2.2	0.9	0.4

MinkLoc3D	Baseline			T-S			Naive Ens.			T-S Ens. (ours)			Mason et al. [22]		
Datasets	R@1	R@5	R@10	Δ1	Δ5	Δ10	Δ1	Δ5	Δ10	Δ1	Δ5	Δ10	Δ1	Δ5	Δ10
Oxford	92.4	97.9	98.8	0.9	0.2	0.1	-0.3	-0.3	-0.3	1.3	0.3	0.1	2.2	0.5	0.2
U.S.	84	94.5	96.4	0.7	0	0.3	1.9	0	-0.1	3.1	1.3	0.9	4.9	2	1.4
R.A.	75.9	89.8	93.1	4.2	3.5	2.1	4.5	3	2.1	6.6	4.4	2.8	9.5	5	3.4
B.D.	80	93.3	96.3	1.6	-0.2	-0.3	0.1	-0.6	-0.5	3.1	0.7	0.2	5.7	1.7	0.9
DCC	76.9	86.4	89.5	2.1	-0.6	-1.3	3.5	1.8	1	2.3	-0.4	-1.2	4.5	2	1.2
Riverside	56.4	69.1	74.9	-0.1	-1.9	-2.4	0.4	0.5	-0.5	0.8	-0.7	-2.1	2.1	1	0.7

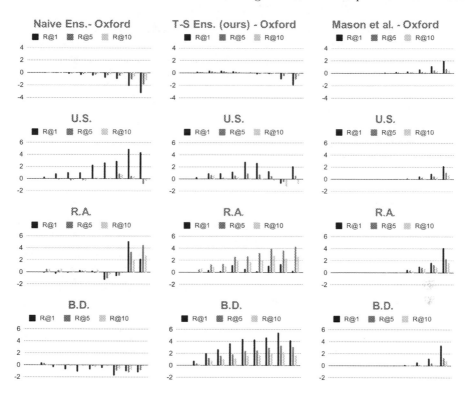

Fig. 3. Uncertain queries removal test on Oxford [21] and InHouse [25] datasets. x-axis represents the percentage of query removed in the interval of $[0\%, 90\%]$, while y-axis reports the $\Delta\%$ R@1, R@5 and R@10. We compare Naive Ensemble (Left), Ours (Centre) and [22] (Right) approaches.

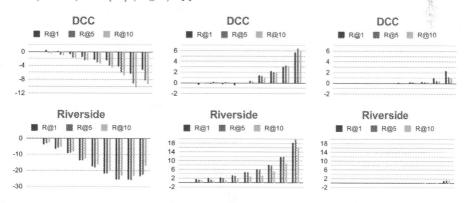

Fig. 4. Uncertain queries removal test on MulRan [13] dataset. x-axis represents the percentage of query removed in the interval of $[0\%, 90\%]$, while y-axis reports the $\Delta\%$ R@1, R@5 and R@10. We compare Naive Ensemble (Left), Ours (Centre) and [22] (Right) approaches. Due to the worse recall obtained by all the reported methods, we consider this dataset more challenging.

In general, the approach of Mason et al. [22] slightly outperforms the other methods. However, with this method we need to maintain separated replicas of the database and queries implying n simultaneous searches to extract the most likely match, where n represents the number of ensemble members. Furthermore, as we will report in the next section, while this method achieves higher recall, it produces lower quality uncertainty.

4.5   Localization Failures Detection

A desirable behavior from an uncertainty-aware system is to provide the possibility of detecting possible failures. In the context of place recognition, we would like to decide whether a prediction is reliable or not to perform localization, *i.e.,* by fixing a threshold on the total feature uncertainty and discard EVs accordingly.

We use a similar evaluation protocol of Sect. 4D. However, for each dataset and each traversal, we order queries in descending order according to the total uncertainty computed with Eq. (1), and we progressively discard queries to observe the presence of an increasing trend in terms of R@1, R@5, R@10. Since we compute a new ordering for each run, the results show the average recall obtained by simulating multiple traversals of a vehicle within the navigation map. We aim to observe the recall capability of our system on a subset of queries that we label as reliable. We report the results in Fig. 3 and Fig. 4 by splitting the evaluation datasets into two groups. If our deep ensemble approach achieves a R@1 $\geq 80\%$ on a particular dataset, we label such dataset as *trivial* and *challenging* in the opposite case. Our goal is to observe the uncertainty quality of the considered approaches in the presence of those two different scenarios. From the results obtained with our approach (center column), it is possible to determine a strong relation between high uncertainty and wrong matches. In fact, by gradually removing uncertain queries we are able to ensure a better recall capability of our system. Furthermore, our method shows excellent results within challenging scenarios as reported in Fig.4. The approach of Mason et al. also shows improvements but after discarding a considerable amount of queries. This suggests that feature-wise variance is more powerful than similarity variance to represent the model's uncertainty. As expected, uncertainty extracted with a Naive Ensemble does not produce the desired results.

5   Conclusions

In this work, we provide an in-depth study of the deep ensemble effect in LiDAR-based place recognition. In particular, we propose a deep ensemble implementation that exploits a knowledge-distillation approach to approximate a unique feature space between members, and we compare it with the method of Mason *et al.* [22], which instead relies on different feature space replicas. From our extensive experimental activity, we can conclude that both strategies increase the overall system recall. In particular, the approach of Mason *et al.* achieves slightly better performance, but our method better associates wrong predictions to high uncertainty estimates. Furthermore, our feature-level uncertainty demonstrates its effectiveness especially in challenging scenarios never represented in the training set, and we perform query-to-database search only once since we exploit a unified feature space. Finally, since our method estimates uncertainty directly on EV, it enables the discovery of features that generate anomalies giving a better introspection of the neural network model. This aspect put the basis for future works to improve the explainability of such systems.

References

1. Amini, A., Schwarting, W., Soleimany, A., Rus, D.: Deep evidential regression. In: Larochelle, H., Ranzato, M., Hadsell, R., Balcan, M., Lin, H. (eds.) Advances in Neural Information Processing Systems, vol. 33, pp. 14927–14937. Curran Associates, Inc. (2020). https://proceedings.neurips.cc/paper_files/paper/2020/file/aab085461de182608ee9f607f3f7d18f-Paper.pdf
2. Arandjelovic, R., Gronat, P., Torii, A., Pajdla, T., Sivic, J.: NetVLAD: CNN architecture for weakly supervised place recognition. In: Proceedings of the IEEE Conference on Computer Vision and Pattern Recognition (CVPR) (2016)
3. Arandjelovic, R., Zisserman, A.: All about VLAD. In: Proceedings of the IEEE Conference on Computer Vision and Pattern Recognition, pp. 1578–1585 (2013)
4. Cai, K., Lu, C.X., Huang, X.: STUN: self-teaching uncertainty estimation for place recognition. In: 2022 IEEE/RSJ International Conference on Intelligent Robots and Systems (IROS), pp. 6614–6621 (2022). https://doi.org/10.1109/IROS47612.2022.9981546
5. Cattaneo, D., Vaghi, M., Fontana, S., Ballardini, A.L., Sorrenti, D.G.: Global visual localization in lidar-maps through shared 2D–3D embedding space. In: 2020 IEEE International Conference on Robotics and Automation (ICRA), pp. 4365–4371 (2020). https://doi.org/10.1109/ICRA40945.2020.9196859
6. Cattaneo, D., Vaghi, M., Valada, A.: LCDNet: deep loop closure detection and point cloud registration for lidar slam. IEEE Trans. Rob. **38**(4), 2074–2093 (2022). https://doi.org/10.1109/TRO.2022.3150683
7. Deng, H., Bui, M., Navab, N., Guibas, L., Ilic, S., Birdal, T.: Deep bingham networks: dealing with uncertainty and ambiguity in pose estimation. Int. J. Comput. Vision **130**, 1–28 (2022)
8. Denker, J., LeCun, Y.: Transforming neural-net output levels to probability distributions. In: Lippmann, R., Moody, J., Touretzky, D. (eds.) Advances in Neural Information Processing Systems, vol. 3. Morgan-Kaufmann (1990). https://proceedings.neurips.cc/paper_files/paper/1990/file/7eacb532570ff6858afd2723755ff790-Paper.pdf
9. Hausler, S., Garg, S., Xu, M., Milford, M., Fischer, T.: Patch-NetVLAD: multiscale fusion of locally-global descriptors for place recognition. In: Proceedings of the IEEE/CVF Conference on Computer Vision and Pattern Recognition (CVPR), pp. 14141–14152 (2021)
10. Hermans, A., Beyer, L., Leibe, B.: In defense of the triplet loss for person re-identification. arXiv preprint arXiv:1703.07737 (2017)

11. Jégou, H., Douze, M., Schmid, C., Pérez, P.: Aggregating local descriptors into a compact image representation. In: 2010 IEEE Computer Society Conference on Computer Vision and Pattern Recognition, pp. 3304–3311 (2010). https://doi.org/10.1109/CVPR.2010.5540039

12. Kendall, A., Cipolla, R.: Modelling uncertainty in deep learning for camera relocalization. In: 2016 IEEE International Conference on Robotics and Automation (ICRA), pp. 4762–4769 (2016). https://doi.org/10.1109/ICRA.2016.7487679

13. Kim, G., Park, Y.S., Cho, Y., Jeong, J., Kim, A.: MulRan: multimodal range dataset for urban place recognition. In: 2020 IEEE International Conference on Robotics and Automation (ICRA), pp. 6246–6253 (2020). https://doi.org/10.1109/ICRA40945.2020.9197298

14. Kingma, D.P., Salimans, T., Welling, M.: Variational dropout and the local reparameterization trick. In: Cortes, C., Lawrence, N., Lee, D., Sugiyama, M., Garnett, R. (eds.) Advances in Neural Information Processing Systems, vol. 28. Curran Associates, Inc. (2015). https://proceedings.neurips.cc/paper_files/paper/2015/file/bc7316929fe1545bf0b98d114ee3ecb8-Paper.pdf

15. Knights, J., Moghadam, P., Ramezani, M., Sridharan, S., Fookes, C.: Incloud: incremental learning for point cloud place recognition. In: 2022 IEEE/RSJ International Conference on Intelligent Robots and Systems (IROS), pp. 8559–8566. IEEE (2022)

16. Komorowski, J.: MinkLoc3D: point cloud based large-scale place recognition. In: Proceedings of the IEEE/CVF Winter Conference on Applications of Computer Vision (WACV), pp. 1790–1799 (2021)

17. Komorowski, J.: Improving point cloud based place recognition with ranking-based loss and large batch training. In: 2022 26th International Conference on Pattern Recognition (ICPR), pp. 3699–3705 (2022). https://doi.org/10.1109/ICPR56361.2022.9956458

18. Lajoie, P.Y., Beltrame, G.: Self-supervised domain calibration and uncertainty estimation for place recognition. IEEE Robot. Autom. Lett. **8**(2), 792–799 (2023). https://doi.org/10.1109/LRA.2022.3232033

19. Lakshminarayanan, B., Pritzel, A., Blundell, C.: Simple and scalable predictive uncertainty estimation using deep ensembles. In: Guyon, I., et al. (eds.) Advances in Neural Information Processing Systems, vol. 30. Curran Associates, Inc. (2017). https://proceedings.neurips.cc/paper_files/paper/2017/file/9ef2ed4b7fd2c810847ffa5fa85bce38-Paper.pdf

20. Lin, T.Y., Dollár, P., Girshick, R., He, K., Hariharan, B., Belongie, S.: Feature pyramid networks for object detection. In: Proceedings of the IEEE Conference on Computer Vision and Pattern Recognition, pp. 2117–2125 (2017)

21. Maddern, W., Pascoe, G., Linegar, C., Newman, P.: 1 Year, 1000 km: the Oxford RobotCar dataset. Int. J. Robot. Res. (IJRR) **36**(1), 3–15 (2017). https://doi.org/10.1177/0278364916679498

22. Mason, K., Knights, J., Ramezani, M., Moghadam, P., Miller, D.: Uncertainty-aware lidar place recognition in novel environments. arXiv preprint arXiv:2210.01361v1 (2022)

23. Neal, R.M.: Bayesian Learning for Neural Networks, vol. 118. Springer, Heidelberg (2012)

24. Qi, C.R., Su, H., Mo, K., Guibas, L.J.: PointNet: deep learning on point sets for 3D classification and segmentation. In: Proceedings of the IEEE Conference on Computer Vision and Pattern Recognition (CVPR) (2017)

25. Uy, M.A., Lee, G.H.: PointNetVLAD: deep point cloud based retrieval for large-scale place recognition. In: Proceedings of the IEEE Conference on Computer Vision and Pattern Recognition (CVPR) (2018)
26. Vaghi, M., Ballardini, A.L., Fontana, S., Sorrenti, D.G.: Uncertainty-aware DNN for multi-modal camera localization (2023)
27. Zhang, W., Xiao, C.: PCAN: 3D attention map learning using contextual information for point cloud based retrieval. In: Proceedings of the IEEE/CVF Conference on Computer Vision and Pattern Recognition (CVPR) (2019)

Enhancing LiDAR Performance: Robust De-Skewing Exclusively Relying on Range Measurements

Omar Ashraf Ahmed Khairy Salem$^{(\boxtimes)}$ iD, Emanuele Giacomini iD,
Leonardo Brizi iD, Luca Di Giammarino iD, and Giorgio Grisetti iD

Dipartimento di Ingegneria informatica, automatica e gestionale,
Sapienza University of Rome, Rome, Italy
salem@diag.uniroma1.it

Abstract. Most commercially available Light Detection and Ranging (LiDAR)s measure the distances along a 2D section of the environment by sequentially sampling the free range along directions centered at the sensor's origin. When the sensor moves during the acquisition, the measured ranges are affected by a phenomenon known as "skewing", which appears as a distortion in the acquired scan. Skewing potentially affects all systems that rely on LiDAR data, however, it could be compensated if the position of the sensor were known each time a single range is measured. Most methods to de-skew a LiDAR are based on external sensors such as IMU or wheel odometry, to estimate these intermediate LiDAR positions. In this paper, we present a method that relies exclusively on range measurements to effectively estimate the robot velocities which are then used for de-skewing. Our approach is suitable for low-frequency LiDAR where the skewing is more evident. It can be seamlessly integrated into existing pipelines, enhancing their performance at a negligible computational cost.

Keywords: Range Sensing · Sensor Calibration · Mapping

1 Introduction

Accurate and reliable mapping, localization, and navigation are essential for a wide range of robotics applications from autonomous driving, logistics, search and rescue, and many others. To this extent, Light Detection and Ranging (Li-DAR) sensors are a popular choice since they allow us to sense both the free space and the location of obstacles around the robot. A planar LiDAR measures the distance of an object by deflecting laser beams around the sensor's axis of rotation.

In this work we focus on low-grade 2D LiDARs such as the InnoMaker-LD-06 or the RPI-Lidar A1 which at the time of writing can be bought for less than 100 Eur. The major shortcoming of these devices is their relatively slow angular speed

This work has been supported by PNRR MUR project PE0000013-FAIR

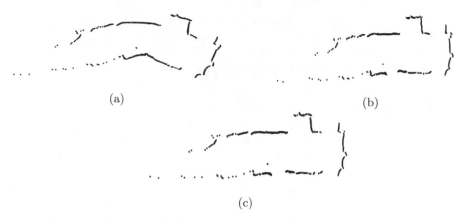

(a)   (b)

(c)

Fig. 1. Effect of de-skewing. (a) Unprocessed (raw) scan acquired by a rotating robot, while (b) is the corresponding ground truth scan, and finally (c) is the same scan in (a), processed (de-skewed) using our proposed approach.

which results in a full sweep of measurements becoming available at a frequency between 5 to 10 Hz. In contrast to more expensive models, these devices are not equipped with an inertial measurement unit or other means to estimate the proprioceptive motion of the sensor while it moves. In such devices, the scan acquisition(a full sweep of laser beams around the vertical axis of the sensor) is not instantaneous, hence when the robot carrying the LiDAR moves, the origin of the beam in the world frame changes for each sensed range. Neglecting this fact, and assuming that all measurements gathered during one rotation are sampled at the same time resulting in a distorted or skewed scan as shown in Fig. 1. Despite this consideration, most perception subsystems in a navigation stack treat the scans as rigid bodies, however, the effect of skewing leads to undesirable decay in accuracy that can result in failures as analyzed by Al-Nuaimi *et al.* [1].

A common way to compensate for the motion of the LiDAR is to integrate external proprioceptive measurements (dead reckoning and/or Inertial Measurement Unit (IMU)), to estimate the origin and orientation of the laser beam each time a range is acquired [4,7,13]. High-end 3D LiDARs already contain a synchronized IMU, which is not available on the inexpensive models previously mentioned.

In this paper, we propose an approach to estimate the velocities of the robot carrying the LiDAR, based *solely* on the range measurements, that are processed as a stream. Our method is based on a non-rigid plane-to-plane registration algorithm, where the velocity of the platform carrying the sensor is estimated by maximizing the geometric consistency of the stream of ranges. We conducted several statistical experiments on synthetic and real data. Results verify that our de-skewing method is effective in estimating the motion of the robot, at negligible computation.

In Fig. 1 we illustrate the effects of our approach on measurements acquired with a constantly rotating LiDAR, with a rotational velocity 3 rad/s. In the remainder of this paper, we first review the related work in Sect. 2, subsequently we describe in detail our de-skewing method for 2D LiDAR data Sect. 3. We conclude the paper by presenting some synthetic and real results in Sect. 4, that show the ability of the proposed system. And finally, we draw some conclusions on the benefits and the limitations of our approach.

2   Related Work

In this section, we review the most recent approaches to de-skew LiDAR data. Existing approaches for de-skewing mostly use either wheeled odometry or IMU to estimate the relative motion of the sensor/robot while a scan is being acquired. This process involves motion integration relying on estimators that process the raw proprioceptive data such as a filter or an integrator that directly provides an estimate of the sensor position each time a single range is measured.

These methods fall in the class of *loosely-coupled*, since they do not use the LiDAR information to refine the proprioceptive estimate. Among this class, we find the work of Tang *et al.* [9] that proposes to match subsequent scans to compute the relative motion, where the initial relative orientations are provided by an IMU. Subsequently, He *et al.* [4] proposed a method to estimate relative motion between IMU poses and de-skew subsequent ranges by using these smoothed poses.

In contrast to loosely-coupled approaches, *tightly-coupled* methods jointly process LiDAR and IMU. These methods are typically based on either smoothing or filtering. Wei *et al.* [11] uses a pre-integration scheme to estimate the LiDAR's ego-motion based on the inertial measurements, and updates the IMU biases in the correct step of an iterative EKF whenever a scan is completed. Shan *et al.* [8] includes the states of IMU in the factor-graph, updating IMU biases through the optimization process, adapting a well-known computer vision work [3] to the LiDAR case. These ideas have been further extended in [10,12] where the authors resort to full factor-graph optimization to obtain a state configuration that is maximally consistent with all the IMU measurements and LiDAR ranges.

For coupled approaches, accurate time synchronization between the sensors is essential. Unfortunately, this is not straightforward to obtain on inexpensive small devices due to the unpredicted communication latencies that affect the communication channels. These issues, however, can be completely avoided when using only LiDAR data to perform de-skewing. At their core LiDAR only methods have a registration algorithm, which aims to compute the velocities of the sensor while the robot moves. The basic intuition is that if the correct velocities were found, the sequence of range measurements could be assembled in a maximally consistent scan. In this context, Moosman *et al.* [6] propose to linearly interpolate scans between the last known pose, and the currently estimated pose, de-skewing the scan at both poses. However, this double approximation might hinder the accuracy when the initial registration fails, resulting in even worse estimates.

Al-Nuaimi *et al.* [1] propose a weighting schema based on their adapted Geometric Algebra LMS solver, where they assume that consecutive relative translation and angular motion are equal, which might be inaccurate due to the existence of drift and friction.

In this paper, we propose a planar LiDAR-only approach that addresses the de-skewing problem by continuously registering the sequence of range measurements. The registration is carried on by estimating the LiDAR's planar velocity, which iteratively minimizes a plane-to-plane metric between the de-skewed endpoints. Our results demonstrate that our methodology is accurate in estimating the velocity of the robot, only based on the laser measurements.

3   Our Approach

Our method leverages some mild assumptions about the motion of the sensor mounted on the robot and the structure of the environment to operate on a continuous stream of range measurements. More specifically we assume to have a 2D slow LiDAR sensor, hence, we define each measurement as $\mathbf{z}_i = \langle r_i, \alpha_i, t_i \rangle$. Here, r_i is the range, α_i is the angle of the laser beam with respect to the origin of the sensor and t_i is the timestamp. We assume the environment consists of a locally smooth surface and that the robot velocities change mildly within a LiDAR beam revolution.

Our method estimates these velocities by registering the stream of measurements $\{\mathbf{z}_i\}$ onto itself. The most likely velocities are the ones that if applied for de-skewing renders the measurement maximally consistent. Consistency is measured by a plane-to-plane metric applied between the corresponding LiDAR endpoints. More formally, let $\mathbf{x} = (v \ \ \omega)^T$ be the translational and angular velocity of the robot we want to estimate $\mathbf{x}^*$, such that

$$\mathbf{x}^* = \underset{\mathbf{x}}{\operatorname{argmin}} \sum_{\langle i,j \rangle \in \mathcal{C}} \rho \|\mathbf{e}(\mathbf{x}, t_i, t_j)\|^2. \tag{1}$$

Where $\mathbf{e}(\mathbf{x}, t_i, t_j)$ denotes an error vector between two planar scan patches computed around two corresponding range measurements at the time t_i and t_j. The optimization step estimates new velocities $\mathbf{x} = (v \ \ \omega)^T$ under the current set of correspondences $\mathcal{C}$, using Iterative Reweighted Least-Squares (IRLS). In Eq. (1) ρ denotes the Huber robust estimator.

Our algorithm is an instance of Iterative Closest Point (ICP) since it proceeds by alternating between the data association and optimization steps. In the data association step, the corresponding endpoints are found using the nearest neighbor strategy based on current velocity estimates. In the optimization step, the velocities are refined from the new correspondences found by the data association.

3.1   Velocity Based De-Skewing

Whereas our approach can be applied to more complex kinematics, for the sake of simplicity we detail the common case of a unicycle mobile base. Our goal is to estimate the location $\mathbf{T}(\mathbf{x}, t_i) = \left(x_i \ y_i \ \theta_i \right)^T$ of the mobile base at time t_i, assuming it starts from the origin and progresses with constant translation and angular velocities over sampling time $\mathbf{x} = (v \ \omega)^T$. After a time t_i, the robot would have traveled for a distance $l_i = v \cdot t_i$ and its angle is $\theta_i = \omega \cdot t_i$. The base will move along an arc of radius R, such that:

$$R = \frac{v_i}{\omega_i} = \frac{l_i}{\theta_i}. \tag{2}$$

From this consideration, we can easily compute $\mathbf{T}$ as

$$\mathbf{T}(\mathbf{x}, t_i) = \begin{pmatrix} R \sin\theta_i \\ R(1 - \cos\theta_i) \end{pmatrix} = \underbrace{v \cdot t_i}_{l_i} \begin{pmatrix} \frac{\sin\theta_i}{\theta_i} \\ \frac{1 - \cos\theta_i}{\theta_i} \end{pmatrix} \tag{3}$$

Assuming the sensor (LiDAR) is located at the center of the mobile base, if at time t_i the beam has a relative angle α_i and reports a range measurement r_i, we can straightforwardly find the 2D laser endpoint $\mathbf{p}_i$ as follows:

$$\mathbf{p}_i(\mathbf{x}, t_i) = \mathbf{R}(\theta_i + \alpha_i) \begin{pmatrix} r_i \\ 0 \end{pmatrix} + \begin{pmatrix} x_i \\ y_i \end{pmatrix}. \tag{4}$$

Here $\mathbf{R}(\theta_i + \alpha_i) \in SO(2)$ is 2D rotation matrix of $\theta_i + \alpha_i$. Applying this process to all the measurements and mapping all reconstructed points back to the pose where the acquisition of the current scan was started, results in the desired de-skew operation.

3.2   Error Metric

To evaluate a plane-to-plane distance the algorithm needs to compute the normal vectors, which are based on the endpoints. Since the position of the endpoints is a function of the estimated velocities $\mathbf{x}$, also the normal vectors are. Hence the algorithm has to recompute both endpoints and normals at each iteration. Furthermore, when subsequent endpoints are too close, the noise affecting the range might result in an unstable normal vector, which hinders the error metric. To lessen this effect, before each iteration, we regularize the scan to retain only temporally subsequent measurements that are sufficiently far from each other to ensure a stable normal. In our experiments, we set this threshold to 0.15 m. Similarly, if there is a large distance gap between two subsequent endpoints (>0.4 m), likely, the surface is not continuous at that point, hence we drop those measurements too. At the end of this regularization step, we end up with a set of reasonably stable measurements we can use for the remainder of the computation. For each temporally subsequent pair of endpoints, we compute a planar patch $\mathbf{m}_i = \langle \mathbf{c}_i, \mathbf{n}_i, t_i \rangle$, characterized by a center $\mathbf{c}_i$, a normal vector $\mathbf{n}_i$, and a timestamp t_i, such that:

$$\mathbf{c}_i = \frac{1}{2} \left(\mathbf{p}_{i+k} + \mathbf{p}_i \right), \tag{5}$$

$$\mathbf{n}_i = \begin{pmatrix} 0 & 1 \\ -1 & 0 \end{pmatrix} \frac{\mathbf{p}_{i+k} - \mathbf{p}_i}{\| \mathbf{p}_{i+k} - \mathbf{p}_i \|}, \tag{6}$$

$$t_i = \frac{1}{2} \left(t_{i+k} + t_i \right). \tag{7}$$

Here, the index $k > 0$ accounts for endpoints suppressed during regularization. If two planar patches $\mathbf{m}_i$ and $\mathbf{m}_j$ corresponds to the same portion of the environment, we can calculate an error vector $\mathbf{e}(\mathbf{x}, t_i, t_j)$ accounting for both their differences in position and orientation. The error vector is a function of the velocities, since the patches $\mathbf{m}_i$ and $\mathbf{m}_j$ are computed based on the endpoints. The latter is related to the velocities by (4).

Let $\mathbf{e}(\mathbf{x}, t_i, t_j) \in \mathbb{R}^3$ be the error vector, whose components are defined as follows:

$$\mathbf{e}(\mathbf{x}, t_i, t_j) = \begin{pmatrix} \frac{1}{2} (\mathbf{c}_i - \mathbf{c}_j)^T (\mathbf{n}_i + \mathbf{n}_j) \\ \mathbf{n}_j - \mathbf{n}_i \end{pmatrix}. \tag{8}$$

Here the first dimension accounts for the distance between two corresponding planar patches $\mathbf{m}_i$ and $\mathbf{m}_j$ projected along the average of their normals. The other two account for the difference between the normal vectors. (8) is differentiable in the velocities $\mathbf{x}$, hence we can minimize (1) by Iterative Reweighted Least Squares.

3.3 Data Association

To determine the correspondence we proceed at each iteration by de-skewing the sequence of measurements, to get a set of updated endpoints $\mathbf{p}_i$. Subsequently, we apply the regularization to discard those measurements whose endpoints fall either too close or too far from their temporal neighbors. This gives us a set of sequential stable measurements we can use to extract the planar patches. Figure 2 demonstarates the data association procedure.

Once this is done, for each $\mathbf{m}_i$ we seek for those other patches $\mathbf{m}_j$ that fulfill all the following criteria:

- their centers are close enough $|\mathbf{c}_i - \mathbf{c}_j| < \tau_{\mathbf{c}}$,
- their normals are sufficiently parallel $\mathbf{n}_i \cdot \mathbf{n}_j > \tau_{\mathbf{n}}$,
- their timestamp are sufficiently distant $|t_i - t_j| > \tau_t$.

Within this set we select as correspondence for $\mathbf{m}_i$, which is the $\mathbf{m}_j$ having the smallest projective distance $(\mathbf{c}_i - \mathbf{c}_j)^T (\mathbf{n}_i + \mathbf{n}_j)$.

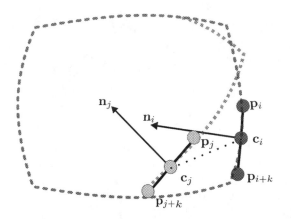

Fig. 2. Illustration of the planar patches calculation and the correspondence search between two matching patches $\mathbf{m}_i$ and $\mathbf{m}_j$.

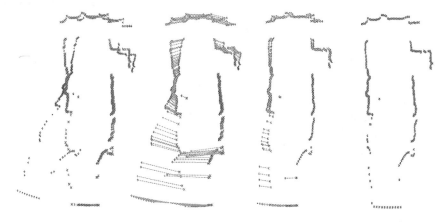

Fig. 3. Iterative evolution of the de-skewing process. Purple points represent skewed points, green points are the ground truth points, and blue lines represent the data association. Initial configuration, instance of full scan acquisition, with RMSE = 0.4 m. After 4 iterations of processing (de-skewing) the raw scan with the proposed approach, with decreased RMSE error to = 0.2 m. After 20 iterations, we ended up with a de-skewed scan closer to the ground truth, with RMSE = 0.074 m. (Color figure online)

4   Experimental Validation

In this section, we present quantitative evaluations to demonstrate the accuracy of the velocities estimated by our approach, and its effect on the processed data, using only LiDAR measurements. To this extent, we carried out statistical experiments under changing velocities.

The goal of the first experiment is to compare the velocities of the robot calculated by our approach with the ground truth applied. As mentioned before utilizing the estimated velocities by our approach, renders measurements geometrically consistent as seen in Fig. 3.

Virtual synthetic scans were created with a skewing effect based on the addressed velocities. We proceed by de-skewing twice, the first time we compute the ground truth measurement by setting the applied velocities, and the second time we compute the de-skewed scan by using our velocity estimate. The consistency is measured as the distance between corresponding endpoints in the two scans. In Table 1 each cell contains 3 rows in which: The first row is the estimated translational velocity$(v) \pm std(m/s)$, while the second row is the estimated angular velocity$(\omega) \pm std(rad/s)$, and finally the third row is the point to point Root Mean Square Error (RMSE) (m) for the de-skewed/skewed respectively with respect to their ground truth counterpart, for each combination of velocities.

Table 1. Evaluation of the proposed approach using different combinations of translation and angular velocities.

$v(m/s)$ \ $\omega(rad/s)$	-2.000	-1.000	-0.500	0.500	1.000	2.000
-2.000	-1.936 ± 0.090	-0.950 ± 0.068	-0.471 ± 0.050	0.470 ± 0.047	0.962 ± 0.052	1.910 ± 0.092
	-1.952 ± 0.081	-1.933 ± 0.115	-1.958 ± 0.066	-1.962 ± 0.052	-1.952 ± 0.070	-1.932 ± 0.103
	0.090/0.404	**0.083**/0.399	**0.059**/0.351	**0.061**/0.414	**0.055**/0.460	**0.081**/0.579
-1.000	-1.890 ± 0.131	-0.979 ± 0.031	-0.477 ± 0.035	0.482 ± 0.034	0.946 ± 0.069	1.897 ± 0.073
	-0.949 ± 0.069	-0.986 ± 0.023	-0.973 ± 0.037	-0.979 ± 0.026	-0.953 ± 0.059	-0.950 ± 0.056
	0.067/0.297	**0.058**/0.308	**0.055**/0.296	**0.049**/0.354	**0.054**/0.336	**0.062**/0.399
-0.500	-1.929 ± 0.085	-0.978 ± 0.063	-0.479 ± 0.054	0.492 ± 0.033	0.935 ± 0.064	1.906 ± 0.062
	-0.487 ± 0.020	-0.493 ± 0.022	-0.477 ± 0.035	-0.495 ± 0.009	-0.484 ± 0.026	-0.482 ± 0.022
	0.040/0.308	**0.035**/0.345	**0.041**/0.188	**0.043**/0.200	**0.060**/0.218	**0.084**/0.338
0.500	-1.955 ± 0.024	-0.954 ± 0.044	-0.474 ± 0.071	0.481 ± 0.048	0.969 ± 0.042	$1,967 \pm 0.036$
	0.483 ± 0.012	0.495 ± 0.018	0.476 ± 0.045	0.485 ± 0.026	0.488 ± 0.020	0.496 ± 0.012
	0.119/0.158	**0.029**/0.140	**0.044**/0.112	**0.052**/0.132	**0.059**/0.161	**0.159**/0.271
1.000	-1.844 ± 0.130	-0.976 ± 0.064	-0.472 ± 0.057	0.495 ± 0.028	$0.969 + 0.059$	1.98 ± 0.038
	0.933 ± 0.077	0.976 ± 0.053	0.940 ± 0.053	0.992 ± 0.015	0.970 ± 0.048	0.992 ± 0.017
	0.063/0.261	**0.063**/0.225	**0.024**/0.231	**0.055**/0.302	**0.058**/0.303	**0.039**/0.335
2.000	-1.906 ± 0.116	-0.941 ± 0.076	-0.465 ± 0.081	0.480 ± 0.065	0.940 ± 0.083	1.947 ± 0.069
	1.904 ± 0.142	1.919 ± 0.120	1.912 ± 0.104	1.905 ± 0.137	1.922 ± 0.116	1.963 ± 0.069
	0.074/0.416	**0.071**/0.368	**0.081**/0.358	**0.075**/0.435	**0.076**/0.494	**0.091**/0.424

We repeated this experiment on the real robot and the velocity plots in Fig. 4 confirm that our system can effectively recover the robot's velocities, correctly de-skewing the scan, in real indoor scenarios.

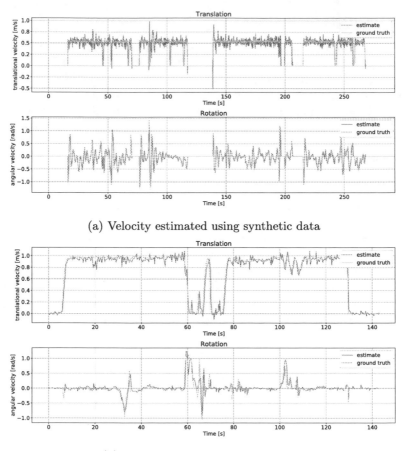

(a) Velocity estimated using synthetic data

(b) Velocity estimated using real data

Fig. 4. Evolution of estimated and real velocities.

4.1 De-Skewing in a SLAM System

In our final experiment, we used our de-skewing mechanism to pre-process the input of our 2D LiDAR Simultaneous Localization and Mapping (SLAM) system [2]. We run SLAM on three different inputs: the raw (skewed) scans, the ones de-skewed by using the proposed approach, and finally the data de-skewed by using the ground truth. We simulated different exploration runs of the same environment while changing the velocity bounds of the robot. Figure 5 illustrates the three different maps obtained.

Furthermore, we measure the Absolute Trajectory Error (ATE) between the ground truth trajectory computed by the simulator and the ones estimated by SLAM using the two types of scans. ATE measures the distance between corresponding points of the trajectories, after computing a transformation that makes them as close as possible. For trajectory registration, we used the Horn

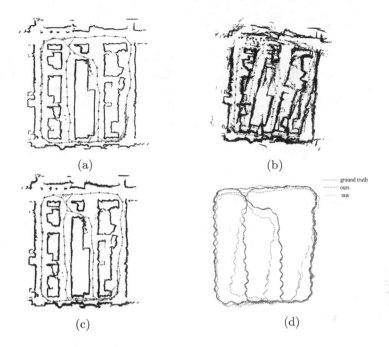

Fig. 5. SLAM Results. (a) Ground truth map (reference). (b) Map constructed using raw scans acquired directly from the LiDAR. (c) Map constructed using processed LiDAR measurements de-skewed by our proposed approach. (d) Estimated trajectories from SLAM, produced by scan matching between consecutive measurements.

Table 2. SLAM comparison

Velocities		ATE(m)	
v_{max} (m/s)	ω_{max}(rad/s)	w/o deskewing	deskewed
0.5	0.5	0.329	**0.113**
0.5	1.0	0.246	**0.232**
1.0	1.0	1.018	**0.977**
1.0	1.5	1.586	**1.520**
2.0	2.0	11.18	**1.805**

method [5], while the corresponding poses are associated based on the times-tamps. The results are summarized in Table 2. Consistently, the trajectories obtained by using de-skewed data are substantially closer to the ground truth compared to their skewed counterpart as shown in Fig. 5d. This is confirmed by the maps generated based on the trajectories and illustrated in Fig. 5. These results are consistent and confirm the importance of the de-skewer since these measurements might induce systematic unrecoverable errors in the registration process.

5   Conclusion

In this paper, we presented a simple and effective planar LiDAR de-skewing mechanism based on plane-to-plane registration criteria. To the best of our knowledge, this is the only de-skewing pipeline that does not rely on additional sensors (i.e. IMU, wheel encoders), targeting specifically slow and inexpensive LiDARs, and enhancing the quality of the scan. For future work, we are planning to integrate the proposed approach in more complex systems, while generalizing the approach for 3D data.

References

1. Al-Nuaimi, A., Lopes, W., Zeller, P., Garcea, A., Lopes, C., Steinbach, E.: Analyzing lidar scan skewing and its impact on scan matching. In: 2016 International Conference on Indoor Positioning and Indoor Navigation (IPIN), pp. 1–8. IEEE (2016)
2. Colosi, M., et al.: Plug-and-play SLAM: a unified slam architecture for modularity and ease of use. In: IROS, pp. 5051–5057 (2020). https://doi.org/10.1109/IROS45743.2020.9341611
3. Forster, C., Carlone, L., Dellaert, F., Scaramuzza, D.: On-manifold preintegration for real-time visual-inertial odometry. IEEE Trans. Rob. **33**(1), 1–21 (2016)
4. He, L., Jin, Z., Gao, Z.: De-skewing lidar scan for refinement of local mapping. Sensors **20**(7), 1846 (2020)
5. Horn, B., Hilden, H., Negahdaripour, S.: Closed-form solution of absolute orientation using orthonormal matrices. JOSA A **5**(7), 1127–1135 (1988)
6. Moosmann, F., Stiller, C.: Velodyne SLAM. In: 2011 IEEE Intelligent Vehicles Symposium (IV), pp. 393–398. IEEE (2011)
7. Shan, T., Englot, B.: LeGO-LOAM: lightweight and ground-optimized lidar odometry and mapping on variable terrain. In: IEEE/RSJ International Conference on Intelligent Robots and Systems (IROS), pp. 4758–4765. IEEE (2018)
8. Shan, T., Englot, B., Meyers, D., Wang, W., Ratti, C., Rus, D.: LIO-SAM: tightly-coupled lidar inertial odometry via smoothing and mapping. In: 2020 IEEE/RSJ International Conference on Intelligent Robots and Systems (IROS), pp. 5135–5142. IEEE (2020)
9. Tang, J., et al.: LiDAR scan matching aided inertial navigation system in GNSS-denied environments. Sensors **15**(7), 16710–16728 (2015)
10. Wang, Z., Zhang, L., Shen, Y., Zhou, Y.: D-LIOM: tightly-coupled direct lidar-inertial odometry and mapping. IEEE Trans. Multimed. (2022)
11. Xu, W., Zhang, F.: Fast-LIO: a fast, robust lidar-inertial odometry package by tightly-coupled iterated Kalman filter. IEEE Robot. Autom. Lett. **6**(2), 3317–3324 (2021)
12. Ye, H., Chen, Y., Liu, M.: Tightly coupled 3D LiDAR inertial odometry and mapping. In: 2019 International Conference on Robotics and Automation (ICRA), pp. 3144–3150. IEEE (2019)
13. Zhang, J., Singh, S.: LOAM: LiDAR odometry and mapping in real-time. In: Fox, D., Kavraki, L.E., Kurniawati, H. (eds.) Robotics: Science and Systems X, University of California, Berkeley, USA, 12–16 July 2014 (2014). https://doi.org/10.15607/RSS.2014.X.007, http://www.roboticsproceedings.org/rss10/p07.html

Can Existing 3D Monocular Object Detection Methods Work in Roadside Contexts? A Reproducibility Study

Silvio Barra[2] , Mirko Marras[1]([✉]) , Sondos Mohamed[1],
Alessandro Sebastian Podda[1] , and Roberto Saia[1]

[1] University of Cagliari, Cagliari, Italy
{mirko.marras,sondoswa.mohamed,sebastianpodda,roberto.saia}@unica.it
[2] University of Naples "Federico II", Naples, Italy
silvio.barra@unina.it

Abstract. Detecting 3D objects in images from urban monocular cameras is essential to enable intelligent monitoring applications for local municipalities decision-support systems. However, existing detection methods in this domain are mainly focused on autonomous driving and limited to frontal views from sensors mounted on the vehicle. In contrast, to monitor urban areas, local municipalities rely on streams collected from fixed cameras, especially in intersections and particularly dangerous areas. Such streams represent a rich source of data for applications focused on traffic patterns, road conditions, and potential hazards. In this paper, given the lack of availability of large-scale datasets of images from roadside cameras, and the time-consuming process of generating real labelled data, we first proposed a synthetic dataset using the CARLA simulator, which makes dataset creation efficient yet acceptable. The dataset consists of 7,481 development images and 7,518 test images. Then, we reproduced state-of-the-art models for monocular 3D object detection proven to work well in autonomous driving (e.g., M3DRPN, Monodle, SMOKE, and Kinematic) and tested them on the newly generated dataset. Our results show that our dataset can serve as a reference for future experiments and that state-of-the-art models from the autonomous driving domain do not always generalize well to monocular roadside camera images. Source code and data are available at https://bit.ly/monocular-3d-odt.

Keywords: Dataset · Object Detection · 3D Vision · Roadside Camera

1 Introduction

Monocular cameras play an important role in urban areas, in which they are commonly used in intersections and other high-risk locations to capture valuable data. Detecting objects in images from monocular cameras is critical for

© The Author(s), under exclusive license to Springer Nature Switzerland AG 2023
R. Basili et al. (Eds.): AIxIA 2023, LNAI 14318, pp. 321–335, 2023.
https://doi.org/10.1007/978-3-031-47546-7_22

developing intelligent monitoring applications that can assist local municipalities in making timely and informed decisions [1–4,15,16]. With such applications, governments can obtain real-time and accurate information regarding traffic patterns, road conditions, and potential hazards. Differently from traditional 2D object detection methods [8,18,21–24,30,31,42], applying 3D object detection approaches offer significant advantages. By providing a more complete understanding of the scene and enabling the detection of occluded objects, they can improve the accuracy and reliability of object detection in complex environments, and better describe object pose and shape. Usually approaches that rely on monocular cameras are also less expensive and can be easily deployed in urban areas, if compared to the more complex *LIDAR* methods [12,20,32,38]. However, 3D object detection from monocular cameras still poses several challenges and shows significant limitations. First, the lack of depth information in 2D images makes it difficult to accurately estimate the size and position of objects; second, environmental factors, such as occlusions, shadows, and weather conditions, can also affect their operational accuracy and reliability.

To overcome such issues, recent advances in autonomous driving solutions have shown promising results, among which the most noteworthy works are *M3DRPN* [5], *Kinematic* [6], *SMOKE* [25], *Monodle* [26], and *FOC3D* [36], to name a few. Additionally, a growing number of datasets [7,10,17,19,27–29,35] are being adopted to further improve the effectiveness of this technology. Notwithstanding these advancements, this field remains an active area of research, and further investigation is necessary to strengthen the performance of monocular camera-based 3D object detection models. Applying such models developed for autonomous driving to roadside cameras is possible, since these cameras usually provide a wider coverage area and greater robustness to occlusion, remain stable for extended periods of time, and are more suitable for event recognition. However, since the scenario is different from that of vehicle use, several questions on their generalizability are open. To improve performance in this context, novel datasets, such as *Ko-PER* [34], *Rope3D* [39], *BAAI-VANJEE* [13], *BoxCars* [33], and *DAIR-V2X* [41] have been proposed, but most of them are not public.

Motivated by the above limitations, in this paper, we designed a novel synthetic dataset, hereafter named as *MonoRoadCam*, with the twofold aim of: a) facilitating the adaptation of 3D object detection methods for use on roadside cameras; b) examine in this context the performance of existing methods borrowed from autonomous driving, in a consistent and unified setting. To generate such a dataset, we opted for the *CARLA simulation environment* [14], for its ability to provide complex data that mimics real-world scenarios. We also employed the widely adopted *KITTI format* [17] in order to guarantee standardization and reproducibility of the evaluation tests. Our contribution is threefold:

– We generated a synthetic dataset for monocular 3D object detection from roadside cameras using the CARLA simulator, compliant with the KITTI format. To provide a fair evaluation, we removed the overlap between the training and validation sets by excluding sequence frames;

– We verified the reproducibility of existing state-of-the-art monocular 3D object detection approaches, originally proposed for autonomous driving, on the roadside context, sharing our framework publicly.
– We conducted a comparative study between 3D object detection datasets from roadside and frontal cameras, observing that state-of-the-art solutions from the autonomous driving domain result in significant potential yet crucial limitations when applied to monocular roadside camera images.

The rest of this paper is organized as follows. Section 2 outlines the research methodology. Section 3 illustrates the obtained results. Finally, Sect. 4 concludes the paper, highlighting the prominent future research directions.

2   Research Methodology

In this section, we describe the reproducibility process, which involves (i) surveying the existing datasets and 3D object detection methods for monocular cameras; (ii) carrying out an analysis of the context, also by collecting the original source codes and adapting them to our unified framework; (iii) generating the MonoRoadCam dataset and adopt it for evaluating the reproduced models.

2.1   Problem Formulation

Given a set of training images $I = \{i_1, i_2, ...i_n\}$ and calibration information P of a monocular camera, where P represents the projection matrix, each image $i \in I$ is represented as a set of 2D projected points. Suppose that $B = \{b_1, b_2, ...b_m\}$ represents a set of bounding boxes for all objects in the image in 3D space, where each $b_i \in B$ included object type C, in addition to $T = (tx, ty, tz)$, $D = (dx, dy, dz)$, and $O = (\vartheta, \Phi, \varphi)$ which represent the centroid, dimension, and orientation of the object, respectively. The goal is to optimize the parameter θ in order to solve $f(i, P, \theta) = B \; \forall i \in I$. Usually, convolution neural networks are used to provide the map, and the optimization is run on θ.

2.2   Paper Collection

In order to gather existing 3D datasets for the study, a systematic search has been conducted about the recent publications in computer vision-related top-tier conferences and journals, such as CVPR, ECCV, ICCV, and IEEE Transactions on Pattern Analysis and Machine Intelligence (TPAMI). Additionally, we searched relevant repositories, such as the Waymo Open Dataset, the KITTI Vision Benchmark Suite, and the ApolloScape dataset. Our search keywords included 3D object detection, monocular 3D object detection, roadside 3D dataset.

Not only datasets providing 3D object information using RGB cameras have been taken into consideration, but also those that used other methods in addition to RGB. Additionally, we limited our search to datasets designed for traffic monitoring using monocular cameras. We excluded datasets that focused on other

Table 1. Comparison of existing publicly available datasets for autonomous driving (AD) and roadside object detection, including their year of release, database type, whether the data is real or simulated, range of data, RGB resolution, number of RGB images, number of 3D boxes, presence of rain/night data, and availability to the public. The last row represents the dataset we propose in this paper.

Dataset	Year	Type	Source	Range	Resolution	Images	3D Boxes	Rain/ Night	Public?
Kitti [17]	2013	AD	Real	70 m	1392 × 512	15K	80K	No/No	Yes
KoPER [34]	2014	Roadside	Real	–	656 × 494	–	–	No/No	Yes
Apollscape [19]	2018	AD	Real	420 m	3384 × 2710	144K	70K	No/Yes	Yes
BoxCars [33]	2018	Roadside	Real	–	128 × 128	116K	116K	No/No	Yes
nuScenes [7]	2019	AD	Real	75 m	1600 × 900	1.4M	1.4M	Yes/Yes	Yes
Argoverse [10]	2019	AD	Real	200 m	1920 × 1200	22K	993K	Yes/Yes	Yes
H3D [28]	2019	AD	Real	100 m	1920 × 1200	27.7K	1M	No/No	Yes
A*3D [29]	2020	AD	Real	100 m	2048 × 1536	39K	230K	Yes/Yes	Yes
Waymo Open [35]	2020	AD	Real	75 m	1920 × 1080	230K	12M	Yes/Yes	Yes
DAiRV2X [41]	2021	AD/Other	Real	200 m	1920 × 1080	71K	1.2M	–/Yes	No
BAAI-VANJEE [13]	2021	Roadside	Real	–	1920 × 1080	5K	74K	Yes/Yes	No
ONCE [27]	2021	AD	Real	200 m	1920 × 1080	7M	417K	Yes/Yes	Yes
Rope3D [39]	2022	Roadside	Real	200 m	1920 × 1200	50K	1.5M	Yes/Yes	No
Ours	2023	Roadside	Simulated	150 m	1280 × 384	15K	39.345K	No/Yes	Yes

tasks or used different data collection methods. After conducting the search and filtering process, we identified *13* relevant datasets that met our criteria for inclusion in our study. Among them, *8* datasets were related to autonomous driving focusing on the frontal view of the road, *4* datasets were based on roadside cameras, and *1* dataset focused on autonomous driving and infrastructure. Table 1 summarizes their general characteristics.

As a second step of our study, we surveyed papers proposing monocular 3D object detection methods. Despite their efficiency, we excluded models that rely on LiDAR and point cloud data [12,20,32,38] from our study, given our focus on contexts with only monocular cameras. Additionally, we excluded models that heavily rely on external sub-networks for performing depth estimation [37] or pseudo point cloud generation [11], given the need of efficiency. Similarly to the dataset selection process, we targeted works from top-tier conferences and journals that propose an approach for monocular 3D object detection and that make that approach reproducible by sharing the source code. Based on these criteria, we were able to select four models: M3DPRN, Kinematic, SMOKE, and Monodel. All of them are autonomous driving-based models. During our search, we also found two roadside models leveraging monocular cameras [43] and [9], but unfortunately the authors did not provide any source code.

2.3   Research Context Analysis

Based on datasets and the monocular 3D object detection models we have examined, we observed that approximately about 68% of them focused on autonomous driving, assuming that DAiRV2X is an autonomous driving dataset. However we also found that only 32% of the work focused on roadside cameras. These models can be useful in various applications, such as sports analysis, traffic monitoring, security systems, road safety, and wildlife monitoring. In addition to this, we found that this area lacks publicly available datasets until the date of this study. Rope3D [39], DAiRV2X [41], BAAI-VANJEE [13] are not publicly available. On the other side, we analyzed the training and testing datasets used by the state-of-the-art models surveyed in our study. From Table 2, we observed that most of surveyed 3D monocular object detection models still rely on the KITTI dataset for their training and testing, despite the availability of diverse publicly available datasets for autonomous driving, especially those that focus on the frontal view. This might be attributed to either the pioneering role of KITTI.

Table 2. Overview of the considered 3D object detection methods.

Method	Year	Type[1]	Status[2]	Datasets	Datasets size[3]
M3DRPN [5]	2019	AD	R	KITTI [17]	3,712-3,769-7,518
Kinematic [6]	2020	AD	R	KITTI [17]	3,712-3,769-7,518
SMOKE [25]	2020	AD	R	KITTI [17]	3,712-3,769-7,518
Monodle [26]	2021	AD	R	KITTI [17]	3,712-3,769-7,518
FCOS3D [36]	2021	AD	R	nuScenes [36]	700-150-150*
UrbanNet [9]	2021	Roadside	$\overline{R}$	Synthetic Only [9]	500-0-100
Zou et al. [43]	2022	Roadside	$\overline{R}$	Real + Synthetic [43]	Synthetic: 64,000/Real: 8,000

Type[1]: AD - Autonomous driving model; Roadside - Roadside model
Status[2]: R - Reproducible model; $\overline{R}$ - Non-Reproducible.
Datasets size[3]: Training set - Validation set - Testing set.
* These values represent the ratio of the scenes instead of the dataset size.

Given all this information, and due to the lack of publicly available datasets for roadside 3D object detection and the convenience of using the same format as in KITTI, we opted to generate our own synthetic dataset with a focus on roadside 3D object contexts and to format it as the KITTI dataset. This allowed us to evaluate state-of-the-art methods (M3DRPN, Monodle, SMOKE, Kinematic - see Table 2) with our dataset smoothly. We chose synthetic data as a reference since it is cost-effective in a preliminary phase and selected Carla [14] as our platform since it is built on a foundation for learning reinforcement and imitation models, making it as simple as possible to resemble the real world.

2.4   Methods Reproduction

Data Generation. We generated the synthetic dataset using the Carla 0.9.13 simulator and placed an RGB camera at an intersection area in TOWN5. Detailed information about the software and hardware specifications can be found in the source code repository (Camera type: RGB Camera; Image resolution: 1280 × 384; Camera location: x = 10 y = 0 z = 10; Camera pitch, yaw, roll: 0; Field of view: 120). Specifically, our synthetic dataset, MonoRoadCam, is composed only of car objects at the intersection area, and includes 7,481 development images and 7,518 test images with annotations provided in the same format as the KITTI dataset. For every frame of both the development and testing sets, we ensured that at least one object is present. Each object in the dataset is defined by its type, size, location, and orientation. For simplicity, we set the occlusion and truncation levels to 0. Notably, the development images are not sequential, and the test images only include 10 continuous frames. This diversity provides a rich set of training and testing data. We extended the diversity of the dataset by incorporating three weather conditions: night, cloudy, and sunny. The statistics for the development and test sets are summarized in Table 3.

Table 3. Object size statistics in our dataset and in KITTI (car objects only).

Dataset	Statistic	Height [m]	Width [m]	Length [m]
KITTI (car object)	Average	1.53	1.63	3.53
Ours (car object)	Average	1.73	1.86	4.47
	Std. Dev.	0.49	0.50	1.38
	Min	1.20	0.33	1.49
	Max	3.83	2.89	8.47

Data Pre-processing. We generated the 3D boxes automatically in Carla. However to ensure that the data is free from any imprecise boxes, we performed data preprocessing in three steps. Firstly, we removed the boxes placed outside the road by determining the boundary of the road. Secondly, we removed too small boxes. Finally, we replaced images that did not contain any objects with other images. Figure 1 explains the data preprocessing phase in detail.

Model Creation. In our experiment, we evaluated two types of monocular 3D object detection methods: anchor-based and keypoint-based.

The anchor-based methods, Kinematic [6] and M3DRPN [5], aim to improve the accuracy of 3D estimation from a monocular camera. Kinematic incorporates uncertainty reduction, Kalman filtering, and ego-motion to extract scene dynamics. M3DRPN is built on the Faster R-CNN [31] concept and uses depth-aware concepts to improve accuracy. Both M3DRPN and Kinematic use predetermined 3D bounding boxes (i.e., *anchors*) and estimate the deviation from the anchor using offsets. On the other hand, the keypoint-based methods, Monodel [26] and SMOKE [25], do not rely on predetermined bounding boxes. Monodel focuses on

Fig. 1. Preprocessing steps for the images included in our dataset. In (a), we removed all the boxes outside the road. In (b), we removed small boxes by setting a threshold. In (c), we detected images not including any objects and replaced them. Blue (red) bounding boxes denote images before (after) preprocessing. (Color figure online)

improving dimension estimation and considering localization errors as a source of 3D detection inaccuracies. SMOKE estimates 3D objects directly without estimating the 2D bounding box. Both methods are anchor-free and use DLA34 [40] as a backbone. Despite the promising results, we decided not to include FCOS3D [36], which separates the 2D and 3D attributes of objects and redefines the centerness of objects based on the 3D center, since it required substantial steps to receive data in our required format, going beyond the scope of this study.

In addition to the monocular 3D object detection methods, we also examined two roadside methods. The first method [43] proposed 3D object detection and tracking using the point detection concept, then estimating the object's 3D pose and size. It predicts the object's 3D bottom center and uses a pre-calibrated plane-to-plane homography to lift the prediction to 3D space. The second method, UrbanNet [9], incorporated urban maps into the image to provide additional information to improve 3D estimation. Both these methods used synthetic datasets. Specifically, the first method used CARLA and UrbanNet used Grand Theft Auto V and KITTI. We excluded these methods from our analysis due to the lack of public source code and data set.

Evaluation. In order to reproduce monocular models in both the KITTI and MonoRoadCam datasets, we followed the same training/validation split protocol as proposed in [11], which is widely accepted in the field as a benchmark for evaluating the performance of monocular models. This protocol consists of 3,712 training and 3,769 validation images, and is commonly used to evaluate the performance of monocular models on the KITTI dataset. For our MonoRoad-Cam dataset, we confirmed that there were no sequential frames, but we still applied the same split protocol as in KITTI to unify the numbers of training and validation sets. This allowed us to perform a fair comparison.

For each trained model, we computed the evaluation metrics proposed and used for the KITTI dataset. Specifically, we included the 11-point and 40-point recall interpolated Average Precision (AP_{11} and AP_{40}) and the Average Orientation Similarity (AOS), which is used to measure the detector performance on rotated rectangle detection. These metrics are defined as follows.

$$AP_{11} = \frac{1}{11} \sum_{r \in 0, 0.1, \ldots, 1} p_{interp}(r), \qquad (1)$$

where $p_{interp}(r)$ is the maximum precision for any recall value $r' \geq r$.

$$AP_{40} = \frac{1}{40} \sum_{r \in 0, 0.025, \ldots, 1} p_{interp}(r), \qquad (2)$$

where $p_{interp}(r)$ is the maximum precision for any recall value $r' \geq r$.

$$AOS = \frac{1}{11} \sum_{r \in 0, 0.1, \ldots, 1} max_{r' \geq r} s(r') \qquad (3)$$

where $s(r)$ is the orientation similarity.

$$s(r) = \frac{1}{|D(r)|} \sum_{i \in D(r)} \delta_i \cdot \frac{1}{2}(cos\Delta\theta_i^{(i)} + 1) \qquad (4)$$

where $D(r)$ is all object detection at recall rate r, δ_i is a binary variable that is set to 1 if detection i has been assigned to a ground truth bounding box (overlaps by at least 50%), and $\Delta\theta_i^{(i)}$ is the difference in angle between the estimated and ground truth orientation of detection.

It should be noted that AP_{40} provides a more fine-grained evaluation than AP_{11}, by computing the precision at 40 different recall levels. AP_{11} computes precision at only 11 recall levels. Therefore, we used AP_{40} to perform a more detailed comparison of the different models. We used AP_{11} only for M3DRPN.

3   Experimental Results

3.1   RQ1: Status of Reproducibility

In Table 4, we report the full reproducibility results under the KITTI validation set for Kinematic, Monodle, M3DRPN, and SMOKE, together with the original results reported in their respective papers on the same validation set. Regarding M3DRPN, we conducted the same experiment as reported in the paper, using AP with 11 recall points, whereas for the other methods, we used 40 recall points for the AP calculation for the car object.

Our reproduced results showed a drop in performance for all the evaluated methods when compared to the same results reported in the original papers. However, on average, the decrease was not substantial, except for the SMOKE method. We conjecture that the decrease for the latter can be attributed to a misalignment in hyper-parameter values during training and decided to carefully consider this aspect while training models with SMOKE on our dataset.

Table 4. Comparison between the reproduced (*Ours*) and the original (*Orig*) results for the Kinematic, Monodle, M3DRPN, and SMOKE methods on the KITTI dataset, within the car object detection task. We report Average Precision (AP) values for both 3D and Bird's Eye (BEV) views, both at easy, moderate, and hard levels. (*) denotes AP for 11 recall points (40 recall points are used where not otherwise specified).

| Method | AP_{3D} $(IoU \geq 0.7)$ | | | | | | | | | AP_{BEV} $(IoU \geq 0.7)$ | | | | | | | | |
| | Easy | | | Mod | | | Hard | | | Easy | | | Mod | | | Hard | | |
	Ours	Orig	Gap %	Ours	Orig	Gap %	Ours	Orig	Gap %	Ours	Orig	Gap %	Ours	Orig	Gap %	Ours	Orig	Gap %
M3DRPN* [5]	14.37	20.40	−29.56	11.67	16.48	−29.19	9.23	13.34	−30.81	20.94	26.36	−20.56	15.35	21.15	−27.42	16.72	17.14	−2.45
Kinematic [6]	17.76	19.46	−8.74	13.45	14.10	−4.61	10.65	10.45	1.91	25.41	27.83	−8.70	18.79	19.72	−4.72	15.16	15.10	−0.40
SMOKE [25]	0.59	14.76	−96.00	0.58	12.85	−95.49	0.36	11.50	−96.87	1.60	19.99	−92.00	1.26	15.61	−91.93	1.21	15.28	−92.08
Monodle [26]	11.40	17.45	−34.67	9.10	13.66	−33.38	7.55	11.68	−35.36	16.97	24.97	−32.04	13.26	19.33	−31.40	11.89	17.01	−30.10

3.2 RQ2: Influence of the Context

The context in which 3D object detection methods are applied can have a significant impact on their performance. Therefore, we examined the performance of the methods, training models from scratch on our synthetic dataset. We used the Average Precision (AP) metric for both 3D object detection and bird's eye view (BEV) object detection. The results were computed separately for easy, moderate, and hard difficulty levels to provide a comprehensive evaluation.

Table 5. Comparison between the results obtained on the autonomous driving (AD) scenario (i.e., *Ours* in Table 4, calculated on the KITTI dataset) and on the roadside cameras (RC) scenario (i.e., our synthetic dataset) by the considered models, within the car object detection task. We report the Average Precision (AP) for both 3D and Bird's Eye (BEV) views, at easy, moderate, and hard levels. (*) denotes AP for 11 recall points (40 recall points are used where not otherwise specified, as in Table 4).

| Method | AP_{3D} $(IoU \geq 0.7)$ | | | | | | | | | AP_{BEV} $(IoU \geq 0.7)$ | | | | | | | | |
| | Easy | | | Mod | | | Hard | | | Easy | | | Mod | | | Hard | | |
	AD	RC	Gap %	AD	RC	Gap %	AD	RC	Gap %	AD	RC	Gap %	AD	RC	Gap %	AD	RC	Gap %
M3DRPN* [5]	14.37	51.14	255.90	11.67	50.43	332.13	9.23	50.43	446.40	20.94	54.12	158.45	15.35	53.73	250.03	16.72	53.73	221.35
Kinematic [6]	17.76	56.49	218.07	13.45	54.15	302.60	10.65	54.15	408.45	25.41	59.40	133.77	18.79	57.27	204.80	15.16	57.27	277.77
SMOKE [25]	0.59	0.15	−74.58	0.58	1.30	124.14	0.36	1.30	261.10	1.60	0.61	−61.88	1.26	6.20	392.10	1.21	6.20	412.40
Monodle [26]	11.40	10.78	−5.44	9.10	9.91	8.90	7.55	9.91	31.26	16.97	11.89	−29.94	13.26	12.59	−5.05	11.89	12.59	5.89

Table 6. Results on the validation set of our synthetic dataset using the Kinematic, Monodle, M3DRPN, and SMOKE methods. The table reports Average Precision (AP) with 40 recall points in 3D and Bird's Eye View (BEV) - the same results reported in Table 5 - column *RC*, but organized here to ease the comparison across models - and the Average Orientation Similarity (AOS) for the easy, moderate, and hard levels.

| Method | AP (IoU>=0.7) | | | | | | AOS | | |
| | Easy | | Mod | | Hard | | Easy | Mod | Hard |
	AP_{3D}	AP_{BEV}	AP_{3D}	AP_{BEV}	AP_{3D}	AP_{BEV}			
M3DRPN [5]	51.14	54.12	50.43	53.73	50.43	53.73	46.01	46.09	46.09
Kinematic [6]	**56.49**	**59.40**	**54.15**	**57.27**	**54.15**	**57.27**	45.52	46.73	46.73
SMOKE [25]	0.15	0.61	1.30	6.20	1.30	6.20	2.25	8.56	8.56
Monodle [26]	10.78	11.89	9.91	12.59	9.91	12.59	**61.53**	**63.75**	**63.75**

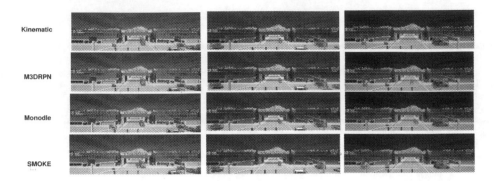

Fig. 2. Qualitative comparison across models on the validation set of our dataset.

Comparing results across contexts (autonomous driving and roadside views) in Table 5, it can be observed that most of the methods perform better on our synthetic dataset (RC) compared to our experiment in the original KITTI dataset (AD). For example, the Easy mode in the Kinematic method exhibited a substantial gap, with a score of 56.49 in our dataset compared to 17.76 in KITTI. However, it is crucial to consider the variations in object diversity between the two datasets, particularly concerning object boundaries in our CARLA environment. We specifically tested the intersection area of a single scene. Although we took precautions to prevent overlap between the training and validation sets, and even in the training and validation phases, by excluding sequential frames, it is possible that the inherent boundary characteristics from our CARLA setup could still influence the results. Furthermore, it can be observed that the performance of all methods decreases as the difficulty level increases in both datasets. This is expected as the difficulty levels correspond to objects with smaller sizes (we avoided occlusion and truncation in our dataset).

Comparing results across models (Kinematic, Monodle, M3DRPN, SMOKE) in Table 6, it can be observed that Kinematic achieved the highest performance in both AP 3D and AP BEV, with the best result being 59.40 in the Bird's Eye View easy mode. M3DRPN ranked second with strong AP scores. Conversely, despite having lower AP scores compared to Kinematic and M3DRPN, Monodle showcased impressive results in terms of AOS (63.75) under moderate and hard difficulty levels. SMOKE reported the lowest overall performance, consistently scoring lower in all metrics and difficulty levels among the four methods. Based on such results, we concluded that the models exhibit effectiveness in the roadside scenario of our synthetic dataset, especially when Kinematic is used.

3.3   RQ3: Qualitative Inspection

We finally conducted a qualitative comparison of the models, by employing specific challenging images chosen from the validation set. Images in Fig. 2 cover various scenarios involving big and small cars as well as cars in close proximity.

We found that Kinematic exhibited good projection accuracy, by accurately localizing objects within the scenes. On the other side, M3DRPN displayed a few false positives in some images (see columns 1–3). When it comes to Monodle, we noticed limitations in terms of IOU scores in columns 1–2, indicating that it struggles to precisely capture object boundaries. Furthermore, Monodle generated a false negative in column 3. Interestingly, both M3DRPN and Monodle detected truncated objects in column 2. As for SMOKE, we observed some limitations in terms of IOU scores, false positives, and false negatives. Notably, the latter faced noticeable challenges in accurately detecting larger cars.

4   Conclusions and Future Work

In this study, we shed a light on the scarcity of publicly available datasets for 3D object detection from monocular cameras in roadside contexts. To address this issue, we introduced a synthetic dataset generated through the CARLA simulator, which is compatible with the popular KITTI format and can be seamlessly integrated into existing frameworks. Furthermore, we showed the feasibility of our dataset by verifying the reproducibility of state-of-the-art monocular autonomous driving models on roadside contexts, yielding promising initial results.

Our findings suggest that our synthetic dataset could serve as a valuable resource for researchers and practitioners in the field of autonomous driving, facilitating the development and evaluation of 3D object detection algorithms for roadside scenarios. Therefore, as next steps, from a data perspective, we plan to extend the generated dataset with more examples and situations and to explore innovative ways for gathering real-world annotated datasets. From a methodological perspective, we plan to devise models that can lead to more effective and efficient computation under the considered roadside scenario. Finally, to assess the impact of our work on the real world, we plan to run applicative studies involving local municipalities.

Acknowledgements. We acknowledge financial support under the National Recovery and Resilience Plan (NRRP), Mission 4 Component 2 Investment 1.5 - Call for tender No.3277 published on December 30, 2021 by the Italian Ministry of University and Research (MUR) funded by the European Union - NextGenerationEU. Project Code ECS0000038 - Project Title e.INS Ecosystem of Innovation for Next Generation Sardinia - CUP F53C22000430001- Grant Assignment Decree No. 1056 adopted on June 23, 2022 by the MUR.

References

1. Atzori, A., Barra, S., Carta, S., Fenu, G., Podda, A.S.: HEIMDALL: an AI-based infrastructure for traffic monitoring and anomalies detection. In: 19th IEEE International Conference on Pervasive Computing and Communications Workshops and other Affiliated Events, PerCom Workshops 2021, Kassel, Germany, 22–26 March 2021, pp. 154–159. IEEE (2021). https://doi.org/10.1109/PerComWorkshops51409.2021.9431052

2. Atzori, A., Fenu, G., Marras, M.: Explaining bias in deep face recognition via image characteristics. In: IEEE International Joint Conference on Biometrics, IJCB 2022, Abu Dhabi, United Arab Emirates, 10–13 October 2022, pp. 1–10. IEEE (2022). https://doi.org/10.1109/IJCB54206.2022.10007937

3. Atzori, A., Fenu, G., Marras, M.: Demographic bias in low-resolution deep face recognition in the wild. IEEE J. Sel. Top. Signal Process. **17**(3), 599–611 (2023). https://doi.org/10.1109/JSTSP.2023.3249485

4. Balia, R., Barra, S., Carta, S., Fenu, G., Podda, A.S., Sansoni, N.: A deep learning solution for integrated traffic control through automatic license plate recognition. In: Gervasi, O., et al. (eds.) ICCSA 2021, Part III. LNCS, vol. 12951, pp. 211–226. Springer, Cham (2021). https://doi.org/10.1007/978-3-030-86970-0_16

5. Brazil, G., Liu, X.: M3D-RPN: monocular 3D region proposal network for object detection. In: 2019 IEEE/CVF International Conference on Computer Vision, ICCV 2019, Seoul, Korea (South), 27 October–2 November 2019, pp. 9286–9295. IEEE (2019). https://doi.org/10.1109/ICCV.2019.00938

6. Brazil, G., Pons-Moll, G., Liu, X., Schiele, B.: Kinematic 3D object detection in monocular video. In: Vedaldi, A., Bischof, H., Brox, T., Frahm, J.-M. (eds.) ECCV 2020, Part XXIII. LNCS, vol. 12368, pp. 135–152. Springer, Cham (2020). https://doi.org/10.1007/978-3-030-58592-1_9

7. Caesar, H., et al.: nuScenes: a multimodal dataset for autonomous driving. CoRR abs/1903.11027 (2019). https://arxiv.org/abs/1903.11027

8. Cao, J., Cholakkal, H., Anwer, R.M., Khan, F.S., Pang, Y., Shao, L.: D2Det: towards high quality object detection and instance segmentation. In: 2020 IEEE/CVF Conference on Computer Vision and Pattern Recognition, CVPR 2020, Seattle, WA, USA, 13–19 June 2020, pp. 11482–11491. Computer Vision Foundation/IEEE (2020). https://doi.org/10.1109/CVPR42600.2020.01150

9. Carrillo, J., Waslander, S.L.: UrbanNet: leveraging urban maps for long range 3D object detection. In: 24th IEEE International Intelligent Transportation Systems Conference, ITSC 2021, Indianapolis, IN, USA, 19–22 September 2021, pp. 3799–3806. IEEE (2021). https://doi.org/10.1109/ITSC48978.2021.9564840

10. Chang, M., et al.: Argoverse: 3D tracking and forecasting with rich maps. In: IEEE Conference on Computer Vision and Pattern Recognition, CVPR 2019, Long Beach, CA, USA, 16–20 June 2019, pp. 8748–8757. Computer Vision Foundation/IEEE (2019). https://doi.org/10.1109/CVPR.2019.00895

11. Chen, X., et al.: 3D object proposals for accurate object class detection. In: Cortes, C., Lawrence, N.D., Lee, D.D., Sugiyama, M., Garnett, R. (eds.) Advances in Neural Information Processing Systems 28: Annual Conference on Neural Information Processing Systems 2015, 7–12 December 2015, Montreal, Quebec, Canada, pp. 424–432 (2015). https://proceedings.neurips.cc/paper/2015/hash/6da37dd3139aa4d9aa55b8d237ec5d4a-Abstract.html

12. Chen, Y., Liu, S., Shen, X., Jia, J.: Fast point R-CNN. In: 2019 IEEE/CVF International Conference on Computer Vision, ICCV 2019, Seoul, Korea (South), 27 October–2 November 2019, pp. 9774–9783. IEEE (2019). https://doi.org/10.1109/ICCV.2019.00987

13. Deng, Y., et al.: BAAI-VANJEE roadside dataset: towards the connected automated vehicle highway technologies in challenging environments of china. CoRR abs/2105.14370 (2021). https://arxiv.org/abs/2105.14370

14. Dosovitskiy, A., Ros, G., Codevilla, F., López, A.M., Koltun, V.: CARLA: an open urban driving simulator. In: 1st Annual Conference on Robot Learning, CoRL 2017, Mountain View, California, USA, 13–15 November 2017, Proceedings. Proceedings of Machine Learning Research, vol. 78, pp. 1–16. PMLR (2017). https://proceedings.mlr.press/v78/dosovitskiy17a.html

15. Fenu, G., Marras, M.: Controlling user access to cloud-connected mobile applications by means of biometrics. IEEE Cloud Comput. **5**(4), 47–57 (2018). https://doi.org/10.1109/MCC.2018.043221014

16. Fenu, G., Marras, M., Medda, G., Meloni, G.: Causal reasoning for algorithmic fairness in voice controlled cyber-physical systems. Pattern Recognit. Lett. **168**, 131–137 (2023). https://doi.org/10.1016/j.patrec.2023.03.014

17. Geiger, A., Lenz, P., Urtasun, R.: Are we ready for autonomous driving? the KITTI vision benchmark suite. In: 2012 IEEE Conference on Computer Vision and Pattern Recognition, Providence, RI, USA, 16–21 June 2012, pp. 3354–3361. IEEE Computer Society (2012). https://doi.org/10.1109/CVPR.2012.6248074

18. He, K., Gkioxari, G., Dollár, P., Girshick, R.B.: Mask R-CNN. CoRR abs/1703.06870 (2017). https://arxiv.org/abs/1703.06870

19. Huang, X., et al.: The ApolloScape dataset for autonomous driving. In: 2018 IEEE Conference on Computer Vision and Pattern Recognition Workshops, CVPR Workshops 2018, Salt Lake City, UT, USA, 18–22 June 2018, pp. 954–960. Computer Vision Foundation/IEEE Computer Society (2018). https://doi.org/10.1109/CVPRW.2018.00141

20. Lang, A.H., Vora, S., Caesar, H., Zhou, L., Yang, J., Beijbom, O.: PointPillars: fast encoders for object detection from point clouds. In: IEEE Conference on Computer Vision and Pattern Recognition, CVPR 2019, Long Beach, CA, USA, 16–20 June 2019, pp. 12697–12705. Computer Vision Foundation/IEEE (2019). https://doi.org/10.1109/CVPR.2019.01298

21. Law, H., Deng, J.: CornerNet: Detecting Objects as Paired Keypoints. In: Ferrari, V., Hebert, M., Sminchisescu, C., Weiss, Y. (eds.) ECCV 2018, Part XIV. LNCS, vol. 11218, pp. 765–781. Springer, Cham (2018). https://doi.org/10.1007/978-3-030-01264-9_45

22. Li, Y., Chen, Y., Wang, N., Zhang, Z.: Scale-aware trident networks for object detection. In: 2019 IEEE/CVF International Conference on Computer Vision, ICCV 2019, Seoul, Korea (South), 27 October–2 November 2019, pp. 6053–6062. IEEE (2019). https://doi.org/10.1109/ICCV.2019.00615

23. Lin, T., Goyal, P., Girshick, R.B., He, K., Dollár, P.: Focal loss for dense object detection. In: IEEE International Conference on Computer Vision, ICCV 2017, Venice, Italy, 22–29 October 2017, pp. 2999–3007. IEEE Computer Society (2017). https://doi.org/10.1109/ICCV.2017.324

24. Liu, W., Anguelov, D., Erhan, D., Szegedy, C., Reed, S., Fu, C.-Y., Berg, A.C.: SSD: single shot multibox detector. In: Leibe, B., Matas, J., Sebe, N., Welling, M. (eds.) ECCV 2016, Part I. LNCS, vol. 9905, pp. 21–37. Springer, Cham (2016). https://doi.org/10.1007/978-3-319-46448-0_2

25. Liu, Z., Wu, Z., Tóth, R.: SMOKE: single-stage monocular 3D object detection via keypoint estimation. In: 2020 IEEE/CVF Conference on Computer Vision and Pattern Recognition, CVPR Workshops 2020, Seattle, WA, USA, 14–19 June 2020, pp. 4289–4298. Computer Vision Foundation/IEEE (2020). https://doi.org/10.1109/CVPRW50498.2020.00506

26. Ma, X., et al.: Delving into localization errors for monocular 3D object detection. In: IEEE Conference on Computer Vision and Pattern Recognition, CVPR 2021, virtual, 19–25 June 2021, pp. 4721–4730. Computer Vision Foundation/IEEE (2021). https://doi.org/10.1109/CVPR46437.2021.00469

27. Mao, J., et al.: One million scenes for autonomous driving: ONCE dataset. In: Vanschoren, J., Yeung, S. (eds.) Proceedings of the Neural Information Processing Systems Track on Datasets and Benchmarks 1, NeurIPS Datasets and Benchmarks 2021, December 2021, virtual (2021). https://datasets-benchmarks-proceedings.neurips.cc/paper/2021/hash/67c6a1e7ce56d3d6fa748ab6d9af3fd7-Abstract-round1.html

28. Patil, A., Malla, S., Gang, H., Chen, Y.: The H3D dataset for full-surround 3D multi-object detection and tracking in crowded urban scenes. In: International Conference on Robotics and Automation, ICRA 2019, Montreal, QC, Canada, 20–24 May 2019, pp. 9552–9557. IEEE (2019). https://doi.org/10.1109/ICRA.2019.8793925

29. Pham, Q.H., et al.: A*3D dataset: towards autonomous driving in challenging environments. In: Proceedings of the International Conference in Robotics and Automation (ICRA) (2020)

30. Redmon, J., Divvala, S.K., Girshick, R.B., Farhadi, A.: You only look once: unified, real-time object detection. In: 2016 IEEE Conference on Computer Vision and Pattern Recognition, CVPR 2016, Las Vegas, NV, USA, 27–30 June 2016, pp. 779–788. IEEE Computer Society (2016). https://doi.org/10.1109/CVPR.2016.91

31. Ren, S., He, K., Girshick, R.B., Sun, J.: Faster R-CNN: towards real-time object detection with region proposal networks. In: Cortes, C., Lawrence, N.D., Lee, D.D., Sugiyama, M., Garnett, R. (eds.) Advances in Neural Information Processing Systems 28: Annual Conference on Neural Information Processing Systems 2015, 7–12 December 2015, Montreal, Quebec, Canada, pp. 91–99 (2015). https://proceedings.neurips.cc/paper/2015/hash/14bfa6bb14875e45bba028a21ed38046-Abstract.html

32. Shi, S., et al.: PV-RCNN: point-voxel feature set abstraction for 3D object detection. In: 2020 IEEE/CVF Conference on Computer Vision and Pattern Recognition, CVPR 2020, Seattle, WA, USA, 13–19 June 2020, pp. 10526–10535. Computer Vision Foundation/IEEE (2020). https://doi.org/10.1109/CVPR42600.2020.01054

33. Sochor, J., Špaňhel, J., Herout, A.: BoxCars: improving fine-grained recognition of vehicles using 3-D bounding boxes in traffic surveillance. IEEE Trans. Intell. Transp. Syst. **PP**(99), 1–12 (2018). https://doi.org/10.1109/TITS.2018.2799228

34. Strigel, E., Meissner, D.A., Seeliger, F., Wilking, B., Dietmayer, K.: The Ko-PER intersection laserscanner and video dataset. In: 17th International IEEE Conference on Intelligent Transportation Systems, ITSC 2014, Qingdao, China, 8–11 October 2014, pp. 1900–1901. IEEE (2014). https://doi.org/10.1109/ITSC.2014.6957976

35. Sun, P., et al.: Scalability in perception for autonomous driving: waymo open dataset. CoRR abs/1912.04838 (2019). https://arxiv.org/abs/1912.04838

36. Wang, T., Zhu, X., Pang, J., Lin, D.: FCOS3D: fully convolutional one-stage monocular 3D object detection. In: IEEE/CVF International Conference on Computer Vision Workshops, ICCVW 2021, Montreal, BC, Canada, 11–17 October 2021, pp. 913–922. IEEE (2021). https://doi.org/10.1109/ICCVW54120.2021.00107

37. Xu, B., Chen, Z.: Multi-level fusion based 3D object detection from monocular images. In: 2018 IEEE Conference on Computer Vision and Pattern Recognition, CVPR 2018, Salt Lake City, UT, USA, 18–22 June 2018, pp. 2345–2353. Computer Vision Foundation/IEEE Computer Society (2018). https://doi.org/10.1109/CVPR.2018.00249
38. Yan, Y., Mao, Y., Li, B.: SECOND: sparsely embedded convolutional detection. Sensors **18**(10), 3337 (2018). https://doi.org/10.3390/s18103337
39. Ye, X., et al.: Rope3D: the roadside perception dataset for autonomous driving and monocular 3D object detection task. In: IEEE/CVF Conference on Computer Vision and Pattern Recognition, CVPR 2022, New Orleans, LA, USA, 18–24 June 2022, pp. 21309–21318. IEEE (2022). https://doi.org/10.1109/CVPR52688.2022.02065
40. Yu, F., Wang, D., Darrell, T.: Deep layer aggregation. CoRR abs/1707.06484 (2017). https://arxiv.org/abs/1707.06484
41. Yu, H., et al.: DAIR-V2X: a large-scale dataset for vehicle-infrastructure cooperative 3D object detection. CoRR abs/2204.05575 (2022). https://doi.org/10.48550/arXiv.2204.05575
42. Zhou, X., Wang, D., Krähenbühl, P.: Objects as points. CoRR abs/1904.07850 (2019). https://arxiv.org/abs/1904.07850
43. Zou, Z., et al.: Real-time full-stack traffic scene perception for autonomous driving with roadside cameras. In: 2022 International Conference on Robotics and Automation, ICRA 2022, Philadelphia, PA, USA, 23–27 May 2022, pp. 890–896. IEEE (2022). https://doi.org/10.1109/ICRA46639.2022.9812137

Embedding Shepard's Interpolation into CNN Models for Unguided Depth Completion

Shambel Fente Mengistu[ID], Mara Pistellato[✉][ID], and Filippo Bergamasco[ID]

DAIS, Università Ca'Foscari Venezia, 155, via Torino, Venezia, Italy
{shambel.mengistu,mara.pistellato,filippo.bergamasco}@unive.it

Abstract. When acquiring sparse data samples, an interpolation method is often needed to fill in the missing information. An example application, known as "depth completion", consists in estimating dense depth maps from sparse observations (e.g. LiDAR acquisitions). To do this, algorithmic methods fill the depth image by performing a sequence of basic image processing operations, while recent approaches propose data-driven solutions, mostly based on Convolutional Neural Networks (CNNs), to predict the missing information. In this work, we combine learning-based and classical algorithmic approaches to ideally exploit the performance of the former with the ability to generalize of the latter. First, we define a novel architecture block called IDWBlock. This component allows to embed Shepard's interpolation (or Inverse Distance Weighting, IDW) into a CNN model, with the advantage of requiring a small number of parameters regardless of the kernel size. Second, we propose two network architectures involving a combination of the IDW-Block and learning-based depth completion techniques. In the experimental section, we tested the models' performances on the KITTI depth completion benchmark and NYU-depth-v2 dataset, showing how they present strong robustness to input sparsity under different densities and patterns.

Keywords: Shepard's Interpolation · Inverse Distance Weighting · Depth Completion · CNN · Sparse convolution

1 Introduction

A dense and accurate depth map is beneficial to many computer vision tasks such as 3D object detection [3,23,33], and reconstruction [21,22,24], optical flow estimation [26,41], and semantic segmentation [37,39]. The popular LiDAR depth sensors produce reliable observations, and are widely employed in real-world applications such as autonomous driving [14] or in industrial setups [34]. However, the resulting depth maps are too sparse, with about 5% of the acquired pixels having a valid depth value [33]. For several applications such data are not sufficient, and methods aiming at densifying sparse data samples are needed.

R. Basili et al. (Eds.): AIxIA 2023, LNAI 14318, pp. 336–350, 2023.
https://doi.org/10.1007/978-3-031-47546-7_23

In this context, depth completion is usually regarded as the task of recovering an accurate dense depth map from a sparse input. The literature counts several approaches to perform depth completion, ranging from classical algorithmic methods [2,11,29] to learning-based techniques [1,10,32]. Non-learning-based approaches are based on predefined rules, do not require training data and rely only on image processing operations. However some of them, such as [11], outperform learning-based methods. Regarding learning-based approaches, state-of-the-art methods are based on deep convolutional neural networks (CNNs). When the network input is sparse and the values are irregularly distributed, applying conventional convolutions gives inaccurate results since not all the input values are actually observable [8]. There are several approaches designed to solve the input sparsity problem with CNNs. This includes the naive approach which assigns a default value to all missing pixels [12], to more effective approaches that apply sparse convolutions to weight the elements of the kernel according to a validity mask [10,32]. The former method does not lead to optimal results, as the learned filters must be invariant to all possible validity patterns. The method proposed in [32] overcomes the problem by introducing a novel sparse convolution, while Zixuan et al. [10] proposed an extension with a multi-scale encoder-decoder CNN.

In this paper, we revisit the idea of sparsity invariant convolution and propose a family of hybrid CNN architectures that mix learning-based elements and a classic interpolation technique to perform unguided depth completion (i.e. based only on depth data). Specifically, we adopt Inverse Distance Weighted (IDW) interpolation, originally presented in [29], which can be easily reformulated as a convolution operation, and embed it in a CNN. To do so, we define the novel IDWBlock, which is able to adjust IDW parameters during training according to local data sparsity and distribution of observable input samples. Such block is combined with trainable sparse convolution layers in two alternative architectures which effectively mix the two approaches in a single or multi-scale fashion. This enables the proposed hybrid model to generate a dense and accurate depth map with clear boundaries. We tested the two proposed IDW-embedding architectures on the KITTI depth completion benchmark [32] and NYU-depth-v2 dataset [30] and show that they offer a more accurate reconstruction with respect to the simple sparse convolution approach.

2   Related Work

Data Interpolation. The problem of scattered data interpolation consists in fitting a continuous function of two or more independent variables that interpolates values that are measured at some scattered points. The sparse observations can be located in a grid or can be distributed with a non-uniform pattern, making the task even more challenging. A considerable number of methods have been proposed to perform this task, from early approaches [7] to more recent solutions [20]. The inverse distance weighted (IDW) interpolation, also known as Shepard's method [29] consists in computing the values of missing points as a weighted average of the observed points, with weights being a power of the inverse of their distance. The authors of [19] applied inverse distance weighted interpolation for topographic surface modeling, while in [6] it is used for particulate matter (PM) estimation and mapping. Another popular method is based on radial basis function (RBF) [31,36,42]. In these approaches the interpolant is a weighted sum of radial basis functions (e.g. Gaussian, polynomial), that depend only on the distance between the input and a fixed point. Since the technique involves the solution of a linear system that depend on the number of points, it is unpractical in real-world applications due to computational complexity.

Depth Completion. Depth completion task is a specific instance of data interpolation, where observations are scattered depth data and the goal is to recover dense depth maps. Depth completion approaches can be classified into different categories, depending on different criteria. The first categorization for depth completion methods is algorithmic or learning-based. Learning-based approaches are typically based on deep neural networks, whereas algorithmic solutions rely on a sequence of image processing techniques. Ku et al. [11] proposed to use of a sequence of well-known image processing algorithms to transform the sparse input into dense depth maps. The proposed work first utilizes morphological operations, such as dilation and closure, to make the input depth map denser, and then fills holes to obtain the final output. Based on the input data, depth completion algorithms can be divided into *guided* and *non-guided*: the former method works with an aligned RGB image used as a guide in addition to the sparse input, while the latter only works on the sparse input. Fangchang M. et al. [16] used color images as guidance in their proposed model that learns a direct mapping from sparse depth to dense depth. Alex W. et al. [35] introduced a method to infer dense depth from camera motion and sparse depth using a visual inertia odometry system, while other works [27,38] applied a transformer-based architecture to produce a dense depth map from the given RGB image and sparse input. Fabian M. et al. [18] used a segmentation map instead of RGB image as guidance in their vgg05-like architecture. Other papers proposed by Uhrig et al. [32], Huang et al. [10], and Chodosh N. et al. [5] used the sparse depth only for depth completion, and thus are classified as non-guided. To handle sparse inputs and sparse intermediate feature maps, Uhring et al [32] proposed a non-guided sparsity-invariant convolution to replace the conventional convolution in CNNs. The sparsity-invariant CNN involves sparse convolution layers which weight the kernel elements according to the pixel validity. Additionally, a second stream carries information about the pixel validity to subsequent layers. Huang et al. [10] proposed three novel sparsity-invariant operations, based on which, a sparsity-invariant multi-scale encoder-decoder network (HMS-Net) is proposed to handle sparse data at different scales. Additional RGB features could also be incorporated to further improve the performance.

3   Combining IDW and Sparsity-Invariant CNNs

We start by discussing how Shepard's interpolation can be expressed in terms of convolutions. Then, we observe how a recent approach based on Convolutional Neural Network can be seen as a special case of such an interpolation algorithm, but with trainable kernel weights. Therefore, we describe how to combine the two so that the learnable part can be trained with a reduced number of parameters regardless of the network receptive field size.

3.1   Inverse Distance Weighted Interpolation

Inverse Distance Weighted (IDW) interpolation, also known as Shepard's method, is an old yet effective spatial interpolation approach for scattered data [29]. It creates estimates for locations without data based on values at nearby locations. The advantage of IDW interpolation includes its simplicity, ease of use, and fast execution time [13].

Suppose to have a scattered set of 2D point samples $\mathbf{x}_1, \ldots, \mathbf{x}_N$ with associated values $v_1, \ldots, v_N$. Such values can represent any scalar field of interest, from terrain elevation of some topographic data to temperature values measured by an array of thermometers in an area. The IDW principle is to interpolate the value at any point $\hat{\mathbf{x}}$ as a weighted average of the values at the neighboring points. Weights are computed according to the distance between $\hat{\mathbf{x}}$ to each sampling point $\mathbf{x}_i, i = 1, \ldots, N$ as:

$$w_p(\hat{\mathbf{x}}, \mathbf{x}_i) = \frac{1}{\left(\sqrt{\hat{\mathbf{x}}^T \mathbf{x}_i}\right)^p} \tag{1}$$

where $p \geq 0$ is a free parameter that governs the relative importance to the point closer to $\hat{\mathbf{x}}$ with respect to the ones farther away.

To get the interpolated value $\hat{v}$ at a point $\hat{\mathbf{x}}$, IDW simply computes the weighted average:

$$\hat{v} = \begin{cases} \dfrac{\displaystyle\sum_{i=1}^{N} w_p(\hat{\mathbf{x}}, \mathbf{x}_i) v_i}{\displaystyle\sum_{i=1}^{N} w_p(\hat{\mathbf{x}}, \mathbf{x}_i)}, & \text{if } \hat{\mathbf{x}}^T \mathbf{x} \neq 0 \ \forall i \\[4mm] v_i, & \text{if } \hat{\mathbf{x}}^T \mathbf{x} = 0 \text{ for some } i. \end{cases} \tag{2}$$

Note that if $\hat{\mathbf{x}}$ coincides with any of the given points, the interpolated value is given directly by v_i since $w(\hat{\mathbf{x}}, \mathbf{x}_i)$ would be undefined in that case. This also agrees with the mathematical definition of "interpolation" which provides a continuous function passing exactly at the given samples. It is easy to observe that the higher the value of p, the more $\hat{v}$ will converge to the value of the nearest neighbour of $\hat{\mathbf{x}}$, as its relative weight will dominate the others. On the other hand, small values of p tend to produce a smoother interpolation since $\hat{v}$ is averaged among several neighbouring values. In the extreme case, when $p = 0$, all the interpolated values will be equal to the average of the given values $v_1 \ldots v_N$. The original formulation described so far can be used for any scattered point set but involve the computation of distances between the interpolated points and the given data points. Since we are dealing with sparse depth images, point coordinates are restricted to the image lattice. In such a case, we can precompute the weights among pixel pairs at certain distances and perform the same operation in terms of convolutions.

Let S be the size of a sparse depth image I^1. Let M be a binary mask of the same size of I containing 1 for each valid pixel in I and 0 for the missing values. We can compute the $S \times S$ correlation kernel:

$$
\mathcal{K}_{S,p} = \begin{pmatrix} k_{-\frac{S}{2},-\frac{S}{2}} & \cdots & k_{\frac{S}{2},-\frac{S}{2}} \\ \vdots & \ddots & \vdots \\ k_{-\frac{S}{2},\frac{S}{2}} & \cdots & k_{\frac{S}{2},\frac{S}{2}} \end{pmatrix}, \quad k_{i,j} = \begin{cases} 0, & \text{if } i = 0 \wedge j = 0 \\ w_p\left((i\ j)^T, \mathbf{0} \right), & \text{otherwise} \end{cases} \tag{3}
$$

weighting the contribution of the neighbouring pixels with respect to the center of the kernel. For example, $\mathcal{K}_{3,1} = \begin{pmatrix} \frac{1}{\sqrt{2}} & 1 & \frac{1}{\sqrt{2}} \\ 1 & 0 & 1 \\ \frac{1}{\sqrt{2}} & 1 & \frac{1}{\sqrt{2}} \end{pmatrix}$.

It is easy to see that the interpolation in (2) can be expressed in terms of convolution as follows:

$$
\hat{I} = M \cdot I + (1 - M) \cdot \frac{I \star \mathcal{K}}{M \star \mathcal{K}} \tag{4}
$$

Since $\mathcal{M}$ is a binary mask, $\mathcal{M} \star \mathcal{K}$ computes the sum of the weights for each given sample used to normalize the weighted average defined in (2). To enforce the resulting value to be equal to v_i at each sample $\mathbf{x}_i$, the interpolated value is overwritten by the original value in I by the linear combination with the binary mask. For this reason, it has to be noted that $\mathcal{K}(0,0)$ can be chosen arbitrarily without affecting the resulting $\hat{I}$ since each produced value is overwritten every time the convolution kernel is centered on a given sample.

Considering IDW in terms of convolutions allows us to modify its formulation providing an additional parameter controlling the resulting interpolation. Indeed, the described operation is well-defined even if the size of the kernel is smaller than S. In that case, instead of computing the value in $\hat{\mathbf{x}}$ as the weighted average of all the given samples, we restrict the average to the neighbouring samples closer to $\hat{\mathbf{x}}$ by half the kernel size. This allows the control of the interpolation "receptive field" to limit the contribution of samples farther away even with low power values. We define the Convolutional-IDW interpolator as follows:

$$
\text{CIDW}_{s,p}(I, M) = M \cdot I + (1 - M) \cdot \frac{I \star \mathcal{K}_{s,p}}{(M + \epsilon) \star \mathcal{K}_{s,p}} \tag{5}
$$

---

[1] We can assume without loss of generality that I is square and that $S = 2a+1, a \in \mathbb{N}$. If that is not the case, I can be padded with zeros to meet such condition.

where $\epsilon > 0$ is a small constant to avoid division by zero. Since $s < S$, CIDW will not produce a valid value if no sample falls within the area encompassed by the convolution kernel. Therefore, the interpolation produced by the function is undefined in all the pixels where the output mask $M' = \text{sign}(M \star \mathcal{K}_{s,p})$ is zero.

3.2 Sparsity-Invariant CNNs

The sparsity-invariant CNNs proposed in [32] is an effective way to modify conventional convolutions in a CNN to handle sparse input feature maps (i.e. when the input layer $\mathbf{x}$ can only be partially observed at the locations in which the binary mask $\mathbf{m}$ is 1). The sparsity-invariant convolution is formulated as:

$$f_{u,v}(\mathbf{x}, \mathbf{m}) = \frac{\displaystyle\sum_{i,j=-a}^{a} m(u+i, v+j) x(u+i, v+j) w(i,j)}{\displaystyle\sum_{i,j=-a}^{a} m(u+i, v+j) + \epsilon} + b \qquad (6)$$

where $\mathbf{w}$ is a learnable kernel of size $(2a + 1) \times (2a + 1)$, b is a scalar bias, and ϵ is again a small constant to avoid division by zero at locations where none of the input values are observed.

Such formulation can be seen as a generalized version of CIDW in which the weights are fully trainable instead of being a function of samples' location as in (1). However, the normalization component is conceptually different. In CIDW we compute the weighted arithmetic mean of input values with the kernel values. In the sparsity-invariant convolution, instead, the linear combination between input and weights is normalized by the number of observed values encompassed by the kernel, regardless of the weights' values. Also in the case of sparse convolutions, some output values might be invalid. The authors propose to produce the output mask by doing a max-pooling operation with a unitary stride and the same kernel size as the one used for the convolution. This produces the same result as computing the output mask M' as we described before.

3.3 IDWBlock: Embedding CIDW in a Sparse CNN

Since the Shepard's interpolation can be formulated in terms of convolutions (as shown in Eq. 5), we studied the idea of embedding such operation into a classical CNN model. In particular, we define a new architectural block, called IDWBlock, with a limited set of parameters that learns the optimal way to combine a set of $CIDW$ outputs performed with different trainable power values $p_1 \ldots p_N$.

The architecture of an IDWBlock is sketched in Fig. 1. The upper part performs several CIDW operations with different combinations of kernel sizes and power values. Kernel sizes are hard-coded into the block architecture and therefore cannot be trained. We observed that 5×5, 17×17, and 37×37 are good values for the most popular datasets for depth completion. For each kernel size, CIDW is executed with a set of different power values. Specifically, the 5×5

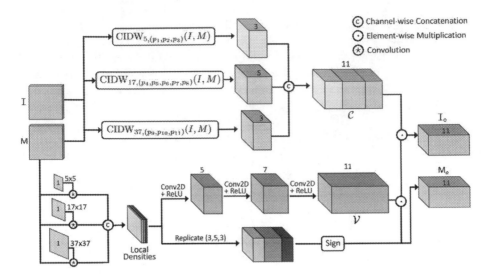

Fig. 1. The Proposed IDWBlock architecture. See text for details.

kernel is applied with 3 power values (p_1, p_2, p_3), the 17×17 with 4 power values and 37×37 with 3. All the $p_1, \ldots, p_{11}$ are randomly chosen at the beginning and optimized during the training together with all other network weights. Outputs of each of the 11 CIDW operations are stacked depth-wise to produce a $W \times H \times 11$ tensor C, where W, H are the width and height of the input image.

The lower part of the block learns the relative importance of the produced CIDW outputs C according to the local density of the given samples. Indeed, we expect that the optimal combination of CIDW kernel size and power value is significantly different if the input samples are very close or far away in a certain region. To approximate the density, we convolve the input binary mask M with unitary (non-trainable) kernels with size 5×5, 17×17, and 37×37. Outputs are stacked together in a $W \times H \times 3$ tensor and processed with a classical feed-forward convolutional network to expand into a $W \times H \times 11$ tensor V representing the relative weight of each CIDW output for each pixel. Since some of the CIDW outputs might be invalid (especially with small kernels), we must force the corresponding weights to zero. The validity information corresponds to pixels where the local density for a certain kernel size is greater than zero. Therefore, we compute the sign of local densities and multiply it element-wise to V. Finally, CIDW outputs are rescaled with the element-wise product $C \odot V$, and the resulting I_o is returned with the per-element validity information M_o.

3.4   Adding IDWBlock into Sparsity Invariant CNNs

We propose two different ways to arrange IDWBlocks in a sparsity invariant CNN. The first (IDWNet) is sketched in Fig. 2 and contains just a single IDW-Block used in parallel with a sequence of sparse convolutions (SparseConv) followed by ReLU activations, as described in [32]. Output images of the IDWBlock are concatenated with the output feature maps of the SparseConvs, as well as the respective output masks. To match the channelwise dimension of the IDWBlock mask, the one-channel SparseConv mask is replicated before concatenation. After the concatenation, the resulting multi-channel I and M tensors are processed with additional SparseConv blocks to obtain the final interpolated image. Note that, at this point, within the SparseConv module the input multi-channel mask is squeezed into a single-channel mask by channel-wise summation followed by sign operation: this is done because a single-channel mask with max-pooling operation is propagated from layer to layer as proposed in [32].

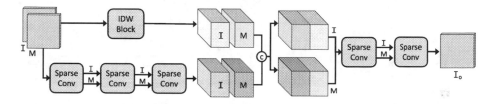

Fig. 2. IDWNet architecture. The input is processed by our IDW block and by a sequence of three trainable sparse convolution layers. Results are concatenated and processed by a second sequence of sparse convolutions.

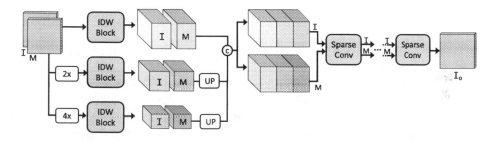

Fig. 3. MS-IDWNet architecture. Input is processed at different scales (original, 2× and 4×) and concatenated. Dense output is produced by a sequence of sparse convolutions.

The second architecture (MS-IDWNet) is shown in Fig. 3. This time we investigated a multi-scale arrangement in which three parallel IDWBlocks are fed with the original input image and a 2×, 4× down-scaled version respectively. Downscaling is performed by doing average pooling on both the image and the mask and then normalizing the obtained image with the down-scaled mask. The effect is equivalent as computing the average only on valid samples. For the up-scaling, we perform a nearest-neighbour interpolation on both the image and the mask. The two operations are not trainable. Finally, outputs of all the IDWBlocks are concatenated and fed to a sequence of sparse convolutions as in the previous architecture.

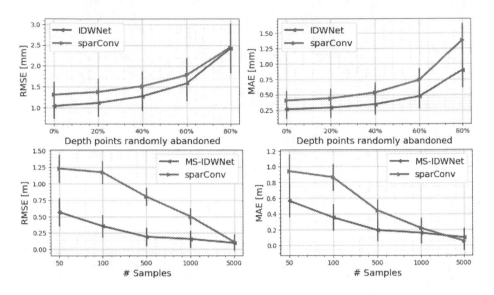

Fig. 4. Testing robustness of our method varying input sparsity levels. First row shows results on KITTI depth completion benchmark: the values on x-axis show the percentage of randomly abandoned input points. Second row shows the same evaluation on NYU dataset for different sparsity levels (number of input samples).

4   Experimental Section

To evaluate our approach, we conducted our experiments on both the KITTI depth completion dataset and NYU-depth-v2 dataset.

KITTI-Depth dataset [32] includes sparse depth maps (5% of the pixels available) from projected LiDAR point clouds that were matched against the stereo cameras. The dataset has 86k training images, 7k validation images, and 1k test set images with no access to the ground truth. We used all the 86k depth maps for training and a validation subset of 1k images for evaluation. As the top part of the images have no valid values, we removed the top 103 rows and center crop for training and validation. For testing, we used the original image size.

NYU-depth-v2 [30] is an RGB-D dataset for indoor scenes, captured with a Microsoft Kinect with size 640 × 480. Similarly to [4,17], we used the official split with roughly 48k images for the training and 654 for testing. Each input image was randomly sampled with a uniform distribution.

We trained both our models on an NVIDIA GeForce RTX 4080 using the Mean Squared Error (MSE) loss function. All parameters were randomly initialized and updated with ADAM optimizer configured with an initial learning rate of 0.01. During the train we applied the Learning rate decaying equation described in [10]. In all our experiments we used the proposed IDWNet (Fig. 2) for the KITTY dataset and MS-IDWNet (Fig. 3) for NYU-depth-v2.

4.1   Evaluation

We started by testing the effect of different input sparsity for our technique. Figure 4 shows the reconstruction error varying the test set sparsity. Plots on the left show Root Mean Squared Error (RMSE), while plots on the right display the MAE. The first row analyses the behaviour when abandoning an increasing number of points on KITTI dataset. The subsampling was performed by randomly deleting samples with an increasing probability (from 0 to 0.8), keeping the points distribution consistent with the original data by performing the operation with a sliding window. We compared our IDWNet (combining CIDW blocks with sparse convolutions) with the sparsity invariant CNN as described in [32]. Our proposed model exhibits a consistent improvement in terms of both MAE and RMSE at any density level. The second row shows the same experiment performed on NYU dataset: since ground truth is dense, we uniformly sampled the data to obtain different sparsity levels (from 50 up to 5000 points per image). Also in this case, our approach performs better with respect to the sparse convolutions approach, since IDWBlock is able to adapt to different sparsity levels, even for significantly sparser samples.

Table 1 reports quantitative results of our IDWNet versus other encoder-decoder and unguided depth completion techniques on the KITTI validation set. We report the RMSE and MAE values (in mm) for U-Net [28], FRRN [25], PSPNet [40], FPN [15], He et al. [9], HMS-Net [10] and SparseConv [32]. Our approach performs better with respect to other methods, and it is comparable with the HMS-Net architecture (especially the MAE), which however involves a complex multi-scale structure. Table 2 reports comparisons on NYU test set while handling very sparse inputs (200 and 500 samples). In this case, we included the Sparse-to-dense [16] and SPN [4] that were designed to work well with a low number of samples (with and without RGB guidance). Also for this case,

Table 1. Comparisons of different methods against the validation set of the KITTI dataset [32]. Data of SegGuided [18] is as reported in the paper, Other competing methods are as reported in [10].

Method	RMSE (mm)	MAE (mm)
U-Net [28]	1387.35	445.73
FRRN [25]	1148.27	338.56
PSPNet [40]	1185.39	354.21
FPN [15]	1441.82	473.65
He et al. [9]	1056.39	293.86
HMS-Net [10]	994.14	262.41
SegGuided [18]	1146.78	278.75
SparseConv [32]	1314.23	409.17
IDWNet (our)	1045.34	265.08

Table 2. Errors by different methods on NYU-DEPTH-V2 test set. The values are taken from their respective papers. "w/RGB" indicates RGB image used.

	Method	RMSE (m)	REL (m)	δ_1	δ_2	δ_3
200 points	SparseConv [32]	1.065	0.257	0.550	0.752	0.880
	Sparse-to-dense [16]	0.259	0.054	0.963	0.992	0.998
	HMS-Net [10]	0.233	0.044	—	—	—
	MS-IDWNet (our)	0.255	0.055	0.955	0.991	0.988
500 points	SparseConv [32]	0.801	0.159	0.739	0.861	0.933
	Sparse-to-dense [16] w/RGB	0.230	0.044	0.971	0.994	0.998
	SPN [4] w/RGB	0.162	0.027	0.985	0.997	0.999
	MS-IDWNet (our)	0.190	0.038	0.975	0.996	0.999

our method shows good results against other state of the art methods while exhibiting a substantially simpler architecture.

Finally, Fig. 5 and Fig. 6 display qualitative outputs on KITTI and NYU datasets respectively. In both the cases, we compare our approach with the sparsity invariant CNN as we did for the experiment shown in Fig. 4. In general, we observe that our multi-scale IDW architecture offers sharper edges with respect to the results obtained from SparseConv.

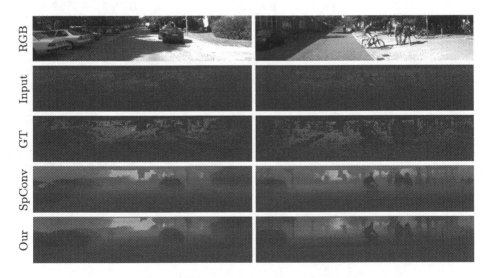

Fig. 5. Visual qualitative example of the result obtained on the KITTI validation set by our method and the Sparsity Invariant CNN (SpConv) [32].

Fig. 6. Visual results for IDWNet and sparseConv [32] from NYU dataset. Our IDWNet produces objects with sharp and clear boundaries.

5 Conclusions

In this paper we proposed two CNN architectures for unguided depth completion. Both models includes the novel IDWBlock, which embeds Shepard's interpolation with sparse convolutions. We show that by mixing algorithmic and learning-based interpolation approaches can offer better performances with a minimal increase in the number of training parameters. Moreover, our approach predicts accurate depths, without requiring different treatment for different sparsity levels. Experimental results showed the advantage of the proposed method for depth completion without adding too much complexity.

References

1. Alhashim, I., Wonka, P.: High quality monocular depth estimation via transfer learning. ArXiv abs/1812.11941 (2018)
2. Barron, J.T., Poole, B.: The fast bilateral solver. ArXiv abs/1511.03296 (2015)
3. Chen, X., Kundu, K., Zhang, Z., Ma, H., Fidler, S., Urtasun, R.: Monocular 3D object detection for autonomous driving. In: 2016 IEEE Conference on Computer Vision and Pattern Recognition (CVPR), pp. 2147–2156 (2016). https://doi.org/10.1109/CVPR.2016.236
4. Cheng, X., Wang, P., Yang, R.: Depth estimation via affinity learned with convolutional spatial propagation network. In: European Conference on Computer Vision (2018)
5. Chodosh, N., Wang, C., Lucey, S.: Deep convolutional compressed sensing for lidar depth completion. ArXiv abs/1803.08949 (2018)
6. Choi, K., Chong, K.: Modified inverse distance weighting interpolation for particulate matter estimation and mapping. Atmosphere **13**(5), 846 (2022). https://doi.org/10.3390/atmos13050846. https://www.mdpi.com/2073-4433/13/5/846
7. Franke, R.: Scattered data interpolation: tests of some methods. Math. Comput. **38**(157), 181–200 (1982)
8. Gasparetto, A., et al.: Cross-dataset data augmentation for convolutional neural networks training. In: 2018 24th International Conference on Pattern Recognition (ICPR), pp. 910–915. IEEE (2018). https://doi.org/10.1109/ICPR.2018.8545812
9. He, L., Wang, G., Hu, Z.: Learning depth from single images with deep neural network embedding focal length. IEEE Trans. Image Process. **27**(9), 4676–4689 (2018)
10. Huang, Z., Fan, J., Cheng, S., Yi, S., Wang, X., Li, H.: HMS-Net: hierarchical multi-scale sparsity-invariant network for sparse depth completion. IEEE Trans. Image Process. **29**, 3429–3441 (2018)
11. Ku, J., Harakeh, A., Waslander, S.L.: In defense of classical image processing: fast depth completion on the CPU. In: 2018 15th Conference on Computer and Robot Vision (CRV), pp. 16–22 (2018). https://doi.org/10.1109/CRV.2018.00013
12. Li, B., Zhang, T., Xia, T.: Vehicle detection from 3D Lidar using fully convolutional network. ArXiv abs/1608.07916 (2016)
13. Li, J., Heap, A.D.: A review of comparative studies of spatial interpolation methods in environmental sciences: performance and impact factors. Ecol. Inform. **6**(3), 228–241 (2011). https://doi.org/10.1016/j.ecoinf.2010.12.003. https://www.sciencedirect.com/science/article/pii/S1574954110001147
14. Li, Y., Ibanez-Guzman, J.: Lidar for autonomous driving: the principles, challenges, and trends for automotive lidar and perception systems. IEEE Signal Process. Mag. **37**(4), 50–61 (2020)
15. Lin, T.Y., Dollár, P., Girshick, R., He, K., Hariharan, B., Belongie, S.: Feature pyramid networks for object detection. In: Proceedings of the IEEE Conference on Computer Vision and Pattern Recognition, pp. 2117–2125 (2017)

16. Ma, F., Cavalheiro, G.V., Karaman, S.: Self-supervised sparse-to-dense: self-supervised depth completion from lidar and monocular camera. In: 2019 International Conference on Robotics and Automation (ICRA), pp. 3288–3295 (2018)

17. Ma, F., Karaman, S.: Sparse-to-dense: depth prediction from sparse depth samples and a single image. In: 2018 IEEE International Conference on Robotics and Automation (ICRA), pp. 1–8 (2017)

18. Märkert, F., Sunkel, M., Haselhoff, A., Rudolph, S.: Segmentation-guided domain adaptation for efficient depth completion. ArXiv abs/2210.09213 (2022). https://api.semanticscholar.org/CorpusID:252918440

19. Mulkal, M., Wandi, R.: Inverse distance weight spatial interpolation for topographic surface 3D modelling. TECHSI - Jurnal Teknik Informatika **11**, 385 (2019). https://doi.org/10.29103/techsi.v11i3.1934

20. Nielson, R., Franke, R.: Scattered data interpolation and applications: a tutorial and survey. In: Hagen, H., Roller, D. (eds.) Geometric Modeling. Computer Graphics – Systems and Applications, pp. 131–160. Springer, Heidelberg (2012). https://doi.org/10.1007/978-3-642-76404-2_6

21. Pistellato, M., Albarelli, A., Bergamasco, F., Torsello, A.: Robust joint selection of camera orientations and feature projections over multiple views. In: Proceedings - International Conference on Pattern Recognition, pp. 3703–3708 (2016). https://doi.org/10.1109/ICPR.2016.7900210

22. Pistellato, M., Bergamasco, F., Albarelli, A., Torsello, A.: Dynamic optimal path selection for 3D triangulation with multiple cameras. In: Murino, V., Puppo, E. (eds.) ICIAP 2015. LNCS, vol. 9279, pp. 468–479. Springer, Cham (2015). https://doi.org/10.1007/978-3-319-23231-7_42

23. Pistellato, M., Bergamasco, F., Albarelli, A., Torsello, A.: Robust cylinder estimation in point clouds from pairwise axes similarities. In: ICPRAM 2019 - Proceedings of the 8th International Conference on Pattern Recognition Applications and Methods, pp. 640–647 (2019). https://doi.org/10.5220/0007401706400647

24. Pistellato, M., Cosmo, L., Bergamasco, F., Gasparetto, A., Albarelli, A.: Adaptive albedo compensation for accurate phase-shift coding. In: 2018 24th International Conference on Pattern Recognition (ICPR), pp. 2450–2455. IEEE (2018). https://doi.org/10.1109/ICPR.2018.8545465

25. Pohlen, T., Hermans, A., Mathias, M., Leibe, B.: Full-resolution residual networks for semantic segmentation in street scenes. In: Proceedings of the IEEE Conference on Computer Vision and Pattern Recognition, pp. 4151–4160 (2017)

26. Ranjan, A., et al.: Competitive collaboration: joint unsupervised learning of depth, camera motion, optical flow and motion segmentation. In: 2019 IEEE/CVF Conference on Computer Vision and Pattern Recognition (CVPR), pp. 12232–12241 (2019). https://doi.org/10.1109/CVPR.2019.01252

27. Rho, K., Ha, J., Kim, Y.: GuideFormer: transformers for image guided depth completion. In: 2022 IEEE/CVF Conference on Computer Vision and Pattern Recognition (CVPR), pp. 6240–6249 (2022). https://doi.org/10.1109/CVPR52688.2022.00615

28. Ronneberger, O., Fischer, P., Brox, T.: U-Net: convolutional networks for biomedical image segmentation. In: Navab, N., Hornegger, J., Wells, W.M., Frangi, A.F. (eds.) MICCAI 2015. LNCS, vol. 9351, pp. 234–241. Springer, Cham (2015). https://doi.org/10.1007/978-3-319-24574-4_28

29. Shepard, D.: A two-dimensional interpolation function for irregularly-spaced data. In: Proceedings of the 1968 23rd ACM National Conference, pp. 517–524 (1968)

30. Silberman, N., Hoiem, D., Kohli, P., Fergus, R.: Indoor segmentation and support inference from RGBD images. In: Fitzgibbon, A., Lazebnik, S., Perona, P., Sato, Y., Schmid, C. (eds.) ECCV 2012. LNCS, vol. 7576, pp. 746–760. Springer, Heidelberg (2012). https://doi.org/10.1007/978-3-642-33715-4_54
31. Skala, V.: RBF interpolation with CSRBF of large data sets. Procedia Comput. Sci. **108**, 2433–2437 (2017)
32. Uhrig, J., Schneider, N., Schneider, L., Franke, U., Brox, T., Geiger, A.: Sparsity invariant CNNs. In: International Conference on 3D Vision (3DV) (2017)
33. Wang, Y., Chao, W.L., Garg, D., Hariharan, B., Campbell, M.E., Weinberger, K.Q.: Pseudo-lidar from visual depth estimation: Bridging the gap in 3D object detection for autonomous driving. In: 2019 IEEE/CVF Conference on Computer Vision and Pattern Recognition (CVPR), pp. 8437–8445 (2018)
34. Wei, P., Cagle, L., Reza, T., Ball, J., Gafford, J.: Lidar and camera detection fusion in a real-time industrial multi-sensor collision avoidance system. Electronics **7**(6), 84 (2018)
35. Wong, A., Fei, X., Tsuei, S., Soatto, S.: Unsupervised depth completion from visual inertial odometry. IEEE Robot. Autom. Lett. **5**(2), 1899–1906 (2020). https://doi.org/10.1109/LRA.2020.2969938
36. Wright, G.B.: Radial Basis Function Interpolation: Numerical and Analytical Developments. University of Colorado, Boulder (2003)
37. Ye, J., Ji, Y., Wang, X., Ou, K., Tao, D., Song, M.: Student becoming the master: Knowledge amalgamation for joint scene parsing, depth estimation, and more. In: 2019 IEEE/CVF Conference on Computer Vision and Pattern Recognition (CVPR), pp. 2824–2833 (2019)
38. Zhang, Y., Guo, X., Poggi, M., Zhu, Z., Huang, G., Mattoccia, S.: Completion-Former: depth completion with convolutions and vision transformers. In: 2023 IEEE/CVF Conference on Computer Vision and Pattern Recognition (CVPR), pp. 18527–18536 (2023)
39. Zhang, Z., Cui, Z., Xu, C., Yan, Y., Sebe, N., Yang, J.: Pattern-affinitive propagation across depth, surface normal and semantic segmentation. In: 2019 IEEE/CVF Conference on Computer Vision and Pattern Recognition (CVPR), pp. 4101–4110 (2019). https://doi.org/10.1109/CVPR.2019.00423
40. Zhao, H., Shi, J., Qi, X., Wang, X., Jia, J.: Pyramid scene parsing network. In: Proceedings of the IEEE Conference on Computer Vision and Pattern Recognition, pp. 2881–2890 (2017)
41. Zhu, A.Z., Yuan, L., Chaney, K., Daniilidis, K.: Unsupervised event-based learning of optical flow, depth, and egomotion. In: 2019 IEEE/CVF Conference on Computer Vision and Pattern Recognition (CVPR), pp. 989–997 (2018)
42. Zou, Y.L., Hu, F.L., Zhou, C.C., Li, C.L., Dunn, K.J.: Analysis of radial basis function interpolation approach. Appl. Geophys. **10**(4), 397–410 (2013)

Performance Evaluation of Depth Completion Neural Networks for Various RGB-D Camera Technologies in Indoor Scenarios

Rino Castellano[ID], Matteo Terreran[✉][ID], and Stefano Ghidoni[ID]

Intelligent and Autonomous Systems Laboratory, University of Padova, Padova, Italy
{rino.castellano,matteo.terreran,ghidoni}@unipd.it

Abstract. RGB-D cameras have become essential in robotics for accurate perception and object recognition, enabling robots to navigate environments, avoid obstacles, and manipulate objects precisely. Such cameras, besides RGB information, allow the capture of an additional image that encodes the distance of each point in the scene from the camera. Popular depth acquisition techniques include active stereoscopic, which triangulates two camera views, and Time-of-Flight (T-o-F), based on infrared laser patterns. Despite different technologies, none of them is yet able to provide accurate depth information on the entire image due to various factors such as sunlight, reflective surfaces or high distances from the camera. This leads to noisy or incomplete depth images. Neural network-based solutions have been researched for depth completion, aiming to create dense depth maps using RGB images and sparse depth. This paper presents a comparison of the data provided by different depth-sensing technologies, highlighting their pros and cons in two main benchmark setups. After an analysis of the sensors' accuracy under different conditions, several state-of-the-art neural networks have been evaluated in an indoor scenario to assess if it is possible to improve the quality of the raw depth images provided by each sensor.

Keywords: Depth completion · RGB-D camera · Image guidance

1 Introduction

Depth images play a crucial role in computer vision research and have various applications in industries like robotics, autonomous driving, and augmented reality (AR). These images provide information about the distance from the sensor of objects in the scene. A common approach to obtain such kind of information is the use of RGB-D cameras, which provide both a color image of the scene and a depth image. RGB-D cameras employ various acquisition modes, such as stereoscopic techniques that capture multiple images from different angles, Time-of-Flight (T-o-F) techniques that project structured infrared (IR) laser

R. Basili et al. (Eds.): AIxIA 2023, LNAI 14318, pp. 351–364, 2023.
https://doi.org/10.1007/978-3-031-47546-7_24

patterns and measure deformations to calculate distance, or LiDAR techniques that employ an 860 nm infrared laser projection. Each acquisition technique has important considerations that can adversely affect the depth image produced: one of the major problems faced by stereoscopic cameras is the presence of noise within the depth image, due to the difficult triangulation of featureless objects (e.g., white walls) or objects more than 3.5m away from the sensor. Another problem, especially for T-o-F and LiDAR cameras, is the invalidation of pixels on object edges or near corners, due to an interference factor between IR beams that can occur around discontinuous surfaces. In cases where a pixel value is invalidated, the camera processor will immediately assign it a value of 0. Various techniques have been proposed to address the issue of incomplete depth maps. These techniques involve filling in invalid pixel holes and reducing noise using dilation [13] or bilateral filtering [20,21]. However, these handcrafted strategies may not fully utilize the geometric information in RGB images and may not be accurate enough for certain applications like autonomous driving. A more sophisticated approach is to use depth completion neural networks [8–10]. Generally, these networks take an incomplete depth image with invalid pixels and estimate a new dense depth map by leveraging geometric information in incomplete depth data, and auxiliary information such as image patterns in RGB images. State-of-the-art depth completion models are typically trained on outdoor datasets, particularly the KITTI dataset [23]. In contrast, indoor datasets, like the NYUv2 Depth Dataset [22], are more limited in availability and often rely on artificially generated data from a dense depth image, where only a small percentage is sampled to generate a new sparse depth image. Currently, there is a lack of indoor datasets that adequately represent the challenges faced by RGB-D cameras, resulting in architectures that have not been extensively trained to handle holes within inhomogeneous depth maps in real-world indoor scenarios.

In this work, the performance of state-of-the-art depth completion networks will be analyzed on specific indoor scenarios, in order to highlight how well networks trained on such limited datasets are suitable for general use on real-world scenarios, and what major performance limitations still exist. Specifically, a main contribution of this work is the proposal of two different benchmarks to analyze in detail the accuracy and robustness of different depth acquisition techniques on indoor data. These benchmarks evaluate several aspects, including measurements' precision as the distance from the sensor increases (Depth Accuracy for indoor scene), as well as the accuracy of depth measurements within a narrower mask of the depth map (Depth Accuracy for objects). For each benchmark, various types of commercial RGB-D cameras were analyzed by highlighting the main causes of errors and holes in the depth image. Based on such results, the performance of current state-of-the-art networks for depth completion are analyzed. Although achieving good performance for poorly scattered or noisy depth images, such methods are generally unable to fill and refine correctly sparse depth images. The paper is organized as follows. Section 2 provides an overview of the most recent works on depth completion. Section 3 explains how common RGB-D cameras technology works. The proposed depth quality benchmarks and results are discussed in Sect. 4 and 5. In Sect. 6 state-of-the-art depth completion have been evaluated on indoor data. Finally Sect. 7 draws the conclusions.

2 Literature Review

The objective of depth completion is to generate a dense depth map by filling in the missing values of a sparse depth map. With a sparse depth map of the image and other potential auxiliary information as inputs, the new depth map needs to have as much smoothness within normal surfaces and a valid geometric consistency around object edges and borders. Hu et al. [8] proposed a taxonomy of the currently used method for depth completion task. Based on the usage of RGB as input throughout the entire training and testing process, the two primary categories of depth completion employing neural networks are defined as follows: i) *Unguided depth completion* [6,10,16,23], which aims at directly completing the sparse depth map, used as input; ii) *RGB guided depth completion* [4,9,17,24], where the neural network requires both the sparse depth map and the RGB of the acquisition as input. Thanks to the use of RGB images it is possible to find more geometrical cues that may help in the identification of semantic information.

RGB-guided networks are valuable for addressing the issue of sparse depth maps with numerous invalid pixels lacking depth information. As a result, unguided depth completion neural networks often struggle in these scenarios, leading to a shift in research focus towards RGB-guided methods. Hu et al. [8] have identified various techniques for RGB-guided depth completion. One such technique is the Early Fusion [11,17] method, which involves concatenating the RGB image and sparse depth and feeding the result as input to the network. Although the Early Fusion technique stands out because of its simplicity and low complexity, its being particularly straightforward makes feature extraction fall entirely within the CNN network. In order to broaden the analysis beyond a single CNN network, the Late Fusion method is employed. This approach involves the fusion of data obtained from RGB and sparse depth inputs into two separate branches: Global and Local Depth Prediction [14,24]. The distinction between the two lies solely in their input sources: the Global branch operates as an Early Fusion network, whereas the Local branch exclusively utilizes sparse depth information. In FusionNet [24], the two branches work in such a way as to obtain two different dense depth maps, with attached confidence maps, that focus on different locations in the image. Further alternatives were also proposed following the Late Fusion scheme such as the Double Encoder-Decoder [9,18]. This gave rise to PENet [9] first and SemAttNet [18] later, an extension of the former network with an additional semantic branch. Fusion modes have also shifted from simple concatenations to more complicated strategies [7], such as the correlation between RGB and depth or fusion at multiple spatial scales [15]. A variant of these fusion techniques is the use of the Spatial Propagation Network-based (SPN) models [3,4,19], which refine an initial sparse depth map through the use of an additional Encoder-Decoder branch, and are currently at the forefront of

RGB-guided depth completion. Already present in the Early Fusion technique, the idea of having to refine an initial coarse sparse depth map resulted useful for a more accurate final depth, especially around corners and edges [5], albeit through the use of an additional Encoder-Decoder branch. The NLSPN [19] is one of the most famous examples of Spatial Propagation Network-based depth completion models that posed most of its computational part in the refinement process.

3   Overview of the Depth Technology

Different technologies have been proposed for estimating depth information with cameras: stereoscopy, Time-of-Flight and LiDAR. In this section, we will explore the characteristics and depth acquisition techniques of different RGB-D cameras, highlighting the strengths and weaknesses of the camera used later in the experiments, namely the Microsoft Kinect V2, Microsoft Kinect Azure, Intel Realsense D455, Intel Realsense L515 (Fig. 1).

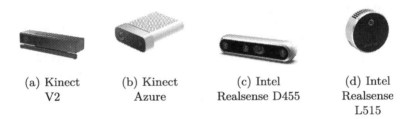

(a) Kinect V2   (b) Kinect Azure   (c) Intel Realsense D455   (d) Intel Realsense L515

Fig. 1. RGB-D cameras used for the benchmark analysis.

Stereoscopic techniques use multiple viewpoints to capture and analyze images, creating a perception of depth. By using cameras with two lenses, these techniques capture the same scene from slightly different perspectives, resulting in disparity between corresponding objects in the images. The Intel RealSense D455 [2] (Fig. 1c) is an RGB-D camera that uses stereo depth technology and active IR pattern projection. One of its major problems faced is the presence of noise within the depth image, which can adversely affect the accuracy and reliability of depth measurements. This noise is particularly prominent when triangulating featureless objects, such as uniform walls or objects located at distances exceeding 3.5 m from the sensor. The Time-of-Flight (ToF) sensors include typically the use of an RGB and infrared camera, as shown with the Kinect V2 (Fig. 1a) [25] and the Azure Kinect (Fig. 1b): an array of IR emitters sends out from the camera a modulated signal that travels to the measured point, then the signal gets reflected and will be received by the CCD of the sensor. The actions of the IR emitter and depth sensor are coordinated by a timing generator inside both the Kinect. The depth image generated by these cameras are accurate but can have some invalidation points when they are outside of the active IR illumination mask due to the saturation of the IR signal and the presence of corners and edges in the image. At the same time, a pixel may be invalidated when the sensor does not receive a signal strong enough. The LiDAR technique uses laser technology to capture high-resolution 3D depth data: projecting an infrared laser at 860 nm wavelength as active light source, the depth 3D data is obtained by measuring the Time-of-Flight (ToF) of the light. The Intel RealSense L515 [1] (Fig. 1d), which follows the LiDAR technique for capturing depth images, emits a continuous beam of laser light that is modulated or "coded" with a specific pattern. There are two main situations that can negatively impact the L515's performance. Firstly, in environments with ambient light, such as sunlight, the camera may struggle to differentiate between the transmitted laser light and the natural light. Secondly, smooth and reflective surfaces, which exhibit specular reflection, can cause noise issues.

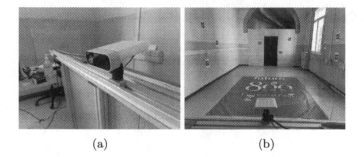

(a)   (b)

Fig. 2. Setup for the experiments a)RGB-D camera; b) view of the setup.

4   Experimental Setup

The setup (Fig. 2) was designed and built: a system of aluminum profiles was designed to analyze the data collected from all cameras, with the same pose framing the same scene without major variations in orientation or proximity to objects (Fig. 3).

   The room used for the acquisition process has windows, allowing the investigation of the sunlight's impact on the depth measurement of the different RGB-D sensors in the experiments. Two benchmarks were proposed to assess the performance of the RGB-D cameras considered in the paper. The first benchmark is the "Depth Accuracy for objects" analysis, which examines the accuracy of the depth map for a plane object placed at various angles, small orientations of 20°, and distances, between 1 and 7 m, within the room. The second benchmark is the "Depth Accuracy for indoor scene" analysis, which evaluates the consistency and reliability of the depth map for planes that move along the depth z-axis.

Fig. 3. RGB and depth images taken of Depth Accuracy benchmark.

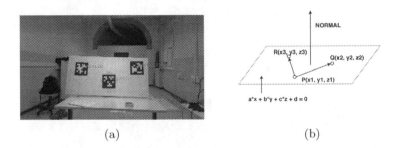

(a)   (b)

Fig. 4. Image of a) the three centers detected found in /tag detections topic; b) synthesized version of plane estimation given three points.

Since the goal of this part of the paper is to analyze the depths obtained with all RGB-D cameras, it was necessary to synthetically construct a ground truth for each acquisition in each benchmark. Three Apriltags [12] markers were utilized for each plane in order to accomplish this, as depicted in Fig. 4, considering as ground truth plane the plane that fits the 3D centers of the three markers.

5   Depth Accuracy Evaluation

It was possible to analyze how much the sensor acquisition method itself can impact the image quality by comparing the various metrics collected during the acquisitions. The metrics analyzed for both the benchmarks are the following Root Mean Squared Error (RMSE) and the custom Percentage of Valid Pixels (PVP), expressed as follows

$$PVP = \frac{total\_valid\_pixel}{total\_pixel} \cdot 100 \qquad (1)$$

where $total\_valid\_pixel = len(\{\hat{y}(i)|\hat{y}(i) \neq 0\}_{i=0}^{N})$. This metric was added as a complementary parameter to the RMSE so that we could know both the quantity and quality of the data.

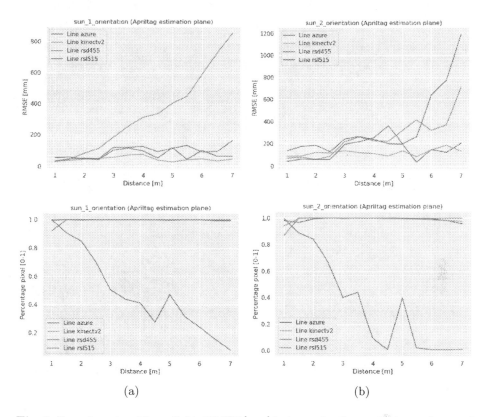

Fig. 5. Experiments with sunlight. RMSE [mm] between depth acquisition and ground-truth plane. a) orientation 1 (0°); b) orientation 2 (+20°).

5.1 Depth Accuracy for Objects Benchmark Results

Figure 5 reports the performance of each camera in the sunlight environment. Time-of-Flight (ToF) cameras regularly maintained average Root Mean Square Error (RMSE) values of less than a few centimeters, together with a high rate of valid pixels, which reached about 98%. In contrast, the RealSense D455, based on stereoscopic technique, experienced a noticeable degradation in RMSE beyond a distance of 3.5 m. However, it consistently maintained 100% valid pixels across all orientations. This behavior was also observed in a neon light environment (Fig. 6), indicating that stereo depth acquisition faced significant noise issues during triangulation. The RealSense L515 displayed a different behavior in different light conditions. For sunlight conditions, the RMSE worsens at distances greater than 6 m for orientations of +20° and -20°, but remains stable for 0° orientation, suggesting that the destructive interference between the LiDAR laser beam and solar beams is mitigated along the optical axis. In neon light conditions, the L515 demonstrated stability and comparable performance to the Kinect V2 and Kinect Azure, even at a distance of 7 m.

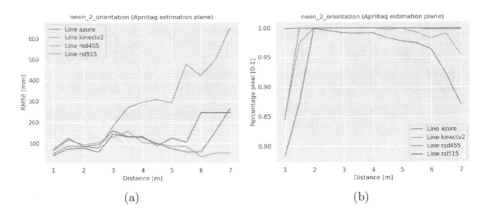

(a)   (b)

Fig. 6. RMSE [mm] and PVP between depth acquisition and plane estimated. (Neon light)

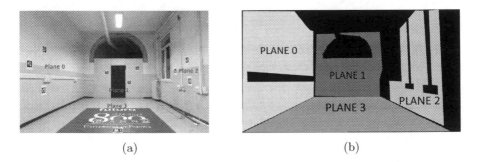

(a)   (b)

Fig. 7. Images of the planes considered inside the Depth Accuracy for indoor scene benchmark in a) input RGB image; b) ground truth annotations.

5.2   Depth Accuracy for Indoor Scene Benchmark Results

Even though analysis at closer ranges can yield greater accuracy, some planes, typically walls and the floor, can especially extend along the depth axis (Fig. 7). The first finding that can be drawn from Fig. 8, is that there is a lot of noise in the RealSense L515 acquisitions when sunlight is present. Regardless of the plane observed, when passing from sunlight to neon light scenario, there is an average decrease in RMSE of 80% and an increase in the percentage of valid pixels of an average 40%. This observation shows that the noise level of the pixels, rather than their number, is what really counts. The RealSense D455 turns out to be the noisiest camera, supporting the conclusions made in the previous section on depth accuracy, especially for planes flying at a distance greater than 3.5 m. The only problem that arises from the analysis of the Kinect V2 is that it works worse on corners. Actually, plane #2 in Fig. 7, which has fewer corners, is the plane where the RMSE performs best. This issue arises because in Kinect V2 camera at corners and intersections of planes, such as in our case between the

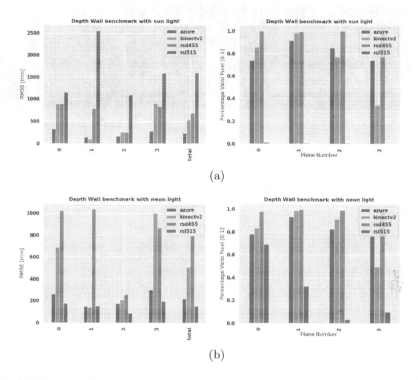

(a)

(b)

Fig. 8. RMSE and PVP of Depth Accuracy for indoor scene benchmark with a)Sun and b)Neon Light

walls and the floor, there is a rounding of the contours and subsequently an incorrect approximation of depth.

6   Depth Completion

Experiments using various sensors have shown that, depending on the technology employed, a variety of issues can appear in the depth images acquired. The most frequent of them are pixel sparsity (for example, LiDAR in sunlight) or inaccurate estimated values (stereo at very large distances). In this section, we investigated whether utilizing the state-of-the-art neural network for depth completion can enhance the depth map's accuracy in relation to the raw data acquired with an RGB-D sensor. It will be analyzed how well the network generalizes the depth completion process with indoor data even when trained with outdoor ones. For this analysis, the neural networks were compared with an additional baseline that uses only morphological operations such as dilation to fill the depth holes. Further analysis will be devoted to the NLSPN network, trained with an outdoor dataset but presenting a homogeneous distribution of valid pixels within the sparse depth map.

(a) Kinect Azure input.   (b) PENet result.   (c) SemAttNet result.

Fig. 9. Depth completion neural network output using Kinect Azure depth.

Table 1. RMSE [mm] of the dense output depth with Sun light source. In **bold** the process with the lowest RMSE [mm], <u>underlined</u> the second lowest RMSE.

SUN LIGHT - RMSE [mm]				
Net	Kinect Azure	Kinect v2	RealSense D455	RealSense L515
FusionNet	2859.00	1793.37	1319.42	3468.13
PENet	2205.68	2443.38	1147.75	4011.12
SemAttNet	1223.40	1457.67	2943.39	2098.36
NLSPN	<u>790.85</u>	<u>859.47</u>	<u>945.09</u>	<u>2754.73</u>
Baseline	**540.32**	**797.28**	**724.87**	**1913.83**

6.1   Neural Network Generalization Performance

When the networks that were trained on the "KITTI depth completion" dataset, PENet [9], FusionNet [24] and SemAttNet [18], are inferenced with indoor data, a decline in RMSE accuracy can be noted in relation to the input raw data (Fig 9). A lack of generalization by the neural network is evident in the generic RMSE in both light source scenarios for all RGB-D cameras (Table 1 and Table 2), which varies from 1200 mm to 4000 mm and performs worse than the baseline technique in every case. The depth range of the "KITTI depth completion" dataset, is the reason for this failure to generalize: unlike acquisitions made in the experiments, which do not go deeper than 7 m, the depth images in the "KITTI depth completion" dataset have a much greater depth range, spanning from 2 to 30 m. As seen in Fig. 9, where there is a hole above the wall at the back of the room, the incorrect pixels denote a higher depth, and the networks overestimate that value anyway, speculating that it might be the bottom of the street, a frequent occurrence in the KITTI dataset. From the analysis in Sect. 5, the RGB-D RealSense L515 camera's depth map is the only one that is affected by sunlight. A large number of invalid pixels have incorrect values with errors larger than 1 m (Table 3) and their influence is inevitably negative for the depth completion task (Table 4).

Table 2. RMSE [mm] of the dense output depth with Neon light source. In **bold** the process with the lowest RMSE, <u>underlined</u> the second lowest RMSE.

NEON LIGHT - RMSE [mm]				
Net	Kinect Azure	Kinect v2	RealSense D455	RealSense L515
FusionNet	2909.21	1864.60	1440.89	4094.90
PENet	2413.49	2466.57	940.38	2978.02
SemAttNet	1568.80	1452.53	3061.97	<u>1491.88</u>
NLSPN	<u>720.98</u>	<u>828.39</u>	<u>885.30</u>	1822.90
Baseline	**515.02**	**802.29**	**758.54**	**451.71**

Table 3. RMSE [mm] of invalid pixels in dense output depth.

SUN LIGHT - RMSE pixel invalid[mm]				
Net	Kinect Azure	Kinect v2	RealSense D455	RealSense L515
FusionNet	3519.45	1656.11	2453.86	3471.50
PENet	3621.58	1905.65	1192.36	4011.47
SemAttNet	1889.90	1193.20	2779.23	**2100.97**
NLSPN	<u>1452.60</u>	<u>1224.46</u>	<u>2040.03</u>	<u>2758.23</u>
Baseline	**1941.41**	**2134.89**	**1164.90**	4813.36

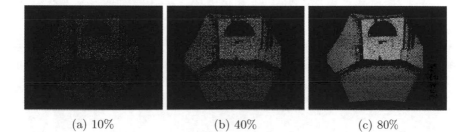

(a) 10%   (b) 40%   (c) 80%

Fig. 10. Sample images with varying density percentages used in NLSPN.

6.2 NLSPN - Different Density Ratio Experiment

Differently from the other models considered, the NLSPN [19] network is trained using an outdoor dataset that presents a homogeneous distribution of valid pixels inside the sparse depth map. In light of this logic, the experiment described below was conducted: how does masking the sparse depth map in the input influence the RMSE of the image when compared to the total number of valid pixels? The RMSE on the total invalid pixels in the input was then checked. More percentages of valid pixels than the total were chosen in the input depth map, ranging from 10% to 100% with a step of 10% (Fig. 10). Except for the RealSense L515, which still has a lot of noise on the majority of its acceptable pixels,

Table 4. RMSE [mm] of invalid pixels in dense output depth using NLSPN net.

NLSPN - SUN LIGHT - RMSE pixel invalid[mm]			
Density Level	Kinect Azure	Kinect v2	RealSense D455	RealSense L515
10%	692.89	889.99	944.84	2893.18
30%	736.76	903.43	952.20	2803.26
50%	787.71	991.82	946.22	2742.17
70%	893.96	962.00	948.66	2709.51
90%	1144.79	1075.77	951.94	2735.17
Full density	1452.60	1224.46	2040.03	2758.23

the RMSE of invalid pixels worsens as data density increases (Table 3). The motivation discovered was that the NYUv2 network was trained with valid pixel depth homogenously distributed throughout the image. The RGB-D Kinect V2 camera was used to capture the dense depth map in the NYUv2 pictures, which were then artificially pre-processed to serve as a sparse depth map for the depth completion benchmark. The pre-processing used is a simple random masking over the entire image of a very precise depth. Our Kinect V2 and Kinect Azure acquisitions have large holes in the image and the only 100% dense depth images we have are from the RealSense D455, which has noisy depth information above 3.5 m. As a result, the model does not generalize with data like the Depth Wall benchmark. Hence, even though the RMSE drops as data density increases, this does not suggest that the error for the invalid pixels decreases as data densities decrease; rather, the average is reduced because a greater number of defective pixels are found among neighbors that contain correct pixels.

7   Conclusions

In this paper, we focused on depth completion. In particular, we investigated how state-of-the-art neural network for depth completion can improve accuracy and overall quality of depth images acquired in real indoor scenarios. Except the RealSense D455, all cameras inevitably produce erroneous pixel holes in depth maps, either as a result of interferences like those in the L515 or as a result of corners and edges for RGB-D cameras made by Microsoft Kinect V2. It is proven that there is no improvement in the network's ability to perceive depth using the current state-of-the-art in depth completion, which prevents tangible results from fulfilling accurate depth map completion and refining. Even if decreased accuracy was expected for neural networks trained on outdoor datasets due to a considerably bigger depth range bias, the accuracy of the NLSPN network trained on indoor datasets does not beat a straightforward dilation technique, as the baseline method. Future research should investigate whether the state-of-the-art depth completion algorithm employs a simple interpolation procedure or if there are more complex mechanisms at play. Evaluating the average inaccuracy in previously invalidated pixels within large and smaller holes using dense data at a 10% ratio, similar to the NLSPN network study, could shed light on this. Additionally, conducting experiments with indoor data to retrain networks like PENet, Fusion-Net, and SemAttNet, or using outdoor data to assess the impact of narrowing the depth range on inference stability, would be valuable.

References

1. Lidar camera l515. https://www.intelrealsense.com/lidar-camera-l515/
2. Stereo depth solution from intel realsense. https://www.intelrealsense.com/stereo-depth/
3. Chen, Y., Yang, B., Liang, M., Urtasun, R.: Learning joint 2D–3D representations for depth completion. In: Proceedings of the IEEE/CVF International Conference on Computer Vision, pp. 10023–10032 (2019)
4. Cheng, X., Wang, P., Yang, R.: Depth estimation via affinity learned with convolutional spatial propagation network. In: Proceedings of the European Conference on Computer Vision (ECCV), pp. 103–119 (2018)
5. Dimitrievski, M., Veelaert, P., Philips, W.: Learning morphological operators for depth completion. In: Blanc-Talon, J., Helbert, D., Philips, W., Popescu, D., Scheunders, P. (eds.) ACIVS 2018. LNCS, vol. 11182, pp. 450–461. Springer, Cham (2018). https://doi.org/10.1007/978-3-030-01449-0_38
6. Eldesokey, A., Felsberg, M., Khan, F.S.: Propagating confidences through CNNs for sparse data regression. arXiv preprint arXiv:1805.11913 (2018)
7. Garnelo, M., et al.: Conditional neural processes. In: International Conference on Machine Learning, pp. 1704–1713. PMLR (2018)
8. Hu, J., et al.: Deep depth completion from extremely sparse data: a survey. IEEE Trans. Pattern Anal. Mach. Intell. **45**, 8244–8264 (2022)
9. Hu, M., Wang, S., Li, B., Ning, S., Fan, L., Gong, X.: PENet: towards precise and efficient image guided depth completion. In: 2021 IEEE International Conference on Robotics and Automation (ICRA), pp. 13656–13662. IEEE (2021)
10. Huang, Z., Fan, J., Cheng, S., Yi, S., Wang, X., Li, H.: HMS-Net: hierarchical multi-scale sparsity-invariant network for sparse depth completion. IEEE Trans. Image Process. **29**, 3429–3441 (2019)
11. Imran, S., Long, Y., Liu, X., Morris, D.: Depth coefficients for depth completion. In: 2019 IEEE/CVF Conference on Computer Vision and Pattern Recognition (CVPR), pp. 12438–12447. IEEE (2019)
12. Krogius, M., Haggenmiller, A., Olson, E.: Flexible layouts for fiducial tags. In: 2019 IEEE/RSJ International Conference on Intelligent Robots and Systems (IROS), pp. 1898–1903. IEEE (2019)
13. Ku, J., Harakeh, A., Waslander, S.L.: In defense of classical image processing: Fast depth completion on the CPU. In: 2018 15th Conference on Computer and Robot Vision (CRV), pp. 16–22. IEEE (2018)
14. Lee, S., Lee, J., Kim, D., Kim, J.: Deep architecture with cross guidance between single image and sparse lidar data for depth completion. IEEE Access **8**, 79801–79810 (2020)
15. Li, A., Yuan, Z., Ling, Y., Chi, W., Zhang, C.: A multi-scale guided cascade hourglass network for depth completion. In: Proceedings of the IEEE/CVF Winter Conference on Applications of Computer Vision, pp. 32–40 (2020)

16. Lu, K., Barnes, N., Anwar, S., Zheng, L.: Depth completion auto-encoder. In: 2022 IEEE/CVF Winter Conference on Applications of Computer Vision Workshops (WACVW), pp. 63–73. IEEE (2022)
17. Ma, F., Karaman, S.: Sparse-to-dense: depth prediction from sparse depth samples and a single image. In: 2018 IEEE International Conference on Robotics and Automation (ICRA), pp. 4796–4803. IEEE (2018)
18. Nazir, D., Pagani, A., Liwicki, M., Stricker, D., Afzal, M.Z.: SemAttNet: toward attention-based semantic aware guided depth completion. IEEE Access **10**, 120781–120791 (2022)
19. Park, J., Joo, K., Hu, Z., Liu, C.-K., So Kweon, I.: Non-local spatial propagation network for depth completion. In: Vedaldi, A., Bischof, H., Brox, T., Frahm, J.-M. (eds.) ECCV 2020. LNCS, vol. 12358, pp. 120–136. Springer, Cham (2020). https://doi.org/10.1007/978-3-030-58601-0_8
20. Qi, F., Han, J., Wang, P., Shi, G., Li, F.: Structure guided fusion for depth map inpainting. Pattern Recogn. Lett. **34**(1), 70–76 (2013)
21. Richardt, C., Stoll, C., Dodgson, N.A., Seidel, H.P., Theobalt, C.: Coherent spatiotemporal filtering, upsampling and rendering of RGBZ videos. In: Computer Graphics Forum, vol. 31, pp. 247–256. Wiley Online Library (2012)
22. Silberman, N., Hoiem, D., Kohli, P., Fergus, R.: Indoor segmentation and support inference from RGBD images. ECCV **5**(7576), 746–760 (2012)
23. Uhrig, J., Schneider, N., Schneider, L., Franke, U., Brox, T., Geiger, A.: Sparsity invariant CNNs. In: 2017 International Conference on 3D Vision (3DV), pp. 11–20. IEEE (2017)
24. Van Gansbeke, W., Neven, D., De Brabandere, B., Van Gool, L.: Sparse and noisy lidar completion with RGB guidance and uncertainty. In: 2019 16th International Conference on Machine Vision Applications (MVA), pp. 1–6. IEEE (2019)
25. Zennaro, S., et al.: Performance evaluation of the 1st and 2nd generation Kinect for multimedia applications. In: 2015 IEEE International Conference on Multimedia and Expo (ICME), pp. 1–6. IEEE (2015)

Hybrid AI

Inference in Probabilistic Answer Set Programming Under the Credal Semantics

Damiano Azzolini[1(✉)] and Fabrizio Riguzzi[2]

[1] Dipartimento di Scienze dell'Ambiente e della Prevenzione, University of Ferrara, Ferrara, Italy
damiano.azzolini@unife.it
[2] Dipartimento di Matematica e Informatica, University of Ferrara, Ferrara, Italy
fabrizio.riguzzi@unife.it

Abstract. Probabilistic Answer Set Programming under the credal semantics (PASP) describes an uncertain domain through an answer set program extended with probabilistic facts. The PASTA language leverages PASP to express statistical statements. A solver with the same name allows to perform inference in PASTA programs and, in general, in PASP. In this paper, we investigate inference in PASP, propose a new inference algorithm called aspcs based on Second Level Algebraic Model Counting (2AMC), and implement it into the aspmc solver. Then, we compare it with PASTA on a set of benchmarks: the empirical results show that, when the program does not contain aggregates, the new algorithm outperforms PASTA. However, when we consider PASTA statements and aggregates, we need to replace aggregates with a possibly exponential number of rules, and aspcs is slower than PASTA.

Keywords: Second Level Algebraic Model Counting · Probabilistic Answer Set Programming · Inference

1 Introduction

Algebraic Model Counting (AMC) [18] is an umbrella term that comprises several well-known tasks, among the other, SAT, #SAT, weighted model counting, and probabilistic inference. All these tasks require to aggregate the models of a program according to a certain criterion. For instance, model counting requires counting the models while probabilistic inference, e.g., in the probabilistic logic language ProbLog [11], requires summing the probabilities associated with the different models. Other tasks, such as decision theoretic inference [7], MAP and MPE inference [4,5,22], and probabilistic inference under the smProbLog language [23], require to aggregate the results obtained via inference, so they need two levels of aggregations. These tasks they were recently identified as Second Level Algebraic Model Counting (2AMC) tasks [17].

Probabilistic Answer Set Programming under the credal semantics (PASP, for short) [2,8] is one of the possible formalisms to express uncertainty in Answer

© The Author(s) 2023
R. Basili et al. (Eds.): AIxIA 2023, LNAI 14318, pp. 367–380, 2023.
https://doi.org/10.1007/978-3-031-47546-7_25

Set Programming (ASP) [14], since it extends ASP with ProbLog probabilistic facts [11]. PASP has been recently adopted in the PASTA framework [3] to encode statistical statements [16], that represent statistical information about a given domain. During inference, these are converted into choice rules and constraints with aggregates [1]. Then, the PASTA solver performs projected answer set enumeration [13]. As a first contribution, we discuss how to represent inference in PASP as a 2AMC task. Then, we implement our approach on top of the state of the art aspmc solver [12], that adopts knowledge compilation [10] to compactly represent a program, and we call it aspcs. Tests on different benchmarks show that when programs do not contain aggregates, aspcs is significantly faster than PASTA. However, aspmc, and so aspcs, currently does not support aggregates, so to represent PASTA statistical statements we manually convert constraints with aggregates into a set of ground rules. In this case, aspcs perform worse than PASTA, probably due to the possibly exponential number of rules that come from the conversion of the aggregates.

The paper is structured as follows: Sect. 2 introduces the needed background knowledge. In Sect. 3 we cast inference in PASP as a 2AMC task and in Sect. 4 we test an implementation on top of the aspmc solver against the PASTA solver. Section 5 concludes the paper.

2   Background

ProbLog *probabilistic facts* [11] are one of the most used syntactical constructs to represent uncertainty within a probabilistic logic program [19]: they are of the form $f_i::\Pi_i$ where f_i is a logical atom and $\Pi_i \in [0, 1]$ is its probability value. Its meaning is that: f_i is true with probability Π_i and false with probability $1 - \Pi_i$. These are considered independent. A choice of a truth value for every probabilistic fact defines a *world* w, whose probability is, according to the Distribution Semantics (DS) [21],

$$P(w) = \prod_{f_i \in w} \Pi_i \cdot \prod_{\neg f_i \in w} (1 - \Pi_i).$$

Every ProbLog program has 2^n worlds, where n is the number of probabilistic facts. The DS requires that every world has exactly one model. A *probabilistic clause* is a clause with a probabilistic fact in the head, such as $0.4::f(X) :- b(X, Y)$. The meaning is that $f(X)$ is true with probability 0.4 if the body $b(X, Y)$, which can also be a conjunction, is true. A probabilistic clause can be translated to a normal clause by inserting in the body a fresh probabilistic fact with the same probability and variables X and Y. The previous clause can be rewritten as $f(X) :- b(X, Y), aux_1(X, Y)$, where aux_1 is a new probabilistic fact with an associated probability of 0.4.

If we consider Answer Set Programming [14], the credal semantics [2,8] gives a meaning to answer set programs extended with probabilistic facts. We use the acronym PASP to denote both Probabilistic Answer Set Programming under the credal semantics and a probabilistic answer set program following the credal semantics. The intended meaning will be clear from the context. Under this semantics, every world w is an answer set program, the one obtained by fixing to true the probabilistic facts true in the world w and by removing the probabilistic facts false in the world w, that has zero or more answer sets (or stable models [14]). Let us denote with $AS(w)$ the set of answer sets for a world w. Furthermore, the probability of a query q, i.e., a conjunction of ground atoms, is characterized by a *lower* and an *upper* probability bound. That is, $P(q) = [\underline{P}(q), \overline{P}(q)]$ where:

$$\underline{P}(q) = \sum_{w_i | \forall m \in AS(w_i),\ m \models q} P(w_i),\ \overline{P}(q) = \sum_{w_i | \exists m \in AS(w_i),\ m \models q} P(w_i). \quad (1)$$

A world w contributes to the lower and upper probability bounds if the query is true in every answer set of w. A world w contributes only to the upper probability bound if the query is true in some of the sets of w. Example 1 shows an example of PASP modeling a scenario where some people buy some products. A crucial point for the credal semantics is that every world must have at least one stable model. If this does not hold, some probability mass is lost. There are alternative semantics that handle worlds without answer sets, such as the credal least undefined semantics [20] or the smProbLog semantics [23], that we do not consider in this paper.

Example 1. This program models a scenario with three different people, Alice, Bob, and Carl, that may shop or not (probabilistic facts *shops/1*), with different probabilities.

```
0.3::shops(alice).
0.2::shops(bob).
0.6::shops(carl).

buy(beans,alice) ; buy(spaghetti,alice) :- shops(alice).
buy(spaghetti,bob) ; buy(steak,bob) :- shops(bob).
buy(tomato,carl) ; buy(garlic,carl) :- shops(carl).

cs(C):- #count{X : buy(spaghetti,X)} = C0,
        #count{X : buy(garlic,X)} = C1,
        C = C0 + C1.
ce(C):- #count{X,Y : buy(Y,X)} = C.

:- cs(S), ce(C), 10* S < 3*C.
```

The three disjuncive rules for *buy/2* state that each one of the three people can buy different products. For instance, the first disjunctive rule stats that if Alice shops she can buy beans or spaghetti. The *cs/1* and *ce/1* rules contain aggregates in the body. The former unifies the number of people that buys spaghetti or garlic to variable C. These two values are computed via the *#count* aggregates. For instance, $\#count\{X : buy(spaghetti, X)\} = C0$ unifies with $C0$ the number of element X such that $buy(spaghetti, X)$ holds. Similarly, *ce/1* unifies with C the number of pairs (X, Y) such that $buy(Y, X)$ is true. Lastly, a constraint

Table 1. Worlds, number of answer sets with the query $q = buy(spaghetti, alice)$ true (#ASq), and total number of answer sets (#AS) for every world of Example 1.

id	shops(a)	shops(b)	shops(c)	P(w)	#ASq	#AS
0	0	0	0	0.224	0	1
1	0	0	1	0.336	0	1
2	0	1	0	0.056	0	1
3	0	1	1	0.084	0	3
4	1	0	0	0.096	1	1
5	1	0	1	0.144	2	3
6	1	1	0	0.024	2	3
7	1	1	1	0.036	4	7

states that at least 30% of the people that buy something buy spaghetti or garlic. We are interested in computing the probability that Alice buys spaghetti. The program has $2^3 = 8$ worlds, listed in Table 1. If we consider the query $q = buy(spaghetti, alice)$, its probability is given by $P(q) = [P(w_4), P(w_4) + P(w_5) + P(w_6) + P(w_7)] = [0.096, 0.096 + 0.144 + 0.024 + 0.036] = [0.096, 0.3]$.

2.1 Statistical Statements

The authors of [3] proposed to represent statistical statements of the form "the fraction of A's that are also C's is between lp and up" with $lp, up \in [0, 1]$ with the syntax $(C \mid A)[lp, up]$ where C is an atom and A a conjunction of literals. All the variables in C also appear in A. They call this language PASTA. For example, if we want to state that at least 60% of the birds ($bird/1$) of a fixed domain fly ($fly/1$) we can write $(fly(X)|bird(X))[0.6, 1]$. To perform inference, a statistical statement is translated into three answer set rules: a disjunctive rule and two constraints with aggregates. The just described example becomes:

$$fly(X); not\_fly(X) :- bird(X)$$
$$:- \#count\{X : fly(X), bird(X)\} = FB, \#count\{X : bird(X)\} = B,$$
$$10 \cdot FB < 6 \cdot B \tag{2}$$
$$:- \#count\{X : fly(X), bird(X)\} = FB, \#count\{X : bird(X)\} = B,$$
$$10 \cdot FB > 10 \cdot B$$

The last rule can be omitted since the value of the variable FB cannot be greater than B. The lb and ub values are multiplied by 10 since ASP does not support floating point values. Note that this example can be rewritten with only one *count* aggregate instead of two, but we stick with the previous notation for clarity.

For a conditional $(C \mid A)[lp, up]$, if at least one of the literals in A is probabilistic, the program is interpreted as a PASP. Thus, we can compute the probability of a query with Eq. 1, leveraging the PASTA solver [3]. The inference process of the PASTA solver is the following: first, probabilistic facts are converted into choice rules. For a query q, PASTA introduces two additional rules, $qr :- q$ and $nqr :- not\ q$. Then, it enumerates the projected answer sets [13] on the (converted) probabilistic facts and $qr/0$ and $nqr/0$ atoms and extracts the probability for every world w where the query is true and the contribution of w to the probability bounds.

2.2 Second Level Algebraic Model Counting

Weighted Model Counting (WMC) consists in summing the weights associated with the models of a given propositional formula (program). Algebraic Model Counting (AMC) [18] generalizes WMC by providing a generic definition based on semirings [15], that can be applied to many different tasks (see [18] for a comprehensive list), such as probabilistic inference. AMC can be solved via knowledge compilation [10], that involves representing the problem in a compact form where the solutions can be efficiently computed. As discussed in [17], some tasks such as decision theory and MAP inference require two levels of AMC, since they need two semirings for two different groups of variables. Thus, they belong to the class of Second Level Algebraic Model Counting (2AMC) [17] problems that can still be solved via knowledge compilation.

Let us introduce 2AMC more formally by following [17]. Given a tuple $A = (\Pi, X_{in}, X_{out}, w_{in}, w_{out}, \mathcal{R}_{in}, \mathcal{R}_{out}, f)$, where X_{in} and X_{out} are a partition of the variables in the propositional theory Π, $\mathcal{R}_{in} = (R^i, \oplus^i, \otimes^i, e^i_\oplus, e^i_\otimes)$ and $\mathcal{R}_{out} = (R^o, \oplus^o, \otimes^o, e^o_\oplus, e^o_\otimes)$ are two commutative semirings, w_{in} and w_{out} are two weight functions associating each atom of the program with a weight, and f is a transformation function from the values of $\mathcal{R}_{in}$ to $\mathcal{R}_{out}$, 2AMC requires solving:

$$
2AMC(A) = \bigoplus^o_{I_{out} \in \sigma(X_{out})} \bigotimes^o_{a \in I_{out}} w_{out}(a) \otimes^o \\
f(\bigoplus^i_{I_{in} \in \delta(\Pi | I_{out})} \bigotimes^i_{b \in I_{in}} w_{in}(b))
\tag{3}
$$

where $\sigma(X_{out})$ are the set of possible assignments to X_{out} and $\delta(\Pi \mid I_{out})$ are the set of possible assignments to Π that satisfy I_{out}. AMC is a special case of 2AMC, where the set X_{out} is empty and the transformation function is the identity function. At a high level, the 2AMC task requires solving an AMC task on the variables X_{in} (inner semiring) for every possible set of assignments of X_{out} (outer semiring). The result of the inner AMC task is converted into an element of the outer semiring (with the function f) and another AMC task is solved, now on X_{out}. 2AMC has been adopted to perform inference in smProbLog [23], an extension of the ProbLog language that allows programs where worlds may have zero or more answer sets. A probability is assigned to every answer set in this way: the probability of a world is equally distributed among its answer sets. The probability of a query is then the sum of the probabilities of the answer sets where the query is true. If we consider a smProbLog program $\Pi = L \cup F$ with Herbrand base H and query q, where F is the set of probabilistic facts and L is the logical part of the theory, $X_{out} = F$, $X_{in} = H \setminus F$, $\mathcal{R}_{in} = (\mathbb{N}^2, +, \cdot, (0,0), (1,1))$, $\mathcal{R}_{out} = ([0,1], +, \cdot, 0, 1)$ (i.e., the probability semiring), w_{in} associates all the literals to $(1,1)$ except for $not\ q$, that is mapped to $(0,1)$, w_{out} associates p and $1 - p$ to respectively g and $not\ g$ for every probabilistic fact $p{::}g$ and 1 to all the remaining literals, and the transformation function is $f(n_1, n_2) = n_1/n_2$ where n_2 is the number of models and n_1 the number of models where the query is true. In other words, the inner semiring counts both the number of models (n_2) and the number of models where the query is true (n_1), the transformation function computes the ratio n_1/n_2, and the outer semiring performs probabilistic inference. In the next section we show how we adapted this formulation to perform inference in PASP.

3   Inference in PASP as 2AMC

Recall from Sect. 2 that the probability of a query in a probabilistic answer set program is given by a range. The worlds in which the query is true in all the answer sets contribute to both the lower and upper bound while the worlds in which the query is true in some of the answer sets only contribute to the upper bound. If all the worlds have exactly one answer set, the task reduces to AMC since we just need to sum the probabilities of the worlds where the query is true. In the general case, the inference task is similar to the one of smProbLog described in the previous section: in smProbLog, the probability of a query is a sharp probability value, and every answer set is weighted by the probability of the world divided by the number of its answer sets. In PASP, we have a probability range, so we need to modify both the transformation function and the outer semiring. We consider a transformation function $f(n_1, n_2)$ that returns a pair of values f_{lp} and f_{up} where

$$f_{lp} = \begin{cases} 1 \text{ if } n_1 = n_2 \\ 0 \text{ otherwise} \end{cases} \quad f_{up} = \begin{cases} 1 \text{ if } n_1 > 0 \\ 0 \text{ otherwise} \end{cases}$$

where n_2 is the number of models and n_1 the number of models where the query is true. f_{lp} is adopted for the computation of the lower probability while f_{up} for the upper probability. We propose as outer semiring $\mathcal{R}_{out} = ([0,1]^2, +, \cdot, (0,0), (1,1))$, which is the probability semiring extended to two dimensions, where the operations $+$ and $\cdot$ are applied component-wise. Now, w_{out} associates (p, p) and $(1 - p, 1 - p)$ to respectively g and $not\ g$ for every probabilistic fact $p{::}g$ and $(1,1)$ to all the remaining literals. In other words, the inner semiring counts the models and computes two values, n_1 and n_2. These are combined according to the above $f(n_1, n_2)$ function that also returns a pair of values. Then, the outer semiring performs the actual probability computation by considering these two values simultaneously and returns the lower and upper probability bounds for the query.

Inference in smProbLog is implemented in the aspmc solver [12] by means of tree decompositions and knowledge compilation with sd-DNNF [9] as target

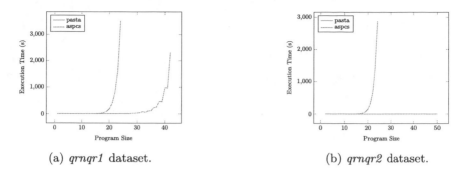

(a) *qrnqr1* dataset.   (b) *qrnqr2* dataset.

Fig. 1. Results for the *qrnqr1* and *qrnqr2* datasets.

language. At a high level, the goal of tree decomposition is to represent a graph as a tree, where each vertex of the tree is a bag, i.e., a subset of the nodes of the graph. Every graph has one or more tree decompositions. The width of a tree decomposition is the size of its largest possible bag minus one. The treewidth of a graph is the minimum width of all its tree decompositions and represents how close a graph is to being a tree, and it is usually a good indicator of the hardness of a task [6]. We modify aspmc for smProbLog inference by introducing the novel transformation function and semiring. The knowledge compilation is still performed once even if the transformation function returns two values, since both are computed on the same semiring, and so the sd-DNNF is traversed only once. We call this algorithm aspcs. A limitation is that aspmc currently does not support aggregates, which are needed to represent PASTA programs. To overcome this, in the experiments of the following section we manually translate aggregates into ground rules. This, however, results in an exponential number of generated rules.

4   Experiments

In this section, we compare the PASTA solver[1] with the previously introduced technique based on 2AMC (aspcs) implemented on top of the aspmc solver [12] on 6 different datasets. For all the datasets, except for the cases where we explicitly describe the instance, the number of probabilistic facts defines the size of the instance. All the considered datasets have at least one answer set for each world, i.e., admit the credal semantics. We use the c2d compiler [9] already available in aspmc. We ran the experiments on a computer with Intel® Xeon® E5-2630v3 running at 2.40 GHz with 8 Gb of RAM and a time limit of 8 h. Execution times are computed with the bash command *time* and reported values are from the *real* field.

The first dataset, *qrnqr1*, consists of programs with an increasing number n of probabilistic facts $a(i)$, where $i \in [0, n-1]$, all associated to a probability

---

[1] Available at: https://github.com/damianoazzolini/pasta.

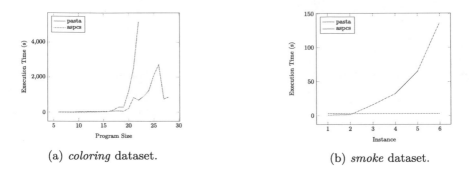

(a) *coloring* dataset.

(b) *smoke* dataset.

Fig. 2. Results for the *coloring* and *smoke* datasets.

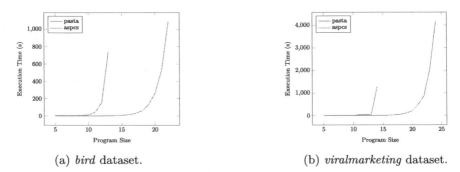

(a) *bird* dataset.

(b) *viralmarketing* dataset.

Fig. 3. Results for the *bird* and *viralmarketing* datasets.

of 0.4. This is an arbitrary value, since the probability of a probabilistic fact does not influence the execution time of the algorithm. For each index i, we include a rule $qr :-\ a(i)$ if i is even and two rules $qr :-\ a(1), not\ nqr$ and $nqr :-\ a(1), not\ qr$ (these are equivalent to the disjunctive rule $qr; nqr :-\ a(i)$) if i is odd. The query is qr. For example, the instance of size 4 is:

```
0.4::a(0).  0.4::a(1).  0.4::a(2).  0.4::a(3).
qr:- a(0).
qr :- a(1), not nqr. nqr :- a(1), not qr.
qr:- a(2).
qr :- a(3), not nqr. nqr :- a(3), not qr.
```

The *qrnqr2* dataset is similar to *qrnqr1*. Given an instance of size n, we have 3 rules: the first rule has qr in the head and all the probabilistic facts $a(i)$ with $i \in [0, n-1]$ and i even in the body. The second rule has qr in the head and all the probabilistic facts $a(i)$ with $i \in [0, n-1]$ and i odd and $not\ nqr$ in the body. The last rule has nqr in the head, all the probabilistic facts $a(i)$ with $i \in [0, n-1]$ and i odd, and $not\ qr$ in the body. The query is qr. For example, the instance of size 4 is:

```
0.4::a(0).  0.4::a(1).  0.4::a(2).  0.4::a(3).
```

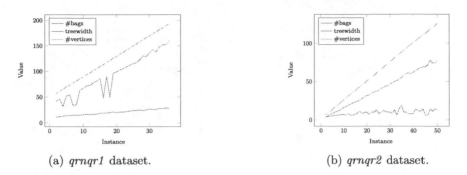

(a) *qrnqr1* dataset.   (b) *qrnqr2* dataset.

Fig. 4. Number of bags (#bags), treewdth, and number of vertices (# vertices) for the *qrnqr1* and *qrnqr2* datasets.

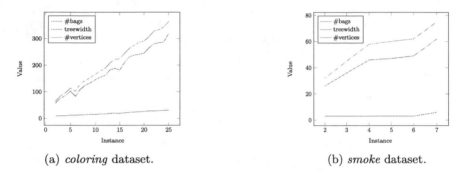

(a) *coloring* dataset.   (b) *smoke* dataset.

Fig. 5. Number of bags (#bags), treewdth, and number of vertices (# vertices) for the *coloring* and *smoke* datasets.

```
qr:- a(0), a(2). qr :- a(1), a(3), not nqr.
nqr :- a(1), a(3), not qr.
```

The *coloring* dataset encodes a graph coloring task, where edges in the graph are associated with a random probability. Some nodes have a fixed color. The program of size 7 is:

```
0.6::edge(1,2). 0.1::edge(1,3).
0.4::edge(2,5). 0.3::edge(2,6).
0.3::edge(3,4). 0.8::edge(4,5).
0.2::edge(5,6).
node(1..6).
red(X) :- node(X), not green(X), not blue(X).
green(X) :- node(X), not red(X), not blue(X).
blue(X) :- node(X), not red(X), not green(X).
e(X,Y) :- edge(X,Y). e(Y,X) :- edge(Y,X).
:- e(X,Y), red(X), red(Y).
:- e(X,Y), green(X), green(Y).
:- e(X,Y), blue(X), blue(Y).
```

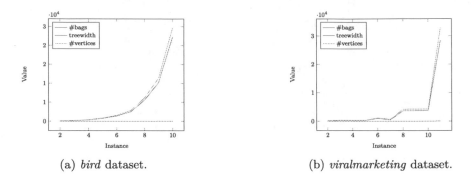

(a) *bird* dataset.   (b) *viralmarketing* dataset.

Fig. 6. Number of bags (#bags), treewdth, and number of vertices (# vertices) for the *bird* and *viralmarketing* datasets.

```
red(1). green(4). green(6).
qr:- blue(3).
```

The query is *qr*. We generate increasing instances of this dataset by adding random probabilistic edges.

The dataset *smokers* is from [23]: it encodes a network of people, indexed with increasing integers starting from 1, where some have asthma (probabilistic rule *asthma*/1), some are stressed (probabilistic rule *stress*/1), and some smoke due to stress (probabilistic rule *smokes*/1), with probability 0.1, 0.3, and 0.4, respectively. If a person Y smokes and influences (probabilistic fact *influences*/2) a person X, then X will also smoke. Smokers have probability of 0.4 to have asthma. Finally, an asthmatic cannot smoke. The base instance, $i1$, is:

```
0.1::asthma(X) :- person(X).
0.3::stress(X) :- person(X).
0.4::smokes(X) :- stress(X).
smokes(X) :- influences(Y,X), smokes(Y).
0.4::asthma(X) :- smokes(X).
:- smokes(X), asthma(X).
person(1). person(2).
0.3::influences(1,2). 0.6::influences(2,1).
```

We are interested in the probability of *smokes*(1). Increasing instances are: $i2 = i1 \cup \{person(3).\}$, $i3 = i2 \cup \{person(4).\}$, $i4 = i3 \cup \{0.2::influences(2,3).\}$, $i5 = i4 \cup \{0.7::influences(3,4).\}$, $i6 = i5 \cup \{0.9::influences(4,1).\}$. PASTA does not support probabilistic rules, so we manually ground the rules, remove the probability in the head and add a probabilistic fact in the body, a different one for every grounding.

We tested the two algorithms also on statistical statements. Since aspmc, and so aspcs, currently does not support aggregates, we manually translate them into ground rules. In the worst case, we get 2^n rules $(\sum_k \binom{n}{k} = 2^n)$, where n is the size of the instance. The *bird* dataset contains an increasing number of probabilistic facts $0.4::bird(i)$, $i \in [0, n-1]$, and a conditional of the form:

```
(fly(X) | bird(X))[0.6,1].
```

which is equivalent to

```
fly(X) :- bird(X), not not_fly(X).
not_fly(X) :- bird(X), not fly(X).
:- #count{X:fly(X),bird(X)} = FB,
   #count{X:bird(X)} = B, 10*FB<6*B.
```

The query is *fly*(1). The instance of size 3 with the constraint with aggregates converted into ground rules is:

```
b1:- bird(1). b1:- bird(2). b1:- bird(3).
:- b1, not fb1.
b2:- bird(1),bird(2). b2:- bird(1),bird(3).
b2:- bird(2),bird(3).
:- b2, not fb2.
b3:- bird(1),bird(2),bird(3).
:- b3, not fb2.
fb1:- fly(1). fb1:- fly(2). fb1:- fly(3).
fb2:- fly(1),fly(2). fb2:- fly(1),fly(3).
fb2:- fly(2),fly(3).
```

Predicate $bk/0$, $k \in \{1,2,3\}$, indicates that at least k probabilistic facts $bird(i)$ are true. Predicate $fbk/0$, $k \in \{1,2\}$ indicates that at least k facts $fly(i)$ are true. Note that the last constraint is :− *b3, not fb2* because given the lower bound 0.6, we have :− $10 \cdot FB < 6 \cdot 3$, so :− $FB < 2$. If the lower bound had been, for example, 0.7, the constraint would have been :− *b3, not fb3* with an additional rule *fb3* :− *fly*(1), *fly*(2), *fly*(3). This translation of the conditionals yields 1420 rules for the instance of size 10, 3048 for size 11, 5694 for size 12, 12301 for size 13, and 22874 rules for size 14.

The *viralmarketing* dataset models a viral marketing scenario, where there is uncertainty on the people (probabilistic facts *person*/1) present in a network. These people advertise (predicate *advertise*/2) a product to other people. A person is reached by the advertisement if it is either directly advertised or advertised by a friend. If advertised, a person can buy or not the product. Finally, a constraint states that at least 70% of the people reached by an advertisement buy an item. The program of size 5 is the following:

```
0.1::person(1). 0.2::person(2).
0.3::person(3). 0.4::person(4). 0.5::person(5).
advertise(1,2):- person(1), person(2).
advertise(2,3):- person(2), person(3).
advertise(2,4):- person(2), person(4).
advertise(3,5):- person(3), person(5).
advertise(4,5):- person(4), person(5).
reach(A,B):- advertise(A,B).
reach(A,B):- advertise(A,C), reach(C,B).
reached(X):- person(X), reach(_,X).
```

```
reached(X):- person(X), advertise(X,_).
{buy(X)} :- reached(X).
:- #count{X:reached(X),buy(X)} = RB,
   #count{X:reached(X)} = R, 10*RB < 7*R.
```

As before, for aspcs, we replace the constraint with aggregates with a set of ground rules. This yields 2016 rules for the instance of size 10, 4055 for size 11, 8141 for size 12, 16322 for size 13, and 32330 for size 14. An instance of size n adds a new individual (person/1 probabilistic fact) and a random connection between two individuals (that are not already connected) to the instance of size $n - 1$. In addition to the execution times (Fig. 1, 2, and 3), we also plotted (Fig. 4, 5, and 6) some statistics of the tree decomposition adopted in aspmc (so aspcs), namely, number of bags, treewidth, and number of vertices.

Overall, when the program does not contain aggregates, aspcs outperforms PASTA in all the datasets. This is due to knowledge compilation adopted in aspmc and so on aspcs. This is particularly evident in Fig. 1b, where the execution time of aspcs seems to be almost constant, possibly because the number of bags, one of the main parameters that drives the construction of the compact form obtained by knowledge compilation, of all the instances is low (77 for the instance of size 50, see Fig. 4). A similar behavior is also present in Fig. 2b. In all the instances, PASTA reaches the time limit. In Fig. 1a, aspcs stops due to the memory limit. When aggregates are present (Fig. 3), aspcs stops due to the memory limit. This can be explained by the statistics of the tree decomposition, where the numbers of bags and vertices increase exponentially (Fig. 6). The biggest instance solved by aspcs for both datasets is 15. For these two datasets, PASTA is faster than aspcs, possibly because enumerating the answer sets is faster than encoding them into a propositional formula and compiling it with knowledge compilation. However, note again that the instance of size 14 of the *viralmarketing* dataset has 32330 rules, so aspcs can handle programs of significant size.

5 Conclusions

In this paper, we proposed aspcs, an algorithm based on aspmc to perform inference in probabilistic answer set programs following the credal semantics via Second Level Algebraic Model Counting. We tested our implementation against the PASTA solver on 6 different datasets. The first four have no aggregates, and aspcs is significantly faster than PASTA. The last two datasets contain statistical statements, and therefore aggregates, which must be manually translated into ground rules, since aspcs does not support them. This translation introduces many more rules, possibly an exponential number, making aspcs slower than PASTA.

Acknowledgements. This work has been partially supported by the Spoke 1 "FutureHPC & BigData" of the Italian Research Center on High-Performance Computing, Big Data and Quantum Computing (ICSC) funded by MUR Missione 4 - Next

Generation EU (NGEU), by TAILOR, a project funded by EU Horizon 2020 research and innovation programme under GA No. 952215, and by the "National Group of Computing Science (GNCS-INDAM)".

References

1. Alviano, M., Faber, W.: Aggregates in answer set programming. KI-Künstliche Intelligenz **32**(2), 119–124 (2018). https://doi.org/10.1007/s13218-018-0545-9
2. Azzolini, D.: A brief discussion about the credal semantics for probabilistic answer set programs. In: Arias, J., et al. (eds.) Proceedings of the International Conference on Logic Programming 2023 Workshops co-located with the 39th International Conference on Logic Programming (ICLP 2023). CEUR Workshop Proceedings, vol. 3437, pp. 1–13. CEUR-WS.org (2023)
3. Azzolini, D., Bellodi, E., Riguzzi, F.: Statistical statements in probabilistic logic programming. In: Gottlob, G., Inclezan, D., Maratea, M. (eds.) LPNMR 2022. LNCS, vol. 13416, pp. 43–55. Springer, Cham (2022). https://doi.org/10.1007/978-3-031-15707-3_4
4. Azzolini, D., Bellodi, E., Riguzzi, F.: MAP inference in probabilistic answer set programs. In: Dovier, A., Montanari, A., Orlandini, A. (eds.) AIxIA 2022. LNCS, vol. 13796, pp. 413–426. Springer, Cham (2023). https://doi.org/10.1007/978-3-031-27181-6_29
5. Bellodi, E., Alberti, M., Riguzzi, F., Zese, R.: MAP inference for probabilistic logic programming. Theory Pract. Logic Program. **20**(5), 641–655 (2020). https://doi.org/10.1017/S1471068420000174
6. Bliem, B., Morak, M., Moldovan, M., Woltran, S.: The impact of treewidth on grounding and solving of answer set programs. J. Artif. Intell. Res. **67**, 35–80 (2020). https://doi.org/10.1613/jair.1.11515
7. Van den Broeck, G., Thon, I., van Otterlo, M., De Raedt, L.: DTProbLog: a decision-theoretic probabilistic Prolog. In: Fox, M., Poole, D. (eds.) Proceedings of the Twenty-Fourth AAAI Conference on Artificial Intelligence, pp. 1217–1222. AAAI Press (2010)
8. Cozman, F.G., Mauá, D.D.: The joy of probabilistic answer set programming: semantics, complexity, expressivity, inference. Int. J. Approximate Reasoning **125**, 218–239 (2020). https://doi.org/10.1016/j.ijar.2020.07.004
9. Darwiche, A.: New advances in compiling CNF into decomposable negation normal form. In: de Mántaras, R.L., Saitta, L. (eds.) 16th European Conference on Artificial Intelligence (ECAI 2004), pp. 328–332. IOS Press (2004)
10. Darwiche, A., Marquis, P.: A knowledge compilation map. J. Artif. Intell. Res. **17**, 229–264 (2002). https://doi.org/10.1613/jair.989
11. De Raedt, L., Kimmig, A., Toivonen, H.: ProbLog: a probabilistic prolog and its application in link discovery. In: Veloso, M.M. (ed.) IJCAI 2007, vol. 7, pp. 2462–2467. AAAI Press (2007)
12. Eiter, T., Hecher, M., Kiesel, R.: Treewidth-aware cycle breaking for algebraic answer set counting. In: Bienvenu, M., Lakemeyer, G., Erdem, E. (eds.) Proceedings of the 18th International Conference on Principles of Knowledge Representation and Reasoning, KR 2021, pp. 269–279 (2021). https://doi.org/10.24963/kr.2021/26
13. Gebser, M., Kaufmann, B., Schaub, T.: Solution enumeration for projected Boolean search problems. In: van Hoeve, W.-J., Hooker, J.N. (eds.) CPAIOR 2009. LNCS,

vol. 5547, pp. 71–86. Springer, Heidelberg (2009). https://doi.org/10.1007/978-3-642-01929-6_7

14. Gelfond, M., Lifschitz, V.: The stable model semantics for logic programming. In: 5th International Conference and Symposium on Logic Programming (ICLP/SLP 1988), vol. 88, pp. 1070–1080. MIT Press, USA (1988)

15. Gondran, M., Minoux, M.: Graphs, Dioids and Semirings: New Models and Algorithms. Operations Research/Computer Science Interfaces Series, 1st edn. Springer, New York (2008). https://doi.org/10.1007/978-0-387-75450-5

16. Halpern, J.Y.: An analysis of first-order logics of probability. Artif. Intell. **46**(3), 311–350 (1990). https://doi.org/10.1016/0004-3702(90)90019-V

17. Kiesel, R., Totis, P., Kimmig, A.: Efficient knowledge compilation beyond weighted model counting. Theory Pract. Logic Program. **22**(4), 505–522 (2022). https://doi.org/10.1017/S147106842200014X

18. Kimmig, A., Van den Broeck, G., De Raedt, L.: Algebraic model counting. J. Appl. Logic **22**(C), 46–62 (2017). https://doi.org/10.1016/j.jal.2016.11.031

19. Riguzzi, F.: Foundations of Probabilistic Logic Programming Languages, Semantics, Inference and Learning, 2nd edn. River Publishers, Gistrup (2023)

20. Rocha, V.H.N., Gagliardi Cozman, F.: A credal least undefined stable semantics for probabilistic logic programs and probabilistic argumentation. In: Kern-Isberner, G., Lakemeyer, G., Meyer, T. (eds.) Proceedings of the 19th International Conference on Principles of Knowledge Representation and Reasoning, KR 2022, pp. 309–319 (2022). https://doi.org/10.24963/kr.2022/31

21. Sato, T.: A statistical learning method for logic programs with distribution semantics. In: Sterling, L. (ed.) ICLP 1995, pp. 715–729. MIT Press (1995). https://doi.org/10.7551/mitpress/4298.003.0069

22. Shterionov, D., Renkens, J., Vlasselaer, J., Kimmig, A., Meert, W., Janssens, G.: The most probable explanation for probabilistic logic programs with annotated disjunctions. In: Davis, J., Ramon, J. (eds.) ILP 2014. LNCS (LNAI), vol. 9046, pp. 139–153. Springer, Cham (2015). https://doi.org/10.1007/978-3-319-23708-4_10

23. Totis, P., De Raedt, L., Kimmig, A.: smProbLog: stable model semantics in ProbLog for probabilistic argumentation. Theory Pract. Logic Program. **23**, 1198–1247 (2023). https://doi.org/10.1017/S147106842300008X

Efficient Modal Decision Trees

F. Manzella[1] , G. Pagliarini[1] , G. Sciavicco[1 (✉)] , and I. E. Stan[2]

[1] University of Ferrara, Ferrara, Italy
federic.manzella@edu.unife.it, {pglgnn,scvgdu}@unife.it
[2] Free University of Bozen-Bolzano, Bolzano, Italy
ioneleduard.stan@unibz.it

Abstract. Modal symbolic learning is an emerging machine learning paradigm for (non)-tabular data, and modal decision trees are its most representative schema. The underlying idea behind modal symbolic learning is that non-tabular (e.g., temporal, spatial, spatial-temporal) instances can be seen as finite Kripke structures of a suitable modal logic and propositional alphabet; from a non-tabular dataset, then, modal formulas can be extracted to solve classic tasks such as classification, regression, and association rules extraction. Although this paradigm has already been proven successful in different learning tasks, a provably correct and complete formulation of modal decision trees has only recently been found. In this paper, we prove that correct and complete modal decision trees are also efficient, learning-wise.

Keywords: Modal symbolic learning · Decision trees · Efficient implementation

1 Introduction

Symbolic learning is the sub-field of machine learning focused on approaching classic tasks (such as classification or regression) via the extraction of logical formulas from data. While often seen as less versatile and statistically accurate, symbolic learning has the advantage of extracting intelligible information that can be later discussed with the domain experts, corrected if necessary, and combined with background knowledge. Out of all possible symbolic learning schemata, *decision trees* are probably the best known ones, and they are also emblematic for a whole range of other symbolic models, such as *decision lists* [13,40], bootstrap aggregation or *bagging* [7], typically based on independent decision trees as in *random forests* [8], *boosting* [25], and, in particular, *gradient boosted trees* (e.g., [12,24]); *hybrid* models combining the strengths of both symbolic and connectionist methods, when based on decision trees, become *neural-symbolic decision trees* [21,44], and *tree-based neural networks* [2,26,33,34,42,43], among others.

The origin of modern decision trees dates back to [3]. In [32] the authors proposed *Automatic Interaction Detection (AID)* as an alternative to functional regression. Whereas AID is used for regression tasks, *Theta AID* [31] and *Chi-Squared AID* [23] extend AID for classification tasks by introducing new impurity *information-based* functions. The *Classification and Regression Trees (CART)* [9] method follows the same greedy approach as the AID-based methods, but adds several features as, for example, pruning techniques to regularize the resulting model to cope with overfitting. Later, Quinlan [37] formalized the development of an inductive process for knowledge acquisition, which resulted in the so-called *Iterative Dichotomizer 3 (ID3)* algorithm, extended with pruning techniques some years later by the same author [39], and improved in terms of learning algorithms with the introduction of C4.5 [38] to cope with the main limitation of ID3 of handling only categorical data. A more complete survey on decision trees can be found, for example, in [18,27,28]. *Modal decision trees* have been introduced in [10], in their temporal form, as a generalization of propositional ones, and later extended and applied to a variety of *non-tabular* data, both in the temporal and in the spatial case, such as respiratory diseases diagnosis [30], land cover classification [35], and electroencephalogram recordings reading and interpreting [16], among others [41]. Modal decision trees, and modal symbolic learning in general, are based on the idea that instances of a non-tabular (that is, temporal, spatial, spatial-temporal, but also text-based and graph-based) dataset can be seen as a set of finite Kripke structures, so that modal (that is, temporal, spatial, and so on) logical formulas can be extracted from such a dataset to solve, for example, classification or regression tasks.

Propositional decision trees are *complete* for the classification task with respect to propositional logic, that is, given a dataset, there always exists an *optimal* tree for it, able to correctly classify each of its instances, whose class is identified by a propositional formula. Learning a *minimal* optimal tree from a dataset is NP-hard [40]; thus, sub-optimal algorithms such as information-based algorithms became the de-facto standard (examples of such algorithms include ID3 and C4.5, mentioned above). In this sense, propositional decision trees are also provably *efficient* in terms of learning, because an optimal (but not necessarily minimal) decision tree can be learned by a polynomial-time information-based algorithm from a dataset. While modal decision trees have already been shown to be able to extract useful, accurate, and interpretable models, their properties have only recently been studied [19]. As it turns out, modal decision trees too are complete for the classification task with respect to modal logic. This solves a problem that was open since the first proposals concerning methods for non-propositional logical formulas extraction from data [5,6,17], but leaves as open the question of whether modal decision trees are also efficient, that is, whether there exists a polynomial-time information-based algorithm that learns an optimal decision tree from a dataset. In this paper, we prove that modal decision tree are *weakly efficient*, which means that there exists a polynomial algorithm that, given a dataset, returns a *t-optimal* tree for it, able to classify in the perfect way each of its instances whose class is determined by a modal formula of length less than or equal to t; we also discuss in detail the problem of minimizing the experimental complexity of an implementation of such an algorithm, by leveraging the nature of the modal formulas that are actually examined during the learning process and by exploiting a suitable memoization approach.

2   Propositional Decision Trees

Definition 1. *A* tabular dataset *is a finite collection of* m *instances* $\mathcal{I} = \{\mathfrak{I}_1, \ldots, \mathfrak{I}_m\}$, *each described by the value of* n *variables* $\mathcal{V} = \{V_1, \ldots, V_n\}$, *and associated to a unique label from a set* $\mathcal{L} = \{L_1, \ldots, L_k\}$.

Several problems are associated to tabular datasets: classification (when labels are categorical – in this case they are also called *classes*), regression (when labels are numerical), association rules extraction (when labels are absent or ignored). In the symbolic context, datasets are naturally associated to a logical alphabet $\mathcal{P}$ of propositional letters (which represents an *inductive bias*, in a learning context), from which formulas are built. While in some cases alphabets are the result of a suitable variable selection and/or domain filtration, from a purely methodological point of view we can always assume that:

$$\mathcal{P} = \{V \bowtie v \mid V \in \mathcal{V}, a \in \mathbb{R}, \bowtie \in \{<, \leq, =, \neq, \geq, >\}\},$$

where $\bowtie$ is a *test operator*; whenever necessary, for a given variable V, we shall refer to its *domain*, defined as the set of all and only distinct values that V takes in a given dataset. Tabular datasets can be also defined as *propositional* datasets, as follows.

Definition 2. *A* propositional dataset *is a finite collection of* m *instances* $\mathcal{I} = \{\mathfrak{I}_1, \ldots, \mathfrak{I}_m\}$, *each described as a propositional model over a given alphabet* $\mathcal{P}$ *and associated to a unique label from a set* $\mathcal{L} = \{L_1, \ldots, L_k\}$.

The purpose of symbolic classification is to extract from a dataset $\mathcal{I}$ a (set of) logical formula(s) to be used as rule(s) for classifying instances of a dataset $\mathcal{J}$ drawn from the same distribution as $\mathcal{I}$. Decision trees allows one to do so in a very convenient way. In the classical setting, formulas are written in *propositional logic*.

Let $\tau = (\mathcal{V}, \mathcal{E})$ be a *full binary directed tree* with *nodes* in $\mathcal{V}$ and *edges* in $\mathcal{E} \subseteq \mathcal{V} \times \mathcal{V}$. We denote by $\mathcal{V}^\ell$ the set of its *leaf nodes* (or, simply, *leaves*), and by $\mathcal{V}^\iota$ the set of its *internal nodes* (i.e., non-root and non-leaf nodes). Given a tree τ, we denote its *root* by $\rho(\tau)$, and its nodes (either root, internal or leaf) by $\nu, \nu_1, \nu_2, \ldots$ and leaves by $\ell, \ell_1, \ell_2, \ldots$ Each non-leaf node ν of a tree τ has precisely two *children*, the *left child* $\mathrel{\lrcorner}(\nu)$ and the *right child* $\searrow(\nu)$, and each non-root node ν has a *parent* $\wr(\nu)$. For a node ν, the set of its *ancestors* (ν included) is denoted by $\wr^*(\nu)$, where $\wr^*$ is the transitive and reflexive closure of $\wr$; we also define $\wr^+(\nu) = \wr^*(\nu) \setminus \{\nu\}$, and we say that if $\nu' \in \wr^+(\nu)$, then ν is a *descendant* of ν'. Moreover, given a tree τ, a *path* $\pi = \nu_0 \rightsquigarrow \nu_h$ in τ of *length* $h \geq 0$ between two nodes ν_0 and ν_h is a finite sequence of $h + 1$ nodes such that $\nu_i = \wr(\nu_{i+1})$, for each $i = 0, \ldots, h - 1$. We denote by $\pi_1 \cdot \pi_2$ the operation of *appending* the path π_2 to path π_1. A *branch of* τ is a path π_ℓ, for some $\ell \in V^\ell$. For a path π and a node ν, π_ν denotes the unique path $\rho(\tau) \rightsquigarrow \nu$. Finally, given two paths π_1, π_2, we denote by $\pi_1 \sqsubseteq \pi_2$ the fact that π_1 is a not necessarily proper prefix of π_2.

Definition 3. *Let* $\mathcal{I}$ *be a dataset with set of classes* $\mathcal{L}$ *and set of associated propositional letters* $\mathcal{P}$, *and define the set of propositional decisions* $\Lambda = \{p, \neg p \mid p \in \mathcal{P}\}$. *Then, a* propositional decision tree *(over* Λ*) is an object of the type:*

$$\tau = (\mathcal{V}, \mathcal{E}, l, e),$$

where $(\mathcal{V}, \mathcal{E})$ *is a full binary directed tree,* $l : \mathcal{V}^\ell \to \mathcal{L}$ *is a leaf-labelling function that assigns a class from* $\mathcal{L}$ *to each leaf node in* $\mathcal{V}^\ell$, $e : \mathcal{E} \to \Lambda$ *is a edge-labelling function that assigns a propositional decision from* Λ *to each edge in* $\mathcal{E}$, *such that* $e(\nu, \swarrow(\nu)) \equiv \neg e(\nu, \searrow(\nu))$ *for all non-leaf node* ν. *For a path* $\pi = \nu_0 \rightsquigarrow \nu_h$ *in* τ, *the path-formula* φ_π *is defined as:*

$$\varphi_\pi = \top \wedge \bigwedge_{\nu_i \in \pi, i < h} e(\nu_i, \nu_{i+1}).$$

For a leaf ℓ, *the* leaf-formula φ_ℓ *is defined as:*

$$\varphi_\ell = \varphi_{\pi_\ell},$$

and for a class $L \in \mathcal{L}$, *the* class-formula *is defined as:*

$$\varphi_L = \bigvee_{l(\ell) = L} \varphi_{\pi_\ell}.$$

Finally, the run *of* τ *on* $\mathcal{I}$ *from* ν, *denoted by* $\tau(\mathcal{I}, \nu)$, *is defined as follows:*

$$\tau(\mathcal{I}, \nu) = \begin{cases} l(\nu) & \text{if } \nu \in \mathcal{V}^\ell; \\ \tau(\mathcal{I}, \swarrow(\nu)) & \text{if } \mathcal{I} \models \varphi_{\pi_{\swarrow(\nu)}}; \\ \tau(\mathcal{I}, \searrow(\nu)) & \text{if } \mathcal{I} \models \varphi_{\pi_{\searrow(\nu)}}, \end{cases}$$

and the run $\tau(\mathcal{I})$ *of* $\mathcal{I}$ *on* τ *is simply* $\tau(\mathcal{I}, \rho(\tau))$. *An instance* $\mathcal{I}$ *is classified into* $L \in \mathcal{L}$ *by* τ *if and only if* $\tau(\mathcal{I}, \rho(\tau)) = L$.

Definition 4. *A decision tree is said to be* optimal *for a dataset* $\mathcal{I}$ *with respect to a logic if and only if, for every instance* $\mathcal{I}$ *whose class is identified by a formula of that logic,* $\tau(\mathcal{I}) = L$ *if and only if* $\mathcal{I}$ *is labelled by* L.

Definition 5. *A family of decision trees is* correct *if and only if every tree classifies every instance into exactly one class. Furthermore, it is* complete *with respect to a logic if and only if, for every dataset, there exists the optimal tree for it with respect to that logic. Finally, it is* efficient *with respect to a logic if and only if there exists a polynomial-time algorithm that, for every dataset, learns an optimal tree for it with respect to that logic.*

It is well-known that the family $\mathcal{DT}$ of propositional decision trees is correct, complete, and efficient with respect of propositional logic.

3 Modal Decision Trees

Symbolic learning is founded on the idea that patterns (in our context, classification patterns) are expressible in propositional logic. Non-tabular data, however, may be too complex to be adequately described using propositional logic. *Modal logic* extends propositional logic by assuming the existence of many propositional *worlds*, connected by *binary relations*. Each world plays the role of a propositional model; in the standard, philosophical formulation, the relation plays the role of *accessibility* among worlds. So, given a set of propositional letters $\mathcal{P}$, formulas of modal logic are generated by the following grammar:

$$\varphi :: = p \mid \neg\varphi \mid \varphi \wedge \varphi \mid \Diamond\varphi,$$

where $p \in \mathcal{P}$. The remaining classic Boolean operators can be obtained as shortcuts; similarly, we use $\Box\varphi$ to denote $\neg\Diamond\neg\varphi$. The *modality* $\Diamond$ (resp., $\Box$) is usually referred to as *it is possible that* (resp., *it is necessary that*), and called *diamond* (resp., *box*). The semantics of modal logic is given in terms of Kripke structures. A *Kripke structure*, over $\mathcal{P}$, $\mathfrak{K} = (\mathcal{W}, \mathcal{R}, \mathfrak{V})$ consists of a non-empty (possible infinite, but countable) set of *(possible) worlds* $\mathcal{W}$, a *binary accessibility relation* over worlds $\mathcal{R} \subseteq \mathcal{W} \times \mathcal{W}$, and a *valuation function* $\mathfrak{V} : \mathcal{W} \to 2^{\mathcal{P}}$, which associates each world w with the set of proposition letters $\mathfrak{V}(w) \subseteq \mathcal{P}$ that are true on it. The *truth (relation)* $\mathfrak{K}, w \Vdash \varphi$, for a (Kripke) model $\mathfrak{K}$, a world w (in that model), and a formula φ, is defined by induction on the complexity of formulas:

$$\mathfrak{K}, w \Vdash p \qquad \text{iff } p \in \mathfrak{V}(w), \text{ for all } p \in \mathcal{P};$$
$$\mathfrak{K}, w \Vdash \neg\psi \qquad \text{iff } \mathfrak{K}, w \nVdash \psi;$$
$$\mathfrak{K}, w \Vdash \psi_1 \wedge \psi_2 \text{ iff } \mathfrak{K}, w \Vdash \psi_1 \text{ and } \mathfrak{K}, w \Vdash \psi_2;$$
$$\mathfrak{K}, w \Vdash \Diamond\psi \qquad \text{iff there exists } w' \text{ s.t. } w\mathcal{R}w' \text{ and } \mathfrak{K}, w' \Vdash \psi.$$

We write $\mathfrak{K} \Vdash \varphi$ as an abbreviation of $\mathfrak{K}, w_0 \Vdash \varphi$, where w_0 is the *initial world* of $\mathfrak{K}$. Modal logic is paradigmatic for propositional temporal, spatial, spatial-temporal logics, as well as description logics, epistemic logics, and many others. Indeed, most classic temporal logics [14,22,36] and spatial logics [1,29] are in fact specializations of modal logic with more than one (possibly non-binary) accessibility relations (and associated modalities), subject to constraints that range from very simple and intuitive ones (e.g., transitivity, antisymmetry) to very complex ones (e.g., when worlds are assumed to be intervals and modalities are assumed to mimic relations between intervals).

Inspired by the generalization from propositional to modal logic, we can now define modal datasets.

Definition 6. *A labelled modal dataset is a finite collection of m instances $\mathcal{I} = \{\mathfrak{I}_1, \ldots, \mathfrak{I}_m\}$, each described as a finite Kripke structure over a given alphabet $\mathcal{P}$ and associated to a unique label from a set $\mathcal{L} = \{L_1, \ldots, L_k\}$.*

The link between non-tabular datasets and modal ones, as well as the role and the nature of the variables in modal datasets can be explained with an example.

Consider the case of temporal data. In its most general setting, a *temporal dataset* is a collection of m temporal instances, where a temporal instance is a *multivariate time series*, described by a set of n temporal variables $\mathcal{V} = \{V_1, \ldots, V_n\}$, each taking a value at each of N distinct instants. A possible way to extract logical information from a temporal dataset is to consider a set of *feature extraction functions* $\mathcal{F} = \{F_1, \ldots, F_s\}$, each defined as $F_i : \mathbb{R} \times \ldots \times \mathbb{R} \to \mathbb{R}$ (e.g., the generalized mean, or the number of local maxima), and then apply them to every *interval* (i.e., to the set of values that a temporal variable takes between an ordered pair of temporal points) of the temporal domain $[1, \ldots, N]$. In this way, each interval can be seen as a world, and the alphabet becomes:

$$\mathcal{P} = \{F(V) \bowtie v \mid F \in \mathcal{F}, V \in \mathcal{V}, v \in \mathbb{R}, \bowtie \in \{<, \leq, =, \neq, \geq, >\}\},$$

and the different relations between any two intervals can play the role of binary accessibility relations, resulting into an instance of *Halpern and Shoham's modal logic for time intervals* (*HS*). Reasoning with intervals is clearly not the only way to extract information from temporal data, but it is a very convenient one; it has been successfully used in [11,30], among others. This approach can be also generalized to spatial data, by considering a multi-dimensional generalization of *HS*, as in [35]. Other types of non-tabular data, such as graph-based data, can be even more naturally treated in the same way, as Kripke structures are, in fact, graphs. However, all kinds of non-tabular data share the notion of variable, so that the above definition of propositional letters ($\mathcal{P}$) can be considered relatively general. Therefore, in the following, we shall assume that a modal dataset is, in fact, characterized by n variables, as it is in the propositional case.

It is natural to ask if, and how, decision trees too can be generalized from propositional to modal logic. This has been first proposed in [10] in the special case of the temporal logic *HS*; in their prototypical version, modal decision trees were not able to express every possible modal formula. Successive extensions have improved several aspects of modal decision trees, but a provably complete version has been proposed only in [19]; notably, other, incomplete, versions of modal decision trees had been proposed earlier, again in the temporal case [6,17]. The idea behind modal decision trees is that the tree structure must be enriched in order to design an information-based learning algorithm that does not need to explore an exponential number of formulas. Completeness and efficiency can be obtained together at the propositional level because propositional formulas can always be expressed in disjunctive normal form. While there are several proposals for modal disjunctive normal forms, they all share a definition of literal whose modal prefix has an arbitrary number of modalities (see, e.g., [4]), and are therefore unsuitable for a straightforward implementation of modal decision trees. At a closer look, it appears evident that the main obstacle on the road to efficiency of modal logic decision trees learning is the fact that diamonds (resp., boxes) do not distribute over conjunctions (resp., disjunctions), that is, modal logic is not *separable*. As a consequence, learning modal formulas in an inductive, information-based fashion, requires building complex formulas along the branches of a tree.

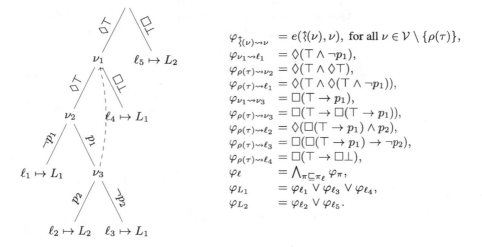

Fig. 1. A modal decision tree τ (right) and all its relevant path-, leaf-, and class-formulas (left). For each node, non-displayed backward-edges and forward-edges are assumed to be self-loops.

Definition 7 ([19], modified). *Let $\mathcal{I}$ be a modal dataset with set of classes $\mathcal{L}$ and set of associated propositional letters $\mathcal{P}$, and define the set of modal decisions $\Lambda = \{p, \neg p, \mid p \in \mathcal{P}\} \cup \{\top, \bot, \Diamond\top, \Box\bot\}$. Then, a modal decision tree (over Λ) is an object of the type:*

$$\tau = (\mathcal{V}, \mathcal{E}, l, e, b, f),$$

where $(\mathcal{V}, \mathcal{E})$ is a full binary directed tree, $l : \mathcal{V}^\ell \to \mathcal{L}$ is a leaf-labelling function that assigns a class from $\mathcal{L}$ to each leaf node in $\mathcal{V}^\ell$, $e : \mathcal{E} \to \Lambda$ is a edge-labelling function that assigns a modal decision to each edge in $\mathcal{E}$, $b : \mathcal{V}^\iota \to \mathcal{V}^\iota$ is a backward-edge function that links an internal node to one of its ancestors, and $f : \mathcal{V} \setminus \mathcal{V}^\ell \to \mathcal{V}^\iota$ is a forward-edge function that links a non-leaf node to one of its descendants, such that, for all $\nu, \nu'\nu'' \in \mathcal{V}$:

1. *if $\nu, \nu' \in \mathcal{V}^\ell$ and $\wr(\nu) = \wr(\nu')$, then $l(\nu) \neq l(\nu')$,*
2. *if $\nu \notin \mathcal{V}^\ell$, then $e(\nu, \nearrow(\nu)) \equiv \neg e(\nu, \searrow(\nu))$,*
3. *if $b(\nu) = \nu'$, then $\nu' \in \wr^*(\nu)$,*
4. *if $b(\nu) \neq \nu$ and $b(\nu') \neq \nu'$, then $b(\nu) \neq b(\nu')$,*
5. *if $b(\nu) = \nu', \nu' \in \wr^+(\nu''),$ and $\nu'' \in \wr^+(\nu)$, then $\nu' \in \wr^+(b(\nu''))$,*
6. *if $(\nu, \nu') \in \mathcal{E}, \nu' \notin \mathcal{V}^\ell,$ and $e(\nu, \nu') \in \{\bot, \Box\bot\}$, then $b(\nu') \neq \nu'$, and*
7. *if $f(\nu) = \nu'$, then $\nu \in \wr^*(\nu)$.*

For a path $\pi = \nu_0 \rightsquigarrow \nu_h$ in τ, with $h > 1$, the contributor of π, denoted by $\zeta(\pi)$, is defined as the only node $\nu_i \in \pi$ such that $\nu_i \neq \nu_1$, with $0 < i < h$, and $b(\nu_i) = \nu_1$, if it exists, and ν_1, otherwise. Moreover, given two nodes $\nu_i, \nu_j \in \pi$, with $i, j < h$, we say that they agree, denoted by $\mathfrak{A}(\nu_i, \nu_j)$, if $\nu_{i+1} = \nearrow(\nu_i)$ (resp., $\nu_{i+1} = \searrow(\nu_i)$) and $\nu_{j+1} = \nearrow(\nu_j)$ (resp., $\nu_{j+1} = \searrow(\nu_j)$); otherwise, we say that they disagree, denoted by $\mathfrak{D}(\nu_i, \nu_j)$. Furthermore, we say that a modal formula φ is implicative if it has the form $\varphi_1 \to \varphi_2$ or $\Box(\varphi_1 \to \varphi_2)$, and we denote by

Im the set of implicative formulas. *The* path-formula φ_π *is defined inductively as* $\top$ *if* $h = 0$, $e(\nu_0, \nu_1)$ *if* $h = 1$, *and, if* $h > 1$, $\lambda = e(\nu_0, \nu_1)$, $\pi_1 = \nu_1 \rightsquigarrow \zeta(\pi)$, *and* $\pi_2 = \zeta(\pi) \rightsquigarrow \nu_h$, *then* φ_π *is:*

- $\lambda \wedge (\varphi_{\pi_1} \wedge \varphi_{\pi_2})$, *if* $\lambda \neq \Diamond\top, \mathfrak{A}(\nu_0, \zeta(\pi))$, *and* $\varphi_{\pi_2} \notin Im$, *or* $\lambda \neq \Diamond\top, \mathfrak{D}(\nu_0, \zeta(\pi))$ *and* $\varphi_{\pi_2} \in Im$;
- $\lambda \rightarrow (\varphi_{\pi_1} \rightarrow \varphi_{\pi_2})$, *if* $\lambda \neq \Diamond\top, \mathfrak{D}(\nu_0, \zeta(\pi))$, *and* $\varphi_{\pi_2} \notin Im$, *or* $\lambda \neq \Diamond\top, \mathfrak{A}(\nu_0, \zeta(\pi))$, *and* $\varphi_{\pi_2} \in Im$;
- $\Diamond(\varphi_{\pi_1} \wedge \varphi_{\pi_2})$, *if* $\lambda = \Diamond\top, \mathfrak{A}(\nu_0, \zeta(\pi))$ *and* $\varphi_{\pi_2} \notin Im$, *or* $\lambda = \Diamond\top, \mathfrak{D}(\nu_0, \zeta(\pi))$, *and* $\varphi_{\pi_2} \in Im$;
- $\Box(\varphi_{\pi_1} \rightarrow \varphi_{\pi_2})$, *if* $\lambda = \Diamond\top, \mathfrak{D}(\nu_0, \zeta(\pi))$ *and* $\varphi_{\pi_2} \notin Im$, *or* $\lambda = \Diamond\top, \mathfrak{A}(\nu_0, \zeta(\pi^\tau))$ *and* $\varphi_{\pi_2} \in Im$.

For each leaf $\ell \in \mathcal{V}^\ell$, *the* leaf-formula φ_ℓ *is defined as:*

$$\varphi_\ell = \bigwedge_{\pi \sqsubseteq \pi_\ell} \varphi_\pi,$$

and for each class L, *the* class-formula φ_L *is defined as:*

$$\varphi_L = \bigvee_{l(\ell) = L} \varphi_{\pi_\ell}.$$

Finally, the run *of* τ *on* $\Im$ *from* ν, *denoted by* $\tau(\Im, \nu)$, *is defined as follows:*

$$\tau(\Im, \nu) = \begin{cases} l(\nu) & if \quad \nu \in \mathcal{V}^\ell; \\ \tau(\Im, \swarrow(f(\nu))) & if \quad \Im \Vdash \varphi_{\pi_{\swarrow(f(\nu))}}; \\ \tau(\Im, \searrow(f(\nu))) & if \quad \Im \Vdash \varphi_{\pi_{\searrow(f(\nu))}}, \end{cases}$$

and the run *of* τ *on* $\Im$, *denoted by* $\tau(\Im)$, *is defined as* $\tau(\Im, \rho(\tau))$. *An instance* $\Im$ *is* classified *into* $L \in \mathcal{L}$ *by* τ *if and only if* $\tau(\Im, \rho(\tau)) = L$.

An example of modal decision tree can be seen in Fig. 1. The idea behind modal decision trees is that backward-edges allow one to add conjuncts and disjuncts to a leaf-formula at any modal depth. Compared with the original definition in [19], the addition of forward-edges straightforwardly allows one to improve the completeness result by formalizing the idea of *lookahead*, that is, the possibility for a modal decision tree to classify using complex formulas on top of simple decisions.

Theorem 1 ([19], modified). *The family* $\mathcal{MDT}$ *of modal decision trees is correct and complete with respect to modal logic.*

As it turns out, a learning algorithm for modal decision trees can still be implemented in an efficient way, but to a lesser extent compared with propositional ones; intuitively, in order to have polynomial time learning, we can only guarantee optimality up to a certain formula length. *ModalCART*, shown in Algorithm 1, is the adaptation of the well-known (family of) algorithm(s) known as *CART*, on which the more famous C4.5, ID3, among many others, are based.

It is an information-based approach to decision tree learning, whose main step is founded on computing the amount of information contained in a dataset (via *entropy*, *Gini index*, or similar measures), which drives a locally optimal choice. The function *SubTrees*, given the set of decisions Λ, a height i and a set of ancestors $\mathcal{N}$, returns all trees of height i with exactly two nodes at any given level greater than 0, with edge labels chosen from Λ, where (consistently with Definition 7) all outgoing backward-edges lead to a node in $\mathcal{N}$, and whose root is linked via forward-edge to the (only) non-leaf node at level $i-1$. Thus, *FindBestSubTree* generalizes the operation of finding the best split to the case of lookahead t; in this way, if a class is determined by a modal formula of length less than or equal to t, such a formula will be certainly found and expressed a branch of the tree, which implies that Algorithm 1 correctly finds a t-optimal tree.

Definition 8. *A decision tree is said to be t-optimal for a dataset $\mathcal{I}$ with respect to a logic if and only if, for every instance $\mathfrak{I}$ whose class is identified by a formula of that logic with length less than or equal to t, $\tau(\mathfrak{I}) = L$ if and only if $\mathfrak{I}$ is labelled by L. A family of decision trees is weakly efficient with respect to a logic if and only if there exists a polynomial-time algorithm that, for every dataset, learns a t-optimal tree for it with respect to that logic when t is constant.*

Algorithm 1: High-level description of *ModalCART*.

---

  function $ModalCART(\mathcal{I}, \Lambda, t)$:
    | $\tau \leftarrow Initialize()$
    | $\rho(\tau) \leftarrow Learn(\mathcal{I}, \Lambda, \emptyset, t)$
    | **return** τ
  end
  function $Learn(\mathcal{I}, \Lambda, \mathcal{N}, t)$:
    | **if** *no stopping condition applies* **then**
    | $\nu \leftarrow FindBestSubTree(\mathcal{I}, \Lambda, \mathcal{N}, t)$
    | $f(\nu).left \leftarrow Learn(\mathcal{I}_{\swarrow(f(\nu))}, \Lambda, \mathcal{N} \cup \{\nu\}, t)$
    | $f(\nu).right \leftarrow Learn(\mathcal{I}_{\searrow(f(\nu))}, \Lambda, \mathcal{N} \cup \{\nu\}, t)$
    | **else**
    | $\nu \leftarrow CreateLeafNode(\mathcal{I})$
    | **return** ν
  end
  function $FindBestSubTree(\mathcal{I}, \Lambda, \mathcal{N}, t)$:
    | $(\epsilon, \epsilon_\nu) \leftarrow (-\infty, nil)$
    | **foreach** $i \in 1, \ldots, t$ **do**
    | **foreach** $\nu \in SubTrees(\Lambda, \mathcal{N}, i)$ **do**
    | $\mathcal{I}_{\swarrow(f(\nu))} \leftarrow$ subset of $\mathcal{I}$ satisfying $\varphi_{\swarrow(f(\nu))}$
    | $\mathcal{I}_{\searrow(f(\nu))} \leftarrow$ subset of $\mathcal{I}$ satisfying $\varphi_{\searrow(f(\nu))}$
    | **if** $\epsilon < Info(\mathcal{I}_{\swarrow(f(\nu))}, \mathcal{I}_{\searrow(f(\nu))})$ **then**
    | $(\epsilon, \epsilon_\nu) \leftarrow (Info(\mathcal{I}_{\swarrow(f(\nu))}, \mathcal{I}_{\searrow(f(\nu))}), \nu)$
    | **return** ϵ_ν
  end

Lemma 1. *Given a dataset $\mathcal{I}$ with m instances, each with n variables and N distinct worlds, a set of nodes $\mathcal{N}$, and given a lookahead amount t, the running time of FindBestSubTree($\mathcal{I}, \Lambda, \mathcal{N}, t$) is:*

$$\mathcal{O}(t(nm^2N)^t mN).$$

Proof. As per Definition 7, a single split in a tree is the result of model-checking one path-formula (and its negation) on every instance $\mathcal{I}$ of the current dataset, at the world w_0; given a generic modal formula φ, one can simply apply a finite model-checking algorithm that labels every world with the truth value of all sub-formulas (in non-decreasing order of length). Using a technique similar to [15], the cost of such a check, for all instances, is $\mathcal{O}(|\varphi|N^2m)$. Approaching *FindBestSubTree* naïvely would imply to repeat such a process for all possible formulas that could be generated at a given step; moreover, with lookahead t, this single step requires trying all sub-trees of height at most t. However, the weak completeness guarantees that one may limit the exploration of incomplete sub-trees with exactly two nodes at each given height. Given a set of ancestors $\mathcal{N}$ to which backward-edges may lead, the number of structurally different such sub-trees, of height $1 \leq i \leq t$, is bounded by $2^{i-1}(|\mathcal{N}| + i - 1)^i$; for each of such sub-trees, we must check $(2nmN + 4)^i$ different formulas which are obtained by choosing a different decision on each edge (observe that, given that one formula differs from another one by at least one of the i decisions, the number of different formulas is determined by the number of decisions $|\Lambda|$; the latter, in turn, is bounded by the number of different variables, n, times the cardinality of the domain of an variable, mN, times 2 different test operators – observe that with numerical variables and finite domains, limiting $\bowtie \in \{\geq, <\}$ suffices to explore all propositional letters, plus 4, which is the cardinality of $\{\lozenge\top, \square\bot, \top, \bot\}$). Summarizing, a naïve implementation of *FindBestSubTree* runs in time:

$$\mathcal{O}(\Sigma_{i=1}^t 2^{i-1}(m + i - 1)^i (2nmN + 4)^i m^2 N^2) = \mathcal{O}(t(nm^2N)^t m^2 N^2),$$

considering that, during the execution, both the number of any set of ancestors and the length of any formula are bounded by m and that every element of the summation can be bounded by $2^{t-1}(m + t - 1)^t (2nmN + 4)^t$. For a small enough t, it makes sense to reduce the above complexity by exploiting the nature of propositional letters via memoization. Observe that at any given step some formulas to be checked have the same structure, only differing by the numerical constants within the propositional letters. By way of example, consider checking a set of formulas $\lozenge(V < a)$ on a single world w of an instance $\mathcal{I}$. The number of worlds that are accessible from w is bounded by N, and the domain of the variable by mN. Thus, a single check of all such formulas takes $\mathcal{O}(mN^2)$. If, instead, we compute and store the minimum of the values for V on every world accessible from w (which takes time $\mathcal{O}(N)$), we can check each of the mN similar formulas in time $\mathcal{O}(1)$, by comparing a with the computed value. Generalizing, consider now the case where $t = 1$. In such a case, the execution of *FindBestSubTree* consists of exploring at most $|\Lambda|m$ different formulas; the factor m depends on the possible backward-edges of the newly formed tree, and the factor $|\Lambda|$ depends on the element that changes from one formula to another. The set of formulas can, then, be partitioned into $2n + 4$ groups. All formulas within a single group are *siblings*, that is, they share the structure of the syntax tree and differ by exactly a numerical constant at a leaf; the groups that emerge from decisions that are not propositional letters are singletons. The key idea is that we can compute, save, and use a single scalar value for each of such groups in order to check all siblings within the group. We now describe a memoization structure, keyed in a triple formed by a formula φ, an instance $\mathfrak{I}$, and a world w, and returning a single number that suffices to check the truth of every sibling formula of φ on $\mathfrak{I}, w$. For a given φ generated by the grammar in Definition 7, we denote the biggest sub-formula that contains the variable part (that is, the single leaf that identifies an element which its group of its siblings) by $\bar{\varphi}$. For convenience, let us define the special values $\top(\geq) = \infty, \top(<) = -\infty, \bot(\geq) = -\infty, \top(<) = \infty$. We inductively define the memoization structure, denoted by T, fixed $\mathfrak{I}$ and w, and fixed V and $\bowtie$ that identify the variable part of φ, as follows:

$$T[\top] = \top(\bowtie) \qquad\qquad T[\lozenge\top] = \begin{cases} \top(\bowtie) \text{ if } |\{(w, w') \in R\}| > 0, \\ \bot(\bowtie) \text{ otherwise} \end{cases}$$

$$T[\bar{p}] = H[\mathfrak{I}, w, V] \qquad T[V' \bowtie' a] = \begin{cases} \top(\bowtie) \text{ if } H[\mathfrak{I}, w, V'] \bowtie' a, \\ \bot(\bowtie) \text{ otherwise} \end{cases}$$

$$T[\varphi \wedge \bar{\varphi}'] = \begin{cases} T[\bar{\varphi}'] \text{ if } \mathfrak{I}, w \Vdash \varphi \\ \bot(\bowtie) \text{ otherwise} \end{cases} \qquad T[\lozenge(\varphi \wedge \bar{\varphi}')] = \begin{cases} \underset{w' \in W(\mathfrak{I}, w, \varphi)}{\zeta} T[\bar{\varphi}'] \text{ if } \mathfrak{I}, w \Vdash \lozenge\varphi \\ \top(\bowtie) \qquad\qquad\text{ otherwise,} \end{cases}$$

where $\zeta = \max$ (resp., min) if $\bowtie = \geq$ (resp., $<$), $W(\mathfrak{I}, w, \varphi)$ is the set of worlds in $\mathfrak{I}$ where φ holds and are accessible from w, and H holds the value of each variable V, at each world w of each instance $\mathfrak{I}$; the missing cases can be treated in a similar way. Fixed a formula $\bar{\varphi}$ that belongs to the group of sibling formulas varying the value a for a specific propositional letter built on V and $\bowtie$ (let us denote such a formula by $\bar{\varphi}_{V,\bowtie}(v)$), it holds that:

$$\mathfrak{I}, w \Vdash \bar{\varphi}_{V,\bowtie}(v) \Leftrightarrow T[\bar{\varphi}_{V,\bowtie}] \bowtie v.$$

As noticed before, within a call to $FindBestSubTree$ the number of structurally different sub-trees of height i that are tested is at most $2^{i-1}(m + i - 1)^i$. Each of the sub-trees gives rise to $2n(2nmN + 4)^{i-1}$ groups of mM siblings, plus $4(2nmN + 4)^{i-1}$ singletons; within each group, the formulas differ from each other by the decision taken at level i. One key observation at this point is that, in order to find the best formula (with respect to a given information measure) from a group of mN sibling formulas induced by $\bar{\varphi}_{V,\bowtie}$, we do not need to check the truth of every one of them on every instance that reached the node. In fact, we only need to check the m formulas that correspond to $\bar{\varphi}_{V,\bowtie}(v)$ with a equal to the corresponding $T[\bar{\varphi}_{V,\bowtie}]$ value of any instance $\mathfrak{I}$; this requires $\mathcal{O}(m^2 N^2)$ time for pre-computing m values $T[\bar{\varphi}]$, plus $\mathcal{O}(m^2 N^2)$ for performing m checks. Therefore, the overall cost becomes:

$$\mathcal{O}(\Sigma_{i=1}^{t} 2^{i-1}(m + i - 1)^i (2nmN + 4)^{i-1}(2n + 4)m^2 N^2) = \mathcal{O}(t(nm^2N)^t mN).$$

Lemma 2. *Given a dataset $\mathcal{I}$ with m instances, each with n variables and N distinct worlds, and given a lookahead amount t, the running time of ModalCART($\mathcal{I}, \Lambda, t$) is:*

$$\mathcal{O}(m^{2(t+1)+1}),$$

in the worst case, and:

$$\mathcal{O}(m^{2(t+1)} \lg(m)),$$

in the average case, assuming constant n, N, and t.

Proof. ModalCART is a recursive procedure whose complexity can be approached via a recurrence; even with lookahead $t > 1$, each step consists, at most, of 2 recursive calls. Assuming constant n and N corresponds to studying the complexity of *ModalCART* as the number of instances grows without changing in nature; assuming constant t is equivalent to fixing a learning parameter. In the worst case, every split of a dataset of cardinality m ends up assigning exactly one instance to a branch and exactly $m - 1$ instances to the other one, so that the recurrence is:

$$T(m) = T(m-1) + \mathcal{O}(m^{2(t+1)}),$$

which ends up being bounded by:

$$T(m) = \mathcal{O}(m^{2(t+1)+1}).$$

In the average case, however, we can assume that all splits are equally likely in terms of relative sizes. Thus the recurrence that describes the time complexity becomes:

$$\begin{aligned} T(m) &= \tfrac{1}{m-1} \sum_{i=1}^{m-1} (T(i) + T(m-i)) + \mathcal{O}(m^{2(t+1)}) \\ &= \tfrac{2}{m-1} \sum_{i=1}^{m-1} T(i) + \mathcal{O}(m^{2(t+1)}). \end{aligned}$$

We claim that $T(m) = \mathcal{O}(m^{2(t+1)} \lg(m))$, and we prove it by substitution, that is, by proving that there exists a constant α such that $T(m) \leq \alpha m^{2(t+1)} \lg(m)$ for large enough values of m. Let us fix $k = 2(t+1)$. Then:

$$\begin{aligned} T(m) &= \tfrac{2}{m-1} \sum_{i=1}^{m-1} T(i) + \mathcal{O}(m^k) \\ &\leq \tfrac{2}{m-1} \sum_{i=1}^{m-1} \alpha i^k \lg(i) + \mathcal{O}(m^k) \\ &\leq \tfrac{2}{m-1} \alpha \lg(m) \sum_{i=1}^{m-1} i^k + \mathcal{O}(m^k) \\ &\leq \tfrac{2\alpha \lg(m)}{m-1} \left(\tfrac{(m-1)^{k+1}}{k+1} + \tfrac{(m-1)^k}{2} + \tfrac{k(m-1)^{k-1}}{12} \right) + \mathcal{O}(m^k) \\ &= \tfrac{2\alpha \lg(m)}{(k+1)(m-1)} \left((m-1)^{k+1} + \tfrac{(k+1)(m-1)^k}{2} + \tfrac{(k+1)k(m-1)^{k-1}}{12} \right) + \mathcal{O}(m^k) \\ &\leq \tfrac{2\alpha \lg(m)}{(k+1)(m-1)} \left((m-1)^{k+1} + \tfrac{(m-1)^{k+1}}{2} + \tfrac{(m-1)^{k+1}}{12} \right) + \mathcal{O}(m^k) \\ &= \tfrac{2\alpha \lg(m)(m-1)^k}{(k+1)} (1 + \tfrac{1}{2} + \tfrac{1}{12}) + \mathcal{O}(m^k). \end{aligned}$$

using (a further bounded version of) the Faulhaber formula [20], and taking into account that assuming constant t implies $k \leq m - 2$, and therefore, $k < k + 1 \leq m - 1$. For large enough values of m, all of the above amounts to proving that:

$$\frac{19}{6(k+1)} \alpha \lg(m)(m-1)^k \leq \alpha \lg(m)m^k,$$

which is implied by:

$$\frac{19}{6(k+1)} m^k \leq m^k,$$

which is true for $k \geq \frac{13}{6}$ that is, $k \geq 3$, which is always true as $t \geq 1$.

Theorem 2. *The family $\mathcal{MDT}$ of modal decision trees is weakly efficient.*

4   Conclusions

In the past few years, modal symbolic learning in general, and modal decision trees in particular, have proven themselves to be a very useful tool for extracting complex knowledge from non-tabular data, in both the temporal and the spatial case. Admittedly, however, current implementations of modal decision trees could not guarantee the completeness of the approach in the logical sense. Building upon a very recent result in which a complete version of modal decision trees has been proposed, in this paper we provided an assessment of their computational complexity, proving that, in fact, modal decision trees are both complete and efficient. Modal decision trees can be seen as prototypical of a large family of symbolic learning tools based on more-than-propositional logics; their development can now rest on a more solid theoretical background. Future work includes the empirical evaluation of their behaviour.

Acknowledgements. We acknowledge the support of the INDAM-GNCS project *Symbolic and Numerical Analysis of Cyberphysical Systems*, founded by INDAM (code CUP_E53C22001930001), as well as that of the FIRD project *Symbolic Geometric Learning*, founded by the University of Ferrara.

References

1. Aiello, M., van Benthem, J.: A modal walk through space. J. Appl. Non-Class. Log. **12**(3–4), 319–364 (2002)
2. Alaniz, S., Marcos, D., Schiele, B., Akata, Z.: Learning decision trees recurrently through communication. In: Proceedings of the 34th IEEE Conference on Computer Vision and Pattern Recognition (CVPR), pp. 13518–13527 (2021)
3. Belson, W.: A technique for studying the effects of television broadcast. J. R. Stat. Soc. **5**(3), 195–202 (1956)
4. Bienvenu, M.: Prime implicates and prime implicants: from propositional to modal logic. J. Artif. Intell. Res. **36**, 71–128 (2009)
5. Blockeel, H., De Raedt, L.: Top-down induction of first-order logical decision trees. Artif. Intell. **101**(1–2), 285–297 (1998)

6. Bombara, G., Vasile, C., Penedo, F., Yasuoka, H., Belta, C.: A decision tree approach to data classification using signal temporal logic. In: Proceedings of the 19th International Conference on Hybrid Systems: Computation and Control (HSCC), pp. 1–10 (2016)

7. Breiman, L.: Bagging predictors. Mach. Learn. **24**(2), 123–140 (1996)

8. Breiman, L.: Random forests. Mach. Learn. **45**(1), 5–32 (2001)

9. Breiman, L., Friedman, J., Olshen, R., Stone, C.: Classification and regression trees. Wadsworth Publishing Company (1984)

10. Brunello, A., Sciavicco, G., Stan, I.E.: Interval temporal logic decision tree learning. In: Calimeri, F., Leone, N., Manna, M. (eds.) JELIA 2019. LNCS (LNAI), vol. 11468, pp. 778–793. Springer, Cham (2019). https://doi.org/10.1007/978-3-030-19570-0_50

11. Caselli, E., et al.: Towards an objective theory of subjective liking: a first step in understanding the sense of beauty. PLoS ONE **8**(6), 1–20 (2023)

12. Chen, T., Guestrin, C.: XGBoost: a scalable tree boosting system. In: Proceedings of the 22nd ACM SIGKDD International Conference on Knowledge Discovery and Data Mining (KDD), pp. 785–794 (2016)

13. Clark, P., Niblett, T.: The CN2 induction algorithm. Mach. Learn. **3**, 261–283 (1989)

14. Clarke, E.M., Emerson, E.A.: Design and synthesis of synchronization skeletons using branching time temporal logic. In: Kozen, D. (ed.) Logic of Programs 1981. LNCS, vol. 131, pp. 52–71. Springer, Heidelberg (1982). https://doi.org/10.1007/BFb0025774

15. Clarke, E., Emerson, E., Sistla, A.: Automatic verification of finite-state concurrent systems using temporal logic specifications. ACM Trans. Program. Lang. Syst. **8**(2), 244–263 (1986)

16. Coccagna, M., Manzella, F., Mazzacane, S., Pagliarini, G., Sciavicco, G.: Statistical and symbolic neuroaesthetics rules extraction from EEG signals. In: Ferrandez Vicente, J.M., Alvarez-Sanchez, J.R., de la Paz Lopez, F., Adeli, H. (eds.) Artificial Intelligence in Neuroscience: Affective Analysis and Health Applications. IWINAC 2022. LNCS, vol. 13258, pp. 536–546. Springer, Cham (2022). https://doi.org/10.1007/978-3-031-06242-1_53

17. Console, L., Picardi, C., Dupré, D.: Temporal decision trees: model-based diagnosis of dynamic systems on-board. J. Artif. Intell. Res. **19**, 469–512 (2003)

18. de Ville, B.: Decision trees. WIREs Comput. Stat. **5**(6), 448–455 (2013)

19. Della Monica, D., Pagliarini, G., Sciavicco, G., Stan, I.: Decision trees with a modal flavor. In: Proceedings of the 21st International Conference of the Italian Association for Artificial Intelligence (AIxIA). in press (2022)

20. Gnewuch, M., Pasing, H., Weiss, C.: A generalized faulhaber inequality, improved bracketing covers, and applications to discrepancy. Math. Comput. **90**, 2873–2898 (2021)

21. Guo, H., Gelfand, S.: Classification trees with neural network feature extraction. IEEE Trans. Neural Netw. **3**(6), 923–933 (1992)

22. Halpern, J., Shoham, Y.: A propositional modal logic of time intervals. J. ACM **38**(4), 935–962 (1991)

23. Kass, G.V.: An exploratory technique for investigating large quantities of categorical data. J. R. Stat. Soc. **29**(2), 119–127 (1980)

24. Ke, G., et al.: LightGBM: a highly efficient gradient boosting decision tree. In: Proceedings of the 31st Advances in Neural Information Processing Systems (NIPS), pp. 3146–3154 (2017)

25. Kearns, M., Valiant, L.: Cryptographic limitations on learning Boolean formulae and finite automata. J. ACM **41**(1), 67–95 (1994)
26. Kontschieder, P., Fiterau, M., Criminisi, A., Rota Bulò, S.: Deep neural decision forests. In: Proceedings of the 2015 IEEE International Conference on Computer Vision (ICCV), pp. 1467–1475 (2015)
27. Loh, W.: Classification and regression trees. WIREs Data Min. Knowl. Discov. **1**(1), 14–23 (2011)
28. Loh, W.: Fifty years of classification and regression trees. Int. Stat. Rev. **82**(3), 329–348 (2014)
29. Lutz, C., Wolter, F.: Modal logics of topological relations. Log. Methods Comput. Sci. **2**(2), 1–41 (2006)
30. Manzella, F., Pagliarini, G., Sciavicco, G., Stan, I.: The voice of COVID-19: breath and cough recording classification with temporal decision trees and random forests. Artif. Intell. Med. **137**, 102486 (2023)
31. Messenger, R., Mandell, L.: A modal search technique for predictive nominal scale multivariate analysis. J. Am. Stat. Assoc. **67**(340), 768–772 (1972)
32. Morgan, J., Sonquist, J.: Problems in the analysis of survey data, and a proposal. J. Am. Stat. Assoc. **58**(302), 415–434 (1963)
33. Murdock, C., Li, Z., Zhou, H., Duerig, T.: Blockout: dynamic model selection for hierarchical deep networks. In: Proceedings of the 29th IEEE Conference on Computer Vision and Pattern Recognition (CVPR), pp. 2583–2591 (2016)
34. Murthy, V., Singh, V., Chen, T., Manmatha, R., Comaniciu, D.: Deep Decision network for multi-class image classification. In: Proceedings of the 29th IEEE Conference on Computer Vision and Pattern Recognition (CVPR), pp. 2240–2248 (2016)
35. Pagliarini, G., Sciavicco, G.: Decision tree learning with spatial modal logics. In: Proceedings of the 12th International Symposium on Games, Automata, Logics, and Formal Verification (GANDALF). EPTCS, vol. 346, pp. 273–290 (2021)
36. Pnueli, A.: The temporal logic of programs. In: Proceedings of the 18th Annual Symposium on Foundations of Computer Science (FOCS), pp. 46–57 (1977)
37. Quinlan, J.: Induction of decision trees. Mach. Learn. **1**, 81–106 (1986)
38. Quinlan, J.: C4.5: Programs for Machine Learning. Morgan Kaufmann, Burlington (1993)
39. Quinlan, J.: Simplifying decision trees. Int. J. Hum. Comput. Stud. **51**(2), 497–510 (1999)
40. Rivest, R.: Learning decision lists. Mach. Learn. **2**(3), 229–246 (1987)
41. Sciavicco, G., Stan, I.: Knowledge extraction with interval temporal logic decision trees. In: Proceedings of the 27th International Symposium on Temporal Representation and Reasoning (TIME). LIPIcs, vol. 178, pp. 9:1–9:16 (2020)
42. Srivastava, N., Salakhutdinov, R.: Discriminative transfer learning with tree-based priors. In: Proceedings of the 26th Advances in Neural Information Processing Systems (NIPS), pp. 2094–2102 (2013)
43. Wan, A., et al.: NBDT: neural-backed decision tree. In: Proceedings of the 9th International Conference on Learning Representations (ICLR), pp. 1–12 (2021)
44. Zhou, Z., Chen, Z.: Hybrid decision tree. Knowl.-Based Syst. **15**(8), 515–528 (2002)

Clique-TF-IDF: A New Partitioning Framework Based on Dense Substructures

Marco D'Elia[1]([⊠])[iD], Irene Finocchi[2][iD], and Maurizio Patrignani[1][iD]

[1] Roma Tre University, Via della Vasca Navale 79, Rome, Italy
{marco.delia,maurizio.patrignani}@uniroma3.it
[2] Luiss Guido Carli, Viale Romania 32, Rome, Italy
finocchi@luiss.it

Abstract. Natural Language Processing (NLP) techniques are powerful tools for analyzing, understanding, and processing human language with a wide range of applications. In this paper we exploit NLP techniques, combined with Machine Learning clustering algorithms, to find good solutions to a traditional combinatorial problem, namely, the computation of a partition with high modularity of a graph. We introduce a novel framework, dubbed *Clique-TF-IDF*, for computing a graph partition. Such a framework leverages dense subgraphs of the input graph, modeled as maximal cliques, and characterizes each node in terms of the cliques it belongs to, similarly to a term-document matrix. Our experimental results show that the quality of the partitions produced by algorithm *Clique-TF-IDF* is comparable with that of the most effective algorithms in the literature. While our focus is on maximal cliques and partitioning algorithms, we believe that this strategy can be generalized to devise AI solutions for a variety of intractable combinatorial problems where some substructures can be efficiently enumerated and exploited.

Keywords: TF-IDF · Graph embedding · Hierarchical clustering · Graph partitioning

1 Introduction

The strictest definitions of community are those based on graph-theoretic properties such as maximal cliques, k-plexes, or γ-quasi cliques (see [26] for a survey). A *clique* is a set of nodes with all the possible edges among them. Although the problem of computing maximal cliques is computationally hard [21], several centralized [4,5,17,22,37] and distributed [7,8,11,40] algorithms are available to efficiently enumerate all the maximal cliques of real-world networks. Unfortunately, there are so many overlapping graph-theoretic communities that it becomes challenging for a user to take advantage of them in order to break down

This research was supported in part by MUR PRIN Projects no. 2022TS4Y3N (EXPAND) and no. 2022ME9Z78 (NextGRAAL).

R. Basili et al. (Eds.): AIxIA 2023, LNAI 14318, pp. 396–410, 2023.
https://doi.org/10.1007/978-3-031-47546-7_27

and analyze a network effectively. In contrast, the definition of community that is most intuitive for the user is that of partition, where the node set is divided into blocks and each node belongs to exactly one block. The target is usually that of maximizing a quality measure, such as the modularity of the partition (see Sect. 2 for a formal definition). The problem of partitioning a network while maximizing modularity is NP-complete [3] and exact algorithms are not possible even if the network is sparse. Therefore, most of the available approaches for network partitioning are heuristics. A state-of-the-art about them is provided in the related work section.

Contributions of the Paper. In this paper, we attempt to bridge the gap between graph-theoretically defined communities, which admit exact algorithms, and node partitions, whose computation relies on heuristics. Our strategy is to use the solutions of the former problem as a hint for an AI approach to solve the latter one. More precisely, we first encode maximal cliques into a matrix, with a row for each node and a column for each clique, which is analogous to the term-document matrix widely used in natural language processing. Second, we perform a weighting operation on the aforementioned matrix analogous to the TF-IDF function: our goal is to obtain higher values for maximal cliques that are both large and weakly connected to the rest of the network. Third, we cluster the matrix rows based on their similarity in order to compute a partition of the network.

An experimental analysis on real-world graphs rounds off the paper. The results are promising and encouraging, showing that the quality of the partitions produced by our approach, called *Clique-TF-IDF*, is comparable with that of the most effective algorithms in the literature. In application contexts where running time is not a major issue, this kind of approach provides high-quality solutions alternative to the traditional ones.

While our focus is on maximal cliques and partitioning algorithms, we believe that this strategy can be generalized to devise AI solutions for a variety of intractable combinatorial problems where some substructures can be efficiently enumerated and exploited. For example, max-cut problems could leverage the efficient computation of maximal bipartite subgraphs. Vertex-coloring of dense graphs could leverage the efficient computation of independent sets. On the one hand, these hybrid approaches would benefit of both combinatorial and AI techniques. On the other hand, they could open up new application areas for multidisciplinary research.

Related Work. The graph partitioning problem has been widely studied, attracting interest in both theoretical and practical circles. Several variants of the problem have been considered in the literature and a few previous works exploit AI techniques to solve different issues. When the input graph has node attributes that must be taken into account in the produced partition, contrastive learning along with graph neural networks make it possible to learn clusterable features and compute a partition that is measurably good with respect a ground truth [16]. More traditional algorithms for partitioning attributed graphs are discussed in [10].

In correlation partitioning edges have quantitative attributes, which may be negative values to indicate dissimilarity, and the measure to be maximized increases when negative edges span different blocks of the partition [1,34]. The online version of these problems has also been considered in [23].

In structural clustering, the blocks of the partition are required to contain nodes that have the same "role" in the graph. Graph neural networks have been widely used in this setting to address various graph-related problems such as node classification and graph classification (see, e.g., [6,15,41]). Other results related to structural embeddings may be indicative of the feasibility of performing cluster analysis [32].

In contrast to the aforementioned works, in this paper we focus on positional clustering of graphs without attributes, where the similarity of the nodes is determined by their adjacencies and the quality of the partition is measured in terms of its modularity. Several combinatorial algorithms have been presented in the literature to solve this problem. The algorithm described in [9] employs an agglomerative hierarchical process aimed at maximizing the modularity measure of the partition. The same approach is pursued, with significant improvements in terms of both efficacy and efficiency, by the algorithm in [2] and its subsequent refinement in [38]. An algorithm based on label propagation can be found in [14]. Random walks in the graph are leveraged to infer good partitions by exploiting a similarity matrix [29] or information theory techniques [33]. Statistical physics models are used by [31]. Other heuristic approaches, which exhibit lower levels of performance, can be found in [19,28,30].

As in the case of structural clustering, node embeddings based on positional information may be exploited for the computation of a good partition of the graph [20,27,41].

Organization of the Paper. The remainder of this paper is structured as follows. Section 2 provides preliminary notation and definitions that will be used throughout the paper. Section 3 describes our approach in detail. Section 4 compares algorithm *Clique-TF-IDF* against a variety of state-of-the-art competitors in terms of both effectiveness and efficiency. Conclusions and future work are discussed in Sect. 5.

2   Background

In this section we provide notation and basic definitions that will be used throughout the paper. Let $G = (V, E)$ be an undirected graph with node set $V = \{v_1, \ldots, v_n\}$ and edge set $E = \{e_1, \ldots, e_m\}$, such that $E \subseteq V \times V$. Let $n = |V|$ denote the number of nodes and let $m = |E|$ denote the number of edges. Let A denote the adjacency matrix of G: for any pair of nodes u and v, A_{uv} (and, symmetrically, A_{vu}) is 1 if u and v are connected, and 0 otherwise. Also, let δ_u denote the degree of node u. A *partition of* G is a subdivision of V into non-empty blocks $\{V_1, \ldots, V_k\}$, such that $\bigcup_{i=1}^{k} V_i = V$ and $V_i \cap V_j = \varnothing$ for every $i \neq j$. The blocks of the partition are meant to represent portions of the graph that are internally dense and weakly connected to the rest of the graph.

Modularity. An effective quality measure for graph partitions is *modularity*, which is defined as follows [9]:

$$Q = \frac{1}{2m} \sum_{i=1}^{k} \sum_{u,v \in V_i} \left(A_{uv} - \frac{\delta_u \delta_v}{2m} \right) \tag{1}$$

Notice that $\frac{\delta_u \delta_v}{2m}$ represents the probability that an edge between nodes u and v exists in a random network model that preserves the vertex degrees of the nodes. The modularity measure Q is defined in the interval $\left[-\frac{1}{2}, 1\right]$, where non-zero values are deviations from randomness and higher values indicate a better community structure.

Even if partitioning a network while maximizing modularity is NP-hard [3], this measure has been widely used in the literature to evaluate the quality of the computed communities, especially in graphs for which ground-truth is not available or its quality has to be validated [2,9,38].

TF-IDF. Let $D = \{d_1, \ldots, d_r\}$ be a collection of r documents that contain overall a set $T = \{t_1, \ldots, t_s\}$ of s terms. Let $\tau_{t,d}$ be the number of occurrences of term t into document d and let δ_t be the number of documents that contain term t. The *inverse document frequency* for a term t is defined as $\gamma_t = \log(\frac{|D|}{\delta_t})$. Finally, the TF-IDF weighting function can be defined with respect to a term t and a document d as $\omega_{t,d} = \tau_{t,d} \cdot \gamma_t$ [25]. The value obtained from the function is higher when term t is frequent in a small subset of documents, and lower when term t is not frequent in document d or is common in D.

Hierarchical Clustering. Let $P = \{p_1, \ldots, p_n\}$ be a set of n points in a d-dimensional space. Given an integer k, the goal of geometric clustering is to partition P into k non-empty clusters $\{P_1, \ldots, P_k\}$ such that $\bigcup_{i=1}^{k} P_i = P$ and $P_i \cap P_j = \varnothing$ for every $i \neq j$.

Hierarchical clustering is a flexible approach to compute clusters in P and it is widely used for its ability to reveal both global and local structures. One of the most used techniques is the so-called agglomerative clustering [36], that starts with individual points as clusters and iteratively merges them into larger ones. This approach requires three main ingredients: (i) the distance or similarity metric between data points, (ii) the "linkage criterion", i.e., the distance metric between clusters that is used to identify those to be merged, and (iii) the stopping criterion to end the computation at a suitable level of the hierarchy. Differently from other alternatives (e.g., centroid-based or density-based), hierarchical clustering guarantees that the output is independent of the initialization phase. Also, it has the advantage of only considering distances, rather than absolute coordinates, which may have a wider range of applications.

3   Methodology

In this section we present our approach to compute a partition of a graph G. We leverage graph-theoretic substructures of G that can be efficiently enumerated.

Overview of the Approach. Our approach for the computation of a partition of the graph consists of a pipeline with the following steps (Fig. 1):

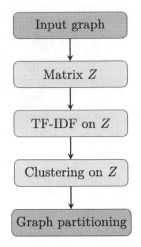

- First, we compute all maximal cliques of the graph and we define a node-community matrix Z, in which values are proportional to the magnitude of each maximal clique.
- Second, we perform a weighting operation on Z analogous to the TF-IDF function. Our goal is to obtain higher values for maximal cliques that are both large and weakly connected to the rest of the network.
- Lastly, the partition of the graph is calculated by clustering the matrix rows, using a binary search strategy based on the modularity measure. In this way the number of clusters, and consequently the number of partitions, can be automatically determined.

Fig. 1. Pipeline of algorithm *Clique-TF-IDF*.

Given a graph G with n nodes, we enumerate all maximal cliques using the algorithm introduced in [4] and improved in [5,37]. Let $C = \{c_1, \ldots, c_d\}$ be the set of all maximal cliques, with $d = |C|$. We use the following data structures.

Clique-incidence Matrix Y. Matrix $Y \in \mathbb{N}^{n \times d}$ is an incidence matrix telling the nodes contained in each maximal clique. More formally:

$$Y_{i\ell} = \begin{cases} 1 \text{ if node } v_i \text{ belongs to maximal clique } c_\ell \\ 0 \text{ otherwise} \end{cases}$$

For example, the graph depicted in Fig. 2(a) contains three maximal cliques c_1, c_2, and c_3 and the corresponding Y matrix is shown in Fig. 2(c). We aim at clustering the rows of Y based on their similarity: if two nodes belong to very similar sets of maximal cliques, they are likely to be in the same partition. For instance, nodes v_1 and v_2 are more similar than nodes v_1 and v_5 in Fig. 2(c).

Co-participation Matrix X. If we used Y as it is, we would not take into account the sizes of the maximal cliques the nodes belong to. Furthermore, nodes that do not share any maximal clique (as nodes v_1 and v_4 of example graph G) would correspond to very different rows even if they had many common neighbors in several maximal cliques (see rows 1 and 4 in Fig. 2(b)). Therefore, we define a *co-participation* matrix $X \in \mathbb{R}^{n \times n}$: intuitively, for each pair of nodes v_i and v_j, X_{ij} is related to the size of the maximal cliques shared by v_i and v_j. More formally, X_{ij} is the sum of the sizes of the maximal cliques including both v_i and v_j. Given a clique c_ℓ, we use as a measure of its size the number of its edges, which we denote by w_ℓ.

Matrix X is symmetric. X_{ii} contains the sum of the sizes w_ℓ of the cliques c_ℓ that node v_i belongs to. For example, in Fig. 2(b), $X_{32} = 6$ because nodes v_3 and v_2 belong to two cliques both of size 3.

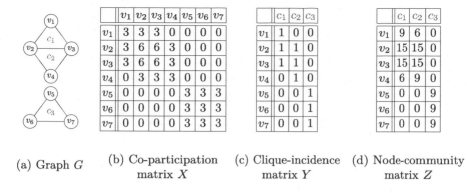

(a) Graph G (b) Co-participation   (c) Clique-incidence   (d) Node-community
matrix X matrix Y matrix Z

Fig. 2. Data structures used in our approach.

Node-community Matrix Z. The *node-community matrix* Z is defined as $Z = X \cdot Y \in \mathbb{R}^{n \times d}$. Observe that the value of $Z_{i\ell}$ is the sum of terms of two distinct types:

- *Direct participation* of node v_i in clique c_ℓ: these terms have value $|c_\ell| \cdot w_\ell$ (see for example Z_{11} in Fig. 2(d), where $Z_{11} = |c_1| \cdot w_1 = 3 \times 3 = 9$).
- *Indirect participation* of node v_i in clique c_ℓ. Namely, for every node $v_j \in c_\ell$ that shares with v_i clique $c_{\ell'}$, we sum to $Z_{i\ell}$ a term $w_{\ell'}$. For example, node v_1 participates indirectly in clique c_2 because of its neighbors v_2 and v_3. Hence, value $Z_{12} = 6$ is the sum of the two terms $X_{12} \times Y_{22} = w_1 = 3$ and $X_{13} \times Y_{32} = w_1 = 3$.

TF-IDF Transformation. Matrix Z can be contrasted with the TF matrix used in Information Retrieval, that traditionally represents the occurrences of terms into documents. In our setting, nodes play the role of documents and maximal cliques play the role of terms. As for the Information Retrieval application domain, it makes sense to consider more relevant the contribution of a clique (term) for a specific node (document) when the clique has very few values different from zero (i.e., when the term is rare). Intuitively, the less the clique intersects with other cliques, the less we would like to split it with the boundary of a block of the partition. Therefore, we compute an IDF vector with as many cells as cliques. Element ℓ of the IDF vector contains the value $\log(\frac{n}{|\delta_\ell|})$, where δ_ℓ, in analogy with the Inverse-Document-Frequency, is the number of non-zero elements of column ℓ of Z. We reassign the values of Z by multiplying each row Z_i of Z with the IDF vector element by element. In the example of Fig. 2, the TF-IDF value for the cell Z_{41} of clique c_1 with respect to node v_4 is $\omega_{1,4} = \tau_{1,4} \cdot \gamma_1 = Z_{41} \cdot \log(\frac{n}{|\delta_1|}) = 6 \cdot 0.8 = 4.8$.

Finally, we normalize each row of Z to obtain an embedding for the nodes of G such that each node corresponds to a vector of length one.

Clustering. Matrix Z can be viewed as a set of n points (the nodes in V) into a d-dimensional space (the cliques). Hence, we can compute a geometric clustering by partitioning the set of n points into a desired number k of clusters. In order to do so we exploit an agglomerative clustering approach [36]: at the beginning, each point falls into a distinct cluster and iteratively the two nearest clusters are joined, where the distance between two clusters is the average distance between their nodes. The process stops when the desired number k of clusters is reached.

Table 1. Real-world networks used in the experimental analysis. Entries labeled with * only refer to the giant component of the networks.

Network	Alias	Nodes	Edges	# Maximal cliques
arenas-email	arenas	1133	5451	3267
ca-grqc*	grqc	4158	13422	3385
ca-hepth*	hepth	8638	24806	9357
ca-hepph*	hepph	11204	117619	14588
citeseer*	cite	2120	3731	2722
email-eu-core*	email	1005	16706	42709
karate	karate	34	78	36
lastfm-asia	lastfm	7624	27806	17957
p2p-gnutella	p2p	10876	39994	38497
sociopatterns	socio	410	2765	1247

Choosing the Number of Clusters. Since the number of clusters k is an input of the above algorithm, we exploit a simple heuristic, based on a binary search on the possible values of k, to choose a value that corresponds to a high modularity measure. The efficiency of such a search is guaranteed by the fact that the agglomerative clustering hierarchy can be computed a single time at the beginning of the process.

4   Experimental Analysis

We performed an experimental study to evaluate the effectiveness and efficiency of algorithm *Clique-TF-IDF*. The source code of our implementation can be found at https://github.com/mdelia17/clique-tf-idf.

4.1   Experimental Setup

We evaluated our approach against a variety of state-of-the-art algorithms, including Walktrap [29], CNM [9], Infomap [33], LP [14], Pott [31], and Leiden [38]. We couldn't compare with [16] because the code is not public available yet.

We also compared the network embedding phase of *Clique-TF-IDF* against other embedding approaches (Node2Vec [20] and DeepWalk [27]) by completing

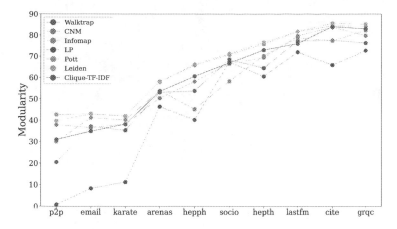

Fig. 3. Effectiveness measures. This figure shows the quality (modularity) obtained by the various algorithms. The networks on the x-axis are ordered based on the average modularity of the algorithms.

them with the two phases of *Clique-TF-IDF* that compute a geometric clustering and that compute the number of clusters.

We used a data set consisting of ten real-world networks of different sizes (from tens to ten thousand nodes) taken from the SNAP repository [24] and typically used as benchmarks in this domain. Their characteristics, including the number of maximal cliques, are listed in Table 1. Since algorithm Pott [31] only accepts connected networks, entries labeled with * refer to the main connected component of the networks (which typically have a giant component which contains a significant proportion of the nodes in the network). All the experiments were performed on a commodity workstation equipped with Intel® Core-i5™ 1135G7 CPU and 8 GB of RAM.

4.2   Experimental Results

Evaluation of *Clique-TF-IDF*. Here we discuss the efficiency and the effectiveness of *Clique-TF-IDF* comparing its performances with those of the algorithms listed in Sect. 4.1.

Our approach is among those that compute partitions with high modularity, although algorithm Leiden, one of the most effective in the literature, is constantly above *Clique-TF-IDF* (see Fig. 3). Algorithm Pott also exhibits a very good performance in terms of effectiveness, at the cost of running times that are at least one order of magnitude higher than those of its competitors.

Figure 4 shows that algorithm *Clique-TF-IDF* has, however, large computation times, even if not as high as algorithm Pott. This is mostly due to the binary search for the best number k of clusters and to the high number of maximal cliques exhibited by some networks. Indeed, a profiling of *Clique-TF-IDF* (see Fig. 5) reveals that the percentage of time spent in Clustering phase dominates

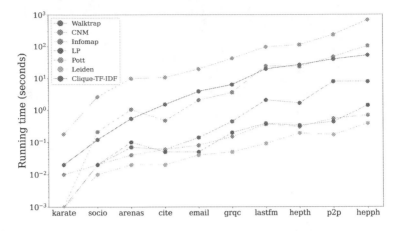

Fig. 4. Efficiency measures. This figure shows the times (in seconds) used by the various algorithms. The networks on the x-axis are ordered based on *Clique-TF-IDF* running time.

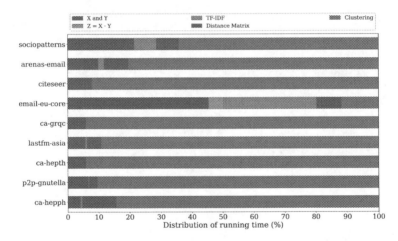

Fig. 5. Percentage of the running time for the phases of algorithm *Clique-TF-IDF*.

the overall running time. There are two notable exceptions to this pattern, i.e., networks `sociopatterns` and, especially, `email-eu-core`. To understand this phenomenon, we analyzed the distribution of the sizes of the maximal cliques. The results of this analysis are shown in Fig. 6, highlighting that these networks have a large number of maximal cliques with a non-scale-free distribution, which resembles a binomial distribution in the case of `email-eu-core`. On these networks, a large percentage of time is spent for maximal clique computation (X and Y matrices in Fig. 5).

Evaluation of the Embedding Phase of *Clique-TF-IDF*. In order to verify that our graph embedding based on maximal cliques is a good starting point

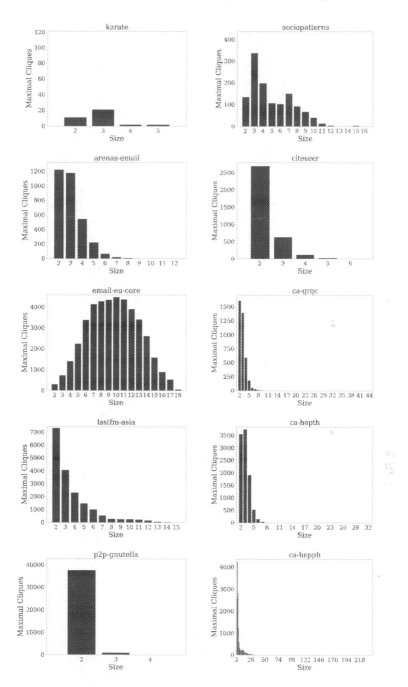

Fig. 6. The distribution of maximal clique sizes for the networks used in the experimental analysis.

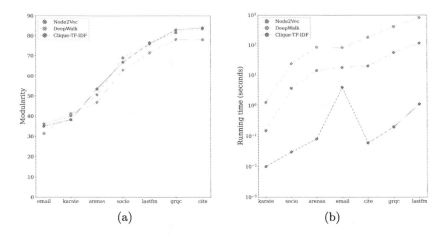

(a)   (b)

Fig. 7. Modularity and running times (restricted to the embedding phase) obtained by replacing DeepWalk and Node2Vec to the clique-based approach of *Clique-TF-IDF*.

to compute a partition, we replaced the first two phases of our pipeline (the synthesis of matrix Z and the computation of TF-IDF on it) with state-of-the-art graph embedding algorithms. Figure 7 shows the results of the experimental comparison obtained with Node2Vec [20] and DeepWalk [27], where the two algorithms have be run with their default parameters. We used a subset of the datasets described in Sect. 4.1, on which the two aforementioned approaches could compute a solution within a time bound of 15 minutes.

As it can be seen in Fig. 7(a), the modularity of the partitions produced by *Clique-TF-IDF* is larger than that of DeepWalk and comparable or larger than that of Node2Vec (with the only exception of the small graph `karate`). In addition, Fig. 7(b) shows that the running times exhibited by DeepWalk and Node2Vec are several order of magnitude higher that those of *Clique-TF-IDF* (we remark that the y-axis of Fig. 7(b) has a logarithmic scale).

In Fig. 8 we repeated the above experiments providing DeepWalk and Node-2Vec with different combinations of parameters. In particular, we varied the dimensionality d of the embedding in the set $d \in \{32, 64, 128\}$ and the length ℓ of the random walks $\ell \in \{20, 40, 80\}$. We fixed to 10 both the number of random walks and the number of epochs. For the remaining parameters we kept the default values. The settings denoted S, M, and L in Fig. 8 correspond to $d = 32$ and $\ell = 20$, $d = 64$ and $\ell = 40$, and $d = 128$ and $\ell = 80$, respectively. As it can be observed in Fig. 8, changes in the parameters do not seem to significantly impact the performances of the algorithms.

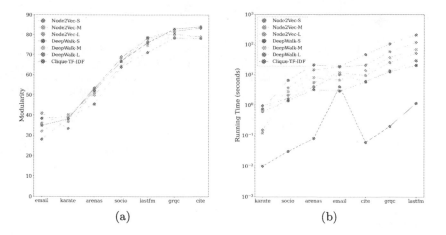

Fig. 8. Modularity and running times measured with different input parameters for DeepWalk and Node2Vec.

5   Conclusions and Future Work

We introduced a novel framework for computing graph partitions. Such a framework leverages dense subgraphs of the input graph, modeled as maximal cliques, and characterizes each node in terms of the maximal cliques it belongs to. Our experimental results show that the proposed approach is promising: the quality of the produced partitioning is comparable with that of the most effective algorithms in the literature. However, this is obtained at the cost of a high computation time. Overall, in application contexts where running time is not a major issue, the approach presented in this paper provides high-quality solutions alternative to the traditional ones. We believe that one of the most intriguing outcomes of our study is that our heuristic, which leverages AI techniques in conjunction with cutting-edge combinatorial algorithms to identify basic structures in the input data, achieved results that are on par with the most advanced algorithms for complex problems that have been the focus of decades of research.

As a future work, we aim at tuning the approach to improve both its effectiveness and its efficiency. We believe that a clique sampling technique might be helpful to reduce the running times on networks with a large number of maximal cliques with a non-scale-free distribution. Also, it would be interesting to apply a similar strategy to the computation of structural clusterings [32,35,41] and to explore other basic dense structures (such as k-plexes [12], fixed-size cliques [13,18] or trusses [39]) instead of maximal cliques as a starting point for the embedding.

References

1. Bansal, N., Blum, A., Chawla, S.: Correlation clustering. Mach. Learn. **56**(1–3), 89–113 (2004). https://doi.org/10.1023/B:MACH.0000033116.57574.95
2. Blondel, V.D., Guillaume, J.L., Lambiotte, R., Lefebvre, E.: Fast unfolding of communities in large networks. J. Stat. Mech. Theory Exp. **2008**(10), P10008 (2008)
3. Brandes, U., et al.: On finding graph clusterings with maximum modularity. In: Brandstädt, A., Kratsch, D., Müller, H. (eds.) WG 2007. LNCS, vol. 4769, pp. 121–132. Springer, Heidelberg (2007). https://doi.org/10.1007/978-3-540-74839-7_12
4. Bron, C., Kerbosch, J.: Finding all cliques of an undirected graph (algorithm 457). Commun. ACM **16**(9), 575–576 (1973)
5. Cazals, F., Karande, C.: A note on the problem of reporting maximal cliques. Theor. Comput. Sci. **407**(1–3), 564–568 (2008)
6. Chen, Y., et al.: SP-GNN: learning structure and position information from graphs. Neural Netw. **161**, 505–514 (2023). https://doi.org/10.1016/j.neunet.2023.01.051
7. Cheng, J., Ke, Y., Fu, A.W.C., Yu, J.X., Zhu, L.: Finding maximal cliques in massive networks. ACM Trans. Database Syst. **36**(4), 21 (2011)
8. Cheng, J., Zhu, L., Ke, Y., Chu, S.: Fast algorithms for maximal clique enumeration with limited memory. In: KDD, pp. 1240–1248 (2012)
9. Clauset, A., Newman, M.E.J., Moore, C.: Finding community structure in very large networks. Phys. Rev. E **70**, 066111 (2004)
10. Combe, D., Largeron, C., Géry, M., Egyed-Zsigmond, E.: I-Louvain: an attributed graph clustering method. In: Fromont, E., De Bie, T., van Leeuwen, M. (eds.) IDA 2015. LNCS, vol. 9385, pp. 181–192. Springer, Cham (2015). https://doi.org/10.1007/978-3-319-24465-5_16
11. Conte, A., De Virgilio, R., Maccioni, A., Patrignani, M., Torlone, R.: Finding all maximal cliques in very large social networks. In: EDBT 2016, pp. 173–184. OpenProceedings.org, Konstanz, Germany (2016)
12. Conte, A., Firmani, D., Patrignani, M., Torlone, R.: Shared-nothing distributed enumeration of 2-plexes. In: CIKM 2019, pp. 2469–2472. ACM, New York (2019)
13. Coppa, E., Finocchi, I., Garcia, R.L.: Counting cliques in parallel without a cluster: engineering a fork/join algorithm for shared-memory platforms. Inf. Sci. **496**, 553–571 (2019)
14. Cordasco, G., Gargano, L.: Community detection via semi-synchronous label propagation algorithms. In: 2010 IEEE International Workshop on: Business Applications of Social Network Analysis (BASNA), pp. 1–8 (2010)
15. Cui, H., Lu, Z., Li, P., Yang, C.: On positional and structural node features for graph neural networks on non-attributed graphs. In: Hasan, M.A., Xiong, L. (eds.) ACM CIKM 2022, pp. 3898–3902. ACM (2022)
16. Devvrit, F., Sinha, A., Dhillon, I.S., Jain, P.: S3GC: scalable self-supervised graph clustering. In: NeurIPS (2022)
17. Eppstein, D., Strash, D.: Listing all maximal cliques in large sparse real-world graphs. In: SEA, pp. 364–375 (2011)
18. Finocchi, I., Finocchi, M., Fusco, E.G.: Clique counting in mapreduce: algorithms and experiments. ACM J. Exp. Algorithmics **20**, 1.7:1–1.7:20 (2015)
19. Girvan, M., Newman, M.E.J.: Community structure in social and biological networks. Proc. Natl. Acad. Sci. **99**(12), 7821–7826 (2002)

20. Grover, A., Leskovec, J.: Node2vec: scalable feature learning for networks. In: Krishnapuram, B., Shah, M., Smola, A.J., Aggarwal, C.C., Shen, D., Rastogi, R. (eds.) ACM SIGKDD 2016, pp. 855–864. ACM (2016). https://doi.org/10.1145/2939672.2939754

21. Karp, R.M.: Reducibility among combinatorial problems. In: Miller, R.E., Thatcher, J.W., Bohlinger, J.D. (eds.) Complexity of Computer Computations. The IBM Research Symposia Series, pp. 85–103. Springer, Boston, MA (1972). https://doi.org/10.1007/978-1-4684-2001-2_9

22. Koch, I.: Enumerating all connected maximal common subgraphs in two graphs. Theor. Comput. Sci. **250**(1–2), 1–30 (2001)

23. Lattanzi, S., Moseley, B., Vassilvitskii, S., Wang, Y., Zhou, R.: Robust online correlation clustering. In: Ranzato, M., Beygelzimer, A., Dauphin, Y.N., Liang, P., Vaughan, J.W. (eds.) NeurIPS 2021, pp. 4688–4698 (2021)

24. Leskovec, J., Krevl, A.: SNAP datasets: stanford large network dataset collection, June 2014. https://snap.stanford.edu/data

25. Manning, C.D., Raghavan, P., Schütze, H.: Introduction to Information Retrieval. Cambridge University Press, Cambridge, UK (2008). https://nlp.stanford.edu/IR-book/information-retrieval-book.html

26. Pattillo, J., Youssef, N., Butenko, S.: Clique relaxation models in social network analysis. In: Thai, M., Pardalos, P. (eds.) Handbook of Optimization in Complex Networks. SOIA, vol. 58, pp. 143–162. Springer, New York, NY (2012). https://doi.org/10.1007/978-1-4614-0857-4_5

27. Perozzi, B., Al-Rfou, R., Skiena, S.: Deepwalk: online learning of social representations. In: Macskassy, S.A., Perlich, C., Leskovec, J., Wang, W., Ghani, R. (eds.) The 20th ACM SIGKDD International Conference on Knowledge Discovery and Data Mining, KDD '14, New York, NY, USA - 24–27 August 2014, pp. 701–710. ACM (2014). https://doi.org/10.1145/2623330.2623732

28. Pizzuti, C.: GA-Net: a genetic algorithm for community detection in social networks. In: Rudolph, G., Jansen, T., Beume, N., Lucas, S., Poloni, C. (eds.) PPSN 2008. LNCS, vol. 5199, pp. 1081–1090. Springer, Heidelberg (2008). https://doi.org/10.1007/978-3-540-87700-4_107

29. Pons, P., Latapy, M.: Computing communities in large networks using random walks (long version) (2005)

30. Prat-Pérez, A., Dominguez-Sal, D., Larriba-Pey, J.L.: High quality, scalable and parallel community detection for large real graphs. In: Proceedings of the WWW 2014, pp. 225–236. Association for Computing Machinery, New York, NY, USA (2014)

31. Reichardt, J., Bornholdt, S.: Statistical mechanics of community detection. Phys.l Rev. E **74**(1) (2006). https://doi.org/10.1103/2Fphysreve.74.016110

32. Ribeiro, L.F.R., Saverese, P.H.P., Figueiredo, D.R.: Struc2vec: learning node representations from structural identity. In: ACM SIGKDD 2017, pp. 385–394. ACM (2017). https://doi.org/10.1145/3097983.3098061

33. Rosvall, M., Bergstrom, C.T.: Maps of random walks on complex networks reveal community structure. Proc. Natl. Acad. Sci. **105**(4), 1118–1123 (2008)

34. Saha, B., Subramanian, S.: Correlation clustering with same-cluster queries bounded by optimal cost. In: Bender, M.A., Svensson, O., Herman, G. (eds.) ESA 2019. LIPIcs, vol. 144, pp. 81:1–81:17. Schloss Dagstuhl - Leibniz-Zentrum für Informatik (2019). https://doi.org/10.4230/LIPIcs.ESA.2019.81

35. Srinivasan, B., Ribeiro, B.: On the equivalence between positional node embeddings and structural graph representations. In: ICLR 2020. OpenReview.net (2020)

36. Tan, P.N., Steinbach, M., Karpatne, A., Kumar, V.: Introduction to Data Mining, 2nd ed. Pearson, London (2018)
37. Tomita, E., Tanaka, A., Takahashi, H.: The worst-case time complexity for generating all maximal cliques. In: Chwa, K.-Y., Munro, J.I.J. (eds.) COCOON 2004. LNCS, vol. 3106, pp. 161–170. Springer, Heidelberg (2004). https://doi.org/10.1007/978-3-540-27798-9_19
38. Traag, V.A., Waltman, L., van Eck, N.J.: From Louvain to Leiden: guaranteeing well-connected communities. Sci. Rep. **9**, 1–12 (2019). https://www.nature.com/articles/s41598-019-41695-z#citeas
39. Wang, J., Cheng, J.: Truss decomposition in massive networks. Proc. VLDB Endow. **5**(9), 812–823 (2012)
40. Xu, Y., Cheng, J., Fu, A.W.C., Bu, Y.: Distributed maximal clique computation. In: International Congress on Big Data, pp. 160–167. IEEE (2014)
41. Zhu, J., Lu, X., Heimann, M., Koutra, D.: Node proximity is all you need: unified structural and positional node and graph embedding. In: Demeniconi, C., Davidson, I. (eds.) SIAM International Conference on Data Mining, SDM 2021, pp. 163–171. SIAM (2021). https://doi.org/10.1137/1.9781611976700.19

Combining Contrastive Learning and Knowledge Graph Embeddings to Develop Medical Word Embeddings for the Italian Language

Denys Amore Bondarenko, Roger Ferrod[(⊠)], and Luigi Di Caro

University of Turin, Turin, Italy
{denys.amorebondarenko,roger.ferrod,luigi.dicaro}@unito.it

Abstract. Word embeddings play a significant role in today's Natural Language Processing tasks and applications. However, there is a significant gap in the availability of high quality-word embeddings specific to the Italian medical domain. This study aims to address this gap by proposing a tailored solution that combines Contrastive Learning (CL) methods and Knowledge Graph Embedding (KGE), introducing a new variant of the loss function. Given the limited availability of medical texts and controlled vocabularies in the Italian language, traditional approaches for word embedding generation may not yield adequate results. To overcome this challenge, our approach leverages the synergistic benefits of CL and KGE techniques. We achieve a significant performance boost compared to the initial model, while using a considerably smaller amount of data. This work establishes a solid foundation for further investigations aimed at improving the accuracy and coverage of word embeddings in low-resource languages and specialized domains.

Keywords: Contrastive Learning · Knowledge Graph Embeddings · Metric Learning · Self-Supervised Learning

1 Introduction

Text has always represented a significant portion of all the clinical data produced every day in the world, from Emergency Room reports to clinical diary of patients, drugs prescriptions and administrative documents. Recent digitalization has paved the way for new applications by leveraging automatic data analysis. It is therefore necessary to develop tools capable of understanding the content of documents and their contextual nuances in order to be able to extract useful information. This is one of the main objectives of Natural Language Processing (NLP), which in recent years – thanks to the deep-learning revolution – has led to extraordinary results.

Many of these successes can be attributed to foundational models, which are large neural networks that have been trained over a vast collection of

---

D. A. Bondarenko and R. Ferrod—These authors contributed equally to this work.

R. Basili et al. (Eds.): AIxIA 2023, LNAI 14318, pp. 411–424, 2023.
https://doi.org/10.1007/978-3-031-47546-7_28

unannotated data. These models can be adapted or fine-tuned to perform various downstream tasks with minimal modifications.

However, it is difficult to train a generic model suitable for every kind of text. For this reason, and starting from a pretrained model of the language of interest, a new specific embedding model is created for a given domain. This is done by continuing the training on a specific selection of texts. Although less expensive than newly training from scratch, there are still many difficulties, especially when dealing with languages with limited resources, such as Italian, which lacks extensive corpora of freely accessible clinical texts. Due to limited resources, these models should be even more capable of operating in contexts of few annotations with regard to downstream tasks. In these cases, a more accurate representation of similarity is therefore necessary and turns out to be useful in many circumstances. For example, in [16] the semantic similarity between medical terms has been exploited to reduce lexical variability by finding a common representation that can be mapped to IDC-9-CM. Starting from this work, and with the aim of improving the measure of semantic similarity, we have applied recent techniques of contrastive learning as a tool for representation learning, by approaching pairs of semantically similar or possibly equivalent terms (i.e. synonyms) and distancing dissimilar pairs.

Born in the Computer Vision field, contrastive learning is increasingly being applied in NLP [23], with still unexplored potential. However, the biggest difficulty lies in the efficient sampling of negative cases and the selection of positive examples, an even more difficult task in a low-resource language such as Italian.

To compensate for the lack of synonyms listed in the Italian vocabularies of the Unified Medical Language System (UMLS)[1], we directly exploit the Knowledge Graph Embedding (KGE) representation derived from the UMLS semantic network. In doing this, we modify the contrastive Multi Similarity (MS) loss [19] so that its parameters are tied to the similarity calculated on KGEs, and we exploit the context surrounding the terms, treating it as an augmented view of the term. To the best of our knowledge, this is the first time that MS loss, contexts and KGE have been combined in a single model. This solution has made it possible to train a new model capable of exceeding the performances of multilingual state-of-the-art models applied to the Italian language. Compared to the original training methodology, our proposal is able to obtain comparable or better results, while using a significantly lower amount of data. Data, source code and pretrained model are available at https://github.com/rogerferrod/MedITA_embeddings.

2   Related Work

In the literature, there are many works that aim to specialize a word embedding model on a specific domain, like [4,5,8]. Similar studies exist for Italian, for example [15], but not for the medical domain. To the best of our knowledge,

---

[1] UMLS is a collection of controlled vocabularies which comprises a comprehensive thesaurus and ontology of the biomedical sciences; it is available at https://www.nlm.nih.gov/research/umls.

there is no publicly available embedding model for the medical domain in Italian. There are several possible strategies to train new pretrained models, such as the possibility of training a model from scratch (like SciBERT [1]) with considerable associated costs, or to continue the pre-training on new domain-specific documents (BioBERT [8]).

In some domains, and in particular in the biomedical field, the knowledge is explicitly distilled in semantic networks (or knowledge graphs) that define entities (e.g. objects, events, concept) and relations between them. Knowledge graphs are usually big, dynamic and incomplete, though. Moreover, their graph structure is not efficient to be traversed, nor is compatible with common machine learning frameworks. For these reasons, various techniques have been proposed to overcome these limitations, introducing the concept of Knowledge Graphs Embeddings (KGEs). In analogy to word embeddings, a Knowledge Graphs Embedding model maps similar entities closer in a dense low-dimensional vector space. TransE [2] was one of the first method proposed, that despite its simplicity is still commonly used today. Then, other models follow, such as DistMult [20], ComplEx [18], RotatE [17] and SimplE [7]. We experiment with these solutions, that differ for their working principle, for encoding the UMLS semantic network.

Our research draws direct inspiration from two key works in the field: SapBERT [9] and CODER [21]. SapBERT was the first to use contrastive learning on UMLS synonyms in order to enhance the representation of biomedical embeddings. On the other hand, CODER integrated relational information from the UMLS semantic graph by incorporating a loss function inspired by DistMult. The authors of CODER have subsequently developed an extension of CODER called CODER++ [22], which introduces dynamic hard pair sampling. This technique leverages the model itself to include the most informative samples in batch. By providing online hard negative pairs to MS loss, CODER++ surpasses previous results and establishes itself as the new state-of-the-art model.

While SapBERT and CODER are limited to decontextualized terms, KRISS-BERT [24] expands upon SapBERT by incorporating contexts, extracted from PubMed, in which the UMLS synonyms are used. This additional contextual information helps manage term ambiguity. Furthermore, KRISSBERT incorporates UMLS relationships, although it focuses exclusively on the taxonomic relationships of the ontology in textual form.

It is important to note that while CODER is available in a multilingual version, and a multilingual extension has recently been released for SapBERT [10], CODER++ and KRISSBERT are currently not compatible with the Italian language.

3   Method

Due to the challenges posed by data scarcity in low-resource languages like Italian, the classical training methods for natural language processing tasks are not easily applicable. Consequently, we propose a synergistic approach that maximizes information extraction from limited textual data and a restricted domain vocabulary using multiple preexisting solutions. Our proposed method revolves around utilizing a domain ontology and an unlabeled text corpus, enabling us to address these challenges effectively and efficiently.

3.1 Self-supervised Mentions

Contrastive learning involves bringing together the representations of different views of a single entity within the representational space. These views are generally called positive samples, and in a case of some previous works the positives were obtained directly from the ontology, leveraging the synonymy relation. However, there are very few Italian synonyms in UMLS, which makes contrastive learning on the terms themselves impossible. Following KRISSBERT [24], that locates the UMLS medical terms in an unlabeled textual corpus, we adopt the same strategy, but focused on a specific subset of the Metathesaurus that encompasses three main Italian vocabularies: ICPCITA, MDRITA, and MSHITA. Furthermore, we narrow down our attention to a subset of semantic categories[2], which we refer to as $UMLS_{ITA}$. Consequently, we conduct a search for all terms belonging to $UMLS_{ITA}$ within our plain text corpus derived from different Italian sources, as reported in Table 1. Upon locating these terms, we extract a fixed-sized context window around each mention. In cases where certain terms overlap, such as "fever" and "hay fever," we always choose the longest matching term. By employing this approach, we successfully identify 2.2 million mentions referring to 26, 432 unique terms.

Table 1. The corpus contains the collection of scientific pages of wikipedia-italian, divulgative web pages of the ministry of health, medical websites and blogs (such as Nurse24, MyPersonalTrainer, Dica33 etc.), material from university medical lectures, the E3C raw-dataset [12] and degree thesis.

Source	Words	
Wikipedia	9,068,684	25%
Ministry of Health	1,120,952	3%
Medical websites & blogs	9,528,004	26%
PubMed	2,242,367	6%
Medical Lectures	958,802	3%
E3C	7,660,558	21%
Medical Degree Thesis	5,762,792	16%
TOTAL	36,342,159	

---

[2] Body Part, Organ, or Organ Component (BP), Body Substance (BS), Chemical (C), Medical Device (MD), Finding (F), Sign or Symptom (SS), Health Care Activity (HCA), Diagnostic Procedure (DP), Laboratory Procedure (LP), Therapeutic or Preventive Procedure (TPP), Pathologic Function (PF), Physiologic Function (PhF), and Injury or Poisoning (IP).

3.2   Contrastive Learning

Once the mentions are obtained, we utilize contrastive learning to train a transformer-based encoder, aiming to bring closer the contextualized mentions of the same entity while pushing mentions of different entities farther apart. A schematic overview of this process is represented in Fig. 2. The mention context m can be formally defined as:

$$[CLS]ctx_l[M_s]mention[M_e]ctx_r[SEP]$$

where ctx_l, ctx_r denote the left and right contexts respectively, [CLS], [SEP] are special tokens, $[M_s]$, $[M_e]$ are special tags delimiting the mention. To encode m, we employ a transformer-based encoder. Subsequently, we obtain the contextualized entity mention representation $\mathbf{e}$ by applying average pooling to the last-layer hidden state of the wordpiece tokens that compose the mention, as illustrated in Fig. 1.

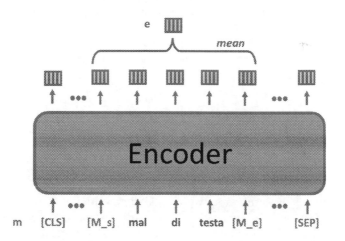

Fig. 1. Mention context encoding

During training, we construct every minibatch by first sampling n entity contexts $[\mathbf{e}_1, ..., \mathbf{e}_n]$. Then, for each anchor $\mathbf{e}_i$ we randomly sample k positives, i.e. the contexts that share the same concept unique identifier (CUI) with the anchor, $[\mathbf{p}_{i1}, ..., \mathbf{p}_{ik}]$. We prioritize selecting positives that use a different synonym, as those samples are more informative. Subsequently, we use a hard sample mining mechanism to retrieve m possibly hard negatives (i.e. samples with the highest cosine similarity with respect to the anchor). The rationale behind this mechanism is that at the beginning of training, many negatives will be included in the top-m similarity set. As training progresses, the model learns to bring positives closer together, saturating this set with positives. Meanwhile, the negatives belonging to the top-m similarity will be the hardest for the model to distinguish, thereby providing the most informative samples for learning. The implementation details of the hard negative sampling mechanism will be further discussed in Sect. 4.1.

3.3 Loss Function

We have chosen to employ the Multi-Similarity (MS) Loss function for our contrastive learning approach, based on its success in biomedical natural language processing tasks. The MS Loss function is defined as follows:

$$\mathcal{L}_{MS} = \frac{1}{m} \sum_{i=1}^{m} \left\{ \frac{1}{\alpha} \log[1 + \sum_{k \in \mathcal{P}_i} e^{-\alpha(S_{ik} - \lambda)}] + \frac{1}{\beta} \log[1 + \sum_{k \in \mathcal{N}_i} e^{\beta(S_{ik} - \lambda)}] \right\}, \quad (1)$$

where λ is a fixed similarity margin, $S_{i,j}$ the similarity of the i, j pair, b the batch size, $\mathcal{P}_i, \mathcal{N}_i$ the positive and negative sets, respectively, and α, β are hyperparameters of the loss function. Furthermore, the multi-similarity loss has an in-batch hard pair mining mechanism built-in. Specifically, a negative pair is selected by comparing it to the hardest positive pair (i.e. with the lowest similarity), while a positive pair is selected by comparing it to a negative pair that has the highest similarity. Formally, given an anchor x_i its positive set $\mathcal{P}_i$ is constructed as follows:

$$x_j \in \mathcal{P}_i \quad \text{if} \quad S_{ij} < \max_{y_k \neq y_i} S_{ik} + \epsilon, \quad (2)$$

likewise for the negative set $\mathcal{N}_i$ holds:

$$x_j \in \mathcal{N}_i \quad \text{if} \quad S_{ij} > \min_{y_k = y_i} S_{ik} - \epsilon, \quad (3)$$

where ϵ is a hyperparameter of the loss function and y the label.

Throughout our experiments, we noticed that splitting the λ-term into two independent thresholds for positive and negative pairs, as it was done in the general pair-based weighting loss [11], led to noticeable improvements. We refer to this modification as MS loss v2:

$$\mathcal{L}_{MSv2} = \frac{1}{m} \sum_{i=1}^{m} \left\{ \frac{1}{\alpha} \log[1 + \sum_{k \in \mathcal{P}_i} e^{-\alpha(S_{ik} - \lambda_p)}] + \frac{1}{\beta} \log[1 + \sum_{k \in \mathcal{N}_i} e^{\beta(S_{ik} - \lambda_n)}] \right\},$$
$$(4)$$

where λ_p, λ_n are independent thresholds for positive and negative pairs respectively.

This observation prompted us to further investigate the role of the threshold in the learning process. Therefore, we aimed to find a more informative replacement for the traditional scalar threshold term. Drawing inspiration from the vast knowledge encoded in the UMLS semantic network, we explored the utilization of similarities between medical entity nodes encoded using the Knowledge Graph Embedding (KGE) technique. The main idea behind this approach is that incorporating these informative similarities can guide the penalization assigned to pairs more effectively, taking into account the underlying relations between terms when pulling them closer or pushing them apart. Therefore, we propose a modified version of the loss function, referred to as MS Loss v3, which is defined as follows:

$$\mathcal{L}_{MSv3} = \frac{1}{m} \sum_{i=1}^{m} \left\{ \frac{1}{\alpha} \log[1 + \sum_{k \in \mathcal{P}_i} e^{-\alpha(S_{ik} - |S_{ik} - S_{ik}^{KGE}|)}] \right.$$
$$\left. + \frac{1}{\beta} \log[1 + \sum_{k \in \mathcal{N}_i} e^{\beta(S_{ik} - (1 - |S_{ik} - S_{ik}^{KGE}|))}] \right\} \tag{5}$$

where S_{ij}^{KGE} is the similarity of the i, j pair in the knowledge graph embedding space. Notably, we do not simply replace the threshold term with S_{ij}^{KGE}; instead, we introduce an agreement-based mechanism. The impact of this mechanism is evident in the weights assigned to pairs. For positive pairs, we calculate the weight contribution as the partial derivative of $\mathcal{L}_{MSv3}$ with respect to a positive similarity S_{ij}:

$$w_{ij}^+ = \frac{1 - \frac{S_{ij} - S_{ij}^{KGE}}{|S_{ij} - S_{ij}^{KGE}|}}{e^{-\alpha(|S_{ij} - S_{ij}^{KGE}| - S_{ij})} + \sum_{k \in \mathcal{P}_i} e^{-\alpha(S_{ik} - S_{ij} + |S_{ik} - S_{ik}^{KGE}| - |S_{ij} - S_{ij}^{KGE}|)}}. \tag{6}$$

Similarly, for the negative pairs:

$$w_{ij}^- = \frac{1 + \frac{S_{ij} - S_{ij}^{KGE}}{|S_{ij} - S_{ij}^{KGE}|}}{e^{\beta(1 - S_{ij} - |S_{ij} - S_{ij}^{KGE}|)} + \sum_{k \in \mathcal{N}_i} e^{\beta(S_{ik} - S_{ij} + |S_{ik} - S_{ik}^{KGE}| - |S_{ij} - S_{ij}^{KGE}|)}}. \tag{7}$$

From these formulas, it is evident that the weight contribution for any sample pair can zero out. For positive samples, this occurs when their similarity exceeds the similarity observed between concepts in the KGE. In our case, this cannot occur, as the KGE similarity will always be 1. Instead, the more interesting case involves negative pairs. For negative samples, the weight contribution is reduced to zero if the pair similarity is less than the KGE similarity. Unlike in the other versions, the pair is not penalized if it is already dissimilar enough. There may be some benefits to this for those negatives related to the anchor, which should not necessarily be penalized as strictly as those not related to the anchor. For instance, given "fever" as the anchor, the negative term "hyperthermia" should not be penalized in the same way as "hypothermia".

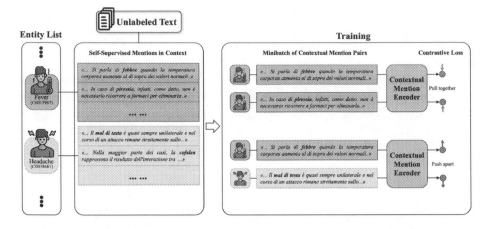

Fig. 2. Overview of the training process; for each medical term available in UMLS_ITA we retrieve its context, taken from our unlabeled corpus, and we exploit the contrastive learning loss for reorganizing the embedding space by approaching positive pairs (i.e. synonyms or different contexts of the same entity) and distancing negative ones. The applied correction depends on the Knowledge Graphs Embedding (KGE) similarity computed on the UMLS semantic network.

3.4   Knowledge Graph Embedding

We train Knowledge Graph Embedding models on a subset of UMLS knowledge graph concerning the entities in UMLS_ITA. We leverage both semantic and taxonomic relationships between these concepts. To ensure the quality of the training data, we applied filtering techniques to exclude rare and inverse relations. This filtering process resulted in a dataset comprising 415, 170 triplets, encompassing 69, 193 entities and 171 distinct relationships.

We then use 90%/6%/4% training/test/validation split ratio. We carefully partitioned the data in such a way that the test and validation sets exclusively consisted of entities and relationships that were already present in the training set.

4   Experiments

To validate our methodology, we apply the techniques described in the previous section to both SapBERT[3] and CODER[4], as illustrated more in details in the following paragraphs.

4.1   Implementation Details

Regarding the hard negative sampling, to find contexts with top-m similarities we would need to perform a matrix multiplication between all contexts in our

---
[3] cambridgeltl/SapBERT-UMLS-2020AB-all-lang-from-XLMR-large.
[4] GanjinZero/coder_all.

dataset. This operation is clearly unfeasible to perform on the fly, therefore we use the FAISS index [6] instead. The index is updated at the start of each epoch using the current state of the model. Specifically, the index we use is IndexFlatIP, which stores all 2.2 million normalized contexts embedding. This choice of index, combined with normalization, enables efficient cosine similarity search.

The training of the model was conducted over four epochs on a single *NVIDIA A40* GPU with 48 GB of memory. At each training step we construct the batch sampling 10 anchor contexts. For each anchor we then sample $k = 20$ positives, and $m = 50$ possible hard negatives. Several experiments were performed to explore different combinations of loss hyperparameters, but no significant improvements were observed. Therefore, we retained the original configuration with $\alpha = 2$, $\beta = 50$, $\epsilon = 0.1$. The remaining hyperparameters were set as follows: a learning rate $2e - 5$, weight decay of 0.01, a maximum gradient norm of 1, and 10,000 warm-up steps. Additionally, during the training, we use gradient accumulation over 8 steps.

In light of an unconventional approach to constructing training batches, where certain samples are selected multiple times during the same epoch, we have opted to minimize the pool from which the anchors are sampled. However, we still sample positives and negatives from the entire dataset. Prior to training, we randomly choose 3 representative contexts for each term and use this subset to sample the anchors. This decision significantly reduces computational burden while ensuring adequate exposure to the complete dataset. Our experiments have demonstrated nearly identical results between training with the entire dataset and training solely with this subset, affirming its efficacy.

4.2   Evaluation Metrics

We evaluated our model on three similarity-oriented metrics: Medical Conceptual Similarity Measure (MCSM), term clustering and semantic relatedness. MSCM is based on the UMLS taxonomy, developed by [3] and used in CODER. It is defined as:

$$MSCM(V, T, k) = \frac{1}{V(T)} \sum_{v \in V(T)} \sum_{i=1}^{k} \frac{1_T(v(i))}{log_2(i + 1)} \tag{8}$$

where V is a set of concepts, T the semantic type according to UMLS, k the parameterized number of neighborhood, $V(T)$ a subset of concepts with type T, $v(i)$ the ith closest neighbor of concept v and 1_T is an indicator function which is 1 if v is of type T, 0 otherwise. Given this formulation and the default settings ($k = 40$ as used in CODER) the score ranges from 0 to 11.09.

Given its importance in low-resource language, where pre-trained tools for entity recognition and linking are lacking, we have also included the term clustering task. Already experimented in [16] to unify lexically different but semantically equivalent terms, the task is defined more formally by CODER++, where two terms are considered synonyms if their cosine similarity is higher than a given threshold (θ) meanwhile true synonyms are taken from UMLS.

For semantic relatedness, since there are no datasets of this kind for Italian and given their development costs (which would require the intervention of several domain experts), we rely on two English datasets, manually translating the entities involved. MayoSRS and UMNSRS were introduced by [14] and [13] with a manual annotation of a relatedness score for 101 and 587 medical term pairs, respectively. The values vary from 1 to 10 for MayoSRS and 0–1600 for UMNSRS. Due to the lack of an appropriate translation for some terms, the number of pairs for the UMNSRS dataset is reduced to 536 tuples.

4.3   Results

Upon initial evaluation of the state of the art, it is observed that SapBERT, and specifically its multilingual version, still outperforms CODER on several tasks, despite CODER having an advantage according to its original publication. Regarding the training of Knowledge Graph Embeddings (KGEs), the outcomes of various models evaluated on link prediction and similarity tasks are presented in the Table 2. Among these, *ComplEx* has been selected as the reference model due to its positive results on similarity datasets and a representation that remains comparable to other models. The remarkable results achieved, as illustrated in Table 4, cannot be solely attributed to a simple fine-tuning process on the Italian biomedical domain. Instead, they can be largely attributed to the significant impact of the MS loss v3. This conclusion is supported by the lack of improvement in the results of the original multi-similarity loss, which was used to continue the pre-training of the SapBERT model. The benefits of the MS loss v3 are clearly shown in Table 3, where we compare the fine-tuning of the Sap-BERT multilingual model with its original loss (MS loss v1) and our proposal (MS loss v3).

Table 2. Evaluations of Knowledge Graph Embeddings over link prediction task (hits@k, Mean Rank, Mean Reciprocal Rank) and similarity tasks (MSCM score and Spearman's coefficient over relatedness scores).

model	hits@1	hits@3	hits@10	MR	MRR	MCSM	MayoSRS	UMNSRS
TransE	0.07	0.21	0.38	1619	**0.17**	9.76	0.45	**0.49**
ComplEx	0.07	0.19	0.34	1918	0.16	**9.96**	**0.55**	0.45
RotatE	**0.14**	**0.25**	**0.42**	**3382**	**0.17**	9.42	0.52	0.40
SimplE	0.09	0.17	0.30	2608	0.16	9.68	0.47	0.41

More in details, Tables 4 and 5 show the model performances on each evaluation task, by comparing the baseline models (mBERT and BERT), the multilingual state of the art used as starting point (SapBERT and CODER) and our proposal. It is not possible to identify a single model capable of obtaining the best results in every task, though. Indeed, we have noticed a different behavior

Table 3. Comparison between SapBERT continual pre-training done with its original MS loss (v1), MS loss with separate margins (v2) and our proposal (v3).

model	MCSM (avg)	Clustering (F1)	MayoSRS	UMNSRS
MS loss v1	6.10	25.00	0.27	0.32
MS loss v2	6.40	**30.10**	0.30	0.34
MS loss v3	**6.71**	28.68	**0.33**	**0.36**

of the model depending on the task on which it is evaluated. In particular, the human annotated semantic relatedness seems to be in contrast with the metrics defined automatically from UMLS: each improvement of human metrics corresponds to a worsening of UMLS-based metrics and vice versa. The choice of the pooling strategy is also not optimal for every task. By replacing the mean pooling with the CLS tag, both during training and validation, we obtain higher than state-of-the-art scores on the MayoSRS and UMNSRS datasets, yet this choice is ineffective for MSCM and term clustering. The chosen hyperparameters, therefore, represent a compromise between the different evaluation tasks.

Table 4. Evaluation of baselines, state of the art and our models with the MSCM similarity score.

Model	BP	BS	C	MD	F	SS	HCA	DP	LP	TPP	PF	PhF	IPs	AVG
mBERT	3.19	0.76	8.98	2.36	6.65	3.72	4.02	3.43	3.04	6.17	9.07	2.85	6.27	4.65
BERT	2.97	0.78	8.72	2.57	6.3	3.27	3.84	3.81	2.86	6	9.07	2.66	6	4.53
SapBERT	6.06	1.79	10.19	4.38	7.54	4.82	**5.48**	6.69	4.39	7.92	9.52	4.46	6.98	6.17
+ MS loss v3	**6.81**	**2.1**	**10.41**	**5.68**	**8.02**	**5.02**	5.47	**7.64**	**5.52**	**8.89**	**9.8**	**4.51**	**7.36**	**6.71**
CODER	4.1	1.22	9.63	2.99	6.57	3.94	4.95	4.01	3.2	6.04	9.08	3.29	5.87	4.99
+ MS loss v3	5.54	1.41	10.23	4.68	7.44	4.36	5.31	5.53	4.64	7.74	9.66	3.87	6.83	5.93

Table 5. a) Results of the term clustering task (i.e. automatic detection of synonyms), with the θ threshold optimized with respect to the F1 score; b) Spearman's coefficient over two semantic relatedness datasets: MayoSRS (with 1–10 range) and UMNSRS (0–1600).

Model	θ	A	F1	P	R
mBERT	0.93	100	6.4	4.8	9.59
BERT	0.94	100	7.91	5.52	13,94
SapBERT	0.88	100	**33,92**	**35,83**	32.21
+MS loss v3	0.89	100	28.68	30.32	27.21
CODER	0.87	100	**32.24**	**31.86**	**32.64**
+MS loss v3	0.88	100	28.44	25.88	31.55

(a) Term Clustering

Model	MayoSRS	UMNSRS
mBERT	0.00	0.14
BERT	0.12	0.19
SapBERT	**0.37**	0.33
+MS loss v3	0.33	**0.36**
CODER	0.44	**0.48**
+MS loss v3	**0.45**	0.40

(b) Relatedness score

5   Conclusion and Future Works

In this paper, we present a novel approach to address the lack of domain-specific word embeddings for the Italian language by combining pre-existing state-of-the-art solutions with a new variant of the Multi-Similarity loss. Our method leverages the Knowledge Graph Embedding (KGE) representation derived from the semantic network to compensate for the scarcity of controlled medical terms and synonyms, effectively reorganizing the embedding space and improving performance on semantic similarity-related tasks.

With regard to metric learning and representation learning, contrastive learning is currently the most suitable and widely adopted method. We used the Multi-Similarity loss, its hard pairs mining and the dynamic sampling mechanism, combined with KGE and contexts. Indeed, unlike other works, language models trained on the Italian language have to overcome more substantial challenges, due to limited resources available. The use of contexts has proved to be essential, not only to capture different nuances of the same term, but more in general to expand the number of positives, which would have been not enough for a successful training if we had limited ourselves to synonyms. To overcome these difficulties, and leverage as much as possible the information available, we have exploited to our advantage the information contained in the KGEs, by adapting the MS loss in order to take into account the similarity computed on them. This contribution represents the major novelty of this work, since – to the best of our knowledge – such an initiative had never been proposed before.

Our proposed method demonstrates comparable or superior results to the current state-of-the-art approaches. However, there are still several limitations that need to be addressed. Firstly, limited computing power restricts the number of samples that can be utilized and impedes further development. Additionally, the quality and availability of domain-specific texts are crucial factors. The collected corpus is skewed towards blogs and informative articles, which often lack specific terms and medical jargon found in medical records. Finally, considering the relevance and usefulness of multilingual models, it would be interesting to extend this work to multilingual environment once the aforementioned limitations have been overcome.

We hope that this work could ultimately promote the advancement of new domain-specific word embeddings in low-resource languages, paving the way for future research directions in the Italian NLP community.

References

1. Beltagy, I., Lo, K., Cohan, A.: Scibert: a pretrained language model for scientific text. In: EMNLP (2019)
2. Bordes, A., Usunier, N., Garcia-Duran, A., Weston, J., Yakhnenko, O.: Translating embeddings for modeling multi-relational data. In: Burges, C., Bottou, L., Welling, M., Ghahramani, Z., Weinberger, K. (eds.) Advances in Neural Information Processing Systems, vol. 26. Curran Associates, Inc. (2013). https://proceedings.neurips.cc/paper_files/paper/2013/file/1cecc7a77928ca8133fa24680a88d2f9-Paper.pdf

3. Choi, Y., Chiu, C.Y.I., Sontag, D.A.: Learning low-dimensional representations of medical concepts. AMIA Summits Transl. Sci. Proc. **2016**, 41–50 (2016)
4. Gu, Y., et al.: Domain-specific language model pretraining for biomedical natural language processing. ACM Trans. Comput. Healthc. **3**(1) (2021). https://doi.org/10.1145/3458754
5. Huang, K., Altosaar, J., Ranganath, R.: Clinicalbert: modeling clinical notes and predicting hospital readmission. ArXiv abs/1904.05342 (2019)
6. Johnson, J., Douze, M., Jégou, H.: Billion-scale similarity search with GPUs. IEEE Trans. Big Data **7**(3), 535–547 (2019)
7. Kazemi, S.M., Poole, D.: Simple embedding for link prediction in knowledge graphs. In: Proceedings of the 32nd International Conference on Neural Information Processing Systems, pp. 4289–4300. NIPS'18, Curran Associates Inc., Red Hook, NY, USA (2018)
8. Lee, J., et al.: Biobert: a pre-trained biomedical language representation model for biomedical text mining. Bioinformatics **36**, 1234–1240 (2020)
9. Liu, F., Shareghi, E., Meng, Z., Basaldella, M., Collier, N.: Self-alignment pretraining for biomedical entity representations. In: NAACL (2021)
10. Liu, F., Vulić, I., Korhonen, A., Collier, N.: Learning domain-specialised representations for cross-lingual biomedical entity linking. In: Proceedings of ACL-IJCNLP 2021, August 2021
11. Liu, H., Cheng, J., Wang, W., Su, Y.: The general pair-based weighting loss for deep metric learning. arXiv preprint arXiv:1905.12837 (2019)
12. Magnini, B., Altuna, B., Lavelli, A., Speranza, M., Zanoli, R.: The e3c project: European clinical case corpus. In: SEPLN (2021)
13. Pakhomov, S., McInnes, B., Adam, T., Liu, Y., Pedersen, T., Melton, G.: Semantic similarity and relatedness between clinical terms: an experimental study. In: AMIA ... Annual Symposium Proceedings/AMIA Symposium. AMIA Symposium 2010, pp. 572–576, November 2010
14. Pakhomov, S.V.S., Pedersen, T., McInnes, B.T., Melton, G.B., Ruggieri, A.P., Chute, C.G.: Towards a framework for developing semantic relatedness reference standards. J. Biomed. Inform. **44**(2), 251–65 (2011)
15. Polignano, M., Basile, P., Degemmis, M., Semeraro, G., Basile, V.: Alberto: Italian BERT language understanding model for NLP challenging tasks based on tweets. In: CLiC-it (2019)
16. Ronzani, M., et al.: Unstructured data in predictive process monitoring: lexicographic and semantic mapping to ICD-9-CM codes for the home hospitalization service. In: Bandini, S., Gasparini, F., Mascardi, V., Palmonari, M., Vizzari, G. (eds.) AIxIA 2021 – Advances in Artificial Intelligence. AIxIA 2021. LNCS, vol. 13196, pp. 700–715. Springer, Cham (2022). https://doi.org/10.1007/978-3-031-08421-8_48
17. Sun, Z., Deng, Z., Nie, J., Tang, J.: Rotate: Knowledge graph embedding by relational rotation in complex space. In: 7th International Conference on Learning Representations, ICLR 2019, New Orleans, LA, USA, 6–9 May 2019. OpenReview.net (2019). https://openreview.net/forum?id=HkgEQnRqYQ
18. Trouillon, T., Welbl, J., Riedel, S., Gaussier, E., Bouchard, G.: Complex embeddings for simple link prediction. In: Balcan, M.F., Weinberger, K.Q. (eds.) Proceedings of The 33rd International Conference on Machine Learning. Proceedings of Machine Learning Research, vol. 48, pp. 2071–2080. PMLR, New York, New York, USA, 20–22 June 2016. https://proceedings.mlr.press/v48/trouillon16.html

19. Wang, X., Han, X., Huang, W., Dong, D., Scott, M.R.: Multi-similarity loss with general pair weighting for deep metric learning. In: 2019 IEEE/CVF Conference on Computer Vision and Pattern Recognition (CVPR), pp. 5017–5025 (2019)
20. Yang, B., Yih, W., He, X., Gao, J., Deng, L.: Embedding entities and relations for learning and inference in knowledge bases. In: Bengio, Y., LeCun, Y. (eds.) 3rd International Conference on Learning Representations, ICLR 2015, San Diego, CA, USA, 7–9 May 2015, Conference Track Proceedings (2015). https://arxiv.org/abs/1412.6575
21. Yuan, Z., Zhao, Z., Yu, S.: Coder: knowledge infused cross-lingual medical term embedding for term normalization. J. Biomed. Inform. 103983 (2022)
22. Zeng, S., Yuan, Z., Yu, S.: Automatic biomedical term clustering by learning fine-grained term representations. In: BIONLP (2022)
23. Zhang, R., Ji, Y., Zhang, Y., Passonneau, R.J.: Contrastive data and learning for natural language processing. In: Proceedings of the 2022 Conference of the North American Chapter of the Association for Computational Linguistics: Human Language Technologies: Tutorial Abstracts, pp. 39–47. Association for Computational Linguistics, Seattle, United States, July 2022. https://doi.org/10.18653/v1/2022.naacl-tutorials.6, https://aclanthology.org/2022.naacl-tutorials.6
24. Zhang, S., et al.: Knowledge-rich self-supervised entity linking. ArXiv abs/2112.07887 (2021)

Applications of AI

Recognizing the Style, Genre, and Emotion of a Work of Art Through Visual and Knowledge Graph Embeddings

Giovanna Castellano⬛, Raffaele Scaringi$^{(\boxtimes)}$⬛, and Gennaro Vessio⬛

Department of Computer Science, University of Bari Aldo Moro, Bari, Italy
{giovanna.castellano,raffaele.scaringi,gennaro.vessio}@uniba.it

Abstract. Recognizing attributes of unknown artworks relies on more than visual information: prior knowledge and emotional context can play a crucial role. Building an AI system mimicking this perception requires a multi-modal model integrating computer vision and contextual factors. In this paper, we propose a new model that uses vision transformers and graph attention networks to learn new artworks' visual and contextual features and predict their style, genre, and emotion. Contextual features are acquired from an extended version of our *ArtGraph* knowledge graph, enriched with emotion information from the *ArtEmis* dataset. Our inductive end-to-end multi-task architecture enables real-time execution and resilience to graph evolutions. Combining computer vision and knowledge graphs could facilitate a deeper understanding of the fine arts, bridging the gap between computer science and the humanities (The new version of the graph is available at https://doi.org/10.5281/zenodo.8172374, while the code is available at https://github.com/CILAB-ArtGraph/multi-modal-end-to-end-art-classifier).

Keywords: Computer vision · Deep learning · Digital humanities · Emotion recognition · Knowledge graphs

1 Introduction

The digitization of art collections has practical implications for computer vision applications in areas such as automatic indexing and cultural heritage analysis. This intersection of computer vision and art has the potential to deepen our understanding of the fine arts and make them more accessible to a broader audience. In particular, recent advances in deep learning have demonstrated the potential of artificial intelligence systems in art, including predicting style, genre, and emotion [6,9,20,22]. However, pure computer vision methods have limitations in capturing the "contextual" knowledge needed for a complete understanding of art. Artworks are influenced by historical, social, and contextual factors, contributing to a richer interpretation beyond the visual aspect.

R. Basili et al. (Eds.): AIxIA 2023, LNAI 14318, pp. 427–440, 2023.
https://doi.org/10.1007/978-3-031-47546-7_29

Recent research has explored integrating contextual information into knowledge graphs (KGs) to improve computer vision methods in various domains, including art [13–16]. However, the existing literature mainly adopts a "transductive" approach, which requires costly re-training and relies on how test data are distributed and linked to the KG. These limitations hinder real-time applications, especially when it comes to predicting the attributes of individual test instances. In our previous work [5], we addressed some of these limitations by proposing an "inductive" method that used the features of our art KG, *ArtGraph*. However, our approach used a projection mechanism, preventing an end-to-end architecture and neglecting the contextual features of new artworks. Moreover, our model focused only on predicting style and genre, neglecting the important attribute of evoked emotions.

The availability of digital image collections has sparked interest in automatic methods for inferring viewers' emotions, with applications ranging from semantic retrieval of images to aesthetic evaluation and opinion mining [19,21]. However, the emotion classification of images is a challenge because of human feelings' complex and subjective nature. This difficulty is amplified in the fine arts domain, where works are abstract and may lack easily identifiable subjects, making it more difficult to discern the artist's intentions [1,10]. Developing an automated system with a high-level understanding of the fine arts requires addressing the challenges of incorporating affective skills.

In this paper, we contribute in the following ways:

- We present an updated version of *ArtGraph*, which now incorporates emotions by integrating information from the *ArtEmis* dataset [1]. A preliminary study of this integration was reported in [2].
- We develop an end-to-end classification model that combines visual and knowledge graph embeddings to recognize artworks' style, genre, and emotion. The model follows an entirely inductive strategy, which makes it suitable for real-time applications.
- Experimental results demonstrate the effectiveness of the proposed model, which exceeds the current state-of-the-art. Moreover, our model proves robust when operating on a graph enriched with its own predictions, simulating a real scenario in which the graph "evolves".

The rest of the paper is structured as follows. Section 2 reviews related work. Section 3 explains the data used and the steps required to extend *ArtGraph*. Section 4 illustrates the proposed classification method. Section 5 discusses the experimental results. Finally, Sec. 6 concludes the article and outlines potential future research directions.

2   Related Work

Deep neural networks have shown promise in deriving complex patterns from art. Previous methods (e.g., [17,22,23]) have used convolutional neural networks

(CNNs) to recognize attributes of artworks, such as the school of painting. However, recognizing specific attributes from visual content alone remains challenging because of their high variability.

Researchers have incorporated contextual information encoded in knowledge graphs alongside visual features to address this challenge. One approach, *ContextNet* [16], combines visual and contextual features by representing the artwork using ResNet50 for visual features and node2vec for contextual ones. However, this method has limitations because it uses contextual knowledge only to "adjust" the visual features and does not consider the content of the graph nodes.

To improve attribute prediction, a new model called *GCNBoost* [14] extends *ContextNet* by incorporating graph convolutional networks (GCNs). It performs a preliminary prediction using *ContextNet* and then extends the KG using the predicted attributes as "pseudo-labels". The GCN is then used to determine the final result. Although this approach overcomes some limitations of *ContextNet*, the generation of the extended knowledge graph can be complex and inefficient.

In our previous work [5], we addressed these problems by proposing a multimodal model based on graph attention networks (GATs). During training, we extract visual and contextual features from our proposed KG, *ArtGraph*. The embeddings are then concatenated, and the resulting feature vector is used for prediction. Since contextual information is unavailable during testing, we use a "projection" function to project the visual features into the pre-optimized context space. This approach follows an inductive strategy and allows us to develop a real-time predictive model that predicts attributes based solely on the visual appearance of an artwork. However, the projection mechanism prevents using an end-to-end architecture, as it requires pre-training of the GAT. In addition, the model in our previous work predicts only style and genre attributes.

Regarding predicting emotions evoked by works of art, Achlioptas et al. [1] introduced the *ArtEmis* dataset and proposed a method based on a pre-trained ResNet32 to minimize the KL divergence between the predicted and empirical user distributions. They also explored sequence models based on textual descriptions. Fine-grained emotion prediction proved to be more challenging than binary classification. Bose et al. [4] developed transformer-based models using textual descriptions and visual features, outperforming methods with separate embeddings but requiring descriptions at the time of testing. We also tried to tackle the problem of emotion recognition in the fine arts domain by combining visual and contextual information. In a previous study [2], we harnessed the capabilities of ResNet50 for visual feature extraction, combined with TransE [3] for contextual representation learning. However, although TransE leverages the logic schema of the graph for the learning process, it does not handle a real scenario in which the graph grows over time since it learns the embeddings in an unsupervised manner.

We aim to develop an inductive method for real-time style, genre, and emotion prediction based on visual and contextual features. Unlike our previous work [5], we enrich *ArtGraph* by integrating emotional data from *ArtEmis*. Our approach avoids artifacts such as projection functions and exploits the graph's style, genre, and emotion nodes for predictions, enabling end-to-end training.

3   Materials

3.1   *ArtGraph*

ArtGraph [5] is a KG in the art domain that can represent and describe many concepts related to artworks and artists. For example, regarding artwork nodes, the hyperlink to the image, the date of creation, and where it is exhibited are encoded. In addition, much information is included as connections between nodes, such as an artist's influence on another. To build the graph, we scraped WikiArt, and since this encyclopedia does not provide rich information about artists, we also exploited DBpedia to retrieve artists' metadata. *ArtGraph* is modeled as a Neo4j database, which can be used to perform information retrieval and knowledge discovery tasks even without explicitly training a learning algorithm.

3.2   *ArtEmis*

In its first released version, *ArtGraph* did not include emotion information. To fill this gap, we exploited *ArtEmis* [1]. It is a large-scale dataset that associates artworks with human emotions and contains natural language explanations of the motivations behind each emotion triggered. The dataset was built on WikiArt and contains $80,031$ unique artworks by $1,119$ artists covering 27 styles and 45 genres. The authors collected emotions by asking at least five annotators to express their dominant emotional reactions. Specifically, after looking at an artwork, the annotators were asked to indicate their dominant reaction by choosing from *anger, disgust, fear, sadness, amusement, awe, contentment, excitement,* and *something else*. This is thus the categorical emotional model proposed by Mikels et al. [18], expanded with the ninth category *something else*, indicating a neutral emotion. As mentioned, the annotators were also asked to explain their choice, but our study did not use these data.

3.3   Combining *ArtGraph* and *ArtEmis*

To enrich the graph with emotions, we integrated the emotion labels provided by *ArtEmis* into *ArtGraph*. We identified the artworks in both datasets, obtaining $65,236$ distinct artworks spanning 30 styles and 18 genres. The *ArtEmis* dataset contains various details for each entry, including the artwork, the emotion elicited, an annotator's explanation of the choice of emotion, and a score indicating the level of arousal. Accordingly, as schematized in Fig. 1, we added in *ArtGraph* an edge between each "artwork-emotion" pair to represent the dominant emotional reaction as reported by the evaluators. However, since multiple annotators recorded their choices for each artwork, we used a majority approach

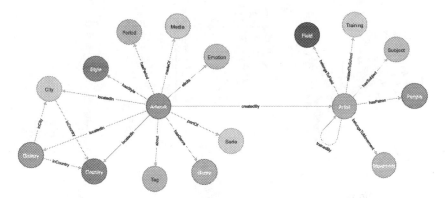

Fig. 1. Logic schema of *ArtGraph* after integrating emotions.

Table 1. Comparison of *ArtGraph* and the new version with emotion nodes.

KG	# nodes	# edges	# artists	# artworks
ArtGraph	135, 038	875, 416	2, 501	116, 475
ArtGraph + *ArtEmis*	135, 047	1, 092, 544	2, 501	116, 475

to select the dominant emotion with the highest score. Specifically, in this study, while incorporating all triggered emotions into the graph, we focused on predicting the most recurrent reaction for the emotion recognition task. To illustrate the evolution, we provide a comparison between the previously published version of *ArtGraph* [5] and the extension presented in this article in Table 1. Significantly, emotions were added only to artworks in both datasets, while those exclusive to one dataset were not considered for emotion recognition. Finally, integrating emotion information into *ArtGraph* provides significant benefits to end users by enabling them to perform information retrieval and knowledge discovery tasks using the graph. For example, users can navigate the graph to search for artworks or artists based on dominant emotions. Currently, *ArtGraph* is one of the most extensive knowledge graphs on art, encompassing 116, 475 artworks by 2, 501 artists, comprising 32 styles, 18 genres, and metadata describing them.

4 Methods

We propose a new multi-task classification method that combines graph representation learning and visual features to predict artworks' style, genre, and emotion simultaneously. Our multi-modal architecture, depicted in Fig. 2, integrates visual and contextual features for improved prediction. By leveraging multiple inputs, a multi-modal and multi-task approach captures different perspectives on artworks, enhancing performance in understanding art-related attributes.

Our previous work [5] surpassed the state-of-the-art but had limitations. It involved a two-step process, learning graph embeddings and then a projection

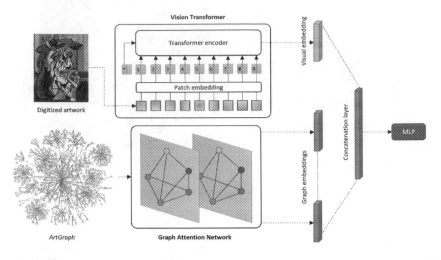

Fig. 2. Architecture of the proposed model. The artwork is encoded using ViT. All class "prototypes" are encoded using a GAT. Then, using a concatenation layer, the visual and contextual embeddings form a single feature vector that is finally fed into a classification head ("MLP") to provide the final output.

encoder, which required contextual embedding at test time. In the method proposed here, we encode all styles, genres, and emotions as contextual embeddings and concatenate them with visual features for prediction. This approach offers advantages such as using *true* contextual embeddings during testing, avoiding surrogate features, and leveraging the knowledge graph as background knowledge, which remains applicable even with new data. In contrast, extracting contextual embedding for a specific artwork relies heavily on the feature projector and lacks handling the data drifts commonly found in this domain.

In the following subsections, we provide a more detailed description of our multi-modal and multi-task approach, focusing on embedding generation and the specific inductive inference method employed.

4.1 Visual Embedding Generation

As for the visual embeddings, each three-channel artwork image is first resized to 224 × 224 pixels and then encoded by a vision transformer (ViT) [12] pretrained on ImageNet and fine-tuned on the artworks in $\mathcal{A}rt\mathcal{G}raph$. ViT consists of a transformer-like architecture, which considers an image a series of patches. The patches are linearly embedded and added to position embeddings. Then, the resulting features are fed into a standard transformer encoder. It is worth noting that, to perform fine-tuning, a supervised learning task is usually solved. To this end, the chosen task was style recognition since the features learned for style may be more general than those learned for genre or emotion. Indeed, while style is usually independent of the content of an artwork, the same genre can be expressed through many styles. Emotions, on the other hand, are highly subjective. For this reason, as a common practice, we first fine-tuned the network by freezing all the layers except the classification head to prevent the loss magnitude from destroying previously learned weights. Then, we unfroze the last feature extraction layer to improve feature representativeness. As a result, we take the final output learned features which result in a visual embedding $\mathbf{h}_v \in \mathbb{R}^{128}$.

4.2 Context Embedding Generation

We use a graph attention network (GAT) [24] to extract contextual embeddings from $Art\mathcal{G}raph$. The GAT learns iterative node representations, where each node embedding $\mathbf{h}_g$ is computed based on the node's neighborhood and attention coefficients. The GAT captures the importance of different neighbors in representing each node by performing message passing and aggregation.

A GAT is particularly useful for our heterogeneous graph, as it considers multiple types of information and relationships. By aggregating information from the linked artwork nodes, we encode the nodes representing style, genre, and emotion. This allows us to capture contextual knowledge and enhance the representativeness of the embeddings. The GAT's non-linear transformation and attention mechanism improve the representativeness of the aggregation, considering particular neighbors more than others during classification. For the *artwork* nodes, we use the same features extracted by ViT as a content representation, while scalar features are used for other node types. This approach accommodates the addition of new nodes and edges to the graph without requiring the retraining of the encoder module.

Unlike our previous work [5], all features have been refined along with ViT to solve the same classification task. As a result, the output of the GAT encoding is a set of node embeddings $\mathbf{h}_g \in \mathbb{R}^{128}$ for each node in the graph. Unlike node2vec, which encodes embeddings solely based on topology, our approach treats encoding as a supervised task within an end-to-end model. The GAT learns the most suitable embeddings for the defined task, enhancing their feasibility.

4.3 Model Inference

When adopting an inductive approach, a significant challenge arises in providing contextual features to the model during testing, especially for "isolated" target artworks where only visual information is available. Previous methods have employed pseudo-labels [14] or projection strategies [5, 16] to address this issue and maintain contextual features during inference. This paper proposes a novel approach that extracts embeddings from class nodes, including styles, genres, and emotions. As mentioned above, the GAT produces a set of node embeddings, and our method considers all embeddings related to styles, genres, and emotions. These features serve as "prototypes" representing each genre, style, and emotion in $Art\mathcal{G}raph$. By doing so, we enable the model to handle unseen artworks without relying on their specific contextual information during testing while encoding the contextual information as background knowledge.

This approach offers several practical advantages. Firstly, it utilizes *true* embeddings encoded in the graph rather than surrogate features, improving performance. Secondly, it eliminates the need to differentiate the model's behavior between the training and testing phases, as previously done. Consequently, we can build an end-to-end architecture that simultaneously refines all features, including the GAT and the final classification layer. Lastly, the class prototypes can adapt and refine as the graph evolves with the addition of new nodes, facilitating the encoding of new knowledge and enabling the model to learn increasingly generalizable patterns in a "continual" learning setting.

Specifically, after encoding the visual features with ViT, we concatenate them with the context embedding of each class, represented by the GAT. This results in a combined feature vector $[\mathbf{h}_v, \mathbf{h}_{g_1}, \ldots, \mathbf{h}_{g_C}] \in \mathbb{R}^{7,680}$, where C denotes the number of classes for the three tasks. These features are fed into a softmax-activated fully-connected output layer, with as many neurons as there are classes to predict. Thus, to optimize the model, we use a multi-task loss function:

$$\mathcal{L} = \sum_{t=1}^{T} \sum_{c=1}^{C} \ell\left(y_{tc}, \hat{y}_{tc}\right),$$

where T is the number of tasks, i.e. three, y_{tc} is the ground truth for task t and class c, $\hat{y}_{tc}$ is the corresponding model prediction, and $\ell\left(y_{ti}, \hat{y}_{tc}\right) = -y_{tc}log(\hat{y}_{tc})$ is the classic cross-entropy loss.

5   Experiments

To evaluate the effectiveness of the proposed model, some experiments were performed. In this section, we describe the experimental setup and discuss the results obtained.

5.1   Experimental Setup

The experiments were conducted on a desktop PC with an AMD Ryzen 7 3700X processor, 16 GB of RAM, and an NVIDIA RTX 3070 GPU. The proposed model was compared with three baselines:

- ViT: it is the backbone of our proposed model and uses only visual features to determine the target attribute of a given artwork [12].
- *ContextNet*: proposed by Garcia et al. [16], this model aims to predict artwork attributes by exploiting visual and contextual knowledge. Visual features are extracted using ResNet50, while contextual features are obtained through node2vec.
- Our previous method: presented in [5], this method involved concatenating the visual features extracted with ViT solely with the contextual feature vector of the artwork. Visual features were projected into the context space during testing to provide a "proxy" for graph embeddings. Because this method did not consider emotions, the output level was adjusted to predict emotions.

In addition, the proposed model was evaluated in two settings: single-task and multi-task. In the single-task setting, separate models were trained to recognize each attribute. On the other hand, a single model was trained in the multi-task setting that could simultaneously predict all three attributes, i.e., style, genre, and emotion. The original model, as proposed, operates in the multi-task setting. All models were implemented in Python using the popular PyTorch and PyTorch Geometric libraries, which are well-suited to graph architectures. It is important to note that we did not include methods that employ a transductive strategy since they are not suitable for real-time applications, and their performance depends on the characteristics and topology of the test graph. In other words, during testing, we assumed that the model knew only the visual appearance of the artwork.

It is crucial to consider that learning graph embeddings by considering the whole graph could introduce a bias into the model. To mitigate this problem, we used an inductive approach, partitioning the whole graph into separate training, validation, and test graphs. Specifically, the training set forms an interconnected graph, while the validation and test sets are only composed of isolated nodes. We adopted an 80/10/10 partitioning criterion, ensuring that the division was stratified by class. In this way, we ensured that the distribution of classes in the training set was approximately preserved in the validation and test sets.

As for preprocessing the artworks, we resized them to a standardized size of 224×224 pixels and performed normalization using the mean and standard deviation values of the ImageNet dataset. For optimization, we used the Adam optimizer with a learning rate of 10^{-4} and a batch size of 128. Dropout regularization was applied to both the contextual encoding and final classification layers, with a dropout probability of 0.25. An early stopping with a patience of 2 and a learning rate schedule based on reducing the learning rate on the plateau were also employed to avoid overfitting. The validation set helped tune other hyperparameters. In particular, we found that the most effective activation function for the graph encoder is tanh, while the leaky-ReLU function was chosen for the final classification layer.

The problem concerns multi-class classification. In addition, we introduced a *coarse-grained* emotion classification, grouping emotions into positive and negative classes and treating *something else* as a distinct class. The result was a ternary classification. To evaluate the effectiveness of the method, we used several performance metrics. Top-1 and top-2 accuracy were calculated to determine the frequency with which the correct class appeared among the first two predicted classes. Moreover, we used the macro F1-score, which involves calculating the F1-score for each class and the subsequent average.

To simulate a realistic execution of the method, in which the knowledge graph is dynamically adjusted after each prediction of new artworks, we conducted experiments to study the impact of "updating" the graph. This updating process involved adding links between the test artworks and their predicted outputs (style, genre, and emotion), thus incorporating this new knowledge into the graph and updating the embeddings accordingly. Although this approach introduces the possibility of noise and potential performance degradation, it allows us to measure the *resilience* of the graph to evolving content and assess its ability to adapt to and learn from new information.

5.2   Results

The results of the proposed method and the baselines in the single-task setting are presented in Table 2. Analyzing the results, some observations can be made. First, integrating contextual features consistently improves performance over relying solely on visual features. This finding supports previous studies in the literature that have highlighted the benefits of leveraging visual and contextual features for attribute prediction [5,16]. In particular, this improvement is most evident in the style classification task, indicating that style recognition greatly benefits from the knowledge encoded within the graph. On the other hand, the impact on genre and emotion classification is relatively minor, suggesting that visual features more influence these tasks. In other words, while visual stimuli play a crucial role in classifying genre and emotion, prior knowledge appears to be less critical. Second, the proposed method consistently outperforms all baselines, including our previous work. This result indicates that the new end-to-end inductive strategy allows the model to learn more effective representations. This improvement validates the effectiveness of the proposed approach and highlights the importance of the new learning framework employed.

Regarding the multi-task strategy, presented in Table 3, quantitative results show that this learning strategy is generally preferable to the single-task approach. The simultaneous prediction of style, genre, and emotion allows the tasks to help each other synergistically. Particularly noteworthy is the influence of the other tasks on the recognition of evoked emotions, suggesting a correlation between them. However, as expected, classifying coarse-grained emotions was much easier than fine-grained ones, considering all labels. It is worth noting that, to have a fair comparison between the single- and multi-task setting, we excluded all artworks for which there was no label related to the emotion elicited. Notably, all methods were trained, validated, and tested using the same split.

As for the update strategy tested, the model performance remains constant or even improves as new, albeit uncertain, knowledge is introduced into the graph. This is a promising result, considering the potential real-world application where the graph evolves and the model needs to self-improve. In the case of contemporary art, for example, which lacks extensive annotations and requires a well-defined taxonomy, this fact is particularly relevant. Also, because we use a graph attention network to compute contextual features, there is no need to retrain, unlike other algorithms like node2vec. This aspect further highlights the efficiency of our approach.

Finally, in addition to presenting quantitative results, our model was subjected to a qualitative evaluation. Figure 3 shows examples of the predictions made for three distinct works of art. The first artwork, entitled "The Seine at Argenteuil", received correct classifications in all labels, confirming the overall effectiveness of the proposed model. However, the remaining paintings did not

Table 2. Comparison between the state-of-the-art and the proposed model in the single-task setting. The best result for each metric per task in both tables is in bold.

Method	Style			Genre			Emotion (multi-class)			Emotion (ternary)		
	Top-1	Top-2	Macro F1	Top-1	Top-2	Macro F1	Top-1	Top-2	Macro F1	Top-1	Top-2	Macro F1
Fine-tuned ViT	47.21	65.91	33.05	66.19	81.90	50.20	39.23	57.25	21.92	61.10	85.24	47.31
ContextNet [16]	48.12	67.58	33.16	65.11	80.90	46.90	40.95	59.37	20.29	63.17	87.55	43.19
Previous work [5]	53.27	71.24	40.69	68.78	84.27	54.74	42.06	59.91	22.17	62.94	86.73	44.76
This work (no update)	63.12	80.65	**48.60**	74.48	88.13	61.94	44.75	63.23	25.66	65.90	89.09	48.23
This work (with update)	63.11	**80.70**	48.57	74.52	88.47	62.06	44.84	63.18	25.66	65.90	88.07	48.56

Table 3. Comparison between the state-of-the-art and the proposed model in the multi-task setting. The best result for each metric per task in both tables is in bold.

Method	Style			Genre			Emotion (multi-class)			Emotion (ternary)		
	Top-1	Top-2	Macro F1	Top-1	Top-2	Macro F1	Top-1	Top-2	Macro F1	Top-1	Top-2	Macro F1
Fine-tuned ViT	57.14	64.28	32.55	64.28	78.71	47.89	42.85	57.14	**27.49**	75.00	85.71	42.48
ContextNet [16]	46.34	65.11	29.76	64.04	79.60	43.72	41.74	60.36	21.03	63.41	87.18	43.33
Previous work [5]	44.44	70.37	36.12	74.07	81.48	57.61	40.74	**66.66**	15.53	**77.77**	**96.29**	44.27
This work (no update)	**63.29**	80.49	47.43	**75.35**	**88.50**	**63.80**	45.42	63.90	27.29	66.32	87.93	50.43
This work (with update)	**63.29**	80.52	47.45	75.32	**88.50**	63.69	**45.51**	63.86	27.32	66.31	88.04	**50.44**

(a)	(b)	(c)
"The Seine at Argenteuil" by Claude Monet	*"The Night Responds to My Complaints"* by Konstantinos Parthenis	*"The Wahdoosee Question"* by Nzante Spee

P: impressionism, landscape, contentment   P: abstract expressionism, abstract, something else   P: expressionism, landscape, excitement
GT: impressionism, landscape, contentment   GT: cubism, symbolic painting, sadness   GT: surrealism, figurative, sadness

Fig. 3. Comparison between model predictions (P) and ground truth (GT): in (a), an ideal scenario is represented in which our model accurately recognizes the correct attributes for all three tasks; (b) presents a case of misclassification, in which the model assigns a class that is semantically similar to the correct class, but still incorrect; (c) shows a case in which the model completely fails to predict the correct labels for the tasks. The labels follow the order of style, gender, and emotion.

fare as well. In particular, in the case of "Night Responds to My Complaints", the model generated incorrect predictions for all tasks. However, it is worth noting that the model's predictions closely resembled the ground truth, indicating that it had difficulties with ambiguous classifications comparable to humans. The complexities arising from ambiguous class membership are evident in the consistently higher top-2 accuracy than top-1. The third painting, titled "The Wahdoosee Question", further highlights the intricate nature of the heritage domain. In this case, the model predictions were inaccurate, and the correct classes differed significantly from those predicted.

6   Conclusion

In this paper, we have focused on the prediction of artwork attributes by introducing a method that combines visual and contextual features, where the latter are derived from a knowledge graph. Our central hypothesis is that incorporating knowledge of past artworks could improve the performance that visual features alone could achieve. We have taken a significant step in this direction by supplementing our previously proposed *ArtGraph* with the *ArtEmis* dataset. Leveraging the potential of graph neural networks and the increasingly popular vision transformers, we have developed a new predictive model for analyzing art. This model is based on a fully inductive end-to-end architecture, enabling real-time predictions when only visual information of new artworks is available. However, we recognize that fine-grained classification of emotions remains a challenging task. Categorizing the specific emotion evoked by a work of art is inherently complex, as emotion labels are subjective in nature. To address this, future work could explore unsupervised or semi-supervised learning approaches to better identify emotion categories without relying solely on personal and potentially conflicting human labels [7]. Furthermore, investigating mechanisms based on attention or patches [11] could be a promising avenue to explore. In paintings, for example, artists often incorporate specific details to evoke particular emotions in viewers, and these mechanisms can help capture those nuances more effectively.

In future work, we aim to explore an additional task that is highly relevant in this domain: artwork captioning [8]. The framework we have developed, which combines visual and knowledge graph embeddings, could also incorporate textual descriptions for a deeper understanding of the semantic aspects of art. This way, our model could not only predict evoked emotion but also generate expressive and historically informative descriptions of the perceived artwork. Integrating knowledge bases into computer vision systems can help bridge the gap between the humanities and computer science communities, enabling better understanding and collaboration in this interdisciplinary field. This integration can improve interpretability and provide meaningful insights into artworks, fostering a deeper appreciation of art from a computational perspective.

Acknowledgment. The research of Raffaele Scaringi is funded by a Ph.D. fellowship within the framework of the Italian "D.M. n. 352, April 9, 2022" - under the National

Recovery and Resilience Plan, Mission 4, Component 2, Investment 3.3 - Ph.D. Project "Automatic analysis of artistic heritage via Artificial Intelligence", co-supported by "Exprivia S.p.A." (CUP H91I22000410007).

References

1. Achlioptas, P., Ovsjanikov, M., Haydarov, K., Elhoseiny, M., Guibas, L.J.: ArtEmis: affective language for visual art. In: Proceedings of the IEEE/CVF Conference on Computer Vision and Pattern Recognition, pp. 11569–11579 (2021)
2. Aslan, S., Castellano, G., Digeno, V., Migailo, G., Scaringi, R., Vessio, G.: Recognizing the emotions evoked by artworks through visual features and knowledge graph-embeddings. In: Mazzeo, P.L., Frontoni, E., Sclaroff, S., Distante, C. (eds.) Image Analysis and Processing. ICIAP 2022 Workshops. ICIAP 2022. LNCS, vol. 13373, pp. 129–140. Springer, Cham (2022). https://doi.org/10.1007/978-3-031-13321-3_12
3. Bordes, A., Usunier, N., Garcia-Duran, A., Weston, J., Yakhnenko, O.: Translating embeddings for modeling multi-relational data. Adv. Neural Inf. Process. Syst. **26** (2013)
4. Bose, D., Somandepalli, K., Kundu, S., Lahiri, R., Gratch, J., Narayanan, S.: Understanding of Emotion Perception from Art. arXiv preprint arXiv:2110.06486 (2021)
5. Castellano, G., Digeno, V., Sansaro, G., Vessio, G.: Leveraging knowledge graphs and deep learning for automatic art analysis. Knowl.-Based Syst. **248**, 108859 (2022)
6. Castellano, G., Vessio, G.: Deep learning approaches to pattern extraction and recognition in paintings and drawings: an overview. Neural Comput. Appl. **33**(19), 12263–12282 (2021)
7. Castellano, G., Vessio, G.: A deep learning approach to clustering visual arts. Int. J. Comput. Vis. **130**(11), 2590–2605 (2022)
8. Cetinic, E.: Towards generating and evaluating iconographic image captions of artworks. J. Imaging **7**(8), 123 (2021)
9. Cetinic, E., Lipic, T., Grgic, S.: Fine-tuning convolutional neural networks for fine art classification. Expert Syst. Appl. **114**, 107–118 (2018)
10. Cetinic, E., Lipic, T., Grgic, S.: A deep learning perspective on beauty, sentiment, and remembrance of art. IEEE Access **7**, 73694–73710 (2019)
11. David, L., Pedrini, H., Dias, Z., Rocha, A.: Connoisseur: provenance analysis in paintings. In: 2021 IEEE Symposium Series on Computational Intelligence (SSCI), pp. 1–8. IEEE (2021)
12. Dosovitskiy, A., et al.: An image is worth 16×16 words: transformers for image recognition at scale. arXiv preprint arXiv:2010.11929 (2020)
13. Efthymiou, A., Rudinac, S., Kackovic, M., Worring, M., Wijnberg, N.: Graph neural networks for knowledge enhanced visual representation of paintings. arXiv preprint arXiv:2105.08190 (2021)
14. El Vaigh, C.B., Garcia, N., Renoust, B., Chu, C., Nakashima, Y., Nagahara, H.: GCNBoost: artwork classification by label propagation through a knowledge graph. In: Proceedings of the 2021 International Conference on Multimedia Retrieval, pp. 92–100 (2021)
15. Eyharabide, V., Bekkouch, I.E.I., Constantin, N.D.: Knowledge graph embedding-based domain adaptation for musical instrument recognition. Computers **10**(8), 94 (2021)

16. Garcia, N., Renoust, B., Nakashima, Y.: ContextNet: representation and exploration for painting classification and retrieval in context. Int. J. Multimed. Inf. Retr. **9**(1), 17–30 (2020)
17. Karayev, S., et al.: Recognizing image style. arXiv preprint arXiv:1311.3715 (2013)
18. Mikels, J.A., Fredrickson, B.L., Larkin, G.R., Lindberg, C.M., Maglio, S.J., Reuter-Lorenz, P.A.: Emotional category data on images from the international affective picture system. Behav. Res. Methods **37**(4), 626–630 (2005)
19. Rao, T., Li, X., Zhang, H., Xu, M.: Multi-level region-based convolutional neural network for image emotion classification. Neurocomputing **333**, 429–439 (2019)
20. Sandoval, C., Pirogova, E., Lech, M.: Two-stage deep learning approach to the classification of fine-art paintings. IEEE Access **7**, 41770–41781 (2019)
21. Song, K., Yao, T., Ling, Q., Mei, T.: Boosting image sentiment analysis with visual attention. Neurocomputing **312**, 218–228 (2018)
22. Strezoski, G., Worring, M.: Omniart: a large-scale artistic benchmark. ACM Trans. Multimed. Comput. Commun. Appl. **14**(4) (2018)
23. Van Noord, N., Hendriks, E., Postma, E.: Toward discovery of the artist's style: learning to recognize artists by their artworks. IEEE Signal Process. Mag. **32**(4), 46–54 (2015)
24. Veličković, P., Cucurull, G., Casanova, A., Romero, A., Lio, P., Bengio, Y.: Graph attention networks. arXiv preprint arXiv:1710.10903 (2017)

Combining Genetic Algorithms and Temporal Constraint Satisfaction for Recommending Personalized Tourist Itineraries

Federica Cena[(✉)] [ID], Luca Console[ID], Marta Micheli[ID], and Fabiana Vernero[ID]

Dipartimento di Informatica, Università di Torino, Turin, Italy
{federica.cena,luca.console,marta.micheli,fabiana.vernero}@unito.it

Abstract. In this paper we propose an approach that combines genetic algorithms and temporal constraint satisfaction for generating personalized tourist itineraries. Not only does the personalization process take into account user preferences about the places to visit but also a number of temporal constraints (e.g., opening hours, time for visiting each place, time to move among places) and time-related user preferences (e.g., number of days of the visit, preferring a dense schedule vs having a lot of free time, variety of the types of attractions during a day of visit). In the paper, we discuss our approach and the results of a preliminary evaluation of a prototypical implementation that generates personalized itineraries for the city of Turin.

Keywords: Recommender Systems · Tourist Itinerary Recommendation · Genetic Algorithms · Temporal Knowledge and constraints

1 Introduction

Planning an itinerary is a very common activity when organizing a visit to a tourist location. In doing that we usually take into account a number of dimensions. On the one hand, we consider the Places of Interest (PoI in the following) to be included based on our tourist interests. On the other hand, we take into account a variety of (i) temporal constraints such as the opening hours of the PoIs, the amount of time for visiting each PoI, the time to move from each PoI to the others, information about crowding at different times and (ii) temporal preferences such as the desire to visit as many PoIs as possible or to be more relaxed, the desire to have a lot of free time to stroll, the different alternatives for moving among PoIs.

Tourist recommender systems have been developed to support this process [1,2]. In particular, the combination of PoIs in an itinerary attracted a lot of attention in the last decades, with the main objective to recommend an itinerary

R. Basili et al. (Eds.): AIxIA 2023, LNAI 14318, pp. 441–452, 2023.
https://doi.org/10.1007/978-3-031-47546-7_30

that maximizes a global profit/reward and can be completed within a specific budget [10,17,18].

Although many recommender systems based the creation of itineraries on the popularity of the attractions [26,27], a number of approaches that generate personalized itineraries by considering incorporating *user interests and preferences* can be found in the literature [5,11,13,14,30].

In this paper, we propose an innovative approach for generating personalized itineraries that combines different aspects.

First of all, our proposed approach can inter-operate with any tourist recommender. The module that generates the itineraries takes a ranked list of PoIs as its input and we do not make any assumption on how this list is generated. It could be the output of any recommender that generates it based on any type of user preferences about PoIs. The advantages of this choice, especially as regards the evaluation of the approach, will be discussed later in the paper.

Second, we consider a number of time-related user preferences. We carried out a user study to understand which of these dimensions are relevant and how they are taken into account by different types of users [6]. The dimensions we considered range from the density of the itinerary (some users prefer to visit as many PoIs as possible while others prefer to visit fewer PoIs in more depth), the preference to visit PoIs when they are less crowded, the preference of having a lot of free time vs that of having a completely scheduled plan, the preference of mixing PoIs of different types vs that of having homogeneous itineraries with PoIs of the same type.

Third, we consider a number of temporal constraints such as the time to move between each pair of PoIs, the opening hours, the estimated minimum and maximum time to visit a PoI and the number of days of the visit. We thus include a temporal constraint propagation and satisfaction module in the itinerary generator.

Finally, we decided to design our itinerary generation module using genetic algorithms. These types of algorithms are very suitable for the problem we are facing which can be seen as a constrained optimization one. Indeed, genetic and evolutionary algorithms have already been used for this task in the literature, see for example [8,27–29,34]. A peculiarity of our approach is that the temporal preference dimension will play an essential role in the evaluation function of the genetic algorithm and constraint satisfaction will be used to prune itineraries that violate them and thus are not temporally consistent.

The paper is structured as follows. In Sect. 2, we provide an overview of the relevant state-of-the-art work. Section 3 discusses the temporal dimensions that we take into account in the generation of itineraries and introduces the structure of the temporal knowledge base. In Sect. 4, we discuss our genetic algorithm that generates itineraries taking into account temporal preferences and knowledge, while Sect. 5 illustrates the design and implementation of our prototype and its evaluation. Finally, in the last part of the paper, we discuss limitations and future works.

2   State of the Art

Recommender systems for itinerary generation have a long history in the state of the art. As seen in the introduction, much research has aimed to recommend an itinerary that maximizes a global profit within a specific budget [10,17,18].

In recent years, more proposals have incorporated *user interests and/or specific preferences* to personalize the construction of itineraries [5,9,11,13,14,19, 24,26,27,30]. Other approaches aim to recommend itineraries that consider personalized requirements such as attractions visit sequence [16], mandatory attraction categories [20] or group interest satisfaction [15,21].

Time is a crucial aspect to be managed in recommenders for tourism [3,23,31] and especially in the case of itinerary recommendations. However, time is usually considered as a *constraint* more than an *object of user preference* as other aspects (categories of place, time of accommodation, etc.). To our knowledge, very few works consider user preferences on temporal dimensions [32,33].

Evolutionary algorithms have been adopted in the literature for generating touristic itineraries. One of the first works in which a genetic approach was used to solve the itinerary planning problem was that of Chen et al. [8]. In their recommender system, a list of 30 PoIs is produced through a collaborative filtering method and then two distinct genetic algorithms are used: the first one to limit the number of recommended places to 10, minimizing the sum of expenses without exceeding the total available time; the second one to sort them minimizing the travelled distance. Representing a first attempt to use GAs in this domain, the proposed solution was only able to produce a path consisting of an ordered set of PoIs; following researchers tried to include in the recommendation a number of constraints and factors such as real visiting times, places' opening hours, etc.

Other works designed algorithms to generate itineraries where the number of PoIs is not determined in advance. For example, Ostrowski [22] proposed a system which takes into account attractions' opening hours and estimated travel times by walk or bus. Zheng et al. [34] also introduced two additional factors (aesthetic fatigue and the variable sightseeing value) in the profit formula, adopting a combination of a GA with a differential evolution algorithm.

The work in [28] investigated for the first time the insertion of restaurants in trips generated by a genetic-based recommender system. In their work, the opening hours of the tourist places and the location at which the user wants to start and end the trip are considered as constraints, while the only parameter taken into account to calculate the results' fitness is the ranking value of the attractions and restaurants.

Compared with previous work, Tarantino et al. [25] developed an evolutionary-based recommender system that includes a greater number of preferences on context features (break intervals, PoI category) and various item characteristics, such as the location accessibility for disabled people and the type of PoI to be preferred (indoor/outdoor depending on the weather forecast). Furthermore, travel times are estimated taking into account the tourist's walking speed and the queues at the PoIs.

Tenemaza et al. [27] tried to create multi-day itineraries by separating the itinerary recommendation problem in two parts: in their work, a k-means algorithm (with k equal to the number of available visiting days) is first used to cluster the best PoIs depending on their location and then a genetic algorithm is exploited to optimize the visit schedule for each geographical sector.

Yochum et al. [29] used an adaptive genetic algorithm to personalize touristic itineraries based on the quantity of PoIs present in the solution, their popularity, their overall rating, their cost and the user desire to visit certain places.

With respect to the works discussed in the literature, the genetic algorithm we propose recommends travel itineraries taking into account a wide range of temporal factors modelled as user preferences (e.g., the travel time, the presence of free time, the avoiding of estimated hours in which attractions are crowded) and constraints (e.g., the estimated visiting time for each PoI, the opening hours of recommended places, the start and end dates of the trip and the lunch breaks). The aspects that are personalized according to user preference also cover other factors, including the variety and quantity of PoIs, the desire to visit specific places and the ranking of the recommended PoIs. The advantages of considering user preference for all these factors are presented in Sect. 5. Furthermore, our recommender system is able to produce both single-day and multiple-day itineraries; in the latter case, itineraries presenting imbalances between the single days are assigned a penalty score and thus are unlikely to be suggested. In this way, especially for long trips, we expect the various visit days to be equally enjoyable for the user.

3   Temporal Dimensions and Temporal Knowledge Base

In this section we discuss the temporal dimensions that we take into account in the generation of itineraries and we present the structure of the temporal knowledge base.

We assume that the following temporal information about PoIs is available:

- Opening hours for each PoI, for each day of the week.
- Spatial coordinates of each PoI and thus time to transfer (on foot, by public transport or by car) between each pair of PoIs.
- The average time for visiting each PoI, expressed either as an average duration or as an interval distinguishing between minimal time for a quick view and maximum time for an extensive visit.
- (Qualitative)   information about estimated crowding (e.g., "low","medium","high") at different times of each day.

All the pieces of information above are available or can be easily obtained from the Internet. Indeed, in order to design our prototype for the city of Turin we extracted all the information from Google services. Opening and closing times are then expressed as points on the time line, crowded times can be expressed as time intervals, while the time to move between PoIs and visiting times are expressed as bound on differences [12], which is thus the formalism we adopted to represent all the temporal constraints in the knowledge base [4].

As regards users' temporal preferences, the following dimensions are taken into account:

- Time (e.g., number of days) available for the visit: date and time of arrival and date and time of departure.
- User preference on maximizing the number of PoIs to be included in the itinerary. Some people may be interested in visiting as many places as possible, while others may prefer to have more relaxed times between the planned activities.
- User interest in visiting heterogeneous PoIs. If this information is provided by the individual, the itinerary recommender will try to include different types of PoIs in (each day of) the itinerary (e.g., natural parks, museums, religious places, historical places and buildings, etc.).
- Willingness to avoid crowding, i.e., whether the user desires to keep away from crowded PoIs or at least crowded times of the day.
- Willingness to have some free time during the day, i.e., whether the user prefers dense or sparse itineraries. In the latter case, a break interval is added to each day of the itinerary.
- User preference concerning means of transport and the desire of minimizing transfer times.

These pieces of information constitute the User Model which will be exploited by our algorithm to generate itineraries. We carried out a study on whether these preferences can be correlated to user's personality and how the personality traits can be used to shape itinerary factors in recommender systems [6].

In the prototype, we derived the user model from a simple questionnaire filled out by the users.

4 Combining Genetic Algorithms and Constraint Satisfaction for Generating Itineraries

In this section, we discuss the algorithm that generates a ranked list of itineraries that are most suitable for a given user. The approach relies on a genetic algorithm which exploits constraint satisfaction in the evaluation process, as we will clarify in the following subsections.

4.1 Inputs to the Algorithm

The algorithm starts by taking the following inputs:

- A list L of PoIs, ranked according to the user's interests. As we noticed in the introduction, our itinerary generation process can be coupled with any tourist recommender. We only assumed that a ranked list is produced in some way. This assumption allowed us to decouple the analysis (and evaluation) of the itinerary recommender from one of the algorithms that suggest to a user the PoIs that are most suitable for her/him. Moreover, in this way, our system can inter-operate with any tourist recommender.

- The temporal knowledge base, as discussed in the previous section.
- A user model with user preferences concerning the temporal dimensions, as discussed in the previous section.

4.2   Genetic Algorithm

The genetic algorithm works on a population of itineraries. Thus an itinerary is an individual in our approach. In more detail, an itinerary is an allocation of PoIs along the timeline whose extension depends on the duration of the visit to be planned. An itinerary is valid if it is temporally consistent, i.e., if the time constraints concerning the opening times of the PoIs, the time to move from a PoI to the next one in the itinerary and those concerning the visit times are consistent.

The genetic algorithm starts with an initial population of random valid itineraries and loops producing subsequent generations until the "quality" of the population is "satisfactory". Let us analyze the process in more detail.

Evaluating the Fitness of Individuals. An individual, i.e. an itinerary receives a fitness evaluation taking into account two aspects:

- The evaluation of the PoIs in the itinerary according to the ranking in the list L. In this way, an itinerary containing PoIs that have a higher ranking in L receives a better evaluation.
- The evaluation of the itinerary according to the user temporal preferences. Each type of preference is considered separately and we adopted a number of heuristic evaluation criteria:
  - The itineraries are ranked according to the number of PoIs they contain; this ranking contributes positively to the evaluation of an itinerary if the user expressed a preference for maximizing PoIs during the visit, negatively otherwise.
  - Similarly, itineraries are ranked as regards the amount of free time and also in this case the ranking can contribute positively or negatively based on the user's preference.
  - The presence of PoIs visited during crowded times can impact negatively the evaluation if the user prefers to avoid crowding.
  - The heterogeneity of PoIs contributes positively if the user prefers this type of itinerary, and negatively otherwise.
  - High transfer times can impact negatively if this dimension is relevant to the user.
  - In case planning involves multiple days, balancing among days is taken into account. Itineraries where the fitness in each day is similar are evaluated better than the others. Those that are unbalanced receive a penalty score that negatively impacts the fitness value. Fitness similarity is calculated using standard deviation.

As a result each itinerary receives an evaluation which allows us to rank them inside the population.

Crossover: Generating Descendant Individuals. At each iteration, some individuals in the current population are combined to generate individuals in the new population. The higher the fitness value of the individuals the more likely they are to be combined. Given two individuals I_1 and I_2, a descendant I_3 can be generated in different ways combining parts of I_1 with parts of I_2; for example, the algorithm may take the morning parts of I_1 and the afternoon parts of I_2 or it can alternate PoIs from I_1 to PoIs from I_2. We analyzed both of these strategies and in the current implementation, we selected the first one mentioned above that seemed to provide better results.

Aborting Temporally Inconsistent Individuals. When a new individual I_3 is generated, we run the constraint satisfaction algorithm to check whether it is temporally consistent. If it is not, the individual is aborted and it will not be part of the new population.

Mutations. Periodically some mutations are introduced in the population. An individual I is mutated by randomly selecting some PoIs in the itinerary and replacing them with other ones (possibly with better ranking). Mutated individuals must pass the constraint satisfaction check to enter the new population.

Termination and Solutions. The process above is iterated producing a number of generations. We made experiments with two termination strategies: (i) a fixed number of iterations and (ii) iterating until there is no significant improvement in the evaluation of the best itineraries in the population (see Sect. 5). When the process is terminated a ranked list of itineraries is produced and can be presented to the user.

5   Prototype: Recommending Itineraries in Turin

In order to evaluate our approach, we developed a prototype providing personalized recommendations of itineraries for our town. The goal of the prototype is twofold. On the one hand, it was used to make experiments with and tune the algorithm. On the other hand, it was exploited to perform a preliminary user evaluation.

To this aim, we fist developed a knowledge base with 30 PoIs in Turin, including a variety of attractions (museums, parks, churches, historic buildings, historic squares . . .). We then collected all temporal information about the PoIs thus creating the temporal knowledge base.

Tuning of the Algorithm. During the design of the algorithm, we made many experiments varying the dimensions of the population, the crossover and mutation rate, and the number of iterations, so as to find the optimal parameter

Fig. 1. Two example PoIs for users to evaluate in our prototype

setting for our application case. This allowed us to tune the algorithm, with the aim of providing optimal results through our prototype. As far as the number of iterations is concerned, we observed that 30 iterations produce stable rankings, but we cannot claim that this can be generalized. Thus, we believe that further experiments should be carried out to better assess the approach and its sensitivity to changes.

Preliminary User Tests. In order to evaluate our approach, we designed an online experiment consisting of several steps, where participants are asked to evaluate different sets of itinerary recommendations. We carried out a preliminary evaluation with 20 people, aged from 18 to over 60, recruited among the acquaintances of the authors using a convenience sampling strategy. Participants were asked to explicitly express their preferences (i) about the PoIs in our knowledge base (see Fig. 1), and (ii) about temporal dimensions (namely: minimization of transfer times, maximization of the number of PoIs per itinerary, maximization of the heterogeneity among PoIs in a certain itinerary, maximization of the number of PoIs they have a strong preference for, the inclusion of free time slots, busy hours avoidance), using a Likert-like scale ranging from 1 (minimum) to 5 (maximum) in both cases.

Then, we ran the itinerary recommender to generate personalized itineraries for each user (Fig. 2): once excluding temporal dimensions (R0), once taking such dimensions into account, but with predefined weights (R1), equal for all participants, and, finally, once considering participants' preferences over the temporal dimensions (R2). Each participant was therefore presented with three alternative itinerary recommendations (randomized to avoid order effects) and was asked to assess, for each of them, how good the recommended itinerary is on the whole (overall evaluation).

The results we obtained are encouraging. In fact, itinerary recommendations generated taking into account participants' preferences over the temporal dimensions (R2) were evaluated more positively than the other two types of recommendations. More specifically, R2 recommendations obtained an average score of 3.4 (st. dev: 0.94) for the "overall evaluation" aspect, which is higher than the scores obtained by R1 (avg: 3.1, st. dev: 1.07) and R0 (avg: 3.2, st. dev: 0.89) recommendations.

Itinerario

Attività per il giorno 2023-02-17	Attività per il giorno 2023-02-18
1. Alle: 8:30 **Partenza**	1. Dalle: 9:00 alle 10.00 **Superga**
2. Dalle: 9:00 alle 11:00 **Museo dell'Automobile**	2. Dalle: 10:50 alle 12:50 **Musei Reali**
3. Dalle: 12:00 alle 12:20 **Piazza Castello**	3. Dalle: 13.00 alle 14:00 **Pranzo**
4. Dalle: 13:00 alle 14:00 **Pranzo**	4. Dalle: 14:20 alle 16:20 **Mole Antonelliana** ⚠ *Può essere affoliato*
5. Dalle: 14:45 alle 16:45 **Museo Egizio**	5. Dalle: 16.55 alle 18:55 **Parco del Valentino**
6. Dalle: 17.00 alle 18:00 **Museo Archeologico**	6. Alle: 19.30 **Rientro**
7. Dalle: 18:20 alle 19:20 **Gallerie d'Italia**	
8. Dalle: 19:30 alle 8.30 **Rientro in albergo**	

Fig. 2. An itinerary example

6   Concluding Remarks

In this paper, we presented an approach for generating personalized tourist itineraries using genetic algorithms coupled with temporal constraint satisfaction. The approach is independent of the way PoIs are ranked based on user's interest and can thus be coupled with any tourist recommender providing this ranking. This choice was motivated by the aim of focusing on evaluating the approach for building itineraries independently of the approach for ranking PoIs. The approach we proposed uses a number of heuristics in the evaluation of the suitability of an itinerary with respect to user's temporal preferences. These heuristics could be improved in many different ways and indeed we are currently studying the impact of changing the heuristics.

The preliminary evaluation we performed with the prototype provided very encouraging results: in fact, recommendations which take into account temporal dimensions appear to be better in terms of their overall evaluation. A more extensive evaluation will be carried out with a larger number of participants, following the same experimental protocol, in order to confirm these results and test for their statistical significance.

Furthermore, as future work, we will work on incorporating negative preferences in order to fine-tune our personalized algorithm [7].

References

1. Abbasi-Moud, Z., Vahdat-Nejad, H., Sadri, J.: Tourism recommendation system based on semantic clustering and sentiment analysis. Expert Syst. Appl. **167**, 114324 (2021)
2. Borràs, J., Moreno, A., Valls, A.: Intelligent tourism recommender systems: a survey. Expert Syst. Appl. **41**(16), 7370–7389 (2014)
3. Botti, L., Peypoch, N., Solonandrasana, B.: Time and tourism attraction. Tour. Manag. **29**(3), 594–596 (2008)
4. Brusoni, V., Console, L., Terenziani, P.: On the computational complexity of querying bounds on differences constraints. Artif. Intell. **74**(2), 367–379 (1995). https://doi.org/10.1016/0004-3702(95)00008-3
5. Cai, G., Lee, K., Lee, I.: Itinerary recommender system with semantic trajectory pattern mining from geo-tagged photos. Expert Syst. Appl. **94**, 32–40 (2018)
6. Cena, F., Console, L., Likavec, S., Micheli, M., Vernero, F.: How personality traits can be used to shape itinerary factors in recommender systems for young travellers. IEEE Access **11**, 61968–61985 (2023). https://doi.org/10.1109/ACCESS.2023.3285258
7. Cena, F., Console, L., Vernero, F.: How to deal with negative preferences in recommender systems: a theoretical framework. J. Intell. Inf. Syst. **60**(1), 23–47 (2023). https://doi.org/10.1007/s10844-022-00705-9
8. Chen, J.H., Chao, K.M., Shah, N.: Hybrid recommendation system for tourism. In: 2013 IEEE 10th International Conference on e-Business Engineering, pp. 156–161 (2013). https://doi.org/10.1109/ICEBE.2013.24
9. Chen, L., Zhang, L., Cao, S., Wu, Z., Cao, J.: Personalized itinerary recommendation: deep and collaborative learning with textual information. Expert Syst. Appl. **144**, 113070 (2020)
10. De Choudhury, M., Feldman, M., Amer-Yahia, S., Golbandi, N., Lempel, R., Yu, C.: Automatic construction of travel itineraries using social breadcrumbs. In: Proceedings of the 21st ACM Conference on Hypertext and Hypermedia, pp. 35–44 (2010)
11. De Choudhury, M., Feldman, M., Amer-Yahia, S., Golbandi, N., Lempel, R., Yu, C.: Constructing travel itineraries from tagged geo-temporal breadcrumbs. In: Proceedings of the 19th International Conference on World Wide Web, pp. 1083–1084 (2010)
12. Dechter, R., Meiri, I., Pearl, J.: Temporal constraint networks. Artif. Intell. **49**(1–3), 61–95 (1991). https://doi.org/10.1016/0004-3702(91)90006-6
13. Di Bitonto, P., Di Tria, F., Laterza, M., Roselli, T., Rossano, V., Tangorra, F.: Automated generation of itineraries in recommender systems for tourism. In: Daniel, F., Facca, F.M. (eds.) ICWE 2010. LNCS, vol. 6385, pp. 498–508. Springer, Heidelberg (2010). https://doi.org/10.1007/978-3-642-16985-4_48
14. Fogli, A., Micarelli, A., Sansonetti, G.: Enhancing itinerary recommendation with linked open data. In: Stephanidis, C. (ed.) HCI 2018. CCIS, vol. 850, pp. 32–39. Springer, Cham (2018). https://doi.org/10.1007/978-3-319-92270-6_5
15. Garcia, I., Sebastia, L., Onaindia, E.: On the design of individual and group recommender systems for tourism. Expert Syst. Appl. **38**(6), 7683–7692 (2011)
16. Gionis, A., Lappas, T., Pelechrinis, K., Terzi, E.: Customized tour recommendations in urban areas. In: Proceedings of the 7th ACM International Conference on Web Search and Data Mining, pp. 313–322 (2014)

17. Hsieh, H.P., Li, C.T., Lin, S.D.: TripRec: recommending trip routes from large scale check-in data. In: Proceedings of the 21st International Conference on World Wide Web, pp. 529–530 (2012)
18. Li, X.: Multi-day and multi-stay travel planning using geo-tagged photos. In: Proceedings of the Second ACM SIGSPATIAL International Workshop on Crowdsourced and Volunteered Geographic Information, pp. 1–8 (2013)
19. Lim, K.H., Chan, J., Karunasekera, S., Leckie, C.: Personalized itinerary recommendation with queuing time awareness. In: Proceedings of the 40th International ACM SIGIR Conference on Research and Development in Information Retrieval, pp. 325–334 (2017)
20. Lim, K.H., Chan, J., Leckie, C., Karunasekera, S.: Personalized tour recommendation based on user interests and points of interest visit durations. In: Twenty-Fourth International Joint Conference on Artificial Intelligence (2015)
21. Lim, K.H., Chan, J., Leckie, C., Karunasekera, S.: Towards next generation touring: personalized group tours. In: Proceedings of the International Conference on Automated Planning and Scheduling, vol. 26, pp. 412–420 (2016)
22. Ostrowski, K.: An effective metaheuristic for tourist trip planning in public transport networks. Appl. Comput. Sci. **14**(2), 5–19 (2018). https://doi.org/10.23743/acs-2018-09
23. Pearce, P.L.: Tourists' perception of time: directions for design. Ann. Tour. Res. **83**, 102932 (2020)
24. Refanidis, I., et al.: MYVISITPLANNER ^{GR}: personalized itinerary planning system for tourism. In: Likas, A., Blekas, K., Kalles, D. (eds.) SETN 2014. LNCS (LNAI), vol. 8445, pp. 615–629. Springer, Cham (2014). https://doi.org/10.1007/978-3-319-07064-3_53
25. Tarantino, E., Falco, I., Scafuri, U.: A mobile personalized tourist guide and its user evaluation. Inf. Technol. Tour. **21**, 413–455 (2019). https://doi.org/10.1007/s40558-019-00150-5
26. Taylor, K., Lim, K.H., Chan, J.: Travel itinerary recommendations with must-see points-of-interest. In: Companion Proceedings of the The Web Conference 2018, pp. 1198–1205 (2018)
27. Tenemaza, M., Luján-Mora, S., De Antonio, A., Ramírez, J.: Improving itinerary recommendations for tourists through metaheuristic algorithms: An optimization proposal. IEEE Access **8**, 79003–79023 (2020). https://doi.org/10.1109/ACCESS.2020.2990348
28. Wibowo, B.S., Handayani, M.: A genetic algorithm for generating travel itinerary recommendation with restaurant selection. In: 2018 IEEE International Conference on Industrial Engineering and Engineering Management (IEEM), pp. 427–431 (2018). https://doi.org/10.1109/IEEM.2018.8607677
29. Yochum, P., Chang, L., Gu, T., Zhu, M.: An adaptive genetic algorithm for personalized itinerary planning. IEEE Access **8**, 88147–88157 (2020). https://doi.org/10.1109/ACCESS.2020.2990916
30. Yoon, H., Zheng, Yu., Xie, X., Woo, W.: Smart itinerary recommendation based on user-generated GPS trajectories. In: Yu, Z., Liscano, R., Chen, G., Zhang, D., Zhou, X. (eds.) UIC 2010. LNCS, vol. 6406, pp. 19–34. Springer, Heidelberg (2010). https://doi.org/10.1007/978-3-642-16355-5_5
31. Zalatan, A.: The determinants of planning time in vacation travel. Tour. Manag. **17**(2), 123–131 (1996). https://doi.org/10.1016/0261-5177(95)00115-8. https://www.sciencedirect.com/science/article/pii/0261517795001158

32. Zhang, C., Liang, H., Wang, K.: Trip recommendation meets real-world constraints: POI availability, diversity, and traveling time uncertainty. ACM Trans. Inf. Syst. (TOIS) **35**(1), 1–28 (2016)
33. Zhang, C., Liang, H., Wang, K., Sun, J.: Personalized trip recommendation with POI availability and uncertain traveling time. In: Proceedings of the 24th ACM International Conference on Information and Knowledge Management, pp. 911–920 (2015)
34. Zheng, W., Liao, Z., Qin, J.: Using a four-step heuristic algorithm to design personalized day tour route within a tourist attraction. Tour. Manag. **62**, 335–349 (2017). https://doi.org/10.1016/j.tourman.2017.05.006. https://www.sciencedirect.com/science/article/pii/S0261517717301061

Towards Automatic Digitalization of Railway Engineering Schematics

Stefano Frizzo Stefenon[1,2]([✉]) [ID], Marco Cristoforetti[1] [ID],
and Alessandro Cimatti[1] [ID]

[1] Fondazione Bruno Kessler, Via Sommarive 18, 38123 Trento, Italy
{sfrizzostefenon,mcristofo,cimatti}@fbk.eu
[2] Department of Mathematics, Computer Science and Physics, University of Udine,
Via delle Scienze 206, 33100 Udine, Italy

Abstract. Relay-based Railways Interlocking Systems (RRIS) carry out critical functions to control stations. Despite being based on old and hard-to-maintain electro-mechanical technology, RRIS are still pervasive. A powerful CAD modeling and analysis approach based on symbolic logic has been recently proposed to support the re-engineering of relay diagrams into more maintainable computer-based technologies. However, the legacy engineering drawings that need to be digitized consist of large, hand-drawn diagrams dating back several decades. Manually transforming such diagrams into the format of the CAD tool is labor-intensive and error-prone, effectively a bottleneck in the reverse-engineering process. In this paper, we tackle the problem of automatic digitalization of RRIS schematics into the corresponding CAD format with an integrative Artificial Intelligence approach. Deep learning-based methods, segment detection, and clustering techniques for the automated digitalization of engineering schematics are used to detect and classify the single elements of the diagram. These elementary elements can then be aggregated into more complex objects leveraging the domain ontology. First results of the method's capability of automatically reconstructing the engineering schematics are presented.

Keywords: Computer vision · Deep learning · Engineering drawings

1 Introduction

Engineering Drawing (ED) is derived from descriptive geometry, which is the science that aims to represent three-dimensional objects in the plane (drawing sheet, drawing board, etc.), thus allowing the resolution of infinite problems on the paper plane. For many years, technical EDs have been made by hand, requiring designers to spend a considerable amount of time developing the drawing and editing it. Nowadays, technical drawings for engineering are developed in Computer-Aided Design (CAD) software, where it is possible to make alterations

---

Supported by Fondazione Bruno Kessler.

easily and quickly. However, the projects that were made before the popularization of CAD software remain archived on paper [1].

When it is necessary to use a not digitized project, a big effort goes into interpreting what has been designed and redesigning the project in CAD. For this reason, many authors have been researching ways to interpret EDs through computer vision methods, and in particular deep learning-based techniques show promise for accomplishing this task [2].

In digitizing EDs through deep learning, several techniques can be applied to improve the model's ability to classify objects in the projects. In this context, preprocessing is performed to highlight the image variations; for this purpose, thresholding techniques can be applied. After preprocessing, shape detection can be performed in specific or holistic categories, features extracted, and the classification process is conducted [3].

According to Günay, Köseoğlu, and Yıldırım [4] Convolutional Neural Networks (CNNs) may be applied to classify drawings made by hand, their research shows that CNNs perform well in the classification of electrical circuit drawings. One of the major challenges in identifying electrical components in hand-drawn drawings is the great difference between designs since there is no linear pattern of hand-drawing development [5]. Classification accuracy using CNNs can achieve acceptable results in this task applied to EDs.

In the railway signaling domain, the Railway Interlocking Systems (RIS) control the movement of trains, allowing or denying their routing according to safety rules. Relay diagrams are a commonly used abstraction for modeling relay-based RIS, describing such systems by graph-like schematics that show the connections between the electrical components. However, verifying these diagrams for safety is challenging due to their complexity and the lack of tools for automatic verification [6].

Several EDs of the RIS remain on paper because these systems were designed before the popularization of CAD. With models based on CNN becoming increasingly faster and capable of classifying images with high accuracy, the interpretation of ED of RIS becomes relevant research. From a model that can interpret the drawings, transform this information into matrices, and verify the semantics, it will be possible to have a tool that will help update these projects. So far, the application of machine learning related to railways is based on the analysis of RIS automation or improved timetable analysis [7], having room and need for ED evaluation using deep learning techniques, as presented here.

The proposed method presented in this paper has a combination of several techniques, its overall workflow is: Initially, the You Only Look Once (YOLO) [8] Deep Neural Network is applied for object detection, and based on the found objects a new drawing without them is used to focus especially on the segments. To identify the segments, the Probabilistic Hough Transform (PHT) [9] combined with the Density-Based Spatial Clustering of Applications with Noise (DBSCAN) [10] is applied. Based on the segments found a graph is built to evaluate the electrical circuits of the EDs.

The contributions of this work to the digitization of EDs for RIS are summarized in the following:

- developing an automatic method for digitizing engineering schematics. The proposed approach is capable of redrawing EDs that are printout and is faster than the manual labor required to render these EDs in executable machines.
- improving segment detection using the Density-based Spatial Clustering of Applications with Noise in the Probabilistic Hough Transform. Using a clustering method, it is possible to group overwritten segments, improving the quality of the digitalization of these elements.
- proposing a graph problem based on the electrical connections of the RIS. Building on the ontological characterization of the domain, this paper proposes a graph-based problem to aggregate the basic elements into more complex objects.

The remainder of this paper is organized as follows: Sect. 2 brings a literature review on works related to EDs. Section 3 presents the applied methodology. Section 4 brings the evaluation of the proposed approach. Finally, Sect. 5 presents a conclusion and discusses future works.

2 Related Works

Technical drawings have a large application in industrial processes because they provide important information about the structure where the project is applied, besides interconnections between equipment. EDs are used in different industries, such as oil and gas, mechanical, construction, and other fields of engineering [11]. Nowadays, digitizing these designs is becoming extremely important, and to update the projects, it is necessary to have them digitized.

In industrial projects, the specific identification of components is difficult to achieve since there is a similarity between the standard graphic symbols used. According to Yun et al. [12], to perform the object identification process in EDs, it is necessary to have a structure composed of several steps: region proposal evaluation, feature extraction, and classification. From the results of this evaluation, it is possible to classify the proposed regions and extract the symbolic information by means of dummy detection.

To recognize and extract important information from engineering diagrams, it is necessary to perform a preprocessing stage in which the alignment of the drawing, the removal of outer edges, and the title box withdrawal are performed [13]. This information can make it difficult to identify objects and, at this stage does not contribute to the classification since, in the initial analysis, the object is not related to the place where it is installed.

The relationship between the location of the object and the place where it belongs is important as soon as there is global knowledge of the project, so it is possible to make a validation of what has been identified. Mani et al. [14] presented a strategy using graph search to traverse a diagram through its lines and discover interconnected symbols.

An essential aspect to be considered is that CNNs may perform well for object classification; however, they may have difficulty identifying text characters, lines, and tables. For this reason, to improve the interpretability of EDs, it is promising to use combined models, in which part of the network is used specifically for character detection, making the solution more powerful [15]. Deep learning-based models can be used especially for classification, making the network more accurate for this task.

In the work of Kim et al. [16] the interpretation of EDs is conducted using high-resolution images through specialized models for symbol detection and text recognition after preprocessing the images. The selection of symbols into labels makes object identification a clearer task to be performed. The Generalized Focal Loss (GFL) and feature selective anchor-free methods can show slightly better results for localizing objects in projects compared to other CNNs. Using different backbones applied to GFL can further improve the results in symbol identification, highlighting the Residual neural Network (ResNet) using 50 layers has resulted in an accuracy of 0.970 for this task.

Specialized models such as the Character Region Awareness For Text detection (CRAFT) proposed by Baek et al. [17] and the Convolutional Recurrent Neural Network (CRNN) presented by Shi, Bai, and Yao [18] stand out for text recognition. With this, Kim et al. [16] showed that to have a better performance in the analysis of EDs, it is required to use specific techniques for text detection, such as CRAFT and CRNN, and other techniques for object identification, such as GFL. Even with a large number of classes, this approach results in a complete and robust solution for interpreting EDs.

Li, Yuhui, and Xiaoting [19] developed a CNN-based analysis for classifying EDs using three categories: mechanical EDs, text drawings, and electrical EDs. In their study, argumentation techniques were applied to increase the size of the dataset by rotating, slicing, and including random noise. This practice is common due to the need for a large database to train the CNN model. The results showed that it is possible to have an accuracy of up to 0.987 for the classification of different project types. For their application, the use of four convolutional layers resulted in higher accuracy than using three.

An important issue to take into account in ED classification is the large number of different classes with a little variation and imbalance that makes this even more challenging. In the research of Elyan, Jamieson, and Ali-Gombe [20], a combined approach is proposed to deal with all these challenges. In the proposed method, bounding box detection is initially performed to locate and recognize symbols. A deep generative adversarial neural network is used to deal with class imbalance. From this approach, it is possible to train the network with a small number of images and achieve highly accurate results.

To deal with the problem of the small database faced in this type of analysis, Bickel, Schleich, and Wartzack [21] presented an approach to augment the dataset based on randomly creating symbols and illustrations. From this, a deep learning network can be used to test the dataset and recognize the symbols in the EDs using more images. Since there are a large number of classes to be classified, a promising strategy in the first stage is to group similar circuit components, and in the next stage, the circuits belonging to the same group can be classified using CNN-based models. According to Dey et al. [22], using a 2-stage structure with 20 classes of circuit components, a classification accuracy of 0.973 can be achieved, which is higher than single-stage models.

Since Relay-based RIS (RRIS) contain thousands of combinations of component instances, the interpretation of ED manually is a hard task. In this context, deep computer vision is an outstanding solution. Since besides object detection it is also needed to detect segments, this paper proposes a method that combines techniques to achieve this goal, which is innovative for this application, the proposed method is explained in the next section.

3   Proposed Method

The method proposed in this paper combines deep learning-based models with probabilistic methods and clustering techniques. To meet the project goal, the eighth generation of the You Only Look Once (YOLOv8) is applied for object detection, and the PHT combined with the (DBSCAN) are employed for segment detection.

3.1   Data Preparation

The EDs of the Italian railway company (*Rete Ferroviaria Italiana* - RFI) have high-resolution, reaching more than 30,000 pixels wide by 4,000 pixels high, with images having different electrical connections from different parts of the railway stations. The first step in this project, in order to be able to apply machine learning models, was to make standardized cutouts of the engineering drawings. The 640, 1280, and 2560-pixel cutouts were considered, as in the examples in Fig. 1.

Since drawings have different sizes (height and width), with horizontal dimensions larger than vertical dimensions it is necessary to standardize the images to be considered. Therefore, it was standardized to use 640-pixel cutouts, and with this, the dataset for training and validation of the model was created and organized. Given this size variation, the number of cutouts depends on each project's original size.

The cutouts are disjoint from the complete ED, and then for the training the symbols that were not wholly presented were not considered. Since not complete symbols were disregarded the model was trained based on identifying only whole symbols as needed for the reconstruction of the EDs. After identifying all symbols and labels, a reconstruction of the entire drawing is performed and objects in the borders are manually evaluated.

Training the model using images only of each symbol (from a pallet) did not have effective results in the testing phase (inference). For this reason, no dataset augmentation was used. In the initial experiments, including augmented data reduced the model's ability to be effective for real applications. Since the best

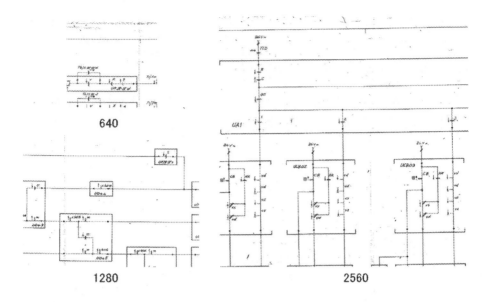

Fig. 1. Engineering drawing of a relay-based railway interlocking system.

results were obtained using real images, only this type of image was used to improve the applicability of the proposed model.

Symbols are the main objects to be identified in the project since electrical connections occur between them. The labels and specifiers are additional information that is attached to the symbols. The specifiers, labels, and connection points (dots) were annotated to obtain a complete dataset. The total classes considered in the project are 133: letters [0 to 9, a to z, A to Z], dots [0 to 11 variations], specifiers [arrows up or down], and symbols [C00 to C56]. Regarding the letters, the Tesseract Optical Character Recognition (OCR) [23] was used as a baseline comparison to the YOLO results.

3.2   Object Detection Method

The YOLO is a single-shot algorithm, meaning the detection and classification are performed in a single run. The model has been improved over the years, and the latest version released by Ultralytics [24] is the eighth generation (YOLOv8).

The images under consideration are divided into a $S \times S$ grid, where each grid square predicts the object's bounding box, corresponding to its degree of confidentiality [25]. Thus, the confidence of classes (cl) of objects (obj), is denoted by:

$$pr(cl_i \mid obj) \cdot pr(obj) \cdot IoU_{pred}^{truth} = pr(cl_i) \cdot IoU_{pred}^{truth}. \tag{1}$$

where i is the respective class under evaluation, considering the intersection over union (IoU) of the predicted ($pred$) bounding boxes compared to the ground truth ($truth$) [26]. In this paper, 133 classes are considered. Once the image is divided into grids, a class probability map is computed to identify the target objects and bounding boxes to determine if the desired objects are situated in this confidence region.

3.3 Segment Detection to Create Connections

The Hough Transform (HT) is employed to determine the parameters of features as lines in an image [27]. In EDs of the RFI, the lines (segments) are used to connect electrical components (symbols) and create a logic for the control of the RIS. It should be noted that the symbols have rules to be connected; thus, there is a need to identify the segments properly. Therefore evaluations of the system logic can be performed to improve the safety of the RIS.

To apply the HT, a binary image is used as input, where each active pixel is part of an edge feature, and the HT maps every pixel in the Hough space. The Canny edge detector was applied to have the input image binarization [28]. For line detection, a single edge pixel is mapped to a sinusoid in parameter space (θ, p), representing all possible lines that could pass through the point in the image. If several points are collinear, their sinusoids in parameter space will intersect. Finding the points in parameter space where most of the sinusoids intersect provides the parameters for the lines in the input image. The process is referred to as the search stage [29].

The standard HT returns lines that cross the entire image, then the PHT is used to have the start and end points of the segments. The PHT is defined as the logarithm of the probability density function of the output parameters, taking into account all input features [30].

Let's consider an input image with a set X_n of feature $x_1, x_2, ..., x_n$ and a specified point in the parameter space y. The probability density function in Hough space $H(y)$ is $p(y \mid X_n)$ and then the PHT is denoted by:

$$H(y) = \ln[p(y \mid X_n)] \qquad (2)$$

which, by the Bayes' rule, is

$$H(y) = \sum_{i=1}^{n} \ln[p(x_i \mid y)] + \ln[p(y)] + C \qquad (3)$$

where the probability distribution $p(y)$ is considered uniform and C is the arbitrary constant. The PHT result may have short segments instead of a complete segment since preprocessing using canny edge detection is required before computing the PHT. Therefore, the detection may be a set of small segments that can be nearby and overwritten, based on which clustering of the segments must be performed.

In this paper, DBSCAN is applied to connect segments that are close apart or overwritten. This method is a non-parametric density-based clustering algorithm. Taking a set of points in a given space, it clusters the close points, scoring as outliers the points that are isolated in low-density regions [31]. Therefore, combining DBSCAN with PHT is promising for reconstructing the detected segments. The complete architecture applied here is presented in Fig. 2.

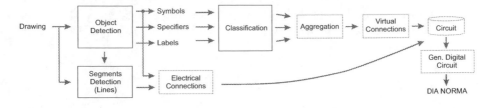

Fig. 2. Architecture of the proposed method.

4 Results and Discussion

In this section, the results of the application of the proposed method will be presented. An analysis will be performed regarding the use of a CNN, focusing on the detection of labels, electrical connections, specifiers, and symbols. The detection of labels will be compared to the well-established Nanonets and Tesseract OCR. From the identification of the objects under evaluation, the results of segment detection, clustering, and the final outcome of the automatically reconstructed drawing will be presented.

4.1 Experiment Setup

The proposed approach is based on the PyTorch library using Python programming language. The experiments were conducted on a cluster, with a Graphics Processing Unit (GPU) NVIDIA Tesla V100 and 32 GB of random-access memory. To maximize processing time, the experiments of random initialization were run in parallel using five GPUs, with the same requirements to be computed. The performance evaluation measures are the standard for this kind of task: precision, recall, F-measure, and mean Average Precision (mAP).

4.2 Object Detection and Classification

The YOLOv8 (nano) is evaluated considering all considered 133 classes being these labels (letters), electrical connections (dots), specifiers, and symbols. For the training of the models, five RFI projects were considered, containing 850 cutouts of 640 pixels in which 2,323 symbols are shown having their respective labels and specifiers.

The results presented here are relative to the model validation scores, since in the test phase using inference images the used metric is confidence in the predictions given a threshold. For a complete assessment, the maximum (max), minimum (min), mean, median (med.), and standard deviation (std dev.) of the performance measures are computed. In Table 1 the influence of starting weights is presented considering 50 experiments with different random seeds.

The major goal of this model is to detect the objects to continue with image processing, for this reason, the average of the mAP@[0.5] equal to 0.80276 is an acceptable value. There was a difference of 4.32% comparing the highest

Table 1. Statistical analysis considering different seeds.

Measure	Max	Min	Mean	Med.	Std dev.
Precision	0.83	0.72	0.78	0.79	2.82×10^{-2}
Recall	0.81	0.74	0.77	0.77	1.89×10^{-2}
F1-score	0.81	0.74	0.78	0.77	1.37×10^{-2}
mAP@[0.5]	0.82	0.78	0.80	0.80	1.01×10^{-2}
mAP@[0.5:0.95]	0.39	0.34	0.38	0.38	8.09×10^{-3}

and lowest mAP values. This result shows that there may be some variation in the model due to network initialization, however, this is acceptable for object detection needed at this stage.

To avoid the influence of the data selection, the k-fold cross-validation using 5-folds was used. The results of this evaluation are presented in Table 2. An observation to be made is that when images with higher levels of noise are used for validation, the training time becomes considerably longer.

Table 2. Evaluation of cross-validation.

Measure	Max	Min	Mean	Med.	Std dev.
Precision	0.78	0.69	0.74	0.76	3.95×10^{-2}
Recall	0.80	0.57	0.72	0.73	7.60×10^{-2}
F1-score	0.79	0.63	0.73	0.75	5.59×10^{-2}
mAP@[0.5]	0.82	0.64	0.75	0.78	6.29×10^{-2}
mAP@[0.5:0.95]	0.47	0.36	0.42	0.42	3.64×10^{-2}

The utilization of noisy data to perform the model validation resulted in an average reduction of mAP@[0.5] of 4.93%. Although this is a high reduction in mAP, this variation is given by the characteristics of the data used. Even with high noise data, the model is still capable of achieving an average mAP@[0.5] equal to 0.75349.

The output of the model is a text file that has the class of the found object, the bounding box that determines the geometric position of the object, and the prediction confidence of the detection. The resulting text file is used as a reference for segment detection since the objects identified in this phase should not be considered when segment detection is performed.

4.3   Evaluation of Standard OCR Methods

For comparison, an experiment is conducted using Tesseract and Nanonets for character recognition on EDs of the RFI. The preliminary results showed that because these standard models were trained for text identification based on standard fonts, character identification using these techniques was inefficient.

Using the Tesseract engine, the results were under 40% for both precision and recall, by using the Nanonets, the results were under 55% for these same metrics. It was observed that these methods were suitable only for identifying characters in the project legends. Based on these results, the YOLO is defined for label recognition, where all characters are new classes.

4.4   Results of Segment Detection

To detect the segments properly, the symbols, specifiers, electrical connections, and labels are removed. In this procedure, the output of the YOLO is used as a reference to define the locations that should not be considered segments because they are objects. A new image is then created in which the bounding boxes of the identified objects are redrawn blank and are disregarded in the segment detection. Then, the PHT is applied as presented in Fig. 3A.

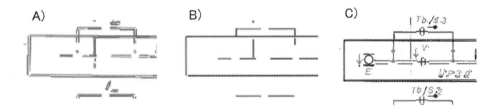

Fig. 3. Probabilistic Hough Transform applied in the ED of the RFI: A) original PHT, B) DBSCAN applied to the PHT, C) reconstructed ED.

The use of PHT results in the detection of multiple segments, instead of one complete segment, i.e. instead of identifying a connection between two symbols the method overwrites segments. For this reason, DBSCAN was applied, whereby segments that have a short distance between them and are in the same direction (vertical or horizontal) are clustered. The result of the application of this technique in the PHT is presented in Fig. 3B.

Using this clustering approach to join smaller segments, the proposed method had acceptable results and can be applied even to other engineering problems. After defining the new segments, the drawing can be reconstructed, considering the position of the identified objects beyond the segments. The results of this combination are presented in Fig. 3C.

The misclassification in object detection is not a problem for segment detection considering that only the position of the bounding box is used to remove the objects and apply the PHT and DBSCAN. Missing objects can be a problem given that the PHT would recognize them. To solve this issue only horizontal and vertical segments are considered with a maximum variation angle of 5°.

4.5   Electrical Connection Graph

To improve the meaning of the connection of the identified objects, logical reasoning rules can be applied to validate the connection of the symbols. Since
symbols are the focus of electrical connections, specifiers and labels can be considered as additional information. To build the graph of electrical connections,
Identifier Numbers (IDs) are defined for each identified object and segment, as
presented in Fig. 4.

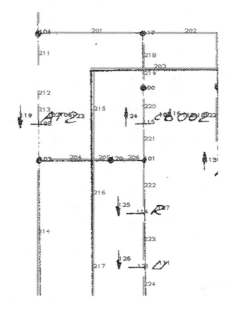

Fig. 4. Drawing with IDs of segments and objects. (Color figure online)

For standardization, the object IDs are shown in blue with values between
100 and 199, and the segment IDs are shown in red and have values between 200
and 299. Due to the low sharpness of some segments of the schematics, these
may not be identified using this method, such as the segment below the symbol
ID 108 (Fig. 4). This characteristic is related to the available dataset and makes
the task even more challenging.

In general, the method is able to identify in an acceptable way the segments
and objects under consideration, especially the symbols which are the focus of the
analysis. Based on the proximity of the segment to the edges of the bounding
boxes of the symbols and the electrical connections (points in the drawing) a
graph is created, as shown in Fig. 5.

In the presented example of the resulting graph all the connections were
identified, this occurred mainly because, in the distance calculation, the edges
of the bounding boxes were considered, preliminary evaluations using the center
of the symbols resulted in lower accuracy. In this example, the detected graph
meets the expectations in comparison with the ground truth.

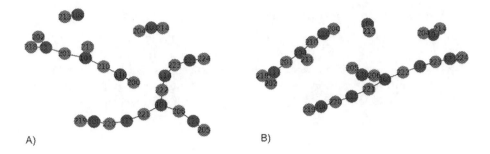

Fig. 5. Electrical connection graph: A) ground truth, B) detected connections.

5   Conclusion and Final Remarks

The digitization of engineering drawings is a necessity in many fields since many projects come from a legacy in which they were originally hand-designed. Identifying text is a challenge because handwritten drawings do not follow a font standardization, making this challenge even more difficult. Established OCR techniques are not enough to solve this task, therefore it is necessary to train specific models for the identification of each character.

The proposed method successfully had the ability to identify text, symbols, specifiers, and segments in EDs. With a mean F1-score of 0.77513, and a mean mAP@[0.5] of 0.80276, considering 50 experiments, the YOLOv8 had acceptable results to be applied in the field. Especially for segment detection, the segmentation and clustering techniques were combined, resulting in a promising approach to automate the redrawing EDs.

These results highlight that the redraw of ED based on deep learning methods is flexible. The presented method returns the symbols and label positions with acceptable results, being a functional approach that represents the original EDs. Given the importance of accuracy in reconstructing EDs of the RRIS, the verification and approval of an expert is still necessary, therefore the proposed method aims to speed up the manual task of redrawing from scratch.

In future work, the electrical connections between symbols can be used to strengthen the specification of electrical components. Furthermore, using graphs, a more adequate determination of labels and specifiers can be achieved since their use in the projects follows a pattern, and using logical reasoning graphs can improve the redrawing of the projects, besides being a tool for verification and validation of what is being presented.

References

1. Rica, E., Moreno-García, C.F., Álvarez, S., Serratosa, F.: Reducing human effort in engineering drawing validation. Comput. Ind. **117**, 103198 (2020). https://doi.org/10.1016/j.compind.2020.103198
2. Mizanur Rahman, S., Bayer, J., Dengel, A.: Graph-based object detection enhancement for symbolic engineering drawings. In: Barney Smith, E.H., Pal, U. (eds.)

ICDAR 2021. LNCS, vol. 12916, pp. 74–90. Springer, Cham (2021). https://doi.org/10.1007/978-3-030-86198-8_6

3. Moreno-García, C.F., Elyan, E., Jayne, C.: New trends on digitisation of complex engineering drawings. Neural Comput. Appl. **31**(6), 1695–1712 (2019). https://doi.org/10.1007/s00521-018-3583-1

4. Günay, M., Köseoğlu, M., Yldrm, ŏ.: Classification of hand-drawn basic circuit components using convolutional neural networks. In: 2020 International Congress on Human-Computer Interaction, Optimization and Robotic Applications (HORA), Ankara, Turkey, vol. 1, pp. 1–5. IEEE (2020). https://doi.org/10.1109/HORA49412.2020.9152866

5. Günay, M., Köseoğlu, M.: Classification of hand-drawn circuit components by considering the analysis of current methods. In: 2020 4th International Symposium on Multidisciplinary Studies and Innovative Technologies (ISMSIT), Istanbul, Turkey, vol. 4, pp. 1–5. IEEE (2020). https://doi.org/10.1109/ISMSIT50672.2020.9255047

6. Huang, L.: The past, present and future of railway interlocking system. In: International Conference on Intelligent Transportation Engineering (ICITE), Beijing, China, vol. 5, pp. 170–174. IEEE (2020). https://doi.org/10.1109/ICITE50838.2020.9231438

7. Huang, P., Li, Z., Wen, C., Lessan, J., Corman, F., Fu, L.: Modeling train timetables as images: a cost-sensitive deep learning framework for delay propagation pattern recognition. Expert Syst. Appl. **177**, 114996 (2021). https://doi.org/10.1016/j.eswa.2021.114996

8. Stefenon, S.F., Singh, G., Souza, B.J., Freire, R.Z., Yow, K.C.: Optimized hybrid YOLOu-Quasi-ProtoPNet for insulators classification. IET Gener. Transm. Distrib. **17**(15), 3501–3511 (2023). https://doi.org/10.1049/gtd2.12886

9. Ahmad, R., Naz, S., Razzak, I.: Efficient skew detection and correction in scanned document images through clustering of probabilistic Hough transforms. Pattern Recogn. Lett. **152**, 93–99 (2021). https://doi.org/10.1016/j.patrec.2021.09.014

10. Chen, Y., Zhou, L., Bouguila, N., Wang, C., Chen, Y., Du, J.: BLOCK-DBSCAN: fast clustering for large scale data. Pattern Recogn. **109**, 107624 (2021). https://doi.org/10.1016/j.patcog.2020.107624

11. Elyan, E., Garcia, C.M., Jayne, C.: Symbols classification in engineering drawings. In: International Joint Conference on Neural Networks (IJCNN), Rio de Janeiro, Brazil, vol. 1, pp. 1–8. IEEE (2018). https://doi.org/10.1109/IJCNN.2018.8489087

12. Yun, D.Y., Seo, S.K., Zahid, U., Lee, C.J.: Deep neural network for automatic image recognition of engineering diagrams. Appl. Sci. **10**(11), 4005 (2020). https://doi.org/10.3390/app10114005

13. Yu, E.S., Cha, J.M., Lee, T., Kim, J., Mun, D.: Features recognition from piping and instrumentation diagrams in image format using a deep learning network. Energies **12**(23), 4425 (2019). https://doi.org/10.3390/en12234425

14. Mani, S., Haddad, M.A., Constantini, D., Douhard, W., Li, Q., Poirier, L.: Automatic digitization of engineering diagrams using deep learning and graph search. In: Conference on Computer Vision and Pattern Recognition Workshops (CVPRW), Seattle, USA, pp. 673–679. IEEE (2020). https://doi.org/10.1109/CVPRW50498.2020.00096

15. Kang, S.O., Lee, E.B., Baek, H.K.: A digitization and conversion tool for imaged drawings to intelligent piping and instrumentation diagrams. Energies **12**(13), 2593 (2019). https://doi.org/10.3390/en12132593

16. Kim, H., et al.: Deep-learning-based recognition of symbols and texts at an industrially applicable level from images of high-density piping and instrumentation

diagrams. Expert Syst. Appl. **183**, 115337 (2021). https://doi.org/10.1016/j.eswa. 2021.115337

17. Baek, Y., Lee, B., Han, D., Yun, S., Lee, H.: Character region awareness for text detection. In: Conference on Computer Vision and Pattern Recognition (CVPR), Long Beach, USA, pp. 9357–9366. IEEE (2019). https://doi.org/10.1109/CVPR. 2019.00959

18. Shi, B., Bai, X., Yao, C.: An end-to-end trainable neural network for image-based sequence recognition and its application to scene text recognition. IEEE Trans. Pattern Anal. Mach. Intell. **39**(11), 2298–2304 (2017). https://doi.org/10.1109/ TPAMI.2016.2646371

19. Li, L., Yuhui, C., Xiaoting, L.: Engineering drawing recognition model with convolutional neural network. In: International Conference on Robotics, Intelligent Control and Artificial Intelligence, pp. 112–116. Association for Computing Machinery, New York (2019). https://doi.org/10.1145/3366194.3366213

20. Elyan, E., Jamieson, L., Ali-Gombe, A.: Deep learning for symbols detection and classification in engineering drawings. Neural Netw. **129**, 91–102 (2020). https:// doi.org/10.1016/j.neunet.2020.05.025

21. Bickel, S., Schleich, B., Wartzack, S.: Detection and classification of symbols in principle sketches using deep learning. Proc. Des. Soc. **1**, 1183–1192 (2021). https://doi.org/10.1017/pds.2021.118

22. Dey, M., et al.: A two-stage CNN-based hand-drawn electrical and electronic circuit component recognition system. Neural Comput. Appl. **33**, 13367–13390 (2021). https://doi.org/10.1007/s00521-021-05964-1

23. Kumar Garai, S., Paul, O., Dey, U., Ghoshal, S., Biswas, N., Mondal, S.: A novel method for image to text extraction using tesseract-OCR. Am. J. Electron. Commun. **3**(2), 8–11 (2022). https://doi.org/10.15864/ajec.3202

24. Ultralytics: YOLOv8 in PyTorch. https://github.com/ultralytics/ultralytics. Accessed 4 Aug 2023

25. Souza, B.J., Stefenon, S.F., Singh, G., Freire, R.Z.: Hybrid-YOLO for classification of insulators defects in transmission lines based on UAV. Int. J. Electr. Power Energy Syst. **148**, 108982 (2023). https://doi.org/10.1016/j.ijepes.2023.108982

26. Singh, G., Stefenon, S.F., Yow, K.C.: Interpretable visual transmission lines inspections using pseudo-prototypical part network. Mach. Vis. Appl. **34**(3), 41 (2023). https://doi.org/10.1007/s00138-023-01390-6

27. El Hajjouji, I., Mars, S., Asrih, Z., El Mourabit, A.: A novel FPGA implementation of Hough Transform for straight lane detection. Eng. Sci. Technol. Int. J. **23**(2), 274–280 (2020). https://doi.org/10.1016/j.jestch.2019.05.008

28. Lu, Y., Duanmu, L., Zhai, Z.J., Wang, Z.: Application and improvement of canny edge-detection algorithm for exterior wall hollowing detection using infrared thermal images. Energy Build. **274**, 112421 (2022). https://doi.org/10.1016/j.enbuild. 2022.112421

29. Zhao, K., Han, Q., Zhang, C.B., Xu, J., Cheng, M.M.: Deep Hough transform for semantic line detection. IEEE Trans. Pattern Anal. Mach. Intell. **44**(9), 4793–4806 (2022). https://doi.org/10.1109/TPAMI.2021.3077129

30. Wang, L., Yang, Y., Shi, J.: Measurement of harvesting width of intelligent combine harvester by improved probabilistic Hough transform algorithm. Measurement **151**, 107130 (2020). https://doi.org/10.1016/j.measurement.2019.107130

31. Li, S.S.: An improved DBSCAN algorithm based on the neighbor similarity and fast nearest neighbor query. IEEE Access **8**, 47468–47476 (2020). https://doi.org/ 10.1109/ACCESS.2020.2972034

Election Manipulation in Social Networks with Single-Peaked Agents

Vincenzo Auletta, Francesco Carbone, and Diodato Ferraioli[✉]

Università degli Studi di Salerno, 84084 Fisciano, SA, Italy
{auletta,dferraioli}@unisa.it, f.carbone41@studenti.unisa.it

Abstract. Several elections run in the last years have been characterized by attempts to manipulate the result of the election through the
diffusion of fake or malicious news over social networks. This problem
has been recognized as a critical issue for the robustness of our democracy. Analyzing and understanding how such manipulations may occur
is crucial to the design of effective countermeasures to these practices.

Many studies have observed that, in general, to design an optimal
manipulation is usually a computationally hard task. Nevertheless, literature on bribery in voting and election manipulation has frequently
observed that most hardness results melt down when one focuses on the
setting of (nearly) single-peaked agents, i.e., when each voter has a preferred candidate (usually, the one closest to her own belief) and preferences of remaining candidates are inversely proportional to the distance
between the candidate's position and the voter's belief. Unfortunately,
no such analysis has been done for election manipulations run in social
networks.

In this work, we try to close this gap: specifically, we consider a setting for election manipulation that naturally raises (nearly) single-peaked
preferences, and we evaluate the complexity of the election manipulation
problem in this setting: while most of the hardness and approximation
results still hold, we will show that single-peaked preferences allow to
design simple, efficient and effective heuristics for election manipulation.

1 Introduction

Nowadays, online social networks have become a ubiquitous, fast, easily accessible source of information: e.g., Matsa and Shearer [31] showed that about
one-fifth of American adults consults social media to read news. Interestingly a
significant part of the interviewed people declared that social media news somehow altered their opinion [31]. This makes social networks a powerful tool that
can be exploited to manipulate people's minds about a particular theme, spreading targeted news to specific users. Indeed, this spread of information has been
apparently exploited in many recent elections [2,18,26,27]. The most prominent

Supported by the Italian MIUR PRIN 2017 Project ALGADIMAR "Algorithms,
Games, and Digital Markets" and by "GNCS-INdAM".

example has been the 2016 U.S. election: in the campaign preceding this event, fake news spreading has been so relevant that some commentators argued that the election's outcome could have changed if the campaign had been fair [2].

The relevance of the topic leads the AI community to investigate about the problem of manipulating elections by spreading information over social networks. Specifically, the problem has been modelled as follows: let $G = (V, E)$ be a graph representing the (online) social network of the voters, with V being the set of voters and E being the set of (possibly directed) social relationships between voters. Each voter $v \in V$ has a political opinion that somehow implies particular preferences over the set C of candidates that, in turn, imply a particular vote according to the voting rule that controls the election. The manipulator has a (possibly unlimited) budget B to spend to hire some voters, bribe them, and make them act as influencers to spread some news in favour of or against a target candidate $c^* \in C$. As a result of such influence, some voters (depending on their influenceability and the effectiveness of the hired influencers) will update their opinions and change their votes in favour of or against the target candidate. The aim of the manipulator is to choose the best set of influencers (not violating the budget constraint) to optimize a specific objective function that encodes the chances of victory of the target candidate c^*. Wilder and Vorobeychik [35] have been the first to deal with this problem. They indeed prove that it is hard to compute both the set of influencers that maximizes the probability of victory of c^*, and the one that optimizes the expected difference between the number of votes of c^* and the number of votes of the best candidate different from c^*. However, for the latter problem there is a greedy algorithm that computes a constant approximation of the optimum [35]. These results have been extended to more complex settings, focusing, e.g., on different models of information diffusion, different voting rules, and different messages to spread [1,19,20].

These works complement the large literature in AI and social choice about bribery in elections [12–14,23]: they focus on ways of altering the outcome of an election by changing the preference of a few voters. Anyway, all these works do not take into account the possibility that manipulators could use voters' social relationships to spread the manipulation. Most of the results in these works imply that it is computationally hard to compute the best way to alter an election. Still, most of these hardness results have been showed to melt down when the preferences of voters satisfy the realistic hypothesis of being *single-peaked* or nearly single-peaked [16,24,25,33], where single-peakedness implies that candidates can be seen as ordered (e.g., along the political spectrum), voters have a preferred candidate (e.g., the one that is closest to their own political belief) and the preference towards remaining candidates decreases as the distance between their position and the one of the preferred candidate increases.

Our Contribution. Election manipulation involving information spreading in social networks has not been explicitly studied for the setting in which preferences are single-peaked. In this work we address this issue, by studying the problem of election manipulation through social influence in single-peaked scenarios. Specifically, we will build over known models of election manipulation in order to embed into them the principles of single-peakedness. Namely, in our model, each voter has an opinion on the topic of the voting and their ranking of alternatives depends on the distance between the candidates' positions and the voter's belief. Here, the diffusion of information has the effect to change the opinion of the voter, and hence it may alter her ranking, but still guaranteeing it to be single-peaked. This model can be also easily extended to encompass nearly single-peaked preferences: these, indeed, may simply arise from voters having a noisy view of candidates' position. Given this model, the problem is to find, subject to a budget constraint, the set of "seeds" from which to start the information campaign that maximizes the margin of victory of the desired candidate.

It is not hard to check that previous hardness results extend also to this setting. Moreover, we show that there exists an approximation algorithm for the problem guaranteeing to return a set of seeds able to achieve at least a constant fraction of the margin of victory that would be achieved by selecting the optimal set of seeds whenever the target candidate is the one that receives the largest benefit from the campaign[1]. The proposed algorithm is based on a greedy approach, and it is built on Monte Carlo simulations in order to estimate the performance of a seed selection [28]. Unfortunately this algorithm, even if it guarantees a polynomial time complexity, turns out to be computationally expensive, even for very small instances of the problem.

This motivates the need to design more efficient algorithms, trying to speed up computations while preserving the effectiveness of the manipulation. To this aim, this work proposes and compares several fast heuristics to identify the best voters to influence the electorate; we experimentally show that the best of these heuristics is a variant of the standard PageRank. We show that the performance of this approach overwhelms the one of the approximation algorithm, improving execution times by a factor of (up to) 3000 on average. And this improvement comes with a relatively small loss in terms of effectiveness. Moreover, the proposed heuristics turn out to be robust against altered voters' views of candidates' positions generating only nearly single-peaked preferences: the performances of the heuristics clearly degrade with the amount of noise in the voter's view, but they are very close to the single-peaked case when this noise is limited.

Other Related Works. The problem of election manipulation over social networks has been only recently formalized in [35]. However, several works considered similar issues. E.g., [32] studies a plurality voting scenario in which the voters can vote iteratively and shows how to modify the relationship among voters to make the desired candidate win an election. [4–6] show that in some scenarios, when there are only two candidates, a manipulator controlling the order in which information is disclosed to voters can lead the minority to become a majority. [9] shows that a similar manipulator can lead a bare majority to consensus. These results do not extend to more than two candidates [8,10]. [17] shows how

---

[1] For example, this may not occur when a message is spread in favour of an extremist party when there are few supporters of an half-extreme party and many supporters for a moderate party: the message causes many votes to move from the moderate towards the half-extreme party, while few votes are conquered by the target party.

this manipulator must select the seeds diffusing information in a two-candidate election. [22] considers a similar issue, but its model does not directly embed the diffusion of information over networks. Our model for election manipulation is also largely inspired by models of election manipulations under metric preferences [3,36].

2 The Model

Consider an election with a set of *voters* V and a set of *candidates* (or alternatives) $C = \{c_0, c_1, ..., c_{m-1}\}$. Let $c^* \in C$ be a special *target* candidate such that we want to alter the election in her favour. We consider a *plurality* voting rule: the voters cast a single vote for their preferred candidate (we assume that they do not misreport the preferred candidate to alter the election outcome), and the winner of the election is the candidate receiving the largest number of votes.

A candidate c is associated with a position x_c (e.g., their position on the political spectrum). For simplicity, we assume henceforth, that positions are included in $[-1, 1]$. Each voter v also is associated with a position x_v in $[-1, 1]$ reflecting her belief. The preference of v over candidates depends on her position x_v and her *view* of the candidates' positions. Indeed, we assume that voters may not have a clear picture of the political positions of the parties. For instance, a pure moderate party can be perceived as moderate-left by some voters and moderate-right by others. To model this, we associate with each candidate c a random variable X_c that presumably depends on the true position x_c of the candidate; the blurred view of each voter v consists of a random realization x_c^v of X_c. Note that the noisy positions of the candidates in the views are clipped in $[-1, +1]$ to ensure that they remain in the allowed range. Hence, the blurred position of candidate c in the view of voter v can be expressed as $x_c^v = [x_c + \eta(x_c)]_{-1}^{+1}$, where $\eta(x_c)$ is the *noise term* depending on the real position of the candidate, and $[\cdot]_{-1}^{+1}$ indicates the clip operation. We assume that $\eta(x_{c_i})$ and $\eta(x_{c_j})$ are independent, for any $c_i \neq c_j$. We will consider different ways to generate the noise term.

The ranking of voter v with respect to candidate c is then defined with respect to the goal of minimizing the absolute value of the difference between x_v and x_c^v: i.e., the most preferred is the one that minimizes $|x_v - x_c^v|$, the second most preferred one achieves the second smallest value of this function, and so on. It is immediate to check that, whenever the view of voters corresponds to real candidates positions, the preferences built in this way are *single-peaked*, i.e., for each voter v there is a preferred candidate c, and for each pair of candidates c', c'' such that $x_{c'} < x_{c''} \le x_c$ ($x_{c'} > x_{c''} \ge x_c$), c' is less preferred than c'' by v. This method also allows to model nearly single-peaked voters: if the variance of the noise is high, the chances of swapping adjacent candidates on the political spectrum are high, too. Hence, the higher the noise, the higher is the number of swaps necessary to make the resulting ranking single-peaked, a common measure of distance from single-peakedness [21]. We stress that preferences of voter v are always single-peaked according to her own view, even if they are not single-peaked according to the real positions of candidates or other voters' views.

A manipulator can spread information supporting c^* among voters. Formally, we suppose that voters are arranged on the nodes of a social *network* $G = (V, E, p)$, where E is the set of edges (u, v) connecting voter u to voter v, and $p(u, v) \in [0, 1]$ encodes the strength of this relationship, namely how probable is that the information that u sends to v affects the opinion of v. The manipulator is then supposed to select a subset S of voters, of size not larger than a given *budget B*, from which the information is sent. As most of the previous literature about election manipulation through social networks [1,19,35] we assume that information spreads through the network according to the Independent Cascade Model [28]: it starts with $S_0 = S$ and, at each time step t, if S_{t-1} is not empty, each voter u in S_{t-1} sends the information to each neighbor v that has not been yet affected, and this neighbor v is affected, and hence inserted in S_t, with probability $p(u, v)$. When a voter v is affected by the news spread by the manipulator (i.e., v belongs to S_t for some $t \geq 0$), her belief is updated. Specifically, the voter's position is moved by a constant amount δ towards the position (in her view) of the target candidate. If the voter is closer than δ to the position of c^*, then she simply moves to $x_{c^*}^v$. Formally, the voter's new position $\hat{x}_v$ is $\hat{x}_v = x_v + \min(\delta, |x_{c^*}^v - x_v|) \cdot \mathrm{sign}(x_{c^*}^v - x_v)$.

As in previous literature [1,19,20,35], we assume that the goal of the manipulator is to choose the set of seeds S of size at most B that maximizes the increment in the margin of victory of c^*. Specifically, the goal of the manipulator is to maximize the expected change of margin of victory $\Delta MoV(S) = |V_{c^*}^*| - \max_{c \neq c^*} |V_c^*| - (|V_{c^*}| - \max_{c \neq c^*} |V_c|)$, where, by $|V_c|$ and $|V_c^*|$, we mean, respectively, the number of votes for the candidate c before and after the manipulation. Essentially ΔMoV is the increase of the advantage of c^* over its best opponent before and after the manipulation (that is guaranteed to be always non-negative). Note that the manipulator knows exactly the real position of candidates and of the voters, but she does not know the voters'views.

It is not hard to see that by considering the special case of zero-noise, only two candidates and δ large enough to guarantee that the least preferred candidate becomes the most preferred candidate for each voter v activated by the spread of information, our model reduces to the one considered in [35]. Hence, the hardness result described there for the election manipulation problem clearly extends to our model. For this reason, in the rest of this work we only look for algorithms able to approximate the optimal choice of the manipulator. Specifically, we say that an algorithm is α-*approximate*, for $\alpha \leq 1$ if it always returns a set of seeds S such that $\mathbb{E}[\Delta MoV(S)] \geq \alpha \mathbb{E}[\Delta MoV(S^*)]$, where $S^* = \arg\max_S \mathbb{E}[\Delta MoV(S)] : |S| \leq B$ is the optimal seed set.

In this work we will also consider an extension of previous models: we allow the manipulator to run a multi-round campaign, by choosing in each round the seeds from which the information spreads, and the electorate evolves accordingly.

Throughout the rest of the paper we assume the reader is familiar with two tools that will turn out to be particularly useful in the design of our algorithms: *Influence Maximization* approximation algorithms, and *PageRank* measure. Due to page limits, we also omit many proofs and experimental details. For the reader interested in these details, we refer to the full version [7].

3   Approximation Algorithm

We here propose a greedy algorithm, that returns a constant approximation of the optimal solution to the Election Manipulation problem in the setting described above whenever the view of voters corresponds to the real position of candidates. The design of the algorithm directly mimics the ones proposed in [19,35]. The crux of the algorithm is identifying the voters that, if influenced, will change their minds and vote for the target candidate c^*. Then, the problem is solved by simply computing the set of seeds that maximizes the weighted influence maximization [28] for which weights $w(v) = 1$ are assigned to such voters and 0 to all the other nodes. Indeed, nodes that already support the target candidate can be useful for spreading information, but reaching them will not modify the margin of victory of the target candidate; similarly, influencing a voter that cannot be convinced to vote for the target candidate apparently cannot improve the margin of victory. Unfortunately, influencing a voter that will never vote for c^* after the manipulation is not that pointless: even if the number of votes of the target candidate does not increase, this voter may change her preferred candidate and erode votes for the best opponent of the target candidate, possibly increasing the margin of victory of c^*. So we need to prove that, even if this contribution is not accounted by our algorithm (i.e., it only focuses on influencing nodes that can be made to support the target candidate but do not actually do), we still achieve a constant approximation whenever the campaign for the target candidate does not advantage other candidates more than the target itself[2].

Since our approximation algorithm relies on the influence maximization algorithm discussed above, it is easy to see that its computational complexity is $O(B \cdot |V| \cdot MI)$, where B is the budget, $|V|$ is the number of nodes in the graph, and MI is the cost of estimating the marginal influence of a node via Monte Carlo simulations, that depends on the margin of error that one is willing to accept in the computed estimation. It is not hard to check that MI also polynomially depends on the size of the input, allowing us to conclude that our algorithm is polynomial.

Moreover, observe that the set of influencers returned by our algorithm has a size that does not exceed the budget, and hence is feasible. We next show that it returns a constant approximation of the optimal seed set whenever the view of all voters coincides with candidates' real positions and the campaign for the target candidate does not advantage other candidates more than the target itself. Specifically, let $X(S)$ be the expected maximum – among all candidates $c \neq c^*$ – of the number of voters that do not vote for c and they will do after

---

[2] In [35], it is not necessary to account for this case since essentially only two candidates are considered. In [19], instead, this case is considered, but the algorithm is showed to provide a constant approximation on stronger assumptions than in our setting.

receiving a message supporting candidate c^* starting from nodes in S (where the expectation is taken over the probabilities of receiving this message). Then we have the following theorem.

Theorem 1. *The set of influencers $\hat{S} \subseteq V$ returned by our algorithm is such that $\mathbb{E}[\Delta MoV(\hat{S})] + X(\hat{S}) \geq \frac{1}{3} \cdot \left(1 - \frac{1}{e}\right) \cdot max_S \mathbb{E}[\Delta MoV(S)]$ whenever $x_c^v = x_c$ for each $v \in V$ and each $c \in C$. Hence, our algorithm returns a constant approximation whenever $X(\hat{S}) = O(\mathbb{E}[\Delta MoV(\hat{S})])$.*

Note that in case of nearly-single-peaked voters the algorithm still works, but its performances in terms of $\Delta MoV(\cdot)$ depend on the amount of noise: the higher the noise, the more the inconsistency between reality and blurred views of the voters, the lower the effectiveness of the manipulation since the manipulator estimates wrong weights $w(v)$ for each voter $v \in V$.

4   The Heuristics

The approximation algorithm presented in the previous section provides a formal guarantee of the quality of the solution. However, it inherits from the weighted influence maximization algorithm used as black box the drawbacks of being computationally expensive, even if it is polynomial in the size of the input. Specifically, the proposed algorithm requires a large number of simulations in order to estimate the marginal influence of each node. Even if faster algorithms have been proposed for the influence maximization problem (see, e.g., [15]), it is often solved in practice through fast heuristics based only on the structure of the network: they, indeed, assign scores to the nodes in the graph defining their "importance", and then they simply return the nodes with the highest scores.

In this work, we propose to extend this approach in order to encompass the problem of election manipulation. Specifically, this work introduces several heuristics in that sense: they are based on both the structure of the networks and centrality metrics adapted to the election context. We here only present in detail the one that happens to achieve the best experimental performances, namely *SPpagerank1.0_ pos*. This heuristic approach mimics PageRank, by distributing at each time step the rank over voters' neighbors, and updating the rank correspondingly, until rank becomes stable. However, in our heuristics, the rank of node u is not shared uniformly among all its neighbors (as in the standard PageRank), but proportionally to a score $\hat{s}$ assigned to each node. The score $\hat{s}$ of v considers political information about voters in the neighbourhood of v: specifically we define $\hat{s}(v) = 1/d(v, c^*) + \sum_{u \cup :\ (v,u) \in E \text{ and } d(u,c^*) > 0} p(v, u)/1/d(u, c^*)$ for the node v, where $d(u, c^*) = 0$ if u votes for c^*, and otherwise measures the distance on the political spectrum between c^* and voter u. Thus, nodes that are more likely to influence others in favour of c^* are assigned a higher weight.

5   Experimental Results

Experimental Setting. We run extensive experiments to evaluate the algorithms described above both in terms of the effectiveness of the manipulation, as measured by the margin of victory MoV and the change of margin of victory ΔMoV resulting from the simulated manipulations, and the execution time of the algorithms. As for the valuation of the running time, we stress that we compare *Python* implementations run on a single core, without any code optimization.

In general we compared different algorithms in election scenarios with a set of voters of sizes 20, 50, and 100. All the experiments involved five candidates. Both voters and candidates were assigned positions in the range $[-1, +1]$ chosen uniformly at random. This should create scenarios in which all the parties are almost equally supported by the voters. When dealing with nearly-single-peaked electorates, the noise was chosen to be independent of the positions of the candidates, namely $\eta(x_c) = \eta$. Specifically, we considered *uniform noise* $\eta = U(-0.2; 0.2)$; *Gaussian noise with low variance* $\eta = \mathcal{N}(0; 0.08)$; and *Gaussian noise with high variance* $\eta = \mathcal{N}(0; 1)$. These values were chosen to test different levels of nearly single-peaked average swap distances [21]. In fact, when normalized with respect to the number of voters, for an election with 20 voters and 5 candidates randomly placed on the political spectrum, the average distances from single-peaked scenarios are ~0.5, ~1, and ~2 swaps.

As for the parameters describing the power of the manipulator, we consider budget B such that $\frac{B}{|V|} \in \{5\%, 10\%, 15\%\}$; the maximum number of manipulation campaigns was set to 10; the parameter δ that represents the influence-ability of the electorate has been chosen in $\{0.1, 0.2, 0.3, 0.4\}$; the target candidate of the manipulation process was chosen randomly among all the candidates $\{c_0, c_1, c_2, c_3, c_4\}$ unless stated differently.

Monte-Carlo simulations necessary for the approximation algorithm have been repeated 300 times. Moreover, estimates of ΔMoV have been evaluated over a number of simulation sufficient to achieve statistical guarantees.

All the variants of the models and algorithms described above have been tested against both synthetic and real-world networks. Specifically, we used: (i) Watts-Strogatz graphs [34] with nodes uniformly distributed in the 2D square whose side is $\sqrt{\frac{|V|}{20}}$ (thus, the density of the nodes remains the same increasing the size of the electorate); strong ties with a radius $r = 0.13$; $k = 2$ weak ties distributed inversely to the distance with a power law of exponent $q = 2$. Since the density does not change when the number of nodes increases, the degree of each node remains almost the same. (ii) Preferential attachment graphs [11], created by setting the probability of linking preferentially to 0.25 and 0.75.

For these networks, tests were performed on several combinations of parameters. Specifically, for each pair $(|V|, B/|V|) \in \{20, 50, 100\} \times \{0.05, 0.10, 0.15\}$, the simulated scenarios involved (in all the possible combinations): 8 random placements of voters and candidates on the political spectrum; 10 randomly generated graphs (Watts-Strogatz or preferential attachment models); 10 randomly generated sets of diffusion probabilities on edges. This led to $8 \times 10 \times 10 = 800$ electoral scenarios. Due to the large running time of our approximation algorithm, it has been tested only with: 31 random placements of voters and candidates; 5 randomly generated graphs (Watts-Strogatz models only); 5 randomly generated sets of diffusion probabilities. This led to 775 random elections.

The real case study involves a snapshot of the Facebook social network [29] available at SNAP [30]. The network has 4039 nodes and 88234 undirected edges.

Among all the tested algorithms, the best one (considering both manipulation performances and computational complexity) was tested in terms of scalability on very large graphs. The experiment is executed on Watts-Strogatz graphs built as explained above. The tested number of nodes of the graphs are $[200, 500, 1000, 2000, 5000, 10000, 20000]$. The algorithm is allowed to run for three hours for each graph size, repeatedly generating random graphs and elections. This experiment was repeated for $\eta = 0$, $\eta = \mathcal{N}(0; 0.08)$, $\eta = \mathcal{N}(0; 1)$.

Results. We start by comparing the different heuristics on Watts-Strogatz networks, in order to find the one that guarantees the best performances. In Fig. 1 we show the performances of a subset of some of the heuristics that we designed (we refer to the full version of this paper [7] for their details). We can check that the algorithm with the best performances is *SPpagerank1.0_pos*, because it considers the whole network, while almost every other ones focus on local properties of the graph.

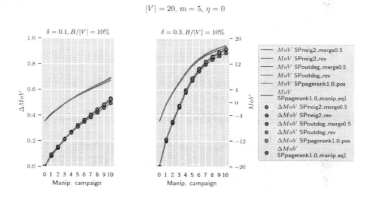

Fig. 1. Performances of the algorithms.

We next compare the best heuristic method and the approximation algorithm. Since the approximation algorithm is computationally heavy (see below), the tests only use the following subset of parameters: $\delta \in \{0.1, 0.3\}$ and $B/|V| \in \{5\%, 10\%\}$. Moreover, in the 75% of the considered instances the approximation algorithm is guaranteed to achieve a constant approximation (i.e., in these instances no candidate is more advantaged than the target candidate by messages in favour of the latter). Performances are graphically shown in Fig. 2. Results show that the approximation algorithm actually performs better than *SPpagerank1.0_pos* only in the initial campaigns. For a higher number of rounds, *SPpagerank1.0_pos* performs better, and on average, after ten campaigns, it gets more votes for the target candidate.

Results in Fig. 3 show the performances of algorithm *SPpagerank1.0_pos* in nearly single-peaked scenarios. Note that the blurred views of the voters make

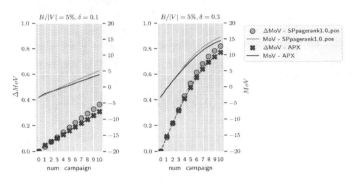

Fig. 2. Performances of *SPpagerank1.0_ pos* and of the approximation algorithm.

the initial MoVs of the simulations different from the initial MoVs in the perfectly single-peaked cases. For this reason, comparisons based on MoV cannot be made. While it may appear that blurred views increase the performances, this only depends on the initial conditions of the simulated scenarios being different. However, this only happens when the noise has low variance: with $\eta = \mathcal{N}(0; 1)$, performances are definitely worse than the single-peaked case (even if the initial MoV is higher). Nevertheless, even with $\eta = \mathcal{N}(0; 1)$ and $\eta = \mathcal{N}(0; 0.08)$ that are very strong noises, performances are not that much worse than the ones in single-peaked scenarios. For this reason, our heuristics has been tested also with noises not having the peak of the probability distribution function in 0, namely $\eta_2 = \frac{1}{2}\mathcal{N}(-0.7; 1) + \frac{1}{2}\mathcal{N}(+0.7; 1)$. The corresponding plots in Fig. 3 show that performances slightly drop when the peak of the distribution of the noise is not 0 (and thus manipulator's estimates of x_c^v are not maximizing likelihood).

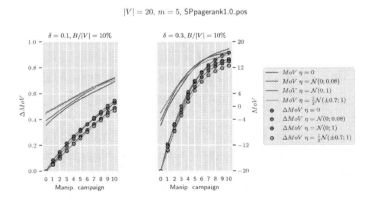

Fig. 3. Performances of *SPpagerank1.0_ pos* for $\eta = \mathcal{N}(0; 0.08)$ and $\eta = \mathcal{N}(0; 1)$ and $\eta = \frac{1}{2}\mathcal{N}(-0.7; 1) + \frac{1}{2}\mathcal{N}(+0.7; 1)$.

Until now, the shown experiments only involved electorates made up of 20 voters. We now analyze how performances change when testing electorates of 20, 50, and 100 voters. The algorithms were only tested with a single, medium budget: 10% of the electorate. Moreover, the target candidate was fixed to the right-most one on the political spectrum. Figure 4 illustrates the results. Note that performances increase when the number of voters increases. Similar results hold even for noisy single-peaked preferences (details in the full version [7]).

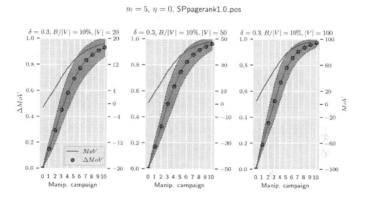

Fig. 4. Performances of *SPpagerank1.0_pos* in perfectly single-peaked scenarios.

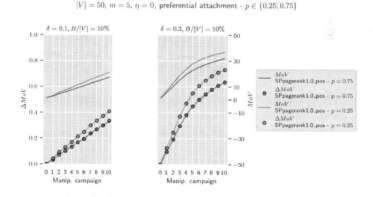

Fig. 5. Performances of *SPpagerank1.0_pos* for $\eta = 0$ and $p \in \{0.25, 0.75\}$.

Next we evaluate whether results showed above are robust against different graphs. We first present the experiments that were performed on preferential attachment graphs. Tests were performed with $\eta = 0$, $|V| \in \{20, 50, 100\}$, $\delta \in \{0.1, 0.3\}$. The target candidate is the right-most one. Since results for different sizes of the electorates were almost identical, only the ones for $|V| = 50$ are displayed. Figure 5 displays the normalized ΔMoV and the MoV. Observe that the manipulator benefits from the rich-get-richer phenomenon.

Finally we show how our heuristics performs on the real Facebook network. The results of the experiment are shown in Fig. 6. Plots only show the margin of victory; ΔMoV can be plotted by simply shifting the curve up, such that the value before the first manipulation campaign is 0.

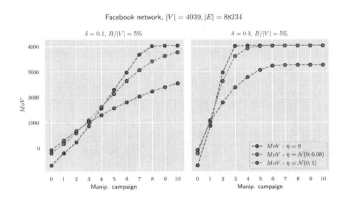

Fig. 6. Average margin of victory for the test on the Facebook network.

Note that candidates are in $\{-1, -0.5, 0, 0.5, 1\}$, and voters are initially placed such that c_2 (at position 0) loses the election; in fact, his margin of victory is negative. Nevertheless, in single-peaked electorates, the algorithm only needs two campaigns (when $\delta = 0.1$) or one campaign (when $\delta = 0.3$) to make c_2 win the election. Moreover, when voters are easily manipulable, the algorithm reaches unanimity in a few campaigns. Even in nearly-single-peaked electorates, the manipulator can make c_2 win, although performances are worse.

Finally, we tested the scalability of $SPpagerank1.0\_pos$ (since its execution time happens to be thousands of times faster than the approximation algorithm) on networks up to 20000 nodes as described above. Interestingly, on a common PC, the algorithm can be executed 15 times in three hours on graphs of 20000 nodes. Since simulations require additional code to prepare the electoral setting and include 10 manipulation campaigns, the number of tests runnable in three hours is even higher: hence, a manipulator would be able to execute the proposed algorithm even on large graphs. A more thorough analysis about the bottleneck of the running time of our heuristics can be found in the full version [7].

6   Conclusion

In this work we considered the problem of election manipulation through social influence when agents have single-peaked or nearly single-peaked preferences.

For this purpose, we first propose a new manipulation model that intrinsically generates single-peaked preferences of the voters. We provided an algorithm with constant approximation guarantees whenever there is no candidate that is more advantaged than the target candidate by a campaign in favour of the latter. We also provided an heuristic approach that has been proved to perform very well in simulations and to be computable very efficiently. These results highlight the huge risk of election manipulation in the single-peaked setting.

It would be desirable to further extend and deepen our analysis. Moreover, it would be interesting to design efficient and effective counter-measures against manipulation. Our analysis, by highlighting those aspects that simplify or complicate the manipulation, may be an useful starting point in this direction.

References

1. Abouei Mehrizi, M., Corò, F., Cruciani, E., D'Angelo, G.: Election control through social influence with voters' uncertainty. J. Comb. Optim. **44**(1), 635–669 (2022). https://doi.org/10.1007/s10878-022-00852-3
2. Allcott, H., Gentzkow, M.: Social media and fake news in the 2016 election. J. Econ. Perspect. **31**(2), 211–236 (2017)
3. Anshelevich, E., Bhardwaj, O., Elkind, E., Postl, J., Skowron, P.: Approximating optimal social choice under metric preferences. Artif. Intell. **264**, 27–51 (2018)
4. Auletta, V., Caragiannis, I., Ferraioli, D., Galdi, C., Persiano, G.: Minority becomes majority in social networks. In: Markakis, E., Schäfer, G. (eds.) WINE 2015. LNCS, vol. 9470, pp. 74–88. Springer, Heidelberg (2015). https://doi.org/10.1007/978-3-662-48995-6_6
5. Auletta, V., Caragiannis, I., Ferraioli, D., Galdi, C., Persiano, G.: Information retention in heterogeneous majority dynamics. In: Devanur, N.R., Lu, P. (eds.) WINE 2017. LNCS, vol. 10660, pp. 30–43. Springer, Cham (2017). https://doi.org/10.1007/978-3-319-71924-5_3
6. Auletta, V., Caragiannis, I., Ferraioli, D., Galdi, C., Persiano, G.: Robustness in discrete preference games. In: AAMAS, pp. 1314–1322 (2017)
7. Auletta, V., Carbone, F., Ferraioli, D.: Election manipulation in social networks with single-peaked agents (2023)
8. Auletta, V., Ferraioli, D., Fionda, V., Greco, G.: Maximizing the spread of an opinion when Tertium Datur Est. In: AAMAS, pp. 1207–1215 (2019)
9. Auletta, V., Ferraioli, D., Greco, G.: Reasoning about consensus when opinions diffuse through majority dynamics. In: IJCAI, pp. 49–55 (2018)
10. Auletta, V., Ferraioli, D., Greco, G.: On the effectiveness of social proof recommendations in markets with multiple products. In: ECAI, pp. 19–26 (2020)
11. Barabási, A.L., Albert, R.: Emergence of scaling in random networks. Science **286**(5439), 509–512 (1999)
12. Bartholdi, J.J., Tovey, C.A., Trick, M.A.: The computational difficulty of manipulating an election. Soc. Choice Welfare **6**, 227–241 (1989). https://doi.org/10.1007/BF00295861
13. Bartholdi, J.J., III., Orlin, J.B.: Single transferable vote resists strategic voting. Soc. Choice Welfare **8**(4), 341–354 (1991). https://doi.org/10.1007/BF00183045
14. Bartholdi, J.J., III., Tovey, C.A., Trick, M.A.: How hard is it to control an election? Math. Comput. Model. **16**(8–9), 27–40 (1992)

15. Borgs, C., Brautbar, M., Chayes, J., Lucier, B.: Maximizing social influence in nearly optimal time. In: SODA, pp. 946–957 (2014)
16. Brandt, F., Brill, M., Hemaspaandra, E., Hemaspaandra, L.A.: Bypassing combinatorial protections: polynomial-time algorithms for single-peaked electorates. J. Artif. Intell. Res. **53**, 439–496 (2015)
17. Bredereck, R., Elkind, E.: Manipulating opinion diffusion in social networks. In: Proceedings of the International Joint Conference on Artificial Intelligence (IJCAI), pp. 894–900 (2017)
18. Bruno, M., Lambiotte, R., Saracco, F.: Brexit and bots: characterizing the behaviour of automated accounts on Twitter during the UK election. EPJ Data Sci. **11**(1), 17 (2022)
19. Castiglioni, M., Ferraioli, D., Gatti, N., Landriani, G.: Election manipulation on social networks: seeding, edge removal, edge addition. J. Artif. Intell. Res. **71**, 1049–1090 (2021)
20. Corò, F., Cruciani, E., D'Angelo, G., Ponziani, S.: Exploiting social influence to control elections based on positional scoring rules. Inf. Comput. **289**, 104940 (2022)
21. Erdélyi, G., Lackner, M., Pfandler, A.: Computational aspects of nearly single-peaked electorates. J. Artif. Intell. Res. **58**, 297–337 (2017)
22. Faliszewski, P., Gonen, R., Koutecký, M., Talmon, N.: Opinion diffusion and campaigning on society graphs. J. Log. Comput. **32**(6), 1162–1194 (2022)
23. Faliszewski, P., Hemaspaandra, E., Hemaspaandra, L.A.: How hard is bribery in elections? J. Artif. Intell. Res. **35**, 485–532 (2009)
24. Faliszewski, P., Hemaspaandra, E., Hemaspaandra, L.A.: The complexity of manipulative attacks in nearly single-peaked electorates. In: TARK, pp. 228–237 (2011)
25. Faliszewski, P., Hemaspaandra, E., Hemaspaandra, L.A., Rothe, J.: The shield that never was: societies with single-peaked preferences are more open to manipulation and control. In: TARK, pp. 118–127 (2009)
26. Ferrara, E.: Disinformation and social bot operations in the run up to the 2017 French presidential election. First Monday (2017)
27. Giglietto, F., et al.: Mapping Italian news media political coverage in the lead-up to 2018 general election. Available at SSRN 3179930 (2018)
28. Kempe, D., Kleinberg, J., Tardos, É.: Maximizing the spread of influence through a social network. In: KDD, pp. 137–146 (2003)
29. Leskovec, J., Mcauley, J.: Learning to discover social circles in ego networks. In: Advances in Neural Information Processing Systems, vol. 25 (2012)
30. Leskovec, J., Sosič, R.: SNAP: a general-purpose network analysis and graph-mining library. ACM Trans. Intell. Syst. Technol. (TIST) **8**(1), 1–20 (2016)
31. Matsa, K.E., Shearer, E.: News use across social media platforms 2018 (2018)
32. Sina, S., Hazon, N., Hassidim, A., Kraus, S.: Adapting the social network to affect elections. In: AAMAS, pp. 705–713 (2015)
33. Walsh, T.: Uncertainty in preference elicitation and aggregation. In: AAAI, pp. 3–8 (2007)
34. Watts, D.J., Strogatz, S.H.: Collective dynamics of 'small-world' networks. Nature **393**(6684), 440–442 (1998)
35. Wilder, B., Vorobeychik, Y.: Controlling elections through social influence. In: AAMAS, pp. 265–273 (2018)
36. Wu, J., Estornell, A., Kong, L., Vorobeychik, Y.: Manipulating elections by changing voter perceptions. In: IJCAI (2022)

Learning to Prompt in the Classroom to Understand AI Limits: A Pilot Study

Emily Theophilou[2]([✉]) [iD], Cansu Koyutürk[1] [iD], Mona Yavari[1] [iD], Sathya Bursic[1] [iD], Gregor Donabauer[1,3], Alessia Telari[1] [iD], Alessia Testa[1] [iD], Raffaele Boiano[4] [iD], Davinia Hernandez-Leo[2] [iD], Martin Ruskov[5] [iD], Davide Taibi[6] [iD], Alessandro Gabbiadini[1] [iD], and Dimitri Ognibene[1,7] [iD]

[1] Dept. Psychology, Università degli Studi di Milano Bicocca, Milan, Italy
dimitri.ognibene@unimib.it
[2] Universitat Pompeu Fabra, Barcelona, Spain
emily.theophilou@upf.edu
[3] University of Regensburg, Regensburg, Germany
[4] Politecnico di Milano, Milan, Italy
[5] Università degli Studi di Milano, Milan, Italy
[6] Istituto per le Tecnologie Didattiche (ITD-CNR), Palermo, Italy
[7] Università of Essex, Colchester, UK

Abstract. Artificial intelligence's (AI) progress holds great promise in tackling pressing societal concerns such as health and climate. Large Language Models (LLM) and the derived chatbots, like ChatGPT, have highly improved the natural language processing capabilities of AI systems allowing them to process an unprecedented amount of unstructured data. However, the ensuing excitement has led to negative sentiments, even as AI methods demonstrate remarkable contributions (e.g. in health and genetics). A key factor contributing to this sentiment is the misleading perception that LLMs can effortlessly provide solutions across domains, ignoring their limitations such as hallucinations and reasoning constraints. Acknowledging AI fallibility is crucial to address the impact of dogmatic overconfidence in possibly erroneous suggestions generated by LLMs. At the same time, it can reduce fear and other negative attitudes toward AI. This necessitates comprehensive AI literacy interventions that educate the public about LLM constraints and effective usage techniques, i.e. prompting strategies. With this aim, a pilot educational intervention was performed in a high school with 21 students. It involved presenting high-level concepts about intelligence, AI, and LLMs, followed by practical exercises involving ChatGPT in creating natural educational conversations and applying established prompting strategies. Encouraging preliminary results emerged, including high appreciation of the activity, improved interaction quality with the LLM, reduced negative AI sentiments, and a better grasp of limitations, specifically unreliability, limited understanding of commands leading to unsatisfactory responses, and limited presentation flexibility. Our aim is to explore AI acceptance factors and refine this approach for more controlled future studies.

D. Ognibene---Lead PI.

R. Basili et al. (Eds.): AIxIA 2023, LNAI 14318, pp. 481–496, 2023.
https://doi.org/10.1007/978-3-031-47546-7_33

Keywords: ChatGPT · Large Language Models · HCI · Prompting · AI Attitude · AI limitations · AI literacy

1 Introduction

Artificial Intelligence (AI) technologies have gained significant prominence in contemporary society, permeating various facets of everyday life. AI is increasingly assuming a vital role in driving progress toward sustainable development worldwide in fields like healthcare, education, climate action [1, 2, 42, 48, 52, 58]. As an example, AI has already contributed to tackling medicine and health issues by improving diagnosis [9], developing new treatments [15, 25, 53], and supporting the overall care process at multiple scales. It also promises to help to deal with the chronic lack of expert personnel that is affecting many developing countries [62] both through training personnel and simplifying the medical procedures [52]. However, with all this potential comes big responsibility. While in the medical domain, the critical lack of personnel reduces the importance of the impact of the issue of jobs loss, several other problems must still be addressed. First, limited AI literacy may limit the gain for the countries where these tools would be more useful. A second issue is patient privacy, as the absence of a transparent and reliable process in place could lead to health data being used for unrelated applications of different entities, e.g. impacting patient access to job, insurance, and financial services [32]. Care must also be taken when applying AI decisions at multiple levels of the healthcare process as they may produce biassed results [41] resulting from biassed objectives and datasets. Moreover, determining the responsibilities in case of bad consequences of AI decisions is a complex topic that has been discussed for decades [37, 67].

With the magnitude of the contrasting positive and negative potential outcomes combined to the astonishing speed and complexity of the AI field, it was to be expected the rise of highly contrasting attitudes toward AI, extending from enthusiasm to phobia. Despite positive outcomes of AI systems, the recent advancements in AI have also sparked fears, anxiety, and negative attitudes particularly when machines begin to perform mindful tasks traditionally associated with humans [13, 22].

Media representations have often amplified these concerns by emphasising the negative consequences of AI and frequently depicting scenarios involving killer robots [30]. Such portrayals contribute to the magnification of AI anxiety. The impact of this negative sentiment toward AI can be dramatic, hindering trust and the acceptance and adoption of AI technologies and blocking the contributions they can provide. For instance, while AI diagnosis performance reaches or surpasses those of expert physicians, it will provide a real clinical benefit only if physicians will take into account its predictions [14]. Thus enabling healthcare professionals to achieve the right balance between trust and suspicion is crucial for achieving the full AI potential in medicine [14, 57]. The same balance is crucial to not miss the important opportunities that AI can provide in many domains and that anxiety-driven rejection or bans would hinder [23, 35, 40]. Understanding the causes of this anxiety is crucial for addressing these concerns. [24] identified three primary factors contributing to AI anxiety: (i) an overemphasis on AI programs without considering the involvement of humans, (ii) confusion regarding the autonomy of computational entities and humans, and (iii) a flawed understanding of technological development. Addressing these factors through targeted literacy interventions is crucial in alleviating public concerns regarding AI advancements. Positive experiences with AI [43] and an understanding of how they work can shape positive attitudes towards AI [50] promoting its usage and acceptance among the public [20, 35]. Moreover, by delving into the inner workings of AI, individuals can develop critical perceptions toward these technologies [54] and become empowered to confidently embrace them.

1.1 The Case of Large Language Models

The recent introduction of Large Language Models (LLM) like ChatGPT to the public may have been the tipping point for exasperating AI attitudes [18, 21]. LLM are machine learning models with a high number of parameters (from hundreds of millions for early models like BERT to hundreds of billions for GPT4) which are pre-trained to create lossy compression of large datasets through simple tasks, e.g. complete a statement or predict the next word, and can perform a variety of domain-independent tasks with little or no specific training and data [40, 59, 66]. LLM functioning is widely different from cognitive processes in biological brains and several LLM limits and vulnerabilities keep emerging [3, 4, 34, 56, 61, 65].

In particular, the tendency to make up responses to factual questions when they are not able to respond [1, 12]. Notwithstanding these limitations, the linguistic capabilities of LLM and ChatGPT have led to the strongest reactions comprising a letter signed by a number of experts calling for a stop of development of large models [2]. However, this call has been considered impractical or even counterproductive for democratic governance of these tools [23, 40] and was not followed even by some of its main authors [39]. However, it still added fuel to the fire of AI phobia and anxiety.

Despite the growing familiarity with ChatGPT and its capabilities, there remains a lingering apprehension about the potential dominance of AI in various aspects of society. Some initial concerns have also emerged regarding its potential impact on educational aspects [17]. Educators, policymakers, and researchers are increasingly voicing concerns about the use of generative AI systems like ChatGPT in educational settings. One major concern revolves around the ethical considerations related to the use of generative AI systems by students [45]. Unethical practices, like using AI-generated content without appropriate attribution or engaging in plagiarism, pose challenges to academic integrity and raise questions about the responsibilities of both students and educators in the AI era. However, excluding ChatGPT from the classroom is not a viable solution, as its inclusion presents a valuable opportunity to familiarise students with the capabilities and limitations of generative AI tools [38, 60]. By explicitly incorporating ChatGPT into classroom activities, educators can provide students with insights and strategies for its proper utilisation, enabling them to effectively utilise this technology within a controlled and educational environment.

Students have a positive view of using ChatGPT as an educational tool, valuing its capabilities and finding it helpful for study and work. While acknowledging its potential for learning, students recognize the need for improvements and are mindful of its limitations [49]. The utilisation of ChatGPT in the classroom opens up opportunities for interactive and engaging learning experiences and prepares students for an increasingly

AI-driven world. ChatGPT's capabilities in the classroom extend far beyond merely familiarising students with AI, as it demonstrates remarkable proficiency in covering diverse learning materials, spanning from coding [46] and microbiology [7] to media-related topics [44]. However, an essential aspect of utilising the full potential of ChatGPT lies in employing effective prompting strategies [64]. Carefully crafted prompts can guide ChatGPT's responses, leading to more accurate and informative outputs. This approach allows educators to align the AI system's responses with specific learning objectives, resulting in more targeted and meaningful interactions [29].

An important target for AI literacy, involving LLM, is defusing the rising and misleading feeling of being able to access and process any form of knowledge to solve problems in any domain with no effort or previous expertise in AI or problem domain. This widespread phenomenon stems from the lack of literacy on the inherent limitations of current LLMs, such as hallucinations, limited understanding, and reasoning constraints [1, 12]. By disregarding the boundaries of LLMs, individuals may fail to recognize the potential risks and inaccuracies that can arise from relying solely on their outputs. The recent widespread acceptance of generative AI LLM tools such as Chat-GPT, highlights the necessity for informative interventions that educate users about realistic and comprehensive understandings of LLMs' capabilities and limitations. Such interventions can encourage users to exercise critical thinking when interpreting and applying knowledge generated by these models. Educators and researchers have been actively exploring and implementing diverse approaches to raise awareness and promote AI literacy within school environments [26, 51]. Recognizing the importance of going beyond theoretical aspects, these efforts aim to provide students with opportunities to expand their learning through hands-on experiences by incorporating practical activities, projects, and real-world applications of AI [26, 31].

As we embrace the new era of accessible AI tools, there is a noticeable lack of research on AI literacy interventions utilising ChatGPT. To address this gap and build upon existing concerns, this study aims to develop and evaluate an intervention focused on AI literacy, providing hands-on experience with ChatGPT. The primary goal is to assess the impact of this intervention on adolescents, exposing them to non-trivial tasks with ChatGPT to demonstrate its limitations while mitigating fears and negative attitudes towards AI. By engaging participants directly with the ChatGPT interface, the intervention aims to foster a deeper and more critical understanding of the technology and its potential limitations. This study specifically focuses on introducing adolescents to the strategy of prompting and examines their perceptions, emotions, interaction evaluations, and opinions toward ChatGPT. By evaluating the effectiveness of this educational approach, the study aims to offer valuable insights into reducing fear and promoting positive attitudes towards AI as well as introducing highly needed educational activities for the classroom about the novel concepts of prompting and LLMs.

2 Methodology

2.1 Participants and Study Design

A pilot study was conducted at a high school in Palermo, Sicily with a sample size of 21 students (n = 21; 33.3% male, 66.7% female; Ages 16 to 18, mean age = 16.3, SD = 0.57). The study was conducted within a formal school setting with students participating in a two hour-long AI workshop. Prior to the study students were informed about the research objectives and the purpose of the workshop and were asked to sign an electronic form to provide their consent to their participation in the study.

2.2 Learning Design and Study Procedure

The pilot study was conducted as an informative educational workshop on AI. The aim of the workshop was to introduce students to the topic of AI and encourage them to explore and question the capabilities and limitations of ChatGPT. The study procedure, depicted in Fig. 1, was designed to facilitate learning through active exploration. In particular, the educational learning plan saw two phases, the first one introduced student to AI and allowed them to freely explore the capabilities and limitations of ChatGPT and the second phase introduced students to prompting techniques to enhance ChatGPT's capabilities.

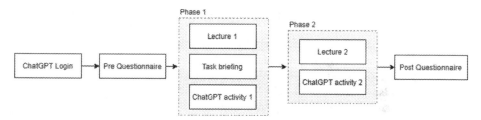

Fig. 1. Study design and educational learning plan.

The study procedure consisted of several key steps. Firstly, to minimize technical incidents influencing the results, students were instructed to access the ChatGPT page before they accessed the pre-questionnaire. After the completion of the pre-questionnaire, the instructor proceeded to deliver a presentation to introduce participants to topics related to AI applications, LLMs, and human intelligence vs artificial intelligence. Students were then provided with instructions for an activity that involved utilising ChatGPT. During this first activity students were asked to instruct ChatGPT to act as a personal teacher to educate in regards to the fundamental concepts of democracy (prior to the study the students had discussed the topic in class due to the Italian National Day and Republic Day, an initial internal trial was also conducted to verify ChatGPT's outputs for accuracy from an educational standpoint). The set of instructions included a variety of key points that the students should have as an outcome of their interaction. A few of the highlighted key points: ChatGPT should interactively explain the main concepts of democracy in a natural and not boring way. It should avoid long bulleted lists and alternate brief explanations with questions addressed to the user. Moreover, students were provided with a set of educational objectives the ChatGPT interaction would eventually generate.

The first ChatGPT activity lasted approximately 20 min and aimed to give first-hand experience to students in regard to the limited ability of ChatGPT to follow complex instructions. At its completion, the instructor proceeded to elaborate the limits of Chat-GPT and then introduced the concept of prompting, providing a few simple examples. After receiving this information, students were given a second opportunity to instruct ChatGPT to act as a personal teacher. The task briefing was the same as in the first activity. At the end of the activity students accessed the post-questionnaire where they could also upload their interaction with ChatGPT.

2.3 Measures

Perceived Level of Realistic and Identity Threat. To measure the perceived level of realistic and identity threat generated by ChatGPT, a set of questions was adapted from the study of [63]. The questions were adapted to AI conversational skills and included items such as "In the long term, artificial intelligence is a direct threat to man's well-being and safety" and "Recent progress in artificial intelligence is challenging the true essence of what it means to be a human being". These sets of questions were part of both the pre and post questionnaires and were rated on a 7-point scale, with responses ranging from Strongly disagree (1) to Strongly agree (7).

Self-reported Emotions After Interaction. We proceeded to measure participants' emotions after their interaction with ChatGPT using the "The Discrete Emotions Questionnaire" adapted from [16]. Participants were then asked to report the degree of emotions they felt after the interaction with ChatGPT (anger, fear, disgust, anxiety, sadness, desire, happiness, joy) The items were anchored with (1) not at all to (7) very much.

Interaction Quality Evaluation (UX). Additionally, in the post-questionnaire, we proceed to collect data regarding the interaction quality. The subscales of "Semantic Differential Pragmatic dimension", "Semantic Differential Hedonic dimension", "Semantic Differential Human likeness", and "Social presence" were used from [19].

Functionality of ChatGPT. Moreover, in the post-questionnaire, a set of measures focused on evaluating students' perception of ChatGPTs functionality was included. Items were included to measure: (a) effort perceived to achieve desired ChatGPT behavior, after their initial interaction with the AI tool, (b) perceived interaction improvement, after being introduced to prompting and engaging to a second interaction with the tool, and (c) ChatGPT capabilities.

Open-Ended Question. Lastly, to collect students' opinions regarding the interaction with ChatGPT, the post-questionnaire included three open-ended questions to collect student's opinions and thoughts in regard to; (a) positive aspects of the interaction, (b) negative aspects of the interaction, and (c) any additional noteworthy thoughts they wished to share.

Besides these measures, we collected students' demographic data, their previous experiences with AI and ChatGPT, and in the post-questionnaire students were requested to paste their ChatGPT chat history.

2.4 Data Analysis

To code and categorize the responses to open questions provided by participants, we used a classical social cognition model, the Stereotype Content Model (SCM), devised to describe the process of impression formation of social actors and groups, traditionally of human beings [10, 11]. According to this theory, humans form and update their impression of others based on two fundamental dimensions: warmth, which involves characteristics such as friendliness, kindness, and trustworthiness – and competence – the ability to reach one's goals effectively. In the last decade, this model was applied to non-human agents like animals [47], brands [27], but also robots [6], chatbots [28], and artificial intelligence [36], showing promising results. In previous studies where people adopted warmth and competence to describe their AI interaction partner, they tend to express more competence-related judgments, and evaluate these agents as more competent than warm [36]. This may also depend on the AI system. In this study, we decided to adopt this approach which summarizes social perception in two main dimensions. Some students' answers, though, were not targeting the perception of the chatbot per se but the whole educational activity and interaction with the composed system, referring to issues like creating an account or the excitement for their first interaction with an AI. Consequently, we devised a third category named "system" aimed at grouping these divergent records.

An attention check was included in each set of questions during data collection, resulting in varying participant counts per questionnaire. The results section provides the number of valid participants who passed the test.

3 Results

Perceived Level of Realistic Threat. To create a composite measure for realistic threat, all five items on the scale were averaged together similar to previous work [13, 63]. Using this measure, a dependent t-test revealed significant differences ($p < 0.05$) between the pre (mPre = 4.17, SD = 1.39) and post (mPost = 3.73, SD = 1.42) questionnaires. This suggests that participants' (n = 20) realistic threat caused by AI decreased after the intervention. A closer look into the individual items, saw a significant decrease in participants' belief that AI is causing work loss for men (mPre = 4.6, SD = 1.05, mPost = 3.3, SD = 1.49, $p < 0.05$). However, participants' belief that AI will not replace workers from their duties remained unchanged after the intervention (mPre = 3.46, SD = 1.25, mPost = 3.46, SD = 1.68, $p > 0.05$). The remaining items saw a non-significant decrease after the intervention.

Perceived Level of Identity Threat. A composite measure was created for identity threat by averaging all five items from the scale similar to previous work [13, 63]. A dependent t-test revealed a significant difference ($p < 0.05$) between the pre (mPre = 4.08, SD = 1.39) and post (mPost = 3.57, SD = 1.54) questionnaires. This finding indicates that participants' (n = 20) AI identity threat significantly decreased after the intervention. A closer look into the individual items, saw a significant decrease in participants' belief that boundaries between man and machine are becoming less clear (mPre = 4.6, SD = 1.29, mPost = 3.73, SD = 1.48, $p < 0.05$). Despite improvements observed in the post-questionnaire, no statistically significant differences were identified among the remaining items of the scale.

Self-reported Emotions After Interaction. Participants (n = 21) exhibited significantly higher positive emotions after their interaction with ChatGPT (mPositive = 3.48, SD = 1.79, mNegative = 1.35, SD = 0.91, p < 0.05). The higher negative emotion was Anger (m = 1.55, SD = 1.43) whilst higher positive emotion was Serenity (m = 3.65,SD = 1.63). The lowest negative emotion was Sadness (m = 1.2, SD = 0.52) and lowest positive emotions were both Desire (m = 3.4,SD = 1.98) and Joy (m = 3.4,SD = 1.81).

Interaction Quality Evaluation (UX). Under the first subscale "Perception of human likeness" students (n = 20) perceived the interaction with ChatGPT more as an interaction with a machine rather than a human (m = 2.9, SD = 1.51), unnatural (m = 3.6, SD = 1.87), and artificial (m = 3.1, SD = 1.95). In the second subscale "Social Presence" the participants gave a substantially below average evaluation to the social aspects of the interaction (m = 3.5, SD = 1.67). With the highest rated item being that the chatbot was efficient in responding to the activities (m = 4.6, SD = 1.49) and the lowest rated item being that the chatbot engaged in a common task with them (m = 2.9, SD = 1.47). In the third subscale "Semantic Differential Hedonic dimension" participants overall found the experience enjoyable (m = 4.75, SD = 1.37) with the adjectives "Elegant, Good Quality, New, Created connections, Innovative, Presentable, and Engaging" receiving higher rating than their negative counter adjectives. In the final subscale "Semantic Differential Pragmatic dimension" the interaction was found predictable (m = 4.85, SD = 1.52) and manageable (m = 5.52, SD = 1.53).

Functionality of ChatGPT. In the first subscale, "Effort perceived to achieve desired ChatGPT behaviour" students' (n = 21) responses indicated a neutral stance, with no strong agreement or disagreement on average. Participants reported that achieving the desired behaviour from ChatGPT required little effort (mean = 3.78, SD = 1.62), somewhat many attempts (mean = 4.47, SD = 1.61), somewhat more attempts were needed to refine the request (mean = 4.63, SD = 1.77), and the desired behaviour required increased understanding of how ChatGPT works (mean = 4.63, SD = 1.53).

After being introduced to the prompting strategies and completing the second activity students were asked to compare the two interactions. Compared to the first attempt, students found the results of the second interaction to be better (mean = 2.45, SD = 1.19), slightly more natural (mean = 4.55, SD = 1.61), and clearer (mean = 5.25, SD = 1.11). However, there was no agreement if the interaction was passively repeating content or more interactive (mean = 4, SD = 1.83).

Finally, in regards to the subscale of "ChatGPT capabilities", participants found ChatGPT intelligent rather than confused (mean = 3, SD = 2.01), intuitive instead of unable to adapt to requests (mean = 3.17, SD = 1.99), understanding of their questions (mean = 3.39, SD = 1.77), knowing what they asked (mean = 3.28, SD = 1.99), adapting to their questions rather than repeating the same mistakes (mean = 3.67, SD = 1.76), however, they reported the interactions as reading from an encyclopaedia rather than communicating with a human (mean = 3.67, SD = 1.76).

Open-Ended Question. The dimension that was most widely covered in the open answers was competence, with the theme that emerged most strongly being that Chat-GPT was responsive and provided answers. This theme was supported by the responses of 8 participants. The responses were characterized by terms such as "immediate," as emphasized by participants P06 and P13, "correct" (P09), "exhaustive" (P04), and "interesting" (P10). A student also observed that the system was able to provide summarizations on request (P06). Another theme that emerged within this dimension with the support of 5 students is the system's usefulness. A student commented that this use of ChatGPT "could be useful for practicality and timing" (P20).

Negative aspects of competence that students commented on were repetitiveness, both in terms of them needing to repeat their questions and ChatGPT repeating responses. These were supported by the writing of 4 students each. The first one of these was mentioned with comments along the lines of "it started repeating the same things" (P06), and the second - along the lines of a student saying they "had to repeat several times to explain [themselves] again and more clearly the topics" (P11). One student also wrote that they had "to repeat [to the system to] to go slowly several times" (P12). Another theme of criticism, related to this need for repetition was supported by 5 students, and represented by writings stating that the system "did not answer as [the student] wanted to questions" (P17) and "the chat was purely notionistic" (P01). When it comes to the warmth dimension, only 3 students provided positive comments, giving a somewhat different spin to similar responses from the competence dimension. The main difference being that the focus in the responses is not on the system sharing its knowledge, but on it complying to students' requests. This is well represented by a student who wrote "that asking it to explain again in a clearer way, it acceded and fulfilled my requests" (P11). Criticisms that fall within the warmth dimension were about ChatGPT not being "natural" enough (P09) and not giving a sense of "a conversation with a human" (P20), "the little feeling in the replies" (P21), supported by 5 students. More precisely, they suggested that it should "briefly answer the questions that are asked" (P09) and it should not provide "answers that are taken from an encyclopedia" (P10), both also suggested it should be more human-like.

Finally, the third dimension that emerged was the perception of the system. Positive comments concerned the possibility to interact with artificial intelligence (supported by 3 students), and with a novel system (7 students). The two points were brought together by a student that expressed satisfaction of "dealing with a new reality, such as that of artificial intelligence" (P03). One student wrote to have found out "how much artificial intelligence can be useful in daily life [...] it helps to save time without being superficial in research" (P08). Others seconded that by writing that it "will surely be used for the future" (P17). In many of their negative comments regarding this dimension, students expressed views that the system needs to be improved, one saying that it's "still at an embryonic stage" (P02).

4   Discussion and Conclusion

This study aimed to develop an AI literacy workshop using ChatGPT to enhance adolescents' understanding of AI limitations and mitigate fears and negative attitudes towards AI. The intervention successfully reduced adolescents' fears related to realistic and identity threats posed by AI advancements. The initial levels in the responses to the corresponding metrics demonstrated the presence of such a fear, similar to previous work [13]. Our study revealed that offering opportunities for guided non-trivial interactions with ChatGPT can effectively reduce the fear associated with AI advancements. A significant decrease was noticed in the items of fear of job loss and belief in the blurring boundaries between humans and machines. This positive shift in attitudes indicates that the exposure of adolescents to generative AI capabilities provided them a better understanding of how AI systems function and the impact they may have on various aspects of society, including the job market and human identity.

Regarding the overall experience, students rated the interaction with ChatGPT as enjoyable, eliciting positive emotions such as desire, serenity, and happiness. In some instances, students reported feelings of anger, which may be attributed to factors beyond the interaction with ChatGPT, such as their difficulties during the registration phase or the survey. This claim is further supported by comments students left in the open-ended responses.

Concerning evaluating the interaction of ChatGPT in terms of human likeness, students perceived ChatGPT as more of a machine than a human-like entity, describing it as unnatural and artificial [29]. This finding was persistent in the open-ended answers with students further describing their interactions with ChatGPT as repetitive. The social presence perceived during the interaction was limited with students reporting that the chatbot did not engage in common tasks with them. However, despite these perceptions, students found the experience enjoyable and manageable. When comparing the two ChatGPT activities, the initial one without prompting strategies and the second one after being introduced to prompting, the students rated the second interaction with ChatGPT clearer, more natural, and better than the initial attempt. A look into students' requests within ChatGPT, we observe more structured prompts as the interactions went on. Due to limitations in collecting the majority of students generated prompts, it was not feasible to derive more concrete results in regards to prompting skills improvement, however students reported perceived improvement in interaction with ChatGPT and understanding of its capabilities. Moreover, the incorporation of prompting strategies in the second ChatGPT activity had a profound impact on students' perceptions and evaluations of the overall interaction. Highlighting the importance of providing users with appropriate guidance and education to fully leverage the capabilities of AI systems [64].

Overall, the findings indicate that participants had a positive view of ChatGPT's capabilities, appreciating its intelligence, understanding, and adaptability similar to previous work [49]. However, despite these positive evaluations of ChatGPT's capabilities, participants perceived the interactions as more akin to reading from an encyclopedia rather than engaging in human-like communication [29]. This suggests that while students recognized the intelligence and adaptability of ChatGPT, they also acknowledged a limitation in its ability to emulate human-like interactions. However, it is essential to consider that this perception may also be influenced by a possible misunderstanding of the question from the students' point of view. The novelty of interacting with ChatGPT might have led them to expect encyclopedic-style answers to their natural language questions.

Findings from the student open-ended responses provide further valuable insights into their experiences and perceptions of ChatGPT in three distinct dimensions: competence, warmth, and system perception. On a warmth level, it was considered low while acceding to help the user, however, this could be part of the alignment fine tuning applied to ChatGPT. Finally, the dimension of system perception received positive comments, centred around the excitement of interacting with AI. Students proceeded to share individual thoughts of how they believed that AI, as represented by ChatGPT, is likely to become increasingly valuable in various aspects of daily life and education. To our knowledge this is the first study that offers an exploration about the need and an approach to learn to prompt with LLMs in the classroom and how this facilitates reflection about AI limits. The qualitative answers to the open questions provide a deep understanding about the aspects under exploration, but they cannot be generalised. Even if in case studies in other contexts we expect similar conditions (e.g., limited current familiarity with ChatGPT), more studies will be needed to determine the generality of our findings.

As with any study we report the following limitations. Our choice of interpretation model for the open questions followed from our data. The concise qualitative answers did not allow for a fine-grained classification like the one proposed by [19] that we adopted in our quantitative interaction quality evaluation. In a naive parallel between these measures, the warmth dimension can efficiently capture the hedonic, social presence, and human-likeness dimensions, while the pragmatic quality dimension aligns with the competence aspect. However, it must be noted that the SCM was mostly designed with human actors and human-level linguistics [5] and functional cognitive capabilities in mind [34]. Instead, [19] proposes measures that were initially applied to classical chatbots whose interaction capabilities were more restrictive, e.g., fixed agent-led instead of mixed-initiative dialog. Those chatbots were designed to effectively complete a specific task with a limited focus on natural and versatile interaction. The pragmatic value for these models usually refers to the complexity of the task and domain at hand, e.g., acquiring all the data necessary from the user and completing the operations requested. This measure may not directly map pragmatic linguistic skills [5], which were too limited in most old commercial chatbots. While later UX chatbot measures like those of [19] have been applied to more complex chatbots, they don't clearly split the perception of different types of linguistic [5] and emotional skills, which may affect items present in all four dimensions: pragmatic quality, hedonic quality, human-likeness, and social presence. SCM would instead collapse in the competence dimension both the semantic and pragmatic linguistic skills while the latter is domain independent and connected to the social domain. The disagreement between these measures was often reflected by disagreement between the annotators. For example, the issues about repetitiveness of responses or need to repeat and reformulate a query were considered by the majority as lack of competence, thus following the selected SCM approach, a minority as social competence, following a line of reasoning more in line with the view of UX chatbot measure. This may explain the contrast between the interaction quality evaluation (that finds the system competent, and the open-ended answers analysis that presents several negative points on this aspect.

The UX chatbot and SCM measures may not be fully suited to cover for both versatility and fragility of modern LLM-based chatbots and the interaction between their broader but fallible capabilities [34] as the tendency to diverge into hallucinations [55], especially during complex natural conversations [29], and the unnatural almost hard-wired safeguard responses they present [8, 33]. To get a more detailed measure of users' perception of ChatGPT skills we added specific semantic differential measures "Functionality of ChatGPT" that non conclusively suggest a positive perception of ChatGPT's capabilities while being still limited in terms of natural interaction. In our future studies, we will extend the measures collected to account for these issues, for example adopting automatic tools for measurement of semantic and pragmatic precision [5]. The study was carried out as a field study within a school environment, but encountered certain challenges related to the accessibility of the ChatGPT website. Additionally, in some instances, students worked in pairs to complete the activity due to malfunctioning of some machines. While most students reported improving quality of the interaction during the activity only nine uploaded their in-class interaction due to technical issues. Only five out of nine interactions showed more than three attempts to improve the conversation modifying the prompts. Moreover, the number of questions in the survey may have tired the students and affected their answers. It is important to note that this was an exploratory pilot study with a relatively small sample size which necessitates caution in generalizing the findings.

In conclusion, our study suggests a significant impact of designing and developing AI literacy workshops with hands-on experience using ChatGPT. While with a limited number of participants, the intervention has shown to be an effective approach in enhancing participants' understanding of ChatGPT limitations and capabilities whilst also diminishing fears of identity and realistic threats caused by AI advancements. Lastly, the study successfully introduced participants to the effective use of prompting strategies, enhancing their interactions with ChatGPT. To conclude, we highlight the need for novel measures of the linguistic aspects of user interaction with LLM based chatbots considering their non-transparent mechanisms and limitations as well as dealing with large amounts of data [5]. In future research, we aim to replicate the study with a larger sample size, enabling more comprehensive analysis and correlation exploration.

Acknowledgements. This work has been partially funded by the Volkswagen Foundation (COURAGE project, no. 95567). TIDE-UPF also acknowledges the support by AEI/10.13039/501100011033 (PID2020-112584RB-C33, MDM-2015-0502) and by ICREA under the ICREA Academia programme (D. Hernández-Leo, Serra Hunter) and the Department of Research and Universities of the Government of Catalonia (SGR 00930). The authors thank Marco Marelli for the useful discussions on pragmatic linguistic skills.

References

1. Bang, Y., et al.: A multitask, multilingual, multimodal evaluation of ChatGPT on reasoning, hallucination, and interactivity. arXiv preprint arXiv:2302.04023 (2023)
2. Bengio, Y., Russel, S., Musk, E., Wozniak, S., Harari, Y.N.: Pause Giant AI Experiments: An Open Letter. Future of Life Institute (2023). https://futureoflife.org/open-letter/pause-giant-ai-experiments/

3. Bishop, J.M.: Artificial intelligence is stupid and causal reasoning will not fix it. Front. Psychol. **11**, 2603 (2021)

4. Borji, A.: A categorical archive of ChatGPT failures. arXiv preprint arXiv:2302.03494 (2023)

5. Bunt, H., Petukhova, V.: Semantic and pragmatic precision in conversational AI systems. Front. Artif. Intell. **6**, 896729 (2023)

6. Carpinella, C.M., Wyman, A.B., Perez, M.A., Stroessner, S.J.: The robotic social attributes scale (RoSAS) development and validation. In: Proceedings of the 2017 ACM/IEEE International Conference on Human-Robot Interaction, pp. 254–262 (2017)

7. Das, D., Kumar, N., Longjam, L., et al.: Assessing the capability of ChatGPT in answering first- and second-order knowledge questions on microbiology as per competency-based medical education curriculum. Cureus **15**(3), e36034 (2023). https://doi.org/10.7759/cureus. 36034

8. Derner, E., Batistič, K.: Beyond the safeguards: exploring the security risks of ChatGPT. arXiv preprint arXiv:2305.08005 (2023)

9. Esteva, A., et al.: Dermatologist-level classification of skin cancer with deep neural networks. Nature **542**(7639), 115–118 (2017)

10. Fiske, S.T., Cuddy, A.J.C., Glick, P., Xu, J.: A model of (often mixed) stereotype content: competence and warmth respectively follow from perceived status and competition. J. Pers. Soc. Psychol. **82**(6), 878–902 (2002)

11. Fiske, S.T., Xu, J., Cuddy, A.J.C., Glick, P.: (Dis)respecting versus (dis)liking: status and interdependence predict ambivalent stereotypes of competence and warmth. J. Soc. Issues **55**(3), 473–489 (1999)

12. Floridi, L.: AI as *agency without intelligence*: on ChatGPT, large language models, and other generative models. Philos. Technol. **36**(1), 15 (2023). https://doi.org/10.1007/s13347-023-00621-y

13. Gabbiadini, A., Ognibene, D., Baldissarri, C., Manfredi, A.: Does ChatGPT pose a threat to human identity? Available at SSRN (2023). https://doi.org/10.2139/ssrn.4377900. https://ssrn.com/abstract=4377900

14. Gaube, S., et al.: Do as AI say: susceptibility in deployment of clinical decision-aids. NPJ Digit. Med. **4**(1), 31 (2021)

15. Gupta, R., Srivastava, D., Sahu, M., Tiwari, S., Ambasta, R.K., Kumar, P.: Artificial intelligence to deep learning: machine intelligence approach for drug discovery. Mol. Divers. **25**, 1315–1360 (2021). https://doi.org/10.1007/s11030-021-10217-3

16. Harmon-Jones, C., Bastian, B., Harmon-Jones, E.: The discrete emotions questionnaire: a new tool for measuring state self-reported emotions. PLoS ONE **11**(8), e0159915 (2016)

17. Haque, M.U., Dharmadasa, I., Sworna, Z.T., Rajapakse, R.N., Ahmad, H.: "I think this is the most disruptive technology": exploring sentiments of ChatGPT early adopters using Twitter data. arXiv preprint arXiv:2212.05856 (2022)

18. Harari, Y.N.: Why technology favors tyranny. The Atlantic **322**(3), 64–73 (2018)

19. Haugeland, I.K.F., Følstad, A., Taylor, C., Bjørkli, C.A.: Understanding the user experience of customer service chatbots: an experimental study of chatbot interaction design. Int. J. Hum. Comput. Stud. **161**, 102788 (2022)

20. Hyesun, C., Prabu, D., Arun, R.: Trust in AI and its role in the acceptance of AI technologies. Int. J. Hum.-Comput. Interact. **39**(9), 1727–1739 (2023). https://doi.org/10.1080/10447318. 2022.2050543

21. Ipsos MORI: Public views of machine learning (2017). https://royalsociety.org/~/media/pol icy/projects/machine-learning/publications/public-views-of-machine-learning-ipsos-mori. pdf. Accessed 20 June 2019

22. Dang, J., Liu, L.: Robots are friends as well as foes: ambivalent attitudes toward mindful and mindless AI robots in the United States and China. Comput. Hum. Behav. **115**, 106612 (2021). ISSN: 0747-5632. https://doi.org/10.1016/j.chb.2020.106612

23. Ienca, M.: Don't pause giant AI for the wrong reasons. Nat. Mach. Intell. **5**, 470–471 (2023)
24. Johnson, D.G., Verdicchio, M.: AI anxiety. J. Assoc. Inf. Sci. Technol. **68**, 2267–2270 (2017). https://doi.org/10.1002/asi.23867
25. Jumper, J., et al.: Highly accurate protein structure prediction with AlphaFold. Nature **596**(7873), 583–589 (2021)
26. Kandlhofer, M., Steinbauer, G., Hirschmugl-Gaisch, S., Huber, P.: Artificial intelligence and computer science in education: from kindergarten to university. In: 2016 IEEE Frontiers in Education Conference (FIE), Erie, PA, USA, pp. 1–9 (2016). https://doi.org/10.1109/FIE. 2016.7757570
27. Kervyn, N., Fiske, S.T., Malone, C.: Brands as intentional agents framework: how perceived intentions and ability can map brand perception. J. Consum. Psychol. **22**(2), 166–176 (2012)
28. Khadpe, P., Krishna, R., Fei-Fei, L., Hancock, J.T., Bernstein, M.S.: Conceptual metaphors impact perceptions of human-AI collaboration. Proc. ACM Hum.-Comput. Interact. **4**(CSCW2), 1–26 (2020)
29. Koyutürk, C., et al.: Developing effective educational chatbots with ChatGPT prompts: insights from preliminary tests in a case study on social media literacy. arXiv preprint arXiv: 2306.10645 (2023)
30. Lemay, D., Basnet, R., Doleck, T.: Fearing the robot apocalypse: correlates of AI anxiety. Int. J. Learn. Anal. Artif. Intell. Educ. (iJAI) **2**, 24 (2020). https://doi.org/10.3991/ijai.v2i2.16759
31. Lomonaco, F., Taibi, D., Trianni, V., Buršić, S., Donabauer, G., Ognibene, D.: Yes, echo-chambers mislead you too: a game-based educational experience to reveal the impact of social media personalization algorithms. In: Fulantelli, G., Burgos, D., Casalino, G., Cimitile, M., Bosco, G.L., Taibi, D. (eds.) HELMeTO 2022, vol. 1779, pp. 330–344. Springer, Cham (2023). https://doi.org/10.1007/978-3-031-29800-4_26
32. Luxton, D.D.: Recommendations for the ethical use and design of artificial intelligent care providers. Artif. Intell. Med. **62**(1), 1–10 (2014)
33. Brundage, M., et al.: Lessons learned on language model safety and misuse (2022). https:// openai.com/research/language-model-safety-and-misuse
34. Mahowald, K., Ivanova, A.A., Blank, I.A., Kanwisher, N., Tenenbaum, J.B., Fedorenko, E.: Dissociating language and thought in large language models: a cognitive perspective. arXiv preprint arXiv:2301.06627 (2023)
35. Marangunić, N., Granić, A.: Technology acceptance model: a literature review from 1986 to 2013. Univ. Access Inf. Soc. **14**(1), 81–95 (2015). https://doi.org/10.1007/s10209-014-0348-1
36. McKee, K.R., Bai, X., Fiske, S.: Humans perceive warmth and competence in artificial intelligence (2021). https://doi.org/10.31234/osf.io/5ursp
37. Mittelstadt, B.D., Allo, P., Taddeo, M., Wachter, S., Floridi, L.: The ethics of algorithms: mapping the debate. Big Data Soc. **3**(2), 2053951716679679 (2016)
38. Montanelli, S., Ruskov, M.: A systematic literature review of online collaborative story writing. In: Nocera, J.A., Lárusdóttir, M.K., Petrie, H., Piccinno, A., Winckler, M. (eds.) Human-Computer Interaction – INTERACT 2023, LNCS, Part III, vol. 14144, pp. 73–93. Springer, Cham (2023). https://doi.org/10.1007/978-3-031-42286-7_5
39. Murgia, M., Bradshaw, T., Kinder, T., Waters, R.: Elon Musk plans artificial intelligence start-up to rival OpenAI. Financial Times (2023). https://www.ft.com/content/2a96995b-c799-4281-8b60-b235e84aefe4
40. Novelli, C., Casolari, F., Rotolo, A., Taddeo, M., Floridi, L.: Taking AI risks seriously: a proposal for the AI act. Available at SSRN 4447964 (2023)
41. Obermeyer, Z., Powers, B., Vogeli, C., Mullainathan, S.: Dissecting racial bias in an algorithm used to manage the health of populations. Science **366**(6464), 447–453 (2019)

42. Ognibene, D., et al.: Challenging social media threats using collective well-being-aware recommendation algorithms and an educational virtual companion. Front. Artif. Intell. **5**, 654930 (2023)

43. Oh, C., Song, J., Choi, J., Kim, S., Lee, S., Suh, B.: I lead, you help but only with enough details: understanding user experience of co-creation with artificial intelligence. In: Proceedings of the 2018 CHI Conference on Human Factors in Computing Systems, Montreal, QC, Canada, pp. 1–13 (2018). https://doi.org/10.1145/3173574.3174223

44. Pavlik, J.V.: Collaborating with ChatGPT: considering the implications of generative artificial intelligence for journalism and media education. J. Mass Commun. Educ. **78**(1), 84–93 (2023). https://doi.org/10.1177/10776958221149577

45. Qadir, J.: Engineering education in the era of ChatGPT: promise and pitfalls of generative AI for education. In: 2023 IEEE Global Engineering Education Conference (EDUCON), Kuwait, Kuwait, pp. 1–9 (2023). https://doi.org/10.1109/EDUCON54358.2023.10125121

46. Rahman, M.M., Watanobe, Y.: ChatGPT for education and research: opportunities, threats, and strategies. Appl. Sci. **13**(9), 5783 (2023). https://doi.org/10.3390/app13095783

47. Sevillano, V., Fiske, S.T.: Warmth and competence in animals. J. Appl. Soc. Psychol. **46**(5), 276–293 (2016)

48. Stahl, B.C.: Artificial Intelligence for a Better Future: An Ecosystem Perspective on the Ethics of AI and Emerging Digital Technologies, p. 124. Springer, Cham (2021). https://doi.org/10.1007/978-3-030-69978-9

49. Shoufan, A.: Exploring students' perceptions of ChatGPT: thematic analysis and follow-up survey. IEEE Access **11**, 38805–38818 (2023). https://doi.org/10.1109/ACCESS.2023.3268224

50. Shin, D.: The effects of explainability and causability on perception, trust, and acceptance: implications for explainable AI. Int. J. Hum.-Comput. Stud. **146**, 102551 (2021). ISSN: 1071-5819. https://doi.org/10.1016/j.ijhcs.2020.102551

51. Sánchez-Reina, J.R., Theophilou, E., Hernández-Leo, D., Medina-Bravo, P.: The power of beauty or the tyranny of algorithms: how do teens understand body image on Instagram? In: Castillo-Abdul, B., García-Prieto, V. (eds.) Prosumidores emergentes: redes sociales, alfabetización y creación de contenidos, pp. 429–450. Editorial Dykinson S.L, Sevilla (2021)

52. Sirmaçek, B., et al.: The potential of artificial intelligence for achieving healthy and sustainable societies. In: Mazzi, F., Floridi, L. (eds.) The Ethics of Artificial Intelligence for the Sustainable Development Goals, vol. 152, pp. 65–96. Springer, Cham (2023). https://doi.org/10.1007/978-3-031-21147-8_5

53. Stokes, J.M., et al.: A deep learning approach to antibiotic discovery. Cell **180**(4), 688–702 (2020)

54. Theophilou, E., Lomonaco, F., Donabauer, G., Ognibene, D., Sánchez-Reina, R.J., Hernàndez-Leo, D.: AI and narrative scripts to educate adolescents about social media algorithms: insights about AI overdependence, trust and awareness. In: Viberg, O., Jivet, I., Muñoz-Merino, P., Perifanou, M., Papathoma, T. (eds.) Responsive and Sustainable Educational Futures. EC-TEL 2023, vol. 14200, pp. 415–429. Springer, Cham (2023). https://doi.org/10.1007/978-3-031-42682-7_28

55. Thorp, H.H.: ChatGPT is fun, but not an author. Science **379**(6630), 313 (2023)

56. Valmeekam, K., Sreedharan, S., Marquez, M., Olmo, A., Kambhampati, S.: On the planning abilities of large language models (a critical investigation with a proposed benchmark). arXiv preprint arXiv:2302.06706 (2023)

57. Verghese, A., Shah, N.H., Harrington, R.A.: What this computer needs is a physician: humanism and artificial intelligence. JAMA **319**(1), 19–20 (2018)

58. Wakunuma, K., Jiya, T., Aliyu, S.: Socio-ethical implications of using AI in accelerating SDG3 in Least Developed Countries. J. Responsible Technol. **4**, 100006 (2020)

59. Wei, J., et al.: Finetuned language models are zero-shot learners. arXiv preprint arXiv:2109. 01652 (2021)
60. Woo, D.J., Guo, K., Susanto, H.: Cases of EFL secondary students' prompt engineering pathways to complete a writing task with ChatGPT. arXiv preprint arXiv:2307.05493 (2023)
61. Xu, L., Chen, Y., Cui, G., Gao, H., Liu, Z.: Exploring the universal vulnerability of prompt-based learning paradigm. arXiv preprint arXiv:2204.05239 (2022)
62. Yan, W., et al.: Association between inequalities in human resources for health and all cause and cause specific mortality in 172 countries and territories, 1990–2019: observational study. BMJ 381, e073043 (2023)
63. Yogeeswaran, K., Złotowski, J., Livingstone, M., Bartneck, C., Sumioka, H., Ishiguro, H.: The interactive effects of robot anthropomorphism and robot ability on perceived threat and support for robotics research. J. Hum.-Robot Interact. 5(2), 29–47 (2016)
64. Zamfirescu-Pereira, J.D., Wong, R.Y., Hartmann, B., Yang, Q.: Why Johnny can't prompt: how non-AI experts try (and fail) to design LLM prompts. In: Proceedings of the 2023 CHI Conference on Human Factors in Computing Systems, pp. 1–21 (2023)
65. Zhang, H., Li, L.H., Meng, T., Chang, K.W., Broeck, G.V.D.: On the paradox of learning to reason from data. arXiv preprint arXiv:2205.11502 (2022)
66. Zhou, C., et al.: A comprehensive survey on pretrained foundation models: a history from BERT to ChatGPT. arXiv preprint arXiv:2302.09419 (2023)
67. Ziosi, M., Mökander, J., Novelli, C., Casolari, F., Taddeo, M., Floridi, L.: The EU AI Liability Directive: shifting the burden from proof to evidence. SSRN Electron. J. (2023). https://doi. org/10.2139/ssrn.4470725

Author Index